ACCESS-RIGHT

ACCESS-RIGHT

THE FUTURE OF DIGITAL COPYRIGHT LAW

ZOHAR EFRONI

OXFORD
UNIVERSITY PRESS

OXFORD
UNIVERSITY PRESS

Oxford University Press, Inc., publishes works that further Oxford University's objective of excellence in research, scholarship, and education.

Oxford New York
Auckland Cape Town Dar es Salaam Hong Kong Karachi Kuala Lumpur Madrid Melbourne
Mexico City Nairobi New Delhi Shanghai Taipei Toronto

With offices in
Argentina Austria Brazil Chile Czech Republic France Greece Guatemala Hungary Italy
Japan Poland Portugal Singapore South Korea Switzerland Thailand Turkey Ukraine
Vietnam

Published by Oxford University Press, Inc.
198 Madison Avenue, New York, New York 10016

Library of Congress Cataloging-in-Publication Data

Efroni, Zohar.
Access-right : the future of digital copyright law / Zohar Efroni.
p. cm.
Includes bibliographical references and index.
ISBN 978-0-19-973407-8 (hardback : alk. paper)
1. Copyright, International. 2. Electronic publishing—Law and legislation. 3. Fair use (Copyright) I. Title.
K1420.5.E38 2010
346.04'82—dc22 2010019397

1 2 3 4 5 6 7 8 9

Printed in the United States of America on acid-free paper

Note to Readers
This publication is designed to provide accurate and authoritative information in regard to the subject matter covered. It is based upon sources believed to be accurate and reliable and is intended to be current as of the time it was written. It is sold with the understanding that the publisher is not engaged in rendering legal, accounting, or other professional services. If legal advice or other expert assistance is required, the services of a competent professional person should be sought. Also, to confirm that the information has not been affected or changed by recent developments, traditional legal research techniques should be used, including checking primary sources where appropriate.

(Based on the Declaration of Principles jointly adopted by a Committee of the American Bar Association and a Committee of Publishers and Associations.)

CONTENTS

FIGURES AND TABLES

ACKNOWLEDGMENTS

In preparing this study I benefited greatly from the financial and institutional support of the Max Planck Institute for Intellectual Property, Competition and Tax Law in Munich, Germany. I am especially indebted to Professor Reto M. Hilty for his faith in the cause of this research, and to Dr. Eva-Marina Bastian for her invaluable assistance and kindness.

This book is dedicated to my mother Linda for being there in times of need and to my three wonderful children, Lian, Miron, and Shira-Mai, for all the joy they bring into my life.

Zohar Efroni
Berlin, June 2010

INTRODUCTION

I. THE INCEPTION OF AN IDEA

This book examines the relations between access to information and copyright protection with special emphasis on access to digital information. Within this field of research and writing, the problem of access and access control under copyright law has been part of broader deliberations over the future of copyright law in the age of digital technology more generally. In 1994, John Perry Barlow famously predicted the demise of copyright law as we know it.[1] In his criticism, Barlow pictured intellectual property protection in the online digital environment as a sinking ship.[2] The gist of his argument was that legal constructs such as copyright law relied on the existence of certain physical conditions and limitations. Those conditions have been prevalent in the analog world, but they no longer existed in cyberspace. In the digital space, information was said to be liberated from the tangible "bottles" in which it has been enclosed for centuries; information is now being transfigured into "voltage conditions darting around the Net at the speed of light, in conditions that one might behold in effect, as glowing pixels or transmitted sounds, but never touch or claim to 'own' in the old sense of the word."[3] Consequently, Barlow predicted the protection of intellectual assets in the network environment would rely far more on ethics and technology than on law.[4]

Around the same time, British lawyer and entrepreneur Simon Olswang published a four-page contribution to the *European Intellectual Property Law Journal* titled "Accessright: An Evolutionary Path for Copyright into the Digital Era."[5] Lamenting about the piecemeal advancement of copyright legislation in the face

1. *See* John P. Barlow, *Selling Wine Without Bottles (1996)* (reprinting *The Economy of Ideas, a Framework for Patents and Copyrights in the Digital Age*, WIRED 2.03 (Mar. 1994).

2. *Id.* at 169.

3. *Id.* at 171.

4. *Id.* at 182–87. Barlow further envisioned that factors such as relationships, servicing, and interactions were more likely to generate economic value than rigid exclusive rights. *Id.*

5. *See* Simon Olswang, *Accessright: An Evolutionary Path for Copyright Into the Digital Era*, 17 EUR. INTEL. PROP. REV. 215 (1995).

of digital piracy threats, Olswang expressed deep dissatisfaction with "the artificial stretching of copyright concepts." Instead, Olswang proposed a "more fundamental approach,"[6] coining the term *Accessright* to describe a meta right that should allow creators to control their creation in the digital domain as it would have the primary purpose of affording them with an exclusive power to authorize or prohibit use. Olswang posited that such right has been necessary in response to the collapsing distinctions between the various exclusive rights in the network environment.[7] The envisioned right should have provided the necessary property platform upon which contractual arrangements could develop to allow access and use, to the extent these activities were authorized by the rights-holder. The "Accessright" should have further afforded the rights-holder with a wide and flexible range of options for fashioning access and use permissions.[8] At the same time, Olswang noted the Accessright should be "limited to permit fair dealing and to maintain the balance between authors and users."[9]

Barlow and Olswang represent two radically different schools of thought that have been grappling with articulation of legal responses to the digital information revolution. This notwithstanding, both approaches are premised on the same basic assumption: that the traditional structure of entitlements under copyright cannot survive the transition to digital technology and global networks communication. Both Barlow and Olswang were skeptical about the capacity of the traditional set of exclusive rights to provide adequate solutions to the newly emerging challenges. Both also shared the recognition the law governing the information economy of the future will maintain a very close relationship to the notion of *access*.[10] However, neither author supported his thesis with extensive empirical or theoretical research, nor did they have any detailed program on how to amend the broken legal system they disparaged.[11]

---

6. *Id.* at 215.

7. "The answer does not lie in further defining the separate acts of infringement: the pace of technological change is too great. Moreover, in a world where technology offers a range of means to reach any end, it may be that we should abandon the notion of discrete acts in favour of a more comprehensive approach." *Id.* at 216.

8. Olswang went so far to suggest a reversal of the traditional burden of proof, creating a presumption that each unauthorized access breached the Accessright unless the user could prove "the copy in question was authorized." *Id.* at 217–18.

9. *Id.* at 217.

10. Barlow admitted that "underlying everything [is] the ability of th[e] market to access your creative services swiftly, conveniently, and interactively." Barlow, *supra* note 1, at 184. He added "[i]n most cases, control will be based on restricting access to the freshest, highest bandwidth information." *Id.* at 185.

11. Barlow cautiously submitted that encryption might play a central role in enforcing licensing schemes. *Id.* at 185–87. Olswang said nearly nothing on how the envisioned "Accessright" could receive concrete and workable outlines.

Much has happened in the copyright scene since the mid-1990s. The debate concerning the future of copyright law in the digital environment fills volumes; a large number of scholarly works are devoted to analyzing the technological changes, the evolution of online markets, and the impact of the copyright systems on society. Despite these considerable efforts, the main issues today are as perplexing as they were a decade or two ago.

Realistically speaking, there is no indication copyright's exclusive rights will disappear any time soon, as Barlow has predicted (or at least hoped). At the same time, many share the observation that simply expanding traditional copyrights to control works in digital formats and cover various network communication activities did not solve the core issues, which comes quite close to Olswang's prediction. Yet among the numerous attempts to fashion solutions to the puzzles digital technology has introduced, Olswang's vision—and the access-based approach generally—have been receiving only rather marginal attention. The bulk of contemporary copyright commentary grapples with the risk of copyright overprotection in the digital environment, which seems quite antithetical to Olswang's proprietary agenda. The main reason is that expansions in the scope and effect of the exclusive rights have been driving commentators to focus on finding ways to protect users and restore balance to the disturbed copyright system, with little tolerance of the prospects of a "mega" exclusive right and its possible affect on the system.

With this background, the present study endeavors to investigate precisely this fairly underdeveloped idea—that of an access-based copyright regulation. A significant portion of the theoretical part is devoted to exploring key aspects of the "access to information" notion in general and its interface with copyright rules. In a nutshell, this book examines the idea of literally premising copyright regulation on the concept of access to digital information and the implications of such a system.

II. STRUCTURE OF THE STUDY

The study is organized in three parts. The *first part* contains three chapters that lay down the theoretical groundwork for the book. Chapter 1 explores the notion of *information*, Chapter 2 investigates the notion of *property*, and Chapter 3 analyzes the notion of *access* to information. These three chapters build together a theoretical framework for the discussion on an information property system based on the concept of access.

The *second part* consists of three chapters as well. Chapter 4 addresses the digital reproduction right, Chapter 5 discusses the digital communication right, and Chapter 6 provides an overview and analysis of anticircumvention regulation. As a whole, the second part scrutinizes the legislative developments in the area of copyright law over the past two decades and describes the digital dilemma, including the prevailing regulative approaches in the United States and Europe. At sharp focus are the tendencies to expand copyright exclusory entitlements to digital formats, infrastructure, and spaces—and the ramifications of that expansion. The discussion is geared to showing how the positive law has been gradually assuming more dominate characteristics of an access right regime.

The *third part* encompasses two chapters: Chapter 7 examines the claim of copyright overprotection and reviews several approaches seeking to ameliorate the effects of overprotection tendencies in the digital setting. Finally, Chapter 8 introduces and explains the outlines of a new framework for dealing with the problem of copyright protection in the digital age. This chapter sketches a model for a copyright system that is designed *for* the digital information environment while introducing the concept of the *access-right* that would replace existing exclusive rights when applied to digital works. Under the proposed regulative framework, digital access to works would become the axis around which both exclusivity entitlements and exceptions are tailored.

III. METHODOLOGY AND TERMINOLOGY

A. Methodology

The first part of the study is largely theory-oriented, the second part focuses primarily on descriptive analysis of the positive law and legislative trends, and the third part analyzes prescriptive aspects of copyright reform. References to copyright's positive rules and doctrines are woven throughout the progression of the study. In this context, the reality of global networks and the rising influence of supranational lawmaking make it difficult to provide a comprehensive analysis of copyright issues from within the narrow quarters of a specific statute or jurisdiction. A broader perspective should consider the spectrum of relevant international and regional legal instruments. At the international level, the study focuses primarily on the provisions of the Berne Convention for the Protection of Literary and Artistic Works (1971) and the WIPO Treaties (1996). European legislative initiatives in the area of copyright law have been robust, and the study occasionally refers to the important European copyright-related directives and their impact on copyright laws of European Union Member States.

The statutory scheme of U.S. copyright law frequently provides the basis for illustrating specific provisions and developments in the positive law. European and U.S. laws furnish the main positive, legislative, and comparative reference points for the discussion. Provisions of the German copyright law offer an additional perspective in two main contexts. First, premised on authors' rights philosophy and tradition, German law provides a comparative contrast to the U.S. "copyright" system. Second, references to amendments to German law serve to illustrate the transposition of European regulation into domestic law.

The study refers predominantly to academic literature from the United States (and other English-speaking countries), as well as European publications in the English language. To supplement the analysis, publications in the German language are cited and discussed. The copyright laws of other countries are mentioned sporadically in specific, narrower contexts. Citation to Internet pages relies on their content as of July 2009.

B. Terminology

The study develops and applies a unique set of terms and concepts. The key terms receive specific definitions as they are first introduced, particularly in the first part. For example, the terms *access-right, rights-of-access, access-conducts, communication-conducts, human-access,* and *technological-access* have a concrete meaning, and each receives a designated definition. This terminology is applied systematically as the discussion proceeds to the second and third parts.[12] Persons holding exclusive rights under copyright are generally referred to as *rights-holders.* Those who do not have exclusive rights in works are generally referred to as *nonowners.* Within the former group, when the distinction between human author and derivative rights-holders is irrelevant, the term *rights-holders* covers both.

Usage of the terms *copyright* or *copyright law* hereinafter is usually insensitive to the distinction between copyright and droit d'auteur systems (unless the distinction is relevant in the specific context, in which case it shall be expressly underscored). The study further refers to copyright's *exclusive rights* mostly without attending to the distinctions between exclusive rights pertaining to works of authorship, exclusive neighboring rights, and exclusive rights attached to other copyright subject matter. When the difference is relevant, it shall receive a focused treatment. Finally, *traditional* copyrights (or the *traditional copyright system*) stand for the core common structure of exclusive rights as stipulated in key international instruments such as the Berne Convention (1971) and the domestic laws of its members until the beginning of the 1990s.[13] In comparison, the notion of *digital copyright* generally describes relatively recent changes in the law that maintain a direct relationship to various efforts and attempts to adjust the traditional copyright system to the digital reality.

---

12. Most of these terms also have a generic meaning. To distinguish between generic terms (such as *access right*) and those defined in this study (e.g., *access-right*), the latter concepts, when composed of more than one word, are often hyphenated.

13. The traditional structure of copyright law also includes core exceptions and limitations to the traditional exclusive rights that are not specifically related to digital technology and the Internet.

IV. THE THESIS

The thesis of this study advances two interrelated propositions. The first proposition posits recent developments in digital copyright law have been altering the nature of copyright by making it an instrument that underlies direct access control. At the basis of this claim is the descriptive observation that the positive law has been undergoing a process of metamorphosis in which copyright entitlements has been changing their character.

The dynamics of transition stem from fundamental changes in the infrastructure of communication systems, and by extension, the haphazard legislative reactions to technological advancements. These reactions, though intended to deal with a new reality, in fact preserve the traditional system: they basically rest on top of centuries-old concepts and rules that are poorly equipped to regulate digital markets and the digital information environment. More than being the result of studied deliberations and strategic policy choices, piecemeal amendments, gap-fillings, and ad hoc expansions of the traditional exclusive rights resulted in the incoherent, overcomplicated, and overprotective copyright regime of today. Thereby, the legislative responses to the challenges posed often failed to present an improvement over the maladies they want to cure.

One consequence of those turbulences has been the creation of de facto entitlements to control individual access to copyrighted works and the lack of appropriate mechanisms to offset the application and impact of such rights, which connects to the second proposition. This (normative) proposition suggests the shift toward access-based regulation is perhaps inevitable by virtue of the technology to which it applies, and in any event, is not objectionable on its face. To be sure, the failure of the traditional legal system to deal with digital challenges is *structural and fatal*, which forces us to rethink the system and evaluate new approaches, one of which is the access-right approach. It shall be contended the deeper reasons for the copyright crisis are indeed rooted in the inherent disparity between the law and the reality subject to its rules. This mismatch between policy goals and legal tools makes achieving the policy goals of copyright increasingly unrealistic.

The prescriptive proposition of this book is that a fundamental change in the legal system is needed, which should incorporate a careful access-based regulative approach as the organizing principle of that change. Perhaps tailoring copyright entitlements around the concept of access indeed could mark the route out of the digital copyright crisis, and at the heart of the prescriptive part is a proposal that outlines such a model. The model examines and applies a strategy of stipulating direct access entitlements both as part of copyright's exclusivity apparatus and of delineating users' legal positions. Defining and allocating formal access entitlements per se as the core modus operandi of digital copyright law and policy will appear a workable, attractive, and future-oriented alternative to the present system.

PART 1

INFORMATION, PROPERTY, ACCESS

1. INFORMATION

I. INTRODUCTORY REMARKS

The study begins with an extended examination of information as a concept. This chapter attempts to define and then refine the notion of information in the context of intellectual property, specifically copyright law. The *ontological* aspect of the discussion does not extend to examining the conditions for the existence of information in the very abstract.[1] Instead, the focus is primarily on the nature and characteristics of information in relation to its interaction with law. Within this framework, situating *information* at the center of the inquiry calls for several preliminary clarifications.

It is common to say that intellectual property law[2] protects information.[3] Put slightly differently, intellectual property protects certain *persons* by supporting

---

1. The following introduction distinguishes between two emphasis points of ontological inquiries:

> As a first approximation, ontology is the study of what there is. [P]roblems in ontology. . . deal with whether or not a certain thing, or more broadly entity, exists. But ontology is usually also taken to encompass problems about the most general features and relations of the entities which do exist. . . . For example the problem how a universal relates to a particular that has it (assuming there are universals and particulars) . . . These kinds of problems quickly turn into metaphysics more generally, which is the philosophical discipline that encompasses ontology as one of its parts. The borders here are a little fussy. But we have at least two parts to the overall philosophical project of ontology: first, say what there is, what exists, what the stuff is reality is made out off [sic], secondly, say what the most general features and relations of these things are.

See Thomas Hofweber, *Logic and Ontology*, *in* STANFORD ENCYCLOPEDIA OF PHILOSOPHY (Edward N. Zalta ed., 2008) (emphasis added). The second set of problems is at focus here. Assuming information "exists," the analysis takes a closer look at the conditions under which it becomes observable, meaningful, and relevant in the universe of property law.

2. The term *intellectual property* hereinafter covers copyright, patent, and trademark laws, as well as other legal disciplines that secure property-like entitlements in intangible subject matter.

3. *See* Thomas Hoeren, *Access Right as a Postmodern Symbol of Copyright Deconstruction?*, *in* ADJUNCTS AND ALTERNATIVES TO COPYRIGHT 348–63 (Jane C. Ginsburg & June M. Besek eds., 2002) ("Copyright protects information, indeed, it is even the Magna Carta of the information law"); Landes and Posner described intellectual property law as protecting "ideas, inventions, discoveries, symbols, images, expressive works . . . or in short any potentially valuable human product (broadly, 'information')." *See* WILLIAM A. LANDES & RICHARD M. POSNER, ECONOMIC STRUCTURE OF INTELLECTUAL PROPERTY LAW 1 (2003). While discussing the political economy of property and commons, Benkler defined

their private claims asserted *against other persons* in disputes concerning information subject matter. The basic distinction between intellectual property and property in tangible resources provides that entitlements secured under real property rights are independent of entitlements in intangibles. The rights to a hardcover book are separate from the rights to the expression it contains. Therefore, being *tangible* or *intangible* predicts the applicable property regime with respect to the resource in question.[4] Indeed, copyright subject matter is per definition intangible as derived from the basic distinction between ownership in works and ownership in the tangible objects embodying them.[5] At the same time, describing copyright law as applying to intangibles and to information is not exactly the same thing. Information is commonly considered as something intangible, but would it be equally plausible to argue that all intangible things are information? Is there a perfect overlap between intangible artifacts that might receive property-like protections on the one hand, and information on the other? If not, what is the relationship between things such as copyrighted works and information? The answers will largely depend on the concept of information one chooses to follow. Either way, it appears intangibility is an *attribute* of information, but not its *essence*. Information is perhaps antonymous to physical objects or spaces in some contexts, but this alone falls short of explaining its notion and distinctive power.

The lack of clarity in this area has not deterred legal scholarship from assuming a profound linkage between information and intellectual property (IP) subject matter. At the same time, information law experts are distinctly hesitant when it comes to drawing definitional boundaries around information.[6]

---

information "colloquially" as "raw data, scientific reports of the output of scientific discovery, news, and factual reports." *See* YOCHAI BENKLER, THE WEALTH OF NETWORKS 313 (2006). This is a good example of the way IP scholars usually refer to "information," namely, as the negation of authorship or originality. *See, e.g.*, Jane C. Ginsburg, *Copyright Protection of Works of Information*, 90 COLUM. L. REV. 1865, 1866 (1990). The discussion in this chapter, however, does not assume that copyright subject-matter definition explains (by negation, if you will) what information is—or what it is not. Quite to the contrary, the notion of information provides the basis for explaining some fundamental aspects of copyright subject matter.

4. *Cf* LIONEL BENTLEY & BRAD SHERMAN, INTELLECTUAL PROPERTY LAW 5 (2004) (referring generally to intellectual property as "intangible property").

5. *See* 17 U.S.C. 202 ("Ownership of a copyright, or of any of the exclusive rights under a copyright, is distinct from ownership of any material object in which the work is embodied.").

6. *See, e.g.*, RAYMOND T. NIMMER, INFORMATION LAW § 1:8 (2007) ("We deal here with a major, transformative phenomenon. We do not need to capture the Genie into a single, confined bottle in order to discuss its consequences in our lives and in the life of the law."); THOMAS HOEREN, INTERNETRECHT SKRIPTUM (2007) §1.1.1 ("Niemand weiß, was Information ist.") *See also* Robert A. Heverly, *Information Semicommons*, 18 BERKELEY TECH. L.J. 1147 (Fall 2003) ("The literature on intellectual property and property rights in

Obviously, it is not only jurists who find this inquiry perplexing,[7] yet this conceptual vacuum is particularly disturbing in the context of IP law to the extent the law assumes (without explaining) the central role information plays in the scenarios to which property rules apply. From a legal-practical standpoint, tinkering with the notional outlines of information might seem unnecessary, as the positive law provides readily available *legal* definitions to the relevant intangible subject matter (for instance, to inventions[8] or works of authorship).[9] As shown below, however, those legal definitions (and specifically copyright law's definition of *works*) are rather open-ended and give only a vague idea of the things they cover. Also after one reads and studies them, the nature of IP subject matter *as information* or as something that *relates to information* remains malleable. Hence, the conceptualization of property subject matter as information could benefit from discussions that are not necessarily legal and not tied to law. Some extralegal sources (primarily information and communication theories) can supplement and corroborate the heuristic understanding of copyright subject matter as information or as a related concept.[10] The broader interdisciplinary perspective this chapter draws on will demonstrate that works (as well as other IP subject matter) are implicitly derived from a more general notion of information.

II. THEORETICAL APPROACHES TO CONCEPTUAL ANALYSIS OF INFORMATION

A. General Classifications

Information is an intricate and multifaceted notion. Outside law, it is subject to various analytical frameworks. To illustrate, Rautenberg summarized several alternatives, conceiving information as (1) a message, (2) the meaning of a message, (3) the effect of the message, (4) a process, (5) knowledge, or (6) an entity

---

information bypass this question [the meaning of 'information'] entirely, even when it is apparent that the notion of information—broad or narrow—could have a distinct effect on the analysis undertaken and the conclusions reached.") (citation omitted).

7. *See* Klaus Krippendorff, *Information Theory*, *in* Communication and Behavior 352 (Gerhard J. Hanneman & William A. McEwen eds., 1975) (noting that information is sometimes considered a "nonanalyzable" quality).

8. *See* 35 U.S.C. § 101 (defining *inventions patentable*).

9. *See* 17 U.S.C. § 102(a) (defining copyrightable subject matter under the Copyright Act).

10. The discussion will invoke several extralegal theories, albeit without elaborating in length on their disciplinary origin and background. It is beyond the scope of this chapter to canvass all the relevant philosophical, social, and communicational critiques that surround the mentioned approaches in the fields in which they were developed. The choice to focus on certain perspectives on information is not arbitrary, however, but part of an effort to achieve a plausible conceptual framework for the present discussion.

in the world.[11] This list is obviously not exhaustive, and treatments of the notion of information vary according to the context of the discussion and discipline to which it is relevant.

At the meta level, analytical approaches to information may be classified in several ways. One classification distinguishes between *static* and *dynamic* analysis. Consideration of information as *content* or as a *mental condition* is reflected in static approaches, whereas information as a cognitive alternation or as a process can be described as dynamic.[12] It is further possible to distinguish between *qualitative* and *quantitative* approaches. Quantitative approaches often address questions concerning the existence of information and related matter by applying objective methods. The influential theory associated with Claude Shannon is a good example of this type of analysis in which information is perceived as an abstract quantity (i.e., the amount of information represented by a given situation or system is derived from probabilities and the degree of freedom to select between alternative symbols or messages).[13] In a similar vein, the amount of information is sometimes said to correspond to the level of *entropy* (or disorder) in a given system.[14] By comparison, qualitative approaches often focus on the relationships between information and subjects, for instance, the communicative qualities of information, meaning, and impact on receivers.[15]

It is important to note these classifications are not necessarily dichotomous as a given treatment of information-related questions may incorporate a number of perspectives (for instance, qualitative and quantitative aspects of the problem). Further, investigating information at the *micro* level (i.e., focusing on a single communication sequence) may inform the *macro* analysis of information as a grand process. The discussion that follows indeed considers some of these aspects in the course of its main quest—namely, articulating a concept of information that is useful for addressing the topics of this study. The model is sensitive to the

---

11. *See* Matthias Rauterberg, *About a Framework for Information and Information Processing of Learning Systems*, *in* INFORMATION SYSTEM CONCEPTS 55 (Eckhard D. Falkenberg & Wolfgang Hesse, eds., 1995). Rautenberg mentioned this list in the context of his learning systems analysis.

12. *Cf.* JEAN M. DRUEY, INFORMATION ALS GEGENSTAND DES RECHTES 3–6 (1995).

13. *See* CLAUDE E. SHANNON & WARREN WEAVER, MATHEMATICAL THEORY OF COMMUNICATION 8–9 (1963) ("[T]his word information in communication theory relates not so much to what you *do* say, as to what you *could* say") (italicization in original). *See also* Krippendorff, *supra* note 7, at 352.

14. SHANNON & WEAVER, *supra* note 13, at 12–13 (explaining the relationship between entropy (the level of disorder in a system) and information as measuring the freedom to choose between alternatives, signified by the probability of selecting a certain message out of a finite set of possibilities).

15. *See* ROBERT L. HEATH & JENNINGS BRYANT, HUMAN COMMUNICATION THEORY 118–20 (2d ed. 2000) (reviewing theories that focus on the impact of the message on receivers).

classifications and distinctions mentioned, but as the same time, it will not follow a single approach or perspective.

B. The Distinction Between Information and Knowledge

Before this framework is introduced, it is helpful to draw an important distinction between *information* and *knowledge*. Colloquially, knowledge is regarded as something morally positive (in the sense that it is good to have it), as something that people seek, and as something that can be subject to a deliberate pursuit. We acquire knowledge through experiencing and experimenting as well as by observing and learning from others. In addition, we assume a relationship between knowledge and truth or accuracy: knowledge must be *true* in order to be considered as such.[16] Yet it is harder to say the same thing about information, which can be false without its falsity negating its being information, including in the legal context.[17] According to some approaches, knowledge is something that reduces subjective uncertainty so that the knowledge acquired by the subject can be "measured" by comparing the degrees of subjective uncertainty at different times.[18] This way of looking at knowledge implies that subjective uncertainty reflects the lack of knowledge, or at least, that knowledge is something *capable of reducing* subjective uncertainty.[19]

Both intuitions about knowledge—the one that connects it to truth and the one that connects it to uncertainty—receive some support from the epistemological angle. Epistemology (the philosophical discipline that studies the nature, origin, and scope of knowledge)[20] tries to answer one basic question: under which conditions does a subject *know* something to be the case?[21] Within this framework, knowledge must meet a series of formal criteria to be considered

---

16. There is a hidden supposition here concerning agreed-upon tests for evaluating the truth-value of a certain claim or a fact, which, philosophically, is a strong assumption indeed.

17. The phrase "false information" is in common use. Some laws even criminalize the act of giving false information in certain situations. A legal database search for the term *false information* yielded approximately 140 results in the U.S. Code alone. *See also* DRUEY, *supra* note 12, at 11 (information is information also when it is uncertain, incomplete, vague, indecisive, or even untrue).

18. Krippendorff, *supra* note 7, at 358–361; *see also* Guy JUMARIE, RELATIVE INFORMATION 46 (1990).

19. *Cf.* Krippendorf, *supra* note 7, at 356. One interesting aspect of this view is that when the recipient's uncertainty concerning a certain matter does not exist, a message about that matter cannot add any knowledge; in other words, the informational value of the message is zero.

20. For an introduction, see Keith DeRose, *What Is Epistemology?: A Brief Introduction to the Topic* (2005) (available at http://pantheon.yale.edu/%7Ekd47/What-Is-Epistemology.htm); Peter D. Klein, *Epistemology*, *in* the ENCYCLOPEDIA OF PHILOSOPHY (E. Craig ed., 2005).

21. DeRose, *supra* note 20.

as such. The classic framework requires three cumulative conditions regarding a given statement be met: it must be true, it must be believed to be true, and that belief must be justified. In short, knowledge is (at least)[22] a justified true belief. Methods and research disciplines that seek to establish knowledge about the world (e.g., in the various fields of science) operate under certain epistemological assumptions relating to these conditions.[23] Among other things, epistemological assumptions imply a notion of truth, and perhaps even more importantly, accepted methods of evaluating justifications for believing that something is true.

Interestingly, some IP fields mirror certain relationships between legal protection and considerations such as truth or accuracy. In trademark law, for instance, the truthfulness of information conveyed by the mark might affect its eligibility for legal protection.[24] In patent law, patentability hinges sometimes among other things on whether the invention *works* in the sense that it must satisfy certain conditions in the physical reality.[25] According to the doctrine of industrial application, it is sometimes required that the invention be operable in the physical world and have a useful purpose.[26] The notions of usefulness and utility similarly imply the invention should faithfully describe a predictable procedure leading to a certain result that is subject to objective verification or rebuttal.[27] In contrast to trademark and patent laws (which are sometimes described as the main branches of *industrial property*), copyright subject matter demonstrates

22. The long-standing postulation that a justified true belief sufficed to constitute knowledge had prevailed since its articulation by Plato until Edmund Gettier published his famous article showing there are situations in which beliefs that are both true and justified are insufficient to constitute knowledge. *See* Edmund L. Gettier, *Is Justified True Belief Knowledge?*, 23 Analysis 121–23 (1963).

23. *See* Alex Rosenberg, Philosophy of Science 106–32 (2005).

24. In trademark law, legal protection has a strong nexus to the informational impact of the mark. *Cf.* Bentley & Sherman, *supra* note 4, at 700–01. Inaccurate or deceptive information that symbols or words convey might disqualify then for trademarks. In the United States, for example, marks that fall under the category of *deceptive* and *deceptively misdescriptive* generally do not qualify for trademark registration. *See* 15 U.S.C. § 1052(a) (absolute registration bar of deceptive marks); 15 U.S.C. § 1052 (e)(1) (a conditional bar on marks that are "merely deceptively misdescriptive"). German trademark law (MarkenG.) imposes an absolute registration bar on marks that might mislead the public regarding, inter alia, their characteristics and geographical origin. *See* § 8(4) MarkenG. For application of the doctrine in the United Kingdom, see Bentley & Sherman at 843–44.

25. The issues discussed by the U.S. Supreme Court in the *Bilski* decision relate in some way to possible limitation on patentable subject matter in conection with the so called "machine-or-transformation test. *See Bilski v. Kappos*, No. 08-964, 130 S.Ct. 3218 (2010).

26. *See* Bentley & Sherman, *supra* note 4, at 385–88 (reviewing the doctrine of industrial application and usefulness in patent law).

27. *Cf.* Mills et al., Patent Law Fundamentals §§ 11:2, 11:3–11:4 (2008) (reviewing utility, usefulness, and operability requirements under U.S. law).

much weaker ties to questions of truth, accuracy, reliability, validity, and the like. The content of a work does not have to subscribe to such or comparable parameters in order to be protected, and subscription to the objective reality does not increase the likelihood of legal protection. In fact, perhaps the opposite is correct: to the extent that an expression merely describes facts, news of the day, processes, or methods, the likelihood of copyright protection would normally decrease (for more discussion, see Sec. V.A.1(c)).

This raises some doubts about the descriptive and explanatory force of knowledge and formal epistemology when it comes to the conceptualization of IP subject matter at a high level of abstraction. Upon second reflection, the framework appears both under- and over-inclusive at the same time. The case of copyright shows why formal conditions to knowledge might turn *under-inclusive*, as epistemology is concerned with *propositional* statements, such as those stating "the water is cold" or "the bridge is safe." The nature of the inquiry is restricted to evaluating a proposition that such-and-such is the case.[28] It is difficult to force expressions that describe emotions, unfold fantasies, or reflect aesthetic tastes into those rubrics. In parallel, the reason formal knowledge criteria might prove in some cases *over-inclusive* connects to the conception of information as a process (this will be explained immediately below). At this point, it suffices to say the concept of knowledge does not mandate communication. Knowledge can be confined to a single subject, such as a Robinson Crusoe who acquires it about his surroundings in isolation from the element of communicating this knowledge to others (until Friday appears). However, the approach introduced below will consider communication as an essential aspect of the notion from which IP subject matter (such as copyrighted works) is derived.

III. INFORMATION AS A PROCESS

A. Introduction to Information As-a-Process

Information has many definitions.[29] To state the obvious, the English etymology of the term *information* cannot provide the basis for a conceptual analysis. However, the English etymology and common definitions do provide useful clues. Consider the English etymology of the noun *information* that suggests a derivation from the action of *informing* in the meaning of shaping (giving *form*)

---

28. *See* Matthias Steup, *The Analysis of Knowledge*, *in* Stanford Encyclopedia of Philosophy (Edward N. Zalta, ed., 2005) ("The concept to be analyzed . . . is commonly expressed using the schema '*S* knows that *p*', where '*S*' refers to the knowing subject, and '*p*' to the proposition that is known. A proposed analysis consists of a statement of the following form: *S* knows that *p* if and only if [certain conditions are fulfilled] . . .").

29. *See, e.g.*, Oxford English Dictionary (2d ed. 1989) (entry for *information*).

to the mind.[30] This is important for emphasizing the assumption of a human subject and for stressing that information is relevant inasmuch as it has an *impact on the human mind.* Can the fact a tree falls deep in the forest—without there being any witnesses, and with this fact remaining outside the sphere of all things of which people are aware—still be called information? Perhaps, but in the present context, it is utterly irrelevant. Facts and phenomena in the objective reality that never penetrate human consciousness are insignificant as regards the problems with which IP deals. Human subjects keep information "alive" in their minds, thoughts, and actions. The notion of "dead information" might explain this proposition further, and for the present purpose the following description seems to hit the mark:

> Information. . . is an intrinsic quality of the material and spiritual reality. . . The organization of the objective reality is transmitted to the subject, and transformed into subjective reality, through perception. . . In this object-subject dialectic, there are two kind[s] of information []: the potential information, which is a "dead" information contained in an object or book; and (2) the actual information, which is "alive" in the person who receives the object or who read the book.[31]

Intellectual property is about information that is alive in this sense of the term, and the human subject is indispensable to it. The information-as-a-process approach assumes a human subject as a necessary (but insufficient) condition to information. This dynamic view of information further reflects continuation and development on the time axis.[32] A common dictionary definition of information represents the same idea: information can be defined as "knowledge communicated concerning some particular fact, subject or event."[33] The "knowledge" component here is a subjective-cognitive condition. The wording "fact, subject or event" are the things to which the subject refers, and the element of *communication* is an essential component to the very notion of information.

B. Micro and Macro Perspectives

In line with these basic recognitions, information can be analyzed at both the micro and macro levels. Micro-level analysis focuses on the smallest, most basic

---

30. *Id.*

31. *See* Nagrib Callaos & Belkis de Callaos, *Definition of Education and Meta-Design of Educational Systems, in* Comprehensive Systems Design: A New Educational Technology 129 (Charles M. Reigeluth et al. eds., 1993).

32. *Id.* ("[I]nformation is a temporal phenomena [sic]; it is dynamic, it changes, it is a flow between receiver and receptor.").

33. Oxford English Dictionary, *supra* note 29 (entry for *information I.3.a*). The Webster's New Collegiate Dictionary (9th ed. 1990) similarly defined information as "the communication or reception of knowledge or intelligence."

communication event, in which a message travels from an originator to a recipient. A macro-analysis studies changes, motions, trends, and currents in the information environment. On that level, information dynamism is characterized by numerous instances of origination, transfer, and reception, as well as their cumulative effect. The focus is on large-scale trends and shifts in the information environment over time. Information as a process implies that early sequences might influence later ones in constantly changing settings of informational exchange. The pre-Socratic Greek philosopher Heraclites is associated with the principle that one cannot step into the same river twice.[34] In a similar vein, every moment in the information process is both different from (and possibly influenced by) an earlier moment.

The model below depicts the single sequence of communication and explains its elements. This is a linear presentation of the sequence that clarifies its basic concepts. The micro-level analysis will support the subsequent discussion on broader questions such as the interface between information and law, as well as the operation of copyright regulation. The relationship between the sequence (micro-level) and the information process (macro-level) can be analogized to the relationship between the basic biological unit—the cell—and the complex organism, which is composed of numerous unique cells that share a common genetic pattern.[35] Studying the operation of the basic unit will later provide clues about the complex structure such units can build.

IV. THE MODEL

A. The Linear Representation

Shannon's classic model, reprinted in Figure 1.1, offers a good illustration of a linear depiction of the single communication sequence. This specific representation contemplates several basic components (such as source, transmitter, receiver, and destination) as well as elements called message, signal, channel, and noise:[36]

34. *See* Daniel W. Graham, *Heraclitus, in* Stanford Encyclopedia of Philosophy (Edward N. Zalta ed., 2007).

35. Dawkins famously analogized information units (which he called *meme*) to the evolution of culture and biological genetic processes. *See* Richard Dawkins, The Selfish Gene 189–201 (1989).

36. Shannon first introduced this model in a paper published in the *Bell Systems Technical Journal* in 1948. *See* Claude Shannon, *A Mathematical Theory of Communication*, Bell Sys. Tech. J. (1948). *See also* Shannon & Weaver, *supra* note 13, at 33–35.

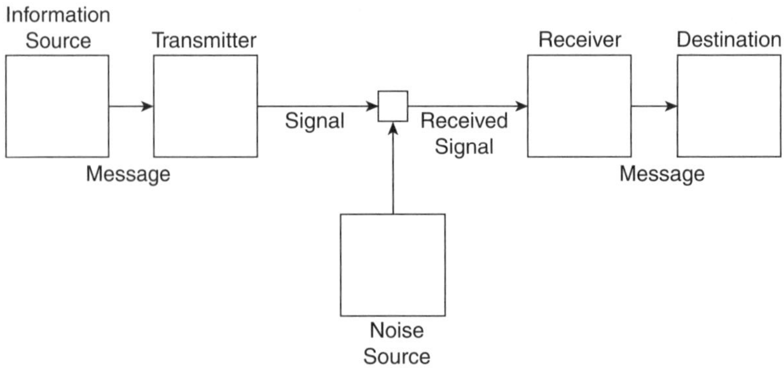

FIGURE 1.1 SHANNON'S CLASSIC MODEL[37]

Other models may differ on the details and terminology in their attempts to describe essentially the same basic sequence. For instance, David Berlo's S-M-C-R model highlighted four main components: Source, Message, Channel. and Receiver.[38] Figure 1.2 below is a development of these models. It applies a unique terminology to accompany the analysis and application that will follow, which is specifically designed to address the questions discussed in this chapter.

It is helpful to think about this linear illustration as a "snapshot" from the information process at a given place and time. For simplification, it ignores for the moment the time dimension and the position of the sequence in relation to other earlier or later sequences. The linear model assumes all relevant operations within a single sequence happen simultaneously, although in reality this is not exactly the case. The sequence has three elementary components: Originator, Message, and Recipient. Both the Originator and the Recipient are human subjects between whom the Message travels.[39] The Message is the objective manifestation of the subjective will to communicate. In turn, the Message qualifies as a *Medial* Message once certain criteria are satisfied, namely the perceptibility and comprehensibility criteria. The zone between the Originator and the Recipient constitutes and contains all the objects and elements that serve to

---

37. Shannon, *supra* note 36. From The Mathematical Theory of Communication. Copyright 1949, 1998 by the Board of Trustee of the University of Illinois. Used with permission of the author and the University of Illinois Press.

38. David Berlo, The Process of Communication 32 (1960). Inter alia, Berlo also mentioned additional components: *encoder* and *decoder*.

39. It is sometimes said that messages are being "transferred" in the course of the sequence, yet "transfer" in this context does not mean that something *leaves* the originator. It only means that something is being passed to the recipient. *Cf.* Colin Cherry, On Human Communication 30 (1978) ("We do not 'send' messages; we always share them. Messages are not goods or commodities, which can be exchanged or sent from one person to another.").

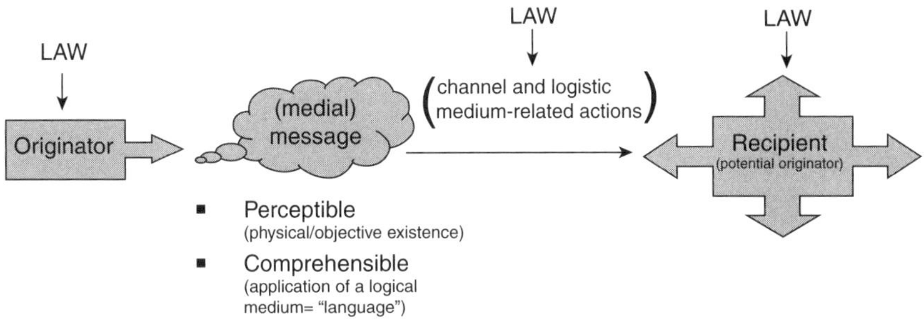

FIGURE 1.2 THE BASIC COMMUNICATION SEQUENCE

mediate between the origination act and the reception act. The model further points to the three main junctions where legal rules might affect the sequence.

The following passages will systematically unpack this rather compact presentation. Yet at this stage it is already possible to identify a key assumption of the model that directly relates to the legal subject matter question: there is a basic distinction between *information* and Messages. Information is a major, broader, dynamic process within which Messages play a key role. This reflects on the subject matter question this way: the intangible artifacts with respect to which the law allocates rights and duties are Messages, not information in the abstract. Obviously, the two are intimately related, though it seems that drawing this distinction may contribute to developing a relatively detailed framework for precisely the "thing" around which exclusive rights are tailored, all within the broader picture of the information process.

B. Originator

The Originator is a human subject who "contains" a cognitive charge (a thought, feeling, state of mind, etc). She is driven by the will to externalize this subjective state, and for this purpose, the Originator launches the sequence by creating objectively detectible signals.[40] This means there are causal relations, first between the subjective will to communicate and communicative action, and second between the communicative action and the existence of the Message. The "volition" attributed to the Originator calls for some explanation: the will to

40. Some existing models use the terms *sender* or *source* to describe a similar function, though they might operate under different assumptions and serve different purposes. In Shannon's model, for instance, the *information source* and the *transmitter* are depicted in two separate boxes. *See* SHANNON & WEAVER, *supra* note 13, at 16–17 (the transmitter receives the message and turns it into an encoded signal.) This separation of tasks relates to Shannon's main focus of telegraph communication. In the present model, it is assumed the originator may fulfill multiple tasks (including the initial creation, encoding, and transmission of signals) with or without the involvement of logistic media.

communicate is crucial both as a reason and as a circumstance that underlies the origination act. The assumption is the driving force behind the Message creation is the individual will, as distinguished from theories that also consider unintentional (or non-volitional) behavior as communicative in the broad sense.[41] This does not mean to challenge the proposition that unintentional behavior also may divulge subjective conditions and thereby "communicate" information to the observer. But for the present purpose, it seems possible to somewhat narrow the communicative act's concept to requiring at least a minimum degree of awareness to the communicative dimension of one's behavior. However, the narrowing effect of this condition is relatively small, as the requirement is weak in the sense it has nothing to do with the way Originators expect others to interpret their communicative behavior. It is only important that Originators be *aware* of the fact others might perceive their acts as communicative and as inviting interpretation. This very awareness to the communicative dimension of one's behavior is likely to affect it and make a Message out of it.[42]

C. Recipient

The Recipient is a human subject situated at the other end of the sequence who absorbs the Message signals through the sensorial systems with which she is equipped. Those signals stimulate various physiological detectors, which (in a process called sensory transduction) are translated into electric pulses that rush through the nervous network to the processing areas in the brain.[43] It should be noted the *existence* of a Recipient simultaneously with origination is an assumption linear models often make. Yet it is not mandatory for qualifying the communicative act as such; it is only necessary the Originator intended someone would receive the signals at a certain point. In this model, both Originators and Recipients are *functions*, not specific individuals, and the person who will *actually* occupy the role of Recipient does not necessarily have to be identified at the moment the Message is created. For this reason, it is also possible the same person will occupy both functions at different points in time with respect to the same communication act (for instance, a writer who keeps her scripts locked in a private drawer without the intention of showing them to anyone as she writes).

---

41. Unintentional, nonverbal cues and gestures can sometimes be considered forms of communication. *See* Heath & Bryant, *supra* note 15, at 47, 52 (discussing theoretical approaches to the question of purpose/intent, and concluding "[t]he key to understanding communication is not found in trying to determine what is intentional or willed, but in acknowledging that the process continues without end. Each conversation builds on previous ones.").

42. Objectively, the same external act (say, nodding one's head) can be either communicative or not. The important question is whether the act has been a result of a choice to share a subjective condition with other persons.

43. *See* E. Bruce Goldstein, Sensation and Perception 1–28 (2002) (providing an introduction to human perception).

The writer may be the Originator while writing the Message (that is intended to be kept private) and a Recipient as she reads it. This does not conflict with the communicative nature of writing, whereas the identity of the Recipient and the circumstances of reception can be ascertained as reception actually takes place.

What then characterizes the reception of signals as it happens? The distinction between low-level sensation and higher-level perception is used sometimes to illustrate two dimensions in the operation and study of human perception. The first (called the *physiological dimension*) focuses on the operation of biological systems and reaction to external stimuli. The second (called the *psychophysical dimension*) relates to the perceptual experience resulting from the processing of sensorial information in the brain.[44] The important point to remember is the complex procedure of perception involves *filtering* and *processing* at various stages and levels. Filtering already begins as a procedure of selecting specific external signals from all the detectible stimuli projected at subjects from the environment, at the center of which is the mechanism called *attention*.[45] At the physiological level, signal processing occurs as neurons "communicate" with one another while transmitting electrochemical pulses across the nervous system.[46] Perception research emphasizes that we do not perceive "the world" as it is; instead, our idea about the external environment is shaped (and limited) by our processing capabilities.[47] In addition to filtering at the signals level, cognitive processing is starkly influenced by the mode in which we experience the environment and the sense we make out of external stimuli.[48] In this respect, higher-level perception that involves cognitive processes attributes special importance to subjective, Recipient-sensitive parameters such as memory, experience, attitudes, and expectations. The ultimate experience of comprehension felt by Recipients is a function of higher-level perception and communication-relevant factors that affect interpretation such as context, relationships, and background.

---

44. *See* Jeremy M. Wolfe et al., Sensation and Perception 6 (2006) (explaining this distinction, but noting it is not always clear-cut). *See also id.* at 8–9.

45. *See* Roy Lachman et al., Cognitive Psychology 183–208 (1979); Wolfe et al., *supra* note 44 (describing attention as a family of selection mechanisms that can pick one out of many stimuli in space); Rauterberg, *supra* note 11, at 57–59 (reviewing theory studies on attention concerning the visual system).

46. Goldstein, *supra* note 43, at 5 (neural processing means operations that change the electrical response of neurons in various ways.) The important insight is that pulses running through a chain of neurons do not remain stable or uniform along the way. The intensiveness of neural firing depends on the activity of neurotransmitters that might inhibit (or rather excite) it.

47. *Id.* at 36.

48. *See generally* Lachman et al., *supra* note 45, at 210–56. For example, in perceiving and recognizing objects, mid-level vision is a *cognitive* stage of interpretation, through which line and colors turn into the experience of seeing a table or an elephant. Wolfe et al., *supra* note 44, at 75–97.

D. Media and the Role of the Channel

Communication—which, in itself, is subject to multiple definitions[49]—is central to the idea of information.[50] This element underscores the key role of media: all the things that mediate between the event of Message creation and the event of its reception for the purpose of facilitating communication between subjects can qualify as media. Next, it is possible to distinguish between logical and logistic media as follows:

1. Logical Media

Logical media is a term referring to encoding methods (or "languages"). It is a general name for the *intangible architecture of communication*. The Originator's choice of which logical media to apply is crucial and is often influenced by various practical and aesthetic parameters such as the type of Message, target audience, artistic considerations, efficiency, and desire to influence people or leave an impact (i.e., to be heard/noticed). The choices involved shed light on the motivation for Message creation, the intention behind it, the purpose of communication, its contemplated Recipients, and so on.

2. Logistic Media

By contrast, *logistic media* refers to the physical conditions surrounding the transfer that enable a passage of signals. When communication theories speak of the *channel* of communication, they often refer to the physical architecture of communication such as objects, devices networks, and physical infrastructure that connect between subjects.[51] The distinction between direct and indirect communication clarifies the nature and operation of various logistic media in different constellations. The difference lies in the role logistic media play in the communication sequence. Direct communication is more intimately interpersonal: the

---

49. Weaver defined *communication* broadly as "all of the procedures by which one mind may affect another." *See* Shannon & Weaver, *supra* note 13, at 3. Communication in general may be regarded as "interaction in all contexts." *See* Heath & Bryant, *supra* note 15, at 89. *Cf.* Cherry, *supra* note 39, at 3–4 ("Communication is essentially a social affair. Man has evolved a host of different systems of communication which render his social life possible, social life . . . in a sense unknown to animals."). Druey suggested viewing communication as intentional with respect to the Originator, personal with respect to the Recipient, and relational with respect to both. *See* Druey, *supra* note 12, at 148.

50. *See* Heath & Bryant, *supra* note 15, at 132 ("Information exchange can be viewed as the basic communication paradigm, that is, people seeking, giving, or exchanging information to reduce uncertainty.") Indeed, we often refer to communication as a process of conveying or exchanging information. For instance, Wikipedia's definition describes *communication* as "the process of conveying information from a sender to a receiver with the use of a medium in which the communicated information is understood by both sender and receiver. It is a process that allows organisms to exchange information by several methods" (available at http://en.wikipedia.org/wiki/Communication).

51. The word *channel* can stand for any means by which a message is sent by a source or obtained by a receiver. Heath & Bryant, *supra* note 15, at 53.

Message signals travel either by physical touching or through natural substances such as air or light. Direct communication has a sense of immediacy to it, as the Message signals do not endure long after their creation, and as the events of origination and reception occur almost simultaneously. By contrast, indirect communication involves physical equipment and objects that "bring" the signals to the Recipient. Depending on the applied technology, Message signals arrive at various speeds and last for a period of time after their initial production.[52] Therefore, the ability to receive the Message is not strictly confined to time and place of origination. Logistic media help to bridge between distant locations and overcome physiological limitations of human perception.[53] The physical architecture of communication facilitates informational exchange in situations where reception would otherwise be unlikely, inefficient, inaccurate, difficult, expensive, or plainly impossible.

3. Multifunctional Media

Multifunctional media combine both patterns of operation with the term standing for technologies that combine logistic and logical functions. A prominent example is digital technology and devices that perform logical functions of translation, interpretation, and signals transmission to multiple remote Recipients. A personal computer is a multifunctional device that can store signals on memory components, detect and emit digital signals, encode sounds and images into binary code, and translate digitized Messages back to sound and images. Multifunctional digital media can detect, receive, transmit, carry, process, manipulate, convert, and translate binary elements of Messages expressed in digital code and bring them to Recipients in a perceptible form. Digital technology has been revolutionizing not only the ways in which human communication operates and societal processes involved, but also those in which law may interfere with the information process.

E. Medial Message

1. Levels of Analysis

Before elaborating on the Message component, it is useful to mention the following taxonomy concerning various levels of communication and Message analysis: The *syntactical* (level A) concerns the accuracy of transmitted symbols from a rather technical viewpoint; the *semantic* (level B) concerns the question how precisely symbols can convey the meaning the Originator has in mind; and the *effectiveness/pragmatic* (level C) concerns questions of impact on Recipients.[54]

---

52. A logistic medium may be a movable object that contains Message signals in a stable manner (for instance, a newspaper carrying ink-printed letters and images on paper sheets). Such logistic media function simply as a container for the signals.

53. For example, a radio set is capable of detecting electromagnetic radiation passing through the air, which it then transforms into audio signals detectable by the human ear.

54. *See* SHANNON & WEAVER, *supra* note 13, at 4–5. Shannon's model focused on level A communication, though Weaver speculated the quantitative methodology perhaps bore some (inverse) relationship to meaning: "One has the vague feeling that information [in

In accordance with this taxonomy, theoretical treatments to the message concept vary according to the respective analytical agenda pursued. The following discussion will focus primarily on semantic and pragmatic aspects of Message creation and the possible nexus between them.

2. Formal and Material Criteria

Figure 1.2 indicates a Medial Message must meet both the perceptibility and comprehensibility criteria:

(a) Perceptibility

The criterion of perceptibility is quite straightforward: in order to furnish a basis for communication, the Message signals must be made perceptible to potential Recipients. A Medial Message is always represented through objectively detectable elements (signs, symbols, shapes, figures, movements, notes, tones, colors, etc.) that manifest the will to communicate. The subjective state of the Originator receives an objective representation via the signals, making the Message discoverable. It follows that quantitative parameters are salient for the question of perceptibility. The focus is on the intensity and physical nature of signals and on whether Recipients *can notice* those signals.[55] Perception research in this context estimates the limits of the human perceptual systems via quantitative methods and empirical studies.[56] It is true the perception of signals might as well be influenced by subjective parameters such as attention, search, and even attitudes.[57] As regards the perceptibility criterion, however, subjective aspects are largely disregarded, with the yardstick being set according to *average* perception faculties.

(b) Comprehensibility

Whereas perceptibility tests whether detectable signals are objectively "there," comprehensibility inquires whether the signals may convey meaning.

---

the quantitative sense] and meaning may prove to be something like a pair of canonically conjugate variables in quantum theory, they being subject to some joint restriction that condemns a person to the sacrifice of the one as he insists on having much of the other." *Id.* at 28.

55. Perception research suggests recipients having identical biological capacities would not necessarily notice environmental stimuli in the same way. *See* GOLDSTEIN, *supra note* 43, at 130–34 (discussing the relationships among attention, the visual system, and attention's effect on neural responding). For the present purpose it should suffice to consider average threshold values as determining perceptibility of external stimuli.

56. A branch in perceptions research seeks to discover the *threshold values* of our biological mechanisms by determining empirically the weakest signals, or the smallest change, humans can detect. *See* WOLFE ET AL., *supra* note 44, at 11–17.

57. For example, psychologists argue that "attitudes and beliefs can influence every step of the information-processing sequence, including attention, encoding, comprehension, interpretation elaboration, and memory." *See* James M. Olson & Mark P. Zanna, *Attitudes and Attitude Change*, ANNUAL REV. PSYCHOLOGY 44, 129 (1993).

The comprehensibility standard is based on several important assumptions; (1) meaning as intended by Originators (Meaning O) and meaning as interpreted by Recipients (Meaning R) may diverge, (2) this fact alone cannot lead to the conclusion the Message is not comprehensible, (3) Originators must always use encoding methods (i.e., logical media) to externalize their subjective state, (4) the nexus between intended and derived meaning depends on a preexisting understanding concerning basic elements and structure of the logical media; (5) comprehensibility hinges on the question of whether the Originator used a coding system, with respect to which intended or potential Recipients could be reasonably expected to have skills and preexisting knowledge to decode. The ensuing discussion will explain and examine these assumptions more closely.

The comprehensibility requirement in fact encapsulates two main propositions: First, the Originator must compose the Message by using a preexisting method or system of encoding. Second, the origination act is done within a certain social, cultural, historical, and communicational setting that furnishes the essential background for communicative behavior.[58] Living in a culture and creating Messages within and from within a certain social-discursive context is premised on general understandings concerning modes of self-expression, the usage of coding systems, and the manner in which we can reasonably expect Recipients to approach the task of interpretation. The first comprehensibility proposition focuses on the system used by the Originator to encode the message. Coding translates thoughts via signals and symbols into something observers can process and grasp.[59] As such, coding is omnipresent—it underlies all conceivable sorts of communication.

The second proposition underscores the relational dimension of Message creation: social conventions and collective knowledge provide indications and instructions on how Originators are likely to *encrypt* their Messages in various communication contexts. In turn, the same background conditions provide guidance concerning the manner in which Messages are to be *decrypted*. It follows that neither decoding nor encoding is completely arbitrary or uniquely esoteric as semiotic relations between notions or ideas and the symbols representing them (as well as rules of *syntax* and *grammar*) guide both types of endeavors.

---

58. The background to the creation of the Message is, to a large extent, the culture from which it emerges. Culture is a fairly open term. Benkler suggested that "[e]ven the simplest intuitive conception of what culture might mean would treat this common frame of meaning as the result of social processes that preexist any individual, and partially structure what it is that individuals bring to the table as they negotiate their lives together, in society or in a polity. Inhabiting a culture is a precondition to any interpretation of what is at stake in any communicative exchange among individuals." *See* BENKLER, *supra* note 3, at 279.

59. *Cf.* CHERRY, *supra* note 39, at 74 ("The writer or speaker does not communicate his *thoughts* to us; he communicates a representation for carrying out this function, under the severe discipline of using only the materials he has, sound and gesture.").

Emitting a random cacophony of signals that are not arranged in any recognizable pattern and which do not fit within existing communicative templates of expression can hardly qualify as a Medial Message. The reason is the likelihood of any nexus, even a faint one, between Meaning O and Meaning R is very slight, so it is difficult to speak of "communication" in the first place. Originators cannot utterly ignore conventions of expression and at the same time still hope to be "understood" in a way that would relate in some way to the mind-set they wished to externalize.

To be sure, this *comprehensibility* criterion leaves significant margins for interpretation about meaning/s. The assumption of preexisting conventions on how to approach Messages in a given communicative setting does not mean Message O must be identical (or even similar) to Message M (though a close match between the two would indicate a high *quality* of communication in some contexts).[60] According to this permissive comprehensibility standard, it is possible to imagine a situation in which the Recipient correctly deciphers the signals but gets the meaning completely wrong (i.e., not as the Originator intended). Gaps between Meaning O and Meaning R are common misunderstandings that in and of themselves principally do not negate the existence of communication. Rather, the Message is comprehensible in terms of the model so long as Recipients can be reasonably expected to interpret it in a manner that yields meaning, and to the extent the interpretation demonstrates some nexus to the mind-set that has motivated the origination act.

In summary, the comprehensibility standard calls for finding an ascertainable linkage between three elements: (1) Meaning O, (2) the logical medium chosen and the way it is applied for expressing the Originator's mind-set, and (3) the expected capability of Recipients to decode the signals in a manner that would identify a relationship between what the Originator wanted to express and the objective manifestation of that intention. This standard obviously allows gaps between Meaning O and Meaning R (i.e., *misunderstandings*), but it would preclude a radical disconnect: an attempt to communicate will not succeed if it cannot facilitate meaning that relates in some way to whatever the Originator wished to externalize.

3. Aspects of Comprehensibility

Indeed, the issue of meaning is central to the comprehensibility criterion. Meaning of symbols and expressive patterns invokes a series of complex issues, which are topics in disciplines such as communication theory, semiotics, linguistics, ethnology, and others.[61] However, consideration of all these aspects

60. *See* Owen Eriksson, *Communication Quality* (1999) (available at http://users.du.se/~oer/forskning/rapporter/er99arap.pdf) (noting information "quality" is high if the sender and interpreter reach a mutual understanding about something in the world).

61. The study of the relationships among signals, symbols, and expressions and their meaning is rich, complex and interdisciplinary. *See*, e.g., CHERRY, *supra* note 39, at 111–23.

is far beyond the scope of the present discussion. Instead, to supplement the notion of the Message and the role comprehensibility plays, the following passages will mention some of the problems that thematically relate to the focus of this chapter.

One difficulty concerns the dominance of qualitative aspects in the study of meaning, which, as compared to objective-quantitative parameters such as threshold values, are very difficult to pin down. There are various facets to qualitative evaluation of Message perception, one of which is the possibility of a syntactical difference between the signals the Originator had created and those that in fact "came across" to the Recipient. An important dimension of this potential gap is the problem of "noise" and its impact on the communication sequence.

(a) The Element of "Noise" and Message Interpretation

Modulations of the sequence sometimes refer specifically to "noise" (e.g., Shannon's model in Figure 1.1 above). *Noise* can be defined as signals that were neither created by the Originator nor meant to play any role in the interpretation process. Noise in this sense includes all environmental signals and circumstances of Message reception that have nothing to do with the manner in which Originators expect Recipients to interpret the Message signals.[62] This definition implies the environment and circumstances of reception might have two contradictory effects on the interpretation process: they might *obscure* or *contribute* to reaching the meaning Originators wanted to convey. For one, environmental signals or circumstances the Originator himself did not create might play an important role in the interpretation of the Message *as intended by the Originator*. For another, noise might create a strong distortion that makes it impossible to identify a relationship between Meaning O and the range of Meanings R. It follows Recipients approaching the Message need to decide which signals/circumstances belong to the Message and which do not. A number of cognitive mechanisms (such as pattern recognition) help us to determine in various situations which elements "belong" to a given object or expressive pattern, and thereby, make sense of our external, stimuli-laden surrounding.[63] This notwithstanding,

---

See also HEATH & BRYANT, *supra* note 15, at 91–128 (surveying multiple communication theory approaches to the question of meaning).

62. Shannon's model focused on engineering and technical aspects of telecommunication (particularly telegraphy). In that context, noise is defined as certain distortions, errors, and extraneous material influencing the message signals as they travel through the channel. *See* SHANNON & WEAVER, *supra* note 13, at 18–19. Perception researchers sometimes use the term *noise* to similarly describe environmental signals that obscure the signal a receiver attempts to detect. *See* WOLFE ET AL., *supra* note 44, at 14–15.

63. Pattern recognition research is an important part of cognitive psychology that is "concerned with systems (man, animal, machine) that convert complex inputs (such as patterns of light and sounds) into recognizable and meaningful words, objects or events." *See* James F. Juola, *Pattern Recognition*, *in* COGNITIVE PSYCHOLOGY AND INFORMATION

it is still very difficult in various communication situations to consider meaning as an objective criterion to Message due to its strong subjective, Recipient-sensitive characteristics. The problem can be referred to as the objective/subjective divide of meaning.

(b) The Objective/Subjective Divide of Meaning

The meaning-making process involves a myriad of subjective and contextual variables such as the circumstances of reception, media, source, relationships, preexisting knowledge, experience, memory, and so on. As suggested above, the Originator and Recipient are both subjects, and the meanings they attribute to Messages inevitably have subjective sides as well. Indeed, according to some views, the meaning of messages is purely subjective, and any attempt to objectivise meaning would be pointless.[64] If this is true, it is hard to see how meaning can help in achieving any testable notion of a Medial Message. Consider, for instance, the view that a Message has meaning to the extent it is capable of reducing Recipients' subjective uncertainty. This implies meaning is determined according to the ability of the expression to answer open questions in the mind of the Recipient.[65] This understanding of meaning would make it very difficult (perhaps impossible) for a set of objective criteria to be forced upon it.[66]

PROCESSING: AN INTRODUCTION 493 (Roy Lachman et al. eds., 1979). Further, "[p]attern recognition is not a simple matter of matching sensory input with memories, because the neural signals arising from stimulation undergo many changes on their way from the senses to the brain." *Id.* Certain perception mechanisms help us to distinguish the relevant signals from other signals (e.g., to perceive an object by distinguishing it from its background). *See* WOLFE ET AL., *supra* note 44, at 84–85.

64. David Berlo, among others, advocated for a purely subjective approach to meaning, which flatly rejected the idea that meaning can receive an objective representation in messages: "[M]eanings are not in messages . . . meaning is not something which is discoverable . . . *meanings are in people* . . . Meanings are learned, we add to them, we distort them, forget them, change them. We cannot *find* them. They are in *us*, not in messages." BERLO, *supra* note 38, at 175 (emphasis in original).

65. Consider the following hypothetical: *A* tells *B*: "Today is a Sunday." *B* already knows that; *B* is not uncertain about which day of the week it is. Thus, *A*'s statement does not answer any open question. However, consider that *A* and *B* often go hiking on Sundays. *B* knows it is a Sunday, and *A* knows *B* knows it is a Sunday. *A*'s statement "Today is a Sunday" is an implied invitation to go hiking together. Although *A* and *B* *often* go hiking on Sundays, *B* is uncertain about *that specific Sunday* on the question of hiking. *A*'s statement could therefore reduce *B*'s uncertainty about *A*'s inclination on the matter. Of course, if *A* and *B* do not think about the same "question," then the message "Today is a Sunday" might not in fact reduce uncertainty, although it theoretically could.

66. The skeptic's critique would argue that, to the extent that any expression *could* "say" something to someone under certain circumstances, meaning is an empty shell, as it cannot concretize the Message concept at all. Imagine one expression delivered to three different subjects, X, Y, and Z. Recipient X attributes meaning A, Recipient Y attributes a different meaning B, and Recipient Z cannot read any meaning and all, so for him the

In an attempt to bridge the divide between the subjective and objective banks of meaning, some communication theoreticians speak of *zones of meaning* they define as "shared understanding or view of some phenomenon . . . These zones are shared meaning."[67] Such zones represent the collective recognitions and views that guide (or at least structure to some degree) the meaning-making process within social-cultural communities. This response to the purely subjective approach to meaning suggests first the *existence* of such zones of meaning, and consequently that some "unconventional" interpretations might fall outside the boundaries of those zones. The possible implication is that certain interpretations (Meanings R) would be considered *implausible* from a communication theory standpoint. This invokes the question of how the boundaries of such zones may be determined and which considerations should guide their delineation. In the specific context of the model, it seems possible to approach the problem of demarcating the zones of comprehensibility by shifting the focus to objective aspects of Message creation. At a minimum, it is worthwhile to examine whether the *extreme points* of comprehensibility could be objectively ascertained.

(c) The Extreme Points of Comprehensibility

The creation of Messages involves the application of an encoding system, or a "language" in the broad sense of the term. In using language, we translate thoughts and subjective cognitive conditions into objectively perceptible expressions. The role of language (or generally, logical media) in the sequence corresponds to its intuitive quality. In order to increase the likelihood a certain expression will carry meaning, the speaker applies a coding system, which, in turn, imposes *structural limitations* on her freedom to use and build symbols, words, and sentences. The number, type, and form of basic components (e.g., the letters of the alphabet), as well as the ways in which the speaker is "allowed" to arrange them to create complex expressions, are not infinite. These *rules of use* are prescribed by conventions prevalent within the community in which the logical system has developed and in which it is used in various communication situations. A communicative act that produces signals not arranged in any recognizable pattern that logical systems would prescribe under the circumstances and within the relevant social, communicational, and cultural setting is not likely to facilitate meaning.

Against this backdrop, consider the application of objective criteria for marking the extreme points of comprehensibility. Some quantitative methodologies refer to information as a measurement of the freedom to choose between potentially available options. The measured quantity maintains a correlative relation to the level of uncertainty concerning the actual choices to be made in creating the expression. In other words, the viewing of information as a quantity considers it

---

expression is utterly meaningless. In such circumstances, do we have *a* Medial Message, *several* Medial Messages, or *none* at all?

67. Heath & Bryant, *supra* note 15, at 129.

as the Originator's level of freedom of choice calculated according to statistical parameters.[68] Accordingly, an expression that is entirely predictable (i.e., with the maximum probability of 1) will deliver zero information. As the degree of uncertainty increases, the expression is said to contain a correlatively increasing amount of information.[69] However, real-life situations where the expression to be delivered is 100 percent predictable are quite rare. The opposite extreme case in which the signals convey zero information is much more interesting for the present discussion, although it often represents a purely theoretical situation. Here, the randomness reflected in the choices involved in the creation of the expression is so great that (from both semantic and pragmatic perspectives) the expression loses its ability to carry *any meaning whatsoever*. This does not mean to say that no Recipient would be able to read into random signals or completely unorganized patterns any meaning at all. Rather, the technique of composing the expression would drive most (if not all) conceivable interpretations beyond the "zone of meaning," and in any event, it would be hard to imagine any relationship between the thought triggering the expression and whatever Recipients can fathom after confronting it.

(d) Meaning, Value, and Relevance

The discussion thus far has suggested it is perhaps possible to identify the objective boundaries to meaning by scrutinizing the way in which speakers apply the most obvious instrument of self-expression: the "language." Extremely unlikely patterns—whether in light of the type of thought the speaker had in mind, the type of language chosen to express it, or the communication conventions in the relevant discursive setting—might render the Message objectively meaningless. The discussion below attempts to supplement the notion of a Medial Message by establishing criteria that are more pragmatic in nature. The basic idea is that in parallel to quantitative benchmarks communicative *value* and *relevance* may also help to develop the comprehensibility aspect.

Consider, for example, the assertion a Medial Message must always be valuable in the sense someone would be willing to invest the resources necessary for its reception. A brief look at reality perception offers an interesting starting point for exploring this argument. Value plays an important role within our perception mechanisms at various levels. To begin with, the processing capacity of our physiological and cognitive systems is limited.[70] Thus, under these limitations,

---

68. *See* John R. Pierce, An Introduction to Information Theory 23–24 (1980); Krippendorf, *supra* note 7, at 358–59.

69. Pierce, *supra* note 68, at 23 ("The amount of information conveyed by the message increases as the amount of uncertainty as to what message actually will be produced becomes greater.").

70. Wolfe et al., *supra* note 44, at 195–203 (reviewing the phenomenon of *change blindness* and experimental evidence to the claim we can attend only to one object, or perhaps only to a very few objects, at one moment).

we process and interpret fewer signals among all the detectable signals the environment projects at us. We apply various mechanisms of selection and filtering that assist us in identifying and focusing on the *important* signals.[71] With natural selection principles in mind, it would appear most important to process those signals crucial for survival in the ecological environment in which we live. Those who possess the skills to channels their limited perceptual resources first and foremost to the important signals are more *fit* (in Darwinian terms) than those who do not have such skills.[72]

Beyond such fundamental matter as survival, selection and filtering play a central role in many other contexts as well. It is reasonable to assume potential Recipients would prefer to allocate their limited perception resources to the processing of certain stimuli while ignoring others. To the extent Recipients can consciously control the allocation of perceptual resources (which, admittedly, is not always the case), it is reasonable to expect them to focus on things they consider important or *relevant*. Relevant Messages, according to these terms, are expressions that Recipients *at a minimum* would not mind absorbing.[73] Relevance can range between this minimum level of being indifferent to knowing the Message and *wanting* to receive it. Pragmatically speaking, Messages that do not pass the minimum bar are of little interest to property law as they are very unlikely to be at the center of legal disputes.[74] Further, describing Messages as

---

71. *Id.* at 177–79.

72. Interestingly, Charles Darwin described his initial use of the term *natural selection* as intended "to mark its relation to man's power of selection." According to this meaning, it might appear to be referring to the human being's power to make choices. However, Darwin accepted that the (now common) meaning used by Herbert Spencer as the "Survival of the Fittest is more accurate, and is sometimes equally convenient." Charles Darwin, The Origin of Species 75 (Signet 2003) (1859).

73. The problem known as Arrow's information paradox can receive only footnote reference here. In connection with his economic analysis of the patent system, Arrow wrote in 1959 "there is a fundamental paradox in the determination of demand for information; its value for the purchaser is not known until he has the information, but then he has in effect acquired it without cost." *See* Kenneth J. Arrow, *Economic Welfare and the Allocation of Resources for Invention* at 12 (1959) Reproduced by the RAND Corporation, California. This is perhaps one of the most difficult problems involved in applying economic analysis to information goods. The paradox is universally applicable and equally troubling concerning ex ante valuation of informational input, and in this context, for making an *informed* decision about devoting necessary reception resources. How can Recipients make rational decisions on whether to incur the costs of reception before knowing the Message, or at least something about the Message? For the purpose of the current presentation, it is assumed for simplification that actual reception indicates a willingness to invest the necessary resources.

74. Philosophers traditionally assume that in the lack of scarcity, the problems concerning the nature of and the justification for property would turn largely irrelevant. *See* Jeremy Waldron, The Right to Private Property 31–32 (1988). Scarcity is a situation

valuable brings to mind economic connotations. The debate on treating information as an economic commodity or good[75] in different contexts is well documented (the discussion on analogizing information to a public good is left to Chapter 2).[76] Messages—like other goods—indeed can have value, whether it be "value in use" or "value in exchange."[77] The modest value requirement here merely suggests a Medial Message is something for which reception is preferable to the Recipient as a matter of utility (broadly conceived)[78] as compared to not receiving it.

What are the implications of saying that Medial Messages must be relevant or valuable? Relevance and value are attributes that mirror one another to a significant degree: messages are viewed as valuable to the Recipients who consider them relevant, but as valueless if they lack any relevance at all. Further, disputes over utility benefits that emanate from value might require the law to provide solutions to the allocation of these benefits.

---

in which the resource is both desired and available in limited quantities. This situation is likely to create competition and bring about conflicts. Clearly, limited availability will not result in conflicts in the absence of demand. Even under the assumption that information is not "scarce" in the same way as apples or land–after all, take away demand for information and the allocation problems legal rights are designed to solve will become insignificant.

75. An economic "good" is generally defined as "an object or service of which consumer would choose to have more." *See* Murray Milgate, *Goods and Commodities, in* 2 The New Palgrave: A Dictionary of Economics 546 (John Eatwell et al. eds., 1987) (citing Harry Johnson's theorem on value theory). Another definition describes goods as "objects or things which confer some advantage or produce some desirable effect upon their owners." *Id.*

76. Many observers warn against this trend, advocating for caution regarding the prevalence of information commodification tendencies. *See* Margaret Jane Radin, *Incomplete Commodification in the Computerized World, in* The Commodification of Information (Neil Netanel & Niva Elkin-Koren eds., 2002) (criticizing the "market rhetoric" of information). Radin defines market rhetoric as "the practice of describing things in terms of market and reasoning about them as one reasons about the functioning of a market." *Id.* at 4. *See also* Dan Schiller, How to Think about Information (2007).

77. *See* Adam Smith, The Wealth of Nations 131 (Penguin Books 1970) (1776). (According to Smith, "value in use" means the utility of some particular object, whereas "value in exchange" represents the power of purchasing other goods which the possession of that object conveys.) He famously stated "[l]abour. . .is the only universal, as well as the only accurate measure of value." *Id.* 139–40.

78. Welfare economics provides a rather generous definition of *utility*, meaning everything that has an impact on human well-being, broadly defined. *See* Louis Kaplow & Stephen M. Shavell, *Fairness versus Welfare*, 114 Harv. L. Rev. 961, 980 (2001) ("The notion of well-being used in welfare economics is comprehensive in nature. It incorporates in a positive way everything that an individual might value—goods and services that the individual can consume, social and environmental amenities, personally held notions of fulfillment, sympathetic feelings for others, and so forth.").

It should be noted the *source* of value associated with a given Message might vary. The important distinction here is between value that directly relates to the communicative dimension of the Message and value that does not. The former is value arising due to the capacity of Messages to carry *meanings*, whereas the former shows no direct relationship to the communication sequence. Accordingly, a popular novel is valuable because of its expressive power and that people want to read it, but it could also be valuable as a source for technical or statistical analysis and indexing that helps search engines to improve their operations and sell context-sensitive advertisements more effectively.[79] In other words, the objective manifestation of the Message can be used for purposes that have little to do with its communicative aspects and its role in the sequence. In accord with this distinction, any saying the Message must be valuable concerns only communication-related utility advantages as distinguished from other types of value. A proposition that emanates from this distinction (and which cannot be explored here in length) is that exploiting purely non-communicative value of Messages or elements of Messages cannot infringe on certain intellectual property rights attached to the Message (for example, copyrights), as the relevant IP rights are not structured to secure such value exclusively to rights-holders.

V. APPLICATION OF THE MODEL TO COPYRIGHT LAW

The three main propositions made thus far can be summarized as follows: (1) It is plausible to view information as a process; (2) the analysis of its basic unit (i.e., the communication sequence) enables extrapolation of the concept of the Medial Message; and (3) this concept underlies in general terms what we often consider as IP subject matter, specifically as to copyrighted works. Application to copyright law begins with adapting the model presented in Figure 1.2 above. Accordingly, Figure 1.3 translates it into the corresponding terms with which copyright law is more familiar:

79. An example are the provisions in the settlement agreement between Google Inc. and those holding rights in books Google uses for its Google Book Project, which confer upon certain beneficiaries the rights to make use of texts unrelated to consuming the content of those books (in terms of the Agreement, to perform "Non-Consumptive Research"). *See* Amended Settlement Agreement (2009) sec. 7(2)(d) (Research Corpus). The Agreement defines Non-Consumptive Research as "research in which computational analysis is performed on one or more Books, but not research in which a researcher reads or displays substantial portions of a Book to understand the intellectual content presented within the Book." *Id.* sec. 1.93.

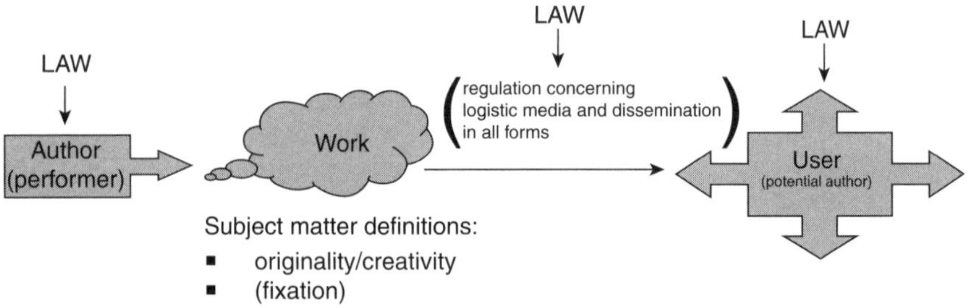

FIGURE 1.3 THE INFORMATION MODEL APPLIED TO COPYRIGHT LAW

The discussion now turns to evaluation of some descriptive and normative aspects of this application along the margins of two basic themes in copyright law, namely the inception of rights in works and violations of the exclusive rights the law attaches to them.

A. Acquisition of Copyrights

1. Work as Message

The present application of the model to copyright law proposes that copyrighted works meet the framework requirements of a Medial Message. To begin with, copyright doctrine is in agreement with the assumptions of the model concerning the origin of works as products of the human mind.[80] Obviously, works must be perceptible to receive legal protection, which is mirrored in domestic statutory fixation requirements or serves as a common sense prerequisite.[81] The comprehensibility requirement seems to be implicit in the concept of work as a logical baseline for various copyrightability rules.[82] The analysis will demonstrate

80. In German copyright law, the "work" concept is derived from its attribute as an imprint of its author's personality. Specific aspects of copyrightability (e.g., the personal creation requirement, the mental content, and the individuality parameters) somewhat concretize the nature of protected works. *See* Ulrich Loewenheim in SCHRICKER URHEBERRECHT KOMMENTAR § 2 nr. 8–40 (2006). In U.S. law, originality encapsulates comparable requirements. *Cf.* MELVILLE B. NIMMER & DAVID NIMMER, 1 NIMMER ON COPYRIGHT §§ 2.01–2.01[A] (2006).

81. Fixation in a tangible medium of expression is a constitutive requirement under the U.S. Copyright Act. *See* 17 U.S.C. §§ 101, 102(a). Also in jurisdictions where copyright laws do not contain a formal fixation requirement, the work must be made perceptible. *See, e.g.*, Loewenheim, *supra* note 80, § 2 nr. 20–22 (work must be perceptible, meaning that it must be made accessible via the human senses ("*Wahrnehmbare Formgestaltung*")). *Cf.* EUGEN ULMER, URHEBER–UND VERLAGSRECHT 13 (1980) ("Der Rechtsschutz setzt aber voraus, daß das Werk in äussere Erscheinung tritt, und die Gebote und Verbote des Rechtes beziehen sich auf Akte, die sinnlich wahrgenommen werden können.").

82. Random, senseless signals that do not demonstrate any expressive pattern are unlikely to pass qualitative thresholds of originality or personal human creativity. Similar

how the Medial Message concept can describe and explain copyright subject matter beyond the common legal definitions and doctrines of copyrightability. The distinction between the expression and the tangible object in which it is embodied[83] essentially exemplifies the model's distinction between the Message and the logical media carrying its signals. Next, the law typically distinguishes copyrighted expressions from other things in four ways that can be described as (1) *general* work categories, (2) *specific* work categories, (3) *negative* categories of expressive elements, and (4) *threshold standards.* The following pages will discuss these four definitional aspects of work and the way in which the model might supplement them.

(a) General Categories: "Literary and Artistic Works"

International and domestic legal instruments often name general categories to describe copyrightable subject matter. These phrases roughly describe the domains of expressions that likely fall within the ambit of copyright protection. For instance, Article 1 of the Berne Convention for the Protection of Literary and Artistic Works provides that copyright protects "literary and artistic works."[84] Variations in national laws refer to "works of authorship"[85] or "works of literature, science and art."[86] To what extent does this help in distinguishing between copyrightable and non-copyrightable expressions? The answer ostensibly depends on the availability of definitions to things such as literature and art. Consider the Berne Convention's clarification stating "[t]he expression 'literary and artistic works' shall include every production in the literary, scientific and artistic domain."[87] This is not very illuminative[88] as it cannot sharpen much further

---

issues are analyzed in German law, inter alia, as the question of minimal degree of formation ("*Gestaltungshöhe*") a work must reflect in order to enjoy copyright protection. *Cf.* Loewenheim, *supra* note 80, § 2 nr. 25.

83. *See* Nimmer & Nimmer, *supra* note 80, at § 2.03[C] (the phrase "original work of authorship" should not be confused with the material objects in which it is fixed).

84. Berne Convention (1971) Art. 1 ("The countries to which this Convention applies constitute a Union for the protection of the rights of authors in their *literary and artistic works*") (emphasis added).

85. *See* 17 U.S.C. § 102(a).

86. *See* Art. § 2(1) UrhG.

87. *See* Berne Convention (1971) Art. 2(1).

88. The words *production* and *domain* have triggered some limited interpretational efforts. *See* Stephen P. Ladas, The International Protection of Literary and Artistic Property § 92 (1938) (referring to the term *production* in Art. 2(1) as implying an element of creation, and therefore, originality); Sam Ricketson & Jane C. Ginsburg, International Copyright and Neighboring Rights: The Berne Convention and Beyond § 8.03 (2006). Then again, this language adds little to the intended content of the qualifiers *literary* or *artistic.*

the rough approximation art and literature already offered.[89] Thus, commentators tend to view the phrases "literary" and "artistic" as having a *permissive* (rather than a limitative) character.[90]

General categories sometimes appear in national statutes as well; for example, the German Copyright Act of 1965 adopted the Berne language almost verbatim.[91] Also at this level of domestic law, the contribution of general categories (such as "artistic" expressions) is quite limited.[92] The problems involved in defining art or literature as contrasting expressions that cannot be considered as such obviously cross disciplinary and jurisdictional borders.[93] In Germany, for instance, the freedom of art is explicitly secured under the federal constitution, which has led courts to grapple with the possibility of legally defining art as part of their attempts to apply the relevant constitutional protections.[94] In many cases

---

89. The Berne Convention generally does not prescribe subject matter rules. Formulation of copyright rules is largely a matter of domestic laws. Protection under the Convention is based on the assumption that such rules exist in the various countries, and foreign rights-holders cannot invoke the Convention with respect to subject matter that the forum state considers noncopyrightable according to its standards.

90. *Cf.* Ricketson & Ginsburg, *supra* note 88, at § 8.06 (noting the term *scientific* in Art. 2(1) of the Berne Convention is largely superfluous, and that "'literary' and 'artistic' are themselves very vague.").

91. *See* § 1 UrhG. *See also* Loewenheim, *supra* note 80, at § 2 nr. 3.

92. *See* Loewenheim, *supra* note 80, at § 2 nr. 1–6 (definitions of art are too uncertain and subjective for the purpose of copyright law; general categories mark only the *approximate* contours of protected subject matter, with their operative function being mainly to distinguish copyright subject matter from technical productions that are typically the subject matter of patent law.) *See also* Christine Fuchs, Avantgarde und Erweiterter Kunstbegriff 50–55 (2000) (emphasizing the difficulty in uniformly defining art in light of the plurality and diversity of ways in which art can be perceived and develop over time). *Cf.* Alexander Peukert, Güterzuordnung als Rechtsprinzip 226–29 (2008) (general categories in German copyright law would still exclude things such as sports performances or scent of perfumes).

93. *See, e.g.*, Gordon Graham, Philosophy of the Arts: An Introduction to Aesthetics 149–58 (1997) (discussing philosophical attempts to define art.) The author suggested "it is better for the philosopher of art to explore the question of art's value than to try to arrive at a definition of art, and . . . that the best explanation of its value lies in explaining the ways in which it makes a contribution to human understanding." *Id.* at 2. This observation fits surprisingly well within the concept of "Message" and the role of value/relevance in it.

94. The freedom of art is expressly protected under Art. 5(3) to the German Constitution. The German Constitutional Court has made several attempts to define the concept of "art" in that context. *See, e.g.*, Mephisto, BVerfGRE 30, 173, 188–89 (Feb. 24, 1971) ("Der Lebensbereich 'Kunst' ist durch die vom Wesen der Kunst geprägten, ihr allein eigenen Strukturmerkmale zu bestimmen. Von ihnen hat die Auslegung des Kunstbegriffs der Verfassung auszugehen. Das Wesentliche der künstlerischen Tätigung ist die freie schöpferische Gestaltung, in der Eindrücke, Erfahrungen, Erlebnisse des Künstlers durch

judicial deliberations yield a *description* of art and artistic endeavors rather than setting legal standards for the concept of art. In the context of a copyrightability analysis, the inclination is to skip such questions and shift to criteria such as originality or creativity.[95]

(b) Specific Categories: Listing Classes of Works

Lists of work categories[96] set forth examples of literary and artistic expressions that are somewhat more specific than general categories, yet remain merely illustrative.[97] For instance, "pictorial, graphic, and sculptural works"[98] are commonly regarded as belonging to the artistic domain. At the same time, a finding that a given expression falls within a given category cannot conclude the copyrightability inquiry as it must in any case also pass the originality/creativity threshold. In fact, specific categories viewed through the lens of copyrightability analysis might turn out to be *over*-inclusive in some cases and *under*-inclusive in others. To illustrate, even if a certain composition qualifies as a "musical work"—a listed category—the lacking of originality will nonetheless deny protection.[99] In such case, the specific category "musical works" is over-inclusive, as not all musical compositions are automatically copyrightable. Also, expressions that cannot be mechanically pigeonholed as belonging to one category or another may still receive copyright protection, which means statutory lists might turn out to be under-inclusive.[100] For a concrete example, consider architectural

---

das Medium einer bestimmten Formensprache zu unmittelbarer Anschauung gebracht werden. Alle künstlerische Tätigkeit ist ein Ineinander von bewußten und unbewußten Vorgängen, die rational nicht aufzulösen sind. Beim künstlerischen Schaffen wirken Intuition, Phantasie und Kunstverstand zusammen; es ist primär nicht Mitteilung, sondern Ausdruck und zwar unmittelbarster Ausdruck der individuellen Persönlichkeit des Künstlers."); *Cf.* Anachronistischer Zug, BVerfGRE 67, 213, 224–26 (July 17, 1984) (the German Constitutional Court doubts whether art is definable in general terms).

95. For example, instead of asking whether a certain avant-garde work is copyrightable *because it is a work of art*, borderline cases such as Malevich's black square depicted against white background or trends in appropriation art are dealt with as problems of sufficient expressiveness. *Cf.* FUCHS, *supra* note 92, at 127–30.

96. *See* Berne Convention (1971) Art. 2(1); 17 U.S.C. § 102(a)(1)–(8); § 2(1)(1)–(7) UrhG.

97. RICKETSON & GINSBURG, *supra* note 88, at § 8.01 (concerning the categories listed in the Berne Convention); NIMMER & NIMMER, *supra* note 80, at § 2.03[A] (The notion of "works of authorship" in the U.S. Copyright Act is not limited to the eight categories listed in Sec. 102(a)); Loewenheim, *supra* note 80, at § 2 nr. 74 (same regarding the statutory catalog in the German copyright statute).

98. *See* 17 U.S.C. § 102(a)(5).

99. *See, e.g.*, NIMMER & NIMMER, *supra* note 80 at § 2.05[D] (discussing the originality requirement as applied to musical works under U.S. law).

100. Consider further the definition of *literary works* in the U.S. Copyright Act, which reads as follows: "'Literary works' are works, other than audiovisual works, expressed in words, numbers, or other verbal or numerical symbols or indicia, regardless of the nature

works,[101] a fairly recent category that was added to the U.S. statute as late as 1990.[102] The law defines architectural works as "the design of a building as embodied in any tangible medium of expression, including a building, architectural plans, or drawings. The work includes the overall form as well as the arrangement and composition of spaces and elements in the design, but does not include individual standard features."[103] This does not mean that any given design, drawing, etc. of a building is copyrightable—it simply means that it *might* be. A drawing of an architectural structure is not protected under copyright *only because* it falls under the respective definition, and it is not ab initio unprotectable if the law does not contain a corresponding definition in the first place.[104] The upshot is that specific work categories (like general categories) provide rough approximations that lack independent definitional force.[105]

(c) Negative Categories

Negative categories is a term used here to describe elements in expressions to which the law does not extend copyright protection. Some laws that articulate statutory lists of such non-protectable elements prominently reflect this

---

of the material objects, such as books, periodicals, manuscripts, phonorecords, film, tapes, disks, or cards, in which they are embodied." 17 U.S.C. § 101. More than explaining what a literary work *is*, this definition clarifies the distinction as to audiovisual works. It further describes *elements* that are typically used for the creation of "literary works." Similarly, in German law, art works (*Werke der bildenden Kunst*) is an undefined, catchall statutory category. *See* Loewenheim, *supra* note 80, at § 2 nr. 131–32. Conceptions of artistic works often refer to criteria such as the use of forms, or form and colors that stimulate aesthetic feelings. *Id.* § 2 nr. 134.

101. *See* 17 U.S.C. § 102(a)(8) (listing "architectural works" as protected subject matter).

102. *See* Architectural Works Copyright Protection Act (1990). This is the newest addition to the U.S. statutory catalog. *See* William Patry, 1 Patry on Copyright § 3:107 (2007) (describing the legislative history).

103. *See* 17 U.S.C. §101 (defining *architectural works*). The relevant legislative bill intended to explicitly ensure protection not only to architectural plans and drawings, but also to the built designs of structures. *See* Patry, *supra* note 102.

104. The German copyright statute does not explicitly mention architectural works as a specific category, yet buildings are principally covered as a subcategory of artistic works. *See* Loewenheim, *supra* note 80, at § 2 nr. 149–55.

105. Still, it has been argued specific categories may provide important guidance. *See* Patry, *supra* note 102, at § 3:60 (noting, with respect to statutorily defined categories, "[t]he definitions of protected subject matter in Section 101 have a significant effect on copyrightability and the scope of protection, since they statutorily set forth the nature of the subject matter covered, and thus how the constitutional and statutory requirement of originality can be satisfied").

strategy,[106] and the U.S. statute provides a good illustration of how the law might seek to negatively define copyright subject matter:

> In no case does copyright protection for an original work of authorship extend to any idea, procedure, process, system, method of operation, concept, principle, or discovery, regardless of the form in which it is described, explained, illustrated, or embodied in such work.[107]

Negative categories exclude elements of expressions that are rather technical, factual, or functional in nature.[108] Such elements are not (and cannot be considered) creative expressions for the purpose of copyright protection, and it is common to emphasize the role of negative categories in drawing a distinction between subject matter of copyright and patent law.[109] Section 102(b) of the U.S. Copyright Act further states this principle, according to which exclusive rights pertain to the "expression" but not to the underlying "idea" represented in that expression.[110]

The way in which these principles should apply is quite controversial. Three difficulties can be mentioned in brief: First, the notion of negative categories seems to be based on the premise that protected ("original") element and non-protectable ("negative") elements in a given expression are separable. The severability of the idea from expressive elements has long been considered as one of the most difficult riddles in copyright law.[111] Second, it is not always clear whether negative categories considerations are relevant for copyrightability analysis, or

---

106. *See, e.g.*, Sec. 5 of the Israel Copyright Act of 2007. Not all copyright systems stipulate negative categories statutorily. In German law, for instance, the noncopyrightability of methods and ideas is derived from general principles and case law. *See* Loewenheim, *supra* note 80, at § 2 nr. 48–52.

107. *See* 17 U.S.C. § 102(b).

108. *See* NIMMER & NIMMER, *supra* note 80, at § 2.03[E] (discussing the noncopyrightability of discoveries); Feist Publishing, Inc. v. Rural Tel. Service Co., 499 U.S. 340, 356–57 (1991) (U.S. Supreme Court held that facts are noncopyrightable); *see also* Pamela Samuelson, *Why Copyright Law Excludes Systems and Processes from the Scope of its Protection*, 85 TEX. L. REV. 1921 (2007) (discussing the exclusion of systems and processes from the scope of protection under U.S. law); Dan L. Burk, *Method and Madness*, 2007 UTAH L. REV. 587 (2007) (discussing the noncopyrightability of methods).

109. *See, e.g.*, PATRY, *supra* note 102, at § 4:42 (reviewing the *Baker v. Selden* decision and the balance between the copyright and patent systems).

110. *See* NIMMER & NIMMER, *supra* note 80, § 2.03[D].

111. Judge Story famously wrote that "[p]atents and copyrights approach, nearer than any other class of cases belonging to forensic discussions, to what may be called the metaphysics of the law, where the distinctions are, or at least may be, very subtile and refined, and, sometimes, almost evanescent." Folson v. Marsh, 9 F.Cas. 342, 344 Case No. 4,901, (C.C.D Mass. 1841).

rather, only as part of the courts' infringement analysis.[112] Third, it is unclear whether negative categories represent an *independent* strategy that defines copyright subject matter "by negation," or rather whether these provisions merge with threshold standards analysis such as originality. In other words, can we say that excluding ideas, facts, methods, etc. is simply the "flipside" of the originality requirement? None of these questions is easy to answer. Yet the notion of "negative" subject matter is a powerful analytical instrument, which, if construed as an independent bar on copyrightability, could greatly influence the scope of copyright protection, especially in the case of software and other highly functional expressions.[113]

(d) Threshold Standards: Originality, Individuality, Creativity

Threshold standards such as originality, creativity, or individuality are the most important and intriguing among all four strategies. The requirement of originality (and its equivalents in various copyright jurisdictions)[114] most distinctively is considered as marking the boundaries of copyright-protected subject matter.[115] Generally speaking, originality does not check for artistic qualities, novelty, or other merits of expressions,[116] yet the precise character and content of this requirement may vary across jurisdictions. Under U.S. law, the originality requirement traditionally has two dimensions: the first refers to the element of

---

112. Nimmer & Nimmer, *supra* note 80, § 2.03[D] (opining the distinction between expression and ideas "constitutes not so much a limitation on the copyrightability of works, as it is a measure of the degree of similarity that must exist between a copyrightable work and an unauthorized copy"). *Cf.* Lexmark Int'l, Inc. v. Static Control Components, Inc., 387 F.3d 522, 538–39 (6th Cir. 2004) (U.S. federal appellate court points out a circuit split on this question, and preferred to apply the idea/expression distinction at the copyrightability stage: "When a work itself constitutes merely an idea, process or method of operation, or when any discernible expression is inseparable from the idea itself, or when external factors dictate the form of expression, copyright protection does not extend to the work.") (citation omitted).

113. *Cf.* Samuelson, *supra* note 108, at 1961–73 (analyzing the application of negative categories in U.S. software cases).

114. German law requires a personal mental creation (*"persönliche geistige Schöpfungen"*) as its threshold standard for copyright protection. *See* § 2(2) UrhG.

115. *See, e.g.*, Feist Publishing, Inc. v. Rural Tel. Service Co., 499 U.S. 340, 345 (1991). ("The *sine qua non* of copyright is originality.") The question of originality is also important for acquisition of rights in derivative works. In that context, the second author must add original elements to the earlier work in order to enjoy an independent copyright in the later work. *See* Patry, *supra* note 102, § 3:50.

116. *See* Nimmer & Nimmer, *supra* note 80, § 2.01[A]–[B]; Bleistein v. Donaldson Lithographing Co., 188 U.S. 239, 251, No. 117 (1903) ("[T]he [copyright] act, however construed, does not mean that ordinary posters are not good enough to be considered within its scope. The antithesis to 'illustrations or works connected with the fine arts' [a definition provided in the old U.S. copyright statute] is not works of little merit or of humble degree, or illustrations addressed to the less educated classes.").

origination, whereas the second is more closely associated with *creation*.[117] Origination is a factual inquiry, asking whether the author is the source of the work in the sense "the work owes its origin to the author."[118] It is crucial this origination act be *independent*, as opposed to one of copying from other sources.[119]

The second dimension of originality is *creativity*. It is helpful to think about creativity as a continuum as opposed to something subject to binary determination (i.e., it can either exist or not).[120] Metaphorically, each expression may be positioned on the creativity continuum, and its particular position on that continuum represents the respective degree of creativity. In this respect, copyright doctrines often apply *quantitative* terminology that gauges the plausibility of legal protection in connection with establishing a *modicum* of creativity.[121] The question is not whether a given expression is "creative" or "not-creative", but whether the expression passes an objective minimum bar of creativity.[122] In practice, this bar is notoriously low as it suffices that an expression exceeds banality and reflects at least a "spark" of creativity.[123] Sufficient creativity is reflected in an expression whose elements are arranged in a way that does not necessarily shock,

---

117. *See Feist*, 499 U.S. at 346 ("originality requires independent creation plus a modicum of creativity") (citing to a previous Supreme Court decision in The Trade-Mark Cases, 100 U.S. 82 (1879)).

118. *See* NIMMER & NIMMER, *supra* note 80, § 2.01[A]; *Feist*, 499 U.S. at 345 (citing Burrow-Giles Lithographic Co. v. Sarony, 111 U.S. 53 (1884)).

119. *See* PATRY, *supra* note 102, §§ 3:28–3:31 (discussing the requirement of independent creation).

120. *Cf. id.* § 4:36 (applying the notion of continuum to the distinction between protectable expression and nonprotectable ideas).

121. *See* NIMMER & NIMMER, *supra* note 80, § 2.01[B] (discussing the *quantum* of originality); PATRY, *supra* note 102, §§ 3:33–34 (explaining the creativity requirement and its rationale in U.S. law.) In German law, the doctrine of *kleine Münzen* applies to works having a low level of demonstrable creativity, which are nonetheless granted some copyright protection. *See* Loewenheim, *supra* note 80, § 2 nr. 38.

122. *See* PATRY, *supra* note 102, § 3:36 (creativity is an objective determination.) For a perspective of Canadian law, see CCH Canadian Ltd. v. Law Society of Upper Canada, 2004 SCC 13, Mar. 4, 2004 at ¶ 25 (the Canadian Supreme Court concluded that "an 'original' work under the Copyright Act is one that originates from an author and is not copied from another work. That alone, however, is not sufficient to find that something is original. In addition, an original work must be the product of an author's exercise of skill and judgment. The exercise of skill and judgment required to produce the work must not be so trivial that it could be characterized as a purely mechanical exercise. While creative works will by definition be 'original' and covered by copyright, creativity is not required to make a work 'original.'")

123. *See* Feist Publishing, Inc. v. Rural Tel. Service Co., 499 U.S. 340, 345 (1991) ("[T]he requisite level of creativity is extremely low; even a slight amount will suffice. The vast majority of works make the grade quite easily, as they possess some creative spark, 'no matter how crude, humble, or obvious' it might be") (quoting the Nimmer treatise).

but rather "touches" the audience.[124] Importantly, applying objective standards regarding the *quantum* of creativity does not yet indicate what exactly those standards measure. Possibly, creativity is a quantitative-objective standard that evaluates the *choices* made by the author, as authors (fulfilling the function of Originators) choose systems of communication (a logical medium or a "language") and make various choices while employing those systems to carry over their subjective condition. The less probable these choices are under the circumstances, the more likely it is the expression will reflect a high degree of creativity.

2. Application to Authorship and Copyrightability

Defining a *work of authorship* is no trivial matter. The law, perhaps intentionally, leaves this concept rather open. As applied to copyright law, the model depicts work as an externalization of a human subjective condition that receives manifestation in the objective reality. Communicative behavior renders this condition or thought perceptible and the object of cognitive interpretation by individual Recipients. The application further suggests an author is a special kind of Originator, whose legal status as the owner of property-like rights lies in the choices he performs in composing the Message. The discussion below develops these threads a little further, first by evaluating authorship under quantitative criteria, and next by applying such criteria to more specific originality questions.

(a) Author as Originator

In *Burrow-Giles*, the U.S. Supreme Court declared "[a]n author . . . is 'he to whom anything owes its origin; originator; maker.'"[125] In this sense, authors fulfill the function of Originators as the *actual source* (or origin) of the work.[126] Assuming that quantitative methodologies are constructive for identifying the extreme points of comprehensibility, application of the insights of the model would propose that creativity is a matter of degree, and further, that similar methodology may supplement the conventional copyrightability analysis. Consider creativity

---

124. *Cf.* Patry, *supra* note 102, § 3:27 ("The spark [of creativity] need not provide a shock, but it must at least be perceptible to the touch.").

125. *See* Burrow-Giles Lithographic Co. v. Sarony, 111 U.S. 53, 57–58 (1884) (constructing the term *Authors* as it appears in the U.S. Constitution), *quoted in Feist*, 499 U.S. at 346.

126. The doctrine of independent creation in copyright confirms this point. Two authors who, through rare coincidence, have created an identical work without knowing about each other's work are both holders of a valid copyright in the respective works. *See e.g.*, Sheldon *v.* Metro-Goldwyn Pictures Corp., 106 F. 2d 45, 54 (2d. Cir. 1939), *aff'd*, 309 U.S. 390 (1940) (in Judge Hand's words: "Borrowed the work must indeed not be, for a plagiarist is not himself pro tanto an 'author'; but if by some magic a man who had never known it were to compose anew Keats's Ode on a Grecian Urn, he would be an 'author,' and, if he copyrighted it, others might not copy that poem, though they might of course copy Keats's.") (citation omitted).

as a problem related in some way to the *quantity of information* represented in a given work. In this vein, consider further authorship as the generation of signals, whereby personal creativity is manifested in the choices made, and specifically, the degree of freedom to make expressive choices under the circumstances of the communicative act. As part of the creative process, authors make at least three kinds of choices: (1) symbols/signals, (2) a system of expression (the code/language), and (3) their preferred way of using symbols and languages to express a thought, idea, emotion etc.

Applying Shannon's information theory at this junction may add an interesting dimension to the conventional copyrightability analysis. According to this approach, information is a quantity represented by the letter *H*, which is a function of statistical probability of choosing a certain signal/symbol among available alternatives.[127] Shannon illustrated the concept of *H* in the following graph:

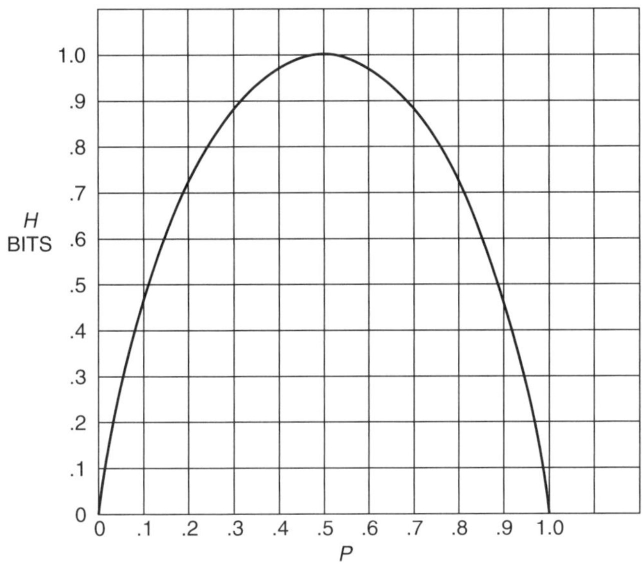

FIGURE 1.4 SHANNON'S CONCEPT OF H[128]

H is measured in units called *bits*, with one bit of information representing exactly 50 percent probability (*p*=.5) of a choice between two possible alternatives. This is an illustration of the simplest scenario in which the choice is

127. *See* SHANNON & WEAVER, *supra* note 13, at 14–16. When a finite number of independent alternative exists, the expression *H* represents the sum-total of their probabilities multiplied by the logarithm:

$$H = -\sum p_i \log p_i$$

128. Reprinted with permission from Shannon, *supra* note 36.

between two alternative symbols, say *a* and *b*. Each alternative has a certain statistical probability (*q*), denoted as *qa* and *qb*, respectively. *H* is a quantitative measurement of the information represented by choosing *a* or *b*. The value of *H* is maximal if *qa*=.5 and *qb*=.5. In that case, the quantity of information represented by choosing *a* or *b* equals one bit.[129] The value of *H* is minimal (zero) when *qa*=1 and *qb*=0 or vice versa. Under such conditions, the freedom to choose between the two alternatives is virtually nonexistent, and choosing *a* will not convey any information at all. In general, *H* can be computed if the relevant probabilities are known (e.g., in so-called stochastic processes).[130]

Copyright scholarship has largely overlooked the possible contribution of quantitative approaches of this sort to the copyrightability question, perhaps under the impression the connection between the fields is quite remote.[131] It is important to emphasize that invoking information theory here does not mean to suggest human creativity can be reduced to statistical calculations and mathematical expression. Notwithstanding, this peculiar perspective can be applied to the problem of creativity in connection with the central role authors occupy in the creative process.

Durham's attempt to apply information theory to copyright law is an interesting move in this direction.[132] He discussed in particular the possible contribution of information theory to analysis of authorship questions in the context of offering alternative models to the "romantic" authorship narrative.[133] He suggested authorship can be thought of as a process of selection between available alternatives, and that a relatively unlikely or unusual choice (i.e., one having only a low probability of taking place) could indicate a higher level of originality.[134]

---

129. *Id.* at 15. Applying this numerical example to the above equation:

$$H = -\left[\frac{1}{2}\cdot\log_2\frac{1}{2}+\frac{1}{2}\cdot\log_2\frac{1}{2}\right]=1$$

130. Weaver explained: "A system which produces a sequence of symbols (which may, of course, be letters or musical notes, say, rather than words,) according to certain probabilities is called a *stochastic process,* and the special case of a stochastic process in which the probabilities depend on the previous events, is called a *Markoff process* or a markoff chain." SHANNON & WEAVER, *supra* note 13, at 11 (italicization in original).

131. *Cf. id.* at 27 ("The concept of information developed in this theory at first seems disappointing and bizarre—disappointing because it has nothing to do with meaning, and bizarre because it deals not with a single message but rather with the statistical character of a whole ensemble of messages, bizarre also because in these statistical terms the two words *information* and *uncertainty* find themselves to be partners.") (emphasis in original).

132. Alan L. Durham, *Copyright and Information Theory: Toward an Alternative Model of "Authorship"*, 2004 BYU L. REV. (2004).

133. *Id.* at 111–23.

134. *Id.* 120–25. Durham was aware of the counterintuitive relationship between the amount of information in the technical sense (represented quantitatively by the concept

Durham's analysis underscores several important points. First, an author takes on a variety of specific functions that information theory handles in more general terms (e.g., source, channel, encoder, and transmitter).[135] Thereby, authors make a series of individual choices. Though authors usually do not create ex nihilo,[136] creating something out of nothing is not the decisive factor of creativity. Originality, individuality and creativity manifest themselves in authorial choices. The less such choices are dictated by the nature of the thought/idea and of the language (i.e., the coding system is less "redundant"),[137] the greater the likelihood becomes of sensing creativity in the expression.

Postmodernist critics might find this perspective attractive for potentially debunking the myth of the author that "romantic authorship" builds on. Accordingly, authorship is nothing more or less than the outcome of compilations and rearrangement of preexisting expressions and basic building blocks of communication and languages.[138] Taken to an extreme, information and communication theories might cast authors themselves as mere channels, with "their" works as artifacts that have no single, individual source at all. However, the present application does not go that far. Proposing that authors "merely" exercise choices (rather than performing God-like creation, as the "romantic authorship" narrative would have it) does not conflict with the recognition that some of the most outstanding examples of human creativity are essentially delivered via a process of choice-making, which (at least to some extent) is circumscribed by available logical systems.[139] All authors are influenced by their

---

of *H*) on the one hand, and meaningfulness of messages on the other. Nonetheless, he concludes: "As a random message embodies the highest level of 'information,' one could argue that it also embodies the highest level of 'originality.' That is not a ridiculous conclusion, if the point of 'originality' is to ensure that exclusive rights to the copyrighted work still leave 'enough and as good' for the use of society and subsequent authors. The least-ordered texts are also the most abundant and probably the least essential as material for the public domain." *Id.* at 124–25 (footnote omitted).

135. *Id.* at 117.

136. *See* Jonathan Lethem, *The Ecstasy of Influence: A Plagiarism*, HARPER'S, Feb. 2007, at 59–71 (providing a powerful analysis of the influence of prior works and authors on subsequent works in the literary field).

137. Weaver described redundancy as "the fraction of the structure of the message which is determined not by the free choice of the sender, but rather by the accepted statistical rules governing the use of the symbols in question." *See* SHANNON & WEAVER, *supra* note 13, at 13.

138. *See, e.g.,* Martha Woodmansee & Peter Jaszi, *Introduction* to THE CONSTRUCTION OF AUTHORSHIP TEXTUAL APPROPRIATION IN LAW AND LITERATURE 1–14 (Martha Woodmansee & Peter Jaszi eds., 1999).

139. *Cf.* Jessica Litman, *The Public Domain*, 39 EMORY L. J. 965, 1011 (1990) ("My characterization of authorship as a combination of absorption, astigmatism, and amnesia is not intended to diminish its merit. Indeed, my position is that this mixture is precisely the process that yields the works of authorship we wish to encourage through the copyright law.

predecessors, and the unique impact of earlier exposures on contemporary creators is reflected in their individual choices through which their unique genius shines.[140] In accordance with the notion of noise, it is perhaps possible to depict those individual creators as "noisy channels"[141] without thereby undermining their achievements. Calling authors channels does not mean to derogate from their status as creators, but rather, to describe them as human filters who produce output sufficiently distinguishable from anything they have ever absorbed in the past. This output—the Messages *they* send to the world—bear the imprint of their own individuality. Suggesting that authors are a class of Originators and works are a class of Medial Messages means, inter alia, that each work is a part of and a stage in a "conversation." Context and background belong to its essence, and creativity is always a function of the particular way in which languages and preexisting elements are being brought together and arranged in a given communicative act.

(b) Application to Copyrightability Questions

Comprehensibility *as a work attribute* implies that authors regularly employ logistic methods to embody their ideas, and that the particular way of using languages should correspond to the general framework of the Medial Message. When the law endows protection to "literary and artistic works," it actually covers classes of Messages in conversations that are characteristic to the cultural domains of literature and the arts.[142] This explains why copyright protection

The strong form of this argument is that all authorship is the product of astigmatic repackaging of others' expression, but this strong form is unnecessary for our purposes. We can rely instead on a milder and hardly controversial variation: All works of authorship, even the most creative, include some elements adapted from raw material that the author first encountered in someone else's works.") (footnote omitted).

140. *Cf. id.* at 696–97 ("The process of authorship, however, is more equivocal than that romantic model admits. To say that every new work is in some sense based on the works that preceded it is such a truism that it has long been a cliche, invoked but not examined. But the very act of authorship in any medium is more akin to translation and recombination than it is to creating Aphrodite from the foam of the sea. Composers recombine sounds they have heard before; playwrights base their characters on bits and pieces drawn from real human beings and other playwrights' characters; novelists draw their plots from lives and other plots within their experience; software writers use the logic they find in other software; lawyers transform old arguments to fit new facts; cinematographers, actors, choreographers, architects, and sculptors all engage in the process of adapting, transforming, and recombining what is already 'out there' in some other form. This is not parasitism: it is the essence of authorship.") (footnotes omitted).

141. *Cf.* Durham, *supra* note 132, at 112–16 (examining an information-theory-inspired authorship model, according to which authors are mere channels who add information to existing messages).

142. Art can be understood in terms of Message-making, and artistic Messages are the quintessential subject matter of copyright protection. The comprehensibility aspect of a

cannot be tethered to experts' or layman's definitions of literature or art, and further, why the legal definition of work *must* remain open-ended: Communication is a dynamic process, in which meanings are being created, exchanged, altered, proliferated, and extinguished over the course of ongoing conversations in a variety of social and cultural settings. Forms, methods, genres, and techniques of expressive endeavors develop and evolve over time; creative individuals reach out and explore new terrains of expressiveness, and this dynamism defeats the confinement of concepts such as art to legal definitions.[143] Art and literature are forms of communication; as such, they invite and accommodate change,[144] whereas stagnancy stands in sharp contrast to the core essence of that dynamism.

At the same time, the diversity and richness of human expressiveness does not necessarily mean that objective criteria in the specific context of the creativity threshold in copyright law are inherently non-articulable. Consider the case of Adib Fricke,[145] an artist who invents words such as *EXPLOM*, *ONOMONO*, or *RITOB*.[146] Are these "word-works" copyrightable? On the one hand, Fricke did not copy them from any preexisting source; in this sense, the artist is the genuine creator and the actual source of his "protonyms."[147] A protonym such as *SMORP*

Message, as explained earlier, does not mean that artists always want to say something concrete or convey their comments, but rather, that the artistic endeavor is always a form of self-expression. *Cf.* Rolf H. Weber, *Press Art–Kunst als Botschaft in* WIRTSCHAFT ZU BEGINN DES 21. JAHRHUNDERTS, FS 1149 (2005) (suggesting art wants to deliver a medial message, without necessarily attempting to comment on anything: "[D]ie Kunst will eine mediale Botschaft vermitteln, ohne dass indessen zwingend eine Kommentierung gegeben werden muss.").

143. The German Constitutional Court used a similar argument in expressing the view that art cannot be confined to formal definitions. *See* Anachronistischer Zug, BVerfGRE 67, 213, 225 (July 17, 1984) ("Daß in der Kunsttheorie jeglicher Konsens über objektive Maßstäbe fehlt, hängt allerdings auch mit einem besonderen Merkmal des Kunstlebens zusammen: die 'Avantgarde' zielt gerade darauf ab, die Grenzen der Kunst zu erweitern. Dies und ein weitverbreitetes Mißtrauen von Künstlern und Kunsttheoretikern gegen starre Formen und strenge Konventionen sind Eigenheiten des Lebensbereichs Kunst, welche zu respektieren sind und bereits darauf hindeuten, daß nur ein weiter Kunstbegriff zu angemessenen Lösungen führen kann.").

144. *See* W. J. McEwen, *Communication Innovation and Change*, in COMMUNICATION AND BEHAVIOR 197 (G. J. Hanneman & W. J. McEwen eds., 1975) (discussing communication theories studying change); FUCHS, *supra* note 92 at 129–35 (discussing different views concerning updating legal conceptions in the face of developments in contemporary art).

145. The artist's Web site is called The Word Company, http://www.thewordcompany.de/start/english.php.

146. *See* the artist's Web site, http://www.thewordcompany.de/start/contents.htm.

147. Fricke's work has been described as follows: "Fricke's protonyms seem to be designed to both annoy and please, combining wry humor and a naive fondness for the potential beauty of the new word-drawing on the avant-garde dream of a creation that transcends the limits of conventional society, language, meaning." Press Release, Harvard

is neither factual nor functional, and thus, it is not squarely non-copyrightable as excluded by virtue of negative categories.[148] On the other hand, single words and short phrases usually do not receive copyright protection.[149] The fundamental problem rests, as expected, on measuring the sufficiency of creativity represented in said protonyms. Can single word-works pass the legal muster for exclusivity protection as a general matter? It seems difficult to provide a ready-made answer; some observers might consider Fricke's invented words highly creative, whereas others might dismiss them as irrelevant nonsense. For the courts it is a case-by-case decision that, in the absence of clear-cut instruction in the law, factors in various policy considerations. But how could anything such as information theory contribute to the legal analysis of copyrightability in such borderline cases?

Consider Fricke's case in terms of information and communication theories. The artist had an idea, and to express that idea he chose an alphabetical-phonetic system. Fricke's protonyms are rich in information (from a syntactical perspective) precisely because his use of the alphabetical system is uncommon and the order of letters is relatively unpredictable.[150] Measured according to technical-quantitative standards, the protonyms are highly creative because they represent a relatively high H value. However, the initial choice of the alphabetic-phonetic system as the expressive platform imposes some structural limitations on the freedom of the artist to "play" with its elements. In case of the Latin alphabet as used in English, the logical system contains twenty-six symbols, of which five are vowels and twenty-one are consonants. This system entails built-in constraints on the way *pronounceable* words can be constructed (information theory calls limitations on the freedom to arrange basic elements *redundancy*). Redundancy *reduces* the *quantity* of information that can be represented by a given expression,[151] so regardless of the Originator's efforts to be creative, a highly redundant logical system would yield relatively low H-value expressions. Indeed, according to the

---

University Art Museums, Feb. 3, 1999, http://www.artmuseums.harvard.edu/press/released1999/wordstowatch.html.

148. Fricke does not claim the words mean or should mean anything at all. He calls them "protonyms"—words with no content or meaning—which in his eyes are simply "beautiful" and "great." *See* Karl Hübner, *Angenehm Sinnfrei* (2004).

149. *Cf.* U.S. Copyright Office, Circular No. 34 (2006) ("Names, titles, and short phrases or expressions are not subject to copyright protection. Even if a name, title, or short phrase is novel or distinctive or if it lends itself to a play on words, it cannot be protected by copyright.").

150. *Cf.* Durham *supra* note 132, at 81–83 (noting the inverse correlation between the amount of information and the level of predictability).

151. *See* Shannon & Weaver, *supra* note 13, at 14–16. Shannon's calculations suggest the redundancy rate in the English language is about 50 percent, meaning that approximately half of the possible letter and word combinations are not subject to free choice, but rather are imposed by the structure of the language. *Id.* at 13.

suggested relation between *H*-value and creativity, the resulting expressions would likely represent a relatively low level of creativity.

Returning to the facts at hand, Fricke's choice of symbols (letters) is not completely random, as it is guided by both *aesthetic* and *functional* considerations. The protonyms are relatively short, pronounceable, and catchy, and they contain common basic combinations of consonants and vowels. Whether such combinations should receive copyright protection due to their artistic merits (despite redundancy) is largely a policy question that should be guided, inter alia, by the following considerations: First, it is reasonable to assume that granting copyright protection to single, pronounceable words (thereby barring their nonconsensual use) would enhance the redundancy of the language in general. Once copyrighted, the probability of such combinations of letters emerging in various communication situations decreases, and the probability of non-copyrighted, pronounceable words will likely increase. For example, if the word *car* were copyrighted and the word *automobile* were not, it is reasonable to expect a broader use of the latter symbol to describe the same referent (or thing) to express a given thought.[152] The upshot is that copyright protection *might* increase the redundancy of a given logical system *in some situations*, quite in contrast to the prevalent intuition of language as a non-exhaustible fountain that allows infinite opportunities and variations of speech. Importantly, this upshot is not necessarily confined to "meaningful" words, that is, to words that *presently* have an objective (dictionary) meaning in the language. Assuming the language provides instructions on how to pronounce written words, it seems the pool of possible, pronounceable words is not boundless after all (after all, what are the chances the combination *ZZTTSYARR* will ever become an official word in the English language?) In this light, copyrighting meaningless yet pronounceable words (such as *QUOBO*)[153] would present a dangerous foray into language, and thus, a dubious policy choice. Exclusivity in pronounceable words is likely to impair the development of the written and spoken language because combinations that strike most people as utter nonsense today might enter common use and acquire general meanings tomorrow.

The legal and policy dilemma is less theoretical and remote than it might appear at first glance. A court decision from 1921 penned by one of America's most influential copyright judges provides a classroom example of the problem and the possible application of information and communication theories in handling it. In *Reiss v. National Quotation Bureau*, Judge Learned Hand upheld the copyrightability of coined, meaningless words published in a code book (called

152. The terms *symbol*, *referent*, and *thought* correspond to their use by Ogden and Richards in their famous semantic triangle. *See* C. K. Ogden & Ivor A. Richards, The Meaning of Meaning 10–11 (Harcourt Brace Jovanovich 1989) (1923).

153. *Cf.* Hübner, *supra* note 148 (Fricke observed the word *QUOBO* had refused to generate any meaning even after a five-year traveling exhibition).

"Simplix' Pocket Blank Code"), to be adapted and given future meaning for the purpose of cable correspondence.[154] The book contained 6,325 coined words of five letters each. Though the words had no known meaning, they were all "susceptible of pronunciation."[155] Judge Hand concluded these words were "writings" in the meaning of the U.S. Constitution, and therefore, they were copyrightable. The concise decision deserves an extended quote here. Hand wrote:

> If the defendants' point is good, it can only be because, to be within the Constitution, the 'writing'must already have a meaning. These words have a prospective meaning, but as yet they have not received, it, like an empty pitcher. Suppose some one devised a set of words or symbols to form a new abstract speech, with inflections, but as yet with no meaning, a kind of blank Esperanto. The case would be approaching the plaintiff's, though not there, because the words would, indeed, express relationship. Mathematics has its symbols, indeed a language of its own, Peanese, understood by only a few people in the world. Suppose a mathematician were to devise a new set of compressed and more abstract symbols, and left them for some conventional meaning to be filled in. Still we should not be quite at the plaintiff's words, but again we should not be far away . . .The distinction is real, but for practical purposes seems to me irrelevant. Not all words communicate ideas; some are mere spontaneous ejaculations. Some are used for their sound alone, like nursery jingles, or the rhymes of children in their play. Might not some one, with a gift for catching syllables, devise others? There has of late been prose written, avowedly senseless, but designed by its sound alone to produce an emotion. Conceivably there may arise a poet who strings together words without rational sequence-perhaps even coined syllables—through whose beauty, cadence, meter, and rhyme he may seek to make poetry . . . Works of plastic art need not be pictorial. They may be merely patterns, or designs, and yet they are within the statute. A patterns or an ornamental design depicts nothing; it merely pleases the eye. If such models or paintings are 'writings,'I can see no reason why words should not be such because they communicate nothing. They may have their uses for all that, aesthetic or practical, and they may be the productions of high ingenuity, or even genius. Therefore, on principle, there appears to me no reason to limit the Constitution in any such way as the defendants require.[156]

Judge Hand was obviously right that *meaning* is not a copyrightability benchmark under the Constitution. Yet the holding significantly underplays the

---

154. *See* Reiss v. Nat'l Quotation Bureau, Inc., 276 F. 717 (S.D.N.Y 1921).
155. *Id.* at 717.
156. *Id.* pp. 718–19.

redundancy problem:[157] the number of available choices is finite, and zero redundancy is purely theoretical in the case of alphabetical-phonetic systems. The court did not consider the impact of copyrighting 6,325 pronounceable words on the freedom to invent new five-letter words in the future. What muddies the water are Hand's analogies to music or ornamental designs, which, in terms of the model, are distinguishable logical systems of expression that afford divergent degrees of freedom to Originators. One of the most powerful lessons information theory can offer is that copyrightability analysis should be adapted to the specific encoding system with which works are expressed, giving weight to their built-in, structural limitations on the freedom to compose expressions. As Judge Hand opined, the result of a copyrightability analysis should not hinge on present or future conceivable "meaning" of the expression. At the same time, parameters such as degrees of freedom, availability of alternatives, and practical ability to make authorial choices should guide judicial decisions in the context of a given logical system.

B. Infringement as Communication

1. The Argument

Application of the model to copyright infringement scenarios underlies the argument that every instance the law considers a violation of copyrights can be identified on the communication sequence (Fig. 1.3). Obviously, not every unauthorized communication of copyrighted material violates exclusive copyrights, but as a descriptive matter, every infringement involves communication or has a communication-related aspect. According to this thesis, the communication dimension of infringement can be localized on the sequence, usually in relation to the origination action and/or communication facilitators located within the media/channel region.[158] An Originator might turn into a copyright infringer to the extent she uses protected elements for the making of her own Message without the permission of rights-holders. In addition, actors who mediate between Originators and Recipients (i.e., their actions are media-related) without securing the necessary permission might also be exposed to copyright liability. From a communication standpoint, the difference between the two types of infringers

---

157. The facts of *Reiss* are actually ideal for a numerical illustration of the point. The number of possible five-letter combinations chosen from the twenty-six letters of the Latin alphabet, assuming that symbols can repeat and that each choice is independent (i.e., order does not matter), is $26^5 \cong 11{,}800{,}000$. The figure of 11.8 million theoretical possibilities seems very high, but it includes combinations such as ZKZLZ, XDRDR, CCNCC, and so on. Pronounceability constraints significantly reduce the number of available word combinations, and exclusive rights being granted in 6,325 pronounceable combinations would restrict the available choices even further.

158. *Cf.* Tim Wu, *Copyright's Communication Policy*, 103 MICH. L. REV. 278 (2004) (proposing to view copyright regulation primarily as an instrument of communication policy rather than promotion of authorship).

rests on their relation to the Message: origination has the character of *self-expression*, whereas mediation or facilitation of communication is essentially functional. Media/channel actors might have various motivations for bringing the Message to the Recipient, though by definition they do not consider their own behavior as expressive. The outlines of this assertion in light of positive infringement rules will now be examined.

2. Economic Rights

Economic rights under copyright law are the legal means to facilitate extraction of economic value from copyrighted Messages. The immediate goal of these rights is to safeguard pecuniary interests. Economic rights are commonly divided into two classes: copy-related and copy-unrelated rights.[159] Copy-related rights control exploitations that involve physical objects, in which signals are fixed in a fairly stable manner. Copy-unrelated rights, by comparison, concern exploitations that do not necessarily involve fixation in tangible objects.[160] This distinction mirrors to some extent the difference between direct and indirect communication (see Sec. IV.D.2). In any case, the *communicative nature* of all potentially infringing acts is salient.[161] The infringements of copy-related and copy-unrelated rights simply involve forms of communication in which media are used in different ways. Prima facie infringements of the economic rights concern the dissemination of valuable works. The impetus of exclusivity is to defend this economic value, as certain acts by unauthorized third parties might put that value at risk. The risk to authors' exploitation opportunities rests precisely in the *communicative value* of actions the law considers potentially infringing because the market value of works emanates from the ability to provide and charge for access. The creation and dissemination of Messages (whether legitimately or illicitly) are actions that potentially generate *pecuniary value* on which the actor seeks to capitalize, and the connection between the communicative and pecuniary value is evident both in cases of legitimate exploitation and

159. *Cf.* Ricketson & Ginsburg, *supra* note 88, § 9A.05 ("The basic economic rights protected in each country have traditionally fallen into two main categories: reproduction of the work in a material form, and public dissemination of the work in a non-material form.").

160. Section 15 of the German copyright statute vividly reflects this division. The first subsection lists only copy-related rights (reproduction, distribution, and public display of certain unpublished works), whereas the second subsection provides a list of copy-unrelated rights, including certain performances, broadcasting, and transmissions. *See* § 15 UrhG.

161. Although to the extent that some language in the copyright statute permits the interpretation that merely "preparing" a derivative work (*cf.* § 106(2) 17 U.S.C.; § 23 UrhG., especially the second sentence) already implicates exclusive rights without any connection to communication (e.g., other persons are not exposed to the work during the process of "preparation"), the normative thrust of the model would strongly advise against this line of interpretation.

of infringement. In other words, there is a direct, unequivocal thread connecting economic value, economic interests, and communication-related behavior.[162]

3. *Moral Rights*

(a) Introductory Remarks

Protection of moral rights is usually independent of economic rights,[163] and their infringement is not necessarily exploitation-based. Though moral rights generally have different rationales, it seems the communication aspect encapsulated in the rules that outlaw their breach is no less prominent. Moral rights protect "ideal" rather than monetary interests.[164] The focus is on "the relationship of authors to their works"[165] and the "sacred bond" between the authors and works.[166] In this case, the linkage between the infringement and communication does not necessarily emanate from the economic value of providing access, but rather rests on the possible *impact* on the Recipient, which, in turn, might shape *the Recipient's image* of the creator. For that reason, it is difficult to think of a violation of moral rights that exists outside the communication sequence and that is divorced from the element of reception and impact on the audience. The analysis below tests this argument against the three core moral rights. The unique contribution of information theory to the discussion is the idea of treating prima facie violations of moral rights as communicative acts, in which infringers occasionally (1) add "noise" to the original Message, or (2) detract some of its components, with both cases being to the disadvantage of the author.

(b) The Three Core Moral Rights

I. THE RIGHT OF DIVULGATION

The divulgation right (also called the "right of first publication" or the "right of disclosure") controls the timing of *initial* dissemination, and occasionally, related issues such as the place and form of initial publication.[167] It seeks to protect authors' entitlement to decide at which stage the work shall be exposed to the

---

162. This is not to say that any act copyright law calls infringement is economically detrimental to rights-holders. Rather, to present an economic risk in the first place (i.e., a risk of the kind economic rights-holders seek to defend), the infringing act must bear some communication insignia.

163. *See* RICKETSON & GINSBURG, *supra* note 88, § 1.16.

164. For an introduction to the concept and function of moral rights, see ELIZABETH ADENEY, THE MORAL RIGHTS OF ARTISTS AND PERFORMERS §§ In. .1–.7. (2006)

165. *See* RICKETSON & GINSBURG, *supra* note 88, § 1.02.

166. *See* Jane C. Ginsburg, *A Tale of Two Copyrights: Literary Property in Revolutionary France and America*, 64 TULANE L. REV. 991, 1007 (1990) (citing Le Chapelier, stating "the most sacred, the most legitimate, the most unassailable, and . . . the most personal of all properties, is the work which is the fruit of a writer's thoughts") (citation omitted).

167. *See* ADENEY, *supra* note 164, §§ 9.69–9.74 (explaining the scope of the right of attribution under German law).

public, if at all.[168] By its terms, the right concerns *publication*, which roughly means large-scale diffusion of the work. In jurisdictions where the divulgation right is explicitly protected, the scope of the right intrinsically relates to the legal definition of publication.[169] Publication is *a form of communication* that is somewhat more restrictive than communication in general; its precise meaning and scope is usually determined by legal definitions found in the respective copyright laws.[170] For instance, a given definition might delineate publication (thereby distinguishing it from communication in general) according to the number and identity of Recipients or to the copy-related or copy-unrelated nature of the dissemination.[171] In any case, the legal notion of publication is *always* nestled within the more general concept of communication. Violation of the divulgation right *must* involve communication, which the law sometimes considers unlawful if at the time of the alleged violation, the author was not yet ready to expose his creative engagement to the public. Therefore, in determining liability one of the critical questions is whether the author has already exhausted the right to be the first to release (or authorize the release of) the work *to the public* prior to the communication act under discussion.[172]

---

168. *Cf.* Cyrill P. Rigamonti, *Deconstructing Moral Rights*, HARV. INT'L L.J. 353, 362 (2006) (noting the right of disclosure's historical importance with respect to the question whether a creditor could force authors to sell their manuscripts or to publish unpublished works).

169. *Cf.* Adolf Dietz in SCHRICKER URHEBERRECHT KOMMENTAR § 12 nr. 7–8 (2006) (discussion of the relationship between first publication and the statutory definition as to publication in the German statute).

170. For example, Art. 3(3) of the Berne Convention provides: "The expression 'published works' means works published with the *consent* of their authors, whatever may be the means of manufacture of the copies, provided that *the availability of such copies has been such as to satisfy the reasonable requirements of the public*, having regard to the nature of the work. The performance of a dramatic, dramatico-musical, cinematographic or musical work, the public recitation of a literary work, the communication by wire or the broadcasting of literary or artistic works, the exhibition of a work of art and the construction of a work of architecture shall not constitute publication." (emphasis added).

171. The law sometimes distinguishes between first publication in the sense of distribution of copies and first publication by making the work publicly available. Section 6 of the German Copyright Act, in subsection (1), refers to published works ("*veröffentlichte Werk*") as works that were made available to the public, whereas subsection (2) refers to published works ("*erschienene Werke*") that involve distribution of copies. *See* § 6(1)–(2) UrhG. The U.S. Copyright Act excludes copy-unrelated disseminations from the statutory definition of publication. *See* 17 U.S.C. § 101 (defining *publication* as "the distribution of copies or phonorecords of a work to the public.").

172. *Cf.* Dietz, *supra* note 169, § 12 nr. 19 (dissemination among small circle of family and friends does not exhaust the right of first publication, and indiscretion *within these circles* would not infringe the right of divulgence as these circles do not satisfy the definition of the public.) In any case, no right can be infringed in the absence of communication.

II. THE RIGHT OF ATTRIBUTION

The right of attribution (or the right of paternity) protects the non-pecuniary interest of authors to be acknowledged as such in connection with their works. Attribution is often relevant in connection with the dissemination of works to the public. Although dissemination is not always a formal, statutory element of violation in jurisdictions that recognize this right, it is difficult to imagine a violation of the attribution right that lacks any communicative dimension whatsoever. Assume arguendo that the author has exercised her right of first publication while making sure her name is properly attached to all legitimate copies. From a communication perspective, the identity of the source is often a very important aspect of Message interpretation and the attribution of value/relevance to it by the Recipient. Omitting or obscuring the identity of the source is likely to have communication-related implications that might in some cases harm the source (namely, the author). The law considers the interest to be associated with the work as its maker warranted and that it deserves protection. Applying the terminology of information and communication theories, violation of the attribution right might introduce noise to the communication, inasmuch as the violator obscures the original Message. This application suggests that when an author publishes a work with her name attached to it, the source element becomes indispensable to the Message itself, as deleting it would impair the Message and the operation of the dissemination process. To the extent that such actions harm authors, this harm would almost certainly occur in communicative constellations, namely, when reception takes place without the Recipients being aware of the identity of the (true) Originator. In other words, there is an unequivocal nexus between the non-pecuniary harm and the infringer's undesired interference with the communication sequence. The magnitude of the harm to authors increases as more Recipients are exposed to the damaging disseminations.[173]

III. THE RIGHT OF INTEGRITY

The analogy of infringement to adding "noise" to the original Message appears even more persuasive in the case of the right of integrity due to the patent linkage between the infringing act and the alteration of Message signals. In the context of the author's right to prevent alterations and mutilations of works, it is possible to view the infringer as a "noisy channel." It is interesting to mention in this context the concept of "negative information," and some information theorists have attempted to expand the application of Shannon's theory to the semantic

173. Consider a situation in which the owner of a book blackens the name of the author on the copy he keeps in his personal library. Would that violate the attribution right? Alternatively, consider an accused infringer who does the same with five hundred copies that are then distributed among secondhand book dealers. Clearly, the injury to the author's attribution interests is much greater in the latter case.

level of communication analysis as well.[174] Negative information (or "negative transinformation") essentially means that certain signals/messages might *increase* (rather than reduce) subjective uncertainty.[175] In this vein, negative information can be thought of as communication elements that obscure or distract from the interpretation and meaning-making process. This is precisely the type of harm the right of integrity seeks to curb. In a typical infringement scenario, the infringer adds and/or removes signals, changes their order or context, or otherwise interferes with the sequence in a way likely to influence the interpretation of the Message. By extension, this interference adversely affects the author's moral interest in preserving the structure of the Message and the intended course in which the sequence flows, as well as the author's reputation as its human source.[176] Also here the relationship between the communicative dimension of the infringing act and the potential injury to the legally protected interests of authors is undeniable. Finally, similarly to violations of the attribution right, a certain positive correlation is likely between the breadth of dissemination and the intensity of the harm.

This being the case, it is also possible to think of prima facie violations of the right of integrity, in which communication might play a relatively minor role. Consider, for instance, the case of an original piece of visual art such as a painting or a sculpture. The piece is sold to a buyer, who becomes the legal owner and possessor of the object. The possessor then alters, mutilates, or otherwise damages the piece, yet the work remains situated on the possessor's privately owned premises, inaccessible to the general public (including the artist himself). The artist, however, finds this behavior offending. Such conflicts usually reflect the collision between the property rights of the owner of the piece in his tangible belongings on the one hand, and the intellectual property right of the artist concerning the integrity of his intangible expression on the other.[177] The voices

---

174. *See* JUMARIE, *supra* note 18, at 44–48.

175. *Id.* at 101–02 (formally defining the concept of subjective entropy and arguing that as compared to Shannon's original model, "negative information" comes closer to meanings and semantic communication analysis).

176. Historically, the right of first disclosure was considered the most basic of all authors' rights, with the right of integrity as an aspect of that basic right. *Cf.* ADENEY, *supra* note 164, § 2.31.

177. Dietz, *supra* note 169, § 14 nr. 15–16 (discussing the question in connection with Sec. 14 of the German Copyright Act.) The hypothetical here does not concern the complete destruction of the piece. The legal analysis may vary in that particular case. *See* Adolf Dietz, *The Artist's Right of Integrity under Copyright Law—A Comparative Approach*, 25 I.I.C. 177, 190–91 (1994) (German law does not extend the right to prevent detrimental modifications to the complete destruction of works); Roberta Rosenthall Kwall, *Copyright and the Moral Right: Is an American Marriage Possible?*, 38 VAND. L. REV. 1, 9 (1985) ("If the artist [is] a painter . . . the right of integrity probably would not allow her to prevent the destruction of one of her paintings by its owner.").

favoring the artist's moral interests in this situation often assume that during the (long) life of copyrights, a large circle of persons *might* be exposed to the mutilated work.[178] This implies the harm to the moral interest of the author remains a *function of the number of persons exposed to the altered work*, in other words, the number of Recipients who have access to it. Without needing to evaluate the plausibility of this view as a matter of (intellectual) property law, the argument is logical enough: the impetus of the integrity right is to protect the honor and reputation of the artist. Reputation, both good and bad, emerges in the course of the information process, meaning it is only earned via circulation of Messages. Without communication, reputation can neither be bolstered nor tarnished.[179]

C. Copyright Policy, Regulation, and Stakeholders

Before concluding this chapter, the discussion turns to analysis of the contribution of the model to broader issues such as copyright policy and the impact of regulation on copyright stakeholders.

1. *Copyright Policy and Regulation*

How could one describe the basic relationship between law and the information process? For one, the information process is extralegal and its existence is independent of law: people engage in communicative exchange for many "non-legal" reasons (e.g., to reduce uncertainty about the world, interact, coordinate activities, shape relationships, express feelings, and be entertained). Law is not the raison d'être of information, and *law itself* is a kind of information.[180] For another, law may certainly influence the information process while targeting communication-related behaviors. For example, legal rules can both *encourage* the creation of Messages and *discourage* certain communicative activities. Copyright policy is part of a larger scheme roughly referred to as *information policy*, for which a given strategy may combine both types of rules to accomplish a certain policy program. Information policy guides regulative efforts to influence the information process and thereby promote certain agendas. The information-as-a-process perspective highlights the factor of unpredictability involved, which renders the regulative efforts to "manipulate" the process (or perhaps better, to "steer" it) a

178. Dietz, *supra* note 169, at nr. 16. (citing commentators who in such conflicts favor the artists' moral interests over possession rights in artworks).

179. *Cf.* Kwall, *supra* note 177 ("Perhaps the underlying rationale for this [destruction] exception is that a work which has been destroyed completely cannot reflect adversely upon the creator's honor or reputation.").

180. "[T]he law runs on information and [] much of law is information. Thus, all of law is not affected by the automobile because law is not composed of automobiles. But law is, in almost all of its parts, dependent on communication and information." *See* M. ETHAN KATSH, LAW IN A DIGITAL WORLD 7 (1995).

very delicate task indeed. At the same time, the main targets of regulation are fairly easy to identify (indicated in Figure 1.2 as Originators and media actors).

As a general matter, whether a given regulation qualifies as an "information regulation" depends on its intended impact on *communication-related behavior.* Information regulation targets certain behaviors due to their communicative aspects. Assuming that regulation generally seeks to guide and occasionally impose restrictions on behavior, and assuming further that it might affect the freedom to engage in communicative activity, almost *any* regulation might have an impact on the information process. Free speech law and theory powerfully illustrate this dilemma: if the state must principally abstain from abridging free expression, and if nearly all regulations (at least indirectly) affect the ability to express oneself via communication,[181] is it at all possible to draw a clear distinction between information regulation and regulation in general?[182] The model helps to refine the distinction in the following manner: Information law rules target the operation of individuals due (or in connection with) the *function they fulfill in the communication sequence.* In other words, the motivation behind the regulation and/or the content of the positive legal provisions should exhibit linkage to the communicative dimension of the regulated behavior. By comparison, it is less plausible to denote "information regulation" laws that have only ancillary impacts on communication (e.g., tax laws that obligate citizens to produce income statements).

Copyright regulation is clearly an important piece of the information policy puzzle. Here the regulator tailors restrictions to behaviors due to the communicative impact of the regulated actions. Infringement rules *discourage* the creation and dissemination of Messages in the short run. It appears that state-supported suppression of communicative behavior must be underpinned by both a solid

---

181. "All laws affect what get said, by whom, to whom and with what effect. In short, all laws have information effect." *See* Larry Alexander, *Trouble on Track Two: Incidental Regulations of. Speech and Free Speech Theory*, 44 HASTINGS L.J. 929 (1993) (challenging the distinction between government regulation focusing on the communicative impact of speech ("track one" cases) and regulation that focuses on public forum aspects and symbolic speech ("track two" cases)).

182. Themes in free speech law address several aspects of this basic problem. In U.S. law, the debate is significantly framed in terms of (1) locating the dividing line between "speech" that is principally eligible of constitutional protections and "non-speech" that principally is not, (2) the distinction between content-neutral and content-specific government regulation, and (3) incidental regulation of speech, particularly as applied to "symbolic" speech. *See, e.g.*, Frederick Schauer, *Must Speech Be Special?* 78 NW. U. L. REV. 1284 (1983) (confronting the question whether constitutionally protected speech is different from any non-protected activities); Kent Greenawalt, *O'er the Land of the Free*, UCLA L. REV. 925 (1990) (discussing the U.S. Supreme Court decision that declared the conviction of a person for burning the national flag as being an unconstitutional violation of the First Amendment).

policy and reasonable strategy. One type of justification of copyright restrictions on communication is the desire to enrich the information environment and accelerate the information process in the long run. For this reason, copyright policy that is forward-looking (e.g., that restricts communicative behavior today *in order to ultimately encourage creation* in the future) would better correspond to the information-as-a-process view as compared to backward-looking, reward-based policies. A utilitarian-consequentialist basis for copyright protection better accounts for information as a dynamic process characterized by relentless progression and relationships between sequences on the time axis. According to utilitarian rationales for copyright exclusivity, both the *justification for,* and the *ultimate mission* of the regulative apparatus are to improve access opportunities in the long run.[183]

Figure 1.3 illustrates the basic options available to the regulator in this respect. In practice, copyright law focuses on restricting authors (in their role as Originators), media-related activities, and to a much lesser degree, acts of users (in their role as Recipients). Regulation of authors and communication facilitators affects access opportunities at later stages of the process. With the policy goal in mind, the law's interference with the delicate set of relationships, dependencies, and synergies that make up our information "ecology"[184] must be excusable. In assessing the success of a given regulative strategy, the critical benchmarks are the quantity and quality of available informational resources as well as the cost and conditions of accessing them.

2. Copyright Stakeholders

The information-as-a-process perspective offers a fresh look at copyright stakeholders and their various (and occasionally conflicting) interests in connection with the operation of copyright regulation. The key point is that the regulator should not necessarily consider these stakeholders as individual actors/entities that fall within traditional categories. Rather, stakeholders should be evaluated primarily according to the *function they fulfill in the process at various stages.* To begin with, every member of society has stakes in copyright legislation, inasmuch as every citizen is being directly or indirectly affected by state-supported restrictions on communication-related activities. It is common to organize

---

183. *See* Chapter 2, Section IV.B(3)(b) *infra.*

184. To illustrate this aspect of information regulation, critical commentators use metaphors of environmentalism, ecology, or ecosystem for describing the effect of regulative intervention. *See, e.g.,* James Boyle, *A Politics of Intellectual Property: Environmentalism for the Net?* 47 Duke L.J. 87, 108–12 (1997); Peter K. Yu, *Intellectual Property and the Information Ecosystem,* 2005 Mich. St. L. Rev. 1, 7 (2005) (arguing "[t]oday, the information ecosystem is heavily depleted, and technology, information resources, and public domain materials have become the new endangered species. If we are to save the information environment, we not only need a new politics, but a new conceptual framework to reframe the public intellectual property debate.").

stakeholders into groups according to certain shared characteristics, interests, and position in the copyright scenario.[185] Classifications are important, inter alia, for assessing the impact of copyright legislation on different groups and sectors and for assessing the overall equilibrium of the system.[186] The idea of copyright balance seems to suggest, among other things, that copyright entitlements should be allocated in a manner that does not overwhelmingly favor one group while neglecting the legitimate interests of other groups.

Regarding the copyright stakeholders as simply authors versus users appears too simplistic.[187] In many respects, stakeholders are much more heterogenic and diverse. Viewing information as a process underscores further that specific actors or entities may assume multiple roles depending on the circumstances of the sequence and the stage of conversation in which they participate. Originators, Recipients, and communication facilitators are *functions*, not individual persons or inherently personal attributes. In any given sequence, persons may fulfill different functions than the same persons have fulfilled in previous sequences. This nearly self-evident observation must still be recalled as the discussion turns to examination of copyright stakeholders and the way in which the law accommodates their interests.

Authors,[188] the first category of stakeholders, all seem to share at least one fundamental common denominator: the will to externalize a thought, an idea, or state of mind from the subjective realm to the objective reality.[189] It may follow that an ideal copyright system would provide authors with the optimal logical and logistic tools for self-expression with which they should be able to exercise personal judgment and be in the best position to make choices in the course of the creative process. If this is true, the lay observer might find it a little odd that the principal way in which the copyright system buttresses the interests of authors is by granting them rights to *suppress* communication-related activities of *others*. The theory behind the formation of private exclusive moral and

---

185. *See, e.g.*, Committee on Intellectual Property Rights in the Emerging Information Infrastructure, The Digital Dilemma: Intellectual Property in the Information Age 61–75 (2000) (naming creators, distributors, educational organizations and research institutions, the general public, as well as subgroups such as governmental organizations, private sector organizations, journalists, and standards organizations).

186. *See generally* Reto M. Hilty, *Urheber in der Informationsgesellschaft: "Wer will was von wem woraus?" Ein Auftakt zum "zweiten Korb"*, ZUM Sonderheft 983 (2003) (describing the difficulties in articulating a balance in the context of contemporary copyright legislation in Germany).

187. *See* Reto M. Hilty, *Vergütungssystem und Schrankenregelungen—Neue Herausforderungen an den Gesetzgeber*, GRUR 820 (2005).

188. In Figure 1.3 the term *author* is sufficiently broad to also include actors who the law might consider as performers. The legal distinction between authors and performers is not directly at issue in this context.

189. *See* Section IV.B.

economic rights and their rationales occupies volumes, and the debate concerning their scope (a topic Chapter 2 will review in some more detail) is as robust today as ever before. At the same time, regardless of the specific rationale behind exclusive rights in Messages, the very function of those legal instruments (especially the exclusive economic rights granted) stands in some tension to the communicative dimension of authorship. This tension is between the author's desire to communicate and reach the target audience as effectively and broadly as possible while maintaining at the same time a certain level of control over dissemination and access that allows the author be compensated.

Copyright law treats authors uniformly by initially granting to all the same level of protection, automatically[190] and regardless of their individual motivations, preferences, and expectations. That level of protection reflects the lawmaker's assessment of authors' legitimate moral and economic expectations *as a group*. Authors who do not care about money and those having entirely other concerns (such as achieving the broadest exposure possible or bringing about a political change) still possess exclusive rights they might not be interested in exercising. In such case, one possible route is to release the work under permissive "public" licenses;[191] however, *actively* licensing the works, even at a zero price (such as under a Creative Commons license) is usually necessary for achieving the maximal distribution the available logistical infrastructure affords. Obviously, authors constitute a much more heterogenic group than their standard set of exclusive rights might imply. At the same time, the regulative strategy of granting uniform protections doubtlessly has pragmatic and information cost advantages; after all, it would be quite inefficient to tailor to each individual work the scope of exclusive protection desired by its individual author. Authors are free to demonstrate their personal preferences later on down the road, as reflected in the permissions they grant (or withhold) and the conditions they set for using and exploiting their works.

Derivative rights-holders (or "publishers") is the next prototypical category of stakeholder, covering commercial actors such as print and music publishers, movie and television producers, theaters, orchestras, and various other employers who engage creative people.[192] Though their contribution to the creative

---

190. The law sometimes imposes technical prerequisites such as fixation or formalities. Note that technical requirements do not concern the conceptual boundaries of the work as a Medial Message.

191. *See* Chapter 7, Section III.A(4)(b).

192. The classic image of the *publisher* in copyright is well known, and even seems to predate the narrative of the individual author itself. *See* LYMAN RAY PATTERSON, COPYRIGHT IN HISTORICAL PERSPECTIVE 42–77 (1968) (providing a detailed account of the Stationer's Copyright in England). At the same time, Patterson cautioned that although authors were not members of the Stationers' Company, "to say that no rights of the author were recognized during the time of the stationer's copyright is . . . too simplistic." *Id.* at 65.

process is sometimes indispensable,[193] their interests in copyright regulation are more heterogenic than authors: in exchange for their involvement in the production of works, derivative rights-holders acquire rights in works (either through exclusive license/rights' transfer contracts or directly via neighboring rights or legal instruments such as work for hire). Though publishers and producers might have various emotional and aesthetic relations to works, their main motivation is economic, and in that sense, derivative rights-holders could be said to generally benefit from a high level of protection of economic interests in "their" works. At the same time, high protection might have a boomerang effect on derivative rights-holders, depending on how much their work takes from existing works and the level of protection covering the copyrighted material needed for producing the new work. High copyright protection for "raw material" will raise the costs of production, and in some cases, prohibitively high clearance costs or insurmountable legal hurdles will curtail the entire enterprise. This is hardly in the best interest of producers in general.

Communication facilitators (or mediators) are persons and entities of which communication-related operations fulfill various channel/media functions. Communication facilitators are usually commercial entities in the business of mediating between Originators and Recipients. Typical examples are companies active in the sectors of telecommunication, Internet services, search engines, mobile telephones, consumer electronics, computer hardware, printers, broadcasters and rebroadcasters, and so forth. Their function is primarily technical-logistical (i.e., to provide communication solutions to respond to the needs of costumers). As such, facilitators favor a regulative scheme that enhances traffic and creates more demand for their products and services. A fairly liberal copyright regulation that has only a moderate impact on the ability of Originators and Recipient to engage in communicative activity (as well as only a limited effect on their own operation as facilitators and their exposure to indirect infringement liability) would serve their interests best. Though facilitators' operations are usually revenue-based and content-indifferent, their role in the information process is obviously crucial, as facilitators can influence the availability, accessibility, form, technical quality, context, speed, location, timing, costs, and other circumstances of reception. For this reason, copyright policy should also be attentive to their special needs and permit them to flourish and innovate.

Lastly, **nonowners** essentially are Recipients in terms of the model (see Sec. IV.C.). This denotation as "nonowners" is intended only to emphasize their lack of formal intellectual property rights in Messages. In the copyright context,

193. By definition, derivative rights-holders are not authors, but they play important and diverse roles in the process of creation. Professional exploiters assist authors to produce and commercialize works; to discover, channel, and unfold their individual talents; and to expose those talents to the world. They also provide the necessary logistical skills, coordination, and financial support necessary for various types of creative endeavors.

nonowners are commonly referred to as *users*. Though their function in the communication sequence is explicable in rather concrete terms, it is most difficult to ascertain or summarize their interests in copyright regulation *as a group*. Arguably, the concept of users in copyright doctrine has been traditionally left under-theorized,[194] yet the fundamental question is whether users in any way represent a category of persons who succumb to a single, "unified" theory or scheme. Positive copyright law considers users for the most part as a residual group—those who do not have exclusive rights in copyrighted information they wish to access or "consume."[195] This does not mean the law *disregards* users, however, as their interests are secured via a series of rules that delimit the scope of exclusive rights (subject matter, duration etc.) as well as various exceptions and defenses that reduce the risk of infringement liability in certain situations. Such copyright rules usually identify specific use interests that, as a policy matter, warrant the attention and protection of the law.

As Recipients, nonowners would prefer to live in an information environment that affords them with optimal opportunities to identify and access interesting, relevant, and valuable Messages. Throwing all users (as a class of stakeholders) into the same basket is very risky as it is probably impossible to generalize their access-related motivations or even the way in which their access needs/expectations are satisfied in reality. Their only common denominator is their dependency on access to Messages they do not legally "own." Nonowners depend on access to information for reasons that range from existential needs to pleasure and happiness and anything in between, including building personal identity and being able to make informed decisions that are important for virtually every aspect of their lives. Access to Messages, whether contemplated, coveted, fortuitous, inadvertent, or serendipitous, is a need and a claim that unites them all.

Finally, it is important to bear in mind that nonowners is a *function* individuals fulfill at a given time and within a given communication sequence. In the next sequence, nonowners might find themselves in the role of Originators.

---

194. *See* Julie Cohen, *The Place of the User in Copyright Law*, 74 FORDHAM L. REV, 347–48 (2005) (arguing that "[c]opyright doctrine . . . is characterized by the absence of the user.") *See also* Joseph P. Liu, *Copyright Law's Theory of the Consumer*, 44 B.C. L. REV. (2003).

195. *Cf.* Jane C. Ginsburg, *Authors and Users in Copyright*, 45 J. COPYRIGHT SOC'Y U.S.A. 1, 3 (1997) (distinguishing between "consumptive" users who use "the entire work" and those who "copy in part or to adapt from preexisting works in the creation of new works.") Ginsburg appears to assume the designation as a consumptive or a transformative user is a personal or a circumstantial attribute, not a contingent function. *Cf.* Liu, *supra* note 194 (challenging the binary division of users into to passive consumers and users who become authors in their own right); Cohen, *supra* note 194, at 370 (defining the *situated user* who appropriates cultural goods found within his immediate environment for four reasons: consumption, communication, self-development, and creative play).

And if every individual Recipient at one point is a potential Originator in a later point, how can the law calibrate these two apparently conflicting sets of interests, which are time and circumstances sensitive? As Recipients today, nonowners arguably benefit from a liberal copyright policy that maximizes access opportunities, yet as authors tomorrow, a more protective scheme might serve them better. Each member of society is an actual or potential Recipient of copyrighted works and an actual or potential author *at the same time*, that is, when the lawmaker is called to strike the balance. This is the crux and pitfall of the copyright balance—namely, the need to achieve a regulative scheme that is fair and reasonable to all stakeholders in an information environment where actors might unpredictably switch roles at any stage. This is also the reason any given copyright legal apparatus is seldom more than a guess about the optimal degree of exclusivity and liberties that need to be allocated to each category of stakeholders.

VI. CONCLUSION

The information-as-a-process approach teaches that copyright law does not protect "information"; rather, it protects individual interests that relate to the creation, communication, and reception of Medial Messages. The nature of the subject matter of copyright can be explored and further investigated through the prism of the Message concept and its role in the communication sequence and the information process at large. In this respect, information and communication theories may offer nonobvious perspectives on copyright law at various levels that have both descriptive and normative force. The approach to information introduced in this chapter and the reference to copyright subject matter as a derivative notion attempts to make a contribution to legal analysis on topics such as the originality threshold, the operation and impact of regulation, and the role of the law in channeling and serving a host of complex and diverse private and public interests. These lessons will inform the progression of this study at later stages and underpin further the theoretical groundwork before the discussion turns to address solutions to the copyright crisis in the digital environment.

2. PROPERTY AND PROPERTY RIGHTS

I. INTRODUCTION

Within the broad question addressed in this study concerning the interrelations between copyright and access, property is a central element. The previous chapter explored the nature of copyright subject matter *as information*. The focus now shifts to examining the set of legal entitlements surrounding the atypical subject matter called *information* (or, in terms of Chapter 1, medial message). The discussion of *access rights* requires an introductory explanation of the study's approach to legal property rights in general. The question whether *A* has a *right* to do (or abstain from doing) conduct *X*, or whether *A* has a *right* to compel *B* to do (or abstain from doing) *X* can be approached at various levels of abstraction. The term *right* is used in different ways and in a variety of contexts: a person may have a right to life, a right to self-defense, a right to earn a living, a right to vote, a right to obtain public records, a right to enjoy public parks, a right to breathe unpolluted air, or a right to keep his personal affairs and related information private. In a given legal system, all the above-mentioned entitlements may be called *rights* in the loose, generic sense of the term. At the same time, the legal situations these (and other) rights represent, as well as the entitlements they entail, may diverge substantially.

As a practical matter, lawyers and courts routinely search for the applicable rights in a given legal dispute in order to ascertain their scope and consequences for litigants. Where do they hope to find those applicable rights? This chapter will mention, but not focus on, related philosophical questions concerning the source, content, authority, and operation of legal rights in general. Yet the discussion on rights will primarily adhere to a *positivistic* methodology and will separate between positive legal rights and ethical questions. This methodology will provide a useful tool for determining the *existence* of legal rights by drawing on man-made institutions and establishments (such as statutes, courts, etc.) as the origin and source of legal rights.[1] In this chapter, natural law, ethics, morality, "soft" social norms and the like—as distinguished from the positive law—will largely remain outside the pool of resources that give rise to legal entitlements.[2]

1. *See* Tom D. Campbell, *Introduction* to Legal Positivism xiii (1999) (enumerating the three spearheads of legal positivism, namely (1) the logical separation between law and morality, (2) the emphasis on historical and institutional origin of the law, and (3) the centrality of rules in the legal system).

2. The term *positive law* here corresponds to its dictionary definition as constituting the black letter, applicable legal rules promulgated by official, competent authorities: "Positive

The question whether *A*, the copyright rights-holder, has a *right* to control access to works will be addressed more closely in Chapters 4–6, which focus on legal analysis of the positive law. However, to set the stage for the descriptive analysis, it is necessary to clarify a concept of *right* that is not biased by moral, political, or normative judgments. It is further necessary to use an objective technique to identify rights in the positive law. To this specific end, the Hohfeldian model of jural relations will provide the analytical framework. After introducing the methodology for identifying and analyzing rights, the discussion will proceed to various conceptualizations of private property, which should help to extrapolate property's paradigmatic characteristics as a legal-social institution. Later, the presentation of property theories and their application in the area of copyright law will underlie the discussion on problems such as the *property metaphor* and the contribution of classic property concepts to the intellectual property debate, as well as selected information cost-theory perspectives.

II. THE HOHFELDIAN MODEL OF JURAL RELATIONS

A. The Model as an Analytical Apparatus

The choice to apply the Hohfeldian model of jural relations has one central thrust. The analytical framework of access rights needs an objective and precise vocabulary for evaluating legal positions under a given legal regime. Throughout this study, the Hohfeldian methodology will guide the search for (and analysis of) rights and other entitlements *as they exist, or may exist in the law.* Wesley Newcomb Hohfeld[3] introduced his model of fundamental jural relations in the early twentieth century. He engineered a logical scheme for analyzing complex legal situations whose key to resolution is reducing legal positions to their lowest common denominators. In striving to articulate these denominators, Hohfeld set forth a strikingly elegant model that reflects a near algebraic, universal rigor.[4] The stated mission of the model is to provide coherent definitions of legal positions and entitlements, thus helping to identify them without reaching normative questions.

The model offers a short and straight answer to the question whether A has a right or not (assuming of course that one knows the relevant facts and applicable

law typically consists of enacted law—the codes, statutes, and regulations that are applied and enforced in the courts. The term derives from the medieval use of *positum* (Latin "established"), so that the phrase positive law literally means law established by human authority." *See* BLACK'S LAW DICTIONARY (4th. ed. 2004).

3. Wesley Newcomb Hohfeld: 1879–1918.

4. *Cf.* STEPHEN R. MUNZER, A THEORY OF PROPERTY 25 (1990) (commenting the Hohfeldian methodology "has the salient advantage of cross-cultural application").

legal rules.)[5] The model hence does not stipulate *the law* or any legal rights; instead, it provides a set of tools for evaluating legal positions in a given legal environment. Further, it does not attempt to answer whether *A* indeed *should* have a right, nor does it offer direct clues concerning the *scope* of rights.

Before reaching the details, it should be noted that despite its modest, nearly matter-of-fact packaging, the Hohfeldian model had a profound impact on modern legal thought[6] and on property law in particular.[7] Legal theorists saw in the model much more than merely an attractive proposal for fixing the legal jargon.[8] Despite its descriptive-formalistic façade,[9] Hohfeld's model and its perspectives on legal relations and conceptions inspired scores of theoreticians. Among them were the founders of legal realism, a movement that, inter alia, has had a major influence on U.S. legal scholarship during the twentieth century.[10] Also intellectual property scholars occasionally apply the Hohfeldian model when analyzing theoretical issues and articulating arguments concerning available and unavailable rights under copyright.[11]

---

5. Munzer considered the inability of the model to answer normative questions or divulge the applicable legal rules as a limitation of the Hohfeldian theory. *See id.* at 20–21. Whether this limitation is severe or not depends on one's expectation from the model. For the present purpose, this limitation may actually be considered an advantage.

6. *See, e.g.*, Nigel E. Simmonds, *Introduction* to Wesley Newcomb Hohfeld, Fundamental Legal Conceptions as Applied in Judicial Reasoning at x (2001) (noting "[f]ew works have made such a lasting contribution to analytical jurisprudence;" Curtis Nyquist, *Teaching Wesley Hohfeld's Theory of Legal Relations*, 52 J. Legal Educ. 238 (2002).

7. One manifestation of this impact in U.S. property law is the adoption of some of the model's basic concepts by the American Law Institute's Restatement of Property. *See* Restatement (First) of Property (1936) § 1 (defining property a property "right" in line with Hohfeld's definition).

8. *See* Joseph William Singer, *The Legal Rights Debate in Analytical Jurisprudence from Bentham to Hohfeld*, 1982 Wis. L. Rev. 975, 989–93 (1982) (reviewing the major theoretical debate invoked by Hohfeld's model and commenting: "The Hohfeldian debate consumed a great deal of paper and energy. Yet I believe that those engaged in it went about it the wrong way. The eight terms presented by Hohfeld were a human invention. Their validity and importance must relate to their utility in solving some problem").

9. *See* Simmonds, *supra* note 6, at x–xi.

10. *See* William Fisher III et al., American Legal Realism 8 (1993) (noting Hohfeld's taxonomy of entitlements was of practical use to the Realists in their efforts to discredit long-standing distinctions and sharpen their critique of classic legal reasoning). For a similar discussion in German legal theory (the so-called "*reine Rechtslehre*") and critique, *see* Alexander Peukert, Güterzuordnung als Rechtsprinzip 857–62 (2008).

11. *See, e.g.*, Wendy J. Gordon, *An Inquiry into the Merits of Copyright: Challenges of Consistency, Consent, and Encouragement Theory*, 41 Stan. L. Rev. 1345 (1989); Thomas P. Heide, *Copyright in the EU and United States: What "Access Right"?* 48 J. Copyright Soc'y. U.S.A. 363, 364–66 (2001); David R. Johnstone, *Debunking Fair Use and Copyduty under U.S. Copyright Law*, 52 J. Copyright Soc'y 345, 359 ff (2005).

TABLE 2.1 THE HOHFELDIAN OPPOSITE POSITIONS

Pair	1	2	3	4
Position	right-claim	privilege	power	immunity
Opposite	no-right	duty	disability	liability

B. The Scheme

As noted, Hohfeld endeavored to clarify the legal vocabulary and render the basic jural terminology more rigorous. He was troubled by finding certain words of critical importance in legal discourse had no agreed meaning, warning that muddled language might lead to muddled thought.[12] He stressed "whether legal or non-legal, chameleon-hued words are a peril both to clear thought and to lucid expression."[13] He then insightfully arranged all legal positions in four pairs, which he denoted "the lowest common denominators of the law."[14] His taxonomy of opposite positions is reprinted in Table 2.1.

Each pair contains two mutually exclusive opposite positions: *A* can have vis-à-vis *B either* a "right-claim" *or* a "no-right" to do a given act (or to compel *B* to forebear from doing an act.) Both the existence and content of the position are determined by the applicable law. For instance, *A* may have either a right to exclude *B* from his land or a no-right to exclude *B* from his land. Similarly, *B* may have either a privilege to enter *A*'s land or a duty to stay off it.[15] Jural relations are always analyzed as between two persons in the bilateral sense, so with respect to each legal position, there is a *correlative* legal position held by another. For example, if *A* holds a right-claim, his opponent *B* by definition holds a duty concerning the act covered by that right-claim. The correlative relationships are represented in the table reprinted in Table 2.2.

1. The Right/Duty and Privilege/No-Right Rubrics

The first two correlative relations denoted as right/duty and the privilege/no-right are of crucial importance. In the Hohfeldian sense, *A* has a *right* when she has an enforceable *claim* against *B*, who is, by definition, a duty holder.

12. While referring to the legalese commonplace in courts, Hohfeld lamented about the "inveterate and unfortunate tendency to confuse and blend the legal and the non-legal quantities in a given problem" as well as about "the ambiguity and looseness of our legal terminology." Wesley Newcomb Hohfeld, *Some Fundamental Legal Conceptions as Applied in Judicial Reasoning*, 23 YALE L.J. 16, 20–21 (1913).

13. *Id.* at 29 (footnote omitted).

14. *Id.* at 58.

15. *Id.* at 32–33.

TABLE 2.2 THE HOHFELDIAN CORRELATIVE POSITIONS

Position	right-claim	privilege	power	immunity
Correlative	duty	no-right	liability	disability

A's having a right means having the legal position to compel *B* to act in accordance with B's duty.[16] Alternatively, if *B* holds a *privilege* against *A* allowing B *to do* X, the logic of the model implies that *B* cannot have a simultaneous *duty* towards *A not to do* X. In this situation, *A* necessarily cannot legally compel *B* not to exercise his privilege regarding act X, which is represented by *A*'s correlative position of "no-right." As Hohfeld stated: "The privilege . . . is the negation of a duty."[17]

There is an additional important point concerning the second scenario of privilege/no-right. In Hohfeldian terms, *A* (the "no-right" holder) does not necessarily owe *B* (the privilege holder) a duty not to interfere with the exercise of *B*'s privilege. In other words, the no-right position held by *A* does not imply a legal obligation to respect *B*'s privilege. To secure the exercise of *B*'s privilege against *A*, *B* then must hold an additional right-claim of noninterference. That means that *B*, by virtue of his privilege per se, does not have a claim against *A* if *A* stands in his way to exercise the privilege. Further, *A* cannot legally enforce her interference (as she is in a no-right position) unless the law grants her a specific right-claim supporting her interference.[18]

Applied to property legal interests, a myriad of complex and intertwined clusters of positions and relations are commonplace. For instance, *A*, the owner of Blackacre, can have a right-claim against *B* to prevent *B*'s unauthorized entry, and *B* has a correlative duty not to trespass on Blackacre. In property jargon, *A* holds a *right-to-exclude B* from *A*'s property. In addition, *A* typically holds a

16. *Id.* at 31–32. *See also* Restatement (First) of Property, *supra* note 7, § 1 com. a. ("The relation indicated by the word 'right' may also be stated from the point of view of the person against whom that right exists. This person has a duty, that is, is under a legally enforceable obligation to do or not to do an act."). Hohfeldian rights are commonly denoted as right-claims or claim-rights, as the existence and scope of the duty determines the existence and scope of the right.

17. Hohfeld, *supra* note 12, at 32.

18. Hohfeld illustrated the situation with his famous shrimp salad hypothetical: "[T]he privilege could, in a given case exist even though the rights mentioned did not. A. B. C. and D, being the owners of [a shrimp] salad, might say to X: 'Eat the salad, if you can; you have our license to do so, but we don't agree not to interfere with you.' In such a case, the privilege exists, so that if X succeeds in eating the salad, he has violated no rights of any of the parties. But it is equally clear that if A had succeeded in holding so fast to the dish that X couldn't eat the contents, no right of X would have been violated." *Id.* at 35.

privilege to enter Blackacre *herself*, correlated to *B*'s no-right to restrict *A*'s privilege to enter. Further, *A* may have a right-claim against *B* that would impose a duty on *B* not to interfere with *A*'s access and use privileges. Such right may cover activities such as entry, exploitation, and enjoyment. Accordingly, *A* (the "owner") holds a bundle of rights and privileges that constitute her legally protected interests in Blackacre.[19]

Often, privileges are not exclusive, which renders the situation of conflicting privileges not unlikely. For instance, *A* can have a privilege to cross over a narrow bridge, whereas *B* is in a position of no-right to prevent it. *B* may have an identical privilege to cross the same bridge, whereas *A* is in a no-right position to prevent it. If the bridge is narrow so only one person can pass at a time, and *A* and *B* wish to exercise their respective privileges simultaneously, the two privileges would collide. To clarify the legal situation, it may be necessary to designate a duty of noninterference as to one of the parties, which would effectively corroborate one of the privileges with a right-claim. As a result, one of the parties will hold both a privilege to cross over and a negative right-claim obligating the other party to stay clear. The Hohfeldian model does not pretend to solve issues such as *when* and *how* to attach duties of noninterference in case of conflicting *privileges* (or *liberties*).[20] To Hohfeld, those were matters of "justice and policy" the model is not designed to resolve.

2. The Power/Liability Rubric

A brief comment on the power/liability constellation is in order. As reflected in the Hohfeldian tables above, a *power* is the jural opposite of disability and the jural correlative of liability. The position of power describes the situation where *A* can volitionally change the legal position of himself and others. Thus, *A*, "whose volitional control is paramount may be said to have the (legal) power to effect the particular change of legal relations that is involved in the problem."[21] Accordingly, owner *A* may have the power to transfer his interests in Blackacre to *B* (e.g., through sale), and by exercising this power he extinguishes his own interests while creating new and corresponding interests in *B*. Hohfeld characterized power as "one's affirmative "control" over a given legal relation as against

---

19. Ownership usually also includes the exclusive entitlement to transfer interests in the res. Such entitlements are Hohfeldian *powers*, discussed below.

20. Hohfeld argued that *privilege* and *liberty* are two names for the same thing, both equally distinguishable from *rights-claims* under the terminology he defined. *See* Hohfeld, *supra* note 12, at 36 ("liberty" or "privilege" per se do not imply a right against third parties to prevent interference).

21. *Id.* at 44. Hohfeld provided various examples of legal powers such as the power of the owner of personal property to extinguish his own legal interests through abandonment, transfer, or contract. Powers are also manifested in agency situations, where the agent is granted a power that can change the position of the principal. *Id.* at 45–46.

another."[22] In the case of *A*'s power to transfer a property interest to *B*, it is likely that before transfer, *A* holds this interest himself, as in order to transfer a good title in Blackacre to *B*, *A* must first hold ownership title. To avoid complications in applying the model, one may assume no agency situation (in which *A* is merely an authorized agent of *C*, who is the actual legal owner of Blackacre). Further, the possibility is set aside that *A* is the government, exercising its power of eminent domain.[23]

In the ordinary situation, *A* cannot transfer a right to exclude others from the res unless *A* himself is entitled to this right in the first place.[24] In general, *A* does not have the *power* to transfer ownership interests to *B* that *A* does not have himself before transfer. The flip side of the same principle is that *A* usually cannot *destroy* entitlements vested in *B* unless he is given the power to do so. If *B* has Hohfeldian immunity, *A* (by definition) is in a position of disability to influence *B*'s affairs, a conclusion derived from the fourth pair of correlative positions. *A*'s power to destroy *B*'s interest is not equivalent to rights/duties relations, as the two situations are represented in two distinguishable rubrics of correlative relations (as Table 2.2 indicates). However, if the law grants *A* the power to destroy *B*'s privilege at will and replace it with duty owed by *B* to *A* himself, the situation is akin to granting a *potential* right-claim. The parties shift from the power/liability rubric to the right/duty rubric if and when *A* resolves to exercise his power. For example, if *B* presently holds a privilege to walk through *A*'s Blackacre, and if *A* has the power to impose a duty on *B* to stay off, one can say that prior to exercising the power, *A* holds a potential right-claim to exclude *B*. To bring an example closer to the central topic of this study, if *B* presently holds a privilege to access a creative work, and if the law grants *A* Hohfeldian power to prohibit *B*'s access at will, *A* was actually granted a potential right-claim to control access to the work. If *A* exercises that power, *B* will be under a duty to respect it.

---

22. *Id.* at 55.

23. Exercising governmental eminent domain powers can alter private property positions. Often, the government is neither the owner of the assets nor a directly authorized agent of the actual owner (Of course, democratically elected/constructed government actors could be said to draw the power to alter private property positions as the legitimate representatives of their constituencies, a topic that goes beyond our focus here on private law, however). For the present purpose, it suffices to assume both actors *A* and *B* are private parties having their private property interests at stake.

24. In some special situations, a person has the power to transfer good title without being the legal owner (e.g., abandonment or transfer to a good faith purchaser in commercial situations). However, the general rule remains that the power to transfer a good title is usually placed in the hands of the legal owner: "A non-owner's power of sale is an exception to the *nemo dat* rule. . . which is the basic property principle that, in general, and for obvious reasons, I cannot transfer to you a property interest I do not have. . . As a non-owner I therefore have no *power* to transfer, *unless I acquire the power from some other source*.") *See* Alison Clarke & Paul Kohler, Property Law: Cases and Materials 24 (2005) (italics in original).

III. PRIVATE PROPERTY

A. Introduction

The colloquial meaning of the word *property* (in the sense of "this is my property!") diverges significantly from its "sophisticated" one. Most property owners are probably unaware of the quandaries with which property theorists have been wrestling for centuries on end concerning this basic term.[25] With regard to property in the legal-specialist context, matters are far from clear.[26] One thorny question has been to articulate the necessary components, or the essential content of private property ownership.[27] Theoretical-definitional inquiries focus, inter alia, on the special characteristics of private property, seeking to ascertain its unique attributes as distinguished from other legal fields. Rumination on the nature of private property is not without practical ramifications, as there is a logical thread connecting the ontological question ("*what is* private property?") and philosophical questions ("*why* private property?")—and further, with normative-political questions ("*how much* private property?") Proposing an answer to one of these questions appears to have an immediate effect on the answer to the others.

It is common to draw a distinction between conceptualist and nonconceptualist approaches.[28] More specifically, some commentators underscore the differences between conceptualism and instrumentalist/economic approaches.[29] In general, conceptualist theories seek to achieve an understanding of the intrinsic *concept* of property by identifying its unique nature and attributes. By comparison, non-conceptualist approaches to legal analysis tend to undermine the importance of the "what *is* property" question. Those following these approaches are suspicious regarding abstract legal concepts in general[30] and are prone to

---

25. *See, e.g.*, Jeremy Waldron, The Right to Private Property (1988) at 30 ("The objects of property—the things which in lay usage are capable of being owned—differ so radically in legal theory, that it seems unlikely that the same concept of ownership could be applied to them all, even within a single legal system.").

26. *Id.* at 26–61 (noting various approaches and setting forth a theoretical-analytical framework for the discussion on private property.) *See also* James E. Penner, The Idea of Property in Law 1–2 (1997) (providing an introduction to property's "identity crisis.").

27. *Cf.* Waldron, *supra* note 25, at 28 (arguing the content of private property (or the bundle of rights) is not constant but rather changing, which creates the difficulty in ascertaining the content of ownership).

28. The latter category includes nominalist, realist, instrumentalist, consequentialist, economic, and neighboring theoretical frameworks.

29. *See, e.g.*, Abraham Bell & Gideon Parchomovsky, *A Theory of Property*. 90 Cornell L. Rev. 531, 534–36 (2005) (underscoring the divide between conceptualist and instrumentalist/economic approaches).

30. For a classic Realist critique on conceptualism, *see* Felix S. Cohen, *Transcendental Nonsense and the Functional Approach*, 35 Colum. L. Rev. 809 (1935).

move directly to more practical aspects of property law and its functions.[31] The differences between theoretical methodologies emerge as one ponders framework questions, such as:

- What *types* of entitlements qualify as "property" entitlements and with regard to *which assets*?
- Against *whom* do property entitlements operate?
- What is the distinctive *content* of property rights?
- What are the *consequences* of property violations (what remedies)?

Consider the owner's legal protection against trespass to land. Is this a *property* right, and if so, why? What is its scope, and who is thereby affected? What are the remedies available to the owner in the case of violation? In which way does the classification of an entitlement as *property right* influence the answers to those questions?

To the conceptualist, protection against trespass to land is a property entitlement first because property law generally defines access and use entitlements of persons with respect to resources (here, between the owner and a plot of land).[32] The conceptualist would further stress that a right to prevent unauthorized entry availing "against the world" is distinctively a feature of property law.[33] The conceptualist could proceed by stating that, in fact, exclusion entitlements are at the very core of private property.[34] The fact the law helps owners to oust uninvited intruders, irrespective of harm or demonstrable damages, can be considered a conceptual dimension of property rights distinguishing them from legal fields such as torts and contracts.

---

31. One may contrast conceptual approaches with functional-nominal approaches to property. Singer explained: "Conceptualism is the belief that concepts at a high level of generality and abstractness are operative, in the sense that they correspond to elements of the real world and are the basis of numerous and concrete subrules that can be deduced from them. . . Nominalism is the belief that concepts at only a very low level of generality and abstractness are operative. Thus general concepts, such as 'law' or 'property' or 'rights,' are seen merely as convenient categorizations of experience." *See* Singer, *supra* note 5, at 1016.

32. *Cf.* Waldron, *supra* note 25, at 31 ("The concept of property is the concept of a system of rules governing access to and control of material resources.") For his discussion on intellectual property rights, *see* Jeremy Waldron, *From Authors to Copiers: Individual Rights and Social Values in Intellectual Property*, 68 Chi-Kent L. Rev. 841 (1993).

33. Section III.B.2 *infra*.

34. *Cf.* Penner, *supra* note 26, at 68 (arguing "property rights can be fully explained using the concepts of exclusion and use" and that "use almost always involves some exclusion of others").

The nonconceptualist addresses the problem differently—for example, by evaluating property rights according to their economic function and operation.[35] Consequentialist theories are less concerned with the question of what property rights *are* as with the question what property rights can or should *do* (e.g., serve as a vehicle for enhancing general utility). Property theories are important for this study because one of the main topics it deals with is clarifying the interrelations between copyright law and access rights with respect to works. Entitlements conferring access control with respect to information subject matter are called "property-like entitlements" due to their suggestive similarities to classic trespass rules; in both cases, controlling access to the resource constitutes the core of private property dominion. The crucial common denominator connecting property theory and access rights to information is the rights-holder's private right to exclude others from the resource, which is an essential element of private property in general. The following passages recount the importance of clarifying the concept of property—or at least, its central conceptual dimensions—as an intermediate step toward explaining how property-like rights in information materialize and operate.

B. Conceptual Dimensions of Property

1. *Property, Its Res, and Thing-Ownership*

Property law traditionally defines relations of persons with regard to physical "things," or relations between persons concerning "things." The intuition of physical relations has a long lineage. Roman law developed its property doctrines around problems of possession and use of physical resources, in which legal and actual-physical relations often merged.[36] Legal scholars and courts have formulated occupancy and possession theories that enshrine physical relations within property doctrines.[37] For instance, possession-oriented theories consider

35. *See, e.g.*, YORAM BARZEL, ECONOMIC ANALYSIS OF PROPERTY RIGHTS 62 (1989) (arguing "[t]he ability to consume commodities. . . implies the possession of rights over them. One cannot expect, then, to discover any evidence of a pre-property rights state, and it is, in fact, not possible to endow a pre-property rights state of affair with meaning"); Daniel H. Cole & Peter Z. Grossman, *The Meaning of Property Rights: Law versus Economics?* 78 LAND ECON. 317 ff. (2002) (contrasting legal and economic approaches to property rights).

36. Stein notes classical Roman law drew a sharp distinction between possession and ownership, whereas in the post-classical law, where everyone could vindicate his possessory claims in the thing, the distinction between physical possession and ownership became unimportant. *See* PETER STEIN, ROMAN LAW IN EUROPEAN HISTORY 25 (1999). Further, mere obligation to convey possessory rights did not affect ownership so long as conveyance had not yet taken place. *Id.* These principles, inter alia, demonstrate the firm nexus between physical and legal relations.

37. *See, e.g.*, Carol Rose, *Possession as the Origin of Property*, 52 U. CHI. L. REV. 73 (1985) (discussing the common law rule of first possession).

original possession in unwonted resources the key for allocating initial ownership rights.[38] Possession and occupancy property doctrines essentially presuppose the existence of an object, or, put in the legal vernacular, a *res*. The res is not simply an element in the property formula; it is its centerpiece. There must always be a *thing*, a resource, with respect of which the property regime creates rules of access and use.

The central importance of res as the signifier of property law is evident in civil code jurisdictions, which occasionally classify property regimes as the "law of things."[39] Mere manifested relations between persons and resources usually do not suffice to confer legal property rights absent social recognition in that person-thing relation. Property is not only a legal, but also a social institution in which members of society make assumptions and claims.[40] Property law regulates behavior of individuals in social settings, where legal rules mirror social conceptions and conventions about the legitimacy of private possession and the duty to respect it. The complex interrelation between the law of private property and social recognition is starkly reflected in theories of social contract or social consent, tracing back to early thinkers such as Grotius, who spread this idea at the dawn of Western liberal thought.[41] Some contemporary scholars similarly emphasize the crucial role of social consent within the foundation of theoretical justification of property.[42]

Grotius and other liberal thinkers derived the social consent requirement from the general proposition that prior to private property, resources are owned

38. *See, e.g.*, Richard A. Epstein, *Possession as the Root of Title*, 13 GA. L. REV. 1221 (1979) (arguing the case for original possession in unowned resources as the baseline to property rights.) *Cf.* Morris R. Cohen, *Property and Sovereignty*, 13 CORNELL L.Q. 8, 15 (1927) (criticizing the normative power of the "occupation" theory, yet admitting "there is a kernel of positive value" in the principle of protecting the first occupant's claim).

39. German law considers property as the broad right to actual and legal control over movable and non-movable "things." *See* OTTO PALANDT, BÜRGERLICHES GESETZBUCH, *introduction* to § 903 BGB nr. 1 (2007) . Property law is organized as the legal field called *Sachenrecht*, in which *Sachen* means (physical) "things." For an analysis of *things* (including intangible things) as a paradigmatic principle for the allocation of exclusive rights in German law, *see* PEUKERT, *supra* note 10, at 212 ff.

40. *See* JIM W. HARRIS, PROPERTY AND JUSTICE 3–5 (1996).

41. *See* HUGO GROTIUS, THE RIGHTS OF WAR AND PEACE, Book II, Ch. II, 2 at 89 (Cosimo 2007) (1625) ("It was not by the act of the mind alone that this change [from common to private property] took place. For men in that case could never know, what others intended to appropriate to their own use, so as to exclude the claim of every other pretender to the same; and many too might desire to possess the same thing. Property therefore must have been established either by express agreement, as by division, or by tacit consent, as by occupancy.").

42. *See, e.g.*, Adam Mossoff, *What is Property? Putting the Pieces Back Together*, 35 ARIZ. L. REV. 371, 379–80 (2003) (recounting Grotius' assertion that required social recognition in manifested relations as a crucial step for the establishment of property ("dominion")).

by mankind in common.[43] Though theorists may disagree about the social contract tenet and its role in *explaining* and *justifying* private property in things, as a practical matter, it seems pointless to speak of private property in the abstract without considering both its social functions and social ramifications—and the manifestation of property entitlements as a part of social life, conventions, and institutions. In that social structure, property is associated most often with physical spaces and/or objects capturing physical space in a world. Scarcity of space and valuable resources generates conflicts for which the law seeks to provide the institutional framework for resolutions. In this light, one central mission of property law is to clarify ownership entitlements and secure the ability of owners to reasonably enjoy, improve, protect, and transfer resources.

At the same time, the *thing* subject to property arrangements need not always be tangible, and the reason for the emergence of property rights in intangible things is not always (and not directly) rooted in scarcity.[44] But either way, it is always about *things*.[45] In this light it is safe to propose that property entitlements have at least two necessary elements. One is the *subject*, which is the person having a claim. The second is the *object*, the property res. Various property systems expressly establish the status of *ownership* or *owner*, denoting the person holding entitlements in the thing over which ownership reigns.[46] Other systems are more ambivalent in their stipulations concerning the content of ownership. Generally speaking, ownership vests in the person(s) holding all or some of the entitlements to the thing.[47] As a rule of thumb, a person is often considered the

---

43. GROTIUS, *supra* note 41, Book II, Ch. II, 2 at 86 ("God gave to mankind in general dominion over all the creatures of the earth.").

44. Section IV. *infra*.

45. For a discussion on *things* and *thingness* in law, with some emphasis on intellectual property, see Michael J. Madison, *Law as Design: Objects, Concepts, and Digital Things*, 56 CASE W. RES. L. REV. 381, 382 & n. 4 (2005) (noting "[p]roperty theorists have recently raised the problem of things in the law, recognizing the paradox that in an era of increasing dephysicalization of the artifacts of our lives, thingness may matter more than ever.") (footnote omitted).

46. The German civil code, for instance, defines ownership entitlements as the general power to do with the thing as one wishes, and to exclude others from the thing. *See* § 903 BGB.

47. The discussion does not address the theoretical problem of defining ownership or its content. The U.S. RESTATEMENT (FIRST) ON PROPERTY, *supra* note 7, reflects some of the confusion surrounding this issue. The "owner" is generally defined as "the person who has *one or more* interests." *See id.* § 10 (emphasis added). Later, the same Restatement provides "[a] person who has the *totality of rights, powers, privileges and immunities* which constitute complete property in a thing. . . is the 'owner' of the 'thing,' or 'owns' the 'thing.'" *Id.* at comment (b) (emphasis added). At the same time, it acknowledges ownership also in cases of diminished interests. *Id.* at comment (c) ("The owner may part with many of the rights, powers, privileges and immunities that constitute complete property

owner if she holds three core interests in the thing: the right to exclude, the privilege to possess/use, and the power of transfer.[48]

2. The Right to Exclude

The right to exclude (*jus prohibendi*) is a keystone element, perhaps the most important among all private property entitlements. Some commentators consider the right to exclude the very essence of private property.[49] In an unruly world, a person having a claim in a resource could still exclude others from it by using physical force or physical barriers. But legal thinkers and common sense predict exclusion that depends solely on self-help measures would furnish a rather "miserable" possession.[50] State-supported exclusory entitlements provide the essential guarantee to owners, with the law ensuring their individual claims shall be respected by their fellow citizens. With legal exclusion rights, owners may expect to have the resource available for use, enjoyment, and transfer without the need to ceaselessly watch for challengers.

The right to exclude is a negative entitlement: it commands third parties to *forbear,* rather than support duties to perform acts.[51] Holders of exclusory entitlements[52] may prevent unauthorized entering, touching, use, and other physical interference with the res. In the absence of the ability to exclude, control over the resource is impaired and its value to the owner is expected to diminish. The right to exclude is often celebrated as the hallmark of ownership, as it provides the necessary underpinning for virtually all (or most) other ownership-related property entitlements.[53] Private exclusion is the most direct measure to combat

---

and his relation to the thing is still termed ownership both in this Restatement and as a matter of popular usage.").

48. In his influential account, Honoré identified multiple *incidents* of ownership, while noting the right to exclusive possession is central: "The right to possess, namely to have exclusive physical control of a thing, or to have such control as the nature of the thing admits, is the foundation on which the whole superstructure of ownership rests." A. M. HONORÉ, OWNERSHIP 113 (1961). Honorè seems to present the right of (positive) possession and the (negative) right to exclude as two "aspects" of the same legal position.

49. *See, e.g.,* Cohen, *supra* note 38, at 12 ("the essence of private property is always the right to exclude others"). *See also* Thomas W. Merrill, *Property and the Right to Exclude,* 77 NEB. L. REV. 730 (1998) (arguing for the primacy of the right to exclude and its status as both a necessary and sufficient condition of property). *Cf.* PENNER, *supra* note 26, at 68–74 (discussing the nexus between exclusion and use in the social setting).

50. *See* Richard Epstein, *Liberty Versus Property? Cracks in the Foundations of Copyright Law,* 42 SAN DIEGO L. REV. 1, 18 (2005) (quoting Bentham).

51. For a statement of this universal principle in German property doctrine, *see* PALANDT, *supra* note 39, § 903 nr. 6.

52. In this study, the term *exclusory entitlements* denotes only negative exclusion entitlements, not positive duties imposed on other persons.

53. Few dispute that exclusion is a necessary aspect of property. *Cf.* HARRIS, *supra* note 40, at 24–25 (arguing that trespassory rules are a necessary but not sufficient condition for property).

the problem giving rise to the need for private property in the first place, namely, competition over valuable resources under conditions of scarcity. Further, as the right to exclude is transferable, it can increase the exchangeable value of the resource.

Negative-exclusory entitlements and positive-use entitlements are often intertwined.[54] The negative right-claim to exclude indirectly secures the rights-holder's opportunity to exercise positive enjoyment privileges herself. Exclusion capacity can be said to encapsulate within itself positive use entitlements, as making positive use often become feasible indirectly by virtue of the ability to exclude strangers.[55] Accordingly, positive use entitlements are implied and inferable from a broad exclusion entitlement.[56] (We do not attend here to situations in which "standing-alone" positive use rights conflict, and where the law's recognition in such positive rights might influence the legal analysis.) In any event, property rights (both negative and positive) are rarely unqualified. Public and private interests of others may trump private ownership rights to use the object where the law considers it more beneficial or just.[57]

3. The In Rem Principle

The in rem principle goes hand in hand with the right to exclude. It addresses the second question mentioned in the introduction to this section: who is affected by the right to exclude? Exclusion in rem usually means the right avails "against the world." The law does not identify or specify duty holders, but every person is generally under a duty to respect the private dominion.[58]

---

54. PENNER (1997), *supra* note 26, at 68–69. Penner argued that "at a theoretical level we understand the right to property equally as a right of exclusion or a right of use, since they are opposite sides of the same coin." *Id.* at 71.

55. Merrill, *supra* note 49, at 740 ("if one starts with the right to exclude, it is possible to derive most of the other attributes commonly associated with property through the addition of relatively minor clarifications about the domain of the exclusion right"). Of course, the ability to exclude others does not *always guarantee* that ability, and not even the legal entitlement to perform *all* imaginable uses of the resource. For instance, the owner of a parcel may have a broad right to exclude, but still be limited by zoning regulations concerning the structures she is allowed to erect on her land.

56. It is true the right to exclude does not always entail a right to positive use by the same person holding the negative entitlement. However, it is safe to assume that empirically, when the right to exclude in rem vests in a person, it ushers in an entitlement to exclusive use by that person more frequently than not.

57. A Hohfeldian solution to problems of conflicting or harmful uses of the resource by the owner to the detriment of another person does not necessitate explicit positive stipulations to the benefit of either party; for instance, the law can simply grant opponents the negative entitlement not to be harmed without needing to directly delineate the positive use rights of owners.

58. In Blackstone's classic formulation: "There is nothing which so generally strikes the imagination, and engages the affections of mankind, as the right of property; or that sole and despotic dominion which one man claims and exercises over the external things

The in rem operation of property exclusion entitlements draws an important distinction between the domains of property and contract law. In the property scenario, duty holders are indefinite and numerous. One of the most important distinctive characteristics of property right connects precisely to that impersonal aspect. Rights-holders do not need to know the duty holders or have a personal connection to them. No less important, duty holders do not need to know the rights-holders or have any connection to them either. This feature is particularly significant in the constellation of exchange. As property rights are usually impersonal, according to the in rem principle, the fact a property interest has changed hands does not affect the obligation of nonowners in general;[59] the only thing nonowners need to know is that the resource is owned by *someone*. Among other things, this aspect of property rights reduces the information cost of nonowners, who need not inquire about the precise identity of rights-holders in order to assess the scope of their duty.[60] Though property rhetoric speaks of rights against the *world*, the circle of persons *actually* affected by property rights held by owner *A* with regard resource *X* clearly does not extend so broadly. Rights in rem actually affect only those nonowners whose activities might conflict with the exclusive rights held by *A*. For analytical purposes, one may classify affected nonowners according to certain distinctions. For example, nonowners who only wish to avoid violation of exclusion rights can be distinguished from those advancing conflicting claims over the resource. Other groups of nonowners are those interested in transactions with rights-holders or those who are adversely affected by the use performed by rights-holders.[61] Most importantly, the in rem principle generally situates all nonowners on an equal footing, and the scope of their duties is initially independent of classifications and subjective inclinations.

4. The **Numerus Clausus** *Principle*

Numerus clausus means literally "closed number." As a legal principle, it reflects the observation that the design of property rights is subject to structural limitations.[62] In the United States, some property scholars have contended that

---

of the world, *in total exclusion of the right of any other individual in the universe.*" *See* 2 William Blackstone, Commentaries Ch. 1 at 56 (1838) (1765–69) (emphasis added).

59. Of course, the status of the specific parties to the transfer is affected, but *only theirs*, despite the possibly broader legal consequences of the transaction.

60. Thomas W. Merrill & Henry E. Smith, *The Property/Contract Interface*, 101 Colum. L. Rev. 773, 802 (2001) ("In rem rights entail lower information costs, at least on a unit-cost basis. To create an in rem right it is necessary only to specify particular resources and to identify one person as the manager (owner) of the resources. The 'deal' here is much simpler. It confers general exclusionary rights on the owner and then leaves it to the owner's discretion to establish use rights.").

61. This classification is discussed in more detail later on. *See* Section II.C.2(a) *infra*.

62. In German law, this principle is known as *Typenzwang* or *Typenfixierung*, which generally means that parties to a contract cannot "invent" new property rights that are effective *in rem*. *Cf.* BGH, V ZB 43/93 (1994) (*Erwerberhaftung für Wohngeldrückstände*)

property rights are limited in number and form, and that this feature is unique to property entitlements. They argue (descriptively) that property rights are fixed and limited in a menu of basic choices.[63] The principle implies structural and quantitative constraints on the possible emergence of property rights in any given scenario. Specifically, private parties cannot create property rights that are not already recognized as such.

The *numerus clausus* principle indicates the property system, with some exceptions, is generally intolerant to the novel, idiosyncratic formulation of interests.[64] That means the law would generally refuse to enforce nonrecognized entitlements against persons who are not in contractual privity with each other. In other words, nonrecognized entitlements usually will not "run with the asset" to bind third parties other than the original parties to an agreement.[65] Commentators generally agree the *numerus clausus* principle is reflected in property systems, though they might disagree about its description and main function. For instance, whereas Merrill and Smith argue the *numerus clausus* principle operates to reduce information costs,[66] Hansmann and Kraakman challenge that view, proposing instead that the principle, in fact, regulates the types and degrees of notice required to establish different property rights, and that its purpose is to

---

(stating the principle, but qualifying its application in cases when the law itself provides the possibility of the creation of new in rem entitlements).

63. *See* Thomas W. Merrill & Henry E. Smith, *Optimal Standardization in the Law of Property: The* Numerus Clausus *Principle*, 110 YALE L.J. 1, 9–24 (2000). *Cf.* Henry Hansmann & Reinier Kraakman, *Property, Contract, and Verification: The* Numerus Clausus *Problem and the Divisibility of Rights*, 31 J. LEGAL STUDIES 373, 376–77 (2002) (interpreting the *numerus clausus* principle as a limitation on rights) This principle has no explicit stipulation in US law, not even a unique "American" name, a fact that contributed to the heated debate on its existence, scope and function.

64. Merrill & Smith, *supra* note 63, at 10–11 (arguing that common law systems follow the principle while treating the recognized forms of property as a closed list that can be modified only by the legislature).

65. *See* Hansmann & Kraakman, *supra* note 63 (arguing the distinction between a property and a contractual entitlement is that the former "runs with the asset").

66. *See* Merrill & Smith, *supra* note 63, at 69 ("the *numerus clausus* makes sense from an economic perspective. By permitting a significant number of different forms of property but forbidding courts to recognize new ones, the *numerus clausus* strikes a balance between the proliferation of property forms, on the one hand, and excessive rigidity on the other. Proliferation is a problem because third parties must ascertain the legal dimensions of property rights in order to avoid violating the rights of others and to assess whether to acquire the rights of others. Permitting free customization of new forms of property would impose significant external costs on third parties in the form of higher measurement costs").

facilitate verification of ownership of rights offered for conveyance.[67] In any event, both views offer an economic-functional explanation to the *numerus clausus* principle, which focuses on information-related dimensions and consequences of property rights on such costs.[68]

5. Property Rule

Calabresi and Melamed articulated in thier well-known account the distinction between property and liability rules and its implications in the following manner:

> In our framework, much of what is generally called private property can be viewed as an entitlement which is protected by a property rule. No one can take the entitlement to private property from the holder unless the holder sells it willingly and at the price at which he subjectively values the property. Yet a nuisance with sufficient public utility to avoid injunction has, in effect, the right to take property with compensation. In such a circumstance the entitlement to the property is protected only by what we call a liability rule: an external, objective standard of value is used to facilitate the transfer of the entitlement from the holder to the nuisance.[69]

---

67. Hansmann & Kraakman, *supra* note 63, at 347. These authors' disagreement with Merrill and Smith is both descriptive and normative:

> At bottom, [the] difference between property rights and contract rights reflects the relative ease of aligning the interests of multiple claim holders who deal with each other directly as compared with the substantial costs, both private and social, of aligning the expectations of rights holders who are strangers, and of providing evidence of those expectations to a court. *This difference between contract and property is quantitative rather than qualitative.* Just using the ordinary tools of contract, it is possible with sufficient effort to fashion nonpossessory rights in an asset that will bind third-party purchasers. The rules of law that offer explicit recognition of particular types of property rights *simply reduce the costs of establishing those rights.* Consequently, it is not quite right to say that the law limits the kinds of property rights that can be created. Rather, it is more accurate to say that there are only limited kinds of property rights whose creation the law affirmatively facilitates.

Id. at 419 (emphasis added).

68. For a rather different Continental-European perspective on the *numerus clausus* principle (with special focus on intellectual property), see Ansgar Ohly, *Gibt es Numerus clausus der Immaterialgüterrechte?*, *in* PERSPEKTIVEN DES GEISTIGEN EIGENTUMS UND WETTBEWERBSRECHTS (2005). The application of that principle in various intellectual property contexts depends on the classification of those rights as thing-related (*dinglich.*) For a discussion on this classification in the context of intellectual property licensing agreements, see RETO M. HILTY, LIZENZVERTRAGSRECHT 108–16 (2001).

69. *See* Guido Calabresi & A. Douglas Melamed, *Property Rules, Liability Rules, and Inalienability: One View of the Cathedral*, 85 HARV. L. REV. 1089, 1105–06 (1972) (footnote omitted).

Calabresi and Melamed identified a typological distinction between legal rules endowing holders a priori veto powers to suppress unapproved use on the one hand, and on the other legal rules that excuse unapproved action, but mandate *ex-post* compensation. Significantly, Calabresi and Melamed constructed an economic framework for their analysis. For example, they explain the existence of liability rules as buttressed by a straightforward economic efficiency rationale.[70] At the same time, they did not neglect to mention noneconomic rationales to liability rules (e.g., distributional reasons).[71]

The distinction between property and liability rules receives concrete outlines when one closely examines the legal-positive formulation of a given legal entitlement. Does the law grant to the rights-holder an in rem veto power to prevent actions, or rather, does it create a compensatory cause of action valid against wrongdoers? An important aspect (or rather, a consequence) of having a property entitlement is the availability of injunctions to the rights-holder, which is a typical characteristic of a property regime. Property rules, as identified by Calabresi and Melamed, signify property entitlements, whereas liability rules exhibit a deviation from the common property formulation of rights and duties. As noted, their perspective gives much weight to legal remedies and their impact on stakeholders (i.e., the legal *consequences* of violations).[72] Injunctions and super-compensatory (punitive) damages are typical consequences of property rules' violations, whereas judicial awards of compensation to remedy violations by stipulating monetary damages based on approximate market value or actual harm are more typical of liability rules.

Calabresi and Melamed suggested that a liability rule is generally preferable when transaction costs are high, whereas a property rule is preferable when transaction costs are low.[73] The economic rationale behind this proposition is elementary: when a property rule controls a situation in which high transaction costs prevented a more efficient allocation through contracting, it is more

70. *Id.* at 1106 ("Often the cost of establishing the value of an initial entitlement by negotiation is so great that even though a transfer of the entitlement would benefit all concerned, such a transfer will not occur. If a collective determination of the value were available instead, the beneficial transfer would quickly come about.").

71. *Id.* at 1110.

72. Other scholars also underscored the substantive role of remedies in the definition of the legal rights they corroborate. *See, e.g.*, Epstein, *supra* note 38 (noting the question about the nature of rights and the question of remedies are very much intertwined); Henry E. Smith, *Property and Property Rules*, 79 N.Y.U. L. Rev. 1719, 1749 & n. 116 ("Property rules and liability rules are properly thought of as different ways of defining the *scope of entitlements* in the domain of transfer, rather than simply as 'remedies' protecting entitlements") (citing to respective literature) (emphasis added). Of course, the recognition that defining legal rights mirrors the legal consequences of their violations (or, that the duty is the mirror image of the right) is a tenent of the Hohfeldian model.

73. *See* Calabresi & Melamed, *supra* note 69, at 1106–08.

efficient to shift to a liability rule, under which nonowners are allowed to extract utility without consent, but must pay compensation that would approximate a hypothetical efficient transaction. Thus, when transaction costs are prohibitively high, or in holdouts and strategic behavior situations, it would be generally more efficient to follow a liability rule.[74] The contribution of the property/liability rule distinction to the conceptualization of property is important, as it helps to identify private property entitlements according to their general adherence to the property rules scheme. According to this scheme, the legitimacy of using a privately owned resource depends on its owner's consent most of the times and for most purposes, and consent is the key to extracting enjoyment and utility from the res. Infringement of private property rights is likely to entail severe legal consequences in the form of injunctions and overcompensatory damages awards.

C. The Concept of Property and the Information Cost Theory

1. Property's Conceptual Erosion

The five characteristic aspects enumerated above roughly outline the picture of what property rights are about and how they find expression in the law. In this context, the countermovement led by nonconceptualists should be mentioned. Hohfeld's project was a jurisprudential milestone within a larger movement that antagonized conceptualism and high-level categorizations.[75] For his part, Hohfeld launched a direct attack on the in rem and in personam concepts, which were traditionally used to distinguish between property law and the law of obligations. Specifically, he rejected the notion of in rem rights due to its conceptual fuzziness and proposed instead the term *multitial* rights, which are the practical equivalent of bunching together a multiplicity of in presonam rights.[76] Hohfeld also implicitly challenged the prominence of the right-to-exclude in the property scenario. He began with drawing a sharp distinction between physical relations and jural relations,[77] then insisted property rights, like any other rights (whether

---

74. *See* Smith, *supra* note 72, at 1733–34.

75. For a detailed account on the "decline" of property in Anglo-American scholarship during the twentieth century, see Thomas W. Merrill & Henry E. Smith, *What Happened to Property in Law and Economics?* 111 Yale L.J. 357 (2001). *See also* Bell & Parchomovsky, *supra* note 29, at 543–47.

76. Hohfeld suggested in rem rights are nothing other than the aggregation of numerous in personam rights (which he called "paucital" rights). Hohfeldian multitial rights are held by one person (or a group of persons) and are good against "persons constituting a very large and indefinite class of people." *See* Wesley Newcomb Hohfeld, *Fundamental Legal Conceptions as Applied in Judicial Reasoning,* 26 Yale L. J. 710, 718 (1917) (footnote omitted).

77. "A man may indeed sustain close and beneficial *physical* relations to a given *physical thing*; he may *physically* control and use such thing, and he may *physically* exclude others from any similar control or enjoyment. But, obviously, such purely *physical* relations could

in rem or in persoman) define the relationships *between individuals,* not between persons and things.[78] Hohfeld identified no particular hierarchy among the various possible entitlements consisting of the legal position of a person,[79] while deemphasizing the thing-ownership concept by focusing on the legal persons who have legal positions against each other and not against things.[80] To Hohfeld, there was no real qualitative distinction between a multitial right against trespass and a multitial right not to be a victim of battery.[81] In his twin articles, Hohfeld sewed the seeds for what Grey more than sixty years later proclaimed as the "disintegration" of property:

> We have gone, then, in less than two centuries, from a world in which property was a central idea mirroring a clearly understood institution, to one in which it is no longer a coherent or crucial category in our conceptual scheme. The Concept of property and the institution of property have disintegrated.[82]

As a result, the property "orthodoxy" reigning supreme in the Anglo-American legal scholarship views property as nothing more (and nothing less) than a bundle of rights or "sticks."[83] According to this view, property is a composite of legal interests such as rights, privileges, and powers. Metaphorically, the entitlement beneficiary holds her stick(s) at one end, while another person (the Hohfeldian correlative partner), holds the stick(s) at the other end. Property is an amalgam of Hohfeldian entitlements in which the content, number, size, or length of the sticks in a given bundle is contingent. No conceptual framework can outline the notion and boundaries of property "ownership," as the property bundle may theoretically assume any shape and form.

2. The Information Cost Theory

(a) Information Cost: In General

The broad acceptance of the "bundle" theory in the Anglo-American property jurisprudence did not mark the end of the property debate. In recent years, some scholars have developed a theoretical rejoinder to the bundle theory and

---

as well exist quite apart from, or occasionally in spite of, the law of organized society: physical relations are wholly distinct from jural relations." *Id.* at 721 (emphasis in original) (footnote omitted).

78. *Id.* at 720–21.

79. *Id.* at 723 (arguing the obligation to keep a contractual promise and an obligation not to commit trespass are not intrinsically distinguishable).

80. *See* Merrill & Smith, *supra* note 75, at 364 (arguing "Hohfeld failed to perceive that in rem property rights are qualitatively different in that they attach to persons insofar as they have a certain relationship to some thing").

81. *See* Hohfeld, *supra* note 76, at 719.

82. *See* Thomas C. Grey, *The Disintegration of Property, in* PROPERTY: NOMOS XII. 69, 74 (J. Roland Pennock & John.W. Chapman eds., 1980).

83. *Id.* at 69–71. *See also* MUNZER, *supra* note 4, at 22–24.

its problems, which, based on economic analysis, *reinforces* (rather than liquidates) the conceptual dimensions of property law. At first blush, one might suspect a tension between information cost's functional orientation and property conceptualism. However, property scholars (most significantly Merrill and Smith) showed that to the extent made, this assumption is rebuttable.

The emerging literature has begun to identify and explain the core traditional features of private property within the framework of an information cost paradigm. Information cost theory is premised on the universal proposition that regulation always imposes certain economic costs. One sort is information costs. In the context of property entitlements, the legal rule generally carries with it two types of information costs: The first type concerns information about the res itself, its conceptual and physical boundaries, its attributes, qualities, and so on. These costs relate to ascertaining what the "thing" is and what distinguishes it from other objects.[84] The second type of information costs relates more directly to the legal entitlements surrounding the res.[85] It includes first information about the fact the object *is* a private property res, and second, information concerning the content and scope of the property entitlements surrounding the object. As a practical matter, nonowners need to know (at least) what they can and cannot do without talking to rights-holders first.

As noted earlier, nonowners facing in rem rights scenarios can be classified according to their idiosyncratic agendas, intentions, and information cost they need to obtain to make rational decisions. The three main groups of nonowners affected by property regulation can be called avoiders, challengers, and transactors.[86] **Avoiders** are likely to make up the largest group. Avoiders simply wish to keep away from infringing on others' private property rights and minimize the risk of incurring liability. Accordingly, they must be able to identify the object and comprehend their set of negative abstention duties concerning that object. It is possible to view avoiders' information cost as *externalities* resulting from the allocation of property rights to rights-holders.[87]

---

84. *See* Clarisa Long, *Information Costs in Patent and Copyright*, 90 VA. L. REV. 465, 474 ff (2004) (noting the distinction between information costs related to the thing (the object) and those concerned with legal relations).

85. *Id.* at 474–76. *See also* Henry E. Smith, *Exclusion Versus Governance: Two Strategies for Delineating Property Rights*, 31 J. LEGAL STUDIES S453, S454–55 (2002).

86. Long proposed a taxonomy classifying nonowners (in the intellectual property context) into avoiders, transactors, and builders. *See* Long, *supra* note 84, at 489–92. Note classifications here are analytical and not mutually exclusive, as in reality, a single nonowner may exhibit attributes of one or more groups. Long makes a similar point (*id.* at 492).

87. Externalities can be described as "side effects" of economic activity. Standard economic analysis distinguishes between consumption and production externality. *See* HAL R. VARIAN, INTERMEDIATE MICROECONOMICS 602–03 (2003). If property rights are the "good" in the focus, then "consumption" by rights-holders (i.e., the exercise of rights)

Challengers vindicate antagonistic claims with respect to the res. As a logical preliminary step, they should be able to resolve information uncertainties so as to realize they *are* challengers in the first place. In other words, they need to know what the object is and what rights are attached to it in order to ascertain conflict with their own expectations regarding the same res. Next, they need information about the scope of their opponents' rights to formulate their own claims.

Transactors endeavor to acquire property rights via consensual exchange. They obviously need to valuate the object. To make an accurate assessment, transactors need detailed information about the attributes of the res (e.g., its quality, age, origin, functionality, or marketability). They further need to know who their potential contractual partners are and what rights they hold in order to assess what rights the potential partners can legally transfer.[88] In the course of ascertaining rights and identifying rights-holders, information about challengers' actual and potential claims and the prospects of successfully undermining the legal position of the rights-holders are relevant factors in the decision-making process. In this respect, information costs are a central component in the overall transaction costs involved in dealing with economic goods.[89]

In order to act rationally, parties affected by the allocation of property rights must acquire information relevant to their profile—but acquiring this information is costly. The basic idea of the information cost theory is that the legal rule, which imposes lower net information costs, is better than a rule imposing higher net information costs. The net information costs entailed by each alternative regulation depend on multiple variables (e.g., the number of persons affected by the rule, the attributes of the res, and the complexity of the property arrangement surrounding it).

---

imposes negative (information) externalities on duty holders. This application might seem rather plastic, though it suffices for explaining the general point of information costs that attach to legal rights. Note the notion of *externalities* in economic theory intimately relates to the notion of transaction costs. *See, e.g.*, Carl J. Dahlman, *The Problem of Externalities*, 22 J.L. & Econ. 141–42 (1979) (explaining the reason externalities are not fully internalized by wealth-maximizing economic agents must be rooted in high transaction costs).

88. As already mentioned in a different context, rights-holders generally have the power to transfer only entitlements they already have. *See* Section II.B.2 *supra*.

89. As Coase explained: "In order to carry out a market transaction it is necessary to discover who it is that one wishes to deal with, to inform people that one wishes to deal and on what terms, to conduct negotiations leading up to a bargain, to draw up the contract, to undertake the inspection needed to make sure that the terms of the contract are being observed, and so on. These operations are often extremely costly, sufficiently costly at any rate to prevent many transactions that would be carried out in a world in which the pricing system worked without cost." Ronald H. Coase, *The Problem of Social Cost*, 3 J.L. & Econ. 1, 15 (1960).

Smith described the regulation dilemma as the choice between two strategies, an *exclusion* strategy and a *governance* strategy.[90] According to Smith, in exclusion, "decisions about resource use are delegated to an owner who, as gatekeeper, is responsible for deciding on and monitoring specific activities with respect to the resource. To set up such rights, rough proxies like boundaries and the *ad coelum* rule are used. These exclusion rights are used when the audience (of duty holders) is large, and their simplicity reduces the processing costs that would be high for such a large and anonymous audience."[91] By contrast, Smith describes governance rules as picking out specific uses and users. As governance rules contain more details, they impose a greater informational burden on a definite group of duty holders.[92] Any given legal rule generally falls somewhere on the spectrum between the exclusion and governance poles.[93]

(b) Information Cost and Property Concepts

Information cost theory has been applied to provide an economic rationale to the existence and justification of long-standing property concepts—a kind of antithesis challenging the "disintegration" thesis. The paradigmatic example of exclusion strategy is the prevalence of the right to exclude in positive property law. According to Smith, "property proper includes a basic exclusionary regime with refinements of the governance type."[94] Instead of positively specifying in detail the uses exclusively reserved to the owner—thereby imposing correlative duties on nonowners to respect them—the law employs a rough proxy, bunching all those uses under the simple norm stipulating negative exclusion from making *any* unauthorized use of the resource. Nominally, the information costs of knowing a simple negative rule are expected to be lower than those of knowing a complex positive regulation. The information cost theory would justify the right to exclude if rough exclusion proxies (sending on/off signals telling uninvited nonowners always to stay clear) are more efficient than refined proxies contemplated under a governance rules (e.g., nonowner *X* is prevented from doing *A*, *B*, and *C* under *Y* and *Z* circumstances.) Exclusion rules are less precise on the one hand, but are cheaper to process and enforce on the other. By comparison,

---

90. *See* Smith, *supra* note 85.

91. *Id.* at 454–55 (footnote omitted).

92. *Id.* at 455.

93. Smith writes: "The theoretical limit, achievable only under conditions of zero transaction costs, would be one in which every potential Hohfeldian legal relation (right/duty, privilege/no right, and so on) is specified between every pair of members of the society. At the opposite extreme would be a total absence of specification of rights (anarchy or complete open access). In between are situations in which rights are specified, but they bunch together what would be separate rights in the fully specified zero-transaction-cost world, and so fall further toward the exclusion end of our spectrum." *Id.* at 473 (footnote omitted).

94. *Id.* at 456.

governance rules are more precise but entail more processing and enforcement cost.[95] It follows there is an inevitable trade-off between the preciseness of the rule and the information costs it imposes. It is equally obvious exclusion strategy is not always "better" than governance simply because it lowers net information costs. More accurate proxies may be necessary both as a matter of economic efficiency and broader policy considerations. The information costs argument only underlines its unique focal points as such that might help to shape the legal rule among other factors that should guide lawmakers.

Information cost analysis indeed offers an attractive explanation of the in rem principle. It helps to show why in rem patterns are necessary for private property and identifies situations in which it would make sense to grant in rem rights. When developing their information cost analysis, Merrill and Smith built on (and modified) Hohfeld's taxonomy of *paucital* versus *multital* rights while adding four clarifications/qualifications to Hohfeld's explication of the nature of in rem rights: (1) in rem rights are characterized by an indefinite and large number of duty holders; (2) in rem rights are *qualitatively different* from a simple aggregation of in personam rights by virtue of their relationship to a particular *thing*; (3) from the perspective of a duty holder, rights-holders of in rem entitlements are also numerous and indefinite; and finally, (4) in rem always require duty holders to abstain (*negative* entitlements) rather than imposing a positive duty to perform an act.[96]

The first clarification led Merrill and Smith to articulate a typology counting four species of rights, among which the attributes of indefiniteness and numerousity are diverse. The two polar cases are the Hohfeldian paucital (or pure in personam) rights and pure in rem rights.[97] In the middle range, the phrase *compound paucital* rights has been coined, the duty holders of which are definite but numerous (as in the case of standard-form contracts), and *quasi-multital* rights, the duty holder of which is indefinite but singular (as in the case of assignment of a right under a lease).[98] The important insight behind this taxonomy is that the in rem concept can be refined in a manner that would invite an information costs analysis of such rights. According to this framework, information costs considerations influence the type of rights designated to their holders. Pure in rem rights are defined as negative duties (which according to the fourth clarification, demand abstention) that are imposed on numerous and indefinite duty holders. Under an information cost analysis, in rem exclusion rules make sense when the number of persons who must know about the entitlement is great and the rules can be phrased in simple, unsophisticated terms. This reflects the classic Blackstonian in rem scenario, in which (i) negatively defined exclusion duties are directed (ii) against "the world."

95. *Id.* at 473–75.

96. *See* Merrill & Smith, *supra* note 60, at 783 ff.

97. *Id.* at 785.

98. *Id.*

Smith also explored the application of the information cost framework to the Calabresi/Melamed distinction between property and liability rules.[99] Smith notes Calabresi and Melamed initially did not mean the term *property rule* to necessarily accompany or be associated with the classic concept of property;[100] to them, the term was a derivative of economic conditions. At the same time, Smith brings forth an argument linking property rule and property law based on information costs analysis. Smith argued the information cost theory, as applied to the distinction between property and liability rules, helps to "capture[] the deep connection between 'property rule' treatment and the traditional notion of property as an in rem right to a thing."[101] Smith's central contention is that what Calabresi and Melamed defined as *property rules* is prevalent in property law as a response to information cost problems.[102] Smith further argues property rules are naturally paired with the right to exclude, which he conceives as the predominant property entitlement. It is worthwhile to recite Smith's argument in its original formulation:

> [E]xclusion, property, and property rules fit together. Resources in the world are multidimensional and not homogeneous from one token to the next. But producing information about the things in the world is costly and thus things tend to be grouped by type, even though the tokens in those types are not equally suited to various uses . . . If delineation and evaluation—the production of information—were costless, then the response to the problem of heterogeneous tokens would be to measure the valued attributes of the tokens—at zero cost—and set up new, more fine-grained types. This process would continue until marginal benefit declined to zero. At this point, the homogeneity of assets and services would be reestablished, with smaller groupings of assets and services under one price . . .
>
> Human minds, however, cannot know or process every detail of the environment; the mind segments the environment into things and things into classes based on similarities. Thus, in many cases, significant differences exist among the seemingly interchangeable assets and services, from the oranges in a grocer's bin to toasters to haircuts, that are grouped under the same type. These differences are economically significant because the attributes are valued; the different levels of these attributes in the tokens cause the various tokens to differ in value. . .different actors will have differing abilities to

99. *See* Smith, *supra* note 72.

100. *Id.* at 1791 ("In their article, Calabresi and Melamed coined the term 'property rule' but without relating property rules to the traditional notion of property. Instead, following in the Realists'—and Coase's—footsteps, they ignored property as an in rem right to a thing in favor of 'entitlements,' which have no antecedent character until filled in by judges resolving use conflicts between plaintiffs and defendants.") (footnote omitted).

101. *Id.*

102. *Id.* at 1753 ff.

> develop and act on this information. Property responds to uncertainty over uses by bundling uses together and delegating to the owner the choice of how to use the asset, thus avoiding the need to specify uses at any stage.[103]

Smith posits that liability rules, which impose a "price" on unapproved use, are more typical to governance regulative strategy, whereas property rules, which impose "sanctions" as a response to violations, are more typical of exclusion strategy.[104] Exclusion is an inextricable feature of property, and one should expect property rules to dominate the structure and allocation of property rights. Information costs analysis provides an explanation of the advantage of property rules within the exclusion strategy by relying on rough and low-cost signals.[105] To complete the picture, Smith argued information cost theory also corroborated property law's essential attribute as thing-related regulation:

> Protection of a large and indefinite class of uses by delineating a thing and giving the owner a right to exclude others from the thing is a strategy well suited to situations in which it is not economical to decide first-order questions of use on a use-by-use basis. Instead, the right to exclude from a thing—property in the classic sense—is the result of a second-order delegation to the owner to choose among any uses, known or unknown, of the thing.[106]

To summarize the main points, information cost theory underscores and reinforces the economic-functional rationales of traditional property concepts. Property law is about the regulation of access and use of (i) resources ("things"), making an intensive use of an apparatus called (ii) the right to exclude, which avails against (iii) the rest of the world, of which violation entails (iv) injunctions and other legal sanctions. All these basic features of property law reemerge as the discussion proceeds to the area of intellectual property, at times yet with greater vigor. It shall be shown the persuasive force of information costs perspectives is also reinforced when the property res is stripped from any physical attributes—namely, when the res is intangible.

IV. INTELLECTUAL PROPERTY

A. Proprietary Entitlements in Information

Chapter 1 showed that information subject matter can be thought of as a medial message, which is the perceptible manifestation of communicative activities within the information process. In the intellectual property context, the message

103. *Id.* at 1727–28 (footnotes omitted).
104. *Id.* at 1750–53.
105. *Id.* at 1753 ff.
106. *Id.* at 1754.

is the "thing" around which property-like entitlements are tailored,[107] forming the conceptual convergence point between information and property. In its prevalent contemporary meaning, intellectual property is an umbrella notion covering patent, copyright, and trademark laws, as well as other legal branches securing exclusivity in immaterial objects.[108] The bulk of intellectual property theoretical and practical problems concern the application of property-like exclusion regimes to domains of intangible artifacts.[109] Two assumptions strongly underlie intellectual property law, with one being pragmatic and the other normative: it is assumed that at least in principle, protection of property-like entitlements in messages is both *feasible* and *warranted*, with neither assumption being self-evident.[110] A number of theoretical and normative justifications for intellectual property are discussed in the next section,[111] and matters concerning the design of property-like rights in information are explored in Chapter 3 infra. First addressed are several issues concerning the uneasy transition from the corporeal property res to the incorporeal.

1. *Information as "Public Good"*

Due to its informational nature, a message is an unusual candidate for being considered property res. This peculiarity is frequently expressed in conjunction with the economic notion of *public good*.[112] The description of immaterial subject

---

107. The denotation *property-like* is used to indicate the distinction between property ownership in the conventional sense, and the set of entitlements protected under intellectual property law.

108. *See* Peter K. Yu, *Intellectual Property and the Information* Ecosystem, 2005 MICH. ST. L. REV. 1, 2–6 (2005) (reviewing common usage of the term *intellectual property* in legal scholarship.) *See also* WIPO Web site, *What Is Intellectual Property*? ("Intellectual property refers to creations of the mind: inventions, literary and artistic works, and symbols, names, images, and designs used in commerce") (available at http://www.wipo.int/about-ip/en/). One textbook generally described intellectual property as covering "the creation, use and exploitation of mental or creative labour." *See* LIONEL BENTLEY & BRAD SHERMAN, INTELLECTUAL PROPERTY LAW 1 (2004) (citation omitted). *Cf.* ROBERT P. MERGES ET AL, INTELLECTUAL PROPERTY IN THE NEW TECHNOLOGICAL AGE 1, 24 (2006) (avoiding a general definition).

109. *See, e.g.*, Mark Lemley, *Property, Intellectual Property, and Free Riding* 83 TEX. L. REV. 1031 (2005) (criticizing the application of real property legal norms, rationales, and terminology to areas of intellectual property).

110. *Cf.* Wendy J. Gordon, *Intellectual Property, in* THE OXFORD HANDBOOK OF LEGAL STUDIES 618–19 (P. Peter Cane & Mark Tushent eds., 2003) (the accuracy of both the *intellectual* and the *property* labels contained in the term *intellectual property* can be questioned).

111. Section IV.B *infra*.

112. *See* WILLIAM M. LANDES & RICHARD A. POSNER, THE ECONOMIC STRUCTURE OF INTELLECTUAL PROPERTY LAW 14 (2003) ("[intellectual property] is a 'public good' in the economist's sense that consumption of it by one person does not reduce the consumption by another.").

matter as public goods has become so prevalent in the literature that its fundamental assumptions are seldom questioned,[113] though the fuzziness of this labeling already manifests itself at the level of definitions. Economic literature describes a "pure" public good as having two characteristic features: it is nonexcludable, and its consumption is nonrival.[114] First, non-excludability means it is impossible to provide the good to one person and prevent the provision of the good to others. Classic examples are the benefits of a lighthouse and national defense. Second, enjoyment from (or consumption of) tangible goods is considered rivalrous, meaning that enjoyment derived by one person diminishes the ability of other persons to do the same. Classifying goods as non-rivalrous means consumption of the good by one person does not diminish the supply available for consumption by others.[115] In economics vernacular, the marginal cost involved in extracting marginal utility from such goods is zero.[116]

Many intellectual property scholars view in these features the most critical distinction between physical and incorporeal resources.[117] Yet some aspects of the treatment of information goods as public goods are controvertioal, for instance the question of whether one or rather both pure public good features accurately describe the intangible subject matter of property. Some legal scholars believe intellectual property subject matter is both non-excludable and non-rivalrous.[118] Others insist such subject matter is non-rivalrous but excludable

---

113. For one notable exception, see Christopher S. Yoo, *Copyright and Public Good Economics: A Misunderstood Relation*, 155 U. Penn. L. Rev. 635 (2007). Yoo critically observed that much of the scholarship on the economics of copyright has been considering works as pure public goods. *Id.* at 644 ff.

114. This terminology is widespread but not universal. For instance, Demsetz objected to the notion that public goods are nonexcludable *per* definition. Instead, he proposed that such goods can be nonrival but excludable, and called goods that meet both conditions "collective goods." *See* Harold Demsetz, *The Private Production of Public Goods*, 13 J.L. & Econ. 13 292, 295 (Oct. 1970).

115. *See, e.g.*, Andrew Gowers, Gowers Review of Intellectual Property ¶ 1.2 ("Unlike physical property, knowledge, ideas and creations are partial 'public goods.' Knowledge is inherently non-rivalrous. That means one person's possession, use and enjoyment of the good is not diminished by another's possession, use and enjoyment of the good.").

116. *Cf.* Landes & Posner, *supra* note 113, at 19–20.

117. *See, e.g.*, Merges et al., *supra* note 109, at 2 ("The fact that the possession and use of ideas is largely 'nonrivalrous' is critical to intellectual property theory because it means that the traditional economic justifications for tangible property does not fit intellectual property.").

118. *See, e.g.*, Tom G. Palmer, *Intellectual Property: A Non-Posnerian Law and Economics Approach*, 12 Hamline L. Rev. 262, 275–76 (1989) (arguing "ideal objects" satisfy both pure public good conditions, as namely, they are both nonexcludable and nonrivalrous: "My consumption of an idea or of a process, for example, does not in the least diminish the consumption of another, while, since the cost of reproduction of an idea is virtually

upon investment of some effort and expense for fencing.[119] Yoo has recently proposed a perspective for the debate by returning to Samuelson's original analysis, which was particularly interested in the optimal production of public good by the *government*.[120] Yoo notes Samuelson saw the peculiarity of public goods not in their non-excludability and non-rivalrous consumption, but in the way consumers signal their preferences and valuation. Whereas in the case of private goods (which are provided and consumed individually, with consumers revealing their preferences by purchasing a given quantity at a given price), in the case of public good, consumers reveal idiosyncratic preferences by their willingness to pay a given price for one quantity *unit*, which is in fact the *whole* product.[121]

These and other divergent views on the public good problem yield divergent approaches to legislative solutions and the legal protection of intellectual property in general. Those who believe intangible subject matter is *inherently* non-excludable are often hostile to legal fencing in the form of strong intellectual property protection.[122] Others believe fencing is necessary to alleviate the systematic malfunction of markets in which the marginal cost of producing the next unit is zero (or near zero) and consumption is non-rivalrous.[123] Yoo's analysis shifts the focus to the "Samuelson condition," requiring expansion of the production of public goods so long as the aggregate marginal benefits derived by all consumers exceed the marginal cost of that production.[124] Though it is arguably impossible to determine the aggregate marginal value to consumers of a public good, Yoo argues that analyzing ideal objects (in that case, copyrighted works)

---

zero (as it need only by thought), it can be very difficult, if not impossible, to exclude non-purchasers from enjoying the benefits of their production. Thus, ideal objects may qualify as truly archetypical cases of pure public goods.").

119. *See, e.g.*, Patrick T. Croskery, *Institutional Utilitarianism and Intellectual Property*, 68 CHI.-KENT L. REV. 631, 635 ff. (1993) (preferring the term *information goods* that are excludable and non-rival to describe IP subject matter).

120. *See* Paul A. Samuelson, *The Pure Theory of Public Expenditure*, 36 REV. ECON. & STAT. 387 (1954) (defining *collective consumption goods* as being that "each individual's consumption of such a good leads to no subtraction from any other individual's consumptions of that good").

121. *See* Yoo, *supra* note 113, at 638–39 ("Indeed, each person who purchases the public good simultaneously consumes the entire output of the public good. This characteristic gives rise to an interesting inversion of the conditions for the efficient allocation of private goods. For private goods, consumers pay the same price and signal the different valuations that they place on the good by purchasing different quantities. For pure public goods, consumers consume the same quantity of production and signal the intensity of their preferences by their willingness to pay different prices.") (footnote omitted).

122. *See* Palmer, *supra* note 119, at 303.

123. Economic perspectives on copyright law will be briefly discussed in Section IV.B.3(b) *infra*.

124. Yoo, *supra* note 113, at 639.

as impure public goods, which nonetheless must satisfy the Samuelson condition, has a major doctrinal payoff.[125]

Much of the trouble is rooted in the seemingly inherent contradiction between the essence of messages and property-like exclusion strategies and the proper response to that contradiction. How can a message (as defined in Chapter 1) fit in the traditional property framework? As to the first pure public good feature (concerning excludability), if one were given complete freedom to shape factual circumstances, it would seem possible to also selectively provide products such as air or information.[126] To some extent, a similar conclusion may follow if one could freely shape the legal landscape in connection with the view considering intellectual property laws as a form of legal fencing, thus effectively enhancing the excludability of ideal objects. The main instruments of the law to achieve a degree of excludability are enforcement of exclusory entitlements, and no less significantly, deterrence.

Theoretically, there are several ways to achieve selective provision of the message ex post initial communication by the originator. One obvious way is to impose legal sanctions on recipients who recommunicate the message without permission. The legal basis for such rule could be intellectual property law, but also others such as contract, privacy, libel, or national security. A second strategy piggybacks on real property rights. Ownership of physical spaces (e.g., keeping the sole exemplar of a work in a domestic safe), or ownership of tangible objects (possessing the sole copy of a manuscript) can serve to impede unwanted reception by unauthorized individuals. A third strategy, which shall be explored in length in the next chapters, is exercising control over the functionality of logical and logistic media.

As to the second pure public good feature (concerning nonrival consumtion), it is broadly accepted that often the costs involved in marginal reception by the marginal recipient of a message are zero (or near zero) while the marginal utility effect is positive.[127] Consumption itself may be non-rivalrous; however, the consumption of *input resource* invested to create the message may very well be rivalrous,[128] which appears to be the main rationale behind providing legal fencing under the incentive theory. It should be noted the term *consumption* in this

---

125. *Id.* at 683 ff.

126. *Cf.* Bell & Parchomovsky, *supra* note 29, at 580–82 (providing a hypothetical fact pattern in which a resource such as air is provided selectively).

127. Note that although production costs may be zero, the overall costs (production, consumption, and opportunity costs) are greater than zero. Reception consumes resources such as time and attention span. Economists may call them positive opportunity costs. In addition, the crowding of the channel (congestion) caused by marginal reception might have a negative impact on net utility.

128. *See* Henry Smith, *Intellectual Property as Property: Delineating Entitlements in Information*, 116 Yale L.J. 1742, 1744 (2007).

context might be misleading as messages obviously are not "consumed" as are food, water, or physical commodities.[129] (Still, a message might "expire" if nobody knows its content, and if all feasible routes to recover it have been exhausted.)[130] Nor are messages subject to natural-biophysical processes or the transformation of energy into matter and vice versa.[131] Indeed, information can be "used" (as distinguished from being "consumed").[132] One can think of three paradigmatic ways to use messages. First and most basically, **reception** itself is a type of use, such as reading a book or listening to music. The second is **recommunication** (i.e., incorporating the message or elements thereof in one's own expression). Finally, the third is **action upon (or according to) information**, such as purchasing stocks of a publicly traded company after receiving insider information. This observation is illustrated in Figure 2.1 below:

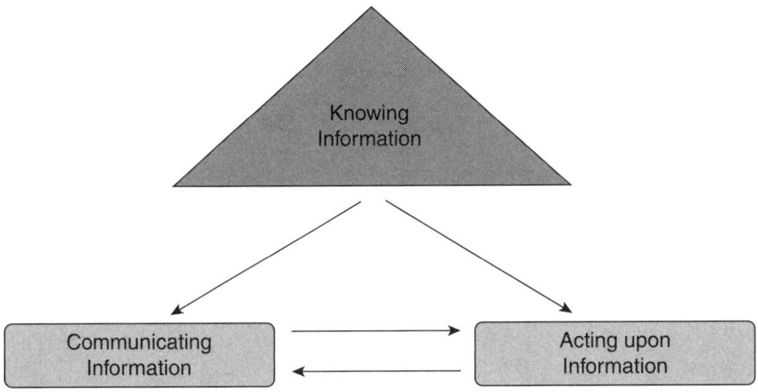

FIGURE 2.1 THE INFORMATION PYRAMID

Figure 2.1 illustrates the three types of information use (or use of a medial message) and the relationships between them. Knowledge (or reception of the

129. *See* Niva Elkin-Koren, *Making Room for Consumers under the DMCA*, 22 BERKELEY TECH. L.J. 1119, 1137 (2007) ("We do not 'consume' a book in the same way we 'consume' chocolate. Both reading a book and eating a piece of chocolate may involve pleasure, but the novel—the copyrighted informational work that is embodied in a book—is never consumed. It can never be used up like all other tangible goods. Consumption of informational works does not exhaust the resource.") (footnote omitted).

130. Chapter 1, Section 2.A *infra.*

131. *See* Klaus Krippendorff, *Information Theory, in* COMMUNICATION AND BEHAVIOR 351 (Gerhard J. Hanneman & William A. McEwen eds., 1975).

132. *Cf.* Yochai Benkler, *From Consumers to Users: Shifting the Deeper Structures of Regulation Towards Sustainable Commons and User Access,* 52 FED. COMM. L.J. 561, 565–70 (2000) (objecting to the term information *consumers* and favoring the term *users* to underscore perspectives of democracy, personal autonomy, and communication).

message) is a precondition to both recommunication and action upon information. In turn, acting-upon may have communicative dimensions, and communication may have acting-upon dimensions. In other words, the two secondary types of use are not inherently separable. Either way, the nature and consequences of each type of message use imply important differences as compared to use of corporeal resources. Due to *lack* of use, messages might be forgotten, expire, cease from being circulated, and consequently dissolve into nonexistence (at least for any practical purpose). Paradoxically, the only reason for the expiration of messages is not overuse but a lack of use, precisely the opposite of the wear-and-tear effect of overuse in the case of real resources. It follows that though messages do not carry in their concept the promise of endurance through eternity their basic *communicative* value is unlikely to be exhausted *through use.* At the same time, if strangers are allowed to access the message, communicate it, and act upon it without limitations, this might adversely affect the claimant's opportunity to do the same with "his" message, most relevantly, in the context of drawing related economic and reputational advantages.

2. Information and Possession

Commentators and courts attending to issues of intellectual property as public good often quote Thomas Jefferson's famous words objecting to natural rights in ideas. Jefferson observed:

> It would be singular to admit a natural and even an hereditary right to inventors. . .It would be curious. . .if an idea, the fugitive fermentation of an individual brain, could, of natural right, be claimed in exclusive and stable property. If nature has made any one thing less susceptible than all others of exclusive property, it is the action of the thinking power called an idea, which an individual may exclusively possess as long as he keeps it to himself; but the moment it is divulged, it forces itself into the possession of every one, and the receiver cannot dispossess himself of it.
>
> Its peculiar character, too, is that no one possesses the less, because every other possesses the whole of it. He who receives an idea from me, receives instruction himself without lessening mine; as he who lights his taper at mine, receives light without darkening me. That ideas should freely spread from one to another over the globe, for the moral and mutual instruction of man, and improvement of his condition, seems to have been peculiarly and benevolently designed by nature, when she made them, like fire, expansible over all space, without lessening their density in any point, and like the air in which we breathe, move and have our physical being, incapable of confinement or exclusive appropriation.[133]

---

133. *See* Thomas Jefferson, *Letter to Isaac McPherson,* Aug. 13, 1813, *in* 13 THE WRITINGS OF THOMAS JEFFERSON (Andrew A. Lipscomb ed., 1903). The cited letter was

The relevant part of this quote denotes the problem of consolidating between the conventional notion of possession and the immaterial subject matter of property. As noted, the classic concepts of property law evolved out of life situations and conflicts related to physical possession.[134] In the quoted excerpt, Jefferson's objection focuses precisely on the fundamental difference between the nature of possessing *ideas* as compared to material resources. Actual possession of physical resources has provided the necessary background for the emergence and formation of traditional property conceptions and arrangements in which the act of taking possession is both *declarative* and *prohibitive*: it is a declaration of an individual claim, which occasionally imposes actual barriers on possession and use by other claimants. Taking possession is an open act in the physical world that can be observed and evaluated by members of the community. It puts others on notice with regard to subjective claims and invites them to submit their objections (if they have any).[135]

The central importance of actual possession in the classic property narrative is frequently mirrored also in modern positive property law (for instance, in adverse possession law or finders law).[136] Possession is noticeable, affirmative, and declarative. It demarcates the physical space or thing of which the claimant seeks to deprive others. It is fairly undisputed today, as Jefferson lucidly articulated two centuries ago, that the rationales for recruiting public resources (adjudication, enforcement etc.) for the sake of securing private claims over valuable resources cannot be transplanted as-is into intellectual property doctrines. Often, the problems intellectual property law must confront differ radically. For example, possession by its nature simply cannot fulfill the same functions in the information good scenario. To "have" information (or knowledge, or an idea) is at its core a subjective condition, a cognitive circumstance. So long as this condition remains purely subjective, it cannot single out any intention or claim.

---

quoted in length and clearly influenced the U.S. Supreme Court in Graham v. John Deere Co., 383 U.S. 1, 7 ff (1966).

134. In making a similar point, Palmer argued that unlike traditional property, patents and copyrights are "not the product of an evolutionary process of interaction among interested parties that is later ratified through legal sanctions." *See* Palmer, *supra* note 118, at 280.

135. *See* Carol M. Rose, *Possession as the Origin of Property*, 52 U. Chi. L. Rev. 73, 81 (1985) ("Possession as the basis of property ownership, then, seems to amount to something like yelling loudly enough to all who may be interested. The first to say, 'This is mine,' in a way that the public understands, gets the prize, and the law will help him keep it against someone else who says, 'No, it is mine.' But if the original communicator dallies too long and allows the public to believe the interloper, he will find that the interloper has stepped into his shoes and has become the owner.").

136. *See, e.g.*, Thomas W. Merrill, *Property Rules, Liability Rules, and Adverse Possession*, 79 Nw. U. L. Rev. 1122, 1226 ff (1984) (explaining adverse possession law in the United States).

As Jefferson pointed out, others become aware someone "possesses" a message upon communication, which in fact, has precisely the opposite effect of physical possession, namely, of occupying the thing for one's self in order to exclude others from its benefits. Instead of declaring an exclusivity claim, the immediate effect of communication is that other persons become new "possessors" of the message.[137]

The relationship between information (as a public good) and the role of possession are commonly invoked to emphasize the *discrepancies* between information subject matter and common conceptions of real property. Those skeptical about intellectual property protection attack the *property metaphor*, which draws analogies from real property conceptions in analyzing exclusivity in ideal objects.[138] With this debate in mind, it might not be necessary to flatly reject "conventional" property principles when one comes to explore the issue of rights in messages—perhaps as representing "nonconventional" subject matter. The analogy to real property (or, the "property metaphor") could be valuable for theoretical analysis, but in any case, it shoud be handled with caution, as the issue of possession illustrates. More refined sub-analogies must take into consideration the conceptual differences between real and information reasources for the purpose of applying property principles to messages.

B. Theoretical Approaches to Intellectual Property

Thomas Jefferson did not object to intellectual property per se—his critique targeted the natural law justifications to property-like entitlements in ideas.[139]

---

137. This does not mean to argue that communication of the message is the *only* way to let the world know an individual possesses information, as it is perhaps possible to communicate information *on* the message rather that the message *itself*. Further, acting upon information may signal the actor has information. In the example above, the inside trader does not need to tell the authorities he has been acting according to insider information in order to be identified—and possibly convicted. Illuminating a different aspect of the same point (but in a different context), Gordon wrote: "Once put into the cultural stream by an initial creative person, intellectual products may be impossible for others not to use. Consider someone trying independently to invent a paper clip after having seen one. Some inventions 'infect' one immediately with knowledge of their workings." *See* Wendy J. Gordon, *A Property Right in Self Expression: Equality and Individualism in the Natural Law of Intellectual Property*, 102 YALE L.J. 1533, 1582 (1993).

138. *Cf.* Julie E. Cohen, *Cyberspace And/As Space*, 107 COLUM. L. REV. 210, 230–32 (2007) (critiquing the property metaphor within a broader critique concerning cyberspace as a "place").

139. Thomas Jefferson wrote: "Inventions then cannot, in nature, be a subject of property. Society may give an exclusive right to the profits arising from them, as an encouragement to men to pursue ideas which may produce utility, but this may or may not be done, according to the will and convenience of the society, without claim or complaint from anybody. . . The exclusive right to invention [is] given not of natural right, but for the benefit of society." Jefferson, *supra* note 133. For a recent critique of Jefferson's approach

In the above excerpt, he used a metaphor of fire to describe the information process.[140] Jefferson's fire metaphor is powerful: It encapsulates the nature of information as a dynamic process mobilized by thinking and communication energy. It also implies information is not a "natural" object of exclusion rights, and that when such rights are nonetheless granted, there must be compelling underlying arguments justifying legal protection.

The main projects of intellectual property theory have been to *explain* the positive law and *justify* property-like entitlements in information goods. On the prescriptive level, a further objective has been to propose an optimal (or at least a better) design of the positve law. Pondering the very basic justifications to intellectual property protection has remained a vibrant topic in legal scholarship, which continuesly produce new theories.[141] Some of the most influential approaches—those that now form the conventional basis to argue about intellectual property—originally did not focus on ideal objects at all. Also today, most leading arguments draw heavily on philosophical traditions primarily designed to underpin private property *in general*, occasionally with a mix of influences from other legal fields such as torts, restitution, and unfair competition.[142] Often, intellectual property rhetoric blends arguments having their roots in various theoretical traditions, and justifying legal protection is flanked with snippets put together, but that do not necessarily "belong" together.[143]

---

to patents, *see* Adam Mossoff, *Who Cares What Thomas Jefferson Thought About Patents? Reevaluating the Patent "Privilege" in Historical Context*, 92 CORNELL L. REV. 953 (2007).

140. *Id.* ("[Information] seems to have been peculiarly and benevolently designed by nature, when she made them, like fire, expansible over all space, without lessening their density in any point.").

141. *See, e.g.*, LIOR ZEMMER, THE IDEA OF AUTHORSHIP 8–21 (2007) (listing six to seven leading categories of theoretical justifications to copyright law).

142. *See* Gordon, *supra* note 110, at 624 (noting the influence of tort, restitution, and unjust enrichment theories).

143. *See, e.g.*, Eldred v. Ashcroft, 537 U.S. 186, 212, n. 18 (2003) (U.S. Supreme Court suggesting a complementary relationship between natural law and utilitarian justifications, noting that both types of underlining principles—protection of authors and achieving utilitarian maximization of welfare—are not "mutually exclusive."). In Europe, a strong utilitarian influence is felt in the field of copyright law after the adoption of the European Copyright Directive (EUCD) (2001). *See* Recital 4 EUCD (using rhetoric of incentives and consequentialist theories to justify harmonization at a high level of protection); *see also* Kamiel J. Koelman, *Copyright Law and Economics in the EU Copyright Directive: Is the Droit d'Auteur. Passé?*, 35 IIC 603 (2004) (criticizing the Directive's economic-utilitarian stance). In connection with the competition between instrumentalist and normative arguments, Hughes observed "the instrumental argument often seems to be treated as a 'proof' of the normative argument." *See* Justin Hughes, *The Philosophy of Intellectual Property*. 77 GEO. L.J. 287, 303 (1988).

Fisher, among others, is skeptical concerning the capacity of any single theoretical approach to explain, justify, and model positive intellectual property regimes.[144] At the same time, he noted theoretical approaches are important for helping to identify "nonobvious attractive resolutions" to particular problems, as well as to foster "valuable conversations" among stakeholders involved in the legislative process.[145] Hughes referred to a "mirroring" effect between theoretical principles and the positive law, noting the "two things are becoming more acceptable by mirroring one another."[146] With this optimistic-yet-cautious view on the role of theory in shaping positive rules, the following passages focus on three of the most significant theoretical narratives and their application to copyright law.

1. The Lockean Argument

(a) Locke's Labor Justification of Property

The works of John Locke profoundly influenced modern property theories.[147] Locke is famous, inter alia, for his labor-based justification of private property rights. The theory proclaims a natural right to property born out of exercising labor upon not-yet-appropriated resources found in the state of nature.[148] Locke's initial premise is that to extract utility, persons must exercise labor upon natural raw resources. The raw resources in the state of nature are held in common by all mankind until appropriation via labor occurs, as labor morally justifies a reward. The laborer's claim for reward furnishes the core normative justification for the grant of an exclusive property right in the resources he has extracted from the state of nature.

Locke's argument is complex and intriguing,[149] inspiring vast literature debating its meaning, correctness, and robustness. The discussion here focuses

---

144. *See* William Fisher, *Theories of Intellectual Property*, *in* New Essays in the Legal and Political Theory of Property 177 (Stephen Munzer ed., 2001): "Ambiguities, internal inconsistencies, and the lack of crucial empirical information severely limit the[] prescriptive power [of IP theories]".

145. *Id.* at 194.

146. Hughes, *supra* note 143, at 289 (arguing "[t]he existing law supports, to varying degrees, the credibility of different theories of property and [] these theories support, to varying degrees, the validity of existing laws.").

147. *See* Ian Shapiro, *Introduction: Reading Locke Today*, to John Locke, Two Treatises of Government and a Letter Concerning Toleration (Yale Univ. Press 2003) (1690).

148. For a detailed discussion and critique on the Lockean justification to private property, see Waldron, *supra* note 25, at 137 ff. Waldron classified the Lockean argument as a natural, special rights-based justification to property in that property rights are "acquired rights [] as a result of actions and transactions that men undertake on their own initiative." *Id.* at 137–38.

149. *See* Shapiro, *supra* note 147, at ix (indicating Locke's central arguments are sufficiently complex to invite disputes about their true meaning).

mainly on one critical point, namely, the *baseline problem* (asking "where property in information begins?" or "what is the information commons from which information is appropriated?") and its relation to copyright.

Locke begins with proposing that a person has a property right over his own body.[150] He describes the state of nature as containing resources given to mankind from God in "common." However, these resources cannot be utilized or enjoyed in their natural state—instead, individuals must exercise labor upon them.[151] When a person mingles his efforts (the "labour of his body, and the work of his hands") with the raw, uncultivated materials of nature, thereby removing them from the state of nature, the resulting product should to be his.[152] Mixing labor with a natural resource endows property rights in the resource and distinguishes it from the common.[153] The status of resources in the state of nature as "common" suggests the appropriation applies to resources not yet appropriated through labor by someone else.[154] Locke suggested that appropriation through labor of common resources is justified under two main conditions (provisos). The enough-and-as-good proviso requires that in ex post appropriation, there are enough and as good resources left in common for others to exercise labor upon.[155] In other words, appropriation should leave the world with similar appropriation opportunities as it has been ex ante. Locke also introduced the no-waste proviso condemning excessive accumulation of property leading to destruction of goods before they can be utilized.[156]

---

150. *See* John Locke, Two Treatises of Government, Second Treatise [ST], Ch. V § 26 (Yale Univ. Press 2003) (1689), ("every man has a 'property' in his own 'person.'") Munzer questioned this axiom, concluding a person has a limited package of property rights in his body that does not amount to full "ownership." *See* Munzer, *supra* note 4, at 37 ff.

151. Locke, *supra* note 150, §§ 26–27.

152. *Id.*

153. *Id.* § 26 ("Whatsoever, then, he removes out of the state that Nature hath provided and left it in, he hath mixed his labour with it, and joined to it something that is his own, and thereby makes it his property.").

154. Locke's use of the term *common* seems to denote the opposite of (private) property. *Id.* § 24.

155. *Id.* § 26 ("For this 'labour' being the unquestionable property of the labourer, no man but he can have a right to what that is once joined to, at least where there is enough, and as good left in common for others.") Locke elaborates on this proviso also in §§ 32–33 as a justification for the appropriation of land and other resources for the purposes of improving them.

156. *Id.* § 30 ("As much as any one can make use of to any advantage of life before it spoils, so much he may by his labour fix a property in. Whatever is beyond this is more than his share, and belongs to others. Nothing was made by God for man to spoil or destroy.").

Theorists often classify Locke's argument as a natural law justification of private property.[157] The argument emphasizes the "pains" suffered by the laborer, which renders his claim superior to the expectations of residual claimants, who anyway are left with enough-and-as-good appropriation opportunities.[158] At the same time, Locke makes several assertions having instrumental-utilitarian flavor.[159] Importantly, Locke seems to have strayed away from the path marked by early natural law thinkers such as Grotius and Puffendorf by questioning the theory of social agreement/tacit consent. Grotius, for instance, insisted natural property rights must be based on the community's acknowledgement.[160] By contrast, Locke did not seem to condition appropriation out from the common with the consent of all commoners or society in general.[161] Locke warned that if private use of natural resources depended on the consent of all mankind, "man had starved, notwithstanding the plenty God had given him."[162]

The numerous important objections to the Lockean justification cannot be reviewed here.[163] One significant point is Locke appears to have downplayed the

---

157. According to Locke, property is a "natural" right not in the sense that persons are born with that right, but that their individual endeavors give rise to the right, as opposed to dependency on positive stipulation by the state. *See* WALDRON, *supra* note 25, at 138.

158. LOCKE, *supra* note 150, § 33 ("He that had as good left for his improvement as was already taken up, needed not complain. . . if he did, it is plain he desired the benefit of another's *pains*, which he had no right to.") (emphasis added).

159. *See, e.g., id.* §§ 38–39. Michelman argued that, on the one hand, desert theory such as Locke's "makes no assertion that property is desirable because it leads to consequences which can be regarded as good for society 'as a whole.'" *See* Frank Michelman, *Property, Utility, and Fairness*, 80 HARV. L. REV. 1165, 1203–04 (1967). On the other hand, Michelman admitted Locke's theory can be perceived simultaneously as a social utility theory. *Id.* at 1204, n.80 ("Locke's theory may, with at least equal plausibility, be understood as a social utility theory.").

160. *See* GROTIUS, *supra* note 41, Ch. II, Sec. 2(5).

161. LOCKE, *supra* note 151, § 27: "And will any one say he had no right to those acorns or apples he thus appropriated because he had not the consent of all mankind to make them his? Was it a robbery thus to assume to himself what belonged to all in common? If such a consent as that was necessary, man had starved, notwithstanding the plenty God had given him." This part of Locke's argument gave rise to the *social utility* interpretation of the labor justification. It seems Locke sought to fill the void left after dropping Grotius' social consent principle by inserting the general utility factor.

162. *Id.* More than a century after Locke, Blackstone made note of this philosophical debate, and although refusing to unequivocally take sides, he seems to position himself closer to Locke while upholding the occupancy theory. *See* 2 BLACKSTONE, *supra* note 58, at 5–6 & n. 1. For a modern critique of this aspect of Locke's argument, see Epstein, *supra* note 38, at 1127–28.

163. For a critical analysis of occupation, labor-based as well as other natural law principles and theories as the foundation of property law—as distinguished from theories that uphold the social contract idea and the emanating legislative power of the state as reflected in the positive law, see PEUKERT, *supra* note 10, at 772–84.

obvious problem of scarcity, that is, taking from the common under scarcity conditions almost inevitably diminishes the opportunity of other commoners to do the same. A possible solution to this problem resides in Locke's enough-and-as-good proviso, yet to serve this purpose, the proviso must be sustainable under real-life conditions. In Locke's reality, exploring the vast, uncultivated plains of the New World[164] or drinking from an ever-rushing pond that is permanently generating water to quench the thirst of men,[165] served as examples of appropriation that left enough-and-as-goods resources in common. It is clear, however, that natural resources are more often scarce and exhaustible than otherwise. Simple logic warrants that under scarcity conditions, *any* taking from the commons would reduce the quantity of remaining resources left for others. It also follows that a taking from the commons *necessarily* affects others' ability to appropriate for themselves.[166] If the taking is done unilaterally without requiring even the tacit consent of the injured commoners, how can one ethically justify this result?[167]

Nozick proposed a modification to Locke's argument based on a lenient interpretation of the enough-and-as-good proviso. Accordingly, appropriating from the commons does not *necessarily* worsen the position of other commoners under scarcity conditions, and persons whose *overall situation* is improved by the *existence of property rights protection in general* cannot complain about being impoverished via individual acts vesting private property rights in certain assets labored upon.[168]

---

164. LOCKE, *supra* note 150, § 36.

165. *Id.* at § 32.

166. It is open to debate whether the proviso strictly requires that commoners shall have enough and as good *appropriations* opportunities, or whether they shall merely have enough and as good opportunities to use/enjoy/benefit from resources. Locke's own formulation, requiring "there is enough, and as good *left in common* for others," seems to better correspond to the first alternative because it does not include enjoyment from resources *not* in common ownership any longer. The first alternative is obviously more difficult to satisfy in practice.

167. It appears that solving the allocative dilemma and the moral problem rooted in unilateral allocation of scarce resources via enacted positive rules—while considering the government the authorized agent of the injured commoners—would still be in tension with the enough-and-as-good proviso.

168. *See* ROBERT NOZICK, ANARCHY, STATE AND UTOPIA 174 ff (1974). Nozick suggested the increase in social products resulting from the private property right can alleviate the problem of applying the proviso under scarcity conditions. Nozick is careful to distinguish between his proposed modification to the proviso and utilitarian interpretations, as his does not seem to consider the labor rationale (including its provisos) as part of the normative justification of private property.

A second well-documented critique of Locke's property rationale relates to the problem of *proportion*. Locke seems to hold the laborer is entitled to private ownership in the entire product or resource he has labored upon.[169] However, there is no clear indication the intensity or scope of property rights earned are commensurate with the intensity or amount of labor invested, or that their scope should be proportional to the value added to the resource through labor. In an imaginary reality of inexhaustible resources, this might not amount to a serious distributional problem. However, under scarcity conditions, there is a strong sense of unfairness if the investment of minimal input, say, pouring a Nozickian can of tomato juice into the ocean, could buy one the ocean, and this to the detriment of all other would-be appropriators.[170] Correction of this problematic outcome possibly should include a mechanism for determining the scope of property rights according to the amount of self-resources invested (i.e., labor) and the amount taken away from the commons (i.e., the value of expropriated common resources, possibly offset by the *benefit* to the public resulting from the appropriation). Or at the very least, it seems this is what a moral labor-based system of property rights would need.

(b) Labor Justification of Copyright

It is debatable whether Locke himself intended his argument to underpin property rights in intangible resources.[171] The Lockean argument itself does not contain elements that would a priori foreclose application to ideal objects, perhaps to the contrary: some property theorists find the argument particularly attractive in the context of intellectual property.[172] Echoing these sentiments, Epstein writes:

> Indeed, the labor theory of acquisition seems, if anything, stronger here precisely because intellectual property does not require any form of mixing with tangible forms. Rather, these types of property appear to be the result of pure

---

169. In chapter V of the SECOND TREATISE, Locke frequently uses the term *enclosure* to describe the distinction between private property and common resources, which indicates that via labor, the laborer acquires the right to exclude others from the *entire* resource. *Cf.* LOCKE, *supra* note 150, §§ 25, 32, 34, & 38.

170. NOZICK, *supra* note 168, at 175.

171. Epstein seems to propose a negative answer: "To be sure, Locke did not offer any explicit treatment one way or the other of intellectual property rights, which adds to his charm." *See* Epstein, *supra* note 50, at 21. *Cf.* ZEMMER, *supra* note 141, at 147–77 (reaching the opposite conclusion in the context of copyright law after consulting other writings by Locke).

172. For two leading treatments, *see* Hughes, *supra* note 143, at 297–330; Gordon, *supra* note 137. For an articulate objection to the Lockean argument in the intellectual property context, see Seana Valentine Shiffrin, *Lockean Arguments for Private Intellectual Property, in* NEW ESSAYS IN THE LEGAL AND POLITICAL THEORY OF PROPERTY (Stephen Munzer ed., 2001).

> labor, which the creator, therefore, cannot keep because first possession of a tangible object allows him only to protect the paper on which the draft is written, rather than the draft itself. Yet by the same token, the author has not taken anything else out of the commons and so does not run into the joint contribution objections that undermine the power of the first possession rule for tangible objects. The only function of legal intervention here is to protect that investment in labor without any expropriation.[173]

This passage encapsulates the essential points. Authors do not expropriate commoners by acquiring exclusive rights in works they have created, and the enough-and-as-good proviso can be more easily satisfied, depending on the scope and nature of exclusive rights granted.[174] For example, if copyright protection extends *only to the original elements of the work*, arguably the position of other would-be authors ex post appropriations is not worse as a result of copyright exclusivity relating to nothing more than that. According to this view, later-day authors enjoy *at least* the same number and quality of informational resources as compared to their position before copyrights have been acquired. To the extent a system of property rights in expression *improves* the position of later-day authors (e.g., by enriching their intellectual heritage and sources of inspiration), the objection based on questioning the viability of the enough-and-as-good proviso might lose much of its vigor.[175]

Additionally, it might be possible to view copyright's exceptions and limitations on exclusive rights as a response to the proportionality problem highlighted by Nozick and others. At least in theory, according to the idea/expression distinction, authors receive protection proportional to the amount of creativity they have injected into existing informational resources. Preservation of the commons is achieved by protection not attaching to "negative categories" such as ideas, facts, or methods. Its limited duration renders copyright a weaker form of property and provides the lawmakers with fine-tuning tools, with fine-tuning-by-duration rules allowing monitoring of the amount (or value) taken from society as a result of exclusive copyrights by setting an "expiration date" to copyright protection. As far as the no-waste proviso is concerned, it has been argued that

---

173. Epstein, *supra* note 50, at 21.

174. *See* Hughes, *supra* note 143, at 329 ("Intellectual property systems, however, do seem to accord with Locke's labor condition and the 'enough an [sic] as good' requirement. In fact, the 'enough and as good' condition seems to hold true only in intellectual property systems. That may mean that Locke's unique theoretical edifice finds its firmest bedrock in the common of ideas.") (footnote omitted).

175. *Cf.* Hughes, *supra* note 143, at 316–19 (arguing that appropriating ideas could in fact increase the "ideas commons" left for others ex post).

unlike apples, information does not "spoil" over time,[176] nor does it become barren if neglected the way a pasture might.[177]

(c) The Baseline Problem: What is the Information Commons?

Application of the information model's terminology and methodology to the Lockean argument reveals some doubts concerning Locke's basic assumptions. Locke's argument follows a clear temporal and logical order: In the beginning, God gave the earth and all natural resources on it to mankind in common,[178] and persons had property rights *only* to their own bodies.[179] As human subsistence and prosperity depend on labor, labor will emerge, and as the laborer has a natural claim to the resources he has labored upon, he may exclude others from them. According to this depiction, it is easy to imagine the world in its primal phase, where unowned resources simply exist "out there," with their existence depending neither on labor nor on mankind in general. Because mankind *does* exist, labor directed against those untouched resources will be exercised. Labor then is a *constituting event*: it creates a division between privately owned resources and whatever resources are left in the common pool. However, if informational messages are the resource at issue, this order cannot be sustained.

To illustrate the point, it is useful to consider two different types of informational input. The first type is unrelated to human communication—it is the bird in the sky, the view of the ocean, the sound of the waves, the tree in the forest, and so on. These impressions are dubbed here "natural input," or **N-input**. The second type is communication-related impressions, referring to all the *messages* to which the author is exposed, called **M-input**. The information environment surrounding the author consists of both N-input and M-input elements. Both types may be used by the author for creating his own expression, constituting together the "raw material" labored upon. Consider now the conceptual convergence between labor in the Lockean sense and origination in the meaning of the information model, with origination as a *constituting event*. In that context, origination creates a message, which is essentially the subject matter of copyright. Before origination, the message has been purely a subjective thought,

---

176. *Id.* at 327–29 (discussing the no-waste proviso in the context of intellectual property, and observing "the value lost by hoarding an idea until it becomes obsolete is a very different kind of loss than food spoilage. There is no internal deterioration in the idea and the loss in value is seen only against a social backdrop. The loss is speculative and may be reversible.").

177. *Cf.* Peter Drahos, A Philosophy of Intellectual Property 51 (1996) (pointing out "[a]s abstract objects ideas cannot spoil, but the opportunities that they confer may").

178. Locke, *supra* note, §§ 24–25.

179. *Id.* at § 26 ("Though the earth and all inferior creatures be common to all men, yet every man has a 'property' in his own 'person.' This *nobody has any right to but himself.*") (emphasis added).

whereas now (ex post origination) the message becomes an artifact that is both legally and economically relevant.

To the extent the author used N-input incorporated in the message, these impressions—which are not subject to any property right in themselves—become a component of property subject matter as expressed in the message (provided the originality threshold is met). N-input *may* be used for creating works, but M-input *must* be used for *any* work. All authors must use existing coding systems, formulations, and communication building blocks that cannot qualify as N-input as they are the fruits of others' "labor". Though (input) information broadly conceived is not always man-made (e.g., a tree in the field, a bird in the sky, the whistle of the wind, or the waves of the ocean), authors routinely use ideas, constructions, and formulations that are the result of others' intellectual achievements. Now, the proportion between the intensity of using M-input and N-input for creating a given message does not change the facts that (1) there is no reasonable way to subject N-imput to property rules, and (2) the message will always include M-input that (also under a Lockean worldview) could and sometimes should be subject to property rules.

The most important point is that this M-input does not fit within the Lockean depiction of the common as untouched resources, as a raw gift from God.[180]

---

180. This argument is corroborated by Locke's epistemology as laid out in his essay on human knowledge. *See* John Locke, An Essay Concerning Human Understanding (1849). Locke believed that no knowledge is innate ("No Innate Principles in the Mind") and that all knowledge is acquired throughout life's experience. *Id.* Bk. 1, Ch. II. Locke wrote: "No proposition can be said to be in the mind which it never yet knew, which it was never yet conscious of." *Id.* Bk. 1, Ch. II.5. Persons are borne only with the *capacity* of knowing and senses that allow them to receive impressions from their external environment:

> *Ideas, especially those belonging to principles, not born with children.* —If we will attentively consider new-born children, we shall have little reason to think that they bring many ideas into the world with them. For, bating perhaps some faint ideas of hunger, and thirst, and warmth, and some pains, which they may have felt in the womb, there is not the least appearance of any settled ideas at all in them; especially of ideas answering the terms which make up those universal propositions that are esteemed innate principles. One may perceive how, by degrees, afterwards, ideas come into their minds; and that they get no more, nor other, than what experience, and the observation of things that come in their way, furnish them with; which might be enough to satisfy us that they are not original characters stamped on the mind.

Id. Bk. 1, Ch. IV.2 (italicization in original) Locke continued:

> *All ideas come from sensation or reflection.* Let us then suppose the mind to be, as we say, white paper, void of all characters, without any ideas; How comes it to be furnished? Whence comes it by that vast store which the busy and boundless fancy of man has painted on it with an almost endless variety? Whence has it all the materials of reason and knowledge? To this I answer, in one word, From experience: in that all our knowledge is founded; and from that it ultimately derives itself. Our observation

The information environment consists of messages that owe their existence to the actions of other persons. In this sense, the baseline problem denotes the inability of one to determine when (based on the labor justification) property begins and the information commons ends. Put differently, there is no articulable baseline from which one can be allocating property rights out of the commons to individuals based on the principle of labor on not-yet-labored-upon resources in their "state of nature."

Two recognitions emerge from this baseline problem. First, it is evident the critical challenge is defining the information commons ex ante appropriation. Second, this commons cannot mean untouched resources. Therefore, our conception of ex ante appropriation resources cannot rely on Locke's depiction of the "plenty of natural provisions there was a long time in the world."[181] Yet the Lockean argument appears to heavily rely on the assumption that not-yet-labored-upon resources *do exist* in the world ex ante appropriation.

It could be useful at this point to return to some possible interpretations of the commons in the context of intellectual property theory. Fisher proposed seven information commons candidate categories: the universe of facts, languages (vocabularies, grammar), cultural heritage, non-appropriated ideas already comprehended by at least one person, the set of ideas already apprehended by at least one person, the set of all "reachable" ideas, and the set of all "possible" ideas.[182] Each version of the commons stipulates a different criterion for defining zones of freedom to create new messages under an information property regime. Fisher's portrayal takes into account the possibility information resources could indeed exist independently of human communication. For example, *reachable ideas* are defined as "all ideas that lie within the grasp of people today," and *possible ideas* are defined as "all ideas that someone might think of."[183] According to this interpretation of the commons, amorphous, wholly abstract ideas reside in a metaphysical universe, waiting to be plucked by a genius mind who will endow them with a communicable form.[184] This potential may or may not materialize into an expression.

> employed either, about external sensible objects, or about the internal operations of our minds perceived and reflected on by ourselves, is that which supplies our understandings with all the materials of thinking. These two are the fountains of knowledge, from whence all the ideas we have, or can naturally have, do spring.

Id. Bk. 2 Ch. I.2. (italicization in original).

181. LOCKE, *supra* note, at § 30.

182. *See* Fisher, *supra* note 144, at 186 (listing seven possible ways to define the raw material constituting the common).

183. *Id.*

184. Hughes added a skeptical comment concerning the presumption of a platonic universe of ideas constituting the commons: "The Lockean conception of idea-making provides another ground for treating idea and execution as a single event. Viewing new ideas as plucked from some platonic common may be reification in the extreme. Yet in

The Platonic universe of ideas seems attractive at first hearing for conceptually coming quite close to the Lockean untouched state of nature. However, because each message, regardless of the status of the ideas it represents, contains M-input elements, the baseline problem remains unsolved. To reiterate, unlike in the Lockean world (or, in the Platonic universe of ideas, by comparison), the existence of information raw material is never completely independent of previous human labor.[185] Therefore, the problem of defining the ex ante appropriation commons transforms into that of deciding how much M-input (if any) remains in the commons ex post appropriation, *despite the fact that it is M-input*—namely, the product of someone else's labor.

As shown, approximations and modifications to the original labor argument must be made, as in its original formulation it cannot justify *initial* allocation of property rights in creative messages. The crux of the labor argument is that strangers have a weaker moral claim to a product that costs the laborer with toil and sweat. A modified argument will have to explain why the claim of the author is superior *despite his usage of M-input.*

To remain faithful to the basic assumptions of the labor argument as applied to information resources, one may assume externalizing thoughts and ideas—and converting them into medial messages—always requires some degree of "labor." The originator is hence a Lockean laborer. The key justification underpinning a moral claim to exclusive rights in the message is not so much the toil of communication as it is the social value added by the author-originator.[186] The next question is *how much* property would be morally justified under the value-added justification. Insoluble questions of measuring and apportionment are involved. First, it would seem unfair to reward the author for elements she has taken from other authors. Second, it is practically impossible to measure the precise individual contribution of value added to information resources as a

---

that view, the ideas already exist and the chief labor is transporting them from the ethereal reaches of the idea world to the real world where humanity can use them. If ideas are thought of as such preexistent platonic forms, the only activity possible is execution, which consists of transporting, translating, and communicating the idea into a form and a location in which humans have access to it." *See* Hughes, *supra* note, at 311–12 (footnote omitted).

185. *Cf.* Gordon, *supra* note 137, at 1558–59 ("[A]lthough the common explicitly discussed in the two Treatises was the physical realm—both that which existed already (land, seas, mountains) or that which was continually in the process of coming into existence without the assistance of humankind (deer, fish, acorns)—applying Locke's analysis to the intangible realm would not do violence to his thought. Admittedly, for the intangible reality of intellectual property, the common must be defined differently.").

186. As Hughes noted, desert theories tend to depart from Locke's naïve depiction of a laborer removing material from the state of nature and move towards instrumentalist and consequentialist arguments. Hughes, *supra* note, at 305–06.

result of producing the message.[187] Messages cannot be dissected precisely according to their original and borrowed elements,[188] and allocation of exclusive rights can never scrupulously correspond to the actual contribution of each and every individual origination in past and present communication sequences.[189] At the same time, the law cannot flatly prohibit any such unauthorized "taking" as the result would be both ridiculous and unjust. Some accommodations and compromises must be made, but either way, a calculus based on moral issues should also factor in authors' moral "debt" to their predecessors.[190]

One practical strategy is to allow some M-input taking and grant exclusive rights in the output, but simultaneously diminish the intensity of the "harm" to others by reducing the intensity of exclusive rights.[191] A modified approach would necessarily apply rough approximations, yet any compromise of this sort seems to diminish the direct relations between labor and reward. Epstein offered a pragmatic solution: he proposed an approximation rationale he named "confession and avoidance." He argued in favor of a practical, rough-justice rule that mixes influences from the added-value approach. Accordingly, he who contributed the lion's share to the finished product, making it worthy of our attention, shall be morally entitled to the entire property claim.[192] Further, Epstein suggested

---

187. *Cf.* Stephen Breyer, *The Uneasy Case for Copyright*, 84 HARV. L. REV. 281, 285–87 (1970) (criticizing value-added justifications to copyright); Hughes, *supra* note, at 309 (questioning the validity of the value-added reasoning for copyright, which grants protection irrespective of the value or non-value of a given work to society).

188. One may argue that a given author labored on her expression as a whole; therefore, she deserves exclusive rights in the entire message, negative categories elements excluded. In this case, the conceptual indivisibility of the message plays to the hands of present authors, who claim exclusive rights in the entire work as one whole.

189. *Cf.* Sheldon v. Metro-Goldwyn Pictures Corp., 106 F.2d 45, 49–51 (2d Cir. 1939) (the court discussed in detail the evidentiary problem of discerning the economic value added to the original work by the creator of a derivative work).

190. *See* Jonathan Lethem, *The Ecstasy of Influence: A Plagiarism*, HARPER'S, Feb. 2007 ("Most artists are brought to their vocation when their own nascent gifts are awakened by the work of a master. That is to say, most artists are converted to art by art itself. Finding one's voice isn't just an emptying and purifying oneself of the words of others but an adopting and embracing of filiations, communities, and discourses. Inspiration could be called inhaling the memory of an act never experienced. Invention, it must be humbly admitted, does not consist in creating out of void but out of chaos. Any artist knows these truths, no matter how deeply he or she submerges that knowing.").

191. For a detailed interpretation of the labor argument through the lens of the obligation not to harm others (in particular with respect to free speech rights), see Gordon, *supra* note, at 1560 ff.

192. *See* Epstein, *supra* note 50, at 22 (suggesting "[t]here is little question that all these [external] influences come to bear on the individual author. But by the same token, it is possible to locate in one person, or a small group of joint authors, the creative spark or hard effort that took these disparate influences and melded them into a coherent work,

the author's property claim could be morally justified if the author contributed an "equal measure" to the common pool of knowledge.[193]

(d) Communication as Labor?

Let us summarize the critique: Proponents of the Lockean labor argument as a justification to copyright protection must come to terms with serious compromises in the initial formulation of the labor justification and the way justifying property rights in expressions operate. So far it has been assumed, without proof, that human communication generally falls within the notion of Lockean "labor" for which originators desrve a reward in the form of property rights. However, this might turn at times a very weak assumption. Often, the originator's primary reward for the "toil" involved in creating a message is purely communicative: the joy and benefit of being socially involved, noticed, and understood by others. To the extent authors-originators contribute to the information process additional (valuable) messages that otherwise would not have existed, assessing their contribution to society seems to better fit within the value-added variation.[194] Indeed, the value-added approach would undermine the "pains" element as the crux of the moral justification for reward[195] and shift the focus to adding value (=adding messages) to the information environment.

At this point we should pause: saying that communication (=adding messages to the information environment) adds value is one thing. Saying that such contributions *morally justify individual reward in the form of exclusive rights in expressions* is yet another. After all, the urge to communicate is a basic human need, and as such, it is not inherently something that automatically creates a societal debt from the collective to the individual communicator.

Even assuming *arguendo* that authors in general deserve a reward for creating messages, and assuming their net contribution to society can be measured, what then should be the ratio between that net contribution and the net social costs of copyright (assuming the net social cost can also be measured)? Should society "pay back" exactly the same value it has received from authors? How does this payback translate into exclusive rights, the commercial value of which is to a

---

worthy of our attention.") This argument demonstrates the clear nexus between the justification to copyright and the perception of the author *as originator* in the meaning of the information model. *See* Chapter 1, Section V.A.2 *supra.*

193. Epstein, *supra* note 50, at 22–23. Alas, this formulation threatens to re-evoke the measurement problem Epstein seeks to avoid.

194. Chapter 1, Section IV.E.3.(d) *supra.*

195. *Cf.* Hughes, *supra* note, at 300–05 (offering a thoughtful discussion on the question whether mental creation can be considered a Lockean labor, and concluding "[t]he issue is not whether idea-making is an absolutely unpleasant activity, but whether it is comparatively less pleasant and less desirable than other activities") (footnote omitted). It appears, however, that communication often cannot be caged within the constraints of such formulation.

large extent initially undeterminable? How can this undeterminable value of a work be distributed among all atomistic authors who have contributed to its creation at various stages of its formation? How strong should the private entitlements be to the whole message? Lockean labor theories do not seem to offer satifying answers to these concerns.

2. The Hegelian Personality Theory

(a) Hegel's Idea of Property

Personality theories of property inspired by the philosophy of Hegel and Kant focus on the relationship among property, autonomy, and personal development of the individual. It is possible to distinguish between development-based and identification-based personality theories. The former category of arguments focuses on the process of personal development and the need to secure the freedom to become a person, whereas the latter focuses on the psychological relationships and dependencies persons develop with respect to things.[196] As one example of identification-based theory, Radin offered a distinction between "personal property" and "fungible property,"[197] with the former type relating to personal autonomy manifested in the object, a recognition having a potential influence on the scope and nature of positive property rights in objects.[198] According to many personality approaches, property is an essential condition for freedom, autonomy, and self-actualization.

Hegel's account of the relations between persons, freedom, and property, as laid out in the *Philosophy of Right* (*Grundlinien der Philosopie des Rechts*), proves remarkably viable in the contemporary theoretical discourse on property law.[199]

---

196. *See* Christian Gero Stallberg, Urheberrecht und Moralische Rechtfertigung 111 ff (2006) (explaining this distinction and analyzing various arguments in the context of justification for copyright protection).

197. *See* Margaret Jane Radin, *Property and Personhood*, 34 Stan. L. Rev. 957, 960 (1982) (describing personal property "as simply a category of property for personal autonomy or liberty. Property for personal autonomy or liberty might be a class of objects or resources necessary to be a person or whose absence would hinder the autonomy or liberty attributed to a person").

198. *Id.* at 978 ff.

199. *See* Peter Gordon Stillman, *Property, Freedom, and Individuality in Hegel's and Marx's Political Thought, in* Property (J. Roland Pennock ed., 1980). For a study on Hegel's ethics in general, see Allen W. Wood, Hegel's Ethical Thought (1990). For a leading analysis in the context of private property, see Waldron, *supra* note 25, at 343 ff. The cursory discussion that follows does not aim at providing a comprehensive account of Hegel's contribution to legal thought. The focus is on Hegel's treatment concerning property as stated in the Philosophy of Right, under the caveat often voiced by Hegel scholars, warning the Philosophy of Right cannot be fully and properly understood without reference to Hegel's previous works, and importantly, as a reply to Kant. *See, e.g.*, David Gray Carlson, *How to Do Things with Hegel* , 78 Tex. L. Rev. 1377, 1381 (2000) (arguing

Property plays a critical role in Hegel's broader political-philosophical discussion[200] while assuming its great importance both as being the initial right of persons and as providing the logical basis for the rights to life and liberty.[201] The logical beginning is the free will—a universal, infinite *potential*.[202] The will is free in the sense that in its abstract, initial mode as "self" it has no physical characteristics;[203] as it has no physical dimensions, free will is not subordinated to natural conditions or needs, even those of time and space.[204] The will is free and true as a "thinking intelligence."[205]

Free will resides in persons who are likewise free in the initial stage of their individual development: "The abstract will, the will which exists for itself, is a person."[206] The will can actualize its abstract freedom only through acts against external objects/things, which, by definition, are not subjects as they do not exist in and for themselves. External objects are distinguished from subjects on the basis that they lack free will of their own.[207] The physical attributes of persons, and the external reality in which they must operate, imposes restrictions on the will. In that reality, through will-driven conducts directed against external things, the personality—initially a shapeless, contentless and abstract entity—progressively develops its *actual* freedom and individuality. Hegel suggested will-driven

---

"[w]ithout knowledge of [Hegel's] Science of Logic, we cannot fathom the Philosophy of Right in the way Hegel meant for it to be read").

200. *See* Wood, *supra* note 199, at 96 (observing "Hegel treats all abstract right as a right of property, even the right to our own life and body, the right over our inner life and conscience, and the right to a social status as free persons").

201. Stillman (1980), *supra* note 199, at 130–31.

202. Georg Wilhelm Friedrich Hegel, Philosophy of Right § 34[A] (S.W. Dyde trans., Batoche Books 2001 (1896) ("The completed idea of the will is found when the conception has realized itself fully, and in such a manner that the embodiment of the conception is nothing but the development of the conception itself. But at the outset the conception is abstract. All its future characters are implied in it, it is true, but as yet no more than implied. They are, in other words, potential, and are not yet developed into an articulate whole.") Note that the Additions (marked as [A]) were written by Hegel's students, and were not supervised by the philosopher himself. At the same time, they provide an important source for understanding the original paragraphs, which are concisely and often cryptically formulated. *Id.* Translator's Preface at 10.

203. *See* Carlson, *supra* note 199, at 1380 ("Such a self is freed of all attributes. It has no property, and it has no 'properties.' In such a state it cannot be perceived at all. It is nothing.") (footnote omitted).

204. Georg Wilhelm Friedrich Hegel, Grundlinien der Philosophie des Rechts §§ 21–22 (1821) (referring to the absolute existence of the will as infinite (*unendlich*)).

205. *Id.* at § 21[N] ("Hier ist der *Punkt, auf welchem es erhellt,* daß der Wille nur als *denkende* Intelligenz wahrhafter, freier Wille ist.") (emphasis in original).

206. Hegel, *supra* note 202, § 35[A].

207. *Id.* §§ 42–44.

conducts executed against external things is a necessary condition for actualization of freedom and personal development: "A person must give to his freedom an external sphere, in order that he may reach the completeness implied in the idea."[208]

In the Hegelian sense "right" is an extension of freedom,[209] and free persons have a "right" to actualize their freedom and develop their individuality via external objects. As noted, in Hegel's philosophy, the subject is an end-in-itself. As such, the person has a right to direct his free will upon every thing and thereby make it his property.[210] Hegel's argument is logical and systematic: as persons have a right to actualize their freedom, and as the only way to do that is to act against external objects, a person must have a right to external objects. Hegel initially speaks of appropriation of unowned things (*herrenlos*).[211] Through taking possession of external objects, the subject seeks to achieve self-recognition; he distinguishes himself thereby from unfree objects and from other subjects with respect to which he seeks to relate himself.

The function of property in Hegel's ethical composition is multifaceted. Property is first and foremost a result of a mental act of willing, a claim that creates rights. Hegel draws at the outset an important dialectic distinction between right in the legal sense and right in the philosophical sense.[212] Further, Hegel defined *abstract right* as having to do with personality,[213] as the proper safeguarding of freedom within the special juridical sense. [214] Abstract right is derived from the personal entitlement to develop and actualize freedom. It is formulated as the general duty to "[b]e a person and respect others as persons."[215] In line with this distinction, the positive (formal) right granted by the state in particular cases may or may not mirror the full spectrum of acts covered by the abstract right.

---

208. *Id.* § 41. In Hegel's original formulation: "Die Person muß sich eine äußere *Sphäre ihrer Freiheit* geben, um als Idee zu sein." *See* HEGEL, *supra* note 204, § 41 (emphasis in original).

209. On the multiple meanings of the term *right* (*Recht*) in Hegelian philosophy, see WOOD, *supra* note 199, at 94.

210. HEGEL, *supra* note 202, at § 44 ("A person has the right to direct his will upon any object, as his real and positive end. The object thus becomes his.").

211. *Id.* §§ 50–51.

212. *Id.* §§ 2–3.

213. *Abstract right* is defined in connection with personality: "Personality implies, in general, a capacity to possess rights, and constitutes the conception and abstract basis of abstract right." *Id.* § 36.

214. *See* WOOD, *supra* note 199, at 94 (explaining that "abstract right" has to do with the property safeguarding of a sphere of arbitrary choices, as distinguished from morality, which is concerned with what ought to be performed).

215. HEGEL, *supra* note 202, § 36.

Further, having a formal-positive right is not proof the rights-holder has an abstract right to begin with.[216]

In *The Philosophy of Right,* Hegel pointed out three external aspects of appropriation. The embodiment of the will occurs in the process of progression thought levels of development—from a purely abstract existence towards objective and external freedom—which is manifested in possession, use/consumption, and alienation. It is possible to think about the three forms as delineating the stages in the evolution of the relations between the person and the object. Possession begins the relation, use or consumption maintains it, and alienation often marks the end of it.

Possession appears to occupy a central role in Hegel's framework: "The reasonableness of property consists not in its satisfying our needs, but in its superseding and replacing the subjective phase of personality. *It is in possession first of all that the person becomes rational.*"[217] For possession to take effect, two necessary conditions need to be fulfilled: first, the subject must have will to appropriate the object, and second, some physical interaction between the will-contained body and the external object must take place.[218] As to the physical-objective phase, possession is manifested partly as *occupancy*, partly as *forming,* and partly as mere *marking.*[219] Interestingly, Hegel refers to marking as a form of possession, and perhaps as its purest, most genuine indication. The rationale is that marking can ideally fulfill the double function of possession: (i) a direct manifestation of physical relation to an object (ii) through which the claim of the will becomes recognizable.[220] This confirms an important operation of possession is to put others on notice about the existence of a subjective claim: "A person's putting his

---

216. *Id.* § 37[A] ("When anyone bases a claim upon his mere formal right, he may be wholly selfish, and often such a claim comes from a contracted heart and mind. Uncivilized man, in general, holds fast to his rights, while a more generous disposition is alert to see all sides of the question. Abstract right is, moreover, the first mere possibility, and in contrast with the whole context of a given relation is still formal. The possession of a right gives a certain authority, it is true, but it is not, therefore, absolutely necessary that I insist upon a right, which is only one aspect of the whole matter. In a word, possibility is something, which means that it either may or may not exist.").

217. *Id.* § 41[A] (emphasis added).

218. *Id.* §§ 51–51[A].

219. *Id.* § 54 ("Taking possession is partly the simple bodily grasp, partly the forming and partly the marking or designating of the object.") It seems that a *continuous* physical interaction is not necessary. It is more important the person continues to grasp the object as dominated by his will with some external manifestation that can be attributed to that relation. *Id.* § 55[A].

220. *Id.* §§ 58–58[A]. The Addition provides: "Of all kinds of possession this by marking is the most complete, since the others have more or less the effect of a mark. When I seize or form an object, in each case the result is in the end a mark, indicating to others that I exclude them, and have set my will in the object. The conception of the mark is that the object stands not for what it is, but for what it signifies." *Id.*

will into an object is the conception of property, and the next step is the realizing of it. The inner act of my will, which says that something is mine, *must be made recognizable for others*. When I make an object mine, I give it a predicate, which *must be manifested in its outer form*, and not remain merely in my inner will."[221]

The thread of external manifestation continues to the next stage of property relations. Use or consumption of the object is recognized through the alteration of the object in some way, where the change in form is attributed to the claim of the will. In Hegel's framework, the nexus between property rights and use/consumption is crucial.[222] This modus of property externalization signifies a direct and immediate relationship between the will and the thing. The thing is openly and unambiguously subject to the individual will; the relational hierarchy between the willing subject and the thing is salient.[223] The subject-object interaction, signified by use (or deformation) of objects, launches a process of recognition-by-negation through which subjects and objects are recognized as such.[224]

In the *Philosophy of Right*, Hegel does not attempt to sketch a model for an ideal legal system.[225] Perhaps this reservation has something to do with Hegel not endeavoring to precisely draw limits on the legitimate power of state intervention regarding conduct of individuals.[226] In this vein, Hegel further did not provide specific guidelines for the proper allocation of property entitlements.[227] At the same time, several commentators read in Hegel the proposition that all persons are entitled to *some* private property rights.[228] This proposition is supported, inter alia, by Hegel's objection to slavery.[229] Accordingly, everyone is entitled to at least a modicum of private property, but we do not know exactly *how much*. A positive legal system should support private property via organizations

---

221. *Id.* § 51A (emphasis added).

222. *See* WALDRON, *supra* note 25, at 365–70.

223. HEGEL, *supra* note 202, §§ 59–59[A].

224. *Id.*

225. *See* Stillman, *supra* note 199, at 133–34.

226. *Cf.* Allen W. Wood, *Editor's Introduction*, to GEORGE WILHELM FRIEDRICH HEGEL, ELEMENTS OF THE PHILOSOPHY OF RIGHT xvi. (Allen W. Wood ed., 1991).

227. It has been argued that personality-based property theories are too vague to have much practical significance in addressing issues concerning the size and shape of property rights. *See* Fisher, *supra* note 144, at 191 ("the conceptions of the self. . . that underlie most avatars of personality theory are too abstract and thin to provide answers to many specific questions").

228. *See, e.g.*, WALDRON, *supra* note 25, at 129 ff.; *see also* Jeanne L. Schroeder, *Unnatural Rights: Hegel and Intellectual Property*, 60 U. MIAMI L. REV. 453, 456 (2006) ("It follows from the fact that the subjectivity created by abstract right is purely formal, that it is only the form of property, and not its content, that is relevant to Hegel's analysis. All that matters is that some minimal private property rights exist.").

229. HEGEL, *supra* note 202, §§ 57[N], 66[N], 66[A].

and political institutions while conducting rational decision-making processes that determine the actual scope and limits of private legal rights.[230]

The possibility of disposing of property rights follows the same rationale for acquiring them in the first place, namely, the relation to the will. When the element of will-driven actions embodied in external objects fades away, so does property.[231] Hegel recognized that some things are inalienable: those elements of the inner self such as personal freedom, morality (*Sittlichkeit*), religious convictions, and life itself.[232] However, Hegel clearly regarded property as alienable in principle, inasmuch as such alienation does not compromise an ongoing, present exchange between the free will and the object.[233] The issue of alienation proved particularly challenging: if the object is indispensable to the self, is it at all transferable, and if so, under which condition? At first blush, if personality (or the autonomy of the person) is imbued in the object, alienation of the object might violate the principle that freedom cannot be relinquished.[234] This appears to be a serious problem if personality interests are said to *justify* property rights in external objects. In this context, Waldron proposed an interpretation "of a dual line of effect from my will to the object and back to my will."[235] Only so long as this dual line exists is the object the property of the person. Hughes pointed out that recognizing a power of alienation might lead to a paradox, as the free will (which no longer relates to the relinquished object) cannot have the power to transfer property rights to others—property rights that it no longer has.[236]

---

230. *See* Wood, *supra* note 199, at 239–41 (discussing Hegel's concept of civil society).

231. Hegel, *supra* note 202, § 65 ("I may relinquish property, since it is mine only by virtue of my having put my will into it.").

232. *Id.* §§ 66, 70.

233. *Id.* § 65 ("I may let a thing go unowned by me or pass it over to the will and possession of another; but this is possible only so far as the object is in its nature something external.").

234. For an argument favoring autonomy-based inalienability rules under copyrights, see Neil Netanel, *Copyright Alienability Restrictions and Enhancement of Author Autonomy: A Normative Evaluation*, 24 Rutgers L.J. 347, 398 ff (1993).

235. Waldron, *supra* note 25, at 370. ("To say, then, that my will is embodied in the chair is to regard the chair as the nexus of this dual relation between will and object, object and will. Now to alienate an object is to terminate one relation of this pair, and thus to withdraw from the object this status as a nexus of relations. . . My will is reflected in the object inasmuch as there is this dual line of effect from my will to the object and back to my will.").

236. "This is the paradox of alienation under the personality model of property. The present owner maintains ownership because he identifies the property as an expression of his self. Alienation is the denial of this personal link to an object. But if the personal link does not exist—if the object does not express or manifest part of the individual's personality—there is no foundation for property rights over the object by which the 'owner' may determine the object's future. An owner's present desire to alienate a piece

In response, the nexus between property and Hegel's idea of the *contract* is crucial, an idea complex and intriguing in itself:

> But property is also a manifestation of will, and the other, for which it exists, is the will of another person. This reference of will to will is the true and peculiar ground on which freedom is realized. The means by which I hold property, not by virtue of the relation of an object to my subjective will, but by virtue of another will, and hence share in a common will, is contract.[237]

Wood noted the dependence of the abstract right on the dialectic of recognition is stated quite clearly here.[238] He explains "[a] self actualizes itself when it makes itself into what it needs to be in order to satisfy its desire for self-certainty . . . a self must become a free person, through participating in a community of recognition or universal self-consciousness, and becoming aware of itself as a free person."[239] Accordingly, neither abstract right nor contract can be understood outside the social context and the idea of free wills that need to interact through mutual recognition in one another's freedom and in one self's.[240] Thus, the

---

of property is connected to the recognition that the property either is not or soon will not be an expression of himself. Thus, the justification for property is missing. This subtle control of the object's future does not jibe with foreseen future denial of the personality stake." *See* Hughes, *supra* note 143, at 345. Schroeder replied that the problem is answered through the Hegelian concept of contract. *See* Schroeder, *supra* note 228, at 476 ff.

237. HEGEL, *supra* note 202, § 71. *See also id.* §§ 40(b), 40[N].

238. *See* WOOD, *supra* note 200, at 91.

239. *Id.* at 92.

240. Carlson argued "[i]n Hegel's account personality is not pre-legal. Contract law is not merely useful to persons. It is the foundation of personality itself. Consent binds because personality is consent to human interrelation." *See* Carlson, *supra* note 199, at 1378 (footnote omitted). Carlson further explains: "If the warriors exchange objects, each confirms whatever the other rightly possesses. A freely bestows property on B—property that B claimed to own previously. B freely bestows property on A—property that A purported to own already. This is true in a very radical sense. When A gives property to B, A gives B all the property B has. Until the contract, Warrior B has nothing. Likewise, B gives A all the property Warrior A has. Until the contract, Warrior A had nothing. Hence, it is wrong to think that A and B 'exchange property.' Property comes into existence for the first time with the contract. What is really exchanged is recognition as such." *Id.* at 1391 (footnote omitted). In this respect, Hegel is perhaps not so distant from Hohfeld, who emphasized the constitutive *relational* aspect of legal positions, though Hohfeld, unlike Hegel, did not insist that "things" are indispensable to the interaction between subjects. *See* HEGEL, *supra* note 204, § 40[N] ("Es ist allerdings nur eine Person, die aus einem Vertrage zu leisten hat, sowie auch nur eine Person, die das Recht an eine solche Leistung erwirbt, aber ein solches Recht kann man darum nicht ein persönliches nennen; *jede* Art von Rechten kommt nur einer Person zu, und objektiv ist ein Recht aus dem Vertrage nicht Recht an eine Person, sondern nur an ein ihr Äußerliches oder etwas von ihr zu Veräußerndes, immer an eine Sache.") (italicization in original). This fundamental subject-object dialectics is absent in the Hohfeldian model.

answer to the alienation "paradox" is that at the intersection of a contract, the will of the transferee *already implicitly exists* in the object, and unlike in the traditional property sense of passing "good title," the property rights of the transferee do not depend on simultaneous existence of precisely the same property rights in the transferor.[241]

(b) Personality Theory and Copyright

Intellectual property scholars have identified in Hegel's discussion on property qualities that significantly enrich the theoretical foundation for property rights in intangible objects. The most direct and obvious attractiveness of Hegel lies in the property res having no intrinsic relation to physical attributes—and that physical attributes do not belong in the definition of property rights' objects.[242] In the case of copyright, personality theories inspired by Hegel's treatment view human creative expressions as the embodiment of the creator's self.[243] Accordingly, an essay or a musical piece can be viewed as a direct and genuine objectivization of the self in the thing. Moreover, in Hegel's framework, incorporeal things are the most natural candidates for becoming objects of private property. Things are defined by negation to subjects; they are external to the self and dominated by it. Things cannot have free will, and they do not need to acquire any *physical* (as distinguished from *external*) form whatsoever:

> The will is a special way of thinking; it is thought translating itself into reality; it is the impulse of thought to give itself reality. The distinction between thought and will may be expressed in this way. When I think an object, I make of it a thought, and take from it the sensible. Thus I make of it something which is essentially and directly mine.[244]

It would seem a thought is the purest object to be considered as *belonging* to the thinking subject. Thinking is an action of the free will in the external world that shapes the external world into objects of property. Thinking out the thought, in the course of the self's endeavors to reach a higher stage of development and recognition, gives it an objective existence and underpins the claim to control it. In paragraphs 68–69 of the *Philosophy of Right*, Hegel reaches the issue of legal

241. *Cf.* Schroeder, *supra* note 228, at 480–81 ("legal relationships relate only to the creation of legal subjects—persons capable of bearing rights and duties. The legal subjectivity mutually constituted with abstract right is, therefore, equally abstract and formal.").

242. Hegel, *supra* note 202, § 43[N] ("Mental endowments, science, art, such matters of religion as sermons, masses, prayers, blessings of consecrated utensils, inventions also, are objects of exchange, recognized things to be bought and sold. It is possible to ask, also, if an artist or scholar is in legal possession of his art, science, or capacity to preach or read mass; and the question is put on the presumption that these objects are things.").

243. For a recent account and critique, see Stallberg, *supra* note 196, at 122 ff.

244. Hegel, *supra* note 202, § 4[A].

rights in intellectual productions (*geistige Produktion*). He begins by identifying the particular nature of such objects:

> What is peculiar to a mental product can be externalized and directly converted into an object, which it is possible for others to produce. When another person has acquired the object, he may make the thought or, it may be, the mechanical genius in it, his own; a possibility which in the case of literary works constitutes the reason and special value of acquisition. But, over and above this, the new owner comes at the same time into possession of the general power to express himself in the same way, and so of making any number of objects of the same kind.[245]

Hegel grappled with the question whether claims in immaterial objects are capable of being conceptually separated from the property rights in physical objects embodying them.[246] He reaches this question is his discussion on relinquishment of property. In that context, Hegel felt obligated to explain whether and how the property holder should be able to alienate copies on the one hand, but on the other reserve for himself (or separately alienate) the exclusive power to make reproductions. Hegel's answer to the "whether" question is positive—and that should be the case due to the special character of intellectual property rights, which are said to be less like possession (*Besitz*) and more like wealth (*Vermögen*).[247] The direct and intended use of an intellectual product is to think it,[248] whereas the indirect, particular power to control use bestowed by intellectual property is indirect, separate, and alienable.

In a lengthy Note to paragraph 69, Hegel continues to struggle with the special nature of intellectual property rights. He notes that through multiple reproductions and modifications, "the profit which the work promised the author or inventor in the first place may be wiped out, or the purpose of both author and imitator may be defeated, or one may be ruined." This notwithstanding, for

---

245. *Id.* at § 58.

246. *Id.* at § 69[N] ("The first question is whether the separation of the object from the power to reproduce, which goes with the object, is allowable in thought, and does not destroy full and free possession.").

247. *Id.* ("Now there is this peculiarity about this power [to reserve the right to allow reproductions] that through it the object becomes not merely a possession, but a means of wealth. . . This new feature is a special kind of external use, and is different and separate from the use to which the object was directly appointed. It is not, as it is called, an *accessio naturalis* as are *foetura*. Hence as the distinction occurs in the sphere of external use, which is naturally capable of being divided, the reservation of one part, while another is being disposed of, is not the retention of an ownership without *utile*.").

248. *Id.* ("But in the case of a mental product the intention is that others should comprehend it, and make its imagination, memory, and thought their own. Learning is not merely the treasuring up of words in the memory; it is through thinking that the thoughts of others are seized.").

Hegel using existing expression in one's own expression (an act he named "plagiarism") was, above all, a violation of the code of honor (*Ehre*).[249] He does not appear to articulate a stronger justification to the prohibition against unauthorized literary reproduction beyond the protection of economic interest. He is further highly skeptical about the feasibility of identifying "plagiarized" elements in new works, which leads him to conclude plagiarism cannot be said to strictly violate property rights.[250] As a logical consequence, Hegel commented that intellectual property rights as expressed in the positive law serve their purpose in granting specific protections to authors and publishers, yet these protections are justifiably very limited in scope.[251]

3. Utilitarian Theories

(a) Utilitarian Approaches to Property

Classic utilitarian thinkers considered utility, welfare, and happiness as bedrock concepts in legal theory and legislation. Jeremy Bentham, for instance, opened the Theory of Legislation with the following statement: "THE PUBLIC GOOD ought to be the object of the legislator; GENERAL UTILITY ought to be the foundation of his reasoning. To know the true good of the community is what constitutes the science of legislation."[252] Bentham applied this principle when speaking about civil law and the allocation of legal rights/obligations in general: "In the

---

249. HEGEL, *supra* note 204, § 69[N] ("Inwiefern nun die in der wiederholenden Äußerung sich ergebende *Form* den vorhandenen wissenschaftlichen Schatz und insbesondere die Gedanken solcher anderer, die noch im äußerlichen Eigentum ihrer Geistesprodukte sind, in ein spezielles geistiges Eigentum des reproduzierenden Individuums verwandle und ihm hiermit das Recht, sie auch zu seinem äußerlichen Eigentum zu machen, gebe oder inwiefern nicht,—inwiefern solche Wiederholung in einem schriftstellerischen Werke ein *Plagiat* werde, läßt sich nicht durch eine genaue Bestimmung angeben und hiermit nicht rechtlich und gesetzlich festsetzen. *Das Plagiat müßte daher eine Sache der Ehre sein und von dieser zurückgehalten werden.*") (emphasis added).

250. Anglo-American copyright commentators who discuss the application of Hegel's idea of property tend to overlook this important aspect of Hegel's treatment (Schroeder—supra note 228— is exceptional in this respect).

251. HEGEL, *supra* note 204, § 69[N] ("Gesetze gegen den *Nachdruck* erfüllen daher ihren Zweck, das Eigentum der Schriftsteller und der Verleger rechtlich zu sichern, zwar in dem bestimmten, aber sehr beschränkten Umfange") (emphasis in original). Schroeder went so far to argue Hegel's discussion of property does not *mandate* positive copyright protection at all. *See* Schroeder, *supra* note, at 502. In copyright terminology, Hegel was probably a "dualist" rather that a "monist" for considering the economic rights so contingent and merely a matter of "commercial law." *See* Leslie Kim Treiger-Bar-Am, *Kant on Copyright: Rights of Transformative Authorship*, 25 CARDOZO ARTS & ENT. L.J. 1059 (2008) (noting the distinction between Kant-inspired monistic systems and Hegel-inspired dualistic systems).

252. *See* 1 JEREMY BENTHAM, THEORY OF LEGISLATION Ch. 1 at 13 (1840).

distribution of rights and obligations, the legislator . . . should have for his end the happiness of society."[253] As concrete legislative ends, Benthan named Subsistence, Abundance, Equality, and Security.[254] Famously, Bentham ferociously rejected natural rights as the basis of law.[255] Moving to discuss property law in his Theory of Legislation, Bentham perceived property entitlements merely as a basis of expectation guaranteed by the law.[256] State protection of property expectations enhances the sense of security among members of the public, thereby contributing to greater happiness.[257] Property protects the basis of expectations that is founded on existing rules—and by securing these expectations through the institution of property, society can expect some level of productivity.[258]

Bentham was deeply influenced by David Hume, who described property as "a *relation* betwixt a person and an. object as permits him, but forbids any other, the free use and possession of it, without violating the laws of justice and moral equity."[259] Justice and morality are indeed central to Hume's social and political philosophy in general. Hume categorically rejected the notion that morality is universal and derivable from reason.[260] Instead, he posited that moral virtues and vices are contingent, and that morality is essentially a matter of the relations between mental (internal) actions such as passion or volition and external objects.[261] Hume suggested both vice and virtue are in this sense equally artificial and "out of nature." He stated "[f]or however it may be disputed, whether the notion of a merit or demerit in certain actions be natural or artificial,'tis evident, that the actions themselves are artificial, and are perform'd with a certain design and intention."[262]

---

253. *Id.* at Pt. 1, Ch. 2 at 119.

254. Id.

255. Jeremy Bentham, Anarchical Fallacies 501 (1843) ("*Natural rights* is simple nonsense: natural and imprescriptible rights, rhetorical nonsense—nonsense upon stilts.") (emphasis in original). In a similar vein, Bentham proclaimed: "All men born free? Absurd and miserable nonsense!" *Id.* at 498.

256. *See* Bentham, *supra* note 252, Ch. 8 at 137–38.

257. *Id.* at 139 ("As regards property, security consists in receiving no check, no shock, no derangement, to the expectation founded on the law, of enjoying such and such portion of good. . . When [the legislature] does not contradict [that expectation], he does what is essential to the happiness of society.").

258. *See* Michelman, *supra* note 159, at 1212.

259. *See* David Hume, Treatise of Human Nature Bk.II., Ch.I., sect.x (e-books@adelaide 2006) (1739).

260. *Id.* Bk.III., Ch.I., sect.i.

261. *Id.* Hume further believed "[v]ice and virtue. . . may be compar'd to sounds, colours, heat and cold, which, according to modern philosophy, are not qualities in objects, but perceptions in the mind." *Id.*

262. *Id.* sect. ii.

Understanding Hume's formulation requires some background. He divided what he called "virtues" into those that are "natural"—in that our approval of them does not depend upon any cultural inventions or social intervention—and those that are "artificial" (i.e., dependent both for their existence as character traits and for their ethical merit on the presence of conventional rules for the common good).[263] Hume's "natural" virtues are more refined and completed forms of human traits, which one could expect to find even in people who belonged to no society but cooperated only within small familial groups.[264] The traits he calls "artificial" virtues are the ones we need for successful impersonal cooperation, but our natural sentiments are too partial to give rise to these virtues without intervention.[265] To Hume, then, morality does not emanate from any higher or natural source other than human nature itself.[266] A moral and just law is neither divine nor universal; morality is an "artifice" and the laws based upon it are artificial rather than natural.[267] Humans must operate in social settings to survive and satisfy their needs; moral distinctions are derived from social conventions necessary for the success of the collaborative effort. Social conventions, on their part, preserve social structures, maintain social life, and enable prosperity under conditions of scarcity and selfish human actors having claims to those resources.[268] Upon the premise of justice as a social artifice, Hume established the justification for property law:

> Our property is nothing but those goods, whose constant possession is established by the laws of society; that is, by the laws of justice. Those, therefore, who make use of the words property, or right, or obligation, before they have explain'd the origin of justice, or even make use of them in that explication, are guilty of a very gross fallacy.[269]

Property is an artificial and necessary circumstance of social life; property law reinforces the prevalent convention concerning property according to the moral

---

263. *See* Rachel Cohon, *Hume's Moral Philosophy*, *in* THE STANFORD ENCYCLOPEDIA OF PHILOSOPHY (Edward N. Zalta ed., 2004).

264. *Id.*

265. *Id.*

266. HUME, *supra* note 259, Bk.III., Ch.II., sect.I ("no action can be virtuous, or morally good, unless there be in human nature some motive to produce it, distinct from the sense of its morality") (emphasis in original).

267. *See* Frederick G. Whelan, *Property as Artifice: Hume and Blackstone*, *in* NOMOS XXII: PROPERTY 101–02 (J. Roland Pennock & John Chapman eds., 1980) (explaining "artifice" is a distinctively Humean term, used to designate something as based on social conventions, rather than being "natural" and independent of nature).

268. HUME, *supra* note 259, Bk. III., Ch.II., sect. i–ii.

269. *Id. See also* Whelan, *supra* note 267, at 108–14 (discussing Hume's justification for property law).

parameters set by society.[270] Hume considered property law and prosperous social life as interlocked in the sense that morality and property mirrored one another. Property law mirrored the contingent standards of morality and justice in human societies, and without conventions about stable ownership supported by property law, societies cannot function and thrive.

Drawing on the insights of Hume, Bentham, Mill, and others, legal utilitarianism scholars generally view the law as an instrument for achieving higher goals. Utilitarian property scholarship generally maintains that private property is justified inasmuch as it positively contributes to social utility. Accordingly, utilitarianism supports a regime of private property that functions as a catalyst of greater welfare. The premise underlying utilitarian approaches is that without private property, society stands to lose as no rational actor would have sufficient incentives to invest in preserving, nurturing, and improving common resources.[271] Utilitarian concepts of property evolved out of the understanding that association is advantageous, yet impossible in the absence of rules governing individual rights to control and enjoy resources. Hume identified the *locus* of the problem of socially collaborating efficiently in the tendency of people to trespass against one other.[272] To combat this tendency, property rights are instated to secure stable possession. Therefore, recognized rules regarding acquisitions and transactions are essential for the very existence of associations and the formation of large-scale social structure and institutions.[273]

Influenced by the tendency to apply economic analysis to law, the utilitarian idea of maximizing social welfare in the law-and-economics literature coincides with a striving toward higher economic efficiency. Economic analysis of the law

---

270. HUME, *supra* note, Bk.III., Ch.II., sect.iii.

271. For the famous modern articulation of this argument, see Garrett Herdin, *The Tragedy of the Commons*, 162 SCIENCE 1243, 1244 (1968).

272. Michelman explained:

> The key is Hume's historical starting point, which posits men initially in an atomistic, nonsocial situation. By his account, sexual attraction and natural affections among family members lead men into a first perception of the advantages of association—the efficiency of combined and divided labor, and the usefulness of sharing. The wish to associate gradually transcends the family group. But as each person approaches association with strangers, cognizant of potential advantages, he carries with him a certain accumulation of possessions. Since it is men's selfishness, not their gregariousness or their sympathy, which turns them towards association, nothing in the process of associating necessarily implies any security of possessions, or any curbs on violations of such security. Yet people realize that no lasting association will be possible as long as they trespass against one another. As a result, there evolves a kind of tentative practice of mutual forbearance, which gradually solidifies into an established set of rules.

See Michelman, *supra* note 159, at 1209–10.

273. *Id.*

has both descriptive and prescriptive claims.[274] In the latter context, economic analysis may attempt to ascertain the legal rule that would bring society to the desired result more efficiently. The central operation of property law under utilitarian-economic approaches is functional: the law facilitates allocative efficiency of valuable resources under scarcity conditions, striving toward wealth maximization, with property ownership being in principle an economically efficient arrangement.[275] Demsetz argued that property rights will emerge when internalization of externalities is cost-effective and that, in fact, "[a] primary function of property is that of guiding incentives to achieve a greater internalization of externalities."[276] Viewed through the prism of economic analysis, a key role of the law is to provide the proper incentives to wealth-maximizing individuals who compete over scarce resources. The strategy for achieving greater societal welfare is to provide incentives to individuals who pursue their selfish agenda, namely, striving toward greater *personal* happiness.

Incentivizing selfish individuals to obtain, preserve, and improve resources by granting them legal rights to control and benefit from these resources is said to offer the answer to the "tragedy of the commons."[277] According to conventional economic wisdom, a regime of property rights is likely to enhance the value of resources in many situations. If markets operate efficiently, resources through free exchange should end up in the hands of the owner who values them the most and who can extract the highest utility. In the aggregate, the market would theoretically stabilize on a Pareto-optimal allocation in which no one is able to further improve his position through voluntary exchange.

However, the issue of externalities makes murky the idealized picture of a perfect resource allocation through voluntary and efficient exchange. Some economists indeed consider externalities as a central impediment to efficiency.[278] Externalities create efficiency problems because the market price of an asset does not reflect its true value. More generally, in an externality situation, not all the costs and benefits involved in a transaction are reflected in the price. Some economic approaches to property law view its central mission as providing the optimal conditions for *internalization* of externalities; more pointedly, one of Coase's greatest contributions to the economic analysis of the law was to shift

---

274. Richard A. Posner, Economic Analysis of Law 24–25 (2007).

275. *See* Harold Demsetz, *Toward a Theory of Property Rights*, 62 Am. Econ. Rev. 347 (1967).

276. *Id.* at 348.

277. *See* Herdin, *supra* note 271.

278. *Externalities* could be thought of for this purpose as the unintended positive or negative utility effects on others, resulting from certain activity, that are not reflected in the market price. A common example of a negative externality is environmental pollution, and a common example of a positive externality is the improved capacity telecommunication systems have with every additional user (network effects).

the focus from externalities in general to transaction costs. Coase famously showed that in a world of zero transaction costs and enforceable contracts, parties would reach an efficient internalization of externalities *regardless of what the legal norm says.*[279] As conditions of zero transaction costs exist only in classroom hypotheticals, the actual mission of the law is to create the conditions for efficient transactions by helping to minimize transaction costs.[280]

(b) Utilitarianism and Copyright

A well-known exposition of the utilitarian stance in the positive law is the Intellectual Property Clause of the U.S. Constitution, vesting in Congress the power to legislate patent and copyright laws "[t]o promote the Progress of Science and useful Arts."[281] This clause exhibits a consequentialist, means-ends relationship between the exclusive rights and the grand project those rights are destined to serve. By contrast to backward-looking reward theories that seek to compensate authors for past achievements such as Lockean labor, utilitarian approaches to copyright aim to encourage the production of creative works in the future. The key assumption is that authors and other rights-holders can be incentivized via exclusive copyrights to create and produce more than what they would otherwise do. With this assumption in mind, an extensive body of theoretical literature deals with applying law-and-economics analysis to intellectual property issues.[282]

Economic analysis of copyright law emerged more-or-less simultaneously with the inception of modern law-and-economics literature.[283] Standard economic analysis of copyright law considers the main task of the law as ameliorating the free-rider problem.[284] Actors who invest economic resources in creating and producing information products should be able to recoup their production

---

279. *See* Coase, *supra* note 89.

280. Landes and Posner argue "[r]educing transaction costs is the very raison d'etre of property rights." *See* LANDES & POSNER, *supra* note 112, at 12–13. For an influential analysis of the U.S. fair use doctrine as a response to transition costs problems, see Wendy J. Gordon, *Fair Use as Market Failure, A Structural and Economic Analysis of the Betamax Case and Its Predecessors*, 82 COLUM. L. REV. 1600 (1982).

281. *See* U.S. Constitution, art. 1, § 8.

282. *See* Peter S. Menell, *Intellectual Property: General Theories, in* ENCYCLOPEDIA OF LAW AND ECONOMICS (Boudewijn Bouckaert & Gerrit De Geest eds., 2001) (providing a law-and-economics introduction to intellectual property and an extensive collection of sources).

283. For a classic treatment, see Robert M. Hurt & Robert M. Schuchman, *The Economic Rationale of Copyright*, 56 AM. ECON. REV. PAPERS & PROC. 42 (1966) (formulating the framework that is still widely followed today concerning weighing effects of regulation on incentives against restrictions on access). *See also* Wendy J. Gordon & Robert G. Bone, *Copyright, in* 2 ENCYCLOPEDIA OF LAW & ECONOMICS 189 (Boudewijn Bouckaert & Gerrit De Geest eds., 2001) (providing an introduction and a collection of sources).

284. *See* Gordon, *Intellectual Property*, *supra* note 110, at 619.

costs. Creators usually cannot compete with a copyist, who only needs to cover the marginal costs of producing an additional copy (which are comparatively very low).[285] Exclusive rights to reproduce, distribute, communicate, etc. provide supercompetitive advantages to rights-holders and are designed to secure a level of protection that will offset the social costs of monopoly with the value generated by providing economic incentives to produce and create new works.

Under the assumption that utility, efficiency,[286] and incentives should serve both as the compass and the conscience of copyright legislation,[287] a number of initial questions call for attention. First, creating effective exclusory rights in intangible resources should be *achievable through state legislation.* It is questionable whether one can build walls around messages in the same way, for the same purpose, and with the same effect as a farmer erecting fences around a pasture in which only her (or only "authorized") cows may graze.[288] As noted in the context of the public good discussion, legislation attempts to provide some fencing designed to mitigate the inefficient results involved in non-excludability that is meant to secure the ability to generate revenues from producing information goods.[289] Second, to be efficient, the net benefits of the copyright system must outweigh its net costs. This general law-and-economics consideration is not unique to copyright, of course, yet in this particular context it warrants special attention. Economists often assess the cost of the copyright system in terms of deadweight loss caused by monopolistic market conditions, which is technically described as reduction in consumer surplus. In this vein, the copyright system is economically justified if the additional aggregate gain of value extracted from creative works outweighs the aggregate loss causes by exclusivity. Property rights

---

285. *See* William M. Landes & Richard A. Posner, *An Economic Analysis of Copyright Law*, 18(2) J.L. & ECON. 325, 326–27(1989).

286. The literature underscores the distinction between consideration of static and dynamic efficiency. Posner explains that static analysis suppresses the time dimension of economic activity, whereas dynamic analysis relaxes the assumption of instantaneous adjustment to change. *See* POSNER, *supra* note 274, § 3.1.

287. For a recent critical analysis of applying Demsetzian principles to copyright law, see Brett M. Frischmann, *Evaluating the Demsetzian Trend in Copyright Law*, 3 REV. L. & ECON. 649 (2007). For a more general analysis on the advantages and disadvantages of positive and normative economic analysis for the allocation and shape of exclusive rights, see PEUKERT, *supra* note 10, § 3.

288. After Herding's *Tragedy of the Commons*, the example of the pasture and the grazing cows became a popular illustration of efficiency problems concerning use of scarce resources in the absence of private property rights. *See, e.g.*, POSNER, *supra* note 274, § 3.1.

289. *Cf.* LANDES & POSNER, *supra* note 113, at 40–41 (cautioning that copyright restriction will not *always* be necessary for recovering the costs of creating works.) For the classic argument in this vein, see Breyer, *supra* note 188. *Cf.* Barry W. Tyerman, *The Economic Rationale for Copyright Protection for Published Books: A Reply to Professor Breyer*, 18 UCLA L. REV. 1100 (1971).

in information goods tend to be more costly due to their monopolistic nature and their non-rivalrous "consumption."[290] The implied assumption is that an accurate cost/benefits analysis is feasible through which contradicting welfare effects of copyright legislation are juxtaposed to yield the *net* social impact. At a minimum, one should be able to determine whether a given copyright rule is Pareto-superior to the alternatives.[291]

However, both sides of the copyright cost/benefit analysis are difficult to determine. Apparently Paul Samuelson himself—the thought leader of the public good problem—was skeptical about the ability to measure the net utility generated from providing non-excludable goods due to the valuation problem,[292] and it should be equally challenging to quantify the utility of which the public is *deprived* (i.e., the reduction in positive externalities) that is the expected result of a given copyright restriction. Indeed, dynamic analysis of alternative copyright regulations poses grave empirical challenges. It would seem insurmountable to assess today the future welfare impact of a legal rule, under the assumption that every stage of the information process depends on the previous one, and assuming also that circulation of messages is a significantly random and unpredictable progression. As Chapter 1 demonstrated, this recognition is derived from the very nature of information, rendering assessments about the ramifications of regulative interventions risky in general. For example, how can one calculate the costs of regulation in terms of the value that has *not been created* yet due to copyright restrictions (e.g., the derivative work that never came to be)? Further, it is likely impossible to achieve sufficient certainty concerning the impact of regulation (or the abstention from regulation) on the creation of a given work.[293] Assessing the cause-and-effect relationship between copyright regulation and the level of creative production always involves a certain degree of guessing, especially where the involvement of derivative rights-holders in the creative process is relatively minor, and more generally, in cases

---

290. *Cf.* LANDES & POSNER, *supra* note 112, at 16–21.

291. *See* VARIAN, *supra* note 87, § 1.9 (if allocation of resources allows some people to be made better off without making anybody else worse off, the allocation is Pareto inefficient). For an alternative approach to cost analysis of copyright law from the perspective of the new institutional economy, see F. Scott Kieff, *The Case Against Copyright: A Comparative Institutional Analysis of Intellectual Property Regimes*, Stanford Law and Economics Olin Working Paper No. 297; Washington U. School of Law Working Paper No. 04-10-01 (available at SSRN: http://ssrn.com/abstract=600802 or doi:10.2139/ssrn.600802) (2004).

292. *See* Yoo, *supra* note 113, at 639–40.

293. Particularly in nonprofessional creative circles (hobbyists, for instance), it seems difficult to determine whether a given work has been created as a response to the legal incentives encapsulated in copyright protection or whether the same work would have been created irrespective of copyright incentives.

where commercial considerations do not play a siginificant role in the creative process.

V. CONCLUSION

This chapter opened by introducing Hohfeld's model of jural relations. The lawyer should find the model helpful for answering his client's questions, which can be roughly framed as follows: "Do I (client) have a right to do this and that?" "Can I refrain from doing this and that?" "Can I force person *X* to do (or refrain from doing) this and that?" Under a Hohfeldian analysis, the charged concept of "right" appears to be reduced to earthy, practical questions of the sort that are determined by the positive law. The Hohfeldian model will play an important role in the descriptive project of this study concerning the positive law's position on access rights questions (Chapters 4–6 infra).

Property conceptualists attack Hohfeld for his contribution to the dissolving of long-standing understandings about property in the theoretical discourse. This said, the discussion in this chapter suggests that making a principal choice between property conceptualism and property nominalism is not necessarily dispositive for evaluating the "property metaphor" and its implications. Contemporary conversations about property in general—and intellectual property more specifically—can draw important insights from both perspectives on private property as a social and legal institution. It was further argued that instrumental-economic approaches to property law might even reinforce the conceptualist's view on property (for instance, under the assumptions and methodology of information cost theory). In the same vein, both traditional property concepts and legal nominalism are constructive for addressing various aspects and complex philosophical, normative, and pragmatic questions of intellectual property law. Especially in the context of copyright protection in the digital environment, high protection proponents tend to uphold the physical property metaphor to support their views,[294] including arguments for a broad right to exclude in rem being applicable to copyrighted works as well. Yet as their critics often maintain, a sweeping analogy between intangible goods and conventional property already bears significant risks at the level of the basic assumptions of that analogy.

As shown in the discussion above, justifying strong copyright protection solely on moral/personality grounds is especially problematic,[295] a recognition

---

294. *Cf.* MELVILLE B. NIMMER & DAVID NIMMER, 3 NIMMER ON COPYRIGHT § 12A.03[D][1] (2006) (demonstrating and critiquing the "breaking and entering" metaphor in the context of U.S. anticircumvention legislation).

295. *See, e.g.*, STALLBERG, *supra* note 196; Tom G. Palmer, *Are Patents and Copyrights Morally Justified? The Philosophy of Property Rights and Ideal Objects*, 13 HARV. J. L. & PUB. POL'Y. 817 (2002).

that has been arising also in jurisdictions such as Germany and France.[296] Among the many discrepancies between classic moral justifications of private property and copyright law, this chapter elaborated on problems in Locke's original labor-based argument as the basis for exclusive rights in works.[297] By comparison, Hegel's position viewing positive intellectual property protection merely as a department of commercial regulation is far less an "ethical" underpinning to copyright as it is often thought to be the case.

At the framework level, no single theoretical approach to copyright is capable of providing conclusive answers to the regulative challenges, and at the same time, neither should be dismissed on its face as plainly "false." In addition, some longstanding conceptual tenets of property, within which the right-to-exclude in rem plays a central role, can provide a useful orientation point for analyzing the nature and function of various property structures, including the one controlling creative works.[298] In the context of digital copyright protection, a clear view of the way in which private property law principally operates is important for understanding the transition of the legal system from regulating works in analog formats to covering digital information. The next chapter will develop a theoretical framework that draws on these insights in more detail.

296. *See, e.g.*, Matthias Leistner & Gerd Hansen, *Die Begründung des Urheberrechts im digitalen Zeitalter*, GRUR (2008) (arguing the classic author-centered justifications for copyright protections are facing a crisis).

297. Section IV.B.1.(c)–(d) *supra*.

298. This principle is not unique to Anglo-American conceptions of property. A recent study established the centrality of subjective *exclusory* (and relational) entitlements within the constitutional concept of property under German law as reflected by the jurisprudence of the German Constitutional Court. *See* PEUKERT, *supra* note 10, at 718; *see also id.* at 860 (objecting to a pure negative approach to property rights and upholding the view that subjective-exclusive rights must have some positive content—the entitlement to *do*, not only to *exclude* others).

3. ACCESS

I. INTRODUCTION

The word *access* commonly describes an action of going or coming to/into something.[1] Other times, access is something that someone *has*—a power of getting near or into contact with something.[2] In the property scenario, the "something" to which the act of access pertains is typically the property res. In this context, private legal entitlements affect the ability to exercise, permit, and proscribe physical interaction such as entry, touching, using, etc. For example, access control guaranteed by trespass rules is inherent to ownership of corporeal assets.[3] Access to physical assets confers material benefits: it enables use and facilitates extraction of value. Usually, enjoyment of physical resources *depends* on the ability to perform the physical interaction that property entitlements secure. Thus, unauthorized physical entries to a privately owned domain (or exceeding the scope of permission granted by the owner) might per se injure possessory interests and trigger legal remedies as well as justify legitimate self-help actions.[4] In Anglo-American common law traditions, injunctions and high damages awards sometimes reflect a punitive reaction of the law to such property violations.[5]

Indeed, the relationships between physical access to resources and use/enjoyment are intense, often inextricable. Ordinarily, before use can even take place, the resource must be *accessible* to the actor, as actual physical access happens simultaneously with use.[6] The role of access in a given property scenario depends on the nature of the asset and of the use/enjoinment sought. For example, mere

---

1. Oxford English Dictionary (2d ed. 1989) (entry *access*: I.1. & I.4.). As a verb, in the sense of "to gain access to," it is often used in the context of data stored in a computer. *Id.*

2. *Id.* at I.2.a.

3. Chapter 2, Section III.B.2 *supra.*

4. *See* Alison Clarke & Paul Kohler, Property Law 286–92 (2005) (reviewing remedies to violation of possessory interests (trespass) under English law, including self-help and criminal sanctions).

5. *See* Jacque v. Steenberg Homes, 563 N.W.2d 154 (Wis. 1997) (Supreme Court of Wisconsin upheld $100,000 punitive damages for intentional trespass as it "recognized that in certain situations of trespass, the actual harm is not in the damage done to the land, which may be minimal, but in the loss of the individual's right to exclude others from his or her property and, the court implied that this right may be punished by a large damage award despite the lack of measurable harm"). *Id.* at 617.

6. For example, if a person wishes to eat an apple, he should be able to touch it, and touching must occur simultaneously or prior to eating. Obviously, eating cannot happen before access is made possible.

physical access to a place, without more, might satisfy the entrant's expectations in full. (Consider the benefit to a climber who mounts a hill for the sole purpose of appreciating the panoramic landscape surrounding it from that altitude). Other times, mere access has no value in itself, yet the ability to access preconditions the ability to draw actual benefits. (Consider a barren parcel of land with arid desert soil that lies over lucrative natural resources underground such as expensive minerals in which extracting the valuable minerals depends on the ability to access the land.) In any event, access control is the key to utilizing property res, and as shown in the previous chapter, access control is indeed a strong and perhaps the most salient indication of ownership.

The case of information res conjures up several distinctions. Concerning information res, Chapters 1 and 2 indicated there are three main ways to utilize information (or a given message): to know it, to act according to it, and to communicate it. First in the order and the most basic is "*having*" or "*knowing*" the message; receiving a message forms its most fundamental "use." In this sense, the notions of "access to information" and reception of a medial message converge to form what Hegel called the "purpose" (*Bestimmung*) of human intangible production: becoming part of the mental-spiritual universe of the recipient.[7] The ability to access information confers actual and/or potential benefits upon the recipient. When reception itself is enjoyable or provides satisfaction (e.g., reading a book or listening to music), access to the message immediately intermingles with its benefits, somewhat similar to the hill climber hypothetical. Further, access may be the first step in making certain other "uses" of information—namely, acting according to it or communicating messages to others.[8] In some situations, merely knowing the message will not confer any immediate advantage, but acting upon/according to it will (e.g., investing in company stock after receiving information concerning a future event likely to increase its value).[9] Finally, the actor may want to communicate the message (or facilitate its

7. *See* Georg Wilhelm Friedrich Hegel, Philosophy of Right § 69[N] (S.W. Dyde trans., Batoche Books 2001) (1896). ("But in the case of a mental product the intention is that others should comprehend it, and make its imagination, memory, and thought their own.").

8. It is possible to draw a distinction between *acting according* to information and *making communicative use* of the content. Both can be considered "using" information, but in the intellectual property context, the former is more relevant to patent law situations, whereas the latter is typical to copyright or trade secrets law. The principle is of general application, however. In the hypothetical involving the underground natural minerals, the person knowing about their approximate location may either extract the minerals himself (i.e., "act upon information") or sell the information to others (i.e., "communicate" a message for a fee or other kinds of consideration).

9. Acting upon information does not have to occur immediately, and at the moment of reception, the recipient cannot always predict in which way and under which circumstances knowing something could later become translatable to actual advantage. Recipients, whether consciously or not, often keep the information "in mind" until the point where they see the benefits of acting.

communication to others) in a manner that would enhance his personal utility or improve his situation.

Information regulation policy is tailored around these basic, seemingly obvious recognitions. In the case of intellectual property (and specifically copyright regulation), designing property-like arrangements raises several questions, some of which have been partly touched upon in the previous chapter:

- Is information *capable* of being subject to trespassory entitlements?
- If so, is it *justified* to grant private rights to exclude others from information, and if so, under which conditions?
- Is it accurate to say traditional copyright rules *already secure* some level of access control with respect to copyrighted information?
- What is the *impact* of *new copyright legislation* concerning digital technology on the answer to the previous question?
- What is the *interplay* between traditional copyrights and new regulation concerning digital technology in the context of legal access control?

The first two questions are part of the general debate over justifications to and scope of intellectual property law. The last three questions target more specifically the complex interrelations between "traditional" and "new" copyright legislation and their impact on access. As indicated, many observers are skeptical about the very notion of "trespassory" rules attached to information.[10] In addressing such and related questions of proprietary control over information, three theoretical variations come to mind:

First Variation: When someone holds trespass-like exclusive entitlements with respect to information, this person has a Hohfeldian right-claim to exclude unauthorized parties from that information. This first variation is similar (but not identical!) to the subjective-negative entitlement of a real estate owner to exclude strangers from his land. It provides the conceptual basis for the *access-right* notion, as defined shortly below.

Second Variation: Having access rights regarding information may mean something quite the opposite of the first variation. The rights-holder is the person having a Hohfeldian right-claim directed against "information possessors." The right imposes an affirmative legal duty on those possessors ordering them to enable access to information in their control upon the rights-holder's demand.[11] To distinguish the second variation from the first, this entitlement shall be called *right-of-access in the strong form*.

---

10. *Cf.* Thomas Hoeren, *Access Right as a Postmodern Symbol of Copyright Deconstruction?*, *in* ADJUNCTS AND ALTERNATIVES TO COPYRIGHT 361 (Jane C. Ginsburg & June M. Besek eds., 2002) (stating "above any intellectual property [is] freedom of information. This meta-rule determines that any information can be used by everybody for free"). Whether or not one agrees with this proposition, it is more difficult to say the same with respect to physical resources in general.

11. In the general property parlance, such an entitlement is akin to having a positive servitude in land law. Positive servitude is defined as "[a] real servitude allowing a person

Third Variation: Somewhere in between the two opposites, a third variation emerges. Here, information is not subject to any private right-claim. A person is entitled to access information *if she can*. In other words, the person having such access entitlement merely holds a Hohfeldian access privilege. By definition, the privilege holder is not in the position to affirmatively enforce it against others. Thus, this third variation shall be called *right-of-access in the weak form*.

This chapter will explained this terminology and its possible contribution to analyzing access rights pertaining to information and the application of these insights to the digital copyright debate.

II. ACCESS TO INFORMATION REVISITED

Applying the information model vocabulary, an individual occasion of access to information is the reception of a medial message in the course of a single communication event. The concept of access implies, inter alia, cognitive processing occurring inside the recipient's mind once exposure to the message signals takes place. Though the information model assumes a human recipient, it is not impossible to imagine reception of signals by a non-human agent. This possibility is especially important in the context of computer programs and digital communication. In those cases, reception of information is rather a technological procedure, which, in its own right might surely entail considerable legal and economic ramifications. The distinction between human and technological access is relevant particularly within the broader debate over anticircumvention laws (discussed in greater detail in Chapter 6 infra). To highlight this distinction, access by human agents is referred to as *human-access*, whereas access by nonhuman agents is termed *technological-access*.

A. Human Access to Information

Human-access to information is an internal, cognitive occurrence that is to a significant degree involuntary.[12] The point is intuitively plausible: once the physical

---

to lawfully do something on the servient landowner's property, such as entering the property.—Also termed affirmative servitude." *See* BLACK'S LAW DICTIONARY (8th. ed. 2004). Perhaps the more precise terminology is of an affirmative easement, which is generally defined as entitling "the owner thereof to use the land subject to the easement by doing acts which, were it not for the easement, he would not be privileged to do." *See* RESTATEMENT (FIRST) OF PROPERTY (1936) § 451.

12. Goldstein explains that some perception theorists associate a critical role to attention in the process of combining features towards perception of the whole object. *See* E. BRUCE GOLDSTEIN, SENSATION AND PERCEPTION 167 (2002). Further, attention is not only necessary for object perception, it often happens automatically "as we focus on things that interest us in the environment." *Id.* Attention illustrates one aspect of perception that may be independent of subjective volition or intention.

signals representing the message (e.g., sound waves or light beams) reach the sensorial receptors of the recipient, they initiate an internal process of recording, processing, and interpreting, at the end of which the percipient can be said to have "accessed information." Human-access involves both sensorial and cognitive processes in reaction to external stimuli. Listening to music, reading a book, looking at an advertisement poster, appreciating a painting in a museum, or watching a play are all examples of human-access to information. Reading a Braille script or smelling perfume are also forms of human-access achieved via the senses of scent and touch.

Regulation can influence the *physical conditions* allowing human-access (e.g., the physical position or location of the subject and/or the object). At the same time, the process of reception triggered by exposure to external stimuli is intrinsically internal and therefore, essentially *non-regulatable*. Access to information creates alteration in the minds of recipients, which, to some extent results in their obtaining "possession" of the message. In this sense, the human recipient becomes a new "possessor" of the information that remains captured in his memory.[13] In this limited context, upon access the recipient "acquires" information in a process that is significantly *irreversible*.[14] Acquisition of information via the mechanisms of the human organism alone has limitations dictated by the imperfect processing and storage capacities of the human brain. Still, in his new status as possessor, the recipient can communicate the message to others directly or with the aid of logistic media.

B. Technological Access to Information

1. General Observations

Warren Weaver opened his essay accompanying Shannon's model by musing on the definition of communication in general:

> The word *communication* will be used here in a very broad sense to include all of the procedures by which one mind may affect another. This, of course, involves not only written and oral speech, but also music, the pictorial art, the theatre, the ballet, and in fact all human behavior. In some connections it may be desirable to use a still broader definition of communication, namely, one which would include the procedures by means of which one mechanism (say automatic equipment to track an airplane and to compute its probable future positions) affects another mechanism (say a guided missile chasing this airplane).[15]

---

13. Chapter 2, Section IV.A.2 *supra*.

14. Irreversible here is meant to distinguish between taking possession of a tangible object, which normally can later be abandoned, returned, or transferred, and "taking possession" of a message in the sense described above. Of course, people forget messages all the time, but they cannot "return" a message to its source after having received it.

15. *See* CLAUDE E. SHANNON & WARREN WEAVER, MATHEMATICAL THEORY OF COMMUNICATION 3 (1963).

The information model anticipates an originator and a recipient that are both human actors, corresponding to Weaver's first, narrower definition of communication. The information model assumes only human agents can originate a medial message as only such actors can have the will and the urge to communicate.[16] Further, the function of the human recipient is to absorb, process, and possibly retransmit message signals. At the same time, it is clear these communicative capacities are not *inherently* human.[17] Non-human agents ("machines" and their "components") can store, manipulate, reproduce, and emit information signals, often at a much higher degree of intensiveness, fidelity, and precision than humans. The term *technological-access* is introduced here to describe the second, broader aspect of Weaver's definition. The underlying assumption is that non-human agents can perform some communication functions (beyond serving as mere conduits) and that these operations are relevant to a fuller conceptualization of the term *access* in the present context. Accordingly, the term *technological-access* describes certain processes in which absorption (and related processing or manipulation) of message signals occur *independently of human-access to a message.*

Consider the operation of multifunctional logistic media,[18] which are capable of performing automated operations on encoded digital messages. Technological-access is largely independent of direct human intervention; instead, operations are executed by software and similar tools, which are designed to interact with machine-readable information. The involvement of a human agent in a given operation may be limited to launching the process executed by the software according to a preprogrammed and predictable pattern. For example, it can be said that technological-access to a message takes place when a computer program identifies, interacts, or operates against information that represents a certain binary-encoded message.

At this stage the notion of technological-access can be put in the context of copyright law and digital works. Every work protected under copyright law is

---

16. Of course, animals communicate too. Communication theorists debate whether *human* communication and languages are unique, and if so, in what respect. *See, e.g.*, Colin Cherry, On Human Communication: A Review, a Survey, and a Criticism 329–36 (1978). The choice to address only human (and not animal) communication in the information model is a practical one, as animals are not likely to have property claims (or be granted such) with respect to the "messages" they generate. In the eyes of the law, animals are for most purposes "things." *Cf.* § 90a BGB (German law distinguishing between animals and "things" as defined in § 90 of the German Civil Code). However, this distinction is considered more declarative than operative. *See* Otto Palandt, Bürgerliches Gesetzbuch, § 90a. (2007).

17. *See* Cherry, *supra* note 16, at 52–62 (reviewing the analogy and distinctions between human information processing and communication capacities on the one hand, and digital machines and networks (or, the operation of "artificial brains") on the other.

18. Chapter 1, Section IV.D.(3) *supra* (defining multifunctional media).

either initially expressed in digital code or can be digitized (whether simultaneously with creation or at a later stage.)[19] Human-access to the naked binary code does not ensure reception because the message is not comprehensible to the recipient expected to decipher the code.[20] Thus, human-access to bits representing a novel or a musical piece does not accomplish the reception of the message as the binary strings of ones and zeros must first be converted into comprehensible elements such as letters, images, and sounds. The conversion process is conducted by machines equipped with appropriate hardware and software, which essentially correspond to the definition of multifunctional media. The process of converting binary digits to intelligible messages involves technological-access to the encoded messages—access that is *performed by computer programs.* Technological-access also takes place as more than one application software interacts with one another to achieve a certain result or perform an operation.[21] In cases where the software can manipulate binary data, or where software can exchange information with another computer program residing locally or remotely, it could be said the software has "accessed" information, or that technological-access has occurred. Human-access may or may not be relevant to such operations. As the following two U.S. court decisions demonstrate, the significance of technological-access and its distinction from human-access for resolving copyright questions is not merely academic.

2. Real-Life Scenarios: The Chamberlain *and* Lexmark *Decisions*

The notion of technological-access appears initially quite alien to copyright questions, yet precisely this issue stood at the heart of two litigation sagas in the United States that yielded important judicial observations. At issue are relatively recent legal norms called copyright anticircumvention laws,[22] which have introduced complicated schemes concerning digital works subject to technological

---

19. Digitization is the process of converting information into a digital format, where information is organized into discrete units of data (called bits) that can be separately addressed, usually in multiple-bit groups (called bytes). This is the binary data computers and similar devices can process. On the distinction between digital and digitized works, *see* Thomas Dreier, *Copyright Digitized: Philosophical Impacts and Practical Implications for Information Exhanged in Digital Networks,* paper presented at World Intellectual Property Organization Symposium on the Impact of Digital Technology on Copyright and Neighboring Rights, Harvard University (March 31–April 2, 1993), manuscript at 3.

20. Judge Kaplan in *Reimerdes* provided an informative introduction to those aspects of digital technology. *See* Universal City Studios v. Reimerdes, 111 F. Supp. 2d. 294, 305–07 (S.D.N.Y. 2000), *aff'd sub nom.* Universal City Studios v. Corley, 273 F.3d 429 (2d. Cir. 2001).

21. An exemplary legal definition of computer programs describes them as "set of statements or instructions to be used directly or indirectly in a computer in order to bring about a certain result." *See* 17 U.S.C. § 101.

22. The U.S. copyright anticircumvention scheme will be discussed in detail in Chapter 6, Section V.

protection measures. At this stage, it should suffice to say both these disputes involved access-related copyright regulation in which access to the copyrighted work was actually performed by a computer program or a digital code rather than human beings. In particular focus are the judicial attempts to interpret the term *access* as to works in technological settings and applications of access-related regulation in real-life disputes.

To this end, the next passages provide a rather detailed description of the fact patterns surrounding both cases and the judicial holdings that followed. It should be noted the disputes were not explicity recognized by the courts reviewing them *as problems of technological-access* and its distinction from human-access. Curiously, in both cases, the courts did not question the assertion that technological-access may count as "access" to works in the meaning of the applicable anticircumvention provisions. Taking a close look at those technologically condensed fact patterns nicely supplements the abstract discussion above and illuminates some practical dimension of the human/technological access distinction.

(a) *The* Chamberlain *Scenario*

I. FACT PATTERN

Plaintiff Chamberlain Group manufactured and sold homeowners' garage doors together with handheld portable transmitters (remote control devices). The technology at issue was the garage door opener system (GDO), which facilitated the opening of the door through a device when a person used a portable transmitter.[23] The opening device mounted on the door consisted of both a receiver with associated signal processing software and a motor performing the opening and closing of the door. A homeowner wishing to open or close the garage door would activate the portable transmitter, which sends a radio frequency signal to the receiver located on the opening device. Only upon receiving a recognized signal from the transmitter would the signal processing software activate the opening device and instruct the motor to open or close the door.[24] Chamberlain employed in its Security+ line of GDO systems a copyrighted "rolling code" computer program that, for enhanced security purposes, constantly changed the transmitter signal required to open the door.[25] As explained by the court, the range of recognized signals was limited, and a user transmitting too many signals might exhaust

---

23. *See* Chamberlain Group, Inc. v. Skylink Techs., Inc., 381 F.3d 1178, 1183 (Fed. Cir. 2004).

24. *Id.* The court further noted that both the opener and the transmitter were sold to consumers by the Chamberlain Group. Replacement or spare transmitters—the so-called "universal transmitters" (which interoperate with GDOs regardless of kind or model)—could be purchased in the aftermarket. The two major dealers in that market were the Chamberlain Group and defendant Skylink. *Id.*

25. *Id.* at 1184. In fact, the program would increase the rolling code by a factor of three each time the user activated the transmitter.

that range. To facilitate multiple use of the transmitter, Chamberlain Group developed a "resynchronization" sequence that would activate the door after comparing and calculating two signals sent one after the other in rapid succession.[26]

Defendant Skylink Technologies, a major competitor for Chamberlain Group's universal transmitters, began marketing and selling transmitters in 1992, then introduced its Model 39 that was designed to interoperate with common GDOs whether or not supported by a "rolling code" computer program.[27] Although the Model 39 did not use "rolling code" technology, it was able to simulate the effect of the rolling code: by sending three codes in rapid succession, the Model 39 transmitter would send the initial (fixed) signal required for activating the door or imitate the operation of the "resynchronization" sequence (with the second and third signals). As a result, one press of the button of a Model 39 transmitter would activate the opening device affixed on Chamberlains' doors.[28]

Two district court decisions preceded the ruling of the Federal Circuit in *Chamberlain*. In the first decision (*Chamberlain I*), the District Court for the Northern District of Illinois denied Chamberlain's motion for summary judgment on its DMCA claims.[29] Specifically, the court refused to grant summary judgment against Skylink for violation of section 1201(a)(2) of the Copyright Act (the "anti-trafficking provision") after identifying "disputes of material fact concerning whether the computer program in Chamberlain's rolling code is a work protected by copyright and whether the owner of a Chamberlain rolling code GDO is authorized to use the Model 39 universal transmitter."[30]

Shortly thereafter, the same district court issued a second decision on the matter (*Chamberlain II*) in which it granted Skylink's motion for summary judgment against Chamberlain's claims of DMCA violations.[31] The district court rejected plaintiff's anti-trafficking allegation, holding (1) the burden of proof was on Chamberlain to demonstrate Skylink's Model 39 transmitter provides an

---

26. *Id.*

27. *Id.* However, one of Skylink's settings for its Model 39 was designed to interoperate only with Chamberlain's rolling code GDOs. *Id.* at n.3.

28. *Id.* at 1184–85.

29. *See* Chamberlain Group, Inc. v. Skylink Techs., Inc., 292 F. Supp. 2d. 1023 (N.D. Ill. 2003) (*Chamberlain I*). In this first action, Chamberlain Group invoked some additional federal and state law claims, including unfair competition and patent infringement. *Id.* at 1024–25. The district court, however, discussed primarily the DMCA claims.

30. *Id.* at 1040. As the court noted, "Summary judgment is warranted where 'there is no genuine issue as to any material fact and the moving party is entitled to a judgment as a matter of law.'" *Id.* at 1033 (citing Fed. R. Civ. P. 56(c)).

31. Chamberlain Group, Inc. v. Skylink Techs., Inc., 292 F. Supp. 2d 1040 (N.D. Ill. 2003) (*Chamberlain II*).

"unauthorized" access to Chamberlain's software,[32] and (2) Chamberlain neither explicitly restricted the ability of purchasers of its GDOs to buy an "unauthorized" replacement (or additional) transmitter from third parties, nor were purchasers implicitly bound to use only "authorized" devices.[33] The court further maintained consumers had a reasonable expectation of having the ability to "replace the original product with a competing, universal product without violating federal law."[34] Chamberlain appealed the *Chamberlain II* decision before the Federal Circuit.

II. HOLDING

On appeal, the Federal Circuit focused on Chamberlain's contentions that (1) both the door opener and the transmitter incorporated computer programs "protected by copyright," and (2) rolling codes were "technological measures" that "control access" to these programs (or, more precisely, to the door opener program), which proved a prima facie violation of section 1201(a)(2) of the U.S. Copyright Act.[35] Though the court eventually rejected Chamberlain's theory of DMCA violation in this situation, it failed to draw a distinction between human and technological access. The court did not question the contention that sending a digital radio sequence (which interacts with a computer program instructing it to perform a certain task) was *access to work* in the meaning of the DMCA.

It is notable that none of these opinions considered the possibility that "access" here was a purely technological-functional operation that did not involve any human-access to any copyrighted expression in any form at any stage of using the universal transmitter. As noted, the target information was copyrighted software mounted on the GDO.[36] Users involvement in the technological process was limited to pressing on the bottom of a remote control to operate the garage door opener. Plainly, no person was ever exposed to a copyright-protected work as a result of using the device in question. Nonetheless, the *Chamberlain* court seems to have tacitly accepted the idea that bypassing a technological access control mechanism under these circumstances (the authentication sequence

---

32. *Id.* at 1044. This statement was given in connection with the section 1201(a)(3)(A) definition of "circumvent[ion] [of] a technological measure" as "descrambl[ing] a scrambled work, to decrypt an encrypted work, or otherwise to avoid, bypass, remove, deactivate, or impair a technological measure, without the authority of the copyright owner." *Id.*

33. *Id.* at 1044–45.

34. *Id.* at 1046 (citation omitted).

35. Chamberlain Group, Inc. v. Skylink Techs., Inc., 381 F.3d 1178, 1185 (Fed. Cir. 2004). Notably, the Chamberlain Group claimed neither copyright infringement of its programs nor contributory copyright infringement committed by Skylink. *Id.*

36. Copyrightability of the software was apparently not challenged by Skylink, and the court did not address this issue.

serves here as the TPM that controls access to the work) *in principle* resulted in an unauthorized access to work.[37]

(b) *The* Lexmark *Scenario*

I. FACT PATTERN

Less than two months after *Chamberlain*, the Sixth Circuit issued its *Lexmark* ruling,[38] in which the problem of technological-access seems to have received a more direct treatment. Subject to appeal before the Sixth Circuit was a decision rendered by the District Court for the Eastern District of Kentucky[39] involving a dispute between Lexmark International and Static Control Components (SCC). Lexmark, a leading manufacturer of laser and inject printers and seller of toner cartridges for its printers, began selling discounted toner cartridges that only Lexmark could refill. Those cartridges contained a microchip designed to prevent Lexmark printers from functioning with toner cartridges Lexmark itself did not refill.[40] The two relevant computer programs incorporated in Lexmark's products were the Toner Loading Program (TLP) and the Printer Engine Program (PEP). The main function of the TLP was to measure the amount of toner remaining in the cartridge while the PEP controlled a variety of the printers' operations such as paper feed and motor control.[41] A Certificate of Registrations from the U.S. Copyright Office covered both programs (the programs were presumably copyrightable),[42] and neither program was encrypted.[43]

Lexmark marketed Prebate and Non-Prebate cartridges, with the former being sold to consumers at an up-front discount. A shrink-wrap agreement was

---

37. Presumably, the court preferred to solve the matter without reaching the meaning of the term 'access', which is not statutorily defined. By declaring simply that technological-access did not fall under the DMCA's concept of access, the court could have prima facie dismissed the claim without even reaching the issue of circumvention.

38. *See* Lexmark Int'l, Inc. v. Static Control Components, Inc., 387 F.3d 522 (6th. Cir. 2004).

39. *See* Lexmark Int'l, Inc. v. Static Control Components, Inc., 253 F. Supp. 2d 943 (E.D.Ky. 2003), *vacated and remanded* by 387 F.3d 522 (6th Cir. 2004) (*Lexmark District Decision*).

40. *Lexmark*, 387 F.3d at 529.

41. *Id.* at 529–30.

42. Registration of a copyright with the U.S. Copyright Office is not a prerequisite for copyright protection. *See* 17 U.S.C. § 408(a). However, Sec. 410(c) creates a presumption of copyright protection that confers a evidentiary advantage in the case of litigation. ("In any judicial proceedings the certificate of a registration made before or within five years after first publication of the work shall constitute *prima facie* evidence of the validity of the copyright and of the facts stated in the certificate. The evidentiary weight to be accorded the certificate of a registration made thereafter shall be within the discretion of the court.") *Id.* § 410(c).

43. *Lexmark*, 387 F.3d at 530.

on the top of each cartridge box mandating purchasers' adherence to its terms.[44] Specifically, the purchaser agreed to use the cartridge only once and then return the empty unit to Lexmark.[45] To ensure adherence to the Prebate agreement, Lexmark employed an "authentication sequence" that performed a "secret handshake" between the printer and the cartridge microchip—a calculation performed by the printer based on data located in the microchip's memory. If the code calculated by the microchip matched the code calculated by the printer, the printer would function normally. If not, the printer would return an error message and not operate.[46]

In addition to the authentication sequence, the printer also performed a second calculation. This process, called "checksum operation," would be performed after the authentication sequence was concluded by downloading a copy of the TLP to the PEP. The function of this process was to ensure the integrity of the data downloaded from the TLP before the printer actually ran it. The printer then would compare the data downloaded from the chip with a "checksum value" located elsewhere on the chip itself. A mismatch between those values would block the operation of the printer.[47]

Defendant SCC was in the business of manufacturing a wide range of technology products, including microchips it sold to third-party companies that, in turn, used the chips in refurbishing toner cartridges.[48] At issue was SCC's "SMARTEK" chip that enabled consumers to satisfy Lexmark's access control system while allowing third party companies to refurbish Lexmark's cartridges by refilling them and replacing the original chip with the SMARTEK chip. Those refilled cartridges were sold to consumers at a price lower than new Lexmark cartridges.[49] To achieve interoperability with Lexmark's printers, SCC copied Lexmark's TLP's code to its own SMARTEK chips.[50] In response, Lexmark filed a lawsuit in the district court alleging (1) copyright infringement for the unlawful reproduction of the TLP on the SMARTEK chip, (2) violation of the DMCA by selling a product that circumvents access control to the TLP, and (3) violation of the DMCA by selling a product that circumvents access control to

44. *Id.*

45. The shrink-wrap agreement read: "This all-new cartridge is sold at a special price subject to a restriction that it may be used only once. Following this initial use, you agree to return the empty cartridge only to Lexmark for remanufacturing and recycling. If you don't accept these terms, return the unopened package to your point of purchase. A regular price cartridge without these terms is available." *Id.* at 563 n.10.

46. *Id.* at 530.

47. *Id.* at 531.

48. *Id.* at 529.

49. *Id.* at 530.

50. *Id.* at 530–31.

the PEP.[51] Lexmark's motion for preliminary injunction was granted on all three counts in the first instance,[52] and SCC appealed.

II. HOLDING

Lexmark contended that selling the SMARTEK chip violated section 1201(a)(2) of the DMCA. It tried to persuade the court the SMARTEK microchip was a "device" that was able to "circumvent" a "technological measure"[53] that "effectively controls access" to the copyright-protected TLP and PEP.[54] Lexmark further argued all three alternative liability tests under the anti-trafficking provision had been met.[55]

The appellate court first rejected Lexmark's assertion the authentication sequence *controlled access* to the PEP. Instead, the court noted printer owners could gain access to the literal code of the PEP (i.e., they could read it directly from the printer's memory) simply by purchasing and possessing the printer, which embodied the non-encrypted literal code of the program.[56] The court agreed a certain form of access was in fact controlled by the authentication sequence to the extent that using the ordinary functions of the printer constitutes "access." However, according to the court, "access control" in the meaning of the statute could not be accomplished where access to the copyrighted work was otherwise available.[57] Further, the court held the (partial) access control achieved by the authentication sequence was not "effective" in the meaning of the statute as it restricted one form of access but left other access routes wide open.[58] Turning next to discussing the TLP, the court emphasized that nothing

---

51. *Lexmark*, 387 F.3d at 522. *Supra* note 29.

52. *Id.* at 974.

53. The technological measure referred to by plaintiff was apparently the authentication sequence, not the checksum operation. *See* Lexmark Int'l, Inc. v. Static Control Components, Inc., 387 F.3d 522, 546 (6th. Cir. 2004).

54. *Id.*

55. *Id. See also* 17 U.S.C. § 1201(a)(2)(A)–(C) (providing three alternative anti-trafficking prohibitions).

56. *Lexmark*, 387 F.3d at 546–47.

57. The court held: "Because the statute refers to 'control[ling] access to a work protected under this title,' it does not naturally apply when the 'work protected under this title' is otherwise accessible. Just as one would not say that a lock on the back door of a house 'controls access' to a house whose front door does not contain a lock and just as one would not say that a lock on any door of a house 'controls access' to the house after its purchaser receives the key to the lock, it does not make sense to say that this provision of the DMCA applies to otherwise-readily-accessible copyrighted works." *Id.* at 547.

58. "[T]he DMCA not only requires the technological measure to 'control [] access' but also requires the measure to control that access 'effectively,.'.. and it seems clear that this provision does not naturally extend to a technological measure that restricts one form of access but leaves another route wide open." *Id.*

in the operation of the SMARTEK chip amounted to "accessing" that program—the SMARTEK in fact *replaced* the TLP.[59] To the extent the TLP was downloaded from the SMARTEK chip to the PEP,[60] this fact alone did not render the DMCA applicable as the relevant work (the PEP code) remained freely accessible.[61] In addition, the court cast doubts concerning the copyrightability of the TLP. To the extent this program was found noncopyrightable in a later court proceeding, the anticircumvention provisions would become inapplicable anyway.

What the *Lexmark* court *did not* say is that the invisible interaction between the TLP and the PEP (both computer programs performing functional operations) *could not constitute access to a work*. Unlike *Chamberlain*, the *Lexmark* court in fact attended to the definitional issue of the term *access*.[62] Importantly, the court did not dismiss the anticircumvention claims because access did not (or could not) occur. Rather, Lexmark's anticircumvention allegations failed due to the judicial finding the technological measure did not effectively block access to the code of the PEP software.[63] The critical language hinting at the importance of the distinction between technological and human access emerged as the court distinguished the present fact pattern from previous rulings in which courts had upheld anticircumvention allegations. The *Lexmark* court explained "copyright protection operates on two planes: in the literal code governing the work and in the visual or audio manifestation generated by the code's execution."[64] *Lexmark* observed that in finding anticircumvention liability, previous courts perceived the relevant technological access control as "restricting 'use' of the work [as] restricting consumers from making use of the copyrightable expression in the work."[65] The court went on to draw the following distinction:

> The copyrightable expression in the Printer Engine Program, by contrast, operates on only one plane: in the literal elements of the program, its source and object code. Unlike the code underlying video games or DVDs, "using" or executing the Printer Engine Program does not in turn create any protected expression.[66]

---

59. *Id.* at 549–50.

60. Recall that in the course of the checksum operation, the PEP would download a copy of the TLP to the printer. The same process occurred when the TLP was downloaded from the SMARTEK chip to which it had been copied by SCC. Hence, one could argue that operating the printer with a SMARTEK chip performs "access" to the TLP.

61. *Lexmark*, 387 F.3d at 550.

62. *Id.* at 546 (recalling the district court's reference to the dictionary definition of the term *access*).

63. *Id.* at 546–47.

64. *Id.* at 548.

65. *Id.* (citations omitted).

66. *Id.*

This comes quite close to clarifying a distinction between a technological measure that prevents access to an intelligible message (i.e., preventing human-access to works) and a measure that prevents an internal, functional, and imperceptible interaction among software, codes, and machine components (i.e., hindering technological-access). Although this point plays a relatively minor role in the reasoning of the *Lexmark* court, it is perhaps the closest courts have ever come to articulating the distinction in the context of copyright law.

C. Access-Conducts and Communication-Conducts

Before proceeding to discuss access rights and rights of access, it is important to clarify another terminological distinction between two types of access-related conducts. Human-access per se is non-regulatable, but human *conducts* related to access are. Most importantly, government regulation intervenes to curtail human-access in two ways by promulgating legal rules that impose restrictions on two categories of conducts called *access-conducts* and *communication-conducts.*

1. Access-Conducts

The term *access-conducts* pertains to actions performed by the human agent before and/or simultaneously with human-access. Access-conducts are carried forth allowing the actor to gain access to information. These conducts place the recipient in a position in which or from which human-access may occur. Broadly perceived, access-conducts can be both intended and unintended. To illustrate, when a person walks into a room in which a copyrighted painting hangs on the wall without previously knowing anything about the existence of the painting, the act of walking into the room is nominally an access-conduct in the broad sense, though the human-access achieved thereby did not motivate the entrance and was not intended by the actor in the first place. Recipients may or may not be aware of access opportunities and the type of information likely to be opened before them as a result of their actions in general. Much of the human-access that takes place on a daily basis is unplanned. The actor does not know the information is "there," and his behavior is not determined by deliberations having anything to do with access to information.[67]

From a legal standpoint, however, the case of *intended* access-conducts is more interesting. Objectively, these conducts place the actor in a human-access position. Subjectively, the actor is at least aware of the fact that access to information would likely result from the contemplated conduct. Further, this awareness might have some influence on the deliberation preceding the act, and in the

67. The human actor here can be thought of as a recipient in terms of the model presented in Chapter 1. The abstract concept of recipient does not prescribe any specific mental state to qualify a person as such.

clearest case, the wish to achieve human-access provides the motivation behind the conduct. Conducts of this latter type appear more likely to subject recipients to state regulation and entail liability.

It follows that access-conducts are relevant in situations in which (unlike the person absentmindedly entering the room with the painting) human-access involves some *deliberation*. At a minimum, the conduct should be accompanied by subjective awareness of the possibility of access as a natural consequence of the act. In the clear case of an intended access-conduct, the would-be recipient takes affirmative, conscious, and target-oriented steps to achieve access to information.

Returning to the hypothetical above, the actor "knows"—in the epistemological meaning of knowledge (i.e., he is justified in believing)—that the painting is located in the room. He further knows (or has justified reasons to believe) that entering this specific room will result in his access to the message placed by the artist on the canvas hanging on the wall. If the door to the room is closed, the actor will need to open it. If the door is locked, he will further need to obtain the key or break the lock in order to enter. All such actions may be considered "access-conducts" as they are premised on the assumption that human-access thereby shall be achieved.[68]

By definition (and unlike human-access), access-conducts always have an immediate external manifestation. Society can observe, evaluate, and regulate such conducts. Should access-conducts become a target for regulation, it is likely questions of subjective mental condition (e.g., whether the actor intended thereby to achieve access to information) will assume a significant weight for establishing liability. Or, legal scrutiny will focus on the intention to perform the access-conduct itself, under the assumption the actor expects to achieve human-access as the natural consequence of her conduct. Assuming access-conduct regulation is not based on strict liability, an external fact finder should be able to evaluate the mental state underlying a given access-conduct according to the legal definition of the regulated act. Indeed, it is unlikely liability will be imposed based on strict liability theories due to the problems of identifying access-conducts as such in a manner unrelated to the mental state of the actor (for example, knowledge or intent regarding the prospects of gaining human-access to the information facilitated by the conduct).

---

68. For the present purpose, access-conducts refer only to acts required to enable access to *information*, not to domains, spaces, or physical articles. Accordingly, the access-conduct is not merely breaking the lock, but breaking the lock *in order to view the painting*.

The conclusion is that access-conducts are principally regulatable.[69] In imposing legal constraints on access-conducts, the law indirectly regulates human-access by reducing access opportunities.[70] Public policy may sometimes justify regulation of access-conducts (e.g., in the case of the right to privacy),[71] and the freedom to pursue access to information, like most other freedoms, is not absolute. The distinction between human-access and access-contacts emphasizes that access regulation may apply to the latter but not the former.

This observation holds with equal force regarding entitlements under copyright law. If the lawmaker resolved to vest in rights-holders a right-claim to exclude others from accessing works (for now such an entitlement is considered merely hypothetical), one practical way would be to define certain *access-conducts,* then subject those conducts to private exclusive right-claims to prohibit them. According to the Hohfeldian terminology, the scope of such hypothetical right is determined by the scope of nonowners' duty *not to perform* access-conducts without permission.

Remaining on the hypothetical level, rights-holders wishing to enforce such right-claims would necessarily have to prevent unintended access to the information they wish to keep under access control. In other words, rights-holders must take steps to fence around the information with respect to which they claim exclusive control. Actual fencing should render inadvertent access impossible,

---

69. An objective legal standard of simple negligence could technically set the minimal level of mental state required. The level of mental state required under the relevant legal norm is a question of policy, depending on the nature of the restriction imposed on the specific access-conduct at question.

70. At this stage, the discussion does not reach normative questions of whether regulating access-conducts is *advisable,* and if so, what the minimum level of required awareness should be.

71. In their seminal article, Brandeis and Warren underpinned the right to privacy, inter alia, with the "right 'to be let alone.'" *See* Samuel D. Warren & Louis D. Brandeis, *The Right to Privacy*, 4 HARVARD L. REV. 193, 195 (1890) (citation omitted). According to some common concepts of the right to privacy, it appears that mere unauthorized penetration to the private sphere per se would injure the protected privacy interest; further communication of private information is not a necessary element of prima facie violations. This point is important as violations of the right of privacy *often* involve and merge with the dissemination of private information. For example, Warren and Brandeis cautioned: "Owing to the nature of the instruments by which privacy is invaded, the injury inflicted bears a superficial resemblance to the wrongs dealt with by the law of slander and of libel, while a legal remedy for such injury seems to involve the treatment of mere wounded feelings, as a substantive cause of action." *Id.* at 197. Libel and slander *per definitionem* involve communication of messages. The question whether violations necessitate a communication element touches precisely upon the critical distinction between access-conducts and communication-conducts, discussed shortly below.

or at least very unlikely. This actual fencing is a crucial condition for any defendable entitlement to control access-conducts as it creates the environmental conditions that *compel* nonowners to perform access-conducts for which they have a duty to ask permission. To the extent such conducts are subject to a duty to abstain unless permission is granted, the outlines of a fairly concrete legal framework begin to emerge under which private exclusive entitlements to control access to information become conceivable.

Concisely stated, the right to control access to information is nothing else but a legal *duty* imposed on strangers to *forbear* from pursuing *unauthorized access-conducts* falling within the ambit of the duty as defined by the law. Before concluding the discussion on the access-conducts notion, one related observation is in order: a homeowner who does not lock the door to his house (or even does not have a door at all) usually will not lose his property right to exclude uninvited strangers *solely due to the fact the door remained unlocked.* By contrast, a rights-holder asserting a legal entitlement to control access to information often *must* deploy some self-help measures to prevent the information from finding its way to unauthorized recipients."[72] A rights-holder who does not impose physical and/or logical obstacles on human-access might lose her actual control over the res together with much of the *legitimacy to enforce exclusivity claims against recipients.*

2. Communication-Conducts

The notion of *communication-conducts* denotes affirmative actions to communicate or transfer a message in various circumstances. Communication-conducts in the broad sense generally cover two types of acts. The first is *message origination* as defined by the information model introduced in Chapter 1.[73] The second is *facilitation conducts* that merely function as communication channels.

(a) Origination of a Message

After access has been achieved, the recipient may attempt to further communicate the message. In this scenario, the recipient becomes the originator and his communication act transfers the received message (or elements thereof enveloped in a new message) to subsequent recipients. As explained earlier, origination

72. Heller suggested, "People seem to know private property when they see it." *See* Michael Heller, The Tragedy of the Anticommons: *Property in the Transition from Marx to Markets,* 111 HARV. L. REV. 621, 660 (1998). This observation cannot apply in this context to information subject matter because persons cannot be expected to respect "trespassory" rights in messages simply as a natural inference from recognizing messages as such. If recipients can inadvertently access messages, any reasonable law would not consider mere access-conducts enabling such access violations of private property rights per se.

73. Chapter1, Section IV *supra.*

is defined as the creation of a perceptible and comprehensible message triggered by the originator's subjective will to communicate.[74]

(b) Facilitation of Message Communication (Facilitation-Conducts)

The term *communication-conducts* covers a broader terrain, including various transfers of the message that are not necessarily accompanied or triggered by a subjective will of the communicator to express *herself*. In this sense, a *facilitation-conduct* generally fulfills a diffusional function; objectively, it may be identical to origination *minus* the subjective nexus to the message content and the element of *self*-expression. Facilitation-conducts are defined as capturing activities performed by persons whose communication-related conducts are not meant to communicate any aspect of their inner sphere, as communication facilitators do not associate themselves with the content of the message. Further, they neither use its elements to express their own message nor wish to add any personal input or comment pertaining to the content. Evaluated through the lens of the information model, these facilitators are mere conduits or fulfill the functions of logistic media located midway between actual communicators. Facilitation-conducts might add "noise" to the message, yet this is a side effect of facilitation activities rather than their main impetus. As noted, facilitators have neither a desire to create a new message nor to modify an existing one; they are simply (noisy) channels that carry the message or agents that bring messages to recipients while possibly making alterations unrelated to any intention to engage themselves as independent originators in communication with recipients.

(c) Controlling Communication-Conducts

Actors who perform communication-conducts enable human-access to recipients. The tendency to describe information goods as nonexcludable relates precisely to the practical difficulties in retaining control over messages ex post initial communication. Information might quickly escape both self-help fencing measures and the grip of legal exclusory rights unless rights-holders are entitled to control communication-conducts *in addition* to access-conducts.

The law can, and indeed it often does define a set of specific communication-conducts that are subject to rights-holders' exclusive power to approve, ban, condition, or alienate. This result is neither surprising nor unprecedented. Chapter 1 demonstrated that granting exclusive rights to control some communications is the central proprietary mechanism in copyright law. In fact, banning certain unauthorized communication-conducts is fundamental to the structure of exclusive copyrights. As shown, all the exclusive rights under copyright law are essentially limitations on behavior that always involves communication and/or transfer of protected messages.[75]

---

74. *Id.* at Section IV.B.

75. Chapter 1, Section V.A.–B *supra*.

III. THE ACCESS-RIGHT AND RIGHTS-OF-ACCESS

Revisiting the general questions articulated in the introduction to this chapter, it appears access to information *is* regulatable and *can* be subject to trespassory rules under the following conditions: (1) the claimant can effectively prevent unintended human-access by deploying self-help measures to actually fence around the message, (2) the claimant is granted legally enforceable right-claims subjecting access-conducts to his exclusive approval power; and (3) the claimant has right-claims to intercept and enjoin communication-conducts in the broad sense (i.e., both unauthorized origination acts and facilitation-conducts). Within this factual and legal framework, a property-trespassory right to control access to information becomes conceivable.

A. The Access-Right

1. The Access-Right: Toward a Definition

The term *access right* penetrated the copyright vernacular concurrently with deliberations over the anticircumvention laws eventually enacted in the United States in 1998.[76] Technically, the access right is a *pseudo* right, as a formal legal entitlement subjecting access to exclusive rights has never been introduced into the positive copyright law.[77] The access right debate has been clouded by uncertainties pertaining to the impact of anticircumvention laws, and by growing apprehension concerning the emergence of information "digital lockup" resulting from their application in practice.[78] New challenges introduced to copyright law by the digital revolution resulted in legislative reactions that were followed by various assessments about their nature and ramifications. Specifically, some commentators identified an implicit "access right" emerging out of the new fabric composed of recent legislative amendments and additions to copyright laws.[79]

---

76. *See* Jessica Litman, *The Exclusive Rights to Read*, 13 Cardozo Arts & Ent. L.J. 29 (1994) (providing an early treatment as to emerging issues concerning the growing tension between the new copyright regulations and access to copyrighted information in digital form).

77. Analysis of the "access right" as a legal copyright concept reflects at times a great deal of confusion. *See, e.g.*, Jon Bing, *The New or Evolving "Access Right"*, *in* Adjuncts and Alternatives to Copyright 288 ff (Jane C. Ginsburg & June M. Besek eds., 2002).

78. *See, e.g.*, Melville B. Nimmer & David Nimmer, 3 Nimmer on Copyright § 12A.06[B][1] (2006) (describing the fears of a "pay-per-use" world in the context of U.S. anticircumvention legislation.) *Cf.* William R. Cornish, Senior Chair's Remarks, *in* Adjuncts and Alternatives to Copyright 80 (2002) (calling new anticircumvention laws in the U.S. and Europe "avowedly experimental").

79. *See, e.g.*, Jane C. Ginsburg, *News from the US*, 180 Revue Internationale du Droit D'Auteur 127, 159 (1999) (drawing a distinction between access to a work and access to a copy of a work, and arguing that the former "is the new right introduced in the

Ginsburg articulated an explicit access-right thesis, proposing in 2003 "[t]he access right is . . . a necessary and integral component of copyright law."[80]

The early scholarly discussion concerning the nature and function of that right naturally yielded several attempts to define it. Amongst the early endeavors confronting this challenge, Olswang suggested "[a]ccessright is a means whereby creators may control access to content . . . the primary purpose of the right will be to allow creators the exclusive right to authorise or prohibit use."[81] In his brief treatment, Olswang devoted a comparatively elaborate discussion to the many advantages of the "accessright" in the digital setting as compared to traditional copyrights.[82]

Ginsburg suggests the right to control access means "the right to control the manner in which members of the public apprehend the work."[83] In a similar vein, it has been contended "[a]ccess can be considered the ability to experience or apprehend a work—in other words, to view, read or listen to it."[84] From this we may derive the access right is defined as the legal entitlement to limit the ability to "experience" or "apprehend" works. But what is the theoretical-doctrinal linkage between access to information (or "experiencing works") and trespass-like rights? How can "experiencing works" be something subject to private property entitlements? Some commentators seem to treat the "access right" (or "the right of access") in the context of copyright law as a self-explanatory notion.[85] Others focus on its pragmatic aspects. For instance, Koelman notes "[i]f a rightholder could bring a (civil) action in court against any person who obtains access without authorisation, it could be said that an additional exclusive-right-like 'right to control access to technologically protected

---

DMCA"); Kamiel J. Koelman, *A Hard Nut to Crack: The Protection of Technological Measures*, 22 Eur. Intell. Prop. Rev. 274, 276 (2000) (observing "the trend seems to be for copyright to slowly move in the direction of granting an exclusive right of access"). For a more recent account, see Jacques de Werra, *Access Control or Freedom of Access?*, Comment *in* Christoph Beat Graber, Digital Rights Management: The End of Collecting Societies? 112–14 (2005).

80. *See* Jane C. Ginsburg, *From Having Copies to Experiencing Works: The Development of an Access Right in U.S. Copyright Law*, 50 J. Copyr. Soc. 113 (2003).

81. Simon Olswang, *Accessright: An Evolutionary Path for Copyright into the Digital Era*, 5 Eur. Intell. Prop. Rev. 215, 217 (1995).

82. *Id.* at 217–18.

83. *See* Ginsburg, *supra* note 80 at 120.

84. *See* June M. Besek, *Anti-Circumvention Laws and Copyright: A Report from the Kernochan Center for Law, Media, and the Arts*, 27 Colum. J. L. & Arts 385, 474 (2004).

85. *See, e.g.*, Michael Landau, *Has the Digital Millennium Copyright Act Really Created a New Exclusive Right of Access?Attempting to Reach a Balance Between Users and Content Providers' Rights*, 49 J. Copyright Soc'y U.S.A. 277–78 (2001) (discussing the "right of access" arguably constituted by the U.S. anticircumvention law).

works' were granted."[86] This approach indeed comes one step closer to articulating a general exclusive right covering access to works.[87]

As noted above, the access-right controversy has been significantly fueled by the debate over legal protection of technological protection measures, a fact that somewhat obscured the more general aspects of this idea regarding copyright protection in the digital setting. The ensuing access-right analysis attempts to follow a more systematic approach. It contemplates a hypothetical right that represents most comprehensively the core idea of the access right. The discussion thus far has already provided most of the necessary components, which now will be arranged to compose the construct called the "access-right". Later, some of the positive and normative implications of access entitlements shall receive a closer review.

2. The Access-Right Defined

The proposed formulation of the access right below is based on the study's set of concepts introduced until this point. The access-right notion brings together elements from the information model, private property law, and the above conceptualization of access to information.

TABLE 3.1 THE ACCESS-RIGHT DEFINED

Access-right is the exclusive right-claim to prevent anyone from performing access-conducts and communication-conducts, without the authorization of the rights-holder, concerning the message to which access is sought, or concerning the message sough to be communicated.

The access-right definition arranges its components according to the logic and structure of legal property entitlements. The rights-holder is granted a legally enforceable in rem exclusive right to exclude others from achieving human-access, and to prevent others from further enabling human-access to third parties without permission. The term *message* represents the subject matter (res) of the right in general. We could just as well replace it with the generic term

86. *See* Koelman, *supra* note 79, at 275.

87. *See, e.g.*, Severine Dusollier, *Electrifying the Fence: The Legal Protection of Technological Measures for Protecting Copyright*, 21 Eur. Intell. Prop. Rev. 285, 291 (1999) ("The protection of technical measures controlling access to works might lead to grant a new right to copyright holders, i.e. the right to control access to works. This new de facto right goes beyond the criteria of exercise of their rights which justified the protection of TM enacted by the WIPO Treaties.").

information or with the specific term *work* in the context of copyright law by adding a requirement that the message be copyrightable.

The concept of the access-right encapsulates important assumptions. As posited above, human-access to information is non-regulatable. However, access-conducts and communication-conducts can be subject to legally binding forbearance duties both in theory and in practice. The access-right targets precisely those elements of access that *are* regulatable. The relevant conducts become subject to Hohfeldian duties of abstention unless a rights-holder's permission is granted. To be effective, the right must engulf various aspects of communication. Therefore, it is initially designed to capture conducts concerning both *achieving* and *providing* (or facilitating) human-access to furnish meaningful legal exclusion. Yet, a perfected access right pertaining to information subject matter cannot depend on law alone, so it is essential the claimant deploys self-help measures designed to prevent inadvertent human-access.

As explained above, actual access obstacles will invite access-conducts by non-owners who contemplate access. Measures restricting human-access must secure two things: First, unauthorized strangers should not be able to access the copyrighted work simply by going about their regular affairs unaware the messages they have received are subject to private trespass-like claims. Second, would-be recipients wishing to access the message must perform access-conducts that will implicate their legal duty not to act without permission. In other words, self-help access restriction measures serve to trigger the access right *once unauthorized parties seek access for themselves*. This is the *first prong* of the access-right.

In addition, having the legal entitlement to curtail unauthorized communication-conducts is an essential component of a perfected access-right. Hence, rights-holders should be able to control communication junctions where *unauthorized persons provide or facilitate human-access to third parties*. Those unauthorized persons include both infringers-originations and mere infringers-facilitators. According to this principle, controlling communication conducts in the broad sense is the *second prong* of the access-right.

It is important to see how the first and second prongs work together to create an integrated whole. Control over individual access, meant to be secured by the first prong, will provide ineffective access control in the absence of the ability to control communications, addressed by the second prong. Rights-holders are put in the position of inhibiting unauthorized communications performed by two prototypical recipients: The first is a recipient who has accessed the work without violating the first prong (e.g., with permission), and the second is a recipient who has achieved access by violating the first prong (e.g., bypassing access control measures). In both cases, to secure access control, the rights-holder must be legally entitled to prevent recommunication. Assuming the work is now distributed in non-protected format, no access prevention measure could any longer effectively enforce the first prong against subsequent recipients. In other words, it would be practically impossible to enforce the first access-right prong once an unencrypted version has "leaked" out. The legal entitlement to inhibit unauthorized communication ensures both permissible access and violations of the first prong remain local. In the first case, communication prohibition imposed on authorized recipients enables differentiation in distribution of information to various individual recipients under different conditions. In the second case, a communication prohibition seeks to keep relatively marginal the economic injury resulting from violations of the first prong.[88] The in rem nature of the access-right ensures isolated violations performed by a small number of dispersed recipients shall not fatally harm the prospects of exercising access control. For example, if an authorized recipient violates his duty not to recommunicate or breaches a corresponding contractual obligation, further recipients remain under a general duty not to communicate without permission.

3. The Access-Right in Positive Copyright Law

After clarifying the general outlines of the access-right, the discussion now turns to examining the relations between theory and positive copyright law. Does copyright law have access-right characteristics? Does copyright law confer entitlements to control access to works? Some commentators seem to uphold precisely this argument,[89] whereas others vehemently object to any general statement of that sort.[90] The access-right definition shows why both arguments have a nucleus of truth. It further serves to refine the two seemingly contradictory propositions beyond what has been stated by their advocates. At this stage of the analysis, anticircumvention laws remain outside the ambit of the discussion; in addressing the foregoing questions, the focus is rather on traditional copyright rules. The basic question reads: do traditional copyright rules contain access-right elements? Chapter 1 demonstrated that, for the most part, all exclusive rights stipulated by copyright law and their violations involve communication elements. The following discussion offers a more pointed scrutiny running along the conceptual margins of the access-right. As the access-right has two prongs, it

---

88. A violator who has already infringed the first prong is perhaps unlikely to be deterred by the legal prohibition on unauthorized communications. However, other downstream recipients may wish to avoid illicit behavior. To deter such actors, legal restrictions on unauthorized re-communication as expressed in the second prong are critical.

89. *See* Ginsburg, *supra* note 80 at 116 ("It does not contend that the access right will or should supplant 'copy' - right. On the contrary, the claim is that the access right is an integral part of copyright.").

90. *See* Thomas P. Heide, *Copyright in the E.U. and the United States: What "Access Right"?*, 48 J. Copyright Soc'y. U.S.A 367 (2001) ("it is key to recall that any 'right against the gaining of unauthorised access' under copyright only exists with the key limiting words 'for the purpose of engaging in uses reserved to the author.'").

appears constructive to proceed by examining the traditional exclusive rights first in terms of access-conducts and then in terms of communication-conducts. The anticipated result is that traditional copyrights partly underpin the latter, but have little to do with the former.

(a) Access-Conducts and the Exclusive Rights

I. ACCESS-CONDUCTS GENERALLY NOT COVERED BY EXCLUSIVE RIGHTS

It is plain traditional copyright rules do not sanction or restrict mere access-conducts as defined above. Simply put, to the extent obtaining human-access to works requires the actor to take an affirmative action, the law does not treat such actions as copyright infringement. Access-conducts per se fall outside the area covered by the duties imposed on nonowners as stipulated in catalogs of traditional exclusive rights. This contention does not require a special proof—it is evident from the statutory language defining exclusive copyrights. Further, human-access is not the type of thing the exclusive rights attempt to regulate, at least not directly. From copyright law's viewpoint, a person is completely free to pursue access so long as her behavior does not involve infringement. Traditionally, access-conducts did not implicate exclusive rights, and thus, the risk of committing copyright violation has been insignificant.[91] At the same time, copyright law does not prevent claimants from attempting to block access to work copies in their possession. Nor does copyright law prevent persons from invoking property rights in the premises where a work is being performed or where copies are stored. In such instances, access prevention to informational resources is made feasible (and possibly also legally enforceable) via access provision to *physical* spaces. Surely, copyright law has little to do with those scenarios as enforcement of control over access-conducts depends on legal entitlements external to copyright law (e.g., property rights in land and chattels).

Next, we might inquire whether copyright law secures an *implicit* right to control access-conduct, or at least allows rights-holders to influence the ability to perform access-conducts. Exercising exclusive rights concerning reproductions, adaptations, distributions, or communication to the public may affect the accessibility of the work.[92] For instance, producing and distributing an additional copy increases the likelihood of human-access to the work. If exclusive rights prevent the production of that extra copy, access opportunities might decline. The same logic applies to communication to the public and other exclusive rights. Importantly, bans on unauthorized reproduction, distribution, communication, etc. assume the work was already made accessible to the potential violator. Such

---

91. It is assumed the statutory catalog of exclusive rights sufficiently demarcates the scope of copyright control. For the present purpose, conducts that are not listed in the catalog of statutory exclusive rights remain outside the reach of the rights-holders.

92. Chapter 1, Section V.C.(1) *supra* (discussing the relationship between regulation and the information process in general terms).

an actor, the Hohfeldian duty holder, is not legally prevented from engaging in any access-conducts, as the definition of his duty is indifferent to the question of how he has gained human-access for himself.

The intermediate conclusion must be that at the formal level of rights-claims and duties, the overlap between traditional exclusive rights and the first prong of the access-right is minimal. To the extent exercising exclusive copyrights might effectively decrease access opportunities in general (e.g., there will be fewer copies available in the market), this represents an *interference* with or influence on access opportunities, not access *control*. The difference is important, and the following passages highlight some of its implications.

II. THE ROLE OF HUMAN-ACCESS IN THE INFRINGEMENT TEST

Examination of the interface between human-access and a given standard infringement test confirms the observation concerning the absence of access-conduct prohibitions in traditional copyright rules. To illustrate the point, we shall consider the infringement test of the reproduction right under U.S. law.[93] The U.S. Copyright Act provides: "Anyone how violates any of the exclusive rights . . . is an infringer of the copyright."[94] In the case of an alleged infringement of the reproduction right, courts have established the plaintiff must show (1) ownership of a valid copyright in (2) a work sufficiently original, and (3) unauthorized copying of the protected element by the defendant.[95] In the absence of direct evidence of copying (which is usually the case), plaintiff may establish the third element by showing (1) access of the defendant to the protected work, and (2) substantial similarity to the copyrighted work.[96] When similarity between the copyrighted work and the content used by the defendant is striking, access may be presumed.[97] Patry writes of the access element:

> Access is the most misunderstood and therefore most misapplied element of the infringement analysis. Access is relevant only at the copying stage; it is not relevant at the later material appropriation (substantial similarity) stage. Access is an element of plaintiff's prima facie burden of proving copying for the common sense reason that no defendant can copy a work to which it does

---

93. Presumably, the law on this narrow issue does not dramatically differ across copyright jurisdictions.

94. *See* 17 U.S.C. § 501(a).

95. *See* WILLIAM PATRY, 3 PATRY ON COPYRIGHT §§ 9:4, 9:6, 9:12, 9:15, 9:16 (2007).

96. *See, e.g.*, Lexmark Int'l, Inc. v. Static Control Components, Inc., 387 F.3d 522, 534 (6th. Cir. 2004) (citing Kohus v. Mariol, 328 F.3d 848, 853–54 (6th. Cir. 2003)).

97. *See, e.g.*, Arnstein v. Porter, 154 F.2d 464, 468 (2d. Cir. 1946) ("If there is evidence of access and similarities exist, then the trier of the facts must determine whether the similarities are sufficient to prove copying. . . . If evidence of access is absent, the similarities must be so striking as to preclude the possibility that plaintiff and defendant independently arrived at the same result.").

> not have access. . .Access cannot be presumed or dispensed with. Access is, however, irrelevant if there are no similarities between the parties' works: Numerous courts have held that no amount of access can lead to infringement in the absence of substantial similarity.[98]

The U.S. doctrine concerning infringement of the reproduction right states the obvious and brings to the forefront the undisputable point concerning the role of human-access in the conventional infringement scenario. On the one hand, human-access *does* fulfill a certain function in the infringement test;[99] on the other hand, human-access is a purely evidentiary element of infringement. Access is by no means an infringement in itself, and human-access as such is not and never has been a copyright violation. In addition, the question of unauthorized access (or the lawfulness of access-conducts) is completely irrelevant to the question of liability under copyright law.

III. SPECIAL COPYRIGHT RULES AFFECTING ACCESS-CONDUCTS

Some copyright rules may influence the ability to perform access-conducts. Consider for instance the remedy allowing rights-holders to have counterfeit copies removed from the market.[100] Once seized and destroyed by rights-holders, no access to the work from those infringing copies can take place. Examples of copyright rules that *specifically address access* are extremely rare, however. One is Section 25 of the German Copyright Act.[101] Under certain limited conditions, the author can demand access to original exemplars or copies of a work she has created that are in the possession of another person for the purpose of making reproductions or derivative works, to the extent the interests of the possessors thereby are not unreasonable prejudiced.[102] The rule emanates from a personality-oriented copyright philosophy focusing on protection of the special bond between authors

---

98. *See* PATRY, *supra* note 95, § 9:22 (citations omitted).

99. *See, e.g.*, Scholz Design Inc. v. Larue, 2008 WL 3827993 (E.D. Ark. 2008) (the court rejected infringement allegations because the plaintiff did not offer sufficient evidence that defendants had actually accessed his copyrighted designs).

100. Seizure remedies are stipulated in the Berne Convention. *See* Berne Convention (1971) Art. 13(3) (seizure of sound recording imported without permission); *id.* at Art. 16(1) ("Infringing copies of a work shall be liable to seizure in any country of the Union where the work enjoys legal protection"). *See also* SAM RICKETSON & JANE C. GINSBURG, INTERNATIONAL COPYRIGHT AND NEIGHBORING RIGHTS: THE BERNE CONVENTION AND BEYOND §§ 11.38, 11.46–11.47 (2006) (noting that though Berne does not stipulate a general exclusive distribution rights, it mandates seizure measures concerning infringing copies that cross borders without rights-holders' consent).

101. *See* UrhG § 25 UrhG.

102. *See* UrhG § 25(1). For commentary on this special copyright rule, see Joachim Vogel, *in* URHEBERRECHT KOMMENTAR § 25 nr. 1 ff (Gerhard Schricker, ed., 3d ed. 2006); Adolf Dietz, in ULRICH LOEWENHEIM, HANDBUCH DES URHEBERRECHTS § 17 (2003).

and their works.[103] The exceptional aspect of this provision relevant for the present discussion is the definition of the possessor's duty, *which directly concerns human-access to works*. Interestingly, the operation of this rule is diametrically opposite to the first prong of the access-right. Section 25 secures a *positive* access entitlement held by the author to access the work *herself*, rather than a negative right to exclude others. In addition, Section 25 presumes duty holders (by definition) already have access to the original exemplar or copy, so the right cannot operate to impose restrictions on *their* access opportunities.[104] The significance of this exceptional rule is to confirm, once again, the first prong of the access-right is not supported by traditional rules, even in the unusual case where the copyright law directly and explicitly regulates human-access.

(b) Communication-Conducts and the Exclusive Rights

Both the acquisition and violation of traditional exclusive rights involve *communication* elements.[105] Only a narrow gap is left to be closed to show that violation of exclusive rights always implicates *communication-conducts* in the meaning of the access-right: the making of an unauthorized copy is communicative in the sense it facilitates reception from the object produced. As explained earlier, whether creating the additional copy is an act of *origination* or mere *facilitation* depends on the mental state of the actor and the circumstances of the act. The second prong of the access-right is defined to cover communication-acts in the broad sense; therefore, it captures both types of activities. The same logic applies to the exclusive rights concerning adaptations, distributions, and other forms of communication and transfer of information assisted by logistic media. Violations of economic rights inherently involve facilitation of receptions, and therefore, any conceivable violation of the traditional economic rights secured under copyright law is controlled by the second access-right prong.

Importantly, the overlap between communication-conducts and copyright violations is not perfect. Communication-conducts in the broad sense obviously make up a larger category than conducts covered by the catalog of exclusive rights. Though every infringement can be considered a communication-conduct, not every communication-conduct may infringe. As a practical matter, the scope of control over communication-conducts supported by positive copyright laws will depend on three main parameters: (1) the scope of exclusive rights to control communications; (2) the enforceability of legal restrictions on communication-conducts; and (3) the breadth of exceptions, including non-voluntary licensing. In any event, the communication-conducts that are in fact subject to copyright exclusivity constitute only a fraction of all possible conducts falling under the definition of the second access-right prong.

---

103. *See* Vogel, *supra* note 102, § 25 nr. 6–7.

104. *See* UrhG § 25(2) (duty holders (possessors) are not obligated to hand over their original exemplar or copy).

105. Chapter 1, Section V.A.–B *supra*.

B. The Right to Access Information

There is a fundamental distinction between the access-right as defined above and what shall be hereinafter called rights-of-access. In many respects, the access-right and rights-of-access represent diametrically opposite legal entitlements. Rights-of-access define the position of *nonowners* regarding access to information subject to property-like entitlements held by rights-holders. Within the rights-of-access spectrum, it should be further differentiated between entitlements in the "weak" and the "strong" form. This vocabulary will be applied systematically throughout this study to present the formal and theoretical distinctions between the two species of access entitlements, namely, those held by rights-holders and those afforded to nonowners.

1. The Right-of-Access Defined

In this discussion, *rights-of-access* is a general name for legal entitlements to access information. Their central mission is to protect nonowners against information "holdouts" by persons who misuse their position as possessors to curtail the dissemination of messages. The purpose of such regulation is also to safeguard sufficient access opportunity when the information is subject to property rights, and to remove legal and physical obstacles preventing human-access.

As a preliminary matter, copyright law does not expressly define rights of access to copyrighted works. In light of the finding establishing the lack of first access-right prong elements under traditional copyright law, the absence of explicit rights-of-access is consistent with the general scheme. In principle, it would seem pointless to articulate formal rights-of-access granted to users of works if the copyright law does not regulate access, or more precisely, does not prohibit unauthorized access-conducts. Rights-of-access are most relevant when another person deliberately creates an artificial barrier inhibiting access opportunities to messages. As a result of those factual barriers, nonowners' access opportunities decline. In cases where the law considers nonowners' access legitimate, intervention in the positions of the parties may be necessary. The central mission of rights-of-access, as entitlements designed to correct such undesirable results, is to order persons to remove obstacles that actually hinder access or otherwise to enable human-access. Accordingly, a *right-of-access in the strong form* is defined as follows:

TABLE 3.2 RIGHTS-OF-ACCESS DEFINED

A right-of-access is a legal entitlement against a person in possession of information, or a person who is otherwise in a position to restrict access to information, to compel that person to facilitate access (for example, by removing physical and logical barriers on communication, as well as other impediments) to enable human-access to the right-holder.

It is possible to think about the right-of-access in its strong form as the dialectic opposite of the access-right. The duty holder is the person capable of restricting human-access to messages after their externalization by originators. This broadly includes anyone who can prevent or intercept reception of a medial message.[106] Accordingly, the beneficiary is the would-be recipient who wishes to actualize his entitlement to achieve human-access to the message.

The distinction between rights-of-access in the strong and the weak form turns on the Hohfeldian distinction between a right and a privilege. A *right-of-access in the strong form* provides a Hohfeldian right-claim against the duty holder to enable access, where the opponent is under the affirmative legal duty to remove access obstacles and otherwise enable human-access. A *right-of-access in the weak form* means the beneficiary holds merely a Hohfeldian privilege to perform access-conducts necessary for achieving access to the message. The opponent does not have a legal *right* to interfere with the beneficiary's access-conduct (i.e., he is in a Hohfeldian "no-right" position). However, in contrast to the first instance, the opponent *may* interfere with the exercise of the privilege, and this interference is not ipso facto unlawful. The privilege beneficiary may attempt to enforce the privilege himself, but he lacks a legally recognized cause of action against potential opponents.

2. *Legal and Normative Sources of Rights-of-Access*

(a) Copyright Law

What are the legal and normative foundations supporting rights-of-access to information? Consider first copyright law itself. At first glance, to the extent rights-of-access directly target access to works, copyright statutes do not seem to contain such norms at all.[107] These statutes traditionally assign rights-claims to copyright holders, as copyright law focuses on defining specifically the rights of those rights-holders; "users" (or nonowners in general) have a residual status.[108]

---

106. Note the duty holder in the general case is not necessarily a copyright holder or anyone holding proprietary-exclusory rights in the information covered by the right-of-access.

107. Limitations on exclusive rights that narrow their scope can be said to support rights of access indirectly. For instance, limitations on duration of copyrights may be viewed as a legal instrument ensuring free and broad access to works after the point where they enter the public domain. In this narrow sense, limitations on duration underpin a right-of-access in the weak form to access public domain works. This rule effectively changes the status of nonowners from duty holders to privilege holders. Note however that copyright limitations of this sort usually do not alter the legal position of parties on an individual basis. The change in the copyright status of the work affects all nonowners and concerns all works whose protection term has elapsed.

108. Some commentators argue the the ultimate goal of exclusive rights is to serve an indefinite group of nonowners or the "public interest." *Cf.* GILLIAM DAVIES, COPYRIGHT AND THE PUBLIC INTEREST (2002). Either way, protecting nonowners under copyright

The exclusive rights are essentially restrictions on communication-conducts directed *against nonowners in general.*

At the same time, the exclusive rights are subject to certain exceptions and limitations designed to balance between the exclusivity interests of rights-holders and the access/communication interests of nonowners. It is possible to intermediately conclude that in the traditional copyright framework, explicit rights-of-access are rare or completely absent. Next, we should consider whether rights-of-access are *implied* by copyright exceptions and limitations. The general problem with this argument is structural, as statutory exceptions are Hohfeldian privileges phrased in a manner that already assumes accessibility of the work to the privilege beneficiary. Because copyright infringement without access cannot take place,[109] the logical inference must be that access is a dispositive assumption in any exception scenario.

I. COPYRIGHT EXEMPTIONS

Copyright exemptions hereinafter broadly describe all copyright rules that restrict the scope and enforcement of exclusive rights both explicitly and implicitly.[110] The status, breadth, and operation of copyright exemptions have been capturing center stage in the copyright debate as overprotection concerns started looming large.[111] Generally speaking, exemptions define or imply situations in which the power of owners to restrict behavior (emanating from their positions as exclusive rights-holders under copyright) is delimited. The lawfulness of exempted acts does not hinge on securing rights-holders' permission, and liability under copyright law does not attach to performing an unauthorized act with respect to copyrighted work. Technically, exemptions often are formulated as Hohfeldian privileges: with regard to a given act, the jural relations between a nonowner and a rights-holder assume the form of privilege/no-right, respectively.[112]

---

statutes is achieved via legal instruments *other than* granting them rights-claims directed against copyright holders.

109. Section III.A.3.(a).ii *supra.*

110. For convenience, the phrase *copyright exemptions* shall be used as a catchall term to cover all recognized limitations, exceptions, and defenses under copyright law.

111. For an internationally oriented study, see Pierre Sirinelli, *Exception and Limits to Copyright* (1999) (available at http://www.wipo.int/meetings/es/details.jsp?meeting_id=3944). The author notes the lack of terminological uniformity in this area. *Id.* at. 2–3. *See also* Christophe Geiger, Right to Copy v. Three-Step Test: *Future of the Private Copy Exception in the Digital Environment,* 1 COMPUTER L. REV. INT'L 7–8 (2005). For a critical analysis of the U.S. fair use doctrine, see William W. Fisher, *Reconstructing the Fair Use Doctrine,* 101 HARVARD L. REV. 1659 (1988).

112. Generally, copyright-implicating conducts can be reduced to a "right-claim/duty" or a "privilege/no-right" situation. Applicable exemptions shift the parties from the first to the latter rubric of correlative legal positions.

This observation applies both to "open" and "closed" systems of exemptions.[113] Exemptions may release nonowners from any liability or obligation whatsoever toward rights-holders in connection with their use. Alternatively, the law may stipulate mandatory payment of royalties to compensate rights-holders for privileged use. For instance, exemptions may create blanket licensing, such as statutory and compulsory licenses. In case of mandatory compensation, levies and collective rights administration are essential elements within the system of exemptions. At bottom, exempted acts basically enjoy the status of Hohfeldian privileges.[114]

The U.S. Copyright Act speaks in terms of "exclusive rights" granted to "owners of copyright" to "do and to authorize" a number of reserved activities enumerated in the statutory catalog.[115] This statute mentions the term *right* almost exclusively in connection with entitlements granted to copyright holders, not with the entitlements of any other classes of stakeholders.[116] By contrast, the language describing statutory exceptions is much weaker: acts covered by statutory exemptions are

---

113. Closed exemptions systems narrowly define the circumstances under which an act is lawful, whereas an open system stipulates standards more generally. The paradigmatic example for an open exemption rule is the U.S. fair use doctrine, which is applicable to violations of all of the exclusive rights as to all nonowners without discrimination under a flexible statutory formulation of circumstances. The difference between open and closed systems is in form, not substance. It concerns the way exempted acts are defined in the law, which does not change the juridical nature of exemptions as Hohfeldian privileges.

114. It is possible of course to reverse the terminological choices and then challenge Hohfeld's definition of the term *privilege*. Bell argues, for example, that exclusive rights are not "rights" but "privileges." *See* Tom W. Bell, *Copyright as Intellectual Property Privilege*, 58 Syracuse L. Rev. 523 (2008). Bell writes: "Does this use of [intellectual] 'privilege' conform with Wesley Hohfeld's influential one? He used the word interchangeably, and confusingly, with 'liberty.' It would surely mislead, however, to call copyrights, 'copyliberties.' If anything, that latter term better describes the rights that each of us enjoys—or, absent the Copyright Act, would enjoy—to freely use others' expressions." *Id.* at 529–30 (footnotes omitted).

115. *See* 17 U.S.C. § 106.

116. There is one noteworthy exception embodied in § 108 of the Copyright Act (concerning certain reproductions by libraries and archives.) *See* 17 U.S.C. § 108. For instance, §§ 108(b) and 108(d) speak of "the right of reproduction and distribution [granted to libraries and archives in certain circumstances under section 108]." *Id.* § 108(b) and (d). Similarly, § 108(c) refers to the libraries' and archives" "right of reproduction" while § 108(f) mentions occasionally "the right of fair use." *Id.* § 108(c) & (f). The terminology of *rights* in connection with copyright exemptions in this context is an unusual formulation within the Copyright Act. In any event, the law does not attach a correlative duty to rights-holders that would secure the exercise of libraries' "right" of reproduction, and therefore, § 108 contains a list of privileges, not rights.

simply "not an infringement of copyright."[117] The same principle is repeated in other copyright statutes as well.[118] Exemptions can constitute releases from infringement liability, but usually, those exemptions are not a legal instrument imposing legal duties. Some courts and commentators consider certain (or all) exemptions as "rights" vested in nonowners, which is known as the "users' rights" approach.[119]

The argument that nonowners' entitlements amount to legal "rights" is largly a normative (not a descriptive) observation that emerges particularly in connection with fair use and fair dealing provisions.[120] Its advocates corroborate their argument with teleological, historical, economic, and constitutional rationales.[121] But it is not necessary to either accept or reject the validity of the users' rights approach on the theoretical-normative level to determine the positive law, *de lege lata,* does not grant nonowners anything more than Hohfeldian privileges. A hotly contested issue in that respect in U.S. copyright circles is the ramifications of the above in connection with the application of the fair use doctrine.

II. FAIR USE AND RIGHTS-OF-ACCESS

Can the fair use doctrine shed a different light on the copyright legal rights/privileges debate? The statutory expression of fair use in Section 107 of the U.S. Copyright Act codifies it as a "limitation" on exclusive rights.[122] Section 107 is structured in two layers, with its preamble first providing an exemplary list of

---

117. *See, e.g.,* 17 U.S.C. § 107 (fair use) & § 110(1) (certain exceptions from performance and display liability done for teaching and educational purposes), § 111(a) (secondary transmission), and § 112 (various exceptions in the case of ephemeral recording).

118. For instance, the German statute speaks of authors' rights (*Urheberrechte*) when referring to the entitlements of initial rights-holders, and of limitations (*Schranken des Urheberrechts*) when listing the casuistic exemptions to exclusive rights.

119. *Cf.* CCH Canadian Ltd. v. Law Society of Upper Canada, 2004 SCC 13 ¶ 48 (2004) (in connection with fair dealing exceptions, the Supreme Court of Canada held that "[p] rocedurally, a defendant is required to prove that his or her dealing with a work has been fair; however, the fair dealing exception is perhaps more properly understood as an integral part of the Copyright Act than simply a defense. Any act falling within the fair dealing exception will not be an infringement of copyright. The fair dealing exception, like other exceptions in the Copyright Act, is a user's right"). *See also* Stanley F. Birch, *Copyright Fair Use: A Constitutional Imperative,* 54 J. COPYRIGHT SOC'Y U.S.A. 139 (2007) (arguing fair use should be considered a users' right other that mere defense to copyright infringement).

120. *Id.*

121. *See* LYMAN RAY PATTERSON & STANLEY W. LINDBERG, THE NATURE OF COPYRIGHT: A LAW OF USERS' RIGHTS (1991).

122. § 107 is captioned: "Limitations on exclusive rights: Fair Use." *See* 17 U.S.C. § 107 (title).

general purposes for which unauthorized use may be lawful. The list includes use of copyrighted works for criticism, comment, news reporting, education, scholarship, and research.[123] Section 107 then articulates a four-factor test instructing courts concerning the circumstances of fair use and how to evaluate the availability of fair use protections to defendants.[124] These factors include the purpose and character of the use, its commercial nature and implications, the nature of the work, and the amount and substantiality of the portion used in relation to the work as a whole.[125] In codifying the fair use doctrine, the U.S. legislature did not articulate a grant of "rights" to fair use in the strict sense. The doctrine is constructed as guidelines to courts regarding the factors to be taken into consideration in a fair use analysis.

Fair use cannot be considered a Hohfeldian right-claim simply because fair use law does not demarcate any formal, pre-adjudication duties. No person is under an affirmative, general legal obligation ex ante to facilitate, assist, enable, or allow acts supposedly qualified under the fair use doctrine. Properly classified, nonowners' entitlements under the fair use doctrine are more like Hohfeldian privileges, or more accurately, *conditional* privileges, as their capability to neutralize the abstention duty is determined after the fact; whether an unauthorized use is lawful or not is generally clarified ex post.[126] Once a court declares a certain use as "fair," the doctrine protects that use in the same way a Hohfeldian privilege protects a privilege holder. Courts survey the "operative facts"[127] surrounding the use at issue, and upon a judicial concluding those facts qualify the act as fair use, the defendant is not liable for

---

123. *Id.*

124. Fair use is considered a one-step inquiry, as distinguished from fair dealing provisions, which predefine the circumstances/purposes where exemption may apply.

125. The four fair use factors read: "(1) the purpose and character of the use, including whether such use is of a commercial nature or is for nonprofit educational purposes; (2) the nature of the copyrighted work; (3) the amount and substantiality of the portion used in relation to the copyrighted work as a whole; and (4) the effect of the use upon the potential market for or value of the copyrighted work." *Id.*

126. It is technically possible to bring the question to court as a motion for declaratory judgment asking the court to determine ex ante (or concurrently) that the use is covered by § 107. *See, e.g.*, 321 Studios v. Metro Goldwyn Studios, Inc., 307 Supp. 2d. 1085 (2004) (plaintiff unsuccessfully pleading for a declaratory judgment to qualify the use as being lawful under fair use).

127. Hohfeld defined *operative facts* as "those which, under the general legal rules that are applicable, suffice to change legal relations, that is, either to create a new relation, or to extinguish an old one, or to perform both of these functions simultaneously." *See* Wesley Newcombe Hohfeld, *Some Fundamental Legal Conceptions as Applied in Legal Reasoning*, 23 YALE L. J. 16, 25 (1913).

copyright infringement.[128] In such case, rights-holders are in a correlative position of "no-right" to enforce their copyrights. At the same time, rights-holders are neither under a general legal obligation to surrender works for fair use purposes nor a duty to otherwise facilitate fair use.[129]

In some respect, fair use is *less* vigorous than a statutory privilege because its protection is contingent and to some degree unpredictable.[130] At least as the law has been applied in U.S. courts so far, all fair uses are technically prima facie infringing until and unless the court rules otherwise. Therefore, relying ex ante on the fair use protections is in some way more risky than relying on more specific statutory exceptions, as it is more difficult to predict in advance a future judicial resolution factoring the circumstances of the case under the multifactor test. Indeed, the U.S. Supreme Court labeled fair use an *affirmative defense* to copyright infringement and such defense only matters after a prima facie violation has been shown.[131] As such, statutory fair use is not a source of affirmative "rights" in the stricter sense of the term.

III. THE UPSHOT

There is strong, perhaps conclusive evidence that copyright law *de lege lata* does not support rights-of-access *in the strong form*. In fact, nonowners for the most part lack affirmative right-claims under traditional copyright law, either concerning mere access-conducts or with respect to any other act. Beneficiaries of copyright exemptions are best described as privilege holders. In addition, in their status as such, their privileges do not concern human-access, but instead, potentially infringing acts such as reproductions, distribution, performance, and other acts covered by the exclusive rights. The exercise of privileges secured under copyright exemptions substantially depends on the ability to first access the work. However, facilitating human-access to the privilege beneficiary *is not the problem traditional copyright exemptions are designed to address*. Even if we accept the contention that statutory exceptions are users' rights, it is plain that if

---

128. The operative facts (sometimes called, as Hohfeld noted, "constitutive," "causal" or "dispositive" facts as distinguished from *evidential* facts) in fair use situations are derived from § 107 and serve to alter the position of the parties once the court has determined the doctrine applies.

129. The point was made by many, including David R. Johnstone, *Debunking Fair Use Rights and Copyduty Under U.S. Copyright Law*, 52 J. Copyright Soc'y 345, 366 (2005).

130. *Cf.* Thomas F. Cotter, *Fair Use and Copyright Overenforcement*, 93 Iowa L. Rev. 1271 (2008) (presenting an economic analysis of fair use factoring in the ex ante uncertainty, which arguably deters use that would otherwise be efficient under transaction costs considerations).

131. Campbell v. Acuff-Rose Music Inc., 510 U.S. 569, 590 (1994) (fair use is an affirmative defense) (citing the previous Supreme Court decision Harper & Row v. Nation Enter., 471 U.S. 539, 561 (1985) and supportive legislative history).

someone resolves to restrict access, invoking the privilege will be to no (or little) avail,[132] as Hohfeld has predicted.[133] The fact copyright statutory privileges are not designed to secure access to facilitate the exercise of exemptions suggests copyright law might fail to adequately safeguard rights-of-access *in the weak form* as well.

A final observation in this context addresses the nature of access-conducts in general, whether or not performed to realize a statutory privilege. The analysis thus far indicates that from a copyright perspective, such conducts can be viewed as non-statutory permissions to act. Access-conducts in general are (1) Hohfeldian *privileges* as the rights-holders have "no-right" to prevent them, and (2) *non-statutory* simply because such entitlements are not expressed in copyright statutes. To the extent rights-of-access are implied in the copyright system, they fall under the general rubric of *non-statutory privileges.* In fact, rights-of-access (especially in the strong form) are rare within private law in general. Explicit rights-of-access in the strong form emerge when special relationships of a special nature between specified parties receive special treatment by the law. The law may recognize an affirmative cause of action to obtain information in situations involving doctor-patient relations, duties owed by manager toward shareholders in publicly traded corporations, or parties to civil litigation.[134] In special situations of that sort, a party may find itself under a legal obligation to surrender information in its possession to the opponent. The answer to the question whether party *X* has an enforceable right-of-access to information held by party *Y* will depend on the identity of the parties, the nature of their relations, the nature of the information, the purpose of access, the purpose of suppressing access, and so forth.

In this context, the distinction between private and public actors plays an important role. Often, the access-seeking party will have more effective rights-of-access against a *public* (or *quasi*-public) entity in control of information than against a private opponent.[135] The discussion now turns to briefly examine

---

132. In 2005, the French Supreme Court (*Cour de Cassation*) held that when a DVD is protected by technological copy control, the statutory privilege to make private copies (*copie privée*) does not provide grounds to circumvent the technological measure, as the provision allowing private copying is a mere exception (*exception*), not a right. *See* the Mulholland Drive Case, French Supreme Court, 1st Civil Chamber, No. 549 (2006).

133. *See* Hohfeld, *supra* note 127, at 35 ff (by definition, there is no cause of action against someone who interferes with the exercise of a mere privilege).

134. Druey provided an analysis of private causes of action concerning information. *See* JEAN NICOLAS DRUEY, INFORMATION ALS GEGENSTAND DES RECHTES 113 ff (1995).

135. The private/public distinction is not always clear-cut, especially in heavily regulated markets such as mass media and broadcasting. *Cf.* E.C. Broadcasting Directive 89/552/EEC (1989); E.C. Television Broadcasting Directive 2007/65/EC (2007) Arts. 3j, 3k. Some broadcasting regulations are perceived as securing a public right of

situations in which information is possessed by the government (or by an equivalent public actor). The purpose of this brief detour is to sharpen the image and illustrate the structure of rights-of-access *as they exist in the positive law.* Public law norms illustrate the core design of legally enforceable right-of-access in general. Further, such norms exemplify the rationales and policies for granting information access-related entitlements. The next passages discuss briefly some public and constitutional norms, and later, human rights aspects of access to information.

(b) Special Public Law Norms

Freedom of information (FOI) regulation represent a potent example of statutory rights-of-access in the realm of public law. Generally, such laws impose obligations on the state to surrender information in its possession when private parties file a request.[136] The policy objectives behind such regulation are, inter alia, to increase government transparency, support the democratic process, and effectively impose the rule of law on state actions.[137] Obligating the state to supply information related to its operation and decision-making processes is essential for a functioning democracy. To some extent, state affairs constitute public information, and as such they should be open to public scrutiny and debate.[138]

Claims under FOI laws often have two basic characteristics: First, the information holder must be a public actor.[139] Second, the information at issue

---

access to certain information under certain conditions. *See, e.g.*, E.C. Television Broadcasting Directive 2007/65/EC, Art. 3.k(1) ("Member States shall ensure that for the purpose of short news reports, any broadcaster established in the Community has access on a fair, reasonable and non-discriminatory basis to events of high interest to the public which are transmitted on an exclusive basis by a broadcaster under their jurisdiction.") At the same time, such provisions usually do not confer private causes of action upon members of the public to enable access. Instead, members of the public are akin to third-party beneficiaries of the arrangements between the regulator and broadcasting organizations (both public and private).

136. *See* PATRICK BIRKINSHAW, FREEDOM OF INFORMATION: THE LAW, THE PRACTICE AND THE IDEAL 1–2 (1996).

137. *Id.* at 18–22 (reviewing political-liberal and philosophical arguments that underlie freedom of information legislation).

138. *See, e.g.*, James A. Goldston et al., *A Nation Less Secured: Diminished Public Access to Information*, 21 Harv. C.R.-C.L. L. Rev. 409, 459 (1986) (noting the U.S. FOIA established an affirmative right to obtain government information directly from executive agencies upon request, based on the premise "if government is to be truly of, by and for the people, the people must know in detail the activities of the government") (quoting a memorandum of the U.S. Department of Justice).

139. For example, the U.S. FOIA (as amended in 1996) speaks of an "agency" defined as including "any executive department, military department, Government corporation, Government controlled corporation, or other establishment in the executive branch of the

is held by the government actor in a manner that prevents reasonable access by members of the public.[140] Often, the applicant does not have to specify any ground for requesting public records. However, the duty of the government to supply the requested information regularly requires a detailed procedure be followed, possibly involving payment of fees. The government's duty is delimited by specific exceptions such as information related to national security.[141] Developments from recent years imposed similar duties on governments specifically concerning environmental information. For instance, a European Union directive from 2003 seeks to harmonize Member States' laws on the issue of access to environmental information.[142] Article 3(1) of that directive provides "Member States shall ensure that public authorities are required, in accordance with the provisions of this Directive, to make available environmental information held by or for them to any applicant at his request and without his having to state an interest."[143] Access to environmental information is a special category of FOI regulation focusing on certain, narrowly defined types of information subject to the government's duty.[144] These illustrative examples unveil common patterns of legal entitlements that directly concern access to information. In fact, these are clear examples of rights-of-access *in the strong form* with the state as the duty holder. Upon request, beneficiaries of FOI provisions hold affirmative Hohfeldian right-claims vis-à-vis governmental authorities to be afforded access.

Government (including the Executive Office of the President), or any independent regulatory agency." *See* 5 U.S.C. § 552(f). The statute further provides a list of agencies and governmental bodies subject to the regulation, including Congress and U.S. courts. *Id.* § 551(1).

140. *Cf.* 5 U.S.C. § 552(a)(2) (U.S. FOIA imposing a limited government duty to provide information "unless the materials are promptly published and copies offered for sale").

141. *See, e.g.*, U.S.C. § 552(c)(3). The duty of the government to open its archives and disclose its decision-making procedures is limited. Birkinshaw noted "[i]nformation is inherently a feature of power. So too is its control, use and regulation. Government . . . is the organisation of information for the use . . . of power in the public interests. Take away the government's preserve on information, and its preserve of when and what to release, then take away a fundamental bulwark of its power.") *See* Birkinshaw, *supra* note 136, at 24.

142. *See* E.C. Directive on Public Access to Environmental Information (2003).

143. *Id.* Art. 3(1). The term *public authority* is defined in Art. 2(2) of the directive.

144. *Id.* Art. 2(1) (provides a detailed list of environmental information relevant for the purpose of the directive).

(c) Free Speech Law—The U.S. Experience

The interface between constitutional norms and copyright law is charged and complex.[145] To begin with, the very competence to legislate copyright laws in the first place may have (or require) an explicit constitutional underpinning.[146] More generally, constitutional texts often safeguard the security of private property[147] or protect private individuals against uncompensated "taking" of private property by the government.[148] Concurrently, democratic constitutions guarantee free speech, and free speech law manifests some critical interface points between copyright regulation and access-to-information issues.

The limited purpose of the following discussion is to point out some problematic junctions where copyright and free speech law questions converge. Additionally, it examines the impact of free speech law on the legal position of nonowners. In fact, the legal position of nonowners participating in the information process is precisely the locus of friction. Nonowners are under a duty not to infringe on copyrights, but at the same time, their rights to communicate freely are constitutionally secured. In the present context, the most relevant aspect of that friction is encapsulated in the question whether—and to what degree—free speech guarantees influence rights-of-access analysis. The following discussion evaluates the problem through the lens of U.S. free speech law and the relationship between the First Amendment to the U.S. Constitution and a public right to receive information.

---

145. For a U.S. law perspective, see NIMMER & NIMMER, *supra* note 78, Ch. A. For a European law perspective, see Bernt Hugenholtz, *Copyright and Freedom of Expression in Europe, in* EXPANDING THE BOUNDARIES OF INTELLECTUAL PROPERTY: INNOVATION POLICY FOR THE KNOWLEDGE SOCIETY (Rochelle Cooper Dreyfuss et al. eds., 2001).

146. For instance, the Copyright Clause of the U.S. Constitution expressly articulates copyright legislative competence, namely "Congress shall have the Power" to enact copyright laws. *See* U.S. Const., art. 1 sec. 8, Cl. 8. The German Constitution lists copyright legislation within the category of topics of exclusive federal legislative competence. *See* Art. 73 Nr. 9 GG.

147. For Germany, see Art. 14.I GG. To the extent exclusive rights under copyright are intellectual "property" (*Eigentum*), legislation that would restrict the ability to exercise the exclusive rights might come under the scrutiny of this provision. *See, e.g.*, Gerhard Schricker in URHEBERRECHT KOMMENTAR Einl. nr. 12 (Gerhard Schricker, ed., 3d ed. 2006) (authors' rights are property in the meaning of Art. 14 GG.) *See also* Eugen ULMER, URHEBER–UND VERLAGSRECHT 7, 63, 65–66 (1980).

148. *See* U.S. CONST. amend. V (". . . nor shall private property be taken for public use, without just compensation").

I. THE FIRST AMENDMENT AND THE RIGHT TO RECEIVE INFORMATION

The First Amendment reads: "Congress shall make no law . . . abridging the freedom of speech, or of the press . . . ."[149] This constitutional free speech guarantee is said to promote a number of important social values such as individual development, personal autonomy, democratic government, social stability, and the search for truth in a heterogenic and diversified marketplace of competing ideas.[150] The right to express or communicate (i.e., to "speak") captures center stage; yet, a right to *receive* information is not explicit in the language of the Constitution. In the celebrated 1979 decision in *Stanley v. Georgia*, the U.S. Supreme Court declared: "It is now well established that the constitution protects the right to receive information and ideas. . . This right to receive information and ideas, regardless of their social worth, is fundamental to our free society."[151] *Stanley v. Georgia* is no isolated occasion in which the U.S. Supreme Court upholds the so-called "right to receive information" under the First Amendment umbrella. In *Board of Education v. Pico* from 1982, the Court held:

> This right [to receive information] is an inherent corollary of the rights of free speech and press that are explicitly guaranteed by the Constitution, in two senses. First, the right to receive ideas follows ineluctably from the *sender's* First Amendment right to send them. . ."The dissemination of ideas can accomplish nothing if otherwise willing addressees are not free to receive and consider them. It would be a barren marketplace of ideas that had only sellers and no buyers". . . More importantly, the right to receive ideas is a necessary predicate to the *recipient's* meaningful exercise of his own rights of speech, press, and political freedom.[152]

---

149. *See* U.S. CONST. amend. I.

150. For a collection of materials on the theoretical foundations on the First Amendment, see JOHN H. GARVEY & FREDERICK F. SCHAUER, THE FIRST AMENDMENT: A READER 35–168 (1996). *See also* Ronald A. Cass, *The Perils of Positive Thinking: Constitutional Interpretation and Negative First Amendment Theory*, 34 UCLA L REV. 1405 (1987) (identifying a pattern of free speech theorization based on four different core values: individual development, democratic government, social stability, and search for truth).

151. *See* Stanley v. Georgia 394 U.S. 557, 564 (1969) (state prohibitions on private possession of obscene materials was held as violating the First Amendment for manifesting the state's desire to control a person's private thoughts based on moral convictions).

152. *See* Bd. of Educ. v. Pico, 457 U.S. 853, 867 (1982) (Brennan, J.) (emphasis in original) (citations omitted.) *See also* Richmond Newspapers, Inc. v. Virginia, 448 U.S. 555, 576 (1980) (in upholding public access to criminal trial proceedings, the Supreme Court declared "[f]ree speech carries with it some freedom to listen"); Renne v. Geary 501 U.S. 312, 330 (1991) ("[a claim to receive information concerning political party endorsements] finds support in our decisions, which have long held that the First Amendment protects the right to receive information and ideas, and that this right is sufficient to confer standing to challenge restrictions on speech") (White, J., dissenting on the issue of standing) (citations omitted); Virginia State Bd. of Pharmacy v. Virginia Citizens

In *Kleindienst v. Mandel*, Justice Marshall observed:

> As the majority correctly demonstrates, in a variety of contexts this Court has held that the First Amendment protects the right to receive information and ideas, the freedom to hear as well as the freedom to speak. The reason for this is that the First Amendment protects a process. . .and the right to speak and hear—including the right to inform others and to be informed about public issues—are inextricably part of that process. The freedom to speak and the freedom to hear are inseparable; they are two sides of the same coin. But the coin itself is the process of thought and discussion. The activity of speakers becoming listeners and listeners becoming speakers in the vital interchange of thought is the "means indispensable to the discovery and spread of political truth." Its protection is "a fundamental principle of the American government." The First Amendment means that Government has no power to thwart the process of free discussion, to "abridge" the freedoms necessary to make that process work.[153]

In *First National Bank vs. Bellotti*, the Court held "the First Amendment goes beyond protection of the press and the self-expression of individuals to prohibit government from limiting the stock of information from which members of the public may draw."[154] The *Bellotti* Court further stressed judicial precedents are based "not only on the role of the First Amendment in fostering individual self-expression but also on its role in affording the public access to discussion, debate, and the dissemination of information and ideas."[155]

The Supreme Court's jurisprudence on the right to receive information and the principal contours of the information process sketched in Chapter 1 mirror similar acknowledgements. In fact, the parallels between the information model vocabulary and the Supreme Court's rhetoric, particularly in *Board of Education v. Pico* and the excerpt above by Justice Marshall in *Kleindienst*, are quite striking. Supreme Court justices repeatedly intuited the critical role of reception within the broad dynamic context of the information process and articulated precise and sensible renditions of these principles. Clearly (as implied in the message concept explained in Chapter 1) the information model can well accommodate free speech concepts.[156] The "message" in the meaning of the information model is "speech." First Amendment protections extend to many kinds of speech, and

---

Consumer Council, 425 U.S. 748, 756–57 (1976) ("where a speaker exists . . . the protection afforded is to the communication, to its source and to its recipients both") (citation omitted).

153. *See* Kleindienst v. Mandel, 408 U.S. 753, 775–76 (1972) (Marshall, J., dissenting, joined by Brennan, J.) (citations omitted).

154. *See* First Nat'l Bank v. Bellotti, 435 U.S. 765, 783 (1978).

155. *Id.* at 783 (footnote omitted).

156. *See* Chapter 1, Section V.C.(1) *supra*.

like messages, the concept of protected speech is not limited to verbal communication alone.[157]

Various types of messages (speech) may receive differentiated degrees of First Amendment protection, though this differentiation often has little to do with the basic *communicative dimension* of the act. First Amendment doctrine initially distinguishes between protected and non-protected speech: some types of speech (such as "obscene" or "libelous" communications) in some circumstances might not be afforded First Amendment protection at all.[158] Further, we can distinguish between more and less intensive speech protections, with some types of speech being granted a comparatively lower level of protection, such as pornographic speech (or "near-obscene" speech) and commercial speech.[159] Also in this case, the rationale for "discriminating against" commercial speech (to the extent discrimination exists) is unrelated to the communicative quality of the act but rather to other factors such as the encouragement of free trade and healthy competition in the marketplace.

As First Amendment theory and the information model rediscover their mutual vocabulary, assumptions, and common recognitions, we should consider the impact of the former on the possibility and scope of a recognized legal right to receive information in connection with the notion of rights-of-access. Due to the special nature of information and communication, free speech law derives a constitutional right *to receive information* (a recipient's right) from the right *to communicate* (the originator's right). This deduction emanates from the recognition that, in the words of Justice Marshall, "[t]he activity of speakers becoming listeners and listeners becoming speakers" is woven into free speech protection rationales, and that, in the words of Justice Brennan, "the right to receive ideas follows ineluctably from the sender's First Amendment right to send them."

---

157. *Cf.* United States v. O'Brien, 391 U.S. 367 (1968) (conviction for burning of Selective Service registration certificates on the steps of a courthouse as an antiwar protest was held constitutionally permissible), *with*, Texas v. Johnson, 491 U.S. 397 (1989) (conviction for burning the American flag as a political protest was held inconsistent with the First Amendment). In any case, nonverbal messages in principle qualify as speech. For a selection of cases covering First Amendment protection of "unconventional" forms of speech, see STEVEN H. SHIFFRIN & JESSE H. CHOPER, THE FIRST AMENDMENT: CASES, COMMENTS, QUESTIONS 184–219 (2001). *See also* THOMAS IRWIN EMERSON, THE SYSTEM OF FREEDOM OF EXPRESSION 80 (1970) ("To some extent expression and action are always mingled; most conduct includes elements of both.").

158. For a case on obscenity, see Miller v. California, 413 U.S. 15 (1973); for libelous speech, see New York Times Co. v. Sullivan, 376 U.S. 254 (1964) (state law granting public figures cause of action to recover damages for publication of defamatory falsehood may be upheld only if they require the element of "actual malice").

159. *See* Jonathan Weinberg, *Constitutional Protection of Commercial Speech*, 82 COL. L.R. 720 (1982) (discussing the development of First Amendment protection for truthful and non-misleading commercial speech).

The freedom of the originator to create messages cannot be divorced from his freedom to receive messages—or at least that is the theory.

II. A CONSTITUTIONAL RIGHT TO RECEIVE INFORMATION: SUBSTANCE, CONTENT, AND CONTEXT

Who is the prototypical beneficiary of the right to receive information? Nonowners are an extremely heterogenic class of stakeholders:[160] as discussed in Chapter 1, the single feature they all seem to share is the lack of exclusive property-like rights in messages thay consider relevant or valuable. One threshold question is whether the right to receive information distinguishes between passive and active recipients.[161] Does it apply only to recipients who actively pursue information—or to idle recipients as well? In other words, does the law also secure access interests of persons who are not engaged in access-conducts driven by the motivation to obtain information, and if so, how do such legal entitlements with respect to inactive persons in this specific context operate?

This distinction appears largely immaterial due to the way access to information occurs and the constitutional values rights-of-access seek to promote,[162] including free speech law's core missions and rationales for protection against unwarranted government intervention.[163] Consider for instance the possible implied distinction between active and passive recipients in the context of "news gathering" concerning the rights of reporters and journalists to access information in various situations and the constitutional protection of their active access-conducts. In *Richmond Newspapers,* discussing the right of the press to attend criminal proceedings, the Supreme Court held:

> It is not crucial whether we describe this right to attend criminal trials to hear, see, and communicate observations concerning them as a "right of access,". . . or a "right to gather information," for we have recognized that "without some protection for seeking out the news, freedom of the press could be eviscerated". . . The explicit, guaranteed rights to speak and to publish concerning what takes place at a trial would lose much meaning if access to observe the trial could, as it was here, be foreclosed arbitrarily.[164]

---

160. Chapter 1, Section V.C.(2) *supra.*

161. As a practical matter, the answer will determine the breadth of the right by defining its beneficiaries according to their access profile.

162. If "obtaining," "receiving," and "accessing" information are qualitatively equivalent, it may be argued the distinction between active and passive rights to receive information is largely semantic. The notion of human-access implies a convergence of reception and access. Human-access, perceived as an occurrence other than a conduct, does not immediately involve volition or intent. Reception of information and access to information therefore appear intrinsically intertwined, or as two names for the same thing.

163. *See* SHIFFRIN & CHOPER, *supra* note 157, at 349–70 (providing resources related to constitutional newsgathering and related rights of reporters).

164. *See* Richmond Newspapers v. Virginia, 448 U.S. 555, 576–77 (1980) (citations and references omitted).

According to the Court's analysis, the activity of "seeking out" information is clearly granted constitutional protection. Should it matter whether the recipient is simply "there" without seeking out anything? It is submitted the distinction between active and passive reception is not a strong one, as protecting the active rights of journalists serves primarily the larger interest of their *audience* to access information, passive and active alike. When the law protects the right of an active information recipient (e.g., a news reporter), it also buttresses the interest of numerous other ("passive") recipients (the public) in receiving news reports (i.e., recipients who participate in the next communication sequence). Indeed, the right to receive information is "an inherent corollary of the rights of free speech and press."[165] And according to the information model's assumptions stated in Chapter 1, recipients per definition do not have to occupy a certain mental state or perform a certain access-oriented conduct in order to be considered as such. By extention, we may assume for the present purpose that the right to receive information generally applies to active and passive recipients alike.

However, the question of the *scope* of the right to receive information has not yet been addressed. To explore the theoretical horizons of that right, we need to clarify the specific duties imposed on the government. Toward this end, three interlocked aspects of state duties should be set forth. First, we should determine whether the state has a duty to *act*, or rather, a duty to *abstain* from action. Second, it should be ascertained as to *which conducts* the duties of action or abstention pertain. Third, it should be clarified under *which circumstances* and with respect to *which beneficiaries* the relevant duties apply.

To provide a framework illustrating the various options, consider a continuum that represents the possible implication of such right on the position of the state. At one extreme of the continuum, the state is obligated to remain completely passive in regard to communicative behavior. This represents a straightforward duty to abstain from burdening originators and from impinging on access-conducts. Such a state obligation shall be called a *duty of inaction*. It is plain a duty of inaction may serve reception interests well. A consistent policy of laissez-faire (zero interference) would leave the information process alone to develop and unfold according to its own intrinsic dynamics and tendencies.

At the other extreme, consider a state duty to mandate communication-conducts in the broad sense (i.e., origination and facilitation), which is designed to increase reception opportunities.[166] For the present purpose, such state obligation shall be called a *duty to coerce*, conceived as a direct policy measure to stimulate the information process and enhance reception.[167] This duty is the

---

165. *See* Bd. of Educ. v. Pico, 457 U.S. 853, 867 (1982).

166. An affirmative obligation to produce messages might sound strange in this context, but it is not unprecedented in others (consider the duty of citizens to submit periodical tax declarations).

167. The idea of the duty to coerce involves a government policy to stimulate the circulation of messages that does not rely exclusively on the individual free will to

diametric opposite of a duty of inaction as it *compels* legislative and administrative initiatives to increase the number of communicated messages circulated and/or spur their dissemination.

In mid-range, consider a state obligation to encourage, facilitate, or support voluntary communication-conducts, particularly the production and communication of medial messages.[168] Such an obligation shall be called a *duty to encourage*. It promotes reception by pursuing strategies to exhaust the potential of voluntary production of messages.[169] The positive impact of such a duty on actual and potential more reception is evident if consequently, more messages will become available to more recipients under more convenient conditions. At this intermediate level, the specific content of the duty (or the particular strategies chosen) remain quite open-ended and subject to government discretion.[170] The successfulness of the strategy can be assessed better or worse reception opportunities in general as compared to access conditions under inaction policy. This thought experiment and its relevancy to the right to receive information is illustrated in Figure 3.1 below:

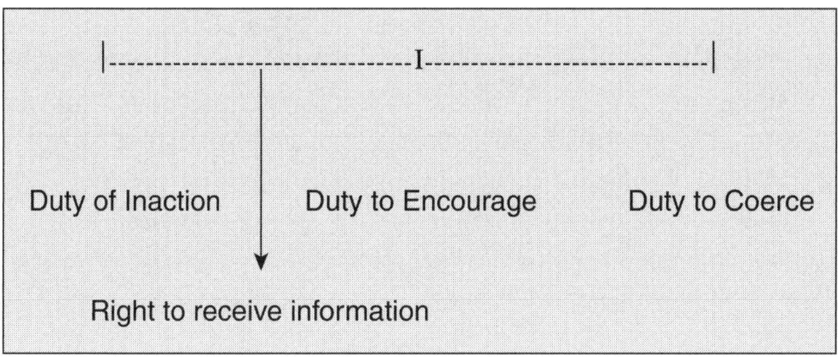

FIGURE 3.1 THE RIGHT TO RECEIVE INFORMATION

communicate or spread information. Regulation that mandates private persons surrender certain information under their control may well be a component of such policy (consider for instance the so-called "must carry rules" in the domain of telecommunication laws.)

168. In actively encouraging speech, governmental incentives to create messages contemplated by this duty to encourage are content-neutral in the sense they do not promote a certain speech based on a point of view, ideology, religious conviction, etc.

169. Possibly, the right to encourage includes a government's duty to produce messages *itself*. Originators could be natural persons who work for the government and its agencies who are assigned originative tasks. In this respect, a government duty to enrich the commons stock of information by producing messages may be part of a broader duty called here the "duty to encourage."

170. The following governmental responsibilities illustrate the kind of actions that may fall under a duty to facilitate and encourage reception: subsidizing and administrating public libraries, fostering education and research, supporting culture and aspiring artists, ensuring telecommunication infrastructure, regulating the price of access to information and communication services, etc.

Figure 3.1 arranges the policy choices on a continuum ranging from inaction to coercion. Clearly, the two extreme poles are theoretical locations rather than practical alternatives. A strict government duty to abstain from any regulation that somehow could restrict the ability to receive information might utterly paralyze the government's ability to fulfill its basic functions. The impossibility of drawing a bright line separating speech acts (where the government must abstain) and nonspeech acts (where the government may regulate) might create a tendency to recognize most regulation as information-relevant, in which event a flat inaction duty would seem ill-advised; fostering communication and access cannot come at the price of anarchy. At the other extreme, coercion of expressions and communication facilitation in general is compatible neither with a democratic government nor with free speech law. First Amendment jurisprudence specifically recognizes the *right to refrain from speaking*, which the Supreme Court read into the constitutional free speech guarantee.[171] The state is further prohibited from interfering with the mental deliberation process and the private thoughts of individuals.[172] Beyond these and other obvious and compelling objections to a hypothetical duty to coerce (e.g., in the area of privacy law), the mechanism of a duty to coerce to enhance access contravenes the very notion of origination. Origination is a free will-driven activity, a manifestation of the subjective desire to communicate[173]—where the effect of a legal duty to speak is likely to have perverse rather than constructive effect on the information process.

As illustrated in Figure 3.1 above, the locus of a constitutional right to receive information likely lies somewhere between a flat government duty of inaction and a duty to encourage voluntary creation, communication, and reception of messages. This position by definition indicates less than a full-range duty to encourage. The reason is that it would seem misleading to assume the core mission of free speech norms centers on compelling the government to actively facilitate production of speech and vigorously encourage communication of messages. The First Amendment is first and foremost a constitutional restriction on governmental speech-abridging actions. In its essence, it is a negative

171. *See* Wooley v. Maynard, 430 U.S. 705 (1977) (U.S. Supreme Court held a state could not constitutionally require an individual to participate in dissemination of an ideological message by displaying it on his private property in a manner and for the express purpose it be observed and read by the public. In particular, it was held the state could not require plaintiffs to display state motto "Live Free or Die" upon their vehicle license plates.).

172. *See* Stanley v. Georgia, 394 U.S. 557, 565 (1969) ("Our whole constitutional heritage rebels at the thought of giving government the power to control men's minds.") The Court further held "[the state] cannot constitutionally premise legislation on the desirability of controlling a person's private thoughts." *Id.* at 566; *but see* Osborn v. Ohio, 495 U.S. 103 (1990) (limiting the application of *Stanley* in cases where the state demonstrated an overriding interest—in this instance, suppression of child pornography).

173. Chapter 1, Section IV.B *supra*.

duty to abstain. The speech the government must not curtail is prone to take place without special encouragement, and free speech law ensures that it in fact will. To be sure, and in light of is negative formulation and characteristics, free speech law typically does not impose *positive* duties on the government, and even according to a generous estimation, the duties it entails concern the government keeping its hands off *free* speech-related activity. As complete abstention has been ruled out as too anarchistic an option, it is likely to find the right to receive information somewhere between the inaction pole and the encouragement middle point.

III. THE TENSION BETWEEN THE FIRST AMENDMENT AND COPYRIGHT LAW

Before we reach the interrelations between free speech law and property rights in information, a preliminary note is advisable. The Hohfeldian methodology structures legal positions in such a way that each entitlement has a correlative position and each entitlement holder has an opponent. The right to receive information is no exception. These analytical assumptions are already built into the present attempt to clarify the scope of that right by seeking to identify the correlative government *duty*. As mentioned, the analysis of access-to-information entitlements varies significantly along the distinction between private and public position holders. The First Amendment imposes limitations directly on *Congress*, and to the extent the First Amendment embodies a right to receive information, the natural duty holder is the public actor. Assuming exclusive rights under copyright law are private entitlements, we may preliminarily inquire whether nonowners attempting to challenge those entitlements can invoke their First Amendment rights in the first place.

In practice, free speech challenges to the enforcement of private entitlements in disputes between private parties often seek to invalidate the opponent's specific claim as irreconcilable with free speech rights.[174] More generally, a litigant may attack the competence of Congress to enact those private entitlements, which arguably conflict with First Amendment principles.[175] As is often mentioned in

174. Analysis of the private/public law interface may vary across legal systems. Hugenholtz commented that European courts are generally reluctant to acknowledge a "horizontal" application of free speech norms, namely, to apply them in private disputes. *See* Hugenholtz, *supra* note 145, at 343 ff & n.12. In U.S. law, a federal court can strike down laws creating private causes of action on First Amendment grounds. *See, e.g.*, The Florida Star *v.* B.J.F., 491 U.S. 524 (1989) (the U.S. Supreme Court held a right of private claim against a newspaper for damages based on invasion of privacy was invalidated by the First Amendment).

175. *See, e.g.*, Eldred v. Ashcroft, 537 U.S. 186 (2003) (petitioners were private actors offering products and services containing public domain works who challenged the Congressional enactment extending copyright protection term by twenty years). Though petitioners' case ultimately failed, they did not fail to state a *recognized* legal claim.

this context, both the free speech rights and federal copyright legislation powers are expressed in the language of the U.S. Constitution. The First Amendment is a categorical command directed at the government not to abridge the freedom of speech and of the press; its language is negative-*affirmative*. By comparison, the Copyright Clause provides an optional mandate; its language is positive-*permissive*.[176] The mere fact the Constitution principally permits exclusive rights in works obviously does not eliminate the possibility of friction between such rights and the free speech guarantee.[177] One related question is whether free speech law imposes any affirmative limitation on the power of the legislature to enact copyright rules, and if so, how both disciplines can operate harmoniously within a single constitutional framework.[178]

The study of potential and actual friction between free speech law and copyright has a relatively brief history, and the U.S. experience in this field is telling: Scholarly attention arose in the early 1970s with the publication of several academic articles that, for the first time, evaluated the prospects of tension between the First Amendment and copyright law.[179] Early Anglo-American property and free speech theories shared a similar historical background—namely, the desire to curtail censorship.[180] Zimmerman suggested both disciplines shared a common vision: the establishment of less paternalistic relationships between

---

176. The Copyright Clause vests in Congress the *power* to enact copyright legislation, but at least from plain reading, the government is not *obligated* to do so under this clause.

177. *See* Diane L. Zimmerman, *Information as Speech, Information on Goods: Some Thoughts on Marketplaces and the First Amendment*, 33 William & Mary L. Rev. 665, 705 n.282 (1992) ("When statutory copyright is at issue . . . the property right is provided for by the Constitution, just as the Constitution guarantees free speech. That both are constitutionally based does not mean, however, that conflicts between them evaporate or can be resolved at will in favor of one or the other.").

178. For an early analysis, see Robert C. Denicola, *Copyright and Free Speech: Limitations on the Protection of Expression*, 67 Cal. L. Rev. 283 (1979).

179. *See* Melville B. Nimmer, *Does Copyright Abridge the First Amendment Guarantees of Free Speech and Press?* 17 UCLA L. Rev. 1180 (1970); Paul Goldstein, *Copyright and the First Amendment*, 70 Colum. L. Rev. 983 (1970); Lionel S. Sobel, *Copyright and the First Amendment: A Gathering Storm?* 19 Copyright L. Symp. (ASCAP) 43 (1971).

180. *See* SunTrust Bank v. Houghton Mifflin Co., 268 F.3d 1257, 1263 (11th Cir. 2001) ("The Copyright Clause and the First Amendment, while intuitively in conflict, were drafted to work together to prevent censorship; copyright laws were enacted in part to prevent private censorship and the First Amendment was enacted to prevent public censorship.") (citations omitted). For a historical background on the First Amendment as a measure suppressing government censorship, see Rodney A. Smolla, Smolla & Nimmer on Freedom of Speech §§ 1.1–1.2 (3d ed. 2008). Not everyone agrees on the "original intent" of the First Amendment and its relevance to free speech law today. *Id.* (suggesting the search for the "original meaning" of the First Amendment is "illusive" and noting the controversy surrounding its "original intent").

the government and citizens.[181] Classic liberal tradition saw no discrepancy between the protection of private property and guaranteeing civil liberties such as free speech.[182] The notion of freedom of speech has rarely been considered a challenge directed against the right to private property, especially regarding more conventional forms of property applied to physical resources.

In the context of the interaction between free speech and copyright law, the "market place of ideas" metaphor ranks high.[183] In this context, so long as copyrights attach only to original expressions and not to the raw material of speech or ideas, the prospects of peaceful coexistence with constitutional speech protection might appear promising, because copyright would not curtail the intellectual market as it leaves the creation and circulation of ideas unaffected by its restrictions.

Reality proved more complicated, however. Defendants in copyright infringement litigations have been experiencing increasing pressure on what they consider their legitimate communicative activities safeguarded by the First Amendment. In the United States, numerous defendants have raised the argument that enforcing copyright law impeded their free speech rights. Birnhack's study investigated the way such arguments fared in U.S. courts by outlining a number of judicial patterns in trying to deal with the problem.[184] One pattern has been to deny the possibility of a conflict based on interpretation of the constitutional structure, historic background, and intention of the Framers.[185] A second approach rejecting the conflict assumed two separate, distinctive areas of the law governed by two separate constitutional norms that always run *parallel*

---

181. Zimmerman, *supra* note 177, at 678 ("[M]ost of the early writings about freedom of speech focused upon problems of prior restraints and the punishment by the government of speech critical of it or damaging to its interests. Insulation of this sort of speech from official sanction was seen, as were protections for private property rights, as securing a changed relationship between citizen and government. A sovereign citizen was entitled to expect the government to respect and guarantee free speech as a right rather than as a revocable privilege and also to respect the freedom to criticize the officials who owed their power to the citizenry.") (footnotes omitted).

182. In words attributed to Thomas Gordon: "The Security of Property; and the Freedom of Speech, always go together; and in those wretched Countries where a Man cannot call his Tongue his own, he can scarce call any thing else his own"). *See* Cato's Letter No. 15, *Of Freedom of Speech: That the Same is Inseparable from Publick Liberty*, Feb. 4, 1720.

183. *See* Abrams v. United States, 250 U.S. 616, 630 (1919) (Holmes, J., dissenting). *See also* SMOLLA, *supra* note 180, § 2:4 ff. (elaborating on the centrality of this idea within First Amendment theory and justification).

184. *See* Michael D. Birnhack, *The Copyright Law and Free Speech Affair: Making-Up and Breaking-Up*, 43 IDEA: J. L. & TECH. 233 (2003).

185. *Id.* at 236 ff. *See also* Michael Birnhack, *Copyright Law and Free Speech after Eldred v. Ashcroft*, 76 UNIV. SO. CAL. L. REV. 1275 (2003).

to each other, not *against* one another.[186] According to this interpretation, the coexistence of speech and property norms in the constitutional scheme implies neither overlap nor friction. Another related method undermining the intensity of the contradiction has been to underscore the common goal of both regimes (i.e., to enrich society's stock of information and knowledge). Thus, in promoting a more robust and diverse "marketplace of ideas," the thrusts of free speech and copyright protection were said to converge. Accordingly, the task of copyright law is to foster the creation of messages, whereas the mission of the First Amendment is to make sure the government does not unduly encroach upon their free circulation. In perhaps the most celebrated formulation of this vision, the U.S. Supreme Court in *Harper & Row v. Nation* stated that by fostering a robust marketplace of ideas and information to the benefit of the public and authors alike, copyright is in fact an "engine of free expression."[187]

A chord sounded in the Supreme Court's free speech/copyright jurisprudence by way of the *Aldred v. Ashcroft* decision, in which the Court explicitly acknowledged the possibility of a conflict.[188] In rejecting the lower court's statement that copyright legislation is "categorically immune from challenges under the First Amendment,"[189] the Court practically abolished the interpretational pattern that ignored any incongruity up-front.[190] The significance of *Eldred* to the ongoing debate is manifold. On some critical issues the Court remained sufficiently ambivalent to preclude informed predictions on the broad ramifications of the decision. That said, two central points were delivered quite straightforwardly. First, the Court recognized the potential for a direct collision between speech interests and copyright norms. Second, it acknowledged the possibility of free speech constraints on copyright legislation.

---

186. *See* Zimmerman, *supra* note 177, at 666–69 & 684 (observing "courts were actively attempting to define and preserve separate spheres for copyright and First Amendment values").

187. *See* Harper & Row v. Nation Enter. 471 U.S. 539, 558 (1985) ("In our haste to disseminate news, it should not be forgotten that the Framers intended copyright itself to be the engine of free expression. By establishing a marketable right to the use of one's expression, copyright supplies the economic incentive to create and disseminate ideas.") This argument somewhat resembles the "duty to encourage" rationale in the context of the right to receive information. Paradoxically, the right to receive information is served by a legal mechanism that reduces access opportunity in the short run. In other words, the enacting of copyright laws is actually conceived as a component of the governmental "duty" (or constitutional mission) to facilitate broader access to information (in the long run). This has been the prevalent approach of the U.S. Supreme Court to the free speech/copyright friction.

188. *See* Eldred v. Ashcroft, 537 U.S. 186 (2003).

189. *See* Eldred v. Reno, 239 F.3d. 372, 375 (D.C. Cir. 2001).

190. Eldred v. Ashcroft, 537 U.S. at 221.

While discussing the friction issue, *Eldred* reiterated the familiar argument depicting a harmonious picture of copyright exclusivity and free speech: "[C]opyright's purpose is to promote the creation and publication of free expression."[191] Citing *Harper & Row*, the *Eldred* Court invoked the metaphor of copyright law as the "engine" of free expression.[192] The majority opinion in *Eldred* stated the copyright law itself incorporates free speech safeguards: "To the extent such assertions raise First Amendment concerns, copyright's built-in free speech safeguards are generally adequate to address them."[193] The two "built-in free speech safeguards" are the so-called idea/expression dichotomy and the fair use doctrine. The former is said to strike a "definitional balance between the First Amendment and the Copyright Act by permitting free communication of facts while still protecting an author's expression."[194] The latter is said to support free speech interests by allowing use of the copyrighted expressions themselves in some situations.[195] The Court depicted these internal copyright mechanisms as constituting copyright's "built-in First Amendment accommodations." Though the Court indicated the built-in safeguards are "generally adequate" to address First Amendment concerns,[196] it seems to have left the door open for *special* situations where this may not be the case. Additionally, the Court held that presently, further First Amendment scrutiny beyond the built-in accommodations is not required as long as Congress does not alter "the traditional contours of copyright protection."[197]

To recap the main Supreme Court's observations, two types of copyright mechanisms secure free speech interests: the classic subject matter rule excluding "negative" information categories (ideas, systems, methods, etc.)[198] and an open mechanism of exceptions (fair use).[199] Some commentators read in this last

191. *Id.* at 219.

192. *Id.*

193. *Id.* at 221.

194. *Id.* at 189 (citing Harper & Row v. Nation Enter., 471 U.S. 539 (1985)).

195. Eldred v. Ashcroft, at 190 ("'Fair use' thereby affords considerable latitude for scholarship and comment . . . and even for parody") (citations omitted). Interestingly, the Court hinted First Amendment protections might bear less heavily when speakers seek to make free use of *other people's* speech: "The First Amendment securely protects the freedom to make—or decline to make—one's own speech; it bears less heavily when speakers assert the right to make other people's speeches." *Id.* at 191.

196. *Id.* at 121.

197. *Id.*

198. Chapter 1, Section V.A.1.(c) (explaining the notion of "negative categories").

199. The Court's analysis begs the following question, which cannot be addressed here in length: what is so special about the fair use and the idea/expression distinction that distinguishes them from other copyright limitations and exemptions in general? Also other exemptions that—from the perspective of their beneficiaries—unchain information

"traditional contours" comment an implied warning to Congress not to substantially deviate from copyright's "traditional contours,"[200] lest copyright legislation be subject to heightened First Amendment scrutiny. To the extent Congress indeed must preserve the traditional contours, the impact of this limitation would obviously depend on the definition of those "traditional contours of copyright protection." Thus far, the issue has been tested three times in federal courts when post-*Eldred* litigants raised the "traditional contours" argument. Two courts rejected the argument,[201] whereas the third was more sympathetic—the Tenth Circuit in *Golan v. Gonzales* agreed to remand the case on the basis that Congress might have stepped outside the constitutional mandate by restoring protection in certain public domain works.[202]

IV. A FIRST AMENDMENT RIGHT TO ACCESS COPYRIGHTED INFORMATION?

The full range of issues entangled with free speech limitations on copyright law cannot be addressed here. This study also does not reach the question whether as the law stands today, the idea/expression distinction and the fair use doctrine (with its stark emphasis on transformativeness)[203] can provide sufficient security to speech interests.[204] The *Eldred* decision may indeed have opened a new chapter, marking a significant turning point in the interrelations between free speech and copyright law in the United States. However, it is equally plausible it has not. The language used by the Supreme Court and its overall treatment makes it difficult to offer a solid prognosis about the law, particularly as the question continues to be litigated in courts. Within the larger debate concerning free speech limitations on copyright law, the right to *receive* information has acquired

---

from private exclusivity entitlements can be said to bolster speech opportunities. Why should the limitation on duration not qualify as a "third" copyright built-in safeguard securing speech interests?

200. *Cf.* Lawrence Lessig, *Does Copyright Have Limits?:* Eldred v Ashcroft *and Its Aftermath*, 5 Queensland Univ. Tech. L. & Justice J. 219, 227 (2005).

201. Both disputes concerned the retroactive coverage of copyright as to foreign works that have already entered the public domain in the United States for failing to meet formalities. In both cases, the courts rejected the argument various legislation had violated the "traditional contours" limitation. *See* Kahle v. Gonzales, 487 F.3d. 697 (9th Cir. 2007); Luck's Music v. Ashcroft, 321 F.Supp. 2d. 107 (D.D.C. 2004).

202. *See* Golan v. Gonzales, 501 F.3d. 1179 (10th Cir. 2007) (Tenth Circuit held the Uruguay Round Agreement Act of 1994 [URAA], particularly its provision restoring copyright protection to certain foreign works that had fallen into public domain, was subject to First Amendment scrutiny). See also, *Golan v. Holders*, 609 F.3d 1076 (10th. Cir. 2010) (holding that the URAA passes intermediate First Amendment scrutiny.)

203. *See, e.g.*, Campbell v. Acuff-Rose Music, Inc. 510 U.S. 569 (1994).

204. *See* Rebecca Tushnet, *Copy This Essay: How Fair Use Doctrine Harms Free Speech and How Copying Serves it*, 114 Yale L.J. 535 (2004) (criticizing the criterion of transformativeness in U.S. fair use doctrine).

only minor significance, if at all.[205] At least in the United States, a situation in which a *nonowner* personally challenges a copyright rule by forwarding the argument that copyright law *violates her right to receive information* hardly ever came under significant judicial scrutiny.[206] Assuming copyright law indeed increases the costs of access to information (sometimes to a prohibitive level), such argument would seem to have at least some persuasive force in light of the relatively weak affirmative protection the Supreme Court has awarded the "right to receive information,"[207] especially when it comes to private disputes in which the right-of-access claimant seeks to justify injury against an established entitlement held by his opponent.[208]

---

205. For a comparative (and similar) assessment by a European commentator, see de Werra, *supra* note 79, at 117 ("there appears to be very limited room for granting access to copyright protected content based on constitutional arguments deriving from freedom of expression and/or freedom of information . . . it should be noted that [] German, French and Austrian court decisions [cited by commentators] relate essentially to the issue of unauthorized . . . use . . . and do not relate to the issue of unauthorized access to the relevant work") (emphasis in original).

206. The facts in *California Satellite Systems* come quite close. In that case, a pay-TV company brought an action against an individual who had circumvented coded transmissions. The district court found this activity in violation of a telecommunication regulation that prohibited circumvention of encrypted transmissions. On appeal before the Ninth Circuit, appellant argued, inter alia, that the injunction violated his First Amendment "right to listen" to a "noninfringing communication." The Ninth Circuit held: "Although the defendant's First Amendment argument may have some validity in the abstract, on the facts of this case we find it unpersuasive . . . Defendant's [signal decryption] equipment was at all pertinent times directed to the plaintiff's transmitter. The district court specifically found that the sole and exclusive use to which the defendant has put his equipment is the unlawful pirating of plaintiff's signal. Defendant enjoys no right of access to this use." California Satellite Sys. v. Seimon, 767 F.2d. 1364, 1368 (9th. Cir. 1985). Note appellant did not challenge copyright law, but rather a general telecommunication-anticircumvention provision. In another case, it took the Ninth Circuit only a brief discussion to reject the argument that certain photographs with news value are precluded copyright protection due to the public's right to access important news information. *See* Los Angeles News Serv. v. Tullo, 973 F.2d. 791, 795–96 (9th. Cir. 1992).

207. *See, e.g.*, Marci A. Hamilton & Clemens G. Kohnen, *The Jurisprudence of Information Flow: How the Constitution Constructs the Pathways of Information*, 25 CARDOZO L. REV. 267, 269–70, 330 (2003) (arguing Supreme Court jurisprudence underpins a weak right to access information and "that information flow is valuable is often a misplaced instinct").

208. In a decision rendered by the Fourth Circuit, the court upheld liability of news reporters for a breach of duty of loyalty and trespass. Those reporters worked for a food company and in the course of their employment gathered information on their employer's controversial practices. The reporters were found liable despite their First Amendment "right to access information" as press persons. *See* Food Lion, Inc. v. Capital Cities, 194 F.3d 505 (4th. Cir. 1999).

The interesting aspect is that even if post-*Eldred* courts attempted in the future to apply the notions of "built-in First Amendment accommodations" and "traditional contours" in this context, they would have to overcome a very serious hurdle: *neither the idea/expression distinction nor fair use provide affirmative protection to a concrete claim to receive information.* To use the terminology explained earlier in this chapter, these doctrines apply solely to communication-conducts, not to access-conducts. Further, there is little indication in copyright law's "traditional contours" that access-conducts should trump valid copyrights. When the giants of copyright exclusivity and free speech law clash, the constitutional entitlement to receive information (insofar as it exists) is too abstract and aloft to play a meaningful role in the struggle. Recipients are likely to discover they have neither standing nor an enforceable cause of action against the state or private rights-holders to vindicate their right to receive information.

If we remember that the exclusive rights are structurally directed to capture communication-conducts rather than access-conducts,[209] this outcome is hardly surprising. Copyright's exclusive rights and the limitations thereto are simply not designed to solve directly the access problem of nonowners. Rather, protection of their access interests is always achieved "over their heads" by discounting the scope of exclusive rights vis-à-vis communicators, which often proves ineffective from the nonowners' standpoint. For most practical purposes, the right to receive information is not much more than a *non-statutory privilege to access information if you can.* In other words, it is a tacit right-of-access in the weak form, bolstered with some constitutional flair. The First Amendment jurisprudence–celebrating reception of information as "fundamental" and "an inherent corollary of the rights of free speech and press" in practice does not change the conclusion the First Amendment (and perhaps free speech law in general) is not necessarily the first place to start digging in the search for effective (and enforceable) rights-of-access.

(d) Human Rights Law

A sense of crisis in the area of intellectual property law has been contributing to the influx of proposals calling for the integration of human rights perspectives. Some intellectual property scholars advocate for shifting the attention to human rights in a quest for guidance and inspiration.[210] The rise of human rights as a

---

209. Section III.A.3.(b) *supra.*

210. Among many others, *see, e.g.*, Audrey R. Chapman, *Intellectual Property and the Right to Culture, in* INTELLECTUAL PROPERTY AND HUMAN RIGHTS, WIPO Panel Discussion to commemorate the 50th Anniversary of the Universal Declaration of Human Rights, Geneva, Nov. 9, 988 (1999) (available at http://www.wipo.int/tk/en/activities/1998/humanrights/papers/word/steiner.doc); Peter Drahos, *The Universality of Intellectual Property Rights: Origins and Development,* INTELLECTUAL PROPERTY & HUMAN RIGHTS, WIPO Publication No. 762(E) (1999); Orit Fischman Afori, *Human Rights and Copyright: The Introduction of Natural Law Considerations into American Coypright Law,* 14 FORDHAM

topic in the intellectual property debate has several explanations, among them being the universal aura of human rights principles and their promise to bestow more consensus and harmony upon vexing and deeply controversial intellectual property issues.[211] Universality, which is inherent to the concept of human rights, has become central also to intellectual property in the wake of globalization trends and the rise of the Internet.[212]

As in numerous other contexts, the unique nature of information and its significance in modern life marks the problematic intersection points between human rights and intellectual property. Freedom of information as a sanctified ideal enjoyed recognition concurrently with the inception of the international movement after World War II striving to establish human rights as a legal discipline.[213] As information came to be considered an essential (or primary) resource in the modern global economy,[214] and upon acknowledgment of information's crucial role in satisfying a variety of human needs ranging from self-subsistence to self-fulfillment, the overlaps between human rights law and private entitlement to information become evident. At the same time, the stakes, importance, and role of property law (and its application to information subject matter) within the human rights rubric are not quite dissimilar, and to the extent intellectual property imposes restrictions on "freedom of information," the potential for conflict between the two species of rights looms large.[215]

Proposals to adopt human rights perspectives for intellectual property often speak in terms of providing a human rights "framework" for intellectual

---

INTELL PROP. MEDIA & ENTM'T 497 (2004); Peter K. Yu, *Reconceptualizing Intellectual Property Interests in a Human Rights Framework*, 40 U.C. DAVIS L. REV. 1039 (2007); Laurence R. Helfer, *Toward a Human Rights Framework for Intellectual Property* 40 U.C. DAVIS. L. REV. 971 (2007); Graeme W. Austin & Amy G. Zavidow, *Copyright Law Reform Through a Human Rights Lens*, *in* INTELLECTUAL PROPERTY AND HUMAN RIGHTS 257 (Paul L.C. Torremans ed., 2008).

211. *See* Drahos, *supra* note 210. Some find the historical separation between human rights and intellectual property law enigmatic in the first place. *See, e.g.*, Laurence R. Helfer, *Human Rights and Intellectual Property: Conflict or Coexistence?* 5 MINN. INTELL. PROP. REV. 47, 49 (2003) (observing "[i]t is something of a mystery why intellectual property and human rights have remained strangers for so long").

212. *Cf.* Drahos, *supra* note 210, at 15–23 (surveying the history and evolution of IP law from the territorial period through the international period into our global period).

213. For example, Resolution 59(I) of the U.N. General Assembly declared: "Freedom of information is a fundamental human right and is the touchstone of all the freedoms to which the United Nations is consecrated." *See* U.N. General Assembly Resolution 59(I) (1946). That resolution further states "[f]reedom of information implies the right to gather, transmit, and publish news anywhere and everywhere without fetters." *Id.*

214. *See* Reto M. Hilty, *Copyright Law and the Information Society—Neglected Adjustments and Their Consequences*, 38 INT'L REV. INDUSTRIAL PROP. & COPYRIGHT L. 135, 136 (2007) (noting that scientific information acquires the character of "essential facility").

215. *Cf.* Drahos, *supra* note 210, at 14.

property law and policy in face of the currently "skeletal and under-theorized" exposition of intellectual property norms in human rights law.[216] Indeed, some scholars have launched considerable efforts to articulate that framework and its ramifications. The primary relevance of this development is rooted in its possible impact on the availability of effective rights-of-access. The issue can be framed as follows: does human right law underpin rights-of-access, and if so, what are the implications in the context of copyright law?

1. UNDERPINNING A HUMAN RIGHT TO ACCESS INFORMATION

Human rights norms are noteworthy for explicitly acknowledging the general right to access or receive information with an affirmative voice that is sometimes absent from domestic constitutional texts. Article 27(1) to the Universal Declaration of Human Rights of 1948 (UDHR) provides that "everyone has the right freely to participate in the cultural life of the community, to enjoy the arts and to share in scientific advancement and its benefits."[217] If access to cultural accomplishments is part of, or a precondition to free participation, enjoyment, and sharing, this language could provide a normative foundation to a right-of-access entitlement. The norm promotes the ideal that culture should be accessible to every person. A recognized entitlement to access cultural achievements is an essential component of the entitlement to *actively* participate in social and cultural exchange. This "access and participation" principle is said to be an important element in the catalog of individual "cultural rights."[218]

One UNESCO document from 1976 provides an important and lucid account of the access entitlement embodied in Article 27(1): "[B]y access to culture is meant the concrete opportunities available to everyone, in particular through the creation of the appropriate socio-economic conditions, for freely obtaining information, training, knowledge and understanding, and for enjoying cultural values and cultural property."[219] The UNESCO recommendations further attribute an affirmative dimension to Article 27(1): "[B]y participation in cultural life is meant the concrete opportunities guaranteed for all—groups or individuals—to express themselves freely, to communicate, act, and engage in creative activities with a view to the full development of their personalities, a harmonious life and the cultural progress of society."[220] It may follow governments are *obligated* to

---

216. *See* Helfer, *supra* note 210, at 976 ff.

217. Universal Declaration of Human Rights (1948), Art. 27(1). The UDRH is said to have "constitutionalized" the human rights regime. *See* Drahos, *supra* note 210, at 24.

218. *See* Afori, *supra* note 210, at 508–09 (providing an overview and collection of sources on the concept of "cultural rights"). *See also* Chapman, *supra* note 210.

219. *See* UNESCO Recommendation on Participation by the People in Cultural Life (1976), Art. I.2(a) (emphasis added).

220. *Id.* Art. I.2(b).

guarantee access opportunities as a matter of their general commitment to secure basic human rights.[221]

The inextricable nexus between the right to receive information and free speech rights also surfaces in the human rights domain. The UDHR articulates free speech rights separately: however. Article 19 to the Universal Declaration provides "[e]veryone has the right to freedom of opinion and expression; this right includes freedom to hold opinions without interference and to seek, receive and impart information and ideas through any media and regardless of frontiers."[222] The apparent overlap between Article 27(1) and Article 19 confirms once again the intimate and complex interrelations between access, communication, and information,[223] with the underlying recognition being that access is the temporal and logical prerequisite for the realization of any speech or cultural participation right.

The International Covenant on Economic, Social and Cultural Rights of 1966 (ICESCR) is yet another key source for human rights norms, and for cultural rights in particular.[224] Ratified by more that 150 nations, the ICESCR builds on the text of the UDHR and proclaims everyone's right "[t]o take part in cultural life"[225] and "[t]o enjoy the benefits of scientific progress and its applications."[226] The ICESCR further instructs states parties to take "steps. . .to achieve the full realization of this right. . .include[ing] those necessary for the conservation, the development and the diffusion of science and culture."[227] These provisions once again reinforce the recognition the full realization of a right to benefit from cultural and scientific progress encapsulates facilitation of access to information by individuals and communities.[228] European human rights law follows closely behind. The European human rights instruments create a complex and elaborate

221. The recommendations to governments concerning specific legislation and regulations are enumerated in Art. II. Among other things, governments must adopt legislation or regulations to "guarantee as human rights those rights bearing on access to and participation in cultural life, in the spirit of the Universal Declaration of Human Rights." *Id.* Art. II.4(a).

222. *See* Universal Declaration of Human Rights (1948), Art. 19.

223. *Cf.* UNESCO Recommendation on Participation by the People in Cultural Life (1976), Art. I.2(c) (defining *communication* as "relations between groups or individuals desirous of freely exchanging or pooling information, ideas and knowledge with a view to promoting dialogue, concerted action, understanding and a sense of community while respecting their originality and their differences, in order to strengthen mutual understanding and peace").

224. *See* International Covenant on Economic, Social and Cultural Rights (1966).

225. *Id.* Art. 15.1(a).

226. *Id.* Art. 15.1(b).

227. *Id.* Art. 15(2).

228. *Cf.* Chapman, *supra* note 210, at 128.

matrix of norms[229] in which cultural rights are also safeguarded. Article 10(1) of the European Convention on Human Rights of 1950 (ECHR) declares: "Everyone has the right to freedom of expression. This right shall include freedom to hold opinions and to receive and impart information and ideas without interference by public authority and regardless of frontiers."[230] This provision exemplifies a free speech norm that equally emphasizes both the right to communicate and the right to receive communication. More recently, Article 11(1) of the European Charter of Fundamental Rights repeats verbatim the quoted language of Article 10(1) of the European Convention.[231]

II. SELECTED CHALLENGES

In drawing on a human rights framework in support of more unyielding rights-of-access, we must address a number of complications. The most obvious hurdle is that many human rights instruments espouse not only access and communication entitlements but explicitly recognize *authors' rights as human rights*. Article 27(2) UDHR champions everyone's "right to the protection of the moral and material interests resulting from any scientific, literary or artistic production of which he is the author."[232] Article 15(1)(c) to the ICESCR obligates states parties to recognize everyone's right "[t]o benefit from the protection of the moral and material interests resulting from any scientific, literary or artistic production of which he is the author."[233] Also, Article 10 to the ECHR, which enshrines the freedom to receive and impart information and ideas, foresees limitations on those rights in the case of conflict with the rights of others.[234] The emerging general picture is that human rights instruments expressly proclaim authors'

229. *See* Christopher McCrudden, *The Future of the EU Charter of Fundamental Rights*, Jean Monnet Working Paper No. 10/012–5 (2002) (providing an informative background on the development of human rights agendas in Europe). As regarding the universal aspiration of European instruments, *see id.* at 6 (noting the European Convention on Human Rights developed as a regional manifestation of an internationalist human rights movement during the days of the cold war).

230. *See* European Convention on Human Rights (1950), Art. 10(1).

231. *See* European Charter of Fundamental Rights (2000), Art. 11(1). The Charter is planned as part of a future European constitution, and Art. 11(1) of the Charter is currently Art. II. 71 of the draft constitution. For background and analysis on the adoption of the Charter, *see* McCrudden, *supra* note 229.

232. *See* Universal Declaration of Human Rights (1948), Art. 27(2).

233. *See* International Covenant on Economic, Social and Cultural Rights (1966), Art. 15(1)(c).

234. European Convention on Human Rights (1950), Art. 10(2) ("The exercise of these freedoms, since it carries with it duties and responsibilities, may be subject to such formalities, conditions, restrictions or penalties as are prescribed by law and are necessary in a democratic society . . . for the protection of the reputation or rights of others, for preventing the disclosure of information received in confidence, or for maintaining the authority and impartiality of the judiciary.") (emphasis added).

rights and principally tolerate limitations on communication and reception rights in the name of intellectual property protection.

The situation in which both access to information and copyright law are simultaneously recognized as human rights raises a concern that may be called the *horizontal interface problem.* In this situation, two or more human rights norms arguably having equal status and weight are on a collision course with each other. But before reaching that concern, it is advisable for us to take a step back and ask once again: Are intellectual property rights indeed human rights at all? Is *private property in general* a human right? A positive answer to the second question enjoys a braod consensus, though is not immune against critical moral and philosophical objections.[235] The critique tends to be more serious as we shift the focus to rights secured under intellectual property legislation. Do such rights deserve the aura of universality and absoluteness attributed to human rights?[236] Would it be appropriate to place copyright's exclusive right to prevent unauthorized copying on the same footing with the most fundamental human rights such as the entitlements to life, food, medicine, or shelter?[237]

As we move to consider the specific domain of copyright law, some aspects of copyright protection appear to have only a weak nexus to human rights, if at all, especially when their exclusive owners are not at all "human" but rather corporations. For instance, how does a doctrine such as work-for-hire (granting initial copyrights to corporate employers) fare under a human rights framework? Without our embarking onto a detailed discussion, human rights analysis often attends to the distinction between entitlements recognized under personality and authors' rights (*droit d'auteur*) approaches on the one hand, and economic

---

235. *See* Leonard W. Levy, *Property as a Human Right,* 5 CONST. COMMENTARY 169, 174 (1988) (noting "Americans of the founding generation . . . regarded property as a basic human right, essential to one's existence, to one's independence, to one's dignity as a person. Without property, real and personal, one could not enjoy life or liberty, and could not be free and independent"). *Compare* Jim W. Harris, *Is Property a Human Right? in* PROPERTY AND THE CONSTITUTION 66, 85–87 (Janet McClean ed., 1999) (observing "[t]he background property right is historically situated. It is not a timeless natural right . . . the background right is now a human right. The well-being of every citizen of a modern state requires that his or her society should maintain a property institution . . . property, in the scale of human well-being, ranks below life, but alongside liberty. Nevertheless, the holdings vested in any particular person at any particular time are stamped, morally, with a contestable and mutable mix of property-specific justice reasons. Only in that presumptive (and weak) sense do I have a human right to my possessions").

236. *Cf.* Paul L. C. Torremans, *Copyright as a Human Right, in* COPYRIGHT AND HUMAN RIGHTS: FREEDOM OF EXPRESSION, INTELLECTUAL PROPERTY, PRIVACY (Paul L. Torremans ed., 2004) (proposing a human rights underpinning to copyright); Michel Vivant, *Le droit d'auteur, un droit de l'homme,* 174 RIDA 71 (1997).

237. *See* Drahos, *supra* note 210, at 30–31 (noting "[h]aving one's artwork copied is not the same as being stripped of one's bedding, food, medicine or other personal possession that for the essentials of daily existence").

rights on the other. The philosophy of universal human rights is said to be moral-natural law based, which endows human rights their universal affinity and sustainability against state legislation and actions that contradict human rights principles. Human rights, as natural rights, subsist in every human individual regardless of nation, nationality, or controlling laws.[238] As such, copyright protection underpinned by personality interests and natural rights seems to ideologically fit better within human rights frameworks as compared to economic-utilitarian based rationales. (The discussion on Article 15.1(c) ICESCR below nicely illustrates the tension between the two families of copyright tradtions in the context of the notion of copyrights as human rights.)

This brief discussion does not attempt to prove or disprove the argument that exclusive rights under copyright are (or have the same status as) human rights. However, the following point should be made: probably the most important potential contribution of a human rights framework to the copyright debate is in crystallizing (perhaps even redefining) the position of *nonowners*. In light of considerable expansion in copyright protection during the past two decades (discussed at length in Chapters 4–6), concerns of copyright's *overprotection* called for a meaningful response—much more than possible under-protection risks.[239] Bluntly put, rights-holders do not seem to need human rights arguments to bring about a mind-shift and bolster their position under the positive law as it stands today.[240] The arsenal of exclusive rights is already quite impressive, and currently shows no signs of deflation. The entitlements of rights-holders are presently carved in numerous domestic, regional, and international legal instruments,[241] and adding human rights rationales and legal instruments on

---

238. *See* Chapman, *supra* note 210, at 132; Afori, *supra* note 210, at 507.

239. For the specific application of human rights perspectives in connection with under-protection arguments related to the rights of indigenous people, *see* Helfer, *supra* note 211, at 52–54. These considerations are left outside the scope of the present discussion.

240. The reference is to rights-holders *in general*. Chapter 1 highlighted the divergent interests of originators/authors on the one hand and derivative rights-holders on the other. Some human rights advocates argue their approach could help to improve the position of authors vis-à-vis commercial exploiters as well as in general. This may be true, but the argument advanced here is that rights-holders *as a group* (as opposed to nonowners *as a group*) do not need human rights to improve their general position against nonowners. The same cannot be said about nonowners, however.

241. Kaplan wrote in 1967: "[W]hen copyright has gone wrong in recent years, it has been by taking itself too seriously. . . I confess myself to be more worried about excessive than insufficient protection." *See* BENJAMIN KAPLAN, AN UNHURRIED VIEW OF COPYRIGHT 78 (1967). These words ring as relevant and as compelling today as they did decades ago. *See also* Reto M. Hilty, *Eldred v. Ashcroft: Die Schutzfrist im Urheberecht—eine Diskussion, die auch Europäer interessieren sollte,* GRUR 201, 204 (2003) (discussing the persistent call both in the United States and Europe for more protection in the context of copyright duration).

top for purpose of showing *why* and *how* exclusive rights should be legally protected might miss the most important role human rights could play in the political and legislative debate. The real significance of human rights rests in their potential impact on the way we perceive rights-of-access, not exclusive copyrights. And the actual impact of human rights-based rights-of-access norms will depend on the extent of their influence on and reflection in the positive law.

This recognition brings us to the *vertical interface* problem, which refers to the tension between "soft" human rights and cultural participation norms on the one hand, and "hard" intellectual property rules on the other.[242] The vertical interface requires legislatures to consolidate their copyright laws with the norms of public access rights and cultural participation. The puzzle lies in determining how far the "universal" access norms could and should affect domestic copyright laws. Problems already begin with the term *cultural rights* itself. Drahos pointed out a possible internal-terminological contradiction, encapsulating two conflicting ideas: one of private "rights" and the other of common, open "culture."[243] Further, "cultural rights" might represent two rather opposite meanings. The first concerns *proprietary* claims of peoples in their cultural heritage, whereas the second concerns cultural *diffusion*, recognizing local cultures as being part of a larger global cultural tradition, a universal common, to which all humans should have some access entitlement.[244] Either way, both meanings do not seem to fit smoothly within Western intellectual property traditions granting private exclusory rights in subject matters named "cultural goods."

One relevant aspect of the vertical interface problem concerns precisely the tension between copyright exclusory entitlements and access entitlements emanating from cultural rights as human rights. A second layer of issues concern textual interpretation of the various human rights norms noted above. One commentator, referring to the wording of the European Charter on Human Rights, described the text as a "combination of pastiche, compromise and studied ambiguity."[245] This observation aptly describes the formulation of human rights provisions in general. To illustrate the last point, consider Article 15.1(a) ICESCR

---

242. *See* Drahos, *supra* note 210. Drahos described human rights instruments as "exist[ing] in the twilight zone of normativity known to international lawyers as soft law." *See also* Afori, *supra* note 210, at 517–20.

243. Drahos, *supra* note 210, at 28.

244. *Id.*

245. McCrudden, *supra* note 229, at 7. Alson identified "norm clarification" as one of the central challenges to the ICESC Committee; *see* Philip Alston, *Out of the Abyss: The Challenges Confronting the New U.N. Committee on Economic, Social and Cultural Rights*, 9 HUM. RTS. Q. 335, 351–55 (1987) ("[o]ne of the most striking features of the Covenant [ICESCR] is the vagueness of the normative implications of the various rights it recognizes").

that stipulates the right of cultural participation.[246] Chapman argues this provision imposes a positive obligation on states parties to guarantee at least the right of equal access to beneficial scientific and technological developments.[247] She argues for a nondiscrimination element protecting, inter alia, against discrimination in the diffusion of knowledge in society on the basis of financial standing.[248] At the same time, copyright protection is based precisely on the idea of securing for rights-holders the opportunity to charge supercompetitive prices for certain acts that facilitate access to works, or prohibit those acts altogether. If the upshot of copyright protection is a higher price being placed on access in general, it will embody a built-in discrimination against the less financially able.

With the range depicted in Figure 3.1 in mind,[249] the question should read: where is the locus of the government's duty to secure cultural rights that depend on access to information on the continuum between a duty of inaction and a duty to encourage? An expansive reading of cultural rights provisions would call for a more active role of the government in securing reception opportunities and access-friendly socioeconomical conditions. The right to receive information would then impose some level of affirmative obligation to facilitate and encourage originating, diffusing, and broadening access to cultural products. Accordingly, the compliance duty under Article 15.1(a) ICESCR (and similar provisions) should effectively shift state obligations closer to the middle of the range—toward a duty to encourage and away from mere duty of inaction.

III. THE CASE OF ARTICLE 15.1(C) ICESCR

The deliberations of the U.N. Expert Committee of Economic, Social and Cultural Rights ("the Committee") and its take on the interface between human rights and intellectual property received intense scholarly attention in recent years. The Committee, established in 1985, is a designated U.N. organ responsible for monitoring compliance with the ICESCR.[250] The Committee further provides interpretation and guidance to states parties regarding the meaning of the

---

246. *See* International Covenant on Economic, Social and Cultural Rights (1966), Art. 15.1(a) (proclaiming everyone's right "[t]o take part in cultural life").

247. *See* Chapman, *supra* note 210, at 134–35.

248. *Id.* at 135 (referring in this context also to Art. 2.2. ICESCR concerning the commitment to guarantee the rights annunciated in the Covenant without discrimination based on race, color, sex religion etc. Interestingly, one basis for impermissible discrimination is "property").

249. Section III.B.2.(c).ii *supra*.

250. The Committee's Web site provides information about its history and responsibilities: http://www2.ohchr.org/english/bodies/cescr/index.htm. *See also* Alston, *supra* note 245, at 335–40 (providing historical background on the establishment of the Committee).

ICESCR provisions. The Committee publishes nonbinding "general comments" on specific ICESCR issues that set forth the important focal points and standards applied in connection with its supervision tasks and compliance assessment.[251]

In 2001, the Committee ventured into issues concerning the interface between human rights and intellectual property by publishing a preliminary Statement,[252] which was followed by a General Comment published in 2005.[253] These documents specifically addressed Article 15.1(c) of the ICESCR securing the moral and material interests of authors in their intellectual productions. Though the specific mandate of the Committee was to consider rights-holders' entitlements under that provision only,[254] it adopted a board perspective, taking note of the ramifications of intellectual property rights on nonowners while underscoring the notion of balance and touching upon cultural participation aspects.[255]

In general, the Committee exhibited a cautious approach that by no means blesses the union between intellectual property rights and human rights as a bond made in heaven.[256] At the outset, the Committee conducted a doctrinal line drawing by highlighting some fundamental distinctions between the two species of rights. Human rights are said to be "timeless expressions of fundamental entitlements of the human person" whereas "intellectual property rights, often with the exception of moral rights, may be allocated, limited in time and scope, traded, amended and even forfeited."[257] Further, "the human right to benefit from the protection of the moral and material interests resulting from one's scientific, literary and artistic productions safeguards the personal link between authors and their creations. . .as well as their basic material interests which are necessary to enable authors to enjoy an adequate standard of living, intellectual property regimes primarily protect business and corporate interests and investments."[258]

This language, and the comment that rights-holders' entitlements under Article 15.1(c) do not "necessarily coincide" with the entitlements they enjoy under positive law, implies a distinction between moral and purely economic interests of rights-holders. Although taking note of the difference between the

---

251. *See* Helfer, *supra* note 210, at 988.

252. *See* ICESCR Committee Statement on Human Rights and Intellectual Property (2001) (offering a "preliminary contribution to the rapidly evolving debate on intellectual property, which remains high on the international agenda"). *Id.* at ¶ 2.

253. *See* ICESCR Committee General Comment No. 17 (2005).

254. The Comment foresaw a separate report specifically targeting Articles 15.1(a)–(b). *See* General Comment (2005), *id.* at ¶ 4 (foreseeing separate general comments dedicated to Art. 15.1 ¶¶ 1(a), 1(b), and 3).

255. General Comment (2005), *id.* at ¶¶ 35, 39(e); Statement (2001), *id.* at ¶¶ 4, 17.

256. For an analysis of the Committee's approach, see Helfer, *supra* note 210, at 987 ff.

257. General Comment (2005), *id.* at ¶ 2.

258. *Id. See also* Statement (2001), *id.* at ¶¶ 5–7.

two types of interets, the way the Committee describes intellectual property regimes has a stark utilitarian-economic flavor, as intellectual property rights are perceived "first and foremost [as] means"[259] and as being "ultimately. . .a social product [having] a social function."[260] Moreover, intellectual property law is said to be "primarily protect[ing] business and corporate interests and investments."[261] In any event, though intellectual property law and the rights stipulated in Article 15.1(c) may cover common territories, the Committee expressly rejected the notion of a perfect overlap.[262]

The Committee's analysis indicates a certain vertical tension between intellectual property and human rights norms in which human rights generally rank higher. Accordingly, intellectual property laws should generally be designed to conform to human rights, not vice versa.[263] Simultaneously, the Committee states the two disciplines are "at the same time mutually reinforcing and reciprocally limitative."[264] Taken together, one possible interpretation of these statements is that as to the vertical interface question, human rights are generally superior, and when it comes to specific clashes on the horizontal interface level, cultural rights may impose some affirmative limitations on the intellectual property regime (but also vice versa).[265]

As to the substantive content of authors' rights from a human rights perspective, the Committee opines that only *natural persons* enjoy Article 15.1(c) protections,[266] and that the human right securing material interests extends only to the *basic* material interests of authors necessary to enable an *adequate* standard of living.[267] Protection of the material interests of rights-holders that go beyond that basic level is not covered by Article 15.1(c), but may conflate with the general protection to property stipulated in other norms.[268] To the extent

---

259. *Id.* General Comment (2005) at ¶ 1.

260. *Id.* at ¶ 35.

261. *Id.* at ¶ 2.

262. The Committee observed "[i]n order not to render [Art. 15(1)(c)] devoid of any meaning, the protection afforded needs to be effective in securing authors the moral and material interests resulting from their productions. However, the protection under article 15, paragraph 1 (c), need not necessarily reflect the level and means of protection found in present copyright, patent and other intellectual property regimes, as long as the protection available is suited to secure authors the moral and material interests resulting from their productions, as defined in paragraphs 12 to 16 below." *Id.* at ¶ 10.

263. *Cf.* Statement (2001), *id.* at ¶ 4.

264. General Comment (2005), *id.* at ¶ 4.

265. *Id.*

266. *Id.* at ¶¶ 7–8.

267. *Id.* at ¶¶ 15, 39(c), & 44.

268. *Id.* at ¶ 15 ("The protection of "material interests" of authors in article 15, paragraph 1 (c), reflects the close linkage of this provision with the right to own property, as recognized in article 17 of the Universal Declaration of Human Rights and in regional human rights instruments, as well as with the right of any worker to adequate remuneration

obligations under Article 15.1(c) and other human rights (i.e., cultural participation or the right to enjoy scientific progress) conflict, the Committee cautiously advocates for a balanced solution.[269] In fact, striking a balance between exclusive rights and cultural rights is said to be a clear *obligation* under the International Covenant.[270]

What is the legal meaning of having an "obligation" under the ICESCR? The "jurisprudence" of the Committee concerning legal obligations stemming from the ICESCR (the so-called "violation approach")[271] conceptualized certain obligations (including the so-called "core obligation") that must be, without delay, "respected, protected and fulfilled" by states parties.[272] Thus, the core obligation imposes affirmative duties on states parties under which states must ensure the satisfaction of (at the very least) the minimum essential levels of each of the rights enunciated in the ICESCR.[273] Such obligations have an immediate effect.[274] Turning to clarify the content of "core obligations" under Article 15.1(c), the Committee states, inter alia, that states parties must "strike an adequate balance between the effective protection of the moral and material interests of authors and States parties' obligations in relation to the rights to food, health, education, as well as the rights to take part in cultural life and to enjoy the benefits of scientific progress and its applications, or any other right recognized in the Covenant."[275] It continues:

> In striking this balance, the private interests of authors should not be unduly advantaged and the public interest in enjoying broad access to their productions should be given due consideration. States parties should therefore

---

(article 7 (a) of the Covenant). Unlike other human rights, the material interests of authors are not directly linked to the personality of the creator, but contribute to the enjoyment of the right to an adequate standard of living (art. 11 para. (1)").

269. *Id.* at ¶¶ 22, 35, & 39(e).

270. *Id.* at ¶ 35 ("States parties are therefore obliged to strike an adequate balance between their obligations under article 15, paragraph 1 (c), on one hand, and under the other provisions of the Covenant, on the other hand, with a view to promoting and protecting the full range of rights guaranteed in the Covenant.").

271. *See* Helfer, *supra* note 210, at 990 (explaining "a 'violations approach' to interpreting the Covenant . . . distinguishes 'core obligations'—minimum essential levels of each right which all states must immediately implement—from other obligations that may be achieved progressively as additional resources become available. These core obligations include three distinct undertakings—to respect, to protect, and to fulfill.") (footnote omitted).

272. General Comment (2005), *id.* at ¶¶ 25, 28.

273. *Id.* at ¶ 39; *see also* Statement (2001), *id.* at ¶ 12.

274. The notion of "immediate effect" is contrasted with the notion of "progressive realization"—signifying an obligation to comply over time. *See* Comment, *id.* at ¶ 25; Statement, *id.* at ¶ 11.

275. General Comment (2005), *id.* at ¶ 39(e).

> ensure that their legal or other regimes for the protection of the moral and material interests resulting from one's scientific, literary or artistic productions constitute no impediment to their ability to comply with their core obligations in relation to the rights to food, health, education, as well as to take part in cultural life and to enjoy the benefits of scientific progress and its applications or any other right set out in the Covenant.[276]

States parties also have a "duty to prevent that unreasonably high costs for access . . . to schoolbooks and learning materials, from undermining the rights of large segments of the population to health, food and education."[277] This statement is particularly intriguing. We may infer a government obligation to intervene in the operation of property-oriented information markets when the inaction policy would lead to price levels on access to particular information goods that are "unreasonably high." It should be remembered that this is not just a polite recommendation but a "core obligation" under the U.N. human rights framework. The practical ramifications of such obligation would necessarily involve (1) making a determination at the state level concerning the point at which market costs of access breach the level of "reasonableness", and (2) determining the appropriate domestic legal measures (perhaps within antitrust laws) that need to be taken to obtain the desired ("reasonable") price level. Finally, the Committee stated clearly that under Article 15.1(c), legal protection to authors must be effective,[278] but at the same time with regard to national legislation, the Committee afforded governments "a considerable margin of discretion in assessing which measures are most suitable to meet its specific needs and circumstances."[279]

IV. IMPLICATIONS

What is the pragmatic payoff in adopting a human rights framework for intellectual property law? Could such framework "correct" copyright law when it fails to achieve its purposes and goals?[280] It is fairly safe to say the human rights framework to copyright law, once accepted, would not permit the domestic legislature to ignore radical effects of exclusive copyrights on access costs, opportunities, and conditions in general. In some situations, lawmakers would have to ensure "affordable access"—with the precise meaning of "affordable" left open

---

276. *Id.* at ¶ 35 (citation omitted).

277. *Id.*

278. *Id.* at ¶31 (stipulating an obligation to "protect" by ensuring effective protections against infringement).

279. *Id.* at ¶ 47.

280. *Cf.* Chapman, *supra* note 210, at 128 (arguing a human rights standard for intellectual property requires the type and level of protection to directly facilitate and promote scientific progress for broadly benefiting members of society on both the individual and collective level).

to interpretation under the domestic legal framework. According to the ICESCR Committee, copyright legislation must be reasonable and balanced. We are left guessing as to how much this observation contributes to the "delicate balance" mantra so familiar from internal intellectual property rhetoric.[281] Even as one agrees to re-evaluate copyright access restrictions through the lens of human rights, it appears governments continue to retain broad discretion regarding the particular design of intellectual property laws, and domestic courts appear thus far unimpressed by arguments demanding human rights be seen as imposing limitations on the adjudication of intellectual property rights.[282] Pragmatic evaluation of this troubled interface tends to discount the effect of human rights norms based on their unclear legal status, location, and force within the domestic norms hierarchy, as well as related interpretation and enforcement questions that remain unresolved by any supranational authoritative body.

To summarize, the problem boils down to the following interrelated questions: (1) To what extent can a human rights approach to intellectual property law *effectively* improve the position of nonowners? (2) In which respect can a human rights approach add to the general commitment to balance already woven into the fabric of intellectual property theory and policy? It has been shown that at least the black letter of human rights norms (alongside constitutional principles) provides an explicit normative basis for rights-of-access. The human rights entitlements of every person to be afforded a proper opportunity to access information have an important declarative value. Comparably clear expressions upholding general rights-of-access are often absent in other legal fields, including various intellectual property legislation.

At the same time, the discussion above has drawn a rather sceptical picture concerning the actual effect of contitutional and human rights norms in the face of the local and global tendency to nonetheless vehemently enforce copyright law. In this light, it appears rights-of-access must receive an affirmative-positive

---

281. For a critical comment on the use of the term *delicate balance* in intellectual property and the prospects of achieving it, see Tom Bell, *Indelicate Imbalancing in Copyright and Patent Law, in* COPY FIGHTS: THE FUTURE OF INTELLECTUAL PROPERTY IN THE INFORMATION AGE (AdamThierer & Clyde Wayne Crews Jr. eds., 2002).

282. Brown reviewed numerous litigation matters in various jurisdictions in which the conflict between human rights law and intellectual property law emerged, concluding: "When human rights and IP appear in conflict, in most cases a middle ground position can be reached, applying the inbuilt exceptions in each. The cynic would say that this simply results in IP prevailing, however in the cases in question, with the likely exception of the United States anti-circumvention cases, an appropriately balanced decision was reached. It cannot be said, so far, that a human rights based approach to interpretation of IP is having any significant effect." *See* Abbe Brown, *Guarding the Guards: The Practical Impact of Human Rights on Innovation and Creativity*, Conference Paper, 20th BILETA Conference: Over-Commoditised; Over-Centralised; Over-Observed: the New Digital Legal World?, 11 (2005).

expression *within copyright legislation* having the same standing as other copyright rules. In other words, the vertical tension between exclusive copyrights and rights-of-access must be reconciled and preferably eliminated within copyright law's own quarters in the form of "ratification" of rights-of-access.

IV. TECHNOLOGICAL PROTECTIONS MEASURES

The discussion leaves rights-of-access for now and returns to the access-right concept. The first access-right prong assumes two things: (1) claimants can use some measures to prevent inadvertent human-access, and (2) those measures allow them to selectively provide and deny human-access to messages on a more-or-less individual basis. In addition, technological means may be used to assist the enforcement of the second access-right prong (namely, the prohibition on unauthorized communication-conducts). This begs a discussion on some technological aspects of access control to digital information. Exercise of supervision and control over conducts covered by the access-rights crucially depends on technological fencing. As the information process unfolds and becomes richer and more sophisticated over time, originators, facilitators, and recipients increasingly rely on the advantages of digital communication networks, digital media, digital devices, and digital logical tools to encode and decode messages. Technological control can be imposed at any one of these junctions and will have various effects on single communication sequences and the process as a whole. The remainder of this chapter will review some basic, largely technical aspects related to technological protection measures and digital rights management systems.

A. Concept and Function

The debate over technological protection measures (TPMs) covers a vast and interdisciplinary cluster of topics concerning complex technological, economic, social, and legal issues.[283] Terminologically, *TPMs* is a general name describing digital technologies, devices, and systems that can restrict or impede operations involving origination and reception of digital information. As such, TPMs can furnish control over access and further use of information in a fashion significantly independent from physical or legal control over physical media and infrastructure. TPMs can enforce predetermined access- and use-restrictions schemes and execute permission platforms; one way to classify TPMs indeed focuses on their principal function.[284] Especially in the context of digital rights management

283. *See* Digital Rights Management: Technological, Economic, Legal and Political Aspects (Eberhard Becker et al. eds. 2003).

284. *See e.g.* Alaine Strowel & Séverine Dussolier, *Legal Protection of Technological Systems*, WCT-WTTP/IMP/2—Workshop on Implementation Issues of the WIPO WCT and the WPPT, Dec. 6–7, 19992–5 (1999).

systems, providers of digital content impose TPM-executed restrictions to preserve permission-upon-payment schemes as well as support various business models and content exploitation strategies.[285] TPMs can support various remuneration models and licensing arrangements—which are tailored to fit the nature of content offered, the needs of content providers, and consumer expectations. Those systems may greatly help to take advantage of technology and facilitate circulation of information while simultaneously allowing an unprecedented level of rights-holders' control.[286]

1. TPMs and DRMS

Digital Rights Management Systems (DRMS) are technologies that support business models by securing trade in digital content.[287] DRMS is not synonymous with TPMs as the former typically involves mass distribution, licensing contracts between end users and content providers, and technology licensing between DRMS developers and manufacturers of devices in which DRMS are embedded.[288] In addition, many DRMS have "surveillance" capacities capable of tracing, recording, and analyzing consumer behavior.[289] By comparison, TPMs are components that *actually enforce* access and use limitations, typically in accordance with terms and conditions retrieved from other DRMS components:[290] though

---

285. *See* Willms Buhse & Amélie Wetzel, *Creating a Framework for Business Models for Digital Content: Mobile Music as Case Study*, *in* DIGITAL RIGHTS MANAGEMENT: TECHNOLOGICAL, ECONOMIC, LEGAL ANDPOLITICAL ASPECTS 271–79 (Eberhard Becker et al. eds., 2003) (describing business models for digital content).

286. *Id.* at 285 (giving as an example the famous "superdistribution" model developed by Ryoichi Mori, who introduced an encryption-based concept for information licensing, allowing free distribution of digital content while controlling access and use, whereby content owners provide the terms).

287. *See* STEFAN BECHTOLD, VOM URHEBERRECHT ZUM INFORMATIONSRECHT 143 (2002); Niels Rump, *DRM—Definition, Aspects, and Overview*, *in* DIGITAL RIGHTS MANAGEMENT: TECHNOLOGICAL, ECONOMIC, LEGAL AND POLITICAL ASPECTS 3–4 (Eberhard Becker et al. eds., 2003).

288. *See* Stefan Bechtold, *Digital Rights Management in the United States and Europe*, 52 AM. J. COMP. L. 323, 325 (2004). *See also* Stuart Haber et al., *If Piracy is the Problem, Is DRM the Answer?* *in* DIGITAL RIGHTS MANAGEMENT: TECHNOLOGICAL, ECONOMIC, LEGAL AND POLITICAL ASPECTS 225 (Eberhard Becker et al. eds., 2003) (the goal of a DRM system is to enforce licenses between content providers and consumers).

289. *See* Ian Kerr, *To Observe and Protect? How Digital Rights Management Systems Threaten Privacy and What Policy Makers Should Do About It*, *in* INTELLECTUAL PROPERTY AND INFORMATION WEALTH: COPYRIGHT AND RELATED RIGHTS 323–24 (Peter Yu, ed., 2007).

290. *See* Rump, *supra* note 287, at 4 (there are two groups of DRM functions: those that are responsible for rights *management* and those that *enforce* exploitation rules). For the present purposes, TPMs fall in the second group, though admittedly the distinction is not always clear.

standing alone, TPMs must not necessarily be a part of any exploitation scheme, business strategy, or support to a certain licensing model.

Another distinction relates to the purpose and intended effect of technology. The term *digital rights management systems* spells out the main purpose of such systems: to facilitate secure distribution platforms of information products. DRMS may operate wholly unnoticed by users, especially when the desired operation is not subject to restriction or when DRMS merely collect and analyze usage information. The term *DRMS* shall be used hereinafter in the particular context of commercial platforms and business strategies, which, in reality, predominantly serve the commercial interests of digital content providers.[291] TPMs more pointedly underscore the technology's end effect (for instance, enforcing access restriction to content). TPMs restrict operations unauthorized users are expected to attempt. The term *TPMs* emphasizes the *actual effect* of technology on the behavior of participants in the information process and their opportunities to access and use information. Accordingly, TPMs, broadly defined, embrace all types of technologies and components that impose actual access/use restrictions with respect to digital content.

2. Protection of Content versus Protection of Rights in Content

As a preliminary note, the term *digital rights management systems* might cause confusion regarding its *right* element, suggesting the technology at issue necessarily applies to information in which content providers have rights. Obviously, DRMS technological restrictions should not be confused with legal intellectual property rights that may concurrently apply to the protected content. It would be a mistake to assume technological restrictions by definition simply prevent violation of property rights. Such technologies do not always enforce recognized intellectual property rights in information, and DRMS do not literally "manage" legal rights. The term *DRMS* originates from technical jargon in which the word *rights* has a different connotation than the legal one. For DRMS engineers, "rights" refer to *permissions* allowing certain operations to take place.[292] DRMS execute "policies," which are explicit, conditional statements specifying how to

291. Commercially oriented platforms do not necessarily entail direct or indirect charging for individual access/use. Free promotion may also be part of a DRMS-supported commercial approach. *See* Rump, *supra* note 287, at 3 & n.7. Using DRMS for purposes that are not commercially oriented (such as confidentiality of internal documents in organization) is also possible, but is not the focus here. *Id.* at 14.

292. Deidre Kathleen Mulligan & Aaron Burstein, *Implementing Copyright Limitations in Rights Expression Languages*, at 2 (2002) (available at http://crypto.stanford.edu/DRM2002/mulligan_burstein_acm_drm_2002.doc (2002) (noting that "rights" in DRM may have no relationship to legal rights, and are more accurately described as "permissions").

handle actions attempted on an information resource by authenticated actors.[293] By contrast, legal rights are generally recognized entitlements concerning an informational resource allocated and controlled inter alia by property and contractual arrangements.[294]

DRMS architecture alone obviously is not the *source* of legal rights, and legal entitlements do not emanate from the DRMS usage platforms unless reinforced by the law. Legal entitlements are principally independent of the capacity of technological systems to impose actual restrictions on human behavior, and attached licensing terms (when applicable) usually provide the legal framework governing usage rules of DRMS-protected content. The license establishes contractual relations between content providers and consumers while stipulating respective mutual obligations. The content, scope, and enforceability of mutual contractual rights and obligations built upon the layer of proprietary entitlements are determined by the applicable law, not by DRMS policies. This point becomes relevant when technological and legal protections do not overlap.[295]

B. TPMs Classifications

There are several ways to classify TPMs based on various distinction keys. One classification focuses on the *type of legal rights* attached to the protected content. For instance, technological measures that protect copyrighted content against infringement are distinguished from systems that protect noncopyrightable data or systems applied to secure online services.[296] Another possibility is to classify them according to the *type of activity* controlled by the technology. Differentiating is common between access-control TPMs on the one hand and "use"- or "copy"-control TPMs on the other.[297] A third distinction targets the *type of technology* used by content providers (e.g., encryption, copy restriction, watermarking, etc.).[298] We may further distinguish between components that actually prevent

---

293. *See* John S. Erickson, *Fair Use, DRM and Trusted Computing*, 46 COMMC'N ACM 34, 36 (2003).

294. *See, e.g.*, BECHTOLD, *supra* note 287, at 16–17 (noting the concept of DRMS is independent of copyright claims in a work).

295. *Cf.* Strowel & Dussolier, *supra* note 284, at 5 ("[T]echnologies being developed at the moment and which copyright holders are likely to subscribe to in order to protect their works have many more marginal functions which in some cases lie far outside the strict bounds of intellectual property itself.").

296. *See* MARTIN TRAYER, TECHNISCHE SCHUTZMASSNAHMEN 22–23 (2003).

297. *See, e.g.*, *id.* at 24; Strowel & Dussolier, *supra* note 284, at 2–3; PETER WAND, TECHNISCHE SCHUTZMASSNAHMEN UND URHEBERRECHT 10–21 (2001).

298. *See, e.g.*, Bechtold, *supra* note 287, at 23–34 (joining under one category both access and use measures that are achieved via encryption, copy-control technologies, and password-control technologies).

something and those that serve broader control schemes (including identification, authentication, integrity of data, and payment).[299]

Such distinctions might assume legal significance when integrated into the regulative scheme, for example, when different legal rules apply to various types of TPMs to achieve certain results based on a variety of policy considerations. In such cases, TPMs taxonomies determine the applicable legal rule (e.g., when the law distinguished between technological "access" controls and "copy" controls).[300] Situations where different laws apply to different technological measures based on the type of content they protect—or based on the measures' purpose or operation—also exemplify the importance of distinctions.[301]

The access-right-related vocabulary and definitions offer an alternative TPMs classification based on the nature of the act they are designed to restrict. Accordingly, we may arrange technological measures in classes of TPMs designed to prevent *unauthorized access-conducts* as distinguished from measures designed to hinder *unauthorized communication-conducts*. Further, the distinction between human-access and technological-access furnishes a basis for categorizing measures according to the specific type of "access" they target.

C. Features of Digital Rights Management Systems

There is no universal definition of DRMS. They range from simple copy control to management schemes that police and detect every single interaction with digital content.[302] Bechtold generally described DRMS as a set of intertwining technologies that may be used to establish a secure distribution chain of digital content.[303] DRMS are deployed in a verity of digital media and services such as compact discs (CDs), DVD players and discs, Pay-TV decoders, online music and

---

299. *Cf. id.* at 34–80 (describing in detail various identification, authenticity, and integrity technologies); WAND, *supra* note 297, at 22; TRAYER, *supra* note 296, at 23–24. Another related distinction is between hardware-based and software-based measures. *See* John A. Rothchild, *Economic Analysis of Technological Protection Measures*, 84 OREGON L. REV. 489, 493–94 (2005).

300. U.S. anticircumvention law, a topic Chapter 6 will discuss in detail, draws such a distinction.

301. Chapter 6 will explain the difference between *copyright* anti-circumvention laws and *general* anti-circumvention law, as well as the distinction between rules that apply to TPMs and those that apply to copyright management information (CMI).

302. *See* Bechtold, *supra* note 288, at 324; Rump, *supra* note 287, at 7–10 (describing various components of DRMS and their functions).

303. Bechtold, *supra* note 288, at 331. *See also* BECHTOLD, *supra* note 287, at 23 (noting a principal goal of DRMS is to control access and use of digital content in order to have users pay for it).

video services, video games, various media players, software, e-books, and mobile devices.[304]

A central feature in many DRMS is the use of encryption technology. Encryption is described as the process of obscuring information to make it unreadable without special knowledge. Digital "envelopes" or "containers" protect data when it is stored on local devices, allowing decryption of content only when authorized processes are performed using a unique decryption key.[305] Some technologies such as "Rights Locker Architectures" enable access to content from various devices in which the authorization is tied to certain users rather than to certain devices. For example, various copy-control mechanisms based on the exchange of information between digital content and copying media may supervise the number of copies allowed to be made. At a higher level of sophistication, the system may determine what "authorized" media may play or run content and control transferability of data between consumer devices.

To manage and identify content in complex distribution models, DRMS contain "identifiers" and "metadata" that allow machine-readable identification of content, content provider, usage, access rules, and users.[306] Content providers use Rights Expression Languages (REL) in metadata to control permissions for numerous operations against the content.[307] As a result, content providers may restrict access and use for certain time periods, locations, devices, and users as well as influence quality and format. Finally, they can condition all the activities above with users' obedience to electronic payment systems.[308]

DRMS are not foolproof in the sense that no system can provide an absolute, hermetic control concerning all types of usage, and all DRMS are vulnerable to attacks and manipulations by hostile actors. Skilled hackers (who "go around" the technological protection system) and crackers (who "break" the protection system) have always been capable of defeating DRM protections, and there is an

---

304. For a comprehensive review, see BECHTOLD, *supra* note 287, at 19–145. *See also* WAND, *supra* note 297, at 7–22; TRAYER, *supra* note 296, at 25–64.

305. BECHTOLD, *supra* note 287, at 26–33; Haber et al., *supra* note 288, at 226–27.

306. For a detailed technical description of DRMS identification and metadata, see Norman Paskin, *DRMS Identification and Metadata Components*, *in* DIGITAL RIGHTS MANAGEMENT: TECHNOLOGICAL, ECONOMIC, LEGAL AND POLITICAL ASPECTS (Eberhard Becker et al. eds., 2003).

307. REL is used to control operations such as "copy, delete, modify, embed, execute, export, extract, annotate, aggregate, install, backup, loan, sell, give, lease, play, print, display, read, restore, transfer, uninstall, verify, save, obtain, issue, possess, and revoke content . . . expressed in a machine-readable form." *See* Bechtold, *supra* note 288, at 345 (footnote omitted).

308. *See* Ahmad-Reza Sadeghi & Markus Schneider, *DRM Electronic Payment Systems*, *in* DIGITAL RIGHTS MANAGEMENT: TECHNOLOGICAL, ECONOMIC, LEGAL AND POLITICAL ASPECTS (Eberhard Becker et al. eds., 2003) (describing in detail electronic payment systems).

inevitable trade-off between the level of security provided by the system and its costs.[309] Additionally, highly sophisticated systems are more susceptible to interoperability and standardization problems. For these and other reasons, there is currently no reasonably functional DRM technology that ensures a perfectly secure environment. This notwithstanding, it is repeatedly called to mind that the main purpose of those systems is to affect and control the behavior and access opportunities of average, unsophisticated users—the bulk of consumers interested in the content and those who constitute a paying market for information goods. So long as this large class of persons continues to be bound by DRM-supported usage terms (and so long as consumers are not thereby discouraged from continuing consumption), the system is likely to achieve its goals. In certain markets for copyrighted works such as computer software, video games, on-demand services, e-books, and mobile devices, DRMS have been and are expected to remain commonly used.

V. CONCLUSION

Two principal missions underlay the discussion in this chapter. *First,* it scrutinized the notion of "access to information" and translated it into a vocabulary that property law can process and analyze. Very little about "access to information" as a property concept is self-explanatory, and even less obvious is the idea law factually can tailor exclusory regimes around this notion. To cement the theoretical foundations of this idea, the concepts called the "access-right" and "rights-of-access" received in this chapter respective legal definitions. These definitions laid the infrastructure for the next stage of the study in which the interrelations between the access-right and digital copyright legislation will be closely investigated. At this point, we may think about the access-right and rights-of-access as analytical tools that integrate the discussion presented in the previous two chapters concerning "information" and "property"—with the two tools being glued together by the element of "access."

Second, the analysis explored three main routes as potential legal sources to rights-of-access: copyright law, free speech law, and human rights law. It concluded positive copyright law itself does not provide a solid and sufficiently explicit basis for such rights. Also the remaining routes have proven to a large extent unable to safeguard rights-of-access, especially when the information at issue is subject to copyright exclusivity. Copyright rules, free speech law, and access to information as a fundamental human right have not been able thus far to counterbalance copyright exclusivity to a satisfactory degree.

---

309. Bechtold, *supra* note 288, at 144.

Concerning copyright, it has been shown that, as a descriptive matter, traditional copyright law does not regulate access in regard to the first access-right prong (control over access-conducts), whereas the notion of access regulation under traditional rules in regard of the second access-right prong (control over communication-conducts) is partly confirmed. This calls for further investigation concerning if and how the necessary protections should be built into the body of copyright law itself. Equipped with these recognitions, the next part of the study (Chapters 4–6) will demonstrate how and why copyright law has been morphing into something that is becoming more similar to an access-right regime.

PART 2

DIGITAL REPRODUCTION, DIGITAL COMMUNICATION, AND ANTICIRCUMVENTION LAW

4. THE DIGITAL REPRODUCTION RIGHT

I. INTRODUCTION

The exclusive entitlement to prevent unauthorized reproductions is perhaps the most basic element of copyright protection.[1] In Anglo-American copyright traditions, the reproduction right has been the first and solitary exclusive right.[2] Traces of legal duties to obtain permission for printing of literary works emerged in temporal proximity to the invention of the printing press technology in the fifteenth century, which revolutionized information markets and gave rise to printing privileges in Europe. In the early days, one of the main purposes of exclusive printing privileges was to secure professional trade monopolies;[3] no less important, the power to allocate exclusive printing permissions also had significant political dimensions. In granting or refusing printing requests, sovereign and local patrons could leverage political power and silence dissenting voices.[4]

Later in the development of copyright, the power to authorize and prohibit printing was transferred to professional printers' guilds that were primarily concerned with preserving their commercial interest and market power.[5] The English Statute of Anne marked a historic turning point, in which by abandoning the guild framework and adopting a general statute directly regulating copyright, the power to control reproductions significantly was transferred to the

1. *See* SAM RICKETSON, THE BERNE CONVENTION FOR THE PROTECTION OF LITERARY AND ARTISTIC WORKS § 8.6 (1987) (describing the reproduction right as "undoubtedly the most fundamental right which has been accorded historically to authors under national legislation").

2. The Statute of Anne, considered the first modern copyright statute, secured only a thin version of the reproduction right *See* Anne, c. 19 (1710). For example, Art. I of the Statute speaks of "printing, reprinting, and publishing, or causing to be printed, reprinted and published [of] books and other writings." *Id.*

3. *See* EUGEN ULMER, URHEBER–UND VERLAGSRECHT 51–54 (1980) (describing the privilege system in Continental Europe).

4. *See* LYMAN RAE PATTERSON, COPYRIGHT IN HISTORICAL PERSPECTIVE 114–42 (1968) (analyzing the relationship between historical printing privileges and censorship in England).

5. *Id.* at 42–77 (reviewing the stationer's copyright system in England). The stationer's copyright "was a right recognized among members of the company entitling one how published a work to prevent any unauthorized printing of the same work." *Id.* at 43–44.

authors themselves.[6] Following that tradition, modern copyright law recognizes an exclusive right initially vested in authors to control production of copies of their intellectual achievements. Authors regularly transfer their exclusive entailments to commercial exploiters such as publishers or employers. Those derivative rights-holders, in turn, may exercise the exclusive right against competitors who "free ride" on creative efforts. Preventing unauthorized printing enables the prices to be charged for copies to substantially exceed marginal production and distribution costs.[7] The standard economic argument for copyright protection purports that this commercial advantage enables amortization of investment in creative production and secures the opportunity to profit from exploitation of works in the marketplace.

Several assumptions furnish the basis for the intended operation and effect of the reproduction right in the economics of information markets. First, it is assumed possessing a physical copy guarantees easy human-access to the work embodied therein.[8] Second, achieving human-access (either directly or by using rendering media) principally does not require the making of additional copies of the work. Third, rights-holders have only a limited power to control downstream transactions in physical copies subsequent to their initial authorized release.

These assumptions and their intuitive appeal stem from the reality and conditions of analog markets. They underlie the shape and structure of virtually all copy-related exclusive rights and the exemptions thereto. The suggestion that controlling initial channels of distribution of copies is crucial for generating exploitation revenues is substantially premised on the recognition it is practically impossible to police human-access facilitated by those copies downstream. The separation between initial and secondary markets for copies underlies exhaustion

---

6. *See* 1 William Patry, Patry on Copyright § 1.5 (2007) (explaining the Statute of Anne was meant to resolve the conflict between the powerful printing guild, the Stationers' Company, which was granted a monopoly via parliamentary legislation (licensing acts), and personal royal printing privileges); Oren Bracha, Owning Ideas: A History of Anglo-American Intellectual Property 176 ff (2005) (cautioning "there is no doubt that Statute of Anne was a significant landmark in the history of copyright. . . [though] the statute's break with the past was less radical than is often realized").

7. *See* Stephen Breyer, *The Uneasy Case for Copyright*, 84 Harv. L. Rev. 281, 294 ff (1970) (analyzing the cost advantage of copiers).

8. This obviously does not mean that works can always be retrieved directly from the physical object without the need for supporting rendering media, which alone does not undermine the easy access assumption. For example, the owner of an audiotape cannot listen to the recorded music without using a player, but such players are widely and cheaply available. The fact the work cannot be perceived directly from the tape does not weaken the easy access assumption conferred upon the possessor of the tape in such circumstances. According to the same logic, when magnetic audiotape players disappear from the market completely, the easy access assumption might be refuted. In that case, it is likely analog magnetic recordings will cease being sold to consumers on a large scale anyway.

(or "first-sale") rules, which generally place copies after their initial distribution beyond the reach of copyright holders. Such rules are central to copyright law and have been cross-jurisdictionally recognized,[9] as copyright restrictions targeting the *initial phase* of information diffusion have been widely considered both realistic and legitimate despite their monopolistic character.[10] One of the reasons is that a limited monopoly power to control the initial market for distribution of copies has not been sufficiently hermetic to severely stifle circulation of information in general. The operation of copyright protection in analog markets fell short of safeguarding an effective monopoly on access per se, and individual access to copies for private enjoyment resided beyond the limits of copyright regulation and enforcement.[11] Both as a matter of law and reason, access per se simply could not violate the exclusive rights.

The analog reproduction right applied to the production of physical articles from which works could be accessed directly (e.g., books or maps printed on paper sheets). Technological advances of the past century raised the issue of "mechanical reproductions," including phonograph recordings and piano rolls. That reproduction rights should cover the manufacturing of mechanical reproductions has not always been self-evident.[12] Yet during the past century, copyright laws expanded toward full coverage of mechanical reproductions irrespective of rendition technology, and it has become rather immaterial for the question of coverage whether reception of work embedded in the "copy" necessitates the operation of some mechanical device.[13] The short-lived historical disagreement

---

9. *See, e.g.*, WCT, Art. 6(2); EUCD (2001), Art. 4(2); 17 U.S.C. § 109.

10. Exclusive copyrights usually do not amount to economic monopoly in the strict sense. *See* Edmund W. Kitch, *Elementary and Persistent Errors in the Economic Analysis of Intellectual Property*, 53 VAND. L. REV. 1727 (2000).

11. *See* Alexander Peukert, *Der Schutzbereich des Urheberrechts und das Werk als öffentliches Gut, in* INTERESSENAUSGLEICH IN URHEBERRECHT, 24–25 (Reno M. Hilty & Alexander Peukert eds., 2004).

12. The Closing Protocol of the 1886 Berne Act declared "the manufacture and sale of instruments for the mechanical reproductions of musical airs in which copyright subsists shall not be considered as constituting an infringement of musical copyright." *See* SAM RICKETSON & JANE C. GINSBURG, INTERNATIONAL COPYRIGHT AND NEIGHBORING RIGHTS: THE BERNE CONVENTION AND BEYOND § 11.07 (2006) (reprinting paragraph 3 of the Closing Protocol of the Berne Act). Such right was first introduced into Berne with the text of the 1908 Berlin Act. *Id.* § 3.17, § 11.08 (referring to Art. 13(1) of the Berlin Act concerning musical works). Interestingly, in exactly the same year the U.S. Supreme Court held that piano rolls were *not* copies within the meaning of the copyright statute. *See* White-Smith Music Publishing Co. v. Apollo Co., 209 U.S. 1, 18 (1908).

13. As a practical matter, the question merges with the definition of a *copy*. In U.S. law, for instance, the respective definition provides that copies are material objects from which the work can be perceived "either directly or with the aid of a machine or device." *See* U.S.C. § 101 (definition of *Copies*).

concerning mechanical reproductions in musical works[14] indeed was a faint prelude to the gathering digital storm. The new opportunities for mediated, indirect communication made possible via objects, devices, and networks have seriously shaken the ground beneath the very basic assumptions concerning "copies" and their communicative dimension.

Consider first the easy access assumption: having a "digital copy" of a work likely means having a component or an object upon which work-representing binary information is mounted. The question of access to that information is separate from the factual inquiry regarding actual possession of a physical object. The "possessor" of a digital copy has the digital representation saved on a personal computer's hard drive or an external data carrier, but such possession does not *guarantee* an easy human-access to the work. The possessor must operate devices that render the digital expression, which are equipped with the appropriate logical tools (software, access permissions, etc.) to enable rendition. Perceptibility of digital copies often depends on the integrity and interoperability of application software and digital machinery. DRM technology such as encryption-based "secure containers" can ensure a sharp division between possessing the data and accessibility of works.[15] As a consequence, content residing on the user's equipment might become useable only upon insertion of an appropriate access key, often subject to restrictive licensing terms.[16] Thus, the easy access assumption might quickly collapse under the sequence of steps and technical operations that must take place before a binary string of data turns into a perceptible message. The main point is that having *physical* control over digital machinery and data carriers, and having *logical* control over the processes they can perform, are two separable (and often actually separate) things.

The second reality assumption collapses after we realize each human-access to a message represented in binary code involves data reproduction(s) of some sort. Human-access to digital copies and reproduction of digital information are,

---

14. Mechanical reproductions of musical works were initially excluded from copyright protection under Berne but were later explicitly covered. With the introduction of the reproduction right in later versions of Berne (currently Article 9(1)), the early text of Art. 13(1) covering mechanical reproductions became redundant. Consequently, Article 13(1) was reshaped into its present form merely to allow compulsory licensing in sound recordings. *See* RICKETSON & GINSBURG, *supra* note 12, §§ 11.21–11.22.

15. Chapter 3, Section IV.A.1 *supra*.

16. *See* Gabriele Spenger, *Authentication, Identification Technique, and Secure Containers—Baseline Technologies*, *in* DIGITAL RIGHTS MANAGEMENT: TECHNOLOGICAL, ECONOMIC, LEGAL AND POLITICAL ASPECTS 78–79 (Eberhard Becker et al. eds., 2003). A secure container is a good example of a situation in which the user "has" a copy saved in his storage device, as this does not guarantee full access opportunities. The content is encrypted and recipients must have a proper key to "unlock" it.

as a practical-technical matter, invariably intertwined.[17] Further, the digital information environment and the possibility of control furnished by DRM technology threaten to supersede the traditional wisdom that trade in physical copies constitutes a *primary* exploitation avenue.[18]

The question troubling copyright experts in the late 1960s and the early 1970s was whether representation of digital information in storage/memory components implicated the reproduction right in the first place.[19] The historical scholarly disagreement about this question suggests the matter was initially rather contested: early on, it was not so obvious that merely creating a "digital copy" without more implicated the reproduction right. Although it was clear digital machinery could later translate strings of binary data into perceptible expressions, the idea of *infringement* via the mere act of digitally duplicating ones-and-zeros data strings *before any rendition could take place* appeared to some observers quite remote from the normal application range of copyright law. At the same time, early supporters of finding copyright-relevant reproduction in such cases insisted these forms of duplication could *ultimately* enable perception from the duplicated information, and therefore, that such duplications were economically significant.[20] In the years that followed, the latter view enjoyed a broad consensus, which was initially formed around the question of *stable storage*: digital reproductions for storage purposes were analogized to more familiar forms of recording as they fulfilled similar functions.[21] The next major step has been to square issues of *non-stable* reproductions with copyright doctrine and policy.

---

17. *See* National Research Council (U.S.), Committee on Intellectual Property Rights and the Emerging Information Infrastructure, The Digital Dilemma: Intellectual Property in the Information Age 6 (2000) (hereinafter The Digital Dilemma) ("In the digital world, even the most routine access to information invariably involves making a copy.").

18. In some sectors (predominantly the music sector), the disappearance of copies as a token of trade is more rapid and drastic than in other industry branches. For a comprehensive review and analysis of the music market and the ways it has been affected by digital technology, see OECD Report on Digital Music: Opportunities and Challenges (2005) (available at http://www.oecd.org/dataoecd/13/2/34995041.pdf).

19. *See* Melvin B. Nimmer, *New Technologies and the Law of Copyright: Reprography and Computers*, 15 UCLA L. Rev. 931 (1968); Eugen Ulmer, *Copyright Problems Arising from the Computer Storage and Retrieval of Protected Works*, 8 Copyright 37 (1972).

20. Nimmer, *supra* note 19, at 1004–17. In 1972, Ulmer contrasted this with the proposition that copyright protection did not attach at the "input" stage of computer operation (i.e., before the work was actually rendered). He concluded: "Storage in the computer. . . must itself be considered as relevant to copyright." Ulmer, *supra* note 19, ¶ 56 at 50.

21. Ulmer, *supra* note 19, ¶¶ 67–74 at 53–54. *See also* Thomas Dreier, *Copyright Digitized: Philosophical Impacts and Practical Implications for Information Exchange in Digital Networks*, *in* WIPO Worldwide Symposium on the Impact of Digital Technology on Copyright and Neighbouring Rights 19 (WIPO ed. 1993) (1993); Second Expert Committee Report on Copyright Problems (1982) ¶ 33 at 242.

This chapter will focus on the second, more controversial question. It describes how non-stable digital representations substantially came to qualify as "copies," rendering the reproduction right omnipresent in digital settings. This chapter will further identify the position and function of the digital reproduction right within the larger transitional process copyright law has been undergoing, and most relevantly, the shift toward an access-right regime.

II. SOME TECHNICAL ASPECTS

A. RAM Reproduction

A message expressed in digital form, like any other message, is composed of signals. The physical manifestation of digital information involves components capable of containing electric or electromagnetic signals. Such components are sometimes integrated into personal computers (e.g., hard drives, RAM chips, and terminals) or in external carriers (e.g., external storage devices, peripheral equipment) as well as network servers and so on. Now the physical representation of digital signals can be roughly divided into stable (nonvolatile) and volatile. Stable representation retains information independent of electric power source, and information is not automatically altered during the normal operation of a computer.

Stable representation is often called *storage*. Some storage components such as PC hard disc drives (HDD) contain digital information embodied on magnetic surfaces. Other storage components apply optical media format to carry data, for example, Digital Versatile Discs (DVDs). Storage components carry information the computer does not immediately need for performing concomitant tasks but may need at some later stage. To summarize the main points, stable expression of digital information has three main characteristics: it is long-term, large in capacity, and persistent. Examples of familiar stable storage components other than HDDs and DVDs are electronic flash cards, USB sticks, Read Only Memory (ROM), floppy discs, and magnetic tapes.

In comparison, volatile components typically contain information only as long as the machine is powered. A common example is computer Random Access Memory (RAM). A RAM component is an integrated circuit ("chip"), which carries evanescent electric pulses. The information is usually erased when the external source of electric power fails or is shut down. RAM contains information actually used by the computer to perform present-time tasks and calculations. The information on the RAM component may be altered, replaced, and deleted automatically as the computer moves along to perform the next task. In general, the scheme of computer operation involves reading stable information, translating it into electric pulses in the RAM, and transferring this information to the Central Processing Unit (CPU), which performs processing procedures according to the instructions of computer programs.

Some types of data representations are purely instrumental and are performed as technical stages in automated operations,[22] with the resulting representation may or may not having a connection to human-access to information. Such automated tasks can take place exclusively within the personal computer (e.g., loading an application computer program from the HDD to the RAM) or as instrumental embodiments occurring in the course of network communication in which transient information resides temporarily on the ISPs' servers and other infrastructure machinery. Both in the case of internal and external operations, instrumental reproductions (as the name suggests) are necessary only as long as a given task is performed; for this reason, they are usually temporary.

B. Streaming Media

Streaming media is a generic name for technologies such as webcasting, simulcasting, and network streaming that are capable of delivering large files containing music, video, and multimedia works through computer networks.[23] Webcasting involves the application and combination of several technologies including data networking, compression, and software application.[24] Streaming differs from downloading in two important respects. First, the media file (song, video) is performed while the file transfer occurs. Second, when the transfer is complete, usually no copy of the file remains, unless the user employs a special program that enables the stream to be saved as a permanent file on the user's hard drive.[25] In this respect, streaming media provides in some cases an alternative to traditional over-the-air (both live and prerecorded) broadcasting. It also facilitates on-demand transmission services over the Internet. Commercial content providers using streaming media technology often deploy technological

---

22. The facts of the *Lexmark* case described above provide a good illustration for such situations. *See* Chapter 3, Section II.B.2.(b) *supra*.

23. The Website Streaming Media provides an informative description: "Streaming media technology enables the real time or on demand distribution of audio, video and multimedia on the Internet. Streaming media is the simultaneous transfer of digital media (video, voice and data) so that it is received as a continuous real-time stream. Streamed data is transmitted by a server application and received and displayed in real-time by client applications. These applications can start displaying video or playing back audio as soon as enough data has been received and stored in the receiving station's buffer." *See* Streaming Media Explained (available at http://www.streamingmedia.com/whatisstreaming.asp).

24. *See* Ha et al., *Broadcast Via the Internet: Technology, Market and the Future*, 11 TREND. COMMUN. 155, 156–59 (2003).

25. *See, e.g.*, Matthew Jackson, *From Broadcast to Webcast: Copyright Law and Streaming Media*, 11 TEX. INTELL. PROP. L.J. 447, 450–52 (2003) (describing the operation of steaming media in the context of music files).

protections to prevent the permanent download of the network transmissions. As one U.S. court explained:

> RealNetworks offers products that enable consumers to access audio and video content over the Internet through a process known as "streaming." When an audio or video clip is "streamed" to a consumer, no trace of the clip is left on the consumer's computer, unless the content owner has permitted the consumer to download the file . . . Streaming is to be contrasted with "downloading," a process by which a complete copy of an audio or video clip is delivered to and stored on a consumer's computer. Once a consumer has downloaded a file, he or she can access the file at will, and can generally redistribute copies of that file to others . . . To guard against the unauthorized copying and redistribution of their content, many copyright owners do not make their content available for downloading, and instead distribute the content using streaming technology in a manner that does not permit downloading.[26]

In the course of streaming media process, two types of temporary reproductions usually take place. First, RAM buffer internal reproductions occur in the computer of the end user.[27] Additionally, external reproductions occur on network servers and other network components in the course of various operations (e.g., routing, cashing, etc.) In both cases, reproductions occur automatically, and they are imperceptible to end-users, who are often completely unaware of those intermediate technical steps.[28]

III. INTERNATIONAL COPYRIGHT LAW AND DIGITAL REPRODUCTION

A. The Berne Convention and the WIPO Treaties

1. Berne Convention

Despite its central role in the historical development of copyright law and its reputation as "the first and perhaps most basic right of a copyright holder,"[29] the reproduction right had not been expressed in the language of the Berne Convention before the Stockholm (1967) and Paris (1971) revisions. Prior to its explicit articulation in Article 9(1) Berne Convention, the reproduction right was

---

26. *See* Realnetworks, Inc. v. Streambox, Inc. 2000 WL 127311 at *1–*2 (W.D. Wash. 2000).

27. *See* Jackson, *supra* note 25, at 450 & n. 6 (in order to perform a streamed song, part of the file is stored in a buffer that theoretically contains no more than a few seconds of the song at any one time and is continuously overwritten).

28. For an overview on technical issues of temporary reproductions, see U.S. Copyright Office Section 104 DMCA Report 107–9 (2001).

29. *See* The Digital Dilemma, *supra* note 17, at 6.

regarded implicit to and derivable from other Berne provisions.[30] Presently, Article 9(1) provides "[a]uthors of literary and artistic works protected by this Convention shall have the exclusive right of authorizing the reproduction of these works, in any manner or form."[31] Article 9(3) clarifies "[a]ny sound or visual recording shall be considered as a reproduction for the purposes of this Convention."[32]

Though now explicitly recognized, Article 9 does not substantively define the reproduction right,[33] and the term *reproduction* leaves some interpretative options open. Uncertainties concerning the scope of obligations under Article 9 have become particularly acute with the arrival of new digital technologies and the sort of "reproductions" they involve. Indeed, the phrase "any manner or form" implies an overarching coverage capturing all instances of duplication regardless of technology, purpose, and technical characteristics. Nonetheless, it was argued the issue of computer reproduction in "invisible form" had not been satisfactorily resolved under the Berne Convention.[34] In that respect, several aspects concerning the scope of the Berne reproduction right call for further clarifications.[35] Most relevantly, the requisite *physical nature* of reproduction and *fixation of signals* are not explicated in the Convention.[36] The most significant

---

30. *See* Ricketson & Ginsburg, *supra* note 12, §§ 11.01–11.03; Ricketson and Ginsburg opined, however, that "the better view is that no such obligation [to provide reproduction right under Berne prior to the Stockholm/Paris Acts] existed." *Id.* § 13.03 at 759. *See also*, Mihály Ficsor, The Law of Copyright and the Internet §§ 3.02–3.10 (2002) (arguing that even before the Stockholm/Paris Acts, Berne members were obligated to grant a reproduction right).

31. *See* Berne Convention (1971), Art. 9(1).

32. *Id.* Art. 9(3). Ficsor noted that this subparagraph is redundant in light of the broad language of paragraph 9(1). Ficsor, *supra* note 30, § 3.15. At the same time, he stressed that subparagraph 9(3) may be useful in clarifying the reproduction right also includes making copies from which works are not directly perceptible. *Id.*

33. *See* Ricketson & Ginsburg, *supra* note 12, § 11.26 (indicating both subparagraphs 9(1) and 9(3) fail to offer clear guidance concerning the actual meaning of "reproduction").

34. In the first edition of his treatise on the Berne Convention, Ricketson indicated that especially in the context of computerized reproductions in "invisible form" the Convention "would benefit from clarification." *See* Ricketson, *supra* note 1, § 8.10.

35. Ricketson & Ginsburg, *supra* note 12, § 11.26.

36. *Id.* § 11.27 (noting "[i]t is open to debate whether the Berne Convention also requires member states to interpret 'any manner or form' to extend to transient digital fixations.") *Cf.* Ficsor, *supra* note 30, §§ 3.17–3.22 (acknowledging the Berne Convention does not define a "reproduction"). Ficsor suggests, however, "clear outlines" of the concept to be understood as "a fixation of a work on the basis of which the work may be indirectly communicated to the public or may further copied (reproduced.)" *Id.* at § 3.21. Three decades earlier, Ulmer opined that any kind of digital reproduction is covered by Article 9 of the Berne Convention, but added that "in the case of internal storage, where

attempt to clarify matters took place shortly before and during the Diplomatic Conference leading to the 1996 WIPO Treaties.[37]

2. The WIPO Internet Treaties

(a) Introduction

The Berne Convention saw its most recent substantive revision at the conclusion of the 1971 Paris Act. Computer technology was in its infancy, and the Internet in its current form was hardly imaginable. As technology kept on racing ahead, a growing need emerged to adapt the international standard to the changing reality. Intensive efforts to harmonize copyright protection continued on two main parallel tracks: the WIPO and the WTO. The latter track culminated in the conclusion of the Uruguay Round and the adoption of the TRIPS Agreement in 1994.[38]

Among other things, the TRIPS Agreement addressed the issue of computer programs by mandating copyright protection (as literary work) of software in any form.[39] Importantly, TRIPS adopts the general formula of the three-step test, initially stipulated in Article 9(2) Berne Convention, as a general benchmark qualifying copyright limitations and exceptions to *all* of the exclusive rights TRIPS covers.[40] Among the rights secured under the TRIPS are neighboring rights granted to performers,[41] producers,[42] and broadcasters.[43] TRIPS further partially harmonized minimum copyright duration among all WTO members.[44]

---

the fixation in the computer memory is only transitory. . .could prove an exception." *See* Ulmer, *supra* note 19, ¶ 69 at 53.

37. During the period between the conclusion of the Paris Act in 1971 and the WIPO discussions launched in early 1990s, the issue of digital reproduction has been intensively discussed in national, regional, and international forums. For an overview on this period, see Ficsor, *supra* note 30, §§ 3.26–3.79.

38. *See* Agreement on Trade-Related Aspects of Intellectual Property Rights ("TRIPS Agreement") (1994).

39. *Id.* Art. 10(1).

40. *Id.* Art. 13 ("Members shall confine limitations or exceptions to exclusive rights to certain special cases which do not conflict with a normal exploitation of the work and do not unreasonably prejudice the legitimate interests of the right holder.") This language is very similar but not identical to Art. 9(2) Berne Convention.

41. *Id.* Art. 14(1).

42. *Id.* Art. 14(2).

43. *Id.* Art. 14(3).

44. *Id.* Art. 12. Despite the language triggering the rule when the term of protection "is calculated on a basis other than the life of a natural person," it also applies to authors that are not natural legal persons (e.g., corporations). The counting of the fifty-years term is oriented by the date of *publication* (as opposed to the Berne minimum protection rule that is oriented by the point of making the work available to the public.) *See* Daniel Gervais, The TRIPS Agreement §§ 2.119–2.120 (2003). *See also* Ricketson & Ginsburg, *supra* note 12, §§ 4.31–4.40.

One of the most important contributions of TRIPS to the shape of international copyright is its subjecting violations of main Berne provisions (and TRIPS additional protections, the so-called "Berne-plus" provisions) to the WTO dispute resolution mechanism and threatening violators with operative trade sanctions.[45] However, in spite of the TRIPS' global ambitions, it neglected—while taking note of the parallel track at WIPO[46]—to address various issues related to digital technology and the rise of the Internet.[47] The Agreement incorporates by reference Articles 1 through 21 of the Berne Convention (1971), except for Berne's moral rights provisions.[48] By swallowing a substantial bulk of Berne as is, TRIPS did not offer solutions to problems associated with adaptation of traditional rules to the information environment.

On the parallel track, the WIPO process assumed the responsibility of tackling the thorny issues and establishing an international minimum standard for copyright protection in the Internet era. The WIPO track started to gain momentum in the early 1990s,[49] accelerated by the adoption of TRIPS in April 1994.[50] Around that time, many shared the observation that the Internet had been fundamentally and irreversibly changing markets and social-behavioural patterns to an extent that required an expedited response in the area of copyright regulation. The WIPO process reached a high peak with the assembly of the Diplomatic Conference in Geneva in December 1996. The so-called WIPO "digital agenda" (developed during the preparatory pre-TRIPS period) listed the burning issues calling for immediate treatment.[51] The negotiations during the Diplomatic

---

45. *See* Ricketson & Ginsburg, *supra* note 12 § 4.38 ("[t]he real steel in the spine of the TRIPs Agreement is provided by the dispute-prevention and dispute-settlement provisions of articles 63 and 64.") *See also* Ficsor, *supra* note 30, § 1.25; William R. Cornish, *Foreword* to Ricketson & Ginsburg, *supra* note 12, at v. ("Before [the TRIPS] Berne may have been little more that [sic] a code of polite behaviour. Suddenly it acquired the voice of positive command.").

46. *See* TRIPS Agreement (1994), Preamble (under the letter (e) expressing a desire "to establish a mutually supportive relationship between the WTO and the World Intellectual Property Organization. . . as well as other relevant international organizations").

47. *See* Marci A. Hamilton, *The TRIPS Agreement: Imperialistic, Outdated, and Overprotective*, 29 Vand. J. Transnat'l L. 613 (1996). Issues such as IP-related electronic commerce received more pointed attention within TRIPS circles only some years after the agreement had entered into force. *See* Gervais, note 44. §§ 1.81–1.82.

48. TRIPS Agreement (1994), Art. 9(1).

49. *See* Ficsor, *supra* note 30, §§ 1.26–1.33 (describing in detail the "New Protocol" and the "New Instrument" processes.) *See also* Ricketson & Ginsburg, *supra* note 12, §§ 4.15–4.18.

50. Ficsor, *supra* note 30, § 1.41–1.55. *See also* Ricketson & Ginsburg, *supra* note 12, § 4.19.

51. *See* Mihály Ficsor, *Copyright for the Digital Era: The WIPO "Internet" Treaties*, 21 Colum.-VLA J.L. & Arts 197, 202 (1997) (summarizing the "digital agenda" issues to be later addressed by the WCT and the WTTP, covering certain definitions, rights applicable

Conference resulted in the adoption of two treaties in December 20, 1996: the WIPO Copyright Treaty (WCT) and the WIPO Performances and Phonograms Treaty (WPPT)].

Article 1(1) WCT clarifies that the treaty is a "special agreement" in the meaning of Article 20 Berne Convention.[52] Nothing in the WCT should derogate existing obligations under the Berne Convention;[53] rather, the WCT is said to supplement existing obligations with additional obligations and clarifications.[54] The preamble to the WCT spells out the desire of the contracting parties to develop and maintain effective and uniform copyright protection under emerging technological changes while recognizing the need to maintain a balance between the rights of authors and larger public interests.[55] The WIPO Treaties adhere to the traditional Berne principle of setting a substantive minimum standard of protection. The contracting parties are principally free to go beyond that level, but protection inferior to the substantive minimum is generally impermissible.[56]

(b) Digital Reproduction in the WCT

Ficsor described the issue of digital reproductions as the most controversial matter on the agenda of the Diplomatic Conference.[57] At the heart of the controversy stood the question of how to treat certain temporary and incidental (often imperceptible) reproductions occurring in the course of digital transmissions and other operations of computer systems.[58] After many tussles and turns, the

---

to storage in digital systems, transmission in digital networks, limitations and exceptions in digital copyright, and legal protection to technological protection measures and rights management information systems).

52. *See* WCT Art. 1(1). Article 20 of the Berne Convention reads: "The Governments of the countries of the Union reserve the right to enter into special agreements among themselves, in so far as such agreements grant to authors more extensive rights than those granted by the Convention, or contain other provisions not contrary to this Convention. The provisions of existing agreements which satisfy these conditions shall remain applicable." For a discussion about the implication of the "special agreement" status of the WCT and the WPPT, see Ficsor, *supra* note 30, §§ 2.12–2.15.

53. WCT, Art. 1(2).

54. *See* Ficsor, *supra* note 30, §§ C1.01–C1.20 (providing an extensive commentary on the interrelations between the WCT and other treaties under Art. 1 WCT).

55. *See* WCT Preamble, ¶¶ 1, 3, & 5.

56. It is unclear whether members of the Berne Union may afford protection where Berne *explicitly limits* or *wholly excludes* protection. *See* Ricketson & Ginsburg, *supra* note 12, §§ 6.110–6.111 (arguing *overprotection* in some cases might also violate Berne obligations). Chapter 6 will return to the maximum protection controversy with a pointed analysis. *See* Chapter 6, Section IV.C.2 *infra*.

57. *See* Ficsor, *supra* note 51, at 203.

58. *See* Ficsor, *supra* note 30, § 3.124 (the debate at the Diplomatic Conference did not concern the question whether digital storage constituted reproduction in general, but

WIPO Committee of Experts presented its Basic Proposal for the substantive provisions of the prospective WCT in August 30, 1996. Draft Article 7 of the Basic Proposal provided:

(1) The exclusive right accorded to authors of literary and artistic works in Article 9(1) of the Berne Convention of authorizing the reproduction of their works shall include *direct and indirect reproduction of their works, whether permanent or temporary, in any manner or form.*
(2) Subject to the provisions of Article 9(2) of the Berne Convention, it shall be a matter for legislation in Contracting Parties to limit the right of reproduction in cases where a temporary reproduction has *the sole purpose of making the work perceptible or where the reproduction is of a transient or incidental nature,* provided that such reproduction takes place in the course of use of the work that is *authorized by the author or permitted by law.*[59]

This text exhibits a tendency to avoid a substantive definition of the concept of reproduction.[60] Even under the assumption of an implicit "fixation" requirement, the proposed provision did not resolve the question as to which reproductions should be considered *sufficiently* fixed and which not. According to the Notes to the Draft WCT, the purpose of Draft Article 7 was, inter alia, "to clarify the widely held understanding that both permanent and temporary reproduction constitute reproduction within the meaning of Article 9(1) of the Berne Convention."[61] In a second statement, somewhat contradictory to the first, the Draft noted the divergent national interpretations of this matter needed to be harmonized.[62]

Draft Article 7 triggered a considerable controversy among the delegations attending the Diplomatic Conference. Ficsor, drawing on various proposals submitted by participants, identified four approaches. One proposed that the Treaties should not cover the temporary reproduction at all. The second approach suggested certain temporary reproductions should be explicitly excluded from the concept of reproduction. A third line insisted exceptions concerning certain temporary reproductions must become mandatory. Suggestions to modify the scope of exceptions in Draft Article 7(2) formed a fourth approach.[63] In the end, the participating delegates were unable to resolve their sharp disagreements,

---

rather, whether certain cases of temporary/transient forms of storage implicated the exclusive reproduction right).

59. *See* WCT Basic Proposal (1996), WCT Draft Art. 7 (emphasis added).

60. Paragraph 7(1) clarifies that Article 9(1) "shall include" certain reproductions. However, it does not stipulate what reproduction *is*. *Id*

61. WCT Basic Proposal (1996), Note 7.05.

62. *Id.* Notes 7.14–7.15.

63. *See* Ficsor, *supra* note 30, §§ 3.105–3.110.

and Draft Article 7 did not find its way into the text of the WCT. Instead, the delegates resolved to enter agreed statements[64] to Article 1(4) WCT:

> The reproduction right, as set out in Article 9 of the Berne Convention, and the exceptions permitted thereunder, *fully apply in the digital environment*, in particular to the use of works in digital form. It is understood that the *storage of a protected work in digital form in an electronic medium* constitutes a reproduction within the meaning of Article 9 of the Berne Convention."[65]

A preliminary voting approved unanimously the first sentence, whereas the second sentence was approved with a substantial majority of the votes.[66] In the final act adopting the texts of the WIPO Treaties, including the agreed statements (the agreed statement concerning Article 1(4) WCT was put to voting as one whole), the participants adopted the agreed statement with a majority vote of fifty-one in favor, five against, and thirty abstaining.[67] The agreed statement obtaining majority support by only a slim margin later raised doubts concerning its binding force. Without reaching this technical issue, the language of the statement poses some interpretational challenges.

B. Scope and Impact of the International Standards

Concerning the question of temporary digital reproductions, both Article 9 Berne Convention and the agreed statement to Article 1(4) WCT left behind ambiguities and some open questions. The next passages briefly introduce the major textual construction lines and the dilemma they reflect.

---

64. On the legal status of "agreed statements" and the extensive use of this instrument in the WIPO Treaties, see *id.* §§ 2.31–2.33.

65. *See* Agreed Statement concerning Art.1(4) WCT (emphasis added). For an extensive historical overview on the emergence of this agreed statement, see Ficsor, *supra* note 30, §§ 3.119–3.127. The problem of temporary reproduction arose also in the context of the WPPT. In its final text, the WPPT secures in Articles 7 and 11 the reproduction right of performers and producers, respectively, as "the exclusive right of authorizing the direct or indirect reproduction of their performances fixed in phonograms/phonograms, in any manner or form." The WPPT also stipulated an agreed statement concerning these rights, providing "[t]he reproduction right, as set out in Articles 7 and 11, and the exceptions permitted thereunder through Article 16, fully apply in the digital environment, in particular to the use of performances and phonograms in digital form. It is understood that the storage of a protected performance or phonogram in digital form in an electronic medium constitutes a reproduction within the meaning of these Articles." *See* WPPT, Agreed Statement concerning Articles 7, 11, and 16.

66. *See* Ficsor, *supra* note 30, §§ 3.125–3.126.

67. *Id.* at § 3.127. Also the Agreed Statement concerning Article 7 WPPT (stating the same regarding use of performances and phonograms in digital form) was adopted by a majority vote. *Id.*

1. The Berne Standard

(a) Minimalist and Maximalist Approaches to Article 9(1) Berne Convention

The debate over the scope of Article 9 Berne Convention underscores the fundamental dilemma of choosing between two basic alternatives. One option is to explicitly recognize a sweeping exclusive right spreading over every conceivable form of reproduction, hereinafter called the *maximalist approach*. Any signals duplication would *principally* implicate the reproduction right. Domestic legislatures may nonetheless limit the scope of exclusivity when necessary by stipulating statutory exceptions covering, inter alia, temporary incidental or instrumental digital reproductions. Alternatively, domestic legislatures may exclude, per definition, certain types and forms of digital representation from the territory governed by the exclusive reproduction right mandated under Berne, called hereinafter the *minimalist approach*.

From a pragmatic perspective, two copyright systems following the two different approaches described above might both consider a given act (e.g., an operation involving transient RAM reproductions that facilitate digital transmission) lawful, but for different reasons. The distinction between the maximalist and the minimalist lines is not merely semantic; the choice between alternatives affects the maneuvering space left for domestic legislatures in shaping liability scope under national laws. Consider for instance the application of the three-step test on the scope of the digital reproduction right. According to the maximalist approach, Article 9(2) Berne Convention controls directly each and every domestic deviation from the all-inclusive exclusivity secured under the broad reproduction right.[68] By comparison, under the minimalist approach, to the extent domestic law excludes certain reproduction from that right ab initio, these rules are not directly subject to Article 9(2) Berne Convention. In other words, the approach chosen by the domestic law underlies the critical distinction between certain domestic rules as copyright exceptions (the maximalist approach), or rather, as definitional limitations to the reproduction right (the minimalist approach) to which Article 9(2) does not apply in the first place. The very same domestic rule exempting temporary reproductions could be considered in Jurisdiction A as a copyright exception and in jurisdiction B as a

68. Domestic statutory exceptions to the reproduction right clearly are directly subject to the three-step test in Article 9(2). The difference between the minimalist and the maximalist approach relates is some way to the terminological and doctrinal distinction between "exceptions" and "limitations" underscored by some authors. *Cf.* MARTIN SENFTLEBEN, COPYRIGHT, LIMITATIONS AND THE THREE-STEP TEST 22 (2004). To be sure, the minimalist approach envisions definitional "limitations" that are *not* controlled by the three-step test.

definitional limitation (provided the approach of Jurisdiction B does not conflict with Article 9(1) mandating protection of the reproduction right *in principle.*)[69]

Under the assumption jurisdiction A follows a maximalist approach, the next question concerns the general principles that should guide the formulations of statutory exceptions. In the context of temporary reproduction, both quantitative and qualitative criteria come to mind. Quantitative criteria examine the duration of reproduction, calling for inquires such as (1) *how long* the representation of signals on the component lasts. For instance, if the representation resides on the component for no longer than a threshold temporal limit before erased, reproduction will be covered by a relevant exception. Another quantitative criterion asks (2) *how much* information, that is, what portion of the work resides on the component during a given time interval before it is erased and replaced by a subsequent block of data representing the next portion of the work. For example, it is possible to imagine a rule determining that when no more than 10 percent of the work data resides simultaneously on the component, the act is covered by a special exception. In the case of quantitative criteria designed to fine-tune the scope of exclusivity, some possibly relevant factors are (1) *purpose* of reproduction, (2) *perceptibility* of reproduction, and its (3) *instrumental function,* asking whether it is merely an intermediate step in a process designed to bring about a certain result. A third (sub-) category of guidelines focuses on the question of independent economic significance (*economic/market criteria*).[70]

In Jurisdiction B that follows the minimalist approach, the legislature would face the challenge of (re)defining the reproduction right as applied to temporary digital representations. To illustrate, the definition may contain a negative clause, for instance, "the reproduction right shall not apply to. . . ." Alternatively, the definition could theoretically stipulate the reproduction right is pertinent only to permanent (or "non-temporary") reproductions.[71]

---

69. Ficsor offered the following observation: Definitional limitations on the reproduction right (minimalist approach) that would perfectly parallel the three-step test (maximalist approach) eliminate any practical difference. According to this logic, domestic regulation adopting the minimalist approach would only "formally" conflict with Article 9(1). *See* Ficsor, *supra* note 30, § C1.55. This analysis implies a minimalist approach would be impermissible if the domestic definition to the reproduction right conflicted with the three-step test. This is somewhat circular, as a definition of the reproduction right under the minimalist approach should determine which acts fall outside its scope, not the other way around.

70. *Cf.* Dreier, *supra* note 21, 20–21 (alluding to the possibility of drawing a bright-line rule asking whether from an economic viewpoint, the reproduction opens up a new additional possibility to use the work, including mere display).

71. *Cf.* Ficsor, *supra* note 30, § 3.106 (describing a Chinese proposal in this spirit introduced at the Diplomatic Conference concerning a suggested amendment of Draft Article 7 WCT). Of course, such a definition might not pass scrutiny under Art. 9(1) Berne Convention.

At bottom, the two regulative frameworks (maximalism versus minimalism) confront similar dilemmas while choosing the appropriate criteria for drawing the line between lawful and unlawful instances of digital reproduction. Before turning to examine these dilemmas more closely, we should first consider whether Article 9 itself demonstrates any preference between a minimalist and a maximalist approach. The answer appears to hinge on the interpretation of the wording "any manner or form" in Article 9(1). Some commentators believe the language of Article 9(1) is broad enough to *mandate* full coverage of digital reproductions.[72] This interpretation draws heavily on the concept of *fixation*. Historically, the issue of fixation surfaced in the context of efforts to define reproduction during the 1967 Stockholm Conference.[73] In fact, these efforts were motivated by the wish (1) to clearly *exclude performance* from the notion of reproduction, and (2) to clarify that reproduction of recorded sounds and images (so-called "indirect" reproductions) were *included*.[74]

In the present context, however, the concept of fixation moves beyond its historical distinguishing function toward constituting a positive-*definitional* element of reproduction. In this context, fixation is perceived generally as a representation having a sufficient degree of stability "so that what is fixed can be perceived, reproduced or otherwise communicated."[75] Admittedly, an unqualified application of this fixation standard to the problem of temporary digital

---

72. *See* JORG REINBOTHE & SILKE VON LEWINSKI, THE WIPO TREATIES 1996 42–43 (2002) (in analyzing the scope of Article 9(1) Berne Convention, the authors state "temporary copies are by definition as much acts of reproduction under copyright as permanent ones. . . technical, incidental, or transient copies made for the purpose of caching, browsing, or storage in electronic memories are equally by definition acts of reproduction in this sense"). *See also* FICSOR, *supra* note 30, § C1.46 ("the scope of [the reproduction right under Article 9(1) Berne Convention]—'by definition' (due to the 'any manner and form' language)—cannot be 'extended' further; there is simply no room for such extension"). Apparently holding a similar view, see Ulmer, *supra* note 19, ¶¶ 67–69.

73. *See* RICKETSON & GINSBURG, *supra* note 12, § 11.19.

74. *Id.*

75. *See* REINBOTHE & VON LEWINSKI, *supra* note 72, at 42–43 (citing the Report of the Second WIPO/UNESCO Committee of Experts 242 (1982)); *Cf.* Ficsor, *supra* note 51, at 205 (citing the same report, but only to show that storage *in general* has for a long time been considered reproduction). Notably, this fixation standard is remarkably similar to the statutory definition under U.S. law. It is questionable, however, whether the U.S. statutory fixation standard can be evaluated separate from its limitation prong ("for a period of more than transitory duration"). Ulmer discussed that issue in 1972, at a time when the current 1976 Copyright Act was only preliminary bill legislation. *See* Ulmer, *supra* note 19, at 47–48. The fixation definition in the bill draft cited by Ulmer is identical to the current statutory definition in the U.S. Copyright Act. Ulmer opined that due to the limitation prong, "[A] transitory fixation in computer does not fall within the term 'copy.'" *Id.* ¶ 50 at 48.

reproduction is a fast track to maximalism.[76] Having that said, it is important to remember Berne *has not adopted so far any binding fixation text*, and therefore, a more restrictive standard as applied to digital transient data representations is equally plausible.[77]

(b) Minimalism: The Better View

Given that Berne leaves open the competition between the maximalist and minimalist views, which one would make a better policy choice? A closer look at the key phrase "any manner or form" is a suitable starting point. The term *manner* seems to be referring to the technical procedure of making a copy; in other words, manner is the reproduction technology. The term *form* seems to be referring to the *representation* of information after the procedure is complete.[78] Obviously, copying technology (manner) largely determines its representation (form). However, it is questionable whether certain evanescent digital reproductions have any "form" whatsoever, at least in the strict sense of the term. If digital data, as a physical phenomenon, subsists merely as fleeting electric pulses, can we confidently assert the work has a discernible material "form"?[79] How can pure energy be "fixed"? Can the notion of *material form*—a key element in various fixation definitions—draw inspiration from physics principles and consider mass and energy interconvertible quantities, and by extension underlie the legal conclusion that electric pulses and paper bearing ink printing are interchangeable qualitatively?

The purpose of raising such questions here is not to press the point ad absurdum but to make a simple observation: a completely "open" fixation test might quickly become all-inclusive, stripping the concept of fixation of its key definitional qualities. In the context of Berne and copyright law more generally, the term *form* should not be elevated to Platonic conceptual altitudes. Form here simply implies the *material* that embodies it is indispensable to the notion of a "reproduction." Thus, considering electric pulses that last milliseconds as "form" might indeed stretch the meaning of a "reproduction" beyond its semantic and conceptual breaking point.

The maximalist view weighs heavily on the proposition that fixation occurs as long as the representation is sufficiently stable so that it can be (1) perceived,

---

76. *Cf.* Reinbothe & Von Lewinski, *supra* note 72, at 43; Ficsor, *supra* note 30, § C1.56.

77. "It is open to debate whether the Berne Convention also requires member states to interpret 'any manner or form' to extend to transient digital fixations." *See* Ricketson & Ginsburg, *supra* note 12, § 11.27.

78. Digital "representation" may take various "forms" such as of magnetic charges, electric pulses, and optic signals.

79. *Cf.* Ricketson & Ginsburg, *supra* note 12, § 11.27 ("the need for the fixation to be in a material form, however, may give rise to different views where the form is invisible . . . Some forms of storage. . . consist simply of a series of invisible electrical impulses").

(2) reproduced, *or* (3) communicated from the material object on which it resides. For convenience, this test shall be referred to hereinafter as the *PRC fixation test*. Its wording requires some minimum level of *stability*—one that might be absent in certain evanescent RAM reproductions. To avoid internal inconsistency, the phrase *perceived-reproduced-communicated* must be read together with the requirement that perception, reproduction, or communication occur *from the material object upon which signals are mounted*. Still, if not delimited by an additional clause, the wording of the PRC test can tolerate an extremely broad reading: is an image reflected in the mirror fixation?[80] It can be *perceived* from the mirror, as the recipient can see it. It is *reproduced* from the mirror if the recipient creates a second reflection by setting a second mirror against the first mirror (or if the light beams returning from the first mirror can be stably captured, for instance by photographic equipment). Finally, an object is *communicated* from the mirror if person *A* situates the object and mirror in a position that enables a second person *B* to observe the image returning from the mirror at *B*'s location. Here again, reductio ad absurdum wants to reemphasize that not every instance where signals can be perceived, reproduced, or communicated from an object is fixation. To effectively serve its purpose as a *test*—distinguishing fixed signals from other things—the PRC formulation *must contain a limitation clause to reinforce the attribute of fixation as having minimal stability*.

After concluding that a naked PRC test borders on meaninglessness for most practical purposes, the next question is whether Berne can be read to *imply* a fixation text, and if so, what its content may be. As noted, there is no explicit language in Berne stating an affirmative obligation to apply reproduction rights only to works that are "fixed" under some certain test or standard. Inasmuch as the 1982 Report of the Second UNESCO/WIPO Committee of Governmental Experts can be considered authoritative, its recommendations in Section 3 refer to "*storage in and retrieval from computer systems*."[81] Using the term *storage* could indicate the drafters of that report, while generally recommending adoption of a fixation test to clarify issues of digital reproductions, did not necessarily mean to include electric pulses that are never "stored" anywhere. Based on this analysis, it appears possible to adopt the following preliminary inference as the baseline for interpretation of the international legal standard: if it is true Berne implies a fixation test, and if an unqualified fixation text would be pointless, Berne should also be read to imply a limitation clause to demarcate the notion of fixation.

---

80. *See* Pamela Samuelson, *The NII Intellectual Property Report*, 37 COMM. ACM 21 (Dec. 1994) (proposing the analogy of a book held against a mirror).

81. *See* Second Expert Committee Report on Copyright Problems 245–46 (1982) (emphasis in text added). This report noted that some delegations emphasized the "functional" side regarding sufficient stability while linking it to the inquiry whether the work can be perceived, reproduced, or otherwise communicated to the public with the aid of a computer system. *Id.* at 242.

Regardless of the specific content of a given domestic limitation clause, it is essential domestic legislatures be allowed to adopt one—which in turn supports the minimalist approach concerning definitional limitations on the reproduction right.

2. The Impact of the Agreed Statements to Article 1(4) WCT

Chronicling the efforts to adopt an internationally binding reproduction definition severely undermines the plausibility of the maximalist approach. Within the Berne/WIPO framework, there have been two noteworthy attempts to substantively define the reproduction right, and twice they have failed.[82] Second and most telling was the episode surrounding Draft Article 7 WCT and the agreed statements to Article 1(4) WCT. The reasons leading to the demise of Draft Article 7 are particularly relevant to assessing the proper approach as that unsuccessful provision was a vivid expression of the maximalist vision: paragraph (1) would have established the broad coverage rule, whereas paragraph (2) would have allowed national exceptions "in cases where a temporary reproduction has the sole purpose of making the work perceptible or where the reproduction is of a transient or incidental nature."[83]

Some delegations expressed concerns vis-à-vis paragraph (2) as it implied a direct application of the three-step test (Article 9(2) Berne Convention) in the case of domestic temporary reproduction rules. Moreover, some attendees feared the explicit enumeration of instances in which exceptions are permissible (i.e., temporary reproduction for the sole purpose of making the work perceptible, and reproduction that is transient/incidental in nature) would render other types of exceptions a contrario impermissible.[84] In relation to that, the fear was such a reading of paragraph (2) would render the scope of Article 9 (1) Berne Convention extremely broad, which could have created tension with some existing domestic laws.

---

82. The first attempt was during the 1967 Stockholm conference. *See* RICKETSON & GINSBURG, *supra* note 12, § 11.19 (especially the proposal of the Austrian delegation). This occasion should be distinguished from earlier attempts to *mention* the reproduction right in the language of the Berne Convention without adding a substantive definition. Attempts of the latter sort had already occurred during the 1948 Brussels revision conference. For more details, see *id.* § 11.05 (describing the proposals of the French and the Austrian delegations.) *See also* BAUM, THE BRUSSELS CONFERENCE FOR THE REVISION OF THE BERNE CONVENTION 59 (1948) (noting the proposal at Brussels to grant authors of motion pictures "*expressis verbis the exclusive right of reproduction, distribution, presentation and public performance of their works*").

83. See WCT Basic Proposal (1996), Draft Art. 7.

84. *See, e.g.*, 2 Records of the WIPO 1996 Diplomatic Conference 612 (1999) ¶ 404 (Singapore delegate expresses concerns with regard to Internet browsing and other legitimate activities); *id.* ¶ 257 at 668 (Denmark delegate objected to Draft Art. 7(2) and suggested deleting it); *id.* ¶ 263 at 670 (Sweden delegate cautioned about the explicit exceptions enumeration in Draft Art. 7(2)).

The drafters of the Basic Proposal were well aware of inconsistencies on the question of temporary digital reproduction among domestic laws: "Today, the countries of the Berne Union may interpret the right of reproduction in different ways. Some countries may consider that temporary reproduction, at least some acts of reproduction the results of which live only a very short time, does not fall under the right of reproduction, whereas other countries may take a contrary interpretation."[85] The stated mission of Draft Article 7 was to change that situation, and indeed, such provision probably would have eliminated the minimalist option completely.[86] Some delegates to the Diplomatic Conference vehemently objected to this provision precisely on this ground,[87] which ultimately spelled its demise, and more generally, expressed the rejection in Geneva of the maximalist approach to digital reproduction.[88]

What survived the Diplomatic Conference was the agreed statement to Article 1(4) WCT.[89] Its first sentence ("[t]he reproduction right, as set out in Article 9 of the Berne Convention, and the exceptions permitted thereunder, fully apply in the digital environment, in particular to the use of works in digital form") is said to merely reflect a long-standing practice.[90] However, the second sentence ("[i]t is understood that the storage of a protected work in digital form in an electronic medium constitutes a reproduction within the meaning of Article 9 of the Berne

---

85. *See* WCT Basic Proposal (1996), Note 7.14.

86. *Id.* Note 7.16 ("The only way to harmonize effectively the interpretation of the scope of the right of reproduction is to confirm that temporary reproduction falls within the scope of the right.").

87. *See* Reinbothe & Von Lewinski, *supra* note 72, at 40–42 (describing the debate at the Diplomatic Conference).

88. *See* Pamela Samuelson, *The U.S. Digital Agenda at WIPO*, 37 Va. J. Int'l L. 369, 392 (1997) ("The most honest thing that can be said about the temporary copying of works in computer memory is that there is no international consensus on this subject.").

89. The binding force and effect of this agreed statement is somewhat unclear as it was not adopted by consensus. *See* Reinbothe & Von Lewinski, *supra* note, at 42 (describing the voting on the agreed statement.) *See also* Ficsor, *supra* note 30, § 2.33, C1.52 (arguing the agreed statement to Article 1(4) WCT is a valid and important source of interpretation).

90. *See* Reinbothe & Von Lewinski, *supra* note 72, at 43; Ficsor, *supra* note 30, § C1.50 ("[t]he first sentence of the agreed statement seems completely unnecessary. . .[t]he is no reason whatsoever for any doubts that 'any manner or form' also covers digital form"); Ricketson & Ginsburg, *supra* note 12, § 11.74 (adding that beyond stating the obvious, the emphasis of the first sentence is to confirm the availability of *exceptions*.) *Cf.* Reinbothe & Von Lewinski, *supra* note 72, at 44 ("this wide definition of the acts of reproduction is without prejudice to the application of appropriate limitations of and exceptions to the right of reproduction. In fact, the digital environment necessitates in many cases a re-evaluation of existing limitations and exceptions. It may also call for new exceptions to the rights concerned").

Convention") proves more controversial among commentators.[91] Proponents of the maximalist approach consider it as reinforcing their view, and generally, as supporting the ubiquity of the reproduction right in the digital domain.[92] Others argue the second sentence has precisely the opposite effect: "[T]he second sentence of the agreed statement muddies the water . . . the text scrupulously avoids detailing the meaning of 'storage' . . . the scope of the reproduction right that emerges from the agreed statement remains open to highly variable interpretation."[93]

As a matter of treaty interpretation, the former view is less convincing as it cannot explain why the WCT uses unnecessary words to indicate what (for the maximalist) is a statement of the obvious. As far as the scope of Article 9(1) is concerned, the agreed statement stirs up confusion. If *storage* of works in digital formats on electronic media constitutes reproduction within the meaning of Article 9 Berne Convention,[94] a representation that is not stored may remain beyond its scope. In using the term *storage* to describe reproduction, the language of the agreed statement in fact better supports the minimalist argument. As noted earlier, storage in the context of digital data often describes information that is *kept*, in contrast to information that automatically evaporates after a moment.[95] When it is said digital information is stored on a component, the ordinary reference is to stable memory, and there is no compelling reason to believe the drafters of the WCT meant otherwise.

IV. DIGITAL REPRODUCTION IN U.S. LAW

The development of the digital reproduction right in the United States is interesting in several respects. Over the long years of debate and deliberations preceding the 1976 copyright reform, digital technology was making its first steps, but had already proved significant enough to considerably influence the legislative process. The 1976 reform culminated in a law that stipulates a statutory fixation

91. *Cf.* RICKETSON & GINSBURG, *supra* note 12, at 44 (the sentence is "controversial" but it does not change "the general understanding concerning the concept of reproduction"); *Cf.* FICSOR, *supra* note 30, § C1.51 ("if we said that the first sentence of the agreed statement seems unnecessary since it states the obvious, we should, in fact, say more or less the same thing about the second sentence. Even without it, what is stated in it would clearly follow from Article 9 of the [Berne] Convention").

92. *See, e.g.*, FICSOR, *supra* note 30, § C1.55.

93. *See* RICKETSON & GINSBURG, *supra* note 12, § 11.75 (footnote omitted).

94. WCT (1996), Agreed Statement to Art. 1(4), second sentence.

95. Some popular definitions of storage in the context of information technology confirm this usage. *See, e.g.*, Webopedia (available at http://www.webopedia.com/TERM/s/storage.html (defining *storage* as the "capacity of a device to *hold and retain* data") (emphasis in text added).

test including an explicit limitation clause, which was intended to address situations of temporary or instrumental digital reproductions. Until recently, however—and notwithstanding that limitation clause—the case law has been showing a strong inclination to dilute the limitation impact of this clause while adhering mostly to the maximalist approach.

A. The Copyright Act

The 1976 U.S. Copyright Act defines *copies* as "material objects, other than phonorecords, in which a work is fixed by any method now known or later developed, and from which the work can be perceived, reproduced, or otherwise communicated, either directly or with the aid of a machine or device."[96] This definition represents the classic PRC (perceived-reproduced-communicated) fixation test. Its limitation clause is located somewhere else, under the statutory definition of fixation: "A work is 'fixed' in a tangible medium of expression when its embodiment in a copy or phonorecord, by or under the authority of the author, is *sufficiently permanent or stable* to permit it to be perceived, reproduced, or otherwise communicated *for a period of more than transitory duration.*"[97] Importantly, fixation in the United States is a substantive protection requirement under federal copyright law.[98] Namely, to enjoy the protections of the 1976 Copyright Act, a work must be "fixed in any tangible medium of expression, now known or later developed, from which they can be perceived, reproduced, or otherwise communicated, either directly or with the aid of a machine or device."[99]

The fixation text plays two central roles, first as a subject matter rule and second as a component in the reproduction right's infringement test. In its role as a *subject matter criterion* for works protected under the Copyright Act in general, the fixation text obviously must also be met when exclusive rights other than the reproduction right are later vindicated with respect to those works. The second relevance of fixation concerns a prima facie showing of infringement, namely, proving violation of the duty not to make unauthorized "copies

---

96. *See* 17 U.S.C. §101 (defining *copies*). In the same section, *phonorecords* are similarly defined as "material objects in which sounds, other than those accompanying a motion picture or other audiovisual work, are fixed by any method now known or later developed, and from which the sounds can be perceived, reproduced, or otherwise communicated, either directly or with the aid of a machine or device. The term 'phonorecords' includes the material object in which the sounds are first fixed." *Id.*

97. *Id.* (emphasis added).

98. State and common law copyright protection may cover non-fixed works under certain circumstances, and when preemption does not apply. *See* PATRY, *supra* note 6, § 3:22 (fixation is a constitutional requirement which, inter alia, provides the dividing line between state and common law protection).

99. *See* 17 U.S.C. § 102(a) (subject matter of copyright).

or phonorecords."[100] In this way, the fixation test penetrates to and is dispositive of the infringement question. An unauthorized reproduction that is not sufficiently fixed does not infringe the reproduction right because it does not produce a "copy."

What qualifies as a "reproduction" under the Copyright Act? The Act does not provide a designated statutory definition of the term; instead, its meaning is derived from the definitions of the terms *copies* and *fixation* read in connection with Sections 106(1) (stipulating the reproduction right) and 501(a) (defining infringement thereof).[101] Interestingly, the legal definition of copies uses the term *fixed*, and the legal definition of "fixed works" uses the term *copy*. Tautologies aside, the definition of *copies* exemplifies a classic PRC fixation text for which the statutory definition of *fixation* sets substantive boundaries. That is, to qualify as a reproduction, the representation must be sufficiently permanent or stable for a period of more than transitory duration.

The legislative history of the Copyright Act speaks in a clear voice about the intended operation of the limitation clause: "[T]he definition of 'fixation' would exclude from the concept purely evanescent or transient reproductions such as those projected briefly on a screen, shown electronically on a television or other cathode ray tube, or captured momentarily in the 'memory' of a computer."[102] House Report 94-1476 quoted above is unequivocal about the intention to conceptually *exclude* some type of temporary reproductions, including certain RAM copying, from the ground exclusive rights principally cover.[103] Concurrently, the statute contained several exceptions concerning reproduction and adaptation in the context of computer programs.[104] This could raise questions concerning the

100. 17 U.S.C. § 106(1) ("the owner of copyright under this title has the *exclusive rights to do and to authorize* any of the following: (1) to reproduce the copyrighted work in copies or phonorecords") (emphasis added).

101. The fixation requirement in Section 102(a) is substantive and pertains to rights-holders. It is clear, however, that in order to infringe the reproduction right the defendant must make a "copy" in which, by definition, the work is "fixed." The Act's legislative history illuminates the meaning of reproduction in the following way: "Reproduction.—Read together with the relevant definitions in section 101, the right 'to reproduce the copyrighted work in copies or phonorecords' means the right to produce a material object in which the work is duplicated, transcribed, imitated, or simulated in a fixed form from which it can be 'perceived, reproduced, or otherwise communicated, either directly or with the aid of a machine or device.'" *See* House Report 94–1476 (1976) at 61.

102. *See* House Report 94–1476 (1976) at 53. This House Report indicates that actually, the purpose of the limitation clause is to clarify the distinction between the reproduction right in Section 106(1) and the public display right stipulated in Section 106(5). *Id.* at 62.

103. *See, e.g.*, Mark A. Lemley, *Dealing with Overlapping Copyrights on the Internet* 22 U. Dayton L. Rev. 547, 551 (1997).

104. The Copyright Act allows owners of software copies "to make or authorize the making of another copy or adaptation of that computer program provided . . . that such a new copy or adaptation is created as an essential step in the utilization of the computer

relationship between the general limitation clause and those narrower statutory exceptions. In a nutshell, it appears special statutory exceptions to RAM reproductions are lex specialis, and the fact they exist does not necessarily indicate a contrario that every digital representation in general implicates the reproduction right. The CONTU Report (discussed immediately below) provides the essential background behind these lex specialis rules.

B. Other Sources

1. CONTU Final Report

The 1976 U.S. Copyright Act was passed into law with the acknowledgment that some unsettled issues concerning computer programs would have to be further investigated at a later time. The National Commission on New Technological Uses of Copyrighted Works (CONTU) was called into existence by Congress as part of the effort to address problems raised by the use of the new technologies of photocopying and computers. Direct focus was put on issues of authorship, distribution, and use of copyrighted works with which the (then-pending) revision bill did not deal. After three years of intensive deliberations, CONTU submitted its Final Report on July 31, 1978.[105] This Report is considered one of the most important legislative history documents pertaining to the 1976 Copyright Act in the area of computer programs.[106]

The CONTU Final Report recommended granting statutory copyright protection to computer programs under the upcoming 1976 Copyright Act.[107] It also recommended enacting provisions exempting rightful possessors of computer programs, inter alia, when reproduction is an essential step in utilizing the computer program in conjunction with a machine.[108] In addition, it proposed creating an exemption concerning reproductions for archival purposes, provided

---

program in conjunction with a machine and that it is used in no other manner." *See* 17 U.S.C § 117(a)(1). Subsection (2) grants certain exceptions to owners regarding archival reproduction. *Id.* § 117(a)(2). In 1998, Title III of the DMCA added two subsections to Section 117 concerning certain exceptions for machine maintenance and repair. *Id.* § 117(c)–(d).

105. *See* CONTU Final Report (1978).

106. For an extended review and critique, see Pamela Samuelson, *CONTU Revisited, The Case Against Copyright Protection for Computer Programs in Machine-Readable Form,* 1984 DUKE L. J. 663 (1984).

107. CONTU Final Report (1978) at 11–12. The recommendations were largely endorsed by Congress and are reflected in the current Copyright Act in § 101 (defining computer programs) and § 117(1)–(2) (providing certain exceptions).

108. *Id.* The Report reasoned: "Because the placement of a work into a computer is the preparation of a copy, the law should provide that persons in rightful possession of copies of programs be able to use them freely without fear of exposure to copyright liability." CONTU Final Report (1978) at 13.

such reproductions are destroyed when possession ceases to be rightful or the title to the original copy is transferred.[109]

The Final Report devoted a sparse (yet important) treatment to the issue of fixation in computer components: "The text of the [Copyright Act] makes it clear that the placement of a copyrighted work into a computer . . . is the preparation of a copy. . . Because works in computer storage may be repeatedly reproduced, they are fixed and, therefore, are copies."[110] This last sentence is accompanied by a footnote in which the drafters specifically refer to the comment of the House Report concerning evanescent or transient reproductions. Footnote 111 in the Report states: "Insofar as a contrary conclusion is suggested in one report accompanying the new law, *this should be regarded as incorrect and should not be followed*."[111] The CONTU report then turns to explain why, as a technical matter, reproduction to a computer memory should be considered fixation:

> When a program is copied into the memory of a computer, it still exists in a form from which a human-readable version may be produced. That is, the copy in the computer's memory may be duplicated, just as a version listed on paper or coded on magnetic tape may be. Only when the program is inserted—instruction by instruction—into the processing element of the computer and electrical impulses are sent through the circuitry of the processor to initiate work is the ability to copy lost. This is true at least under the present state of technology. If it should prove possible to tap off these impulses then, perhaps, the process would be all that was appropriated, and no infringement of the copyright would occur.[112]

The contradiction between the position stated in House Report 94-1476 and the CONTU Final Report is evident. The former opined "purely evanescent or transient reproductions" are to be excluded from the concept of fixation. By contrast, the latter adopted a maximalist approach advocating for a broad exclusive right dotted by statutory exceptions. It endorsed the unbridled PRC fixation test, and the instances mentioned in the House Report as being insufficient for fixation were nonetheless said to be fixations because the data could be reproduced from the computer memory components. Terminologically, the CONTU Report underplayed the distinction between computer *memory* and data *storage*.[113]

---

109. *Id.*

110. *Id.* at 22.

111. *Id.* at n.111.

112. *Id.* at 22.

113. *See* Bradley J. Nicholson, *The Ghost in the Machine: MAI Systems Corp. v. Peak Computer, Inc. and the Problem of Copying in RAM*, 10 HIGH TECH. L.J. 147, 153–54 (1995) (referring to this inconsistency while noting the meaning of the Final Report is "ambiguous because it refers to computer storage without defining or distinguishing it from memory"). *Id.* at 154 (footnote omitted).

Congress subsequently adopted the Final Report's proposal concerning statutory exceptions to the reproduction right, albeit with some minor changes.[114] Though these exceptions address only a small fraction of the issues concerning computer memory and the reproduction right, it is still interesting to note they do not apply *quantitative* criteria, at least not as dispositive considerations. For instance, the Final Report recommended a lawful possessor of a software copy be allowed to make another copy, if such copy is *created as an essential step in utilizing the program in conjunction with a machine.*[115] This is clearly a qualitative criterion in which the duration of reproduction seems to be entirely irrelevant. In addition, the proposed section 117(2), dealing with archival reproduction, provided that all archival copies be "destroyed in the event that continued possession of the computer program should cease to be rightful."[116] Here, the duration of representation is secondary and contingent on a juristic factor testing the legality of possession in the original copy. Also here, asking nominally how long archival copies exist matters less. In proposing the two exceptions, the CONTU Report sought to ensure "persons in rightful possession of copies of programs be able to use them freely without fear of exposure to copyright liability."[117] In this respect, CONTU departs from House Report 94-1476 not only on the general point of choosing between a maximalist or a minimalist approach, but also on the *methodology* of delimiting the scope of the right. Whereas the CONTU Report shows a clear preference for qualitative-normative criteria (such as lawful possession, purpose of use, and instrumentality of reproduction),[118] the limitation clause purported in the House Report is essentially quantitative, at least on its face.

2. The U.S. Green and White Papers

The CONTU Final Report tackled only a handful of early issues at the cutting edge of the newly explored interface between digital technology and copyright law. Due to the speed at which digital technology has been moving ahead and spreading during the late 1980s and early 1990s, it has become clear a more comprehensive response is necessary. The 1994 U.S. Green Paper and the 1995 U.S. White Paper are important milestones in the evolution of that response. In February 1993, the Clinton Administration formed the Information Infrastructure Task Force (IITF) and assigned it the mission to "articulate and implement the

---

114. Copyright Amendment, Pub. L. No. 96–517 (1980) (amending § 101 and § 117 regarding computer programs). One significant alteration in the enacted version is the replacement of the beneficiary from "rightful possessor" to "owner," which arguably narrows its scope.

115. *See* CONTU Final Report (1978) at 12.

116. *Id.*

117. *Id.* at 13.

118. *Id.* at 12–14.

Administration's vision for the National Information Infrastructure [NII]."[119] The IITF's Working Group on Intellectual Property Rights (IP Working Group) was established "to resolve issues of concern to copyright and other intellectual property owners regarding the distribution of their works via the NII."[120] The stated mission of the IP Working Group was to "help develop the NII in a manner that will ensure the integrity of intellectual property rights, make the wealth of information and entertainment products more widely available and accessible than ever before, and provide economic incentives to intellectual property rights owners so that they will make their products available through the NII."[121] The assignment of the Working Group on Intellectual Property Rights was hence broader than the limited agenda of CONTU, as the U.S. government required a panoptic perspective stretching along the entire interface between copyright law and new digital information technologies.

(a) The 1994 U.S. Green Paper

In June 1994, the IP Working Group published a preliminary draft report known as the Green Paper (1994 U.S. Green Paper).[122] The Green Paper followed oral testimonies and written comments from the public and interest groups,[123] then was published to further solicit public comments prior to issuance of the final report. The Green Paper provides some important indications concerning the intermediary position held by the IP Working Group on issues of information technology and intellectual property, putting special emphasis on copyright.[124]

As to the problem of digital reproduction, both the preliminary and final reports walked the maximalist's path. The Green Paper called for subjecting practically all types of digital reproduction to the reproduction right.[125]

---

119. For the background of the IITF, see U.S. White Paper (1995) at 1–2. One official document described the National Information Infrastructure (NII) as "a system of high-speed telecommunications networks, databases, and advanced computer systems that will make electronic information and entertainment products more widely available and accessible to the public than ever before." *See* Request for Comments, U.S. Department of Commerce (1993) at 53917.

120. *See* Request for Comments (1993).

121. *Id.*

122. *See* U.S. Green Paper (1994).

123. *Id.* at 1–5.

124. The Green Paper (quite oddly) described intellectual property as "a subtle and esoteric area of the law that evolves in response to technological changes." *See* U.S. Green Paper (1994) at 5 (footnote omitted).

125. The Green Paper stated:

> [The reproduction right] appears likely to be implicated in innumerable NII transactions . . . For example, when a computer user simply "browses" a document resident on another computer, the image on the user's screen exists—under contemporary technology—only by virtue of the copy that has been reproduced *in the user's computer memory* . . . In each of the instances set out below, one or more copies is made, and, necessarily, in the absence of a proof of fair use or other relevant defense,

It stated: "It has long been clear under U.S. law that the placement of a work into a computer's memory amounts to a reproduction of that work."[126] The rationale supporting this position, here again, is that "the work may be, in the law's terms, 'perceived, reproduced, or . . . communicated . . . with the aid of a machine or device.'"[127] In a different context, while reviewing copyright protection eligibility requirements, the Green Paper alluded to the statutory fixation requirement. It noted first digital "transmissions" principally did not amount to fixation.[128] Here, the Green Paper cited the House Report's comment concerning "purely evanescent and transient" reproductions yet in the same breath clarified that RAM copying was found sufficiently stable to constitute fixation by one district court.[129] As a historical document that provides insights into the controversial questions of the time, the Report indeed reflects contradictory sentiments and views about the issue of temporary digital reproduction. The dilemma of its drafters is mirrored in a text that zigzags between upholding a pure PRC test and recognizing a substantive limitation based on the duration of signals. For instance, the Green Paper stated: "When a work is placed into a computer, whether on a disk, diskette, ROM, or other storage device *or in RAM for more than a very brief period*, a copy is made."[130] In this it seems to have principally accepted the notion of RAM reproductions as relevant for infringing the reproduction right, yet without rejecting the possibility of operative, duration-based limitations on the scope of the right. The qualifier "very brief" saw no further explanation in this Report.

(b) The 1995 U.S. White Paper

The final report of the IP Working Group added little to what the Green Paper had to say on this point. The 1995 White Paper generally echoed the same

---

there is an infringement of the reproduction right:

*When a work is placed into a computer, whether on a disk, diskette, ROM, or other storage device or in RAM for more than a very brief period, a copy is made.

*When a printed work is "scanned" into a digital file, a copy—the digital file itself—is made.

*When other works—including photographs, motion pictures, or sound recordings—are digitized, copies are made.

*Whenever a digitized file is "uploaded" from a user's computer to a bulletin board system or other server, a copy is made.

*Whenever a digitized file is "downloaded" from a BBS or other server, a copy is made.

*When a file is transferred from one computer network user to another, multiple copies are made.

See U.S. Green Paper (1994) at 35–37 (emphasis in original) (footnotes omitted).

126. *Id.* at 36.

127. *Id.*

128. *Id.* at 13–15 (fixation of a transmission occurs only to the extent it is simultaneously recorded).

129. *Id.* at 15 & n.32 (citing Advanced Computer Servs. of Michigan, Inc. v. MAI Sys. Corp., 845 F.Supp. 356, 363 (E.D. Va. 1994).

130. *Id.* at 35–36 (emphasis added).

position, including the heavy reliance on the PRC fixation text. To bolster the persuasiveness of this view, the White Paper cited to additional authorities (not forgetting the 1978 CONTU Final Report) as well as more recent court decisions.[131] Notably, it avoided any explicit reference to the "purely evanescent and transient" language of the House Report. In a slight but not insignificant deviation from the preliminary draft, the White Paper expressed the view that *any* embodiment of works occurring in the course of networks transmission (including activities such as Internet browsing, caching, and e-mail applications) triggered the reproduction right.[132] It mentioned in passing the issue of temporary reproduction, but did not recommend any legislative clarifications on the issue of fixation. In its statement on the current state of the law, the White Paper relied on more recent case law, which at that stage already showed strong maximalist inclinations.

3. Digital Reproduction in the Courts

The dilemma between the maximalist and minimalist approach in the United States thus far has not been clarified via post-1976 legislation. Instead, it was litigation and judicial opinions that quite systematically set aside the minimalist interpretation as a possible tool for delimiting the scope of the digital reproduction right. Shortly before the publication of the White Paper in September 1995 and during the period that immediately followed, courts produced decisions specifically addressing the issue of temporary digital reproduction, with a seminal decision from 1993 by the U.S. Court of Appeals for the Ninth Circuit marking the path numerous courts later followed. The law established in *MAI Systems v. Peak* significantly set the standard for RAM reproductions law in the United States.[133]

(a) The MAI Ruling and Related Case Law

MAI Systems manufactured computers and software and provided service to consumers. Peak provided maintenance service to users of the computers sold by MAI.[134] MAI subjected its consumers to strict licensing terms that permitted them to use the software solely to fulfill their own internal information-processing needs.[135] While servicing MAI's computers, and in order to identify the error log, Peak had to run MAI's software, which caused reproduction of the software on the computer RAM.[136]

MAI contended that by doing so, Peak infringed on its exclusive reproduction rights, and the court agreed. It held the RAM reproductions were sufficiently fixed to create a "copy" because "the copy created in the RAM can be 'perceived,

---

131. *See* U.S. White Paper (1995) at 64–66 & n.202–04.

132. *Id.* at 72 & n. 226.

133. *See MAI Systems*, 845 F.Supp. 356.

134. *Id.* at 513.

135. *Id.* at 517, n.3.

136. *Id.* at 518.

reproduced, or otherwise communicated.'"[137] The court rejected Peak's defense under the exceptions enumerated in Section 117 to the Copyright Act as only "owners" of a copy of the computer program were privileged under this exception, whereas MAI's consumers were mere licensees.[138] It seems the *MAI* court sought to erase whatever wrinkles were left in the aftermath of the CONTU report concerning RAM copying, so after citing to that report and other authorities already recognizing *storage* in computer components as a form of copying, it held:

> We recognize that these authorities are somewhat troubling since they do not specify that a copy is created regardless of whether the software is loaded into the RAM, the hard disk or the read only memory ('ROM'). However, since we find that the copy created in the RAM can be 'perceived, reproduced, or otherwise communicated,' we hold that the loading of software into the RAM creates a copy under the Copyright Act. 17 U.S.C. §101.[139]

At least one pre-*MAI* district court decision implied RAM reproductions should be distinguished from ROM or storage on a floppy disc, which could have blurred the bright line rule *MAI* sought to establish.[140] The *MAI* court referred to that decision in holding: "While we recognize that this language [describing the operation of a RAM component in *Apple v. Formula*] is not dispositive, it supports the view that the copy made in RAM is 'fixed' and qualifies as a copy under the Copyright Act."[141] *MAI* suggested therefore that any RAM copying implicated the reproduction right while remaining silent concerning the possible effect of the statutory limitation clause.

The *MAI* decision (and especially its three-page discussion of the law of RAM copying) has been frequently criticized in the literature,[142] which did little to

---

137. *Id.* at 519. Specifically, the court emphasized the fact that Peak's technicians ware able to read (i.e., "perceive") software error log, and this ability was facilitated by the RAM reproduction.

138. *Id.* at 518–19. Several later courts refused to follow this particular part of the *MAI* decision. *See, e.g.*, DSC Commc'ns Corp. v. Pulse Commc'ns, Inc., 170 F.3d 1354, 1360 (Fed. Cir. 1999) ("Plainly, a party who purchases copies of software from the copyright owner can hold a license under a copyright while still being an 'owner' of a copy of the copyrighted software for purposes of section 117. We therefore do not adopt the Ninth Circuit's characterization of all licensees as non-owners.").

139. *Id.* at 519.

140. *See* Apple Computer v. Formula Int'l Inc., 594 F.Supp. 617, 622 (C.D. Cal. 1984) (implying a distinction between ROM storage and RAM which "would be only temporary fixation").

141. *See* MAI Sys. Corp. v. Peak Computer, 991 F.2d 511, 519 (9th. Cir.1993), *cert. denied*, 510 U.S. 1033 (1994).

142. *See, e.g.*, Lemley, *supra* note 104, at 551 (noting, inter alia, that the *MAI* court ignored the "transitory duration" prong of the fixation text).

undermine its sweeping impact on numerous subsequent rulings.[143] At the same time, at least one appellate court decision voiced a more critical tone in a decision concerning transitory reproductions occurring with Internet service providers functioning as passive conduits. In *Costar v. Loopnet*,[144] the Court of Appeals for the Fourth Circuit upheld the "volition or causation" theory as to direct copyright infringement liability, which concerns the minimum requisite level of knowledge of a direct infringer.[145] In support of its holding, the court revisited the concepts of copying and fixation, noting:

> When an electronic infrastructure is designed and managed as a *conduit* of information and data that connects users over the Internet, the owner and manager of the conduit hardly "copies" the information and data in the sense that it fixes a copy in its system *of more than transitory duration*. Even if the information and data are "downloaded" onto the owner's RAM or other component as part of the transmission function, that downloading is a temporary, automatic response to the user's request, and the entire system functions solely to transmit the user's data to the Internet. Under such an arrangement, the ISP provides a system that automatically transmits users' material but is itself totally indifferent to the material's content. In this way, it functions as does a traditional telephone company when it transmits the contents of its users' conversations. While temporary electronic copies may be made in this transmission process, they would appear not to be "fixed" in the sense that they are "of more than transitory duration," and the ISP therefore would not be a "copier" to make it directly liable under the Copyright Act.[146]

---

143. Most courts followed the *MAI v. Peak* maxim, which substantially upheld reproduction for temporary fixations inasmuch as it could be shown the perceived-reproduced-communicated test was satisfied, without devoting too much discussion to the question of duration of fixation as an independent prong that could negate a legal finding of reproduction. Shortly before the conclusion of this study, the Court of Appeals for the Second Circuit deviated from this pattern significantly. *See* The Cartoon Network L.P. v. CSC Holdings, Inc. 536 F.3d 121 (2d. Cir 2008), *cert denied*, 129 S.Ct. 2890 (June 29, 2009). This decision is antithetical to *MAI v. Peak*, or at least to the way in which *MAI* has been interpreted and applied.

144. *See* CoStar Group, Inc. v. Loopnet, Inc. 373 F.3d 544 (4th. Cir. 2004).

145. *Id.* at 549–50 ("While the Copyright Act does not require that the infringer know that he is infringing or that his conduct amount to a willful violation of the copyright owner's rights, it nonetheless requires *conduct* by a person who causes in some meaningful way an infringement . . . to establish *direct* liability under §§ 501 and 106 of the Act, something more must be shown than mere ownership of a machine used by others to make illegal copies. There must be actual infringing conduct with a nexus sufficiently close and causal to the illegal copying that one could conclude that the machine owner himself trespassed on the exclusive domain of the copyright owner.") (emphasis in original).

146. *Id.* at 550–51 (emphasis in original).

Costar recalled the limitation clause had actually been a dispositive fixation criterion for the purpose of assessing liability in the case of RAM reproductions. In addition, the court mixed a normative criterion into the analysis of direct infringement liability. *Costar* made the customary reference to the *MAI* decision, but only to reiterate the undisputed point that the unauthorized "download" of copyrighted software onto a computer component was likely to be infringing.[147] *Costar* added the following important observation:

> "Transitory duration" is thus both a qualitative and quantitative characterization. It is quantitative insofar as it describes the period during which the function occurs, and it is qualitative in the sense that it describes the status of transition. Thus, when the copyrighted software is downloaded onto the computer, because it may be used to serve the computer or the computer owner, it no longer remains transitory. This, however, is unlike an ISP, which provides a system that automatically receives a subscriber's infringing material and transmits it to the Internet at the instigation of the subscriber.[148]

It is interesting to juxtapose this language with that of *Triad Systems v. Southeastern Express*, a 1994 district court decision,[149] which stated:

> [T]he copyright law is not so much concerned with the temporal "duration" of a copy as it is with what that copy does, and what it is capable of doing, while it exists. "Transitory duration" is a relative term that must be interpreted and applied in context. This concept is particularly important in cases involving computer technology where the speed and complexity of machines and software is rapidly advancing, and where the diversity of computer architecture and software design is expanding at an ever-increasing rate.[150]

The *Triad* district court did not question expert testimony presented in that litigation in which it was stated the RAM reproduction subject to the dispute lasted for only a millisecond. The court nonetheless held the "temporal distinction [the Defendant] is attempting to draw is not probative of the fixation question and does not disturb this Court's finding that the copies [the Defendant] makes are sufficiently fixed to be copies under *MAI* and the Copyright Act."[151] This spells out perhaps most vividly the rejection of a duration-based limitation clause. The decision further implies a possible shift to other criteria that are qualitative in nature, asking "what th[e] copy does, and what it is capable of

147. *Id.* at 551.

148. *Id.*

149. *See* Triad Sys. Corp. v. Southeastern Express Co., 31 U.S.P.Q.2d 1239, 1994 WL 446049 (N.D.Cal. 1994), *affirmed in part, reversed in part on other grounds*, 64 F.3d 1330 (9th Cir. 1995). The reversal in part was for reasons unrelated to the present discussion.

150. *Id.* at *5 (citing the CONTU Final Report (1978)).

151. *Id.*

doing, while it exists." Unfortunately for the defendant, in this case the qualitative criteria led the district court to conclude fixation *did* take place, although the representation vanished before the naked eye of a human being could register it.

(b) Some Reflections

I. QUALITATIVE, QUANTITATIVE, AND ECONOMIC CRITERIA

The fundamental problem courts have been grappling with is how to read the statutory limitation clause and judiciously apply it to disputes concerning temporary digital reproductions. The phrase "more than transitory duration"—both metaphorically and semantically—could embrace anything between zero duration and eternity, excluding both extremes. Courts seeking to translate the language "sufficiently permanent or stable . . . for a period of more than transitory duration" into concrete duration thresholds found this prong highly impractical.[152] This provides a possible explanation for the trend of courts substantially disregarding this language even when it could preclude very brief representations of signals.[153]

Discounting the statutory quantitative criterion can affect the infringement analysis in the two following ways: As the *MAI* court and its progeny were inclined to do, courts could simply apply an unqualified PRC fixation text, which they seem to find appealing as the most practical choice. The far more interesting option, however, is reflected in judicial attempts to read into the limitation clause normative and qualitative criteria. For example, in *Triad Systems*, the court replaced (or supplemented) quantitative-duration inquiries with asking "what

152. In a recent important decision, the Second Circuit concluded a temporary buffer reproduction that lasted for no more than 1.2 seconds did not pass the statutory minimum bar. *See* The Cartoon Network L.P. v. CSC Holdings, Inc. 536 F.3d 121,129–30 (2d. Cir 2008), *cert denied*, 129 S.Ct. 2890 (June 29, 2009). The court did not explain why 1.2 seconds was not fixed "for a period of more than transitory duration" as a matter of law, nor did it proclaim the minimum number of seconds that would have passed the quantitative-temporal bar.

153. Would it be correct to say quantitative criteria *in general* are inapposite for any fixation test? Consider the following proposal: Fixation shall occur only when the copyrighted work *in its entirety* (or a given percentage thereof, say fifty percent) is represented on a computer component *simultaneously* for whatever period of time. This version of a quantitative limitation clause could capture temporary RAM copying of entire computer programs, Web pages, texts, and images, but leave certain streaming media and forms of digital transmissions outside the scope of the reproduction right. It would also exclude a large number of reproductions occurring inside Internet infrastructure machinery, which delivers information in units of packets, not as whole works. *Cf.* Graham Knight, *Internet Architecture*, *in* 1 THE INTERNET ENCYCLOPEDIA 244 (Hossein Bidgoli ed., 2004) (explaining the operation of Internet transmission control protocols (TCP), which send packets of data (or "segments") via different routes to the IP destination). This version of a quantitative limitation clause does not appear to have been significantly explored, possibly due to practical measurement difficulties.

th[e] copy does, and what it is capable of doing." Consider further the qualitative standard applied in *Costar*, which led the court to reconstruct the limitation clause as an inquiry regarding the *situation* of the reproduced signals. Representation is "transitory" not only when and because it is temporary, because transitory can also mean being *in transit* from point A to point B. Reproductions are transitory in the sense they are in the condition of traveling through the maze of automated communication hosts and channels powered by "passive" Internet service providers. In addition, economic/market parameters may also influence the fixation question while substituting in the role of quantitative duration factors. A report prepared by the U.S. Copyright Office articulated the prevailing considerations:

> In establishing the dividing line between those reproductions that are subject to the reproduction right and those that are not, we believe that Congress intended the copyright owner's exclusive right to extend to all reproductions from which economic value can be derived. The economic value derived from a reproduction lies in the ability to copy, perceive or communicate it. *Unless a reproduction manifests itself so fleetingly that it cannot be copied, perceived or communicated, the making of that copy should fall within the scope of the copyright owner's exclusive rights.* The dividing line, then, can be drawn between reproductions that exist for a sufficient period of time to be capable of being "perceived, reproduced, or otherwise communicated" and those that do not. As a practical matter, as discussed above, this would cover the temporary copies that are made in RAM in the course of using works on computers and computer networks.[154]

It is highly questionable whether the criterion advocated by the Copyright Office would have a meaningful limiting effect on the PRC text. The report *merges* the perceived-reproduced-communicated conditions and economic significance, suggesting each reproduction that would satisfy the PRC text is important enough economically to be considered as "fixed." Of course, as a practical matter the Copyright Office here promoted a naked PRC fixation test, as the prospects of excluding unfixed "reproduction [that] manifests itself so fleetingly that it cannot be copied, perceived or communicated"[155] are as slight as those of giving any meaningful reading to this quote.

II. NORMATIVE RIGHT-OF-ACCESS CRITERIA FOR THE FIXATION TEXT

Realistically speaking, amending the relevant fixation provisions in U.S. law through legislation appears remote at the moment,[156] and this study will not

154. *See* U.S. Copyright Office Section 104 DMCA Report (2001) at 111–12 (footnotes omitted) (emphasis added).

155. *Id.* at 111.

156. Samuelson, referring generally to the prospects of a meaningful U.S. copyright reform, commented: "The prospects of copyright reform are perhaps so dim that a reasonable person might well think it a fool's errand to contemplate a reform project of any sort."

elaborate on the proper solution for "fixing" the fixation test. Until a more substantial reassessment of the digital reproduction right takes place, it is still possible to think about normative fixation criteria that would guide courts seeking to promote rights-of-access. For example, a mix of normative and economic criteria could delimit the scope of the reproduction right in cases where the temporary representation of digital signals is purely instrumental and for the purpose of facilitating individual human-access to the copyrighted work. This would place purely instrumental reproductions—those that do not significantly affect the exercise of the reproduction right in general and commercial exploitation of the work—*outside the definition* of fixation and beyond the reach of copyright exclusivity. In this way, nonowners should become less dependent on the applicability of statutory exceptions, fair use, or implied license theories. Admittedly this approach cannot solve the structural problem related to the discrepancies between the notions of fixation and "copies" on the one hand and the network reality on the other. Against an unqualified PRC fixation test, however, we may consider it for the moment to be the lesser evil. As we shall see later on, a mature digital copyright law can do much better without such pre-digital notions in place.

V. DIGITAL REPRODUCTION IN EUROPE

A. Early Developments

1. The 1998 E.C. Green Paper

In June 1988, the European Commission issued a comprehensive report titled "Green Paper on Copyright and the Challenges of Technology—Copyright Issues Requiring Immediate Action" (1988 E.C. Green Paper).[157] This was followed by a second report titled "Follow-Up to the Green Paper" issued in January 1991 (1991 E.C. Follow-Up).[158] These twin reports paved the way for the adoption of several copyright-related directives enacted between 1991 and 1996 on issues such as computer programs, rental/lending rights, duration, satellite broadcasting, and cable retransmission and databases (so-called "first generation" directives).[159]

The 1998 E.C. Green Paper distinguished among three types of copying: home copying, "semi-private" copying (i.e., copying made by institutions such as

---

See Pamela Samuelson, *Preliminary Thoughts on Copyright Reform*, 2007 UTAH L. REV. 551, 556 (2007).

157. *See* E.C. Green Paper (1988).

158. *See* E.C. Follow-Up to the Green Paper (1991).

159. *See* Jorg Reinbothe, *European Copyright–Yesterday, Today, Tomorrow*, *in* DIGITAL RIGHTS MANAGEMENT: TECHNOLOGICAL, ECONOMIC, LEGAL AND POLITICAL ASPECTS 406–08 (Eberhard Becker et al. eds., 2003).

educational establishments), and "piracy."[160] This Green Paper considered Article 9 Berne Convention as providing the international framework norm establishing a broad reproduction right. The report further suggested the Berne three-part test was sufficiently flexible, leaving "fairly wide room for manoeuvre" for domestic legislatures.[161] In laying out the principles for possible legislative responses to technological developments, the Commission generally adopted the maximalist view while simultaneously supporting legalization of copying for "personal use" (provided rights-holders receive monetary compensation).[162] A separate chapter in the 1988 E.C. Green Paper was devoted to computer programs. The report adopted the prevailing view by considering computer programs as protected copyright subject matter,[163] stating the issue should be harmonized in Europe via a special directive.[164] The Commission recommended that copyright should subsist in programs "fixed in any form"[165] and that their reproductions, adaptations, and translations be considered copyright-restricted acts, thus subject to the exclusive rights.[166] The report further supported broad exclusivity concerning digital reproductions and upheld the requirement to obtain rights-holders' consent for all such acts.[167] For cases in which the normal use of programs by legitimate users required performing restricted acts, the Commission trusted that licensing agreements would allow them to take place. The report stated:

> [A] broad use right, either formulated as such or resulting from rights to authorize reproduction, rental, adaptation and translation, seems appropriate given the way software is used in practice . . . authorization to use a program must necessarily imply authorization for all acts inherent in any such use.[168]

Regarding "private copying" of computer programs, the report recommended "the [then-prospective software] directive should contain a provision excluding private copying of computer programs in general. At the same time, the production of a backup copy or copies by a legitimate user would explicitly be made permissible."[169] The picture that emerged was of unyielding coverage of the

---

160. *See* E.C. Green Paper (1988), at ¶ 3.1.1.
161. *Id.* at ¶ 3.3.1.
162. *Id.* at ¶ 3.1.2.
163. *Id.* at ¶ 5.5.13.
164. *Id.* at ¶ 5.6.2.
165. *Id.* at ¶ 5.6.8.
166. *Id.* at ¶ 5.6.10.
167. *Id.* at ¶¶ 5.6.11–5.6.12.
168. *Id.* at ¶ 5.6.14. This formulation may cause some confusion. The term "use right" means a broad exclusive right *to authorize use*, not the rights of consumers to use software.
169. *Id.* at ¶¶ 5.6.18. (emphasis added). Here again, the formulation is somewhat clumsy. The report used the term "excluding" to say that private copying principally falls under the exclusive reproduction right.

reproduction right with respect to computer programs with a narrow window left open for legalizing "back-up" copies, presumably via appropriately stipulated exceptions.[170]

2. The 1991 Software Directive

The Green Paper's strict approach is well-mirrored in the 1991 Software Directive.[171] Article 4(a) stipulates an all-embracing reproduction rule[172] while Article 4(b) covers additional related operations occurring in the process of operating a computer program such as translation, adaptation, and arrangements.[173] In some special cases, the Directive requires Member States to provide exceptions to the reproduction right, for example, when reproductions "are necessary for the use of the computer program by the lawful acquirer in accordance with its intended purpose, including for error correction."[174] The Directive further sets forth a rule allowing a rightful user of a copy of a program "to observe, study or test the functioning of the program in order to determine the ideas and principles which underlie any element of the program if he does so while performing any of the acts of loading, displaying, running, transmitting or storing the program which he is entitled to do."[175] Article 6 to the Software Directive provides an elaborate decompilation exception, allowing under certain conditions restricted acts to be performed in order to achieve interoperability with an independently created program without the need to seek rights-holders' authorization.[176] Domestic exceptions under Article 6 must not "unreasonably prejudice the right holder's legitimate interests or conflicts with a normal exploitation of the computer program."[177]

---

170. *Id.* at ¶ 5.8.2. (specifically under letter (f), stating "the reproduction of a computer program for private purposes should not be permitted without authorization of the right holder whereas the production of back-up copies by a legitimate user should be permitted without authorization").

171. *See* E.C. Software Directive (1991).

172. The exclusive rights in software include "the permanent or temporary reproduction of a computer program by any means and in any form, in part or in whole. Insofar as loading, displaying, running, transmission or storage of the computer program necessitate such reproduction, such acts shall be subject to authorization by the rightholder." *Id.* Art. 4(a).

173. *Id.* Art. 4(b) (covering "translation, adaptation, arrangement and any other alteration of a computer program and the reproduction of the results thereof, without prejudice to the rights of the person who alters the program").

174. *Id.* Art. 5(1). This exception is mandatory and is afforded only "[i]n the absence of specific contractual provisions." *Id.*

175. *Id.* Art. 5(3).

176. *Id.* Art. 6(1)–(2).

177. *Id.* Art. 6(3).

3. The 1995 E.C. Green Paper and Its 1996 Follow-Up

In July 1995, the European Commission published another Green Paper titled "Copyright and Related Rights in the Information Society" (1995 E.C. Green Paper).[178] With several copyright directives already in place, the 1995 Green Paper investigated further needs and alternatives for a more comprehensive harmonization. The notions of "information superhighway" and "information society" repeatedly recur as the report describes the evolving technological environment.[179] The report pointed to the cultural, economic, and social dimensions of electronic networks and digital telecommunication as well as to European and international legal aspects of new technologies. This 1995 Green Paper recommended expanding the reproduction concept adopted by the 1991 Software Directive to all types of works and subject matter protected under copyright.[180] The report stated: "[T]he digitization of works or other protected matter should generally fall under the reproduction right, as should such things as loading on to the central memory of a computer."[181] It further recommended a revaluation of existing exceptions that had been promulgated in the past under Article 9(2) Berne Convention, especially in light of the emerging technical ability to monitor private digital copying.[182] The 1996 Follow-Up report to the 1995 E.C. Green Paper framed the issue of digital reproduction more pointedly:

> In the Information Society environment, traditional forms of reproduction (making of a physical copy) coexist with a multitude of new forms of reproducing works and other protected matter, such as scanning of a printed work, or loading and/or storing of digitised material in a computer memory or other electronic system or device. Reproduction may also arise from incidental and ephemeral acts which occur from normal use of an electronic system, for instance, when transmitting material over the nets, such as the Internet. The question has arisen how far such new acts of reproduction are covered by the traditional reproduction right, which still significantly focuses on the traditional understanding of making copies on paper, tape etc. from print works, phonograms or television.[183]

The brisk solution offered to these subtle and complex issues stands in sharp contrast to their sensitive exposition in the report. The Commission stated any

178. *See* E.C. Green Paper (1995).

179. *Id.* at 3–8.

180. *Id.* at 51–52.

181. *Id.* at 52.

182. The Commission seemed to have lost its confidence in the Berne standard alone: "The scope of the reproduction right is a separate question, because so many exceptions have been made by Member States under Article 9(2) of the Berne Convention. Careful consideration will be needed in order to determine which of these exceptions can continue." *Id.*

183. *See* E.C. Follow-Up to the Green Paper (1996) at 9.

digital representation whatsoever implicated the exclusive reproduction right, yet the scope of actual infringement liability may be fine-tuned via the apparatus of copyright exceptions. The Follow-Up report alluded to the different views held by Member States concerning the question of "transient or ephemeral acts of reproduction" as "restricted acts" (i.e., subject to the exclusive rights).[184] Nonetheless, for setting a European-wide harmonization bar, the 1996 report recommended that all forms of digital embodiment should be subject to the exclusive reproduction right, including "transient or other ephemeral acts of reproduction."[185] The 1996 report reiterated that traditional limitations and exceptions in domestic laws must be reassessed in the process of achieving a more harmonized European framework. To the extent harmonization meant adopting either a stricter or softer approach to the issue of reproduction, the report showed a clear preference for more exclusivity and fewer exemptions:

> In more cases than at present . . . rightholders may enjoy, without limitation, an exclusive right to authorise or prohibit acts of reproduction. Such an approach should be taken where certain acts of reproduction would risk unreasonably prejudicing the rightholders legitimate interests or which would conflict with normal exploitation of his intellectual property. In cases where such a risk is less significant or where such an exclusive right is not enforceable for whatever reason, the exclusive right might be replaced by a legal licence combined with a right to remuneration. For other cases the envisaged legislation will set out closely defined fair use exceptions/limitations to the exclusive right destined to accommodate the interests of users or the public at large. When defining such a limited number of harmonised exceptions/limitations, the guidance offered by Article 9(2) Berne Convention shall be taken fully into account.[186]

B. Digital Reproduction in the 2001 EUCD

1. Article 2 EUCD

Against this backdrop, the maximalist sentiments reflected in the 2001 Copyright Directive come as little surprise. Article 2 EUCD addresses the reproduction right, with the articulation being concise and overarching: "Member States shall provide for the exclusive right to authorise or prohibit direct or indirect, temporary or permanent reproduction by any means and in any form, in whole or in part."[187] Article 2 thus does not explain (or harmonize) the term *reproduction* beyond simply enumerating controversial instances as falling under the concept of reproduction without providing a substantive definition and without reaching

184. *Id.* at 8–9.
185. *Id.* at 11.
186. *Id.* at 11–12.
187. *See* EUCD (2001), Art. 2.

the fixation text.[188] Assuming the intention behind the wording of Article 2 was to capture under the concept of reproduction all forms of digital signals' placements, the lack of a definition of reproduction appears quite understandable. In addition, the wording "in whole or in part" seems to have eliminated the possibility of adopting a domestic quantitative limitation clause based on the portion of the work simultaneously residing on the memory component.

2. Article 5(1) EUCD

The maximalist approach of Article 2 finds expression, inter alia, in the exceptions catalog listed under Article 5 EUCD. To preserve uniformity in the area of exceptions among Member States, Article 5 embodies an exhaustive enumeration of mandatory and elective exceptions. Most relevantly, sub-article (1) provides:

> Exceptions and limitations
>
> 1. Temporary acts of reproduction referred to in Article 2, which are transient or incidental, which are an integral and essential part of a technological process and whose sole purpose is to enable:
>   (a) a transmission in a network between third parties by an intermediary, or
>   (b) a lawful use of a work or other subject-matter to be made, and which have no independent economic significance, shall be exempted from the reproduction right provided for in Article 2.[189]

This wording clarifies beyond any doubt that "temporary" in Article 2 captures all transient, incidental, and instrumental reproductions. The phrase "an integral and essential part of a technological process" remains quite ambivalent, though.[190] The structure of this provision implies that some temporary reproductions, which are "an integral and essential part of a technological process" performed for lawful use, shall be permissible *beyond* those network transmission reproductions between third parties. This leads to a second difficulty—to decipher the phrase "lawful use"—in connection with the provision in subsection 5(1)(b) instructing domestic legislatures to provide exceptions to the reproduction

---

188. The term *fixation* appears no fewer that seven times in the text of the Directive. Still, its drafters have chosen to leave it undefined.

189. *See* EUCD (2001), Art. 5(1).

190. Bechtold noted Art. 5(1) applies to "reproductions that exist due to technical necessities. Internet routers and proxy servers do not exist in order to make reproductions of copyrighted works, but due to network addressing, management and performance issues." *See* Bechtold, *Directive 2001/29/EC (Information Society Directive), in* CONCISE EUROPEAN COPYRIGHT LAW 372 (Thomas Drier & P. Bernt Hugenholtz eds., 2006). But what should "technical necessity" mean? Strictly speaking, most (if not all) temporary reproductions fulfill a technical task, and the general phrasing "integral and essential part of a technological process" cannot apply exclusively to ISPs cashing, network proxy servers, and the like reproductions, as this seems to be a *special* case expressly addressed in Art. 5(1)(a).

right for the sole purpose of enabling "lawful use." What renders a use lawful? And if the use is already lawful, why should it be subject to a mandatory exception? Recital 33 attempts to provide some clarifications:

> The exclusive right of reproduction should be subject to an exception to allow certain acts of temporary reproduction, which are transient or incidental reproductions, forming an integral and essential part of a technological process and carried out for the sole purpose of enabling either efficient transmission in a network between third parties by an intermediary, or a lawful use of a work or other subject-matter to be made. The acts of reproduction concerned should have no separate economic value on their own. To the extent that they meet these conditions, this exception should include acts which enable browsing as well as acts of caching to take place, including those which enable transmission systems to function efficiently . . . A use should be considered lawful where it is authorised by the rightholder or not restricted by law.[191]

Beyond the fact this Recital does not throw new light on the general meaning of the phrase "an integral and essential part of a technological process," it raises the suspicion the phrase "lawful use" is redundant. If "lawful" means either a use authorized by rights-holders or one already covered by statutory exceptions, the law would be the same with or without sub-article 1(b). To avoid this interpretation problem, we must assume a third category of instrumental reproductions that are neither authorized nor covered by exceptions *but are nonetheless lawful*. Even so, the extent to which sub-article 1(b) can liberalize the domestic exceptions apparatus seems rather limited. According to the Directive's maximalist approach, everything is reproduction, and deviations from the general exclusivity principle are possible only via enlisted exceptions, the criteria for which appear in Article 5.

The threshold criterion resembles a general *quantitative* test, requiring the reproduction to be "temporary." This is a generic label denoting all sorts of short-lived digital representations as distinguished from stable storage. Article 5(1) further stipulates a series of cumulative-*qualitative* factors: namely, reproduction must be (1) transient or incidental and (2) an integral and essential part of a technological process; also its (3) sole purpose is to enable transmission or lawful use. Finally, all exceptions are subject to an economic criterion, which is derived from the phrase "which have no independent economic significance" from Recital 33, and from Article 5(5) EUCD.[192]

As to mandatory exceptions warranted under Article 5(1), the formulation criteria are highly restrictive. The narrowness of the framework is expressed, inter alia, by the restricting clauses "for the *sole purpose*" and "no independent

191. *See* EUCD (2001), Recital 33.

192. *See* EUCD (2001), Art. 5(5) (subjecting all elective and mandatory exceptions to the three-part test).

economic significance." Furthermore, the structure of the provision reveals a clear hierarchy among the various factors. Most importantly, normative-qualitative considerations are subordinated to economic significance scrutiny. This means even in the rare case a given reproduction passed the rigorous three-factor normative threshold, economic-market considerations might foreclose it—for instance, in a case in which an independent economic significance of the said reproduction can be shown.

VI. THE DIGITAL REPRODUCTION RIGHT AS ACCESS-RIGHT

A. Access and Reproduction—A Convergence

How and where should the digital reproduction right be situated in the broad access-right framework presented in the previous chapter? In what respect does the broad digital reproduction right drive the copyright system closer to becoming an access-right regime? The alarm bells already started to go off with the publication of the 1994 U.S. Green Paper, as some copyright commentators vehemently warned against the expansion of the reproduction right to paradigmatic human-access situations.[193] Comparing the ability of users to access works from analog media (such as books) to digital media, experts voiced concerns regarding the penetration of copyright exclusivity into private access situations where it has never belonged.[194]

The invocation of these warnings about the resulting *material* upgrade of copyright protection is confirmed as we turn to apply the analytical framework from Chapter 3: to the extent that (1) liability is triggered as nonowners merely operate digital hardware, software, software-based products, browse the Internet, etc., and (2) inasmuch as the sole purpose of such actions is to gain access to works, then a significant convergence between the spectrum of behaviors the reproduction right controls and access-conducts becomes undeniable. Copyright-relevant reproductions and access-conducts turn out to be one and the same thing, as in the digital environment it grows increasingly difficult to separate access-conducts and reproductions both conceptually and practically. Inasmuch as the reproduction right entails a rights-holders' veto power on access-conducts that are necessary for achieving human-access, there is a clear overlap between the *first access-right prong* and the exclusive reproduction right. In other words, the reproduction right in the digital setting is more intimately related to

---

193. *See, e.g.*, Jessica Litman, *The Exclusive Rights to Read*, 13 CARDOZO ARTS & ENT. L.J. 29 (1994); Samuelson, *supra* note 80; Pamela Samuelson, *The Copyright Grab*, 4 WIRED 134 (1996) (criticizing the U.S. 1995 White Paper).

194. *See, e.g.*, THE DIGITAL DILEMMA, *supra* note 17, at 108–09 (warning against blurring distinctions between private and public copyright-relevant activities in the new information environment).

human-access and is less about fixation or distribution of tangible copies. The descriptive conclusion is that the merger between the ground covered by that exclusive right and conducts enabling *human-access* to digital content reinforces the dominance of the access-right characteristics copyright law has been assuming.

B. Toward a Normative Right-of-Access Criterion

As emphasized, it is possible to restrict the scope of the digital reproduction right by introducing a limitation clause to accompany the standard fixation test. Such a clause would accommodate various policy goals that aim at relaxing the grip of copyright exclusivity while stipulating a mix of criteria to mark the desirable boundaries around the fixation concept. Accordingly, lawmakers should build normative constraints into the basic perceived-reproduced-communicated (PRC) fixation test. In cases where digital reproduction and access-conducts substantially converge, the law could *exempt* reproductions that occur for the sole purpose of private perception of copyrighted information.[195] Alternatively, the law could throw such activities outside the domain of copyright protection altogether while declaring access-conducts in private circumstances *copyright irrelevant*.

As a matter of international copyright law, both options are feasible, and the clause's limiting criteria may combine both economic and normative considerations. The former set of considerations would invite a case-by-case inquiry concerning the anticipated economic implication of the suspect act. The latter set of considerations may include questions such as (1) the purpose of reproduction, (2) the technical procedure of gaining access, (3) the automated nature of the process, (4) the awareness of users of the fact that reproductions take place, (5) the possibility of achieving access while avoiding such reproductions, (6) the ability to directly perceive the resulting digital representation, and so on. In contrast to the approach reflected in Article 5 EUCD, the normative considerations *shall not be secondary* to the economic ones, and the specific formulation of the limiting clause can draw on language already existing in international instruments. One source could be Draft Article 7(2) WCT, which proposed "to limit the right of reproduction in cases where a temporary reproduction has the *sole purpose of making the work perceptible.*"[196] Lawmakers may additionally find inspiration in the agreed statement concerning Articles 6 and 7 WCT: "[T]he expressions 'copies' and 'original and copies' . . . refer exclusively to fixed copies *that can be put into circulation as tangible objects.*"[197]

---

195. Among the exempted activities one could mention certain RAM reproductions, as well as other types of digital representations created automatically in the course of the privately operating digital equipment and media.

196. *See* WCT Basic Proposal (1996), WCT Draft Art. 7 (emphasis added).

197. *See* WCT (1996), Agreed Statement concerning Articles 6 and 7 (emphasis added). This wording comes close to a limitation clause on the PRC fixation test. Interestingly,

In this light, temporary reproductions (1) that are performed solely for the purpose of making a work perceptible to humans, (2) that continue only for as long as it is necessary to perceive the work, (3) that have no significant or independent economic value, and (4) that have no more than an insignificant effect on rights-holders' exploitation opportunities should not be curtailed by the exclusive reproduction right. Regarding the last two criteria, economic value and impact on exploitation opportunities are important but not paramount or a priori superior to other considerations.[198] Giving equal weight to economic and access-sensitive normative factors in the course of scrutinizing *all* the relevant interests surrounding the reproduction might produce a balanced law.

C. The Death of the Reproduction Right

An enormous amount of intellectual energy has been spent in recent years on attempts to remodel exemptions to exclusive rights, most relevantly as to the reproduction right, in efforts to prevent overprotection and preserve the "delicate copyright balance."[199] The analysis in this chapter and the limited force of its own modest proposal concerning the question of fixation lead to the conclusion that an exclusive right tailored around the concept of fixation of signals cannot continue to be one of the most basic building blocks of copyright law.[200]

The reproduction right belongs to past chapters in copyright law's evolution; it has grown evidently unsuitable to usher the system into the digital future. The notion of fixation is structurally inimical to contemporary modes and methods

---

this provision embodied a mixture of qualitative and economic considerations according to which representation of signals is considered copyright relevant as a "copy" only inasmuch as the object can be traded and circulated in the marketplace. The next chapter will discuss that provision and its lessons. *See* Chapter 5, Section III.A.2 *infra*.

198. Consider a future automated online DRM-supported payment system that would be able to detect and charge users for each work-bit ever duplicated on their equipment (even if lasting only a millisecond). In such reality, any conceivable duplication of any portion of the work's signals could be said to have a direct and independent economic significance.

199. As a side note, the recurring phrase "copyright balance" is rarely explained in texts that mention it, and attempts to clarify it usually stick to very general formulations. *See, e.g.*, SENFTLEBEN, *supra* note 68, at 35 ("the copyright balance can be characterized as shifting"). This author concluded "copyright's balance has two sides: the side of the authors and the side of users. . . the two 'poles,' in reality, are two sides of the same coin." *Id.* at 41. For a skeptical comment on the conceptual evasiveness of balance in intellectual property law, see Tom Bell, *Indelicate Imbalancing in Copyright and Patent Law*, *in* COPY FIGHTS: THE FUTURE OF INTELLECTUAL PROPERTY IN THE INFORMATION AGE (Adam Thierer & Clyde Wayne Crews Jr. eds., 2002).

200. *See* Ernest Miller & Joan Feigenbaum, *Taking the Copy Out of Copyright* (2002) (available at http://www.cs.yale.edu/homes/jf/MF.pdf). For a discussion questioning the rationale and operation of the reproduction right in context of evaluating the future of copyright law see Paul Edward Geller, *Beyond the Copyright Crisis: Principles for Change*, 55 J. COPYRIGHT SOC'Y U.S.A. 165, 179–81 (2008).

of providing and gaining access to digital information. Fixation, in other words, is the "yesterday" of copyright law. Modern-day legislatures must define and refine alternative concepts around which the apparatus of exclusivity shall be tailored. With this critique in mind, the next chapter will review the digital communication right. As it shall be demonstrated, exclusive communication rights have also been increasingly acquiring dominant access-right qualities.

5. THE DIGITAL COMMUNICATION RIGHT

I. INTRODUCTION

Copyright law has long recognized authors' entitlement to control nonphysical exploitations of certain types of works.[1] The acts controlled by communication rights are typically public performances and other public communications of performable works, both directly and indirectly (i.e., with the aid of logistic media and physical communication channels). Direct communications, in which performers use primarily their own bodies to render the work, have been subject to copyright from the early days.[2] With the arrival of mass media telecommunication and technologies such as radio, television, satellite, and cable, copyright expanded to cover performances that reach numerous remote and disperse recipients using home devices and appliances to receive transmissions.

Infringement of the exclusive rights to communicate a work to the public,[3] or the right of public performance,[4] is generally unrelated to the question of fixation discussed in the previous chapter. Communication rights are delimited in various other ways, inter alia, through non-voluntary licenses concerning certain broadcasts and performances. But the advent of digital transmission seriously confused the distinctions between the fixed and the unfixed, the private and the public. Digital transmission introduced concepts such as webcasting and streaming media that involve mixed elements of both broadcasting and reproduction of electronic signals.[5] Then again, the technical fact transmissions routinely create electronic representations of work signals does not warrant the conclusion that "copies" in the meaning of the reproduction and distribution rights are being made and disseminated. Indeed, new technologies allowing transfer of digital

1. In German law, the exclusive rights concerning exploitation in nonmaterial forms ("communication" rights) are bunched together in a consecutive "block" under §§ 19–22 UrhG.

2. For instance, in the late eighteenth century, French performances of dramatic works were already protected by the vesting in the *Comédie Française* of the exclusive right to perform such works. *See* Jane C. Ginsburg, *A Tale of Two Copyrights: Literary Property in Revolutionary France and America*, 64 TULANE L. REV. 991, 997–98 (1990).

3. For German law, see § 19 UrhG.

4. For U.S. law, see 17 U.S.C. § 106(4) (granting an exclusive public performance right in "literary, musical, dramatic, and choreographic works, pantomimes, and motion pictures and other audiovisual works").

5. *See, e.g.*, Louisa Ha, *Webcasting*, *in* 3 THE INTERNET ENCYCLOPEDIA 674 (Hossein Bidgoli ed. 2004); Herbert Tuttle, *Video Streaming*, *in* 3 THE INTERNET ENCYCLOPEDIA 554 (Hossein Bidgoli ed., 2004).

signals via local and global networks do not fit comfortably within the classic rubrics of traditional copyright as they significantly blur the long-standing distinctions between copy-related rights (such as reproduction, distribution, or rental) and copy-unrelated rights (including various communication rights).

As these recognitions have begun to sink in, the burning question with which lawmakers were engaged was not *whether* to subject digital transmission activities to copyright regulation, but *how* to do so. The debate mainly circled around the applicability of a specific exclusive right (or rights) to the various forms of digital transmission available. One thorny issue concerned on-demand webcasting technology,[6] where transmission of specific content to a specific location happens as individual consumers send specific requests asking for that content. This process differs from traditional notions of broadcasting or communication to the public, and it underlies distinguishable exploitation models. Uncertainties regarding the applicable exclusive rights in such situations also spawned confusion as to the relevant exemptions, for example, the role of exhaustion rules in such situations.

As markets for networked digital transmissions became increasingly lucrative, and as new technologies have been gradually substituting in for traditional mass-media channels such as radio and television, the copyright issues involved began to become pressing. Perhaps the most important milestone in the development of communication rights in recent years was the conclusion of the 1996 WIPO Treaties and the exclusive communication and "making-available" rights they introduced. This chapter discusses the shift from traditional broadcasting media and other forms of analog communications to digital communication and the legal change it brought with it.

II. COMMUNICATION RIGHTS IN THE BERNE CONVENTION

The current text of the Berne Convention entertains several provisions expressing the rights of public performance and communication to the public by transmission. These provisions, generally called "communication rights," cover a range of activities essentially involving large-scale diffusion of works in nonmaterial form. Berne mirrors traditional copyright doctrine, which methodologically distinguishes such activities from copy-related rights,[7] and this distinction is clearly reflected in the structure of the Berne rights. Communication rights cover live

---

6. The term *on-demand* commonly refers to users' ability to control the scheduling and appearance of the content transmitted over the Internet. *See* Ha, *supra* note 5, at 679.

7. *See* Sam Ricketson & Jane C. Ginsburg, International Copyright and Neighboring Rights: The Berne Convention and Beyond § 12.04 (2006) ("[performance] is the opposite of reproduction, in the sense that no "copy" is produced by the performance, although obviously a copy may be necessary in order for it to take place").

performances before an audience within proximity to allow direct perception of the performance (with or without amplifying equipment to enhance sound and images) and performance of recorded works, as well as various kinds of broadcasting of both live and recorded acts. In the case of broadcasting, the performance can reach a very large number of receivers who, on their part, must operate devices capable of capturing and rendering broadcasting signals. The Berne Convention covers such types of communication as long as they are "public." The relevant Convention provisions refer explicitly and consistently only to public acts or acts directed at the public. At the same time, the Convention itself provides little guidance concerning the distinction between public and nonpublic communications, and the key concepts of "public" or "to the public" are determined according to domestic rules.[8]

In Berne vernacular, the term *public performance* means the presentation of a work before a live audience, as distinguished from communication by transmission to a remote audience.[9] Accordingly, it is possible to describe Berne communication rights as falling under one of two general categories: public performance rights or rights of communication to the public. The next pages provide a brief overview on the relevant Berne provisions regarding this distinction.

A. Public Performance Rights

Article 11(1)(i) Berne Convention provides authors of *dramatic, dramatico-musical, and musical* works the exclusive right to authorize public performance of their works by any means or process.[10] The phrase "any means or process" was added to Article 11 to clarify that performances by means of sound recordings, tapes, and other devices are covered by this public performance right.[11] In other words,

---

8. *Id.* § 12.02. The NAFTA Agreement provides an important example of the concept of the public in this context. *See* Art. 1721(2) NAFTA (1992) ("*public* includes, with respect to rights of communication and performance of works provided for under Articles 11, 11bis(1) and 14(1)(ii) of the Berne Convention, with respect to dramatic, dramatico-musical, musical and cinematographic works, at least, any aggregation of individuals intended to be the object of, and capable of perceiving, communications or performances of works, regardless of whether they can do so at the same or different times or in the same or different places, provided that such an aggregation is larger than a family and its immediate circle of acquaintances or is not a group comprising a limited number of individuals having similarly close ties that has not been formed for the principal purpose of receiving such performances and communications of works").

9. *See* Ricketson & Ginsburg, *supra* note 7, § 12.06. *See also* Mihály Ficsor, The Law of Copyright and the Internet § 4.18 (2002).

10. *See* Berne Convention (1971), Art. 11(1)(i) ("Authors of dramatic, dramatico-musical and musical works shall enjoy the exclusive right of authorizing . . . the public performance of their works, including such public performance by any means or process.").

11. *See* Ricketson & Ginsburg, *supra* note 7, § 12.13.

both live performances and recitation of prerecorded works are covered provided the "public" is present where the work is rendered.

Article 11ter(1)(i) Berne Convention secures for authors of *literary works* the exclusive right of authorizing the public recitation of their works by any means or process.[12] This provision creates certain symmetry between rights concerning dramatic/musical works and the rights granted to authors of literary works under Article 11.[13] Article 14(1)(ii) provides authors of *literary and artistic* works are granted the exclusive right of authorizing the public performance and communication to the public *by wire* of *cinematographic adaptations* of their works.[14]

Article 14bis(1) equates the positions of rights-holders in cinematographic works with that of authors of original works, particularly concerning their respective public performance rights.[15] The applicability of Berne public performance rights to digital transmission is limited, which is attributable to the narrowness of the public performance notion. This notion requires the audience to be physically present in the place where the act of performance takes place or where the performance is made simultaneously perceptible to recipients.[16] By comparison, digital transmission (discussed immediately below) often lacks these characteristics.

B. Rights of Communication to the Public

Communication-by-transmission rights are distinguishable from public performance because they lack the requirement the public be present where the communication conduct occurs or where it becomes perceptible. The Berne notion of communication to the public covers over-the-air broadcasting, cables, satellite, and digital network transmissions. However, there is no single provision in the Berne Convention that regulates these activities systematically.

Article 11(1)(ii) grants the owners of *dramatic, dramatico-musical, and musical* works an exclusive right concerning "any communication to the public of the

---

12. *See* Berne Convention (1971), Art. 11ter(1)(i) ("Authors of literary works shall enjoy the exclusive right of authorizing . . . the public recitation of their works, including such public recitation by any means or process.").

13. Ricketson & Ginsburg, *supra* note 7, § 12.14.

14. Berne Convention (1971), Art. 14(1)(ii) ("Authors of literary or artistic works shall have the exclusive right of authorizing . . . the public performance and communication to the public by wire of [cinematographic adaptations of their works].").

15. *Id.* Art. 14bis(1) ("Without prejudice to the copyright in any work which may have been adapted or reproduced, a cinematographic work shall be protected as an original work. The owner of copyright in a cinematographic work shall enjoy the same rights as the author of an original work, including the rights referred to in the preceding Article.").

16. *See* Ficsor, *supra* note 9, § 4.18 (as the public performance right clearly means performance of works in the presence of the public, or at least, in a place open to the public, it lacks direct relevancy to the digital network environment).

performance of their works."[17] The term "any communication" does not include broadcasting, which is regulated separately in Article 11bis of the Convention.[18] Article 11ter(1)(i) grants a similar right to authors of *literary works* concerning *recitations.*[19] Article 11bis(1) grants communication rights that apply to *all work categories* protected under Berne, but specifies three types of protected communications:

Paragraph (1)(i) covers broadcasting of works or the communication thereof to the public "by any other means of wireless diffusion of signs, sounds or images."[20]

Paragraph (1)(ii) covers "any communication to the public by wire or by rebroadcasting of the broadcast of the work, when this communication is made by an organization other than the original one."[21]

Paragraph (1)(iii) covers public communications done "by loudspeaker or any other analogous instrument transmitting, by signs, sounds or images, the broadcast of the work."[22]

Article 11bis(2) allows Berne members to subject certain public communications to compulsory license regimes.[23] However, it is not applicable in cases of communication other than the three types enumerated in Article 11bis(1).[24] Concluding the list of Berne communication rights is Article 14bis(1), which provides the exclusive right of communication to the public *by wire* of *cinematographic works.*[25] Article 14(1)(ii) grants authors of *literary and artistic works* the exclusive right of communication to the public *by wire* of *cinematographic adaptations* of their works.[26]

To summarize, the Berne framework of communication rights yields the following: All work categories enjoy an exclusive right of *wireless* communication to the public,[27] and an exclusive right with regard to wire/wireless secondary transmission.[28] However, the exclusive right of *primary transmission by wire*

---

17. Berne Convention (1971), Art. 11(1)(ii).

18. For further discussion, see FICSOR, *supra* note 9, § 4.19 & §§ 4.23–4.27 (discussing the application of the 1961 Rome Convention to broadcasting activities).

19. Berne Convention (1971), Art. 11ter(1)(i).

20. *Id.* Art. 11bis(1)(i).

21. *Id.* Art. 11bis(1)(ii).

22. *Id.* Art. 11bis(1)(iii).

23. *Id.* Art. 11bis(2). *See also* RICKETSON & GINSBURG, *supra* note 7, § 12.33.

24. For a detailed analysis of Art. 11bis and the types of communication it covers, see *id.* §§ 12.33–12.42.

25. Berne Convention (1971), Art. 14bis(1).

26. *Id.* Art 14(1)(ii).

27. *Id.* Art. 11bis(1)(i) (possibly subject to domestic non-voluntary licensing).

28. *Id.* Art. 11bis(1)(ii).

applies only to: (1) cinematographic works;[29] (2) literary and artistic works to the extent they are adapted into cinematographic works;[30] and (3) literary, musical, dramatic, and dramatico-musical works, but only as *performed or recited*.[31] Consequently, texts of literary works and sheets of musical and dramatic works, as well as still artistic images, are left outside the scope of the exclusive right of primary wired communication.

C. Distribution Rights

As digital transmission involves new reproduction of signals in different places, the exclusive distribution right calls for brief consideration. Generally speaking, the exclusive distribution right affords rights-holders control over the initial market circulation of copies and phonorecords. Despite its prevalence in domestic laws, the current text of the Berne Convention does not stipulate a general distribution right.[32] However, the Convention contains three narrower provisions relevant in this context as affecting dissemination of copyrighted works to the public: Article 14(1)(i) provides an exclusive distribution right only with respect to adaptations and reproductions of cinematographic works.[33] Article 16(1) stipulates a hybrid right/remedy provision—namely, the entitlement to seize infringing copies.[34] (This entitlement can be regarded as a "converse" distribution right because it supports rights-holders' entitlement to *pull out of circulation* infringing copies possessed by others.)[35] Finally, Article 14ter provides an optional right pertaining to original works of art and original manuscripts, which is meant to secure the creator's financial interest in downstream transactions in the genuine piece (*droit de suite*).[36] This peculiar entitlement is neither an "affirmative" exclusive right to authorize distribution of copies nor a "converse" right to eliminate infringing copies: *droit de suite* contains elements of both.[37]

---

29. *Id.* Art. 14bis(1).

30. *Id.* Art. 14(1)(ii).

31. *Id.* Art. 14ter(1).

32. For an overview of efforts to introduce a general distribution right into the Berne text, see RICKETSON & GINSBURG, *supra* note 7, §§ 11.51–11.52; FICSOR, *supra* note 9, §§ 4.05–4.08.

33. Berne Convention (1971), Art. 14(1)(i). For a discussion on the scope of this right, see RICKETSON & GINSBURG, *supra* note 7, § 11.50.

34. *Id.* Art. 16(1) Berne Convention ("Infringing copies of a work shall be liable to seizure in any country of the Union where the work enjoys legal protection.").

35. Seizure of infringing copies is technically a remedy, not a right, as its availability depends on showing a copyright infringement.

36. Art. 14ter(1) Berne Convention (1971) ("The author, or after his death the persons or institutions authorized by national legislation, shall, with respect to original works of art and original manuscripts of writers and composers, enjoy the inalienable.").

37. The term *droit de suite* generally means the author's right to a share in the proceeds of subsequent transactions of the original piece he has created. For an overview, see RICKETSON & GINSBURG, *supra* note 7, §§ 11.53–11.67.

Among these three copy-related provisions, only Article 14(1)(i) mentions the distribution right by name, and only the first two are mandatory under the Berne regime.[38] This is not much, and the Berne regime cannot be said to come any closer to securing an exclusive right to control the distribution of copies. Inasmuch as digital transmission is analogous to the distribution of copies, only Article 14(1)(i) appears to play a relevant role, in which case its application is limited solely to cinematographic adaptations of literary or artistic works. On the one hand, Berne communication rights cover more *work categories* than those stipulated in Article 14(1)(i). On the other, Article 14(1)(i) covers more instances of diffusion than the performance-communication rights as it does not require the works to be performed or broadcasted in any particular way. Generally speaking and regardless of how broadly construed, the communication entitlements secured under Berne have been widely regarded as insufficient.

D. The Need for Reform

Shortly after the conclusion of the 1971 Paris Act, some coverage problems had already begun to surface. In the area of communication rights, Berne offered a complex, incoherent, and often ambiguous treatment of digital disseminations. Further, explicit rights in sound recordings are not mentioned in the Berne Convention at all.[39] Still images of visual art transmitted by wire technology (and importantly, over the Internet) are not covered unless they qualify as a third-party retransmission of a broadcast.[40] Public display rights, which could provide additional tools for controlling communications, are not covered at all. Consequently, texts and notes of literary, musical, dramatic, and dramatico-musical works are generally not protected against unauthorized communication of the text itself.

As to the minimum protections required, Berne accommodates stark differentiations between various work categories, which is often a result of the Convention's historical development rather than a design choice serving any policy objective or following certain logic. Specifically, discrimination concerning minimum protection based on the broadcasting technology is considered anachronistic and incoherent. Further, Berne is ambiguous in cases where the recipient can influence the timing and type of transmitted content. Traditional methods

---

38. Art. 14ter(2) Berne Convention (1971), (the provision in sub-article (1) is subject to the reciprocity rule).

39. Though initial rights in sound recordings of musical works are not stipulated as being exclusive rights of their producers, Berne occasionally provides for permissive exceptions to such exclusive rights and a limited seizure entitlement. *See e.g.*, Arts. 11bis(3) and 13, Berne Convention,. During the pre-WPPT era, the neighboring rights of producers and performers (as well as broadcasting organizations) were substantially governed by the Rome Convention (1961). *See* SILKE VON LEWINSKI, INTERNATIONAL COPYRIGHT LAW AND POLICY § 6.01 ff (2008).

40. *Cf.* Art. 11bis(1)(ii) Berne Convention. *See also* RICKETSON & GINSBURG, *supra* note 7, § 12.44.

of broadcasting and cable communication contemplate large groups of recipients who are almost completely passive. By comparison, new digital transmission platforms allow the user to choose specific contents (on-demand) or select options from a menu offered by content providers (pay-per-view). New services allow the user to control the timing of communication,[41] and to use software-based tools to locate specific content on the Internet simultaneously streamed or uploaded onto servers, ready to be streamed and possibly downloaded upon request.

Against this backdrop, the Berne Convention presented two main coverage problems. The first was uncertainties concerning the application of certain Berne rights to certain technologies/services; the second concerned the public nature of the relevant acts/services. As to the second type of issues, an expansive construction of the "public" or "to the public" notions could solve much of the problem on the domestic level, yet it has been considered questionable whether such construction would bind all Member States.[42] The need to reform the existing structure of copyrights was strongly felt, which is reflected in early policy reports in the United States and Europe. In turn, these fairly early discussions (presented in the next section) significantly influenced the international process heralding the inception of the WIPO Treaties.

III. EARLY DELIBERATIONS IN THE UNITED STATES AND EUROPE

A. The U.S. Green and White Papers

1. The U.S. 1994 Green Paper

The U.S. Copyright Act does not explicitly grant a general exclusive right of communication to the public, a historical consequence (some say "anomaly"[43]) that rendered the digital transmission a particularly acute issue. The IITF IP Working Group identified several problems concerning the application of the customary distribution right to digital transmission, most importantly, the hackled interface with the statutory exhaustion rule (the first sale doctrine).[44]

To sidestep certain "unintended consequences" of the first sale doctrine in this context, the Green Paper simply recommended glossing over it through the

---

41. In the area of streaming media, there is a distinction between "push" technologies, on-demand, live streaming, and pull technologies. For an overview, see Ha, *supra* note 5, at 677–80.

42. For further discussion, see Ricketson & Ginsburg, *supra* note 7, §§ 12.47–12.52.

43. *Cf.* David Nimmer, *Ignoring the Public, Part I: On the Absurd Complexity of the Digital Audio Transmission Right*, 7 UCLA Ent. L. Rev. 189 (2000) (calling a "historical anomaly" the lack of exclusive performance rights in sound recordings under U.S. law prior to the Digital Performance Right in Sound Recordings Act of 1995).

44. *See* U.S. Green Paper (1994) at 120 ff.

creation of a new legal construct. Namely, the IP Working Group advanced the theory a modified distribution right dubbed "distribution by transmission" should cover digital transmissions involving creation of additional copies on recipients' equipment.[45] To achieve the desired effect, it has been proposed to amend the existing definition of the term *transmit*, as well as the first sale doctrine rule as expressed in Section 109(a) of the Copyright Act.[46] According to the proposed amendments, the first sale doctrine would have no impact on "distributions [by transmission] of copies." The rationale for this proposal was that transmitters do not give up possession of their own copy—the same copy from which further reproductions are made in the course of transmission.[47]

The Green Paper did not preclude (in fact, it encouraged) parallel application of exclusive rights other than the distribution right to network transmission. It noted, for instance, that when a "motion picture is literally 'rendered'—by showing its images in sequence—so that users with the requisite hardware and software might watch it *with or without copying the performance*, then, under the current law, a 'performance' has occurred."[48] In addition, the report suggested the statutory definition of "public" performance is sufficiently broad to apply to multiple individual viewers "who may watch a work being performed in a variety of locations at several different times."[49] The report also considered the public display right[50] as an exclusive right that could simultaneously apply to certain digital transmissions: "[W]hen any [Internet] user visually 'browses' through copies of works in any medium . . . a public display occurs. A display is 'public' on the same terms as a 'performance'; therefore, virtually all [Internet] uses would appear to fall within the law's current comprehension of 'public display.'"[51] In addition to its fondness for parallel application of exclusive rights in general, the Green Paper called for the enactment of a new exclusive transmission right in sound recordings, which did not exist at the time in the U.S. Copyright Act.[52]

---

45. *Id.* at 120–24.

46. *Id.* at 121–25.

47. *Id.* at 124 ("It seems clear that the first sale model—in which the copyright owner parts company with a tangible copy—should not apply with respect to distribution by transmission, because under current applications of technology, a transmission involves both the reproduction of the work and the distribution of the reproduction. In the case of transmissions, the owner of a particular copy of a work does not 'dispose of the possession of *that* copy or phonorecord.' A copy of the work remains with the first owner and the recipient of the transmission receives a reproduction of the work.").

48. *Id.* at 42–43 (emphasis in original).

49. *Id.*

50. *See* 17 U.S.C § 106(5).

51. *See* U.S. Green Paper (1994) at 44 (footnote omitted).

52. *Id.* at 131. This right was later codified as Section 106(6) of the Copyright Act. *See* Digital Performance Right in Sound Recordings Act (1995).

2. The U.S. 1995 White Paper

The White Paper maintained this line, and only a few minor alternations are noteworthy. It proposed digital transmission involving electronic reproductions be covered by the modified and expanded version of the distribution right.[53] The White Paper stressed the proposed legislative amendment was not meant to create a "new right."[54] At the same time, amending the statute was necessary to improve the ability of rights-holders to control and trade in exclusive rights *separately* and to expand the coverage of copyright entitlements.[55] In this context, the report rejected the view that as transmission is covered by other exclusive rights (specifically, the public performance and display rights), this justified a narrower application of the distribution right.[56]

It should be noted, however, that the final report has somewhat softened the tone regarding the interface with the first sale doctrine. Unlike the Green Paper, the White Paper did not call for amending the statutory exhaustion rule to explicitly exclude distribution by transmission.[57] In any event, the White Paper's drafters resented the idea that exhaustion rules generally applied in such situations as owners of copies (the transmitters) did not give up possession of their own copies.[58] The White Paper offered yet an additional argument in support of this view by purporting digital transmission does not fulfill the statutory requirement of Sections 109 as it results in copies being made *without the authority* of rights-holders, whereas Section 109 applies only to "lawfully made" copies and phonorecords.[59] Because the copies created in the course of digital transmission arguably violated *the reproduction right,* they could not be regarded as "lawfully made." The first sale doctrine could excuse those reproductions because it is applicable only to violations of *the distribution right,* not the reproduction rights.[60]

---

53. *See* U.S. White Paper (1995) at 213.

54. *Id.* at 213–14.

55. *Id.* at 214–15 ("[T]he fact that more than one right may be involved in infringing activity does not, and should not, mean that only one right should apply. Each of the exclusive rights is distinct and separately alienable and different parties may be responsible for infringements or licensing of different rights—and different rights may be owned by different people.") (footnotes omitted).

56. *Id.* at 214–17.

57. This can be learned from surveying the White Paper's list of proposed amendments, which reveals the IP Working Group retreated from its early recommendation to modify Section 109(a).

58. *See* U.S. White Paper (1995) at 95.

59. Section 109(a) reads: "Notwithstanding the provisions of section 106(3), the owner of a particular copy or phonorecord lawfully made under this title, or any person authorized by such owner, is entitled, without the authority of the copyright owner, to sell or otherwise dispose of the possession of that copy or phonorecord." *See* 17 U.S.C. § 109(a).

60. *See* U.S. White Paper (1995) at 92 ("This provision of the first sale doctrine limits only the copyright owner's distribution right; it in no way affects the reproduction right. Thus, the first sale doctrine does not allow the transmission of a copy of a work (through

The report remained sympathetic to the possibility of multiple exclusive rights simultaneously covering digital transmissions—for instance, the public performance and public display rights would cover digital transmissions either instead or in addition to the distribution right, depending on the nature of transmission and the type of work being transmitted.[61]

The analysis set forth in the White Paper is important for understanding subsequent developments in digital copyright law, and the influence of that report spread far beyond the territorial borders of U.S. jurisdiction alone. The report's significance does not necessarily emanate from the policy or legal soundness of its arguments as it does from the vividness of its expositions. The Which Paper depicts with unmistakable clarity the political line prevailing among U.S. administration and legislative circles immediately before the adoption of the WIPO Treaties and the subsequent enactment of the DMCA. An important aspect of this line is its heavy reliance on the edifice of traditional exclusive rights. The baseline assumption for handling the pressing problems trusted that, for the most part, expanding the application of existing copyrights to digital domains across-the-board was the key to the solution, thereby engulfing new situations, plugging holes, and removing coverage doubts.

Before proceeding to review the parallel process in Europe, a short comment on the White Paper's general approach to distribution can be made. As noted earlier, within the traditional copyright scheme, copy-related rights and copy-unrelated rights are occasionally delimited by different types of exemptions. The two categories of exemptions have a different history and diverse rationales. For example, a number of established rationales support non-voluntary licensing for certain communications and performances with respect to certain copyright-protected subject matter, which are woven into the consensus around granting exclusive rights controlling these conducts in the first place.[62] But those rationales do not necessarily operate in the same way when applied to distribution of copies. Similarly, the rationale for exhaustion limitations does not work well in paradigmatic situations of communication.

These distinctions are reflected in the traditional structure in the sense that many exemptions apply *selectively* to a certain type of exclusive rights, but not to others, and this is precisely the danger in various exclusive rights that simultaneously apply to

---

a computer network, for instance), because, under current technology the transmitter retains the original copy of the work while the recipient of the transmission obtains a reproduction of the original copy (*i.e.*, a *new* copy), rather than the copy owned by the transmitter.") (emphasis in original).

61. *Id.* at 70–72.

62. The commentary on Arts. 11bis(2) and 13(1) Berne Convention provides the historical background. *See, e.g.*, Stephen P. Ladas, The International Protection of Literary and Artistic Property 430–40 (1938); Ricketson & Ginsburg, *supra* note 7, § 12.07 ff.

the same act of digital transmission: applying several exclusive rights this way might result in *mutual neutralization of exemptions* and a significant reduction in their capacity to delimit exclusivity. For instance, if a given transmission of a sound recording implicates the exclusive rights of reproduction, distribution, and public performance, neither exhaustion rules nor traditional non-voluntary licenses are likely to excuse an unauthorized act.[63]

This observation should be put in context: the White Paper perceived coverage by multiple exclusive rights to be a blessing, not a curse, while expressing little concern about the impact of this application on the interests of nonowners. As to fair use, the White Paper questioned the capacity of this doctrine to delimit exclusivity in the Internet environment in general: "Commercial uses that involve no 'transformation' by users and harm actual or potential markets will likely always be infringing, while nonprofit educational transformative uses will likely often be fair."[64] It further envisioned the shrinking of fair use in the face of "technological means of tracking transactions and licensing [that may] lead to reduced application and scope of the fair use doctrine."[65]

B. The European Green Papers

1. The 1988 E.C. Green Paper

The 1988 Green Paper did not devote a separate discussion to digital transmission. Some of the relevant issues are subsumed in its chapter 4 under the title "Distribution Right, Exhaustion and Rental Right."[66] The European Commission focused on the distribution right while noting (rather imprecisely) "[t]his right, where it exists, can be most simply described as the exclusive right to authorize that *a work or copies thereof be made available to the public*."[67] The report took notice of the inconsistency between domestic laws concerning the distribution right, which significantly related to a diversified application of exhaustion rules.[68]

The Green Paper nonetheless did not identify a pressing need to harmonize distribution rights and exhaustion rules on the Community level.[69] The report expressed primary concern with rental rights for audiovisual works such as

---

63. The problems associated with the simultaneous application of exclusive rights to the same act in the network environment are broader than the issue of mutual exceptions neutralization. *See, e.g.*, Mark A. Lemley, *Dealing with Overlapping Copyrights on the Internet*, 22 U. Dayton L. Rev. 547, 567 ff (1997).

64. *See* U.S. White Paper (1995) at 80.

65. *Id.* at 82.

66. *See* E.C. Green Paper (1988) ¶ 4.1. ff.

67. *Id.* ¶ 4.1.1. (emphasis added). This description is imprecise because commonly the distribution right applies exclusively to "copies" and not to "a work" made available to the public.

68. *Id.* ¶¶ 4.1.2.–4.2.3.

69. *Id.* ¶ 4.11.3.

sound and video recordings.[70] Due to the major economic stakes involved, rights-holders wished to preserve control over commercial rental of copies in these secondary markets.[71] Voicing sympathy to the industry's pleadings, the Green Paper recommended introducing a directive[72] that would have secured for authors, performers, and producers exclusive rights concerning commercial rentals in sound recordings.[73] In addition, the report proposed to afford producers of cinematographic works embodied in video recordings (videograms) an exclusive right to authorize commercial rental of copies.[74]

2. The 1995 E.C. Green Paper

In this report, the European Commission shifted the focus from trade in copies in the secondary market to the network environment.[75] While discussing distribution rights and exhaustion rules, the Commission indicated its awareness of the claim that exhaustion doctrines were inapposite for various exploitations over the Internet.[76] The report explained:

> Unlike the distribution right for material items, the different rights attached to services transmitted by electronic means can hardly be made subject to exhaustion. In fact, every service supplied (e.g. broadcasting, rental, or lending) is an act which must be authorised separately, without prejudice to future forms exploitation.[77]

In the section devoted to communication rights, the Commission agreed the concept of "communication to the public" did not have a clear and uniform meaning.[78] It considered the element of the "public" as the key to clarifying the scope of the exclusive communication right.[79] The report went on to explain the

---

70. *Id.* ¶¶ 4.4.11.–4.5.6. In some respect, rental rights are limitations on the exhaustion rule, by allowing rights-holders to control downstream commercial exploitation of copies despite those copies having initially entered market circulation with permission.

71. *Id.* ¶¶ 4.1.1.–4.1.9.

72. *Id.* ¶ 4.12.1.

73. *Id.* ¶ 4.11.1.

74. *Id.* ¶ 4.11.2. On the basis of the 1988 Green Paper (later subject to numerous hearings and discussions described in the 1991 Follow-Up to the Green Paper), the Rental Directive was passed in November 1992. *See* E.C. Rental Directive (1992). This Directive designated exclusive rights, inter alia, "to the author in respect of the *original and copies* of his work." *Id.* Art. 2(1) (emphasis added). Rental of computer programs is regulated separately. *See* E.C. Software Directive (1991), Art. 4.

75. *See* E.C. Green Paper (1995) at 7–8.

76. In referring to works transmitted but not incorporated in material form, the report remarked on interested parties' endeavors to ensure "rights are not exhausted by the information superhighway." *Id.* at 47.

77. *Id.* at 48.

78. *Id.* at 53–54.

79. *Id.* at 53.

fundamental importance of defining "communication to the public" in the network environment:

> [The public] imagines that [it] is to be given access to all the knowledge in the world free of charge, or at any rate for the cost of the call. Thus the definition of private use can be seen as defining the scope actually offered to the public. If it is too broad, rightholders will hesitate to allow their works to be used on the networks. If it is too narrow the public may well stay away from the information superhighway in disappointment.[80]

Accordingly, the report recommended setting forth clarifications concerning the term "communication to the public"—possibly by formulating a uniform definition under Community law.[81] Additional relevant issues were subsumed in the chapter titled "Digital Dissemination or Transmission Right."[82] The report took note of the conceptual vagueness of that "right" and of the demands made by producers and performers to be granted an exclusive "digital dissemination or transmission" right.[83]

The report framed the issue as the problem of formulating a right that would fall somewhere in the range between two extreme cases. At the one extreme was an exclusive right that would cover both point-to-point and point-to-multipoint transmissions, which practically covered all kinds of network transmissions and broadcastings. At that other extreme, there was a right that would be limited only to point-to-point digital transmissions, or at least one that would expressly exclude broadcasting.[84] The Commission refrained from making a proposal at that stage, citing instead some broad definitions of transmission found in existing directives[85] and opining that applying rental and lending rights "by extension" could provide a solution.[86]

At bottom, the Commission identified a clear need to harmonize legal issues concerning copyrights in digital transmission[87] without resolving how exactly

80. *Id.* at 54.

81. *Id.* at 55.

82. *Id.* at 56–60.

83. *Id.* at 56.

84. *Id.* As a terminological matter, digital broadcasting is distinguished from online services: "Community law at present considers a broadcast to be any transmission to the public other than individualized services on demand, whatever the technology used: wire, radio, satellite, analogue or digital." *Id.* at 62. This suggests the Commission was mostly concerned not about the coverage of digital transmissions in general, but the interface between digital online services and existing law controlling broadcasting.

85. *Id.* at 57–59 (mentioning the Rental and Software Directives, and identifying similarities between the rights secured under those directives on the one hand, and the "rental/lending" nature of digital transmission on the other).

86. *Id.* at 59.

87. *Id.* at 58.

this should be achieved. Also with regard to broadcasting, where performers and producers were generally entitled to receive equitable remuneration instead of exclusivity, the report stressed the need for reevaluating (and possibly harmonizing) the appropriateness of existing schemes.[88] The 1995 Green Paper raised and discussed many intriguing questions but was able to answer only a few,[89] leaving unresolved among others the "public" component of the digital communication right.[90]

The Commission was not able to finalize its study before the commencement of the Diplomatic Conference in Geneva, but it managed to release the 1996 Follow-Up report on the eve of the WIPO Conference. During the short interval between the publication of the 1995 Green Paper and its Follow-Up, a "major shift" in the position of the Commission occurred.[91] That shift focused on the treatment given to on-demand network transmissions:

> "On-demand transmissions" are characterised by the fact that a work or other subject matter stored in a digital format is made available to the public or individual members of it in such a way that they may access it and request its transmission individually with respect to time and place to a personal computer or other digital unit "on-demand". This situation is outside broadcasting (consisting of a pre-defined programme) and goes beyond merely private communication.[92]

The Commission acknowledged the possibility of applying existing rules to cover on-demand transmissions, but ultimately rejected that idea. Instead, it recommended introducing a "new" right of communication to the public, which would be based on the traditional concept of communication to the public. The proposed right should have guaranteed rights-holders' exclusivity and importantly, cover acts of "making available to members of the public individual access to works and other subject matters."[93] The 1996 Follow-Up report underscored the necessity of harmonizing exceptions and limitations to this new right, but it did not provide guidelines on how to carry forth this task.[94] It further called for harmonizing the distribution right with respect to all categories of works while emphasizing exhaustion rules should not apply to "on-line services."[95]

---

88. *Id.* at 61.

89. *Cf.* E.C. Green Paper (1995) at 61–64.

90. The report submitted laconically: "Of course the ultimate definition of 'communication to the public' will have a great effect on public perceptions of the information society." *Id.* at 54.

91. *See* Ficsor, *supra* note 9, § 4.76.

92. *See* E.C. Follow-Up to the Green Paper (1996) at 12 (citation omitted).

93. *Id.* at 14.

94. *Id.* The report suggested exceptions to the "making available right" should be limited "to those which are absolutely necessary." *Id.*

95. *Id.* at 19.

IV. THE WCT AND ITS "UMBRELLA SOLUTION"

A. Drafting History

The early reports reviewed above confirm the observation the deliberations focused not on the "IF" but on the "HOW" aspects of copyright protection regarding digital transmissions and communications. The Internet boom and cross-border online communications rendered the calls for more uniformity in domestic copyright laws ever more pressing. Indeed, a broad international consensus existed on the necessity of securing copyright protection for digital transmissions in general, which, to some extent, could be achieved via expansive construction of existing traditional rules. Reproduction, distribution, rental, and performance as well as communication and broadcasting rights could, jointly and severally, capture the most important (if not all) aspects and incarnations of digital transmissions. But still problematic was the heterogenic structure of domestic protection and the fact candidate rights were not uniformly recognized and applied across copyright jurisdictions.

The so-called "umbrella solution" emerged in the mid-1990s in various WIPO fora devoted to issues of copyright protection in the digital environment.[96] The background for discussions was uncertainties concerning the application of traditional rights as well as certain gaps and ambiguities left under the Berne regime. The stated mission of the umbrella solution was to clarify the concept of communication as covering, in addition to acts of actual transmission, acts of merely making the communication accessible to the public. Further, it sought to clarify that factors of interactivity and certain levels of recipients' control over the time and place of communication should not result in under-coverage. As there were no substantial disagreements that exclusive rights should apply, the essence of the umbrella solution was to "identify the said acts, make the necessary clarifications, do away with the gaps . . . but then leave as much freedom as necessary (and reasonable) to national laws concerning the specific legal characterization of the acts (that is, the selection and combination of the specific exclusive rights to be applied)."[97]

1. *Draft Article 8 WCT*

The Basic Proposal introducing the WCT Draft contained several provisions relevant to the problem of communication to the public. As of its distribution, Draft

---

96. The umbrella solution was first outlined in detail at a high-level meeting during the 1995 Mexico City Symposium by the then-presiding WIPO Assistant Director General, Mihály Ficsor, who reposts on the occasion in his treatise. *See* FICSOR, *supra* note 9, § 4.84.

97. *See* Mihály Ficsor, *International Harmonization of the Protection and Management of Copyright and Neighboring Rights*, *in* NAPLES FORUM BOOK 137–138 (1995), *as quoted in* FICSOR, *supra* note 9, § 4.87.

Article 8 WCT presented two alternatives.[98] Alternative A titled "Right of Distribution and Right of Importation" read:

(1) Authors of literary and artistic works shall enjoy the exclusive right of authorizing:
   (i) the making available to the public of the original and copies of their works through sale or other transfer of ownership;
   (ii) the importation of the original and copies of their works, even following any sale or other transfer of ownership of the original or copies by or pursuant to authorization.

(2) National legislation of a Contracting Party may provide that the right provided for in paragraph (1) (i) does not apply to distribution of the original or any copy of any work that has been sold or the ownership of which has been otherwise transferred in that Contracting Party's territory by or pursuant to authorization.

(3) The right of importation in paragraph (1)(ii) does not apply where the importation is effected by a person solely for his personal and non-commercial use as part of his personal luggage.[99]

Alternative B captioned "Right of Distribution" read:

(1) Authors of literary and artistic works shall enjoy the exclusive right of authorizing the making available to the public of the original and copies of their works through sale or other transfer of ownership.

(2) A Contracting Party may provide that the right provided for in paragraph (1) does not apply to distribution after the first sale or other transfer of ownership of the original or copies of works by or pursuant to authorization.

The Notes to Draft Article 8 explain its main purpose was to extend the internationally recognized distribution right and have it uniformly applied to all works and subject matters.[100] The main obstacle to formulating the international standard was divergent views on the issue of exhaustion.[101] Exhaustion rules take

---

98. The WPPT draft contains similar parallel provisions concerning rights of performers and producers of phonograms (sound recordings.) *See* WPPT Basic Proposal (1996), Draft Arts. 9 & 16.

99. *See* WCT Basic Proposal (1996), Draft Article 8, Alt. A.

100. *Id.* Notes 8.02–8.04.

101. *Id.* Note 8.02. The complications sought to be resolved are elaborated on in more detail in Note 8.10:

> The two Alternatives presented in Article 8 reflect the genuine diverging views of many nations in this matter. On the level of an international agreement the Alternatives seem to exclude each other, are apparently contradictory and impossible to reconcile. As an intermediate solution the introduction of agreed conditional limitations of the right of distribution and right of importation, based on Alternative A in Article 8(1), could be explored. National legislation of a Contracting Party could for example provide

three general forms in various jurisdictions: national, regional, or international.[102] In offering two alternatives, Draft Article 8 in fact reflects the different national approaches to the issue of exhaustion. First, Alternative A mirrors a principle of national/regional exhaustion while stipulating an explicit exclusive importation right. Conversely, Alternative B would permit domestic laws to adopt a global exhaustion rule.[103] Either way, Draft Article 8 was not meant to apply to public lending[104] and rental, which were separately addressed in Draft Article 9 WCT.[105]

2. Adoption of Article 6 WCT (Distribution)

Adoption of the final text of the distribution right went quite smoothly.[106] Draft Article 8 was incorporated into the WCT as Article 6 thereof:

> (1) Authors of literary and artistic works shall enjoy the exclusive right of authorizing the making available to the public of the original and copies of their works through sale or other transfer of ownership.
> (2) Nothing in this Treaty shall affect the freedom of Contracting Parties to determine the conditions, if any, under which the exhaustion of the right in paragraph (1) applies after the first sale or other transfer of ownership of the original or a copy of the work with the authorization of the author.[107]

---

that these rights do not apply to the distribution or importation of copies of works that have been sold with the consent of the author anywhere in the world, if copies of that work have not been made available in a Contracting Party in a quantity sufficient to satisfy the reasonable needs of the public, within an agreed period of time, e.g. one year, calculated from the publication of that work outside that Contracting Party. An alternative along these lines has not, however, been presented. Any third alternative would have required extensive international consultations which it would not have been possible to organize during the preparation of the proposed Treaty.

102. For example, in the case of a national exhaustion rule, the distribution right is exhausted only within the country where the work was circulated in the local market with authority of the rights-holder. Importation into that jurisdiction remains an exclusive right even when the work was previously distributed with authority outside the borders of the jurisdiction. In the case of international exhaustion, importation does not require authorization after work copies have initially been released and distributed in the foreign jurisdiction with permission.

103. *See* WCT Basic Proposal (1996), Note 8.04.

104. *Id.*

105. *See* WCT Basic Proposal (1996), Draft Art. 9(1) (stipulating generally exclusive rental rights, subject to some exceptions, in copies of literary and artistic works even after distribution with authorization).

106. *See* Ficsor, *supra* note 9, §§ 4.153–4.154. The parallel provisions concerning the distribution right in the final text of the WPPT are provided in Arts. 8 and 12 WPPT.

107. *See* WCT (1996), Art. 6.

Paragraph (1) introduces a general exclusive distribution right that applies to all Berne-covered work categories.[108] Paragraph (2) solves the issue of exhaustion by delegating complete discretion to national laws.[109] Article 6 WCT is supplemented by an agreed statement, which applies also to the rental right regulated in Article 7 WCT:

> As used in these Articles, the expressions "copies" and "original and copies," being subject to the right of distribution and the right of rental under the said Articles, refer exclusively to fixed copies that can be put into circulation as tangible objects.[110]

This agreed statement was passed with no objections whatsoever.[111] This fact is not insignificant, as the text of the statement in fact provides a quasi-definition of *copies*. Though the agreed statement does not address the issue of fixation directly, it actually stipulates a mixed qualitative-economic criterion for the definition of copies.[112] Accordingly, copies must be things that can be "put into circulation as tangible objects," which would obviously exclude at least some types of digital temporary reproductions. Considering the immense controversy spawned over Draft Article 7 WCT, the broad international concurrence surrounding that agreed statement appears curious.

One possible explanation is that delegates at the Diplomatic Conference did not consider the agreed statements concerning Articles 6 and 7 WCT as having anything to do with the reproduction right. However, this assumption is problematic from a doctrinal viewpoint. Providing a separate definition of "copies" applicable to the distribution right would give rise to severe inconsistency in the structure of copyright law, bringing to the surface the tension with the notion of "copies" for purposes of the reproduction right. Neither copyright theory nor simple logic would justify such a distinction, and even the 1995 U.S. White Paper, while advocating its distribution-by-transmission theory, did not propose to modify the definition of copies, nor did it suggest creating distinctions based on the exclusive right at issue. Creation of separate definitions of "copies"—one for reproduction and the other for distribution—might have at least two negative consequences. First, it would enhance the level of complexity and incoherence, giving rise to interface issues in cases where both rights are involved, but either

108. *See* Jorg Reinbothe & Silke von Lewinski, The Wipo Treaties 1996 at 84–85 (2002) (noting an obligation concerning a general distribution right is unprecedented in the international copyright milieu).

109. For commentary, see Ficsor, *supra* note 9, § C.6.03; Reinbothe & von Lewinski, *supra* note 108, at 85. Reinbothe and von Lewinski note the freedom to choose a domestic exhaustion rule (national, regional, or international) is not subject to the three-part test in Art. 10 WCT. *Id.* at 87.

110. *See* WCT (1996), Agreed Statements concerning Arts. 6 and 7.

111. *See* Ficsor, *supra* note 9, § 4.154.

112. Chapter 4, Section III.B.1 ff *supra*.

requires a distinguishable fixation analysis. More importantly, adopting such an approach would constitute an implicit admonition regarding the concept of digital "copies" in general. Namely, in the digital environment the concept of copies virtually falls apart.

Ficsor purports the agreed statement requires an "appropriate interpretation."[113] Accordingly, it "does not cover the right of reproduction and it is, in fact, an obligation under the WCT . . . also to recognize the making of intangible copies, in particular in electronic memories, as acts of reproduction."[114] Ficsor finds support for this interpretation by pointing out the WCT stipulated only a minimum protection bar. It is thereby implied the requirement of a tangible object in the agreed statement could (or perhaps should) be *ignored* by domestic legislatures wishing to grant greater protection.[115] However, there appears to be some self-contradiction in this approach that must be resolved: On the one hand, the agreed statement is said be *unrelated* to the reproduction right. On the other, it is said to be "in fact, an *obligation* under the WCT (as well as under the TRIPS Agreement and the Berne Convention) also to recognize the making of intangible copies . . . as acts of reproduction."[116] It is perhaps possible to resolve the contradiction in the following way: The first prong of Ficsor's argument suggests that, inasmuch as the agreed statement to Article 6 WCT required a tangible-tradable article, this requirement is inapplicable to reproduction. The second prong is a contrario: according to the language of the agreed statement to Article 6, distribution concerns "fixed copies that can be put into circulation as tangible objects." This indicates "fixed" copies that *cannot* be put into circulation as tangible objects (e.g., certain RAM copies) are irrelevant in the case of distribution, but they are still "fixed" so the reproduction right is triggered.

Reinbothe and von Lewinski attack the problem from a somewhat different angle: "[The agreed statement to Article 6] intends to clarify that these terms ['copies' and 'originals and copies'] be used in the traditional sense, namely as meaning only 'fixed copies' in the form of tangible objects."[117] They continue by suggesting such clarification was necessary to express the WCT's rejection of the

---

113. *Id.* § C.6.04.

114. *Id.* (footnote omitted).

115. If all representations in computer memories of any kind and duration are firmly captured by the WCT reproduction right (as Ficsor believes), it does not seem likely the Agreed Statement to Art. 6 WCT can lower the standard of reproduction in any way. This weakens the contention that the Agreed Statement is meant to stipulate a minimum standard, which could be extended domestically to "*distribution through reproduction through transmission.*" *Id.* The practical upshot of Ficsor's view is that domestic legislatures must simply ignore this definition of copies and its requirement for tangible-tradable objects.

116. *Id.* (emphasis added). The coined phrase "intangible copies" appears quite oxymoronic.

117. *See* Reinbothe & von Lewinski, *supra* note 108, at 87.

U.S. White Paper's distribution-by-transmission approach.[118] This construction seems to implicitly accept a differentiation in the concept of copies depending on the exclusive right applicable to the context in which the problem of fixation is invoked. Accordingly, tangible-tradable objects are required for showing an infringement of the distribution right, but their attribute as tangible-tradable is irrelevant for demonstrating an infringement of the reproduction right.[119] In any event, as a matter of treaty interpretation, we should not simply ignore the agreed statement. The interpreter must presume its language represents the compromise reached in Geneva, which spells out the corresponding positions of the convening parties. Under a certain interpretation, it is not impossible to consolidate the agreed statement with the general WCT structure provided we examine that structure through the correct lens. In general, the language of the agreed statement squares more comfortably with a minimalist approach to the digital reproduction right.[120] Accordingly, the perceived-reproduced-communicated (PRC) fixation text is subject to a limitation clause that reflects both normative-qualitative and economic considerations, and the agreed statement reinforces the plausibility of this solution by stipulating a clear criterion requiring tangibility-tradability of copies.[121]

3. Draft Article 10 WCT

Draft Article 10 WCT articulated a broad communication right expressing the (now familiar) "making available" language:

> Without prejudice to the rights provided for in Articles 11(1)(ii), 11bis(1)(i), 11ter(1)(ii), 14(1)(i) and 14bis(1) of the Berne Convention, authors of literary and artistic works shall enjoy the exclusive right of authorizing any communication to the public of their works, including the making available to the public of their works, by wire or wireless means, in such a way that members of the public may access these works from a place and at a time individually chosen by them.[122]

---

118. *Id. Compare,* Ficsor, *supra* note 9, C.8.09 (arguing the tangible object requirement "does not contradict the applicability of the right of distribution for digital, interactive transmissions in the framework of the 'umbrella solution'").

119. In analyzing the Agreed Statement to Art. 1(4) WCT, Reinbothe and von Lewinsky do not appear to read any such tangibility-tradability limitation. *See* Reinbothe & Von Lewinski, *supra* note 108, at 42–44.

120. *See* Chapter 4, Section III.B.1 ff *supra* (explaining the difference between the maximalist and the minimalist approaches regarding temporary digital reproduction and arguing the minimalist view is preferable).

121. The European Court of Justice has recently adopted such restrictive interpretation concerning the EUCD distribution right while drawing on Art. 6 WCT. *See* Peek & Cloppenburg KG v. Cassina SpA, ECJ Case C-456/06 (April 17, 2008).

122. *See* WCT Basic Proposal (1996), Draft Art. 10. The making-available rights and rights of remuneration for broadcasting and communications to the public granted to

The WCT Basic Proposal provided an extensive commentary on this key provision. It referred to the fragmented protection granted to the communication right under the Berne Convention[123] and the inadequacy of the present structure to meet the challenges of technological developments.[124] The text of the provision followed the European Community's proposal concerning a general communication right,[125] which was structured in two parts. The first part "extends the exclusive right of communication to the public to all categories of works, including any communication by wire or wireless means. It leaves the provisions of Articles 11(1)(ii), 11bis(1)(i), 11ter(1)(ii), 14(1)(i) and 14bis(1) applicable as they are in the Berne Convention."[126] The second part pointedly targets interactive transmissions. The Basic Proposal stated "[t]he relevant act is the making available of the work by providing access to it . . . It is irrelevant whether copies are available for the user or whether the work is simply made perceptible to, and thus usable by, the user."[127] The Notes added the term *public* is used by the provision to exclude "mere private communication."[128] It continued:

> The term "public" has been used in Article 10 as it has been used in the present provisions of the Berne Convention. It is a matter for national legislation and case law to define what is "public". However, the aspects dealt with in Note 1.10 should be taken into account. The "public" consists of individual "members of the public" who may access the works from different places and at different times.[129]

Without commenting on the slight irony in the conceptual convergence of the "public" with "*individual members* of the pubic," the Notes went on to explain the term "any" communication clarified that the right shall be technologically indifferent.[130] Finally, the drafters pointed out "no rights are exhausted in

---

producers of phonograms and performers are stipulated in WPPT Basic Proposal, Draft Arts. 11, 12, 18, & 19.

123. *See* WCT Basic Proposal (1996), *id.* Notes 1.1–1.4.

124. *Id.* Notes 1.5–1.6 (stressing that the Berne communication rights do not apply to all categories of work; in particular, they are not applicable generally to literary works, thereby excluding computer programs).

125. *Id.* at Notes 1.07–1.08.

126. *Id.* at Note 1.09.

127. *Id.* at Note 1.10. A clear intention of the second part to capture interactive on-demand communication and a desire to override a narrow interpretation of the general communication right stated in the first part are expressed in Notes 1.11 and 1.13, respectively. *Id.*

128. *Id.* at Note 1.12.

129. *Id.* at Note 1.17.

130. *Id.* at Note 1.14 ("The technology used may be analog or digital, and it may be based on electromagnetic waves or guided optical beams. The use of the non-restrictive term 'any' in front of the word 'communication' in Article 10, and in certain provisions of

connection with communication to the public. . . Exhaustion of rights is only associated with the distribution of tangible copies."[131]

4. Adoption of Article 8 WCT

The text of Draft Article 10 WCT did not incite much controversy at the Diplomatic Conference.[132] It has been implicitly agreed contracting parties were not obligated to include an explicit provision in domestic law as long as the target activities remained covered by the local protection regime.[133] With some minor alteration in the text of Draft Article 10, Article 8 WCT finally provides:

> Without prejudice to the provisions of Articles 11(1)(ii), 11bis(1)(i) and (ii), 11ter(1)(ii), 14(1)(ii) and 14bis(1) of the Berne Convention, authors of literary and artistic works shall enjoy the exclusive right of authorizing any communication to the public of their works, by wire or wireless means, including the making available to the public of their works in such a way that members of the public may access these works from a place and at a time individually chosen by them.[134]

The concern of telecommunication corporations and Internet service providers about possible liability for facilitating infringing communications passing through their systems yielded agreed statements to Article 8 that were designed to assuage their anxiety:

> It is understood that the mere provision of physical facilities for enabling or making a communication does not in itself amount to communication within the meaning of this Treaty or the Berne Convention. It is further understood that nothing in Article 8 precludes a Contracting Party from applying Article 11bis(2).[135]

Two brief comments concerning this text may follow. First, it releases passive conduits and service providers from *direct* infringement liability, but not from secondary liability. Secondary liability rules remain outside the ambit of this provision and are entirely a matter of domestic law. Second, the permission to apply domestic non-voluntary licensing under Article 11bis(2) Berne Convention is

---

the Berne Convention, emphasizes the breadth of the act of communication. 'Communication' implies transmission to a public not present in the place where the communication originates.").

131. *Id.* at Note 1.20.

132. *See* Ficsor, *supra* note 9, §§ 4.155–4.157.

133. *See* Reinbothe & von Lewinski, *supra* note 108, at 102–04 (describing the discussions at the Diplomatic Conference and noting the clarification made by the U.S. delegation, according to which Article 8 could be implemented into national law by any exclusive right, not necessarily by an explicit right of communication to the public).

134. *See* WCT (1996), Art. 8.

135. *See* WCT (1996), agreed statements concerning Art. 8.

only relevant to traditional Berne situations falling under Article 11bis(1). In general, exemptions to the exclusivity rule governing the broad range of activities covered by Article 8 WCT's communication right are subject directly to the three-step test. The following passages review the scope of this norm in more detail.

B. The WCT Communication-Making-Available Right

1. Scope of Article 8 WCT

The communication right in Article 8 WCT, with its explicit stipulation of the making-available right,[136] is comprehensive. It avidly serves its gaps-filling mission by eliminating uncertainties associated with the fragmented coverage of Berne provisions.[137] Contracting parties are not obligated to adopt the exact wording of the norm provided that acts falling within the purview of Article 8 (particularly making-available conducts) are principally governed by domestic copyright exclusivity rules.[138]

The WCT does not define the term *communication*. As noted, the Basic Proposal indicated the terms "any" and "by wire or wireless means" reflected the intention to create a technology-neutral right.[139] One implication is that although the communication right is intended to cover network transmissions (particularly the Internet), it may apply to *any present and future* communication technology.[140] The norm is "futuristic" in the sense it prepares the copyright system for the advent of the "celestial jukebox"—a global wireless transmission technologies and digital networks making every piece of digitized information available via personal rendition devices.[141]

---

136. The making-available right can be described as an *aspect* of the general, broad right to communicate works to the pubic; it is not an independent right but a subcategory of communication conducts. *Cf.* REINBOTHE & VON LEWINSKI, *supra* note 108, at 108.

137. *See* FICSOR, *supra* note 9, § C.8.03.

138. *See* REINBOTHE & VON LEWINSKI, *supra* note 108, at 108. *Cf.* FICSOR, *supra* note 9, §§ 8.06–8.07 (opining the freedom to choose the domestic structure is only relative, as the idea of the "umbrella solution" does not apply to transmissions that are still controlled by the Berne provisions).

139. *See also* REINBOTHE & VON LEWINSKI, *supra* note 108, at 105; RICKETSON & GINSBURG, *supra* note 7, § 12.54.

140. REINBOTHE & VON LEWINSKI, *supra* note 108, at 109.

141. One of the early references to the "celestial jukebox" notion is found in the U.S. Green Paper: "Transmissions of sound recordings may eventually replace the current forms of distribution of phonorecords. In the very near future, consumers will be able to receive digital transmissions of sound recordings on demand—for performance in the home or for downloading—from the so-called celestial jukebox." *See* U.S. Green Paper (1994) at 131. *See also* PAUL GOLDSTEIN, COPYRIGHT'S HIGHWAY—FROM GUTENBERG TO THE CELESTIAL JUKEBOX 87 ff (2003) (analyzing the celestial jukebox concept and its implication for the copyright system).

Notably, Article 8 does not define the term *public* either. Articulating the borderline between "public" and "private" communication remains a matter of domestic law.[142] However, the making-available prong eliminates the possibility of classifying as "private" acts affording unspecified *members of a group* (beyond the intimate circle of family and acquaintances)[143] the *option* to individually receive communication.[144]

2. External and Internal Limitations

(a) External Limitations

Despite its considerable breadth, the communication right is not borderless. Limitations can be classified as falling under two types: external and internal. The main external source of limitations is the Berne Convention itself. First, the concept of "communication to the public" is derived from and builds on the Berne tradition.[145] This implies the communication right covers only *remote* communications in which the public is not present where communication is originated, performed, and/or made perceptible.[146] Specifically, Berne rules that regulate public performances and the communication right do not apply simultaneously, and to the extent they lead to contradictory results, Article 8 WCT does not control performances.

Second, Berne's restrictions on the WCT communication rights stem indirectly from the relationship between the two instruments, as stated in Article 1 WCT.[147] The WCT cannot be interpreted as derogating Berne obligations,[148] including WCT interpretations that would generally *disturb* the Berne regime and thus count as derogating obligations under Berne. This principle finds explicit formulation in the language of Article 8 itself, in which protection is granted "[w]ithout prejudice to the provisions of Articles 11(1)(ii), 11bis(1)(i) and (ii),

---

142. *See* Reinbothe & von Lewinski, *supra* note 108, at 107.

143. *Id.* at 111 (intranet at home accessible only to family members does not make anything available to the public, but intranet in schools and companies does).

144. *Id,* at 108. *See also* Ricketson & Ginsburg, *supra* note 7, § 12.58.

145. *Cf.* Reinbothe & Von Lewinski, *supra* note 108, at 105 (indicating the notion of "communication to the public" has to be interpreted by taking into account its meaning and use in the various Berne provisions).

146. Reinbothe and von Lewinski argue "remote" communication is not a quantitative question of minimum distance, but rather a qualitative inquiry: "'Transmission' rather implies that a work stored in a server could not be accessed from a certain terminal without transmission to the terminal." *Id.* at 109. This would include making work accessible in local networks even if all terminals are located at the same physical "place." *Id.*

147. *See* WCT (1996), Art. 1(1) (the WCT is a "special agreement" within the meaning of Art. 20 Berne Convention).

148. *Id.* Art. 1(2) ("Nothing in this Treaty shall derogate from existing obligations that Contracting Parties have to each other under the Berne Convention for the Protection of Literary and Artistic Works.").

11ter(1)(ii), 14(1)(ii) and 14bis(1) of the Berne Convention." Thus, Article 8 cannot override or rewrite the structure of rights already formulated in Berne provisions, with broadcasting as a clear example to such situation. As most types of broadcasting as forms of communication to the public[149] are already covered by the Berne communication rights regime, Article 8 has only a limited application in this area.[150]

Importantly, the "without prejudice" clause means also that Article 8 WCT cannot override Berne *limitations* on communication rights.[151] In other words, WCT interpretation cannot give rise to the conclusion that limitations hitherto permissible under Berne are from now on precluded under Article 8 WCT. For example, the broadcasting rights secured under Article 11bis(1) Berne Convention are subject to paragraph (2), allowing Berne members to create non-voluntary licensing provisions.[152] By its terms, Article 8 cannot limit the scope of paragraph (2). To remove any doubt, the agreed statement to Article 8 WCT explicitly preserves the mandate of paragraph 11bis(2) Berne Convention.[153]

Generally, all forms of communications to the public not covered by Berne (e.g., primary transmission by wire of certain works) are governed by Article 8 WCT.[154] In that sense, Article 8 functions as a catchall provision, furnishing a safety net to rights-holders concerned about changing market conditions and rapid technological developments. The communication right is starkly premised on property-like exclusivity,[155] subjecting deviations from this principle to the three-step test stipulated in Article 10 WCT.[156] The common view is that non-voluntary licensing allowed under Article 11bis(2) Berne Convention are generally impermissible with respect to activities falling outside the borders of

---

149. Ficsor argues the first paragraph of Art. 8 WCT confirms broadcasting is "a special form of communication to the public (rather than mere 'emission'"). *See* Ficsor, *supra* note 9, § C.8.04.

150. *See* Reinbothe & von Lewinski, *supra* note 108, at 105–06.

151. *See* Ricketson & Ginsburg, *supra* note 7, § 12.56.

152. *See* Art. 11bis(2) Berne Convention (1971).

153. *See* WCT (1996), agreed statement concerning Art. 8. *See also* Reinbothe & von Lewinski, *supra* note 108, at 107 (Article 8 WCT does not affect Art. 11bis(2) Berne Convention.) *Cf.* Ficsor, *supra* note 9, §§ C8.05–8.06 (offering a limited reading to paragraph (2) as applied to noninteractive transmissions that are globally accessible (e.g., satellite transmissions). To the extent compulsory licensing is permitted under paragraph (2) in such cases, it applies only in the country where the licenses have been prescribed. To the extent services and technologies such as webcasting, simulcasting, streaming, and push services are noninteractive, the same rule applies).

154. For commentary on the scope of Article 8 WCT, see Reinbothe & von Lewinski, *supra* note 108, at 106–07.

155. *See* WCT (1996), Art. 8 ("authors of literary and artistic works shall enjoy the *exclusive right of authorizing*") (emphasis added).

156. *See* Reinbothe & von Lewinski, *supra* note 108, at 108.

Article 11bis(1) and within the scope of Article 8 WCT.[157] Put another way, traditional non-voluntary licensing arrangements do not shift to communication situations covered by Article 8 unless they *independently* pass the WCT's three-step test.

(b) Internal Limitations

The text of Article 8 WCT implies some internal limitations on the communication right in connection with the making-available prong. The clause "from a *place* and a *time* individually chosen by them" is a double qualifier. If individual recipients *cannot choose the timing* of transmission, the making-available right does not apply. Reinbothe and von Lewinski argue the "element of individual choice refers to the on-demand situation and excludes from the making available right any exploitation by way of offering, at specific times, predetermined programs for reception by the general public."[158] Cumulatively,[159] Article 8 requires recipients be able to choose the place of access. The term "place" could be understood both as a physical place (e.g., office, home, library, Internet café)[160] and as a virtual place (i.e., choosing the particular Web site or Internet "location") where work is made available.[161] The interpretation of "place"—physical or virtual—determines to some extent the liability of actors operating as conduits or connectors who are not hosting the work themselves or otherwise making it ready for transmission upon request.

Finally, the agreed statement to Article 8 should be considered. Its first sentence has a very limited application. It does not provide blanket immunity to network operators, ISPs and telecommunication companies, neither for acts covered by the Berne communication provisions nor for those covered by the WCT.[162] The emphasis is on "*mere* provision of physical facilities," which excludes any type of service that goes beyond. Contracting parties are allowed to add conditions to national immunity schemes protecting mere conduits (e.g., a requirement that service providers shall not have actual or constructive knowledge with

---

157. *Id.* at 112–13.

158. *Id.* at 109. The authors exclude from on-demand situations activities such as radio and TV broadcasting, whether by traditional means or by network technologies of radio streaming, webcasting, pay-TV/pay-radio, pay-per-view services, and other instances in which the recipient is dependent on the pre-programming and cannot choose the time of communication. *Id.*

159. The cumulative nature of the twin factors is derived from the connector "place *and* time."

160. *See* Reinbothe & von Lewinski, *supra* note 108, at 111.

161. *See* Ricketson & Ginsburg, *supra* note 7, §§ 12.60–12.61 (mentioning this interpretative option and pointing out the possible impact on liability questions when users are automatically transferred from one Internet location they knowingly visit to another location in cyberspace, where the work is *actually* made available/resides, without their being aware of it).

162. *Id.* § 12.55. *See also* Reinbothe & von Lewinski, *supra* note 108, at 112.

regard to infringements carried out by third parties). Knowledge requirements may help domestic lawmakers to fine-tune liability rules on a case-by-case basis and create appropriate distinctions among direct infringement liability, indirect liability, and immunity.[163] The arrangement of "notice and take down" is also conceivable as part of domestic immunity mechanisms applied to passive service providers.

C. Impact of Article 8 WCT

Though the communication right in Section 8 WCT is comprehensive, a careful scrutiny reveals its limitations. Yet those limitations usually take effect not to create zones of communication freedom but only *to give way to alternative exclusive rights.* Review of the internal and external material constraints makes plain their application often does not result in a diminished capacity to exercise exclusive copyright control over communication conducts, as rights-holders may still invoke alternative exclusive entitlements secured somewhere else under Berne/WCT. As a matter of fact, this is precisely the idea behind the "umbrella solution": to comply with the WCT, it is immaterial which exclusive right controls which communication provided some exclusivity norm applies. The same principle governs the interrelations between the general and the specific elements of Article 8 WCT, as the limitations on the specific making-available prong do not mark the outer boundaries of the exclusive communication right to carve zones of freedom. There is instead an internal division of labor within Article 8 itself, and the choice is mostly between exclusivity under the specific making-available prong or exclusivity under the general communication right.

Non-voluntary licensing, possibly in conjunction with collective rights administration, has been traditionally the central mechanism used to compromise exclusivity's grip in the area of communication to the public. Non-voluntary licensing also remains the single most important candidate for performing the same task under the regime of Article 8, at least in theory. In the limited class of cases where Berne provisions apply directly, the WCT cannot subvert their effect, inter alia in cases of non-voluntary licensing for wireless diffusion of signs, sounds, or images, and in cases of wired communication or over-the-air broadcasting by an organization other than the original (re-broadcasting.)

Yet the role played by Article 11bis(2) Berne Convention in the digital environment is marginal. Non-voluntary licensing is largely disallowed in the case of primary transmissions or broadcastings by wire, including primary transmission

163. *See* Reinbothe & von Lewinski, *supra* note 108, at 112; Ficsor, *supra* note 9, § C.24 (noting that even those who merely provide facilities may be found contributorily or vicariously liable under domestic doctrines).

over the Internet.[164] Paragraph (2) is apparently inapplicable to satellite broadcasting where transmission is communicated to the public in other countries: though wireless satellite transmission might fall under Article 11bis(1), compulsory licensing cannot have extraterritorial effect.[165] In addition, in some situations compulsory licensing generally allowed under Berne becomes impermissible under Article 8 WCT for activities having an interactive element that triggers the making-available prong.

In conclusion, the observation stating the communication right is broad but not borderless should be refined by saying Article 8 WCT covers a very large spectrum of communication activities in the global information environment, and the limitations on this right do not necessarily result in the creation of zones of freedom. This consequence is associated in part with the eroding significance of the public/private distinction and the acceptance that very limited range of communications over the Internet might qualify as "private."[166] In this legal framework, the freedom to communicate copyrighted materials turns out to be the rare. European regulations in this field have so far been pursuing a similar restrictive approach to the digital communication right.

V. COMMUNICATION TO THE PUBLIC IN THE EUCD

A. Substantive Provisions

The 2001 EUCD nicely mirrors the revised position of the European Commission concerning digital transmissions as expressed in the 1996 Follow-Up report. The declared mission of this Directive was to fill all remaining gaps concerning copyright protection in the acquis communautaire, which at the time already consisted of five directives. As discussed in the previous chapter, the EUCD stipulates a broad reproduction right corroborated by a harmonized, pan-European distribution right obligating Member States to provide exclusive rights "to authorise

164. *See* Ricketson & Ginsburg (2006), *supra* note 7, § 13.71 (Art. 11bis(2) does not cover original wired communication (Internet) and retransmissions of works originally communicated by wired transmissions).

165. *Id.* § 13.71 (noting broadcasters may benefit from a compulsory licensing scheme in a certain country if the act of satellite broadcasting is considered completed in the country from which the transmission is made (and where compulsory licenses apply), which is essentially a question of interpretation).

166. Intranets connecting a small number of persons having personal connections, personally directed electronic mail, or instant messaging may still qualify as "private" communications. The effect of excluding these acts from the scope of the communication right is limited. *See, e.g.*, Guido Westkamp, *Transient Copying and Public Communication: The Creeping Evolution of Use and Access Rights in European Copyright Law*, 36 Geo. Wash. Int'l L. Rev. 1057, 1082–86 (2004) (noting the intensified influence of commercial factors on the distinction between private and public communications).

or prohibit any form of distribution [of copies] to the public by sale or otherwise."[167] Directly to the point of communication to the public, the EUCD remains consistently on the maximalist pole:

> This Directive should harmonise further the author's right of communication to the public. This right should be understood *in a broad sense covering all communication to the public not present at the place where the communication originates*. This right should cover any such transmission or retransmission of a work to the public by wire or wireless means, *including broadcasting* . . . The right to make available to the public subject-matter referred to in Article 3(2) should be understood as covering *all acts of making available* such subject-matter to members of the public not present at the place where the act of making available originates.[168]

The broad communication and making-available right is stated in Article 3(1):

> Member States shall provide authors with the exclusive right to authorise or prohibit any communication to the public of their works, by wire or wireless means, including the making available to the public of their works in such a way that members of the public may access them from a place and at a time individually chosen by them.[169]

Similar to the model of Article 8 WCT, the first prong stipulates a broad communication right.[170] Following the same rationale, the second prong intends to ensure "on-demand" transmissions are captured by the exclusive communication right.[171] The making-available right provided to "authors" by the second

167. *See* EUCD (2001), Art. 4(1). The distribution right is subject to a Community exhaustion rule. *Id.* Art. 4(2). Article 4(1) repeats the unfortunate formulation traced back to the 1988 E.C. Green Paper in defining the distribution right as applied "in respect of the original of their works or of copies thereof." *Id.*

168. EUCD (2001), Recitals 23–24. (emphasis added).

169. *Id.* Art 3(1).

170. By comparison, Article 14 WPPT states a producer's exclusive making-available right with respect to *phonograms* without the general "any communication" clause ("Producers of phonograms shall enjoy the exclusive right of authorizing the making available to the public of their phonograms, by wire or wireless means, in such a way that members of the public may access them from a place and at a time individually chosen by them.") *See* WPPT (1996), Art. 14. *See also id.*, Art. 10 (similar exclusive right secured for performers concerning their performance fixed in phonograms).

171. *See* EUCD (2001), Recital 25 ("The legal uncertainty regarding the nature and the level of protection of acts of on-demand transmission of copyright works and subject-matter protected by related rights over networks should be overcome by providing for harmonised protection at Community level. It should be made clear that all rightholders recognised by this Directive should have an exclusive right to make available to the public copyright works or any other subject-matter by way of interactive on-demand transmissions.

prong of Article 3(1) EUCD is further extended in subsection (2) to performers (with respect to fixed performances), producers (with respect to phonograms and films), and broadcasting organizations.[172] Subsection (3) clarifies the exclusive rights provided under Article 3 are not subject to any kind of exhaustion rule.[173]

B. Permissible Exceptions

Article 5(3) provides a list of fourteen permissible specific exceptions (and one general exception concerning analog uses of "minor importance") to the communication right. Those exceptions are also applicable to the reproduction right in Article 2 EUCD. The list is exhaustive, but none of these exceptions in Article 5(3) is mandatory.[174] Providing authors with fair compensation is not strictly required in all cases, though all domestic exceptions must conform to the three-part test.[175] For example, subsection (3)(a) allows an important exception covering "use for the sole purpose of illustration for teaching or scientific research, as long as the source, including the author's name, is indicated, unless this turns out to be impossible and to the extent justified by the non-commercial purpose to be achieved."[176] Many Member States have adopted domestic exceptions in this spirit to limit the communication right in the context of education, research, and learning.[177]

C. Several Interpretation Issues

The term *communication* is undefined, but it is still possible to identify situations *not* controlled by Article 3 EUCD. The provision does not apply to communications where the public is present,[178] and more generally, to public performances in the meaning of the Berne Convention.[179] The act of communication corresponds to the general understanding of the term, namely, generating messages

---

Such interactive on-demand transmissions are characterised by the fact that members of the public may access them from a place and at a time individually chosen by them.").

172. *Id.* Art. 3(2)(a)–(d). In this area there seems to be some overlap between Art. 3(2) WCT and the relevant WPPT provisions.

173. *Id.* Art. 3(3).

174. This can be learned from the language "Member States *may* provide for exceptions or limitations to the rights. . ." *Id.* Art 5(3) (emphasis added).

175. *Id.* Art. 5(5).

176. *Id.* Art. 5(3)(a).

177. For German law, see §§ 52a, 52b UrhG (exceptions to the making-available right for research, teaching and libraries, stipulating equitable remuneration duty).

178. *See* EUCD (2001), Recital 23.

179. *See* Silke von Lewinski & Michel M. Walter, *in* EUROPÄISCHES URHEBERRECHT KOMMENTAR (Michel M. Walter, ed., 2001); Stefan Bechtold, *in* CONCISE EUROPEAN COPYRIGHT LAW 360–61 (Thomas Dreier & P. Brent Hugenholtz eds., 2006).

signals via remote network communication devices and technologies.[180] The communication conduct does not have to be for-profit or be performed with the intention to commercially exploit the copyrighted work.

In addition, the term *public* did not receive a definition in the Directive, and Member States may clarify the public/private distinction in domestic laws under the constraints imposed by the mandatory scope of the making-available prong.[181] The private/public distinction in the general context of the communication right may take into account quantitative factors (e.g., number of recipients) and qualitative factors (e.g., relationship to originator).[182] The making-available prong is a special subcategory of communication to the public, as derived from the word *including* that connects the general communication prong and the making-available prong.

Another question particularly relevant in the context of access-conducts is whether the conducts of *users*, who initiate a request for a transmission of a work made publicly available by another person, are relevant for fulfilling the elements of the making-available prong. As a matter of both policy and common sense the exclusive communication right should in no case affect the lawfulness of requests by end users initiating relevant transmissions.[183] In terms of the access-right framework from Chapter 3, the communication right here should not spill over to cover or control access-conducts.[184]

We may further inquire whether acts that enhance the accessibility of the work already made available to the public by someone else (without actually offering the work) can violate the communication right. This issue is specifically outlined in the case of mere hyperlinking to a work made available in another cyberspace location. The hyperlinking scenario is contested,[185] yet there is a

180. Domestic law probably cannot determine that liability for unauthorized "communication to the public" requires a showing of *actual* reception, or warrant the completion of the transmission process. The making-available clause does not seem to require the communication sequence to be concluded. *See* von Lewinski & Walter, *supra* note 179, at 1130 (merely offering the work for transmission already triggers the making-available right).

181. For a proposed interpretation to the term *public* under the Directive, see *id.* ¶¶ 86–88 at 1053–54.

182. *Cf.* Bechtold, *supra* note 179, at 360–61. Such distinctions would have little impact in the making-available scenario, where the traditional concept of the "public" is largely a fiction.

183. *Id.* at 361 ("The right of making available to the public covers the act of providing a work to the public. If a user subsequently retrieves the work, the user's act is not covered by the right of making available.") *Cf.* Silke von Lewinski, *Der EG-Richtlinienvorschlag zum Urheberrecht und zu verwandten Schutzrechten in der Informationsgesellschaft, in* 1998 GRUR Int. 637, 639–640 (1998) (opining the proposed EUCD provision covered the entire process of transmission, in any event including intermediately carrying signals (*Übertragung*)).

184. The term *access-conducts* is explained in Chapter 3 *supra.*

185. Bechtold, *supra* note 179, at 361–62.

material difference between acts *enhancing accessibility* on the one hand and end users' acts related to *retrieval* on the other. The former type of activities falls systematically under communication-conducts in the broad sense,[186] and in this respect, applying the broad communication rights to linking has some merits, though it would seem preferable to evaluate such conducts under secondary liability theories.[187]

D. Communication Rights in Domestic Laws

1. German Law

The 2003 copyright reform in Germany added to the statute the new Section 19(a) as a special exclusive right of the family of copy-unrelated rights.[188] The new law supplemented existing communication rights and explicitly adopted the wording in the second prong of Article 3(1) EUCD. The statute now expressly secures to rights-holders the exclusive right to makc works available to the public with wire or wireless means in a manner that members of the public can access the work at their chosen place and time.[189]

The reform amended Section 15 and added subsection (2) to express a general exclusive right of communication to the public (*Recht der öffentlichen Wiedergabe*).[190] The newly codified general communication right and making-available right join and supplement the traditional public performance right in Section 19.[191] Section 19a covers remote communication in which (1) members

186. Chapter 3 explained the difference between access-conducts and communication-conducts, as well as the meaning of communication-conducts in the broad sense. *See* Chapter 3, Section II.C *supra*.

187. Proposing that linking to a work unlawfully made available by a third party implicates the communication right does not mean liability for linking will always attach. For example, if the linking party has a reasonable ground to believe the work was made available by the rights-holder or with permission, liability for the act of linking should not apply. Further, under certain theories of implied license, the linking party cannot be found liable if the rights-holder made the work freely available over the Internet. *Cf.* Bundesgerichtshof, I ZR 259/00, GRUR 2003, 958 (2003) ("BGH Paperboy decision") (the German high civil court ruled that deep linking to freely available Web sites does not violate the communication right in Sec. 15 UrhG).

188. *See Gesetz zur Regelung des Urheberrechts in der Informationsgesellschaft* 1774 (2003) (adding § 19a UrhG).

189. *See* § 19a UrhG. For legislative history supporting the bill by stressing the need to adopt the new norm in the face of uncertainties concerning the law of on-demand services, see First Bundle Bill (2002) at 16–17.

190. *See* § 15(2) UrhG. The bill supporting this legislation explained the need to articulate a general communication-to- the-public right. *See* First Bundle Bill (2002) at 17. The bill also proposed adding a definition of *public* that was later codified in Sec. 15(3).

191. *See* § 19 UrhG.

of the public can choose the place and time of reception; (2) unlike Section 19, it applies across-the-board to all work categories.[192]

The 2003 copyright reform also adopted several specific exceptions to the communication rights. Among others, exceptions are stipulated for law enforcement and security,[193] collections for educational and teaching purposes,[194] public speeches,[195] news reporting,[196] citation,[197] and making available for the purpose of teaching and research.[198] Most of these exceptions already limited various traditional communication rights prior to the copyright reform, and the only new exception added during the 2003 revision was the one of making available for teaching and research (Section 52a). The second copyright revision from 2007 added new Section 52b,[199] which applies to electronic reading places in public libraries.[200] In general, exceptions to communication rights are usually accompanied by an obligation to pay equitable remuneration enforced via collection societies.

2. U.S. Law

The U.S. Copyright Act currently does not provide for a general exclusive communication right or making-available right. However, Article 8 WCT communications are controlled for the most part by one or several excusive rights listed in Section 106. For instance, if transmission involves simultaneous performance of a performable work (such as an audio or audiovisual work), Section 106(4) (public performance) may apply.[201] If digital transmission allows recipients to observe the work on a screen, Section 106(5) (public display) may apply.[202] If transmission involves the production of new copies under the broad digital reproduction theory followed by U.S. courts,[203] the reproduction and distribution rights may apply. Finally, in the case of digital transmission of phonorecords, Section 106(6) is directly applicable.

---

192. For an overview on the scope of Sec. 19a, see Joachim von Ungern-Stermberg, *in* URHEBERRECHT KOMMENTAR § 19a nr. 42 ff (Gerhard Schricker ed., 2006).

193. *See* § 45 UrhG.

194. *Id.* § 46.

195. *Id.* § 48.

196. *Id.* § 50.

197. *Id.* § 51.

198. *Id.* § 52a.

199. *See Zweites Gesetz zur Regelung des Urheberrechts in der Informationsgesellschaft* (2007).

200. *Id.* § 52b. For a skeptical comment concerning the effect of this new exception, see Reto M. Hilty, *Der "zweite Korb"—ein erster Schritt in die richtige Richtung* , 7 MMR 713–15 (2004) .

201. *See* 17 U.S.C § 106(4).

202. *Id.* § 106(5).

203. Chapter 4, Section IV.B.3 *supra.*

Some uncertainties remain, however, particularly in the case of the mere *offering* the work for transmission. For example, in *Elektra v. Barker*, a district court in New York reviewed the controversy over the theory that making available acts are captured by the distribution right, concluding that "an offer to distribute . . . for the purpose of further distribution, public performance, or public display" implicated the reproduction right.[204]

In comparison, a district court in Massachusetts offered an extensive analysis of the issue, holding the distribution right covers electronic file transfer, but "merely exposing music files to the internet is not copyright infringement."[205] Continuing this line, a district court in Arizona held that merely making a copy available over peer-to-peer networks did not constitute distribution.[206]

Despite some contradictions on the details among various atypical decisions, the general trend has been to apply one or more exclusive rights to most instances of digital transmission and making available, including peer-to-peer file sharing and various interactive and on-demand services. That said, inconsistency in the case law concerning the making-available-as-distribution continues to spawn uncertainty.[207] In some factual situations, especially for merely offering the work for transmission without evidence of any other copyright violation, the prima facie case of rights-holders in court is more difficult to make.[208] Further, the recent holding of the Second Circuit in *Cartoon Network v. CSC Holdings/*

---

204. *See* Elektra Ent. Group v. Barker, 2008 WL 857527 at *8 (S.D.N.Y. 2008).

205. *See* London-Sire Records, Inc. v. Doe, 2008 WL 887491 at *14–*17 (D. Mass. 2008).

206. *See* Atlantic Recording Corp. v. Howell, 2008 WL 1927353 at *5 ff (D. Ariz. 2008) ("The court agrees with the great weight of authority that § 106(3) is not violated unless the defendant has actually distributed an unauthorized copy of the work to a member of the public. The statute provides copyright holders with the exclusive right to distribute "copies" of their works to the public "by sale or other transfer of ownership, or by rental, lease, or lending.". . . Unless a copy of the work changes hands in one of the designated ways, a "distribution" under § 106(3) has not taken place. Merely making an unauthorized copy of a copyrighted work available to the public does not violate a copyright holder's exclusive right of distribution.").

207. *See, e.g.*, Capitol Records, Inc. v. Thomas, 2008 WL 4405282 (D. Minn. 2008) (the court expressly rejected the theory that merely offering music files over P2P file sharing networks per se infringed the distribution right).

208. *Id.* at *10 ("Equating making available with distribution would undermine settled case law holding that merely inducing or encouraging another to infringe does not, alone, constitute infringement unless the encouraged party actually infringes . . . If simply making a copyrighted work available to the public constituted a distribution, even if no member of the public ever accessed that work, copyright owners would be able to make an end run around the standards for assessing contributor copyright infringement.") (citation omitted).

Cablevision has cast serious doubts concerning the application of the public performance right to certain on-demand transmissions.[209]

VI. THE COMMUNICATION RIGHT AS ACCESS-RIGHT

A. Old/New Communication Rights and Their Access-Right Alter Ego

The communication right—embracing digital transmissions, making-available acts, and interactive services—is the positive law's manifestation of the theoretical construct previously named the "second access-right prong" (Chapter 3, Section III.A(2) supra). The panoply of rights secured under copyright statutes today principally reigns over most forms of unauthorized digital communication. The proliferation and expansion of communication rights render the possibility of access control in the digital environment a real one, at least as a matter of law.

The convergence between the *concept* of the second access-right prong and *actual* copyright exclusivity emanates from the significant overlap between various types and forms of communicative behaviors and the territory exclusive rights cover. The connection between copyright exclusivity and communication is firm, and Chapter 1 has already demonstrated copyright infringement always involves communication or communication-related activity.[210] Indeed, exclusive rights in communication-conducts that target "public" performances of various kinds have been the bedrock of the copyright system from the very beginning. At the same time, traditional communication rights—as applied in the analog domain—have built-in, functioning limitations. They often apply selectively to *certain* work categories and cover only *certain* communication technologies/channels; the requirement of the "public" (or communication "to the public") serves to distinguish commercial infringers that pose eminent threats to rights-holders from noncommercially minded individuals who communicate with each other for whatever reason. Though communications rights have long-standing roots in copyright doctrine, the ramifications of their extension to the Internet reality, and the amount of power they bestow upon rights-holders, are unparalleled by anything the analog past has ever seen. And the lack of coherence in the area of digital *exemptions* to communication rights makes things look even worse from the perspective of nonowners.

B. Coherence and Balance

Perhaps the expansion of communication rights to all corners of cyberspace is inevitable for the preservation of copyright protection in the digital

---

209. *See* The Cartoon Network v. CSC Holdings, 536 F.3d 121, 134–40 (2d. Cir 2008), *cert denied*, 129 S.Ct. 2890 (June 29, 2009).

210. Chapter 1, Section V.A.–B.

environment: the broad digital communication right is a crucial component in copyright's exclusory strategy, a prerequisite without which even a moderate degree of control would be hardly conceivable. At the same time, going too far with proprietary control over communications might be disastrous for the information process that underlies our information society, and no less important, for whatever goal copyright law seeks to accomplish in the long run.

As to the form and structure of the positive law, it is fair to say jurisdictions that have formally introduced a broad communication and making-available right have achieved a significant level of coherence and legal certainty in the area of *coverage*: gaps were filled, doubts removed, and ambiguities vanished. But a functioning copyright system needs coherence also in the area of limitations, which is crucial for copyright's quest for balance, and in the modern world of computer networks, legal distinctions such as the one between private and public communications (or between copy-related and copy-unrelated rights) face a process of disintegration. Where one and the same behavior turns to be banned by multiple exclusive rights, traditional exemptions cannot preserve their old structure and still effectively fulfill their balancing function.

In the end, the sough-after certainty as to coverage of copyright exclusivity has been achieved at a price being paid by exemptions beneficiaries and the general public. Yet effectively securing exclusivity in digital domains *does not warrant* such unbalanced results. The preferable way to address the problem is not to amend/expand traditional exemptions and distinctions, but begin instead at an earlier logical *locus*, namely, with restructuring the exclusive rights themselves. Before turning to examine this option more closely, the study proceeds to the quintessential manifestation of the access-right in the positive law—that is, the bans on circumvention of technological protection measures.

6. ANTICIRCUMVENTION LAWS

I. INTRODUCTION

More than any other development associated with digital copyright lawmaking, the advent of anticircumvention laws has most significantly directed attention to the emerging convergence between access control and copyright exclusivity. It is true legal sanctions against circumvention of access-controls and trafficking in circumvention tools existed before the WIPO Treaties, but these provisions were for the most part copyright-unrelated:[1] Prior to the emergence of *copyright* anticircumvention laws, TPMs circumvention per se generally did not trigger copyright infringement liability.

More recent anticircumvention regulations under copyright have unapologetically introduced the term *access* to the language of copyright statutes. Among the most fiercely contested legislative responses to digital infringement threats, this novelty has been spawning deliberations on the transforming nature and scope of copyright protection as applied to TPM-protected works. This chapter will explain the connection between this controversial annex to copyright law and the first access-right prong (Chapter 3 supra), as well as its central contribution to the transformation process copyright law has been undergoing. Anticircumvention regulation, in tandem with the developments described in Chapters 3 and 4, raises serious doubts concerning the role, function, and efficacy of the traditional copyright regime in modern information markets.

Among other things, it shall be argued that too rigorous anticircumvention prohibitions might conflict with both the letter and spirit of the Berne Convention, which connects to more fundamental questions concerning the interface between anticircumvention regulation and traditional copyrights in general. This chapter will show why both types of regulation cannot be reconciled to build a coherent and harmonious body of law. Rights to control access cannot be "integrated" into the traditional system simply because traditional copyrights conceptually are a *special case* of regulation that bundles together a number of limited, narrow private rights to constrain certain communication-conducts. In other words, the instances covered by traditional law reflect only a small fraction of the rights a full-scaled access-right would embrace, and a

1. See Séverine Dusollier, *Situating Legal Protections for Copyright-Related Technological Measures in the Broader Legal Landscape: Anti Circumvention Protection Outside Copyright*, *in* ADJUNCTS AND ALTERNATIVES TO COPYRIGHT, PROCEEDINGS OF THE 2001 ALAI CONGRESS 123 (Jane C. Ginsburg & June M. Besek, eds., 2002) (providing a study on anticircumvention laws outside copyright).

proprietary framework that captures only certain, special cases of access provision (the so-called "communication-conducts" as defined in Chapter 3) cannot ingest general and much broader access-related entitlements without undergoing a very fundamental process of transfiguring into something else.

Not all copyright scholars share this observation. Some prefer dismissing anticircumvention rules as ancillary, adjunct, or enforcement-like provisions.[2] This chapter brings forward a different perspective, according to which anticircumvention laws are signifiers of a much greater transition that occupy a central position in a shift from the familiar model of exclusive rights to a more explicit access-right regime.

II. EXTERNAL ANTICIRCUMVENTION LAWS

Legal provisions aiming at curtailing TPM circumvention and similar (or related) conducts can be found in unfair competition rules, laws prohibiting the interception of telecommunication data, broadcasting laws, and protections of conditional online services.[3] Some TPMs circumvention and trafficking conducts are further punishable under various criminal provisions.[4]

According to traditional copyright rules, circumvention acts do not independently violate copyrights,[5] and there are several distinctions between modern circumvention prohibitions under copyright and circumvention prohibitions in other legal contexts, called here *external anticircumvention laws*. In the former case, the rules apply only with respect to technological protections of *copyrighted content*. In the latter, the copyright status of protected information is usually irrelevant. External anticircumvention laws are not part of copyright lawmaking and are not designed to promote copyright policy, though they are likely to be part of information policy in the broad sense (e.g., in the case of media and broadcasting law and regulations).

Prohibitions on direct circumvention and preparatory acts are contained in various statutes. In the United States, anticircumvention and anti-trafficking

---

2. For a recent statement of the common view, *see* SILKE VON LEWINSKI, INTERNATIONAL COPYRIGHT LAW AND POLICY § 17.91 (2008) ("obligations concerning technological measures and rights management information constitute novel provisions . . . Unlike minimum rights, they do not grant any direct protection against unauthorized uses, but aim at indirectly protecting the minimum rights by flanking legal measures and thereby indirectly severe the enforcement of the minimum rights.") (footnotes omitted).

3. *See* Dusollier, *supra* note 1, at 124–33.

4. *Id.* at 133–38.

5. The act of circumvention (particularly against software protections) sometimes involves certain reproductions and adaptations that in themselves might violate copyrights. However, in such cases the act is illicit not due to its circumvention element, but its infringement element.

provisions protecting scrambled cable communication and encrypted satellite programming have long been in place.[6] For instance, the Cable Communication Policy Act of 1984 prohibits unlawful interception of cable communication controlled by cable decoders (so-called "black boxes") and trafficking in such devices.[7] The Communications Act of 1934 prescribes civil and criminal liability for those who manufacture and distribute devices that primarily assist in unauthorized decryption of satellite cable programming.[8] In Europe, a recent and prominent example of external anticircumvention regulation in the area of digital network communication is the directive on conditional access (CA Directive), which sets forth anticircumvention regulations targeting electronic access controls to online services.[9] Article 4 of the CA Directive delineates prohibitions concerning the manufacturing, trafficking, installation, and possession for commercial purposes of "illicit devices,"[10] which are defined as "any equipment or software designed or adapted to give access to a protected service in an intelligible form without the authorization of the service provider."[11]

There is a notable tension between the two types of anticircumvention laws that emanates from the practical impossibility of ensuring that copyrighted works remain unaffected by copyright-unrelated regulation. Copyrighted content that is technologically protected by access-control TPMs may be subject to both types of regulation simultaneously, and the problem rests in the fact copyright-unrelated regulations are not sensitive to copyright policy issues.[12] An additional set of complications arises when copyright anticircumvention provisions are used in practice to enforce control over information that does not qualify as copyright subject matter. Specifically, copyright anticircumvention laws can be invoked when TPMs restrict access to noncopyrighted content and to noncopyrightable elements of copyrighted material, as access controls block

---

6. *See* June M. Besek, *Anti-Circumvention Laws and Copyright: A Report from the Kernochan Center for Law, Media, and the Arts*, 27 Colum. J. L. & Arts 385, 438–43 (2004) (reviewing anticircumvention-analogous provisions in cable and satellite regulations, as well as provisions in other federal and state laws that seem to address "circumvention-type situations").

7. *See* 47 U.S.C. § 553(a).

8. *See* 47 U.S.C. § 605(e)(3)–(4).

9. *See* E.C. Conditional Access Directive (1988).

10. *Id.* Art. 4(a)–(c).

11. *Id.* Art. 2(e). German law adopted these provisions in 2002. *See* Zugangskontrolldiensteschutz-Gesetz-ZKDSG (2002).

12. *See, e.g.*, Thomas Heide, *Access Control and Innovation Under the Emerging EU Electronic Commerce Framework*, 15 Berkeley Tech. L.J. 993 (2000); Alaine Strowel & Séverine Dusollier, *Legal Protection of Technological Systems*, WIPO document, WCT-WTTP/IMP/2—Workshop on Implementation Issues of the WIPO WCT and the WPPT 23–24 (1999).

perception of the work in its entirety, including ideas, facts, and public domain materials that are put together in TPM-secured "digital envelopes."

Generally speaking, the main significance of external anticircumvention laws here is in setting precedent for this type of information regulative measures. Such external provisions have been invoked as analogous and as supporting the plausibility of enacting similar rules within copyright's province. For example, the familiar prohibitions on circumvention of encrypted satellite signals were mentioned to downplay the unusual implications of comparable bans as additional protections to copyright holders.[13] In the opposite camp, opponents of anticircumvention laws were alarmed by the risk the copyright law would be transformed into an access control apparatus per se. The next passages provide a panoramic overview and analysis showing how this peculiar type of regulating came to be internationally controlling and prevalent in domestic laws.

III. THE INCEPTION OF COPYRIGHT ANTICIRCUMVENTION LAWS

The pressure to reform copyright law in response to the threats of digital technology as to the interest of copyright holders gained momentum in the United States and Europe in the late 1980s and early 1990s. The spreading acknowledgment digital technology was rapidly changing markets, consumption habits, and long-standing practices fueled sentiments of urgency for adjusting existing laws to the digital reality on both sides of the Atlantic. Considered the world's largest exporter of copyrighted products, the United States felt particularly threatened by the prospects of massive worldwide infringement.[14] In Europe, lawmakers and academics were mainly concerned about how to harmonize domestic copyright laws and formulate a uniform European approach to the new technological challenges.[15] Concurrent with efforts at the domestic and regional levels, interest groups and governments looked to international fora. The twin 1996 WIPO

13. *See* David Nimmer, *A Riff of Fair Use in the Digital Millennium Copyright Act*, 148 U. Penn. L. Rev. 673, 687 (2000) (describing DMCA legislative reports in the U.S. that considered the contemplated anti-trafficking provisions analogous to external provisions: "Building on previous doctrines of law outside the copyright arena (such as those barring manufacture of equipment to receive unauthorized cable television service and decrypting cable programming), the trafficking ban is 'drafted carefully to target 'black boxes,' and to ensure legitimate multipurpose devices can continue to be made and sold)." (footnotes omitted).

14. One recent U.S. Senate resolution stated "the United States is the world's largest creator, producer, and exporter of copyrighted materials." It further expressed "the sense of Congress that United States intellectual property rights must be protected globally." *See* U.S. Senate Concurrent Resolution 87 (2006).

15. *See, e.g.*, Gerhard Schricker et al., Konturen Eines Europäischen Urheberrechts (1996).

Treaties were an important catalyst for passing national anticircumvention laws predominantly in the United States and in Europe, but also in many nations elsewhere.[16]

A. Early Developments in the United States

The antecedents to the enactment of U.S. anticircumvention laws trace back to the early 1990s. The Audio Home Recording Act from 1992 was the preliminary incarnation of anticircumvention law in the copyright statute. As in many other areas of digital copyright, the U.S. Green and White Papers were significant milestones, heralding the anticircumvention provisions introduced by the 1998 Digital Millennium Copyright Act (DMCA.)

1. The Audio Home Recording Act

The Audio Home Recording Act (AHRA)[17] was the first foray of anticircumvention laws into the 1976 U.S. Copyright Act. The AHRA targets a specific digital reproduction technology that was believed at the time to have become widely spread and significantly harmful to the economic interests of rights-holders.

The technology at issue, Digital Audio Taping (DAT), enabled the making of accurate digital reproduction of musical recordings with no traceable derogation in quality. The quality of first generation copies performed with DAT recording devices was, for most purposes, identical to the original recording and to further generations of copies. DAT recording devices could be equipped with a copy-control TPM called a Serial Copying Management System (SCMS). The SCMS imposed technical limitations on the number of second-generation copies users could make.[18] The AHRA articulates statutory prohibitions on trafficking in and manufacturing of DAT machines (called "digital audio recording [DAR] device") made available in the U.S. market that did not conform to the SCMS and similar copy-control systems.[19] Most relevantly, it provided "[n]o person shall import, manufacture, or distribute any device, or offer or perform any service, *the primary purpose or effect of which is to avoid, bypass, remove, deactivate, or otherwise*

---

16. For a review of anticircumvention legislation in Asian countries, see Andy Sun, *Introduction* to THE LAW ON ANTI-CIRCUMVENTION AND DIGITAL RIGHTS MANAGEMENT (2007).

17. The Audio Home Recording Act of 1992 added Chapter 10 to the 1976 U.S. Copyright Act, titled "Digital Audio Recording Devices and Media." *See* Audio Home Recording Act (1992).

18. The Serial Copy Management System (SCMS), when incorporated into a DAT machine, was able to monitor copying by not allowing the making of second-generation digital copies from a digital source. In addition, it was able to allow two generations of digital copying made from an analog source, but a third generation of copying could not be made. For a technical background, see Senate Report 102-294 (AHRA 1992) at 23 ff and 36 ff.

19. *See* 17 U.S.C. § 1002(a).

circumvent any program or circuit which implements, in whole or in part, a system described in subsection (a)."[20]

The AHRA further canvassed a levy system imposed on DAT machines and digital audio recording media.[21] This legislation applies exclusively to DAT technology,[22] and although it is considered today largely an irrelevant appendage to the statute,[23] it brought to the forefront the novel modus operandi of copyright anticircumvention laws, containing all of its three characteristic features: (1) It directly punishes the manufacture and distribution of infringement-*enabling* technologies and devices; (2) the term *circumvention* was introduced for the first time into the statute in connection with copyright violations, and (3) it directly punishes activities "preparatory" to actual circumvention. In fact, the AHRA targets *only* preparatory acts. Actual circumvention of SCMS does not violate its provisions.[24]

2. The 1994 U.S. Green Paper

The Green Paper enthusiastically endorsed the idea of copyright anticircumvention laws as an important element in the legal response to new digital threats, to which a proper response was considered necessary. The report stated:

> The emergence of integrated information technology is dramatically changing, and will continue to change, how people and businesses deal in information and entertainment products and services, and how works are created, owned, distributed, reproduced, displayed, performed, licensed, managed, presented, organized, sold, accessed, used, and stored. This leads, understandably, to a call for change in the law.[25]

The report highlighted the two policy spearheads building the argument in favor of anticircumvention laws. First, there had been a serious concern rights-holders would simply avoid the Internet if they were not feeling sufficiently secure about putting their commercial interests at risk while distributing their works in digital form over computer networks without a sufficient level of technological

---

20. *Id.* at § 1002(c) (emphasis added).

21. *Id.* §§ 1003–07.

22. *See* RIAA v. Diamond Multimedia Sys., Inc., 180 F.3d. 1072 (9th. Cir. 1999).

23. *See* David Nimmer, *Codifying Copyright Comprehensibility*, 51 UCLA L. Rev. 1233, 1332 (2004) ("Instead of DAT products becoming as ubiquitous as Congress imagined when it frantically adopted this legislation, the revolution never occurred. DATs have become standard equipment in American homes to about the same extent as videophones.").

24. The AHRA does not prohibit *actual* SCMS circumvention. Further, it explicitly exempts from infringement liability acts of mere trafficking in, and noncommercial use of, digital audio recording devices and media that conform to the SCMS specifications. *See* 17 U.S.C. § 1008.

25. *See* U.S. Green Paper (1994) at 8.

control. Second, the Green Paper predicted that if, as a consequence of rights-holders' mistrust, the NII (the Internet) did not provide access to a wide variety of works under equitable and reasonable terms, the *public* too would turn its back on the Internet.[26]

To adapt copyright law to the NII environment, the Green Paper suggested a series of adjustments to the Copyright Act. In the field of anticircumvention, the repost recommended introducing new prohibitions concerning technological protection measures (TPMs).[27] The proposal was founded on a number of arguments that have become the standard justification for copyright anticircumvention laws in general. First, TPMs were considered important and desirable considering the ease of committing infringements on the one hand, and the immense difficulties in detecting violations and enforcing copyrights in the digital environment on the other.[28] Second, it was acknowledged TPMs were susceptible to manipulation and could be technologically defeated.[29] Third, in light of the U.S. Supreme Court's *Sony-Betamax* decision from 1984,[30] the IP Working Group opined that relying merely on indirect infringement liability to combat TPMs circumvention and related acts could not ameliorate rights-holders' concerns.[31]

A fourth argument purported that copyright legislation prohibiting circumvention devices would ultimately serve the public interest, as (1) it would reduce the price legitimate users are required to pay, as they otherwise would have to expend more to cover the losses resulting from massive infringement; and (2) the public would have access to more works if copyright protection were more effective.[32] Accordingly, the Green Paper suggested creating a direct trafficking prohibition on circumvention devices and services,[33] targeting devices and services having the "primary purpose or effect" of TPMs circumvention.[34] The prohibited activities included importing, manufacturing, and distributing circumvention devices, as well as offering and performing services with the

---

26. *Id.* at 6–7.

27. *Id.* at 125–30.

28. *Id.* at 125–26.

29. *Id.*

30. *See* Sony Corp. v. Universal City Studios, Inc., 464 U.S. 417 (1984).

31. *See* U.S. Green Paper (1994) at 126.

32. *Id.*

33. *Id.* at 128 ("The Working Group recommends that Chapter 5 of the Copyright Act be amended to include the following new section 512: 'No person shall import, manufacture or distribute any device, product, or component incorporated into a device or product, or offer or perform any service, the primary purpose or effect of which is to avoid, bypass, remove, deactivate, or otherwise circumvent, without authority of the copyright owner or the law, any process, treatment, mechanism or system which prevents or inhibits the exercise of any of the exclusive rights under Section 106.'").

34. *Id.*

primary purpose or effect of TPMs circumvention.[35] The prohibition on trafficking related only to circumvention devices and services that "prevent[] or inhibit[] the exercise of any of the exclusive rights under section 106."[36]

There are four key points in the Green Paper's proposal that undeline the cardinal issues concerning the structure of anticircumvention legislation in general. The proposal (1) concerned *trafficking* activities, not actual circumvention, (2) trafficking prohibitions were connected to the exercise of the exclusive rights under Section 106 of the Copyright Act; (3) prohibited devices and services were those that enabled circumvention *without authority* of the copyright owner *or permitted by law*, and (4) it appears violations of the new trafficking prohibition were to be considered an independent *copyright infringement*.[37]

3. The 1995 U.S. White Paper

The White Paper did not significantly alter the analysis presented in the Green Paper and the proposal for legislative amendment formulated therein. It reiterated the premises for new copyright anticircumvention provisions[38] and recited almost verbatim the text of the proposed anticircumvention provision.[39] The proposed new Section 1201 would have covered only preparatory activities (trafficking in devices and providing services that facilitated TPMs circumvention) in the case when TPMs prevent or inhibit the violation of the exclusive rights under Section 106.[40] The report emphasized the new provision targeted only "unauthorized"

---

35. *Id.*

36. *Id.*

37. This conclusion is drawn from the following language: "The Working Group recommends that Section 501 of the Copyright Act [defining copyright infringement] be amended to read as follows: (a) Anyone who violates any of the exclusive rights of the copyright owner as provided by sections 106 through 118 or of the author as provided in section 106A(a) . . . is an infringer of the copyright or right of the author, as the case may be. *Anyone who violates section 512* [the proposed anti-trafficking provision] *is an infringer of the copyright in a work that utilizes the process, treatment, mechanism or system which the violator's device, product, component or service circumvents.*" *Id.* at 125–30 (emphasis in original).

38. *See* U.S. White Paper (1995) at 230.

39. *Id.* Appendix 1, Proposed Legislation at 6 (introducing the proposed new Section 1201 to be added to the Copyright Act).

40. The text of proposed section 1201 reads: "No person shall import, manufacture or distribute any device, product, or component incorporated into a device or product, or offer or perform any service, the primary purpose or effect of which is to avoid, bypass, remove, deactivate, or otherwise circumvent, without the authority of the copyright owner or the law, any process, treatment, mechanism or system which prevents or inhibits the violation of any of the exclusive rights of the copyright owner under section 106." *Id.* By comparison, the Green Paper would have prohibited trafficking activities that "prevent[] or inhibit[] the *exercise* of any of the exclusive rights under Section 106." (citation omitted) (emphasis added). Replacement of the term *exercise* (which is broader, and arguably includes preventive measures) with the term *violation* (arguably narrower and attached to

activities, and that such authority "may be granted by the copyright owner or by limitations on the copyright owner's rights under the Copyright Act."[41]

As it did in the context of the digital communication right, the White Paper also downplayed fair use concerns in connection with the proposed section 1201. It indicated "if the circumvention device is primarily intended and used for legal purposes, such as fair use, the device would *not* violate the provision, because a device with such purposes and effects would fall under the 'authorized by law' exemption."[42] It further dismissed concerns the new provision would place restrictions on public domain information by clarifying protection systems that lock out public domain content would not qualify under the new provision. Technically, such systems could not be considered as preventing or inhibiting "the violation of any of the exclusive rights of the copyright owner under Section 106."[43]

B. Early Developments in Europe

1. The 1988 E.C. Green Paper and Its Follow-Up

The 1988 E.C. Green Paper addressed TPMs in chapter 3 titled "Audio-Visual Home Copying."[44] At focus was the problem of private copying, considering it was the practice in many European countries to permit private noncommercial reproduction of copyrighted works from copies distributed by rights-holders and off the air.[45] The Commission sympathized with rights-holders' anxiety concerning digital copying technology, particularly DAT machines that enabled "cloning" of works (particularly sound recordings)—a practice the industry feared might replace sales of copies.[46] The Commission was further aware of the already-available and developing technical means to control users' ability to make an unlimited number of perfect digital copies.[47] At the same time, the Commission cautioned whether Community-level intervention was desirable. The Green Paper advised:

> [R]emedies should not be adopted for want of anything better if to do so would simply substitute one set of injustices for another. In matters of legislation,

---

actual infringement) may indicate a wish to tailor the prohibition more closely to formal copyright infringement.

41. *See* U.S. White Paper (1995) at 231 (emphasis added).

42. *Id.* (emphasis in original).

43. *Id.* at 232.

44. *See* E.C. Green Paper (1988). The Commission observed: "Until recently, the audiovisual material in question consisted of sound and video recordings, radio and television broadcasts and cable transmissions. Recent technical developments seem likely to broaden the range of material to include various kinds of information, possibly together with images and sounds, recorded digitally on a support of one kind or another." *Id.* ¶ 3.1.2.

45. *Id.* ¶¶ 3.4.3–3.4.12 (discussing domestic practices of allowing private copying, often in combination with levy systems of recording equipment and media).

46. *Id.* ¶¶ 3.6.1–3.6.2; *see also,* ¶¶ 3.7.1–3.7.5 (presenting the arguments of greater protection advocates).

47. *Id.* ¶¶ 3.15.1–3.15.9.

something is not necessarily better than nothing. Abstention is sometimes the better solution.[48]

The Commission ultimately recommended introducing "mandatory technical solutions" with regard to DAT technology "provided that they are technically feasible and properly balanced in respect of all the interests concerned."[49] It further suggested formulating distinctions between restrictions on DAT machines available in the market for professionals (such as recording studios, broadcasters, and educational establishments) and private users.[50]

Acknowledging that no technological measure is circumvention foolproof,[51] the Commission opted for a three-prong strategy that would (1) require DAT machines to be equipped with technological copy restrictions, (2) ban the distribution of DAT machines that do not conform to the corresponding technical specifications, and (3) ban "the manufacture, importation or sale of devices intended to circumvent or render inoperable the [DAT copy-control] measures."[52]

The 1991 E.C. Follow-Up report added little new substance to the detailed analysis already laid out in the Green Paper. However, a change in the Commission's general tone concerning intervention policy is noticeable. The report opens with a statement of policy indicating protection of copyright "must by *strengthened*" and must, as far as possible, be guided by a "*comprehensive*" approach.[53] Under the aegis of stronger protection, it indicated protection must be better designed to thwart new threats, international conventions "must be adapted," and "new rights must be conferred on authors to prevent their creative efforts and their investments from being unlawfully appropriated by others."[54] After holding several hearings on the recommendations of the 1988 Green Paper concerning issues of home copying, the 1991 Follow-Up reported (1) the intention of drafting a special directive on home copying,[55] and (2) adhesion to the

48. *Id.* ¶ 3.1.4.

49. *Id.* ¶ 3.1.5.

50. *Id.* ¶¶ 3.1.5–3.1.10; *see also,* ¶ 3.13.1(e) (proposing that possession of machines intended for professional or specialist use that do not conform to the copy-control specifications can be possible upon obtaining a license).

51. *Id.* ¶ 3.1.14. ("It is self-evident that no technical solution can ever be guaranteed against deliberate attempts at circumvention. However, if a reasonable degree of security can be achieved together with no derogation in the quality of the product offered to the consumer, and a reduction in the level of sales lost through home copying, then a technical protection system offers a solution which is worthy of consideration.").

52. *Id.* ¶ 3.13.1. Importantly, after a considerable discussion, the Commission did not adopt similar recommendations with respect to video recording.

53. *See* E.C. Follow-Up to the Green Paper (1991) at ¶ 1.4 (emphasis in original).

54. *Id.* ¶ 1.5.

55. *Id.* ¶ 3.4.2.

idea of regulating the market for DAT machines, while adding the preferred anti-copying technology to carry forth the mission should be the SCMS.[56]

2. The 1991 Software Directive

Meanwhile, the Software Directive was promulgated.[57] Among all "first generation" copyright directives, only this one stipulated anticircumvention provisions and only in the narrow context of computer programs. Article 7(1)(c) to the Directive prohibits both the act of putting into circulation and possession for commercial purposes "any means the sole intended purpose of which is to facilitate the unauthorized removal or circumvention of any technical device which may have been applied to protect a computer program."[58]

Article 7(1)(c) is important in several respects. First, it is the first European legislation in the area of copyright law that imposed obligations to introduce domestic prohibitions related to TPMs circumvention.[59] At the same time, the concise formulation of Article 7(1)(c) raised a host of new uncertainties and interpretation challenges, with a language prescribing Member States' obligations in both sweeping and narrow terms. For one, the provision is broad and open-ended in describing TPMs as "any technical device" without further explication, and the preamble to the Software Directive also does not clarify the meaning of this phrase. The only qualification requirement is that the technical device be "applied to protect a computer program."[60] Article 7(1)(c) is vague and broad also in describing illicit circumvention tools, denoted merely as "any means."[61] The Directive's text stipulates that both trafficking in such "means" and the possession thereof for commercial proposes is illicit.

For another, the restrictive aspect of the provision lies in the definition of the nexus between "protection" of a computer program and "means." Namely, the *sole* intended purpose of the act of putting into circulation or commercial possession of the means must be "to facilitate the unauthorized removal or circumvention"

---

56. *Id.* ¶3.4.3.

57. *See* E.C. Software Directive (1991).

58. *Id.* Art. 7(1)(c) ("Member States shall provide, in accordance with their national legislation, appropriate remedies against a person . . . [committing] . . . any act of putting into circulation, or the possession for commercial purposes of, any means the sole intended purpose of which is to facilitate the unauthorized removal or circumvention of any technical device which may have been applied to protect a computer program.").

59. In fact, the Software Directive was the first harmonizing legislation in the area of European copyright law in general. For an overview, see Lionel Bently *in* CONCISE EUROPEAN COPYRIGHT LAW 211 ff (Thomas Dreier & P. Brent Hugenholtz eds., 2006).

60. The requisite that the software must be protected under copyright is not explicit in this provision. However, it may be derived from the general context of the Directive, as covered TPMs must protect *against acts of copyright infringement.*

61. *Cf.* Bently, *supra* note 59, at 235 ("The term 'any means' is clearly intended to be broad and would cover 'devices, products, or components' . . . but would not appear to cover the provision of services.").

of the TPM applied to the software. In other words, trafficking and possession are only banned when there is a clear connection between the functionality of the means as designed to break TPMs and the intention of the actor with respect to this capability. The burden on plaintiffs to show "sole intended purpose" is significant, and it seems multifunctional means generally do not fall under the prohibition. The intended purpose of the act of possession or trafficking could be inferred from the functionality/design of the means, as well as from the circumstances of the accused act. No less important is the fact the Software Directive does not cover acts of actual circumvention at all.

3. The 1995 E.C. Green Paper and Its Follow-Up

The contribution of the 1995 Green Paper to the TPMs debate is rather negligible. It reiterated the threats-opportunities paradigm and mentioned a number of systems that could identify and track data transferred over computer networks.[62] The report recited Article 7 of the Software Directive as precedent for copyright anticircumvention regulation in European law,[63] while stating laconically "[t]he Community may find it advisable to act in order to make technical systems of protection compulsory, on a harmonized basis, once they have been developed and accepted by industry."[64]

With the WIPO process breathing down its neck, the European Commission hastily published the 1996 Follow-Up.[65] In one and the same chapter, this report addressed legal protection of "integrity of technical identification" and "protection schemes."[66] It noted digitization made it "potentially easier to control acts of exploitation by means of access control, identification and anti-copying devices."[67] Further, electronic copyright management and protection systems should improve "[t]he monitoring of the access to, and the use of, works or related subject matters" and "the schemes concerned would also allow for more efficient combating of piracy."[68] In that respect, the Follow-Up opined it was necessary to coordinate and harmonize European national schemes in the area of technological protections.[69]

---

62. *See* E.C. Green Paper (1995) at 79–80. It seems anticircumvention issues were not thoroughly discussed due to the intent to prepare at a later stage a separate green paper to address specifically anticircumvention issues. *Id.* at 80.

63. *Id.* at 81.

64. *Id.* at 82.

65. *See* E.C. Follow-Up to the Green Paper (1996).

66. *Id.* at 15–17.

67. *Id.* at 15.

68. *Id.*

69. *Id.* ("Significant obstacles to trade could arise if some Member States were to impose protection devices, while forbidding the sale of non-protected materials. Finally, the continued absence in Member States of an appropriate legal protection of the integrity of the technical devices and schemes poses a serious threat of intellectual property piracy and is thus a stumbling block for a healthy development of the Information Society within the Community.").

After receiving comments on earlier reports, the Commission concluded "[a]n overwhelming majority of interested circles seeks the adoption of legislative measures providing for the legal protection of the integrity of technical identification and protection schemes."[70] The Follow-Up report gave the impression disagreements among stakeholders concerned not the *necessity* but only the *scope* of new legislation.[71] In general, intervention at the Community level was believed to be necessary, and the report emphasized "[a]ny Community proposal would have to precisely define the scope of [legal] protection and the nature of the act to be covered (such as manufacture, possession in the course of business, putting into circulation, distribution, importation), the way or process of circumvention/deactivation, etc."[72]

Harmonization was also considered desirable in determining the scope of "infringer's liability," specifically in the context of privacy and use of personal data.[73] Finally, the report noted questions of liability for violating anticircumvention laws "might possibly include legitimate defenses to civil liability, and limitations to restricted acts and users' rights have to be taken into account as well. In addition, appropriate civil penalties and/or sanctions may be called for."[74]

IV. ANTICIRCUMVENTION IN THE 1996 WIPO TREATIES

From the outset, WIPO's "digital agenda" placed protection of technological measures and rights management information systems on its high priority list. It favored a policy—hitherto unprecedented in the area of international copyright standard-setting—of adding "collateral" protections to the international obligatory package.[75] The following passages concentrate chiefly on Article 11 WCT and legal protection of TPMs. A concise overview of protection of right management information (RMI) systems stipulated in Article 12 WCT will follow, as well as some issues connected to Article 10 WCT addressing limitations on rights.

A. Drafting History of Article 11 WCT

1. The Emergence of International Anticircumvention Policy

Deliberations within WIPO circles concerning the adjustment of copyright laws to new technological settings had already emerged in the late 1980s.[76] Similar to

70. *Id.* at 16.

71. *Id.*

72. *Id.*

73. *Id.* at 17.

74. *Id.*

75. *See* 1 Sam Ricketson & Jane C. Ginsburg, International Copyright and Neighboring Rights: The Berne Convention and Beyond § 4.27 (2006)

76. Ficsor provides a thorough review of the early phase of discussions, stretching between the late 1980s and the early 1990s (the so-called "guided development"

the debates in the United States and Europe, the advent of machines capable of sampling sounds and converting them from analog to digital signals, storing the information on tapes, and rendering that information computer-processable caused grave apprehensions. The leading technology at the time, the digital audio tape (DAT), distinguished itself by offering a very high quality of digital recording preservable over numerous generations of copying.[77]

WIPO officials were persuaded a "new situation" in copyright had developed in which the harm to rights-holders caused by private copying had become more serious than ever before.[78] The SCMS was deemed a possible solution, provided all DAT machines available on the market were equipped with the SCMS component. This required cross-border, cross-industry cooperation between major players in the phonogram and technology industries—and consensus on the main issues in fact was substantially achieved in the late 1980s.[79] Particularly in this context, international cooperation and a uniform regulative framework to restrict the manufacturing, importation, and sale of DAT machines was vital for the success of the project, and WIPO generally considered legal restrictions on DAT machines coupled with SCMS circumvention prohibitions plausible. However, from an early stage it was clear the scheme must go beyond imposing mandatory SCMS (and similar) specifications on DAT (and similar) digital copying machines. Learnig from the U.S. AHRA experience, the weakness of technology-specific regulation was already well-acknowledged, and the time seemed ripe for a universal, technology-neutral anticircumvention framework to capture various TPMs-supported control systems as such.

2. Draft Article 13 WCT

The idea of TPMs regulation kept being circulated in various WIPO fora prior to the Diplomatic Conference.[80] Those deliberations have set the stage for the initial proposal expressed in Draft Article 13 of the WCT Basic Proposal:

---

period.) *See* Mihály Ficsor, The Law of Copyright and the Internet §§ 6.01–6.22 (2002).

77. *Id.* § 6.08.

78. Rights-holders feared the impact of private copying could no longer be adequately offset by traditional methods of levies on black tapes and copying equipment. *See* addendum to the draft WIPO model provisions for legislation in the field of copyright, document CE/MPC/II/2 (1989), quoted in Ficsor, *supra* note 76. The loss in quality over generations of copies was described as a key assumption rendering levy systems an acceptable compromise. That assumption would have collapsed if DAT recorders were widely used.

79. Ficsor, *supra* note 76, § 6.13.

80. *Id.* §§ 6.40–6.59 (describing the work of the Berne Protocol and the New Instrument Committees); *see also* Jorg Reinbothe & Silke von Lewinski, The Wipo Treaties 1996 135–35 (2002) (describing the work of the WIPO Committee of Experts on proposals to obligate contracting parties to target activities such as circumventions of copy-protection and decrypted broadcast communications).

Obligations concerning Technological Measures

(1) Contracting Parties shall make unlawful the importation, manufacture or distribution of protection-defeating devices, or the offer or performance of any service having the same effect, by any person knowing or having reasonable grounds to know that the device or service will be used for, or in the course of, the exercise of rights provided under this Treaty that is not authorized by the rightholder or the law.
(2) Contracting Parties shall provide for appropriate and effective remedies against the unlawful acts referred to in paragraph (1).
(3) As used in this Article, "protection-defeating device" means any device, product or component incorporated into a device or product, the primary purpose or primary effect of which is to circumvent any process, treatment, mechanism or system that prevents or inhibits any of the acts covered by the rights under this Treaty.[81]

The Notes accompanying Draft Article 13 WCT did not explain why such new obligations were necessary;[82] instead, they focused on the necessity of the knowledge requirement by persons providing circumvention tools or services.[83] Further, the freedom of contracting parties to fashion prohibitions and appropriate remedies according to their respective legal traditions was underscored.[84] It has been clarified "[t]he obligations established in the proposed Article 13 are more akin to public law obligations directed at Contracting Parties than to provisions granting 'intellectual property rights.'"[85] The Basic Proposal explicitly preferred (in subsection (3)) the phrasing "primary purpose or primary effect of which is to circumvent" over "specifically designed or adapted to circumvent" with the specific intention being to provide broader coverage.[86]

The important features of Draft Article 13 can be summarized under the following five points; (1) the text reflected a shift from regulation targeting digital recorders directly (e.g., DAT machines) to regulation banning circumvention tools; (2) it would have prohibited trafficking activities in such tools, but not actual circumvention; (3) a considerable degree of flexibility was afforded to domestic legislatures on how to provide protections and remedies; (4) knowledge was a substantive element in the question of liability, and (5) it offered a

81. *See* WCT Basic Proposal (1996), Draft Art. 13. The Basic Proposal for the WPPT introduced an identical provision. *See* WPPT Basic Proposal (1996), Draft Art. 22.

82. The Notes merely refer to proposals submitted by various countries introduced previously to the WIPO Committee of Experts. *See* Note 13.07 to the WCT Basic Proposal. *See also* Reinbothe & von Lewinski, *supra* note 80, at 137 (the text of Draft Art. 13 was significantly inspired by the proposal made by the European Community).

83. *See* WCT Basic Proposal (1996), Note 13.02.

84. *Id.* Notes 13.04–13.05.

85. *Id.* Note 13.03.

86. *Id.* Note 13.06 (the preferred language was intended to be more comprehensive).

novel legal definition of TPMs, namely as a "protection-defeating device." But a number of delegations (especially the African Group) expressed concerns the text of Draft Article 13 was too vague and overbroad.[87] Their reservations emphasized three edges that needed further sharpening: (1) protected technological measures must be *effective*, (2) they should be used by rights-holders *in connection with the exercise of their rights* under the treaties, and (3) they should restrict acts not authorized by rightholders or *not permitted by law*. The text of Article 11 WCT substantially incorporated all three.

B. The Scope of Article 11 WCT

Article 11 WCT contains several key terms that had never been mentioned in any previous international copyright instrument and rang completely new to the ears of copyright lawyers.[88] The impetus for this provision was to assist rights-holders using TPMs to protect works in digital form against interferences with the function of protection technologies. It sought thereby to encourage rights-holders to use digital formats in disseminating works via computer networks by legally securing their technological "self-help" measures against circumvention.[89] The final text of Article 11 WCT reads:

> Obligations concerning Technological Measures
>
> Contracting Parties shall provide adequate legal protection and effective legal remedies against the circumvention of effective technological measures that are used by authors in connection with the exercise of their rights under this Treaty or the Berne Convention and that restrict acts, in respect of their works, which are not authorized by the authors concerned or permitted by law.[90]

This formulation is concise, leaving considerable margins for interpretation. Understanding the terminology of Article 11 is essential for evaluating its

---

87. *See* Reinbothe & von Lewinski, *supra* note 80, at 137–38; Ficsor, *supra* note 76, § 6.73.

88. One notable precedent of an *external* anticircumvention provision (concerning anti-trafficking bans) is Art. 1707 of NAFTA (entered into force Jan. 1, 1994), which makes it a criminal and civil offense to traffic in satellite decoding devices. NAFTA is an important regional agreement containing provisions that address, inter alia, copyright and neighboring rights protection directly. *See* von Lewinski, *supra* note 2, § 11.11 ff (providing an overview on NAFTA's protections in this area). Art. 1707 falls under Part Six to the NAFTA, captioned "Intellectual Property," though it is structurally separated from other articles in Part Six dealing specifically with copyright, sound recordings, and other intellectual property subjects. This supports the classification of Art. 1707 as an external provision.

89. *See* 2 Ricketson & Ginsburg, *supra* note 75, §§ 15.02–15.03 (describing the policy objectives promoted by Art. 11 WCT).

90. *See* WCT (1996), Art. 11. The final text of the WPPT contains a similar provision. *See* WPPT (1996), Art. 18.

meaning, scope, and implications vis-à-vis domestic laws. As a preliminary matter, the replacement of "rightholder[s]" in Draft Article 13 with "authors" in Article 11 WCT was not intended to limit the category of beneficiaries or the scope of the rule in any way.[91] The term *rightholders* includes authors, as well as successors in title, licensees, agents, and other authorized parties, and therefore can be seen as denoting a broad category of beneficiaries.[92]

1. "effective technological measures"

The meaning of "effective technological measures" is critical for ascertaining *what* must be used by rights-holders to trigger the provision. Unlike the definition in Draft Article 13 of "protection-defeating device" (from which the meaning of technological measures could be derived), Article 11 WCT offers no definitions whatsoever.

Draft Article 13 indicated technological measures were "*any process, treatment, mechanism or system* that prevents or inhibits any of the acts covered by the rights under this Treaty."[93] A more comprehensive and unspecific phrasing than "any process, treatment, mechanism or system" is hardly conceivable, and in this respect, its omission from the final text is not necessarily unfortunate: facing the dilemma of choosing between too-specific a definition of TPMs (as in the case of the SCMS) and a catch-all phrase (as in the case of Draft Article 13), the WCT drafters resolved to provide no definition at all. There is an important insight implicit in this choice suggesting it is quite immaterial *what* rights-holders use. Instead, the crucial questions are for what purpose TPMs are put to use, and to what extent they achieve their intended purpose.[94] The epithet "effective," having no trace in Draft Article 13, nicely squares with this logic. It creates a relationship between the purpose of using the measure and its performance.

Effectiveness first requires ascertaining the intention of rights-holders by asking what exactly they wish to achieve (i.e., to restrict what act, what operations, or what results).[95] The general intention to impose restrictions on free access and use is already manifested in the fact rights-holders invested in and attached TPMs in the first place. The specific acts or results over which rights-holders wish to exercise control are inferable from the features with which the technological protection system is equipped.

---

91. *Cf.* Reinbothe & von Lewinski, *supra* note 80, at 145.

92. *Cf.* Ricketson & Ginsburg, *supra* note 75, §15.12 (the term *authors* includes not only successors in title but the holders of a nonexclusive license to exploit works).

93. *See* WCT Basic Proposal (1996), Draft Art. 13(3) (emphasis added).

94. *Cf.* Reinbothe & von Lewinski, *supra* note 80, at 145 (noting the only indication in Art. 11 of what "effective technological measures" are resides in the reference to their purpose—namely, in connection with the exercise of copyrights).

95. As a matter of simple logic, effectiveness can be neither affirmed nor denied without determining *what is the result sought to be achieved.*

Clearly, mandating effectiveness cannot mean TPMs must be undefeatable.[96] Factoring in several parameters yields the degree of "effectiveness" in a given case. One parameter is the ability of unauthorized parties to perform acts or achieve results rights-holders wish to control (*technical vulnerability*). The system is highly vulnerable when it is easy, cheap, and/or readily feasible for ordinary users to defeat its protections.[97] Other parameters investigate the intensiveness of the nexus between subjective *intent* (to restrict), the *means* deployed (TPMs), the *ends* (curtail infringement) and *effect* (actual prevention of infringements). The ability of the average user having average skills to defeat the *means* without special assistance (and thereby frustrate rights-holders' *intent*) should serve as a yardstick when measuring the *effect*. In the end, the degree of effectiveness of a given TPM is a function of its capacity to make the system less vulnerable to hostile acts seeking to impinge on its intended effect, with the measure being more effective the more difficult it is for the average user to perform an unauthorized act. Passing a threshold of effectiveness on the vulnerability scale (i.e., reaching a sufficient degree of technical robustness) would render the TPM "effective" for the purpose of anticircumvention protections.

But some commentators voiced discomfort concerning the inclusion of the qualifier *effective*.[98] Others offered a narrow reading, according to which a TPM is not effective when it does not "function properly" (in the sense of *broken*), or when it interferes with the "normal functioning" of equipment or services to which it is attached.[99] Hence, according to the restrictive interpretation, a TPM is not "effective" either when it is defective or when the disruption it generates is unrelated to the protection of copyrights. This variety of interpretations of the effectiveness threshold indicates how puzzling the meaning of this requirement might turn out.[100]

---

96. *See* Ricketson & Ginsburg, *supra* note 75, § 15.11 ("['effective'] cannot mean [] 'impervious'").

97. A Finnish court deciding on a criminal prosecution ruled that helping others to circumvent a TPM (the CSS protection for DVD) did not violate the local anticircumvention law. The CSS was held to be no longer "effective" because tools helping to circumvent it were widely available and easily obtainable. *See* Helsinki District Court, Case No. R 07/1004 (May 25, 2007).

98. *See, e.g.*, Ficsor, *supra* note 76, § C11.06 (questioning whether the term *effectiveness* really adds any meaning to Art. 11 WCT).

99. *Cf.* Reinbothe & von Lewinski, *supra* note 80, at 145 (offering the example of a copy-control mechanism that interferes with the playability of programs on a TV set or VCR).

100. *See, e.g.*, Jacques de Werra, *Access Control or Freedom of Access?*, Comment in Christoph Beat Graber, Digital Rights Management: The End of Collecting Societies? 207 (2005). Kamiel J. Koelman & Natali Helberger, *Protection of Technological Protection Measures*, *in* Copyright and Electronic Commerce 172–75, (P. Bernt

Much confusion could be spared should *effective* be perceived as a policy tool. Effectiveness may surely call for a technical inquiry testing technical vulnerability to attacks, but it may also call for a normative evaluation. Effectiveness, as shown, is a threshold condition, and holding a TPM ineffective would deny its eligibility for anticircumvention protections. As such, legislatures (and particularly judges) may use it as an instrument to monitor the breadth of anticircumvention laws. This includes disqualifying TPMs when litigators misuse anticircumvention provisions for purposes inimical to copyright policy.[101]

This interpretative approach considers effectiveness both as a factual inquiry and a normative standard in which the requirement functions as a valve concept for adjusting the scope of protection. For example, because determining the degree of effectiveness requires information about rights-holders' intent, a normative effectiveness test would evaluate that intent and inquire whether it is *legitimate*. For instance, if TPMs are used as a back door for achieving quasi-sui generis protection to non-original databases in jurisdictions where such protection is not granted,[102] the court may refuse to apply anticircumvention law, despite the TPM being rather nonvulnerable as a technical matter. Rights-holders obviously remain free to have all sorts of *intentions* and attempt to restrict any kind of activity with TPMs, yet anticircumvention protection of all such attempts is not guaranteed. Further, it is not inconceivable to hold a measure blocking access to material mostly in the public domain or to generic online services to be ineffective for the purpose of copyright anticircumvention protections as one of several interpretative tools designed to bring anticircumvention protection in line with reasonable copyright policy. The second phrase analyzed below guides normative aspects of Article 11 WCT more explicitly.

2. "in connection with the exercise of their rights under this Treaty or the Berne Convention"

This phrase is of central importance as it explicates the requisite linkage between anticircumvention protection and copyright protection. The technological measure must be deployed by a copyright holder (an "author"), and its use should show a connection to a rightholder's attempts to benefit from rights secured

---

Hugenholtz ed., 2002) (discussing the meaning of "effective" in Art. 11 WCT, as well as in domestic laws implementing that provision).

101. *Cf.* Lexmark Int'l, Inc. v. Static Control Components, Inc., 387 F.3d 522, 547 (6th Cir. 2004); Zohar Efroni, *A Momentary Lapse of Reason: Digital Copyright, the DMCA and A Dose of Common Sense,* 28 COLUM. J.L. & ARTS 249 (2005) (analyzing the *Lexmark* decision and the court's interpretation of the effectiveness requirement in U.S. law).

102. *Cf.* Jane C. Ginsburg, *A Marriage of Convenience? A Comment on the Protection of Databases* 82 CHI.-KENT. L. REV. 1171, 1175–77 (2007) (suggesting that with a copyright "fig leaf" work encrypted together with non-original materials, de facto database protection could be achieved in the United States via anticircumvention laws).

under the Berne Convention and the WCT. For instance, if a rights-holder uses a measure in connection with efforts to prevent unauthorized reproduction of a copyrighted work secured under Article 9(1) Berne Convention, the measure likely meets the in-connection requirement.[103] By contrast, if a rights-holder uses the measure in connection with efforts to prevent the unauthorized reproduction of public domain materials, the measure does not qualify, as neither Berne nor WCT grant exclusive rights in such case.

To benefit from anticircumvention protections, rights-holders hence must fulfill two conditions cumulatively: (1) they must hold the copyrights in the works technologically restricted by the TPM, and (2) they must use TPMs as a means to "exercise"[104] those copyrights. Matters become murkier when access-control TPMs blocking access-conducts are considered.[105] In this context, *infringing* access-conducts must be distinguished from *noninfringing* access-conducts. As to the latter, the preliminary question is whether Berne/WCT cover access-conducts as such.

The answer to this question must be in the negative[106]—unless one views Article 11 WCT *itself* as an implicit grant of exclusivity in access-conducts per se.[107] Such argument, if raised, would be clearly erroneous. First, it would contradict both the clear intention (expressed in Note 13.03 to the Basic Proposal) *not* to create new intellectual property rights. Second, it would ignore the language and structure of the WCT. Article 11 is phrased as *relating* to WCT exclusive rights, which are set forth in *other* provisions and not as an independent source of a new exclusivity norm. Neither Berne nor the WCT provide rights-holders with an exclusive right to prevent access-conducts per se, and therefore, Article 11 cannot relate to such right.

With respect to *infringing* access-conducts, the short answer is that circumvention of TPMs is unlawful under Article 11 WCT because the in-connection requisite is satisfied.[108] In fact, the breadth of this provision correlates with the

---

103. Ficsor opined that use of the term "this Treaty and the Berne Convention" is unfortunate because contracting parties do not have to be members of the Berne Union, but only have to "comply with" Arts. 1 to 21 of Berne according to Art. 1(4) WCT. *See* Ficsor, *supra* note 76, § C.11.08.

104. The term *exercise* is reminiscent of the language proposed in the 1994 U.S. Green Paper. This term arguably implies a broader protection than a provision applicable only when the measure prevents *violation* of copyrights. *See* Section III.A.3 *supra*.

105. Note the distinction between access-conducts and communication-conducts clarified in Chapter 3. *See* Chapter 3, Section II.C *supra*.

106. *Cf.* Ricketson & Ginsburg, *supra* note 75, §§ 15.14–15.15.

107. *Cf.* Reinbothe & Von Lewinski, *supra* note 80, at 142 ("Article 11 WCT does not provide authors with new substantive rights, nor is it, strictly speaking, dealing with the enforcement of rights.").

108. *Cf. id.* at 143 (arguing access-control measures based on encryption, of which circumvention requires decryption, must be granted legal protection under Art. 11 WCT).

breadth of the exclusive rights. For instance, if the exclusive right of reproduction is carefully formulated in a manner designed to exclude the bulk of digital reproductions that are *purely instrumental in facilitating human-access*,[109] the breadth of the anticircumvention ban may shrink correspondingly. Admittedly the option delineated in Chapter 4 to exclude temporary access-facilitating digital reproductions from the scope of the reproduction right could have only a limited impact in this context. First, the convergence problem predicts that technically, only very few (if any) avenues of access to digital works may not involve any type of signals reproduction.[110] Even a narrow legal concept of reproduction that perhaps excludes some of them might not be capable of excluding many other access-facilitating reproductions, particularly those having clear economic significance. Second, the application of important exceptions to the reproduction rights (which may also legitimize access-facilitating reproductions) often cannot be determined ex ante (namely, at the time access-conducts must take place). At that stage, assessing whether a given contemplated access-conduct prima facie implicated the reproduction right may be possible, but it would be more difficult to predict whether anticircumvention laws shall *not* apply because an exception would have excused the prima facie infringing act.[111] Facing this assessment difficulty, it is tempting to simplify matters and assume anticircumvention laws cover a priori both infringing and noninfringing access-conducts; thus, access-control TPMs would generally be covered based on the theory such TPMs still prevent *a lot* of infringement that inevitably depends on initial (noninfringing) access.[112] According to this line, curtailing some noninfringing access opportunities is a necessary evil, and therefore, Article 11 should generally cover access-control TPMs across-the-board. Note, however, that there is an obvious tension between such maximalist interpretation and the in-connection clause.

Both analytically and practically, it appears extremely difficult to articulate a legal norm that would achieve a neat separation between the protection function of access controls and the prevention of copyright-implicating acts. Hence, the dilemma seems to boil down to an all-or-nothing resolution: whether or not access-control TPMs shall principally be covered by anticircumvention law.

---

109. For a proposal going in this direction, see Chapter 4, Section VI.B *supra*.

110. *See* National Research Council (U.S.). Committee on Intellectual Property Rights and the Emerging Information Infrastructure, The Digital Dilemma: Intellectual Property in the Information Age 28 (2000) (hereinafter The Digital Dilemma) ("Access is by Copying").

111. The problem is particularly acute in the case of the fair use defense, but also relevant for other exceptions that call for contextual and circumstantial examination.

112. *Cf.* Ricketson & Ginsburg, *supra* note 75, at § 15.16 ("access controls underpin the reproduction, communication, and distribution rights"). Apparently holding the opposite view, see Strowel & Dusollier, *supra* note 12, at 27 (opining "protection of systems monitoring access seems, in fact, to go beyond the scope of the measures in the WIPO Treaties").

To inject some flexibility into the in-connection clause, it is impotent to view it as a policy instrument. The pragmatic approach to Article 11 interpretation does not try to draw a bright-line rule determining a priori whether access-control TPMs are covered. Instead, it shall be a matter of national laws to determine the meaning of the phrase "in connection with the exercise of [] rights." Domestic laws should be at liberty to articulate the requisite nexus between TPMs circumvention and copyright infringement while bringing general copyright policy into account. Accordingly, to such policy considerations, access-control TPMs that show clear, direct, and unequivocal connection to the prevention of infringement will likely be covered by the domestic norm. Either way, Article 11 cannot be said to *demand* more that this, as far as technological *access control* is concerned. But the pragmatic-policy approach to the interpretation of Article 11's "in connection" clause to access-control TPMs unfortunately does not resolve the problem—it merely postpones it to the later stage of national implementation and application, as shown in the analysis of domestic anticircumvention schemes below.

3. "and that restricts acts, in respect of their works, which are not authorized by the authors concerned"

(a) What "acts"?

There is an interpretation challenge concerning the meaning of the clause "act, in respect of their works." Standing alone, the phrase is broad enough to capture *any* act directed at a TPM-restricted work, including access-conducts performed to render the work perceptible. Yet this clause must be read together with the in-connection clause, a conclusion that derived from the connector "and" placed between both clauses. Thus, the "acts" restricted by the TPM must be connected to the exercise of copyrights secured under Berne/WCT. In other words, the act restricted by technological protections must be part of rights-holders' efforts to prevent copyright infringement.

There are at least two alternative interpretations to this requirement. Narrowly read, Article 11 requires the TPM to restrict acts that *directly* implicate exclusive rights, for instance, copy control measures. Broadly conceived, TPMs that restrict acts that *somehow enable or facilitate* potentially infringing acts are also covered. The same basic dilemma alluded to in the context of the in-connection clause reemerges here and calls for a similar interpretative approach. In this respect, a small wrinkle still needs to be addressed for the sake of consistancey. The meaning given to the in-connection phrase essentially tests the behaviour of the *rights-holder*, whereas "acts" focus on the behavior of an *unauthorized party*. Obviously, the phrase "used by authors in connection with the exercise of their rights . . . and that restrict acts" must receive a harmonious construction, namely, that using TPMs in connection with the protection of copyrights restricts only those acts that jeopardize the enforcement of those rights. A consistent interpretation must therefore consolidate the answers to both questions, which should emanate from the same normative foundation, namely, the need to articulate a requisite nexus between technologically restricted acts and copyright infringement.

(b) The "not authorized" Clause

Two points should be noted in the context of this clause. First, the authorization clause ("which are not authorized by the authors concerned") semantically encompasses *all acts* not authorized by the rights-holder. Alternatively, the authorization clause covers only acts the rights-holders *in fact* prohibit *and can prohibit* considering the scope of their copyright exclusivity mandate. The difference is significant, and the correct alternative must be the one that better conforms to the construction already given to the two previous clauses and to the Article 11 WCT project in general. At first glance, the second alternative seems more attractive, yet it hides the same recurring pitfall: it needs to be decided what acts the rights-holder can prohibit as part of the copyright exclusivity mandate and whether this mandate goes beyond acts that, in themselves, directly and immediately violate exclusive rights.

The second point is whether authorization related directly to the *restricted act* (e.g., "you may reproduce my work") or authorization of the *act of circumvention* (e.g., "you may circumvent my TPM") should satisfy the need to obtain authorization. The syntax of Article 11 seems to tolerate both interpretations, but commentators tend to adopt the first alternative.[113] This raises questions concerning the situation when: (1) the use is authorized, (2) the work is nonetheless technologically protected in a manner that prevents that use, and (3) circumvention is not authorized by the rights-holder. According to the first alternative, authorization of only the copyright-implicating use (say, reproduction) does not automatically legitimize circumvention without permission. A possible solution is to consider the authorization to copy as an implied license to circumvent (to the extent circumvention is necessary) where TPMs prevent the realization of the use permission.[114] Adoption of the second alternative apparently cannot lead to a similar result because it does not follow the same logic. It is perhaps more difficult (yet not inconceivable) to consider an explicit permission to circumvent as indirectly granting a license to perform a copyright-implicating use that thereby turns technically possible.[115]

---

113. *See* Ficsor, *supra* note 76, § C11.10; Reinbothe & Von Lewinski (2002), *supra* note 80, at 146.

114. Evident contradiction between an explicit permission to perform an act and the deployment of TPMs preventing the same act could be attacked on various equitable and contract law doctrines such as lack of good faith.

115. This option is murkier as it is unclear as to how far copyright-implicating acts are authorized merely by virtue of a permission to circumvent a TPM. The scope of permitted acts will likely hinge on the specific terms of the permission to circumvent and the surrounding factual circumstances.

4. "or permitted by law"

The plain meaning of this clause is that performance of generally lawful acts shall not be adversely affected by anticircumvention rules. The ban on circumvention does not extend to TPMs that restrict acts that are not reserved to copyright holders. Accordingly, nonowners who circumvent such measures are unaffected by the norm Article 11 warrants. The term *law* denotes domestic copyright regimes in WCT signatories, under the presumption that their laws, in stipulating permissible acts, conform to international obligations concerning copyright protection and limitations thereto in line with Article 10 WCT.[116]

Under these assumptions, if the act does not violate domestic copyright law (for example, by virtue of an applicable exception), the circumvention of a TPM preventing such act is not unlawful. Assuming compliance with the Berne/WCT minimum protection, contracting parties are free to exempt circumventions that are a necessary step toward exercising copyright exceptions.[117] Indeed, the phrase "or permitted by law" implies that some acts with respect to copyrighted works are not subject to exclusive rights, and that the opportunity to perform them shall not be frustrated by anticircumvention laws. In applying this line of thought, the distinction between acts that are explicitly authorized (*statutory privileges*) and acts that are only implicitly allowed (*non-statutory privileges*) is significant. Assuming copyright laws do not explicitly proclaim the privilege of the public to perform noninfringing access-conducts,[118] are these acts "permitted by law" within the meaning of Article 11 WCT? If so, access-control TPMs that block mere noninfringing access to works are not covered even if they serve to reduce the potential risk of actual infringement. It seems pointless to wrestle with the "permitted by law" riddle in isolation (i.e., separate from the question of copyright coverage in general). Determining what "permitted by law" means intrinsically relates to interpretation questions other clauses of Article 11 invoke. The broader the copyright exclusivity mandate is conceived, the narrower the spectrum of activities "permitted by law" becomes.

5. "circumvention"

The term *circumvention* is yet another novelty not defined in the Treaties. The term entered the WIPO parlance several years prior to the Diplomatic Conference[119] and acquired a generic meaning of removing, breaking, bypassing

---

116. *See* Ficsor, *supra* note 76, § C11.10.

117. *Cf.* Reinbothe & Von Lewinski, *supra* note 80, at 146 (identifying a "rather strong" link between anticircumvention protection and copyright limitations/exceptions, and opining that such domestic limitations/exceptions define acts "permitted by law" in the meaning of Art. 11 WCT).

118. The relationship and distinctions between access-conducts and copyright infringement have been covered in Chapter 3. *See* Chapter 3, Section III.A.3(a) *supra*.

119. Ficsor cited a paper by Charles Clark titled "The Publisher in the Electronic Age" presented during the WIPO Harvard Symposium held in Spring 1993, where Clark

or otherwise interfering with the function of a technological protection measure. Absent explicit definition in the WCT, should they find a definition necessary, contracting parties may define the act of circumvention in national laws as they see fit, where the purpose and logic of anticircumvention laws should provide guidance. The unlawful act of circumvention must have a certain effect on the intended operation of a technological protection system (for instance, an interruption of technological constraints enforcing rights-holders' intention to restrict acts, operations, or results with respect to works).

6. *"adequate legal protection and effective legal remedies"*

This clause articulates the *affirmative obligations* of contracting parties under Article 11. The terms *adequate* and *effective* are relative qualifiers, affording significant maneuvering margins for domestic implementation.[120] A preliminary question is whether contracting parties must introduce anticircumvention schemes within their *copyright* statutes, to which the answer is negative:[121] there is no explicit requirement to fulfill the obligation necessarily by amending the copyright laws. Although the text of Article 11 vastly differs from Draft Article 13, the rationale of formal laxity has nonetheless survived. In light of the intention to afford a high degree of flexibility in applying international obligations (as well as the complexity of the issue), an unequivocal commitment to amend the texts of domestic copyright laws cannot be inferred.[122] In reality, many contracting parties resolved to comply by amending their copyright statutes, rendering the issue largely academic. Still, the question about the obligation to amend domesic *copyright* laws will recur in the context of the controversy over anti-trafficking legislation (discussed immediately below).

(a) The Issue of Trafficking

Does Article 11 mandate adopting domestic provisions targeting trafficking in circumvention devices and technologies (so-called "preparatory" activities)? It shall be argued the answer is no. In supporting this position, a comparison between the text of Draft Article 13 and Article 11 WCT is telling. Draft Article 13 addressed *only trafficking*; namely, it prohibited "the importation, manufacture or distribution of protection-defeating devices, or the offer or performance of

---

introduced suggestions to craft legal prohibitions targeting "removing or circumventing" technological devices. *See* Ficsor, *supra* note 76, at § 6.36.

120. *See* WCT Basic Proposal (1996), Note 13.05. *Cf.* Reinbothe & Von Lewinski, *supra* note 80, at 143 (arguing the language "adequate legal protection" reflects the need to strike a balance between the interests of authors and the interests of others. By "others," the authors specifically refer to "other relevant industries" such as hardware manufacturers).

121. *See* Ricketson & Ginsburg, *supra* note 75, § 15.20. *Cf.* Reinbothe & Von Lewinski, *supra* note 80, at 144 (noting that "effective legal remedies" may also reside in civil, criminal, or administrative law).

122. *See* Strowel & Dusollier, *supra* note 12, at 6 (domestic law has "[c]omplete freedom" in determining how to effectuate their protection).

any service."[123] Conversely, Article 11 WCT mentions *only circumvention* as the prohibited act ("adequate legal protection and effective legal remedies *against the circumvention* of TPMs").[124]

The common view in the literature is that Article 11 still imposes an obligation to introduce protections that specifically target trafficking. The main rationale supporting this view posits that actual circumvention is difficult to trace and enforce.[125] If circumvention tools and services were widely available, the prohibition on actual circumvention would largely become ineffective. Circumvention acts are typically performed in private situations, far from the eye of rights-holders and the arm's reach of legal enforcement. Therefore, many believe national schemes must stipulate trafficking violations lest they fail to meet the adequate-effective protection requirement.[126]

First, it should be reemphasized the choice whether to provide copyright external or internal anticircumvention protections was generally left to domestic laws. This applies with equal force to the specific issue of trafficking. In fact, there are three main alternatives for stipulating direct copyright anti-trafficking bans: (1) imposing liability under *external* anticircumvention regulation, (2) imposing *secondary liability* for assisting *copyright infringement*, and (3) imposing *secondary liability* for assisting direct *circumvention*. Each one of these alternatives could in principle satisfy the adequate-effective protection requirement, including a mixed approach combining those strategies. The claim circumvention activities are hard do detect as they are done "by individuals in their homes" and therefore a "circumvention only" approach would be insufficient[127] should not be overstated. Instead, it should be recognized (as in the context of the digital communication right and the eroding the public/private distinction)[128] that most (if not all) online activities are technically traceable, and application of both legal and technological means to track down illicit acts on the Internet is a noticeable and common way to combat infringements. Internet Protocol (IP) addresses can lead rights-holders, investigators, and enforcement agents to the locations of violations and to the persons committing them. Under certain circumstances,

---

123. *See* WCT Basic Proposal (1996), Draft Art. 13(1).

124. *See* WCT (1996), Art. 11 (emphasis added).

125. *See* Ficsor, *supra* note 76, § 11.12; Reinbothe & Von Lewinski, *supra* note 80, at 141; Ricketson & Ginsburg, *supra* note 75, §§ 15.17–15.19; *cf.* Strowel & Dusollier, *supra* note 12, at 7 (recognizing the greater prejudice to the interests of rights-holders if circumvention measures were widely available in the market, though admitting the WIPO text "appear[s] to concern only the act of circumvention of the technological protection measure itself").

126. *See, e.g.*, Reinbothe & Von Lewinski, *supra* note 80, at 145. The authors caution: "It would appear to be particularly inappropriate to outlaw multipurpose devices, such as computers, only because they may also be used in the context of circumvention." *Id.*

127. *Id.* at 145; *see also* Ricketson & Ginsburg, *supra* note 75, § 15.17.

128. Chapter 5, Section III.C. *supra*.

Internet service provides and administrators of online services face a legal duty to provide identification data about infringing users.[129] Users of some copyright-protected works (predominantly operating system software distributed on persistent remote authentication platforms) simply cannot use counterfeit copies properly on their personal equipment at home.[130]

Also commercial traffickers trading in circumvention tools and technologies cannot effectively operate behind a veil of anonymity—to enjoy commercial success they must promote their goods and services, typically through Internet advertising, online sale points, and download centers.[131] A strategy of pursuing (1) actual circumventors, and (2) traffickers as *indirectly* liable for actual circumventions, could (at least in theory) adequately serve the purpose of anticircumvention laws. The problem significantly boils down not to issues of the *actual feasibility* of discovering and pursuing violators, but to *enforcement costs.* Anti-trafficking bans certainly help rights-holders to reduce their enforcements costs, but unfortunately, this is not their only impact on information markets and innovative industries.

(b) An Argument Against a WCT Anti-Trafficking Obligation

The prevalent view is Article 11 imposes an obligation to provide explicit and direct protections against trafficking activities. The enforcement problem underpinning this view can be broken down into smaller components in the following

---

129. *See, e.g.,* 17 U.S.C. § 512(h). In the ongoing litigation between a major search engine (Google) operating a video-sharing Web site (YouTube) and a major copyright holder (Viacom), a district court in New York ordered defendants to transfer all the log-in data of users who had ever watched videos posed on the YouTube site since its establishment in 2005, as a stage in the litigation between the parties concerning alleged copyright violations connected to users' activity on that site. *See* Viacom Int'l Inc. v. YouTube Inc., 2008 WL 2627388 at 4*–5* (S.D.N.Y. 2008).

130. As Microsoft's Web site explains: "Counterfeit software is more likely than genuine software to contain viruses, spyware, and other unwanted software. Whereas activation provides initial protection for your Windows Vista experience, validation confirms the protection as you continue to enjoy Windows Vista. When your copy of Windows Vista passes validation, you can access optional downloads in the Microsoft Download Center and enjoy the full functionality of your version of Windows Vista. *Validation is an ongoing and easy process* that checks to make sure your system is activated and that *your product key has not been compromised.*" (emphasis added) (available at http://www.microsoft.com/windows/products/windowsvista/buyorupgrade/genuine/default.mspx).

131. One prominent example is SlySoft, which offers over the Internet a myriad of software products considered illicit in some jurisdictions as they are designed to remove DVD protections (available at http://www.slysoft.com/en/) (describing the products offered by the company). Indeed, enforcement problems will arise when potential defendants are incorporated under the laws of Antigua (as in the case of SlySoft). Then again, complications involved in extraterritorial enforcement of Internet-related copyright violations are not unique to trafficking in circumvention tools.

manner: First, the assumption is most users cannot circumvent TPMs themselves. As a result, the role traffickers play in the circumvention scenario is crucial. Second, pursuing a small number of traffickers is more efficient and cost-effective than chasing after numerous individual circumventors. It is sometimes argued that from the perspective of rights-holders, outlawing trafficking activities is of primary concern, while banning actual circumvention is only secondary.[132] This notwithstanding, a number of factors warrant special caution before we conclude there is an international obligation to ban trafficking activities.

I. TREATY INTERPRETATION

The plain text of Article 11 mentions circumvention, not trafficking; hence, anti-trafficking proponents shoulder the burden of persuasion to show why a more expansive reading is mandatory. Yet the drafting history of Article 11 points in the opposite direction. As we have seen, a proposal to ban only trafficking activities turned into a prohibition on actual circumvention. The 180-degree turn in the text of Article 11 as compared to that of the Basic Proposal begs for an explanation.

The in-connection prong of Article 11 importantly establishes the nexus between copyright protection and unlawful circumvention. As this provision does not mention illicit trafficking by name, there was no need to explicate the nexus between illegal trafficking and other violations. Precisely this was attempted in the language of Draft Article 13(3), which provided that "'protection-defeating device' means any device, product or component incorporated into a device or product, *the primary purpose or primary effect of which is to circumvent* any process, treatment, mechanism or system that prevents or inhibits any of the acts covered by the rights under this Treaty."[133] This provision articulated the necessary double nexus, first between the illicit devices or activity and circumvention, and then between circumvention and infringement. *The logical chain connecting trafficking, circumvention, and copyright infringement remains unbroken.*

Had the drafters of Article 11 WCT wished to create an anti-trafficking obligation, it seems most plausible they would have needed to provide instructions concerning the nature of the unlawful acts, but the naked anticircumvention provision in Article 11 provides no such instructions whatsoever. The inference from this article is that a clear obligation to enact domestic anti-trafficking provisions is implausible, as such an obligation would have no definable

---

132. *See* Reinbothe & Von Lewinski, *supra* note 80, at 144 ("[T]he manufacturing and distribution of devices which permit or facilitate circumvention may potentially cause more important prejudice to rightholders than acts of circumvention.").

133. *See* WCT Basic Proposal (1996), Draft Art. 13(3).

contours derivable from the instrument arguably creating them (namely the WCT).[134]

Moving beyond the problem of defining violations, anti-trafficking proponents must further speculate as to what extent domestic law may adjust the scope of liability by promulgating *statutory exemptions* to trafficking liability. For instance, are contracting parties allowed to adopt a "no mandate" clause that would exempt device manufacturers from the obligation to conform to TPMs specifications and standards used by rights-holders?[135] What should the relationship be between the "permissible" framework of anti-trafficking exceptions and copyright policy?[136] Instead of delving into such vexing questions in the context of Article 11 interpretation, the better alternative is simply not to derive such an anti-trafficking obligation in the first place, which would shift the entire bulk of questions concerning coverage and exceptions to the territory of domestic laws. Domestic legislatures can closely evaluate the multiplicity of interests and anticipated impacts on industry players as well as other stakeholders (e.g., consumers). These issues can be better studied, assessed, debated, and resolved on the domestic level. State legislatures are also in a superior position to answer the questions of "if" and "how" to create anti-trafficking provisions, which provides another resoning for the demise of Draft Article 13.

In conclusion, there is no WCT obligation to enact anti-trafficking provisions. Therefore, the lack of express anti-trafficking provisions in the national scheme

---

134. Consider contracting party *A* who has formally enacted an anti-trafficking provision, but created such a strong nexus between unlawful trafficking and actual infringement that there is no practical difference between country *A*'s law and the law of country *B*, which would punish circumvention as a primary violation and trafficking "only" as a secondary violation. To illustrate, the law of country *A* may provide making and trafficking in circumvention tools shall be prohibited if, and only if: (1) copyright infringement facilitated by the circumvention tool can be demonstrated, (2) the tool has no significant purpose or use other than unlawful circumvention, as defined by the law, and (3) the alleged trafficker has actual or constructive knowledge regarding the first two prongs. Alternatively, country *A* may reach a similar result by providing generous statutory exceptions to trafficking violations.

135. *Cf.* Reinbothe & Von Lewinski, *supra* note 80, at 143 (concluding contracting parties should be allowed to make clear that manufacturers of electronic equipment are not obligated to adapt their products to conform to all protection standards).

136. *Id.* at 146 (concluding the link between circumvention and copyright exceptions maintained by the "permitted by law" language does not appear to exist in the context of protection against preparatory acts). According to this approach, it follows that contracting parties are *not* as free to accommodate copyright exceptions into their anti-trafficking law as they are with respect to anticircumvention protection. *Id.* This opens the door to quite absurd situations in which actual circumvention is permissible, but providing tools for such lawful activity is prohibited by virtue of anti-trafficking law. Precisely such discrepancies could be avoided if anti-trafficking constituted branches of *indirect liability*, maintaining an umbilical nexus to the occurrence of the principal violations.

does not constitute an independent ground for stating a failure to provide adequate and effective protections against circumventions as mandated by Article 11 WCT. The adequacy and effectiveness of domestic law should be judged by its *overall* terms and impact.

II. POLICY ISSUES

Codifying anti-trafficking rules essentially creates a *direct* liability for acts that *facilitate circumvention*. Such provisions require the articulation of circumstances in which trafficking is illicit because it facilitates unlawful circumvention. We should not forget provisions against *actual* circumventions are themselves a codification of direct liability for actions that *potentially* facilitate copyright infringement. Therefore, direct liability for trafficking already expands the circle of accountability two degrees further away from actual infringement. Hence, direct prohibitions on trafficking in circumvention tools serve the objective of infringement prevention only in a very abstract—and, one may dare say—speculative manner.[137]

The main problem facing legislatures wishing to provide such protections is to articulate a sensible nexus between trafficking activities on the one hand and illicit circumvention or infringement on the other. In practice, the law should first provide a list of suspect activities such as manufacturing, offering, servicing, importing, marketing, publishing, promoting selling, and possibly possessing circumvention means. Second, the law should judiciously articulate the circumstances in which such activities become illegal. Anti-trafficking law that suffocates research, technological development, and production and distribution of devices simultaneously usable for illicit TPMs circumvention would jeopardize the relevant industries by rendering the legitimacy of their core activities questionable.

From a policy viewpoint, the argument against anti-trafficking laws significantly rests on the danger they pose to competition and innovative industries. The only way to maintain such regulation and still reduce this risk is to articulate the scope of liability under anti-trafficking provisions as precisely as possible. Vagueness, ambivalence, and legal uncertainty are likely to increase the danger

137. One commentator while reviewing the U.S. anticircumvention scheme observed: "What is interesting about this [DMCA anticircumvention] approach is that it tries to define a category of bad tools that are associated with allegedly harmful activities . . . and tries to go after the tools that facilitate the activity, rather than just the harmful activity." *See* Orin S. Kerr, *A Lukewarm Defense of the Digital Millennium Copyright Act*, *in* COPY FIGHTS: THE FUTURE OF INTELLECTUAL PROPERTY IN THE INFORMATION AGE 163, 167 (Adam Thierer & Wayne Crews eds., 2002). Kerr continued: "The first set of questions asks whether the DMCA's goals are worth pursuing. The second set asks whether the DMCA pursues those goals in an effective way." *Id.* at 168. Assuming that the main goal of anticircumvention laws is to curtail copyright *infringement*, it is not at all clear that anti-trafficking regulation is the proper means to that end.

of a chilling effect and harm to technological innovation opportunities. In practice, lawmakers in the United States and Europe bitterly failed in their efforts to formulate anti-trafficking laws that are both coherent and sensible.[138] Legal certainty, to the extent it exists in some cases, comes at the price of overbroadness, which in turn aggravates the danger of overprotection resulting from side and cross effects of such regulation.

C. Related WCT Provisions

1. Application of Article 10 WCT

(a) Substantive Provisions

Article 11 WCT provides no specific instructions concerning the content of the anticircumvention protections it warrants. Either way, it is unlikely a domestic anticircumvention regime would *not* stipulate exceptions to such violations, possibly by coupling them with statutory exceptions to copyright infringement. At this junction, some questions concerning the interface with Article 10 WCT come under scrutiny. Article 10 WCT stipulates the Treaty's exposition of the three-step test controlling domestic limitations and exceptions to exclusive rights covered by the WCT:

(1) Contracting Parties may, in their national legislation, provide for limitations of or exceptions to the rights granted to authors of literary and artistic works under this Treaty in certain special cases that do not conflict with a normal exploitation of the work and do not unreasonably prejudice the legitimate interests of the author.
(2) Contracting Parties shall, when applying the Berne Convention, confine any limitations of or exceptions to rights provided for therein to certain special cases that do not conflict with a normal exploitation of the work and do not unreasonably prejudice the legitimate interests of the author.[139]

The agreed statement to Article 10 WCT provides:

> It is understood that the provisions of Article 10 permit Contracting Parties to carry forward and appropriately extend into the digital environment limitations and exceptions in their national laws which have been considered acceptable under the Berne Convention. Similarly, these provisions should be understood to permit Contracting Parties to devise new exceptions and limitations that are appropriate in the digital network environment.
>
> It is also understood that Article 10(2) neither reduces nor extends the scope of applicability of the limitations and exceptions permitted by the Berne Convention.[140]

---

138. Section V. ff *infra*.
139. *See* WCT (1996), Art. 10.
140. *Id.* agreed statement concerning Art. 10.

The first sentence of Article 10(1) targets domestic limitations or exceptions to "rights granted to authors" exclusively under the WCT.[141] The second stipulates that all such limitations or exceptions should comply with the three-step test. Namely, exemptions to WCT rights may apply in certain special cases, but may not conflict with the normal exploitations of works and may not unreasonably prejudice the legitimate interests of rights-holders. Article 10(2) sets forth a similar rule concerning Berne rights.[142]

The contribution of the agreed statement regarding the interpretation of Article 10 is three-fold. The first sentence clarifies that *all* traditional exemptions permissible under Berne—whether explicit or implicit,[143] mandatory or optional,[144] and whether attached to the reproduction right or to any other Berne/WCT right—may apply in the "digital environment." The second sentence clarifies contracting parties may devise "new" exemptions to Berne/WCT rights inasmuch as they find such new exemptions appropriate in the "digital network environment." The third clarifies application of the three-step test to permitted exemptions under Berne shall not influence their scope.[145] Yet the grip of the three-step text cuts across the entire panoply of Berne/WCT rights: *all* exceptions must pass the three-step test one way or the other. To the extent exceptions are now "extended" and "carried forward" to the digital environment, their application needed to be reevaluated, and possibly remodeled.[146]

(b) Interface with Article 11 WCT

The main interface question is whether Article 10 imposes restrictions on permissible domestic exceptions to anticircumvention violations. The matter requires clarification—for example, when domestic legislatures seek to fashion anticircumvention exemptions to preserve the ability to benefit from traditional copyright exemption. Must such anticircumvention exceptions pass the litmus test articulated in Article 10 WCT? It shall be argued the answer is no. A direct friction between the two provisions does not surface, as Article 10 is *inapplicable*

---

141. *See* Reinbothe & Von Lewinski, *supra* note 80, at 128–30.

142. *Id.* 130–32.

143. *Id.* at 128–30 (explaining the distinction between explicitly and implicitly allowed exceptions to Berne rights).

144. Section IV.C.2(b) *infra*. (discussion of the theory of "mandatory" exceptions under Berne).

145. In other words, the three-step test cannot be used to disqualify an exception that has been permissible according to Berne under the presumption that all such exceptions conform to the three-step test anyway. *Cf.* Reinbothe & Von Lewinski, *supra* note 80, at 134.

146. *Id.* at 133 ("The agreed statement only confirms what has to be the obvious interpretation of Article 10 WCT. It gives no blank cheque 'to carry forward' existing exceptions to, nor does it automatically approve of new ones for, [sic] the digital environment.").

directly to anticircumvention exceptions. Article 10(1) addresses specifically "limitations of or exceptions to the *rights* granted to authors of literary and artistic works under this Treaty."[147] Similarly, Article 10(2) addresses "rights" provided for in the Berne Convention. Because Article 11 neither establishes nor restates any right granted to authors under the Berne/WCT framework, it could follow that Article 10 WCT is irrelevant.

Nonetheless, commentators believe the three-step test applies indirectly to anticircumvention laws.[148] Their argument should be evaluated under the following assumptions: (1) the copyright law contains only exemptions to infringement of Berne/WCT rights that pass the three-step test, because Article 10 so commands; (2) to the extent anticircumvention exemptions seek to accommodate infringement exemptions, they also seek to accommodate the exercise of legitimate acts admissible under the three-step test, as these acts are "permitted by law" within the meaning of Article 11 WCT. In such case, we may wonder why anticircumvention exceptions *again* must be scrutinized under the three-step test, provided that (1) anticircumvention protections themselves do not create formal "rights" belonging to the international substantive minimum, and (2) anticircumvention exceptions are designed to enable conducts that are perfectly legitimate under the three-step test.

Provided these framework assumptions are undisputed, the more elegant outcome is that the three-step test in Article 10 WCT is *wholly inapplicable* to anticircumvention exceptions. This is not to say exceptions that would completely eviscerate Article 11 are permissible. Instead, the substantive strictures imposed by the WCT on domestic anticircumvention models are implied *in Article 11 itself.* Beyond declaring anticircumvention protection obligatory, this provision requires the anticircumvention model be "adequate" and its remedies be "effective." By comparison, Article 11 does not speak in terms of "permissible" or "impermissible" domestic exceptions to anticircumvention prohibitions. The adequate-effective standard refers to the scheme as a whole, including possible specific anticircumvention exceptions. As a matter of treaty compliance, the structure of thoese exceptions should not undermine the legitimacy of the entire domestic anticircumvention model nor should they lower the level of anticircumvention protections below the minimum requisite.

To illustrate the difference, Article 11 does not prescribe that anticircumvention exceptions are only permissible in "certain special cases." Additionally, Article 10's

---

147. *See* WCT (1996), Art. 10(1) (emphasis added in text).

148. *Cf.* RICKETSON & GINSBURG, *supra* note 75, § 15.18 (opining permissible legislating acts transposing Article 11 must "remain consonant with" the scope of exemptions allowed under Art. 10 WCT); REINBOTHE & VON LEWINSKI, *supra* note 80, at 147 ("Any exceptions to the protection of technological measures . . . should . . . (2) be restricted to the balanced application of particularly relevant and important limitations and exceptions in conformity with the condition of the three-step test.") (footnote omitted).

emphasis on prejudice to exploitation opportunities is not explicit in the wording of Article 11. The phrasing of Article 11 radiates balance, whereas the tone of Article 10(2) echoes protectionism.[149] The decision whether to extend the latter (arguably stricter) approach calling for a separate three-step-test scrutiny (with its additional restrictions on the structure of national exceptions) remains in the hands of domestic legislatures. It is purely an internal copyright policy issue whether legislatures and courts should apply the three-step test *directly* when evaluating the *legitimacy and application of anticircumvention exceptions,* when choosing to do so would exceed their international obligations under the WCT. This conclusion applies a fortiori to *anti-trafficking* exceptions. As shown above, Article 11 WCT does not mandate anti-trafficking provisions at all, and in case such protections are granted, contracting parties are completely free to model exceptions as they see fit. Article 10 WCT remains inapplicable.

2. Interface with the Berne Convention: Article 1 WCT

(a) The Provisions of Article 1 WCT

An interesting issue arises when considering the scope of international obligations under Article 11 WCT in tandem with the rather esoteric question of "maximum protection" allowed under the Berne Convention.

Article 1 WCT touches upon the relationship among obligations under the Berne Convention and obligations of contracting parties under the WCT. Article 1(1) clarifies the WCT is a "special agreement" in the meaning of Article 20 Berne Convention. Article 1(2) WCT provides that nothing in the Treaty shall derogate existing obligations under Berne, and Article 1(4) WCT states: "Contracting Parties shall comply with Articles 1 to 21 and the Appendix of the Berne Convention."[150] The Berne substantive minimum protection principle—derived from Article 5(1)[151] and Article 19[152] Berne Convention, coupled with the provisions in Article 20 Berne Convention—indicates WCT contracting parties may not provide *lesser* protection than their substantive minimum obligations under

149. Whether Art. 10 WCT is protectionist may be a matter of interpretation. For a study on the topic, see P. Bernt Hugenholtz & Ruth L. Okediji, *Conceiving an International Instrument on Limitations and Exceptions to Copyright, Final Report* (Mar. 6, 2008) (especially at 20 ff).

150. Concerning the fourth paragraph, it appears WCT contracting parties do not have to be members of the Berne Union. Compliance with the mentioned Berne provisions should suffice as a threshold.

151. *See* Berne Convention (1971), Art. 5(1) ("Authors shall enjoy, in respect of works for which they are protected under this Convention, in countries of the Union other than the country of origin, the rights which their respective laws do now or may hereafter grant to their nationals, as well as the rights specially granted by this Convention.").

152. *Id.* Art. 19 ("The provisions of this Convention shall not preclude the making of a claim to the benefit of any greater protection which may be granted by legislation in a country of the Union.").

Articles 1–21 Berne Convention. These obligations set a minimum bar; domestic laws are at liberty to provide greater protection to foreign rights-holders, but not less.

(b) The Notion of "Maximum Protection" under Berne

Can the Berne Convention be said to set a *maximum* protection bar? This question may acquire some practical relevancy in specific situations (for example, on occasions where Berne specifically denies or limits copyright protection). In such cases, the question is whether providing protection despite the provisions arguably establishing a maximum bar could be considered a violation of Berne. Until recently, the question of overprotection and its consequences in the international law context received only limited attention in the academic literature.[153] The passages below describe the historical debate, the reemergence of the issue in recent years, and its specific relevancy to anticircumvention law.

I. THE ACADEMIC DEBATE

The idea of maximum protection under Berne had already received some scholarly attention before and around the Rome and Brussels revisions. Two prominent advocates of the maximum protection approach were the German jurists Alfred Baum and Willie Hoffmann. Baum referred to several early judicial decisions issued by courts in some Berne members in which the courts refused to grant foreign authors protection while interpreting the Convention as setting a *maximum bar* for copyright protection under the circumstances.[154]

Baum's vantage point was that in the case of collision between domestic laws and material-obligatory Berne provisions, the latter (Berne) must have the upper hand.[155] Following the same logic (and notwithstanding Berne's minimum protection principle), he argued that Berne prevails in situations where the Convention explicitly *excludes* certain instances from the scope of copyright protection—in his example, granting retroactive protraction to mechanical reproductions in contradiction to Article 13(3) Berne Convention (Rome text).[156]

Before we take a closer look at this argument, some historical background is necessary. Concerns national courts would stray too far away from the minimum

---

153. *See* RICKETSON & GINSBURG, *supra* note 75, § 6.110.

154. *See* Alfred Baum, *Berner Konvention und Landesgesetze* 1928 GRUR 684, 687–88 (1928) (earlier versions of Berne and the Closing Protocol of the original Berne Act were interpreted by national courts as denying retroactive protection in the case of mechanical reproduction, and as a consequence, national courts refused to vindicate corresponding infringement claims of foreign authors).

155. *Id.* at 689. Baum generally classified Berne provisions as falling under three groups: (1) provisions that secure for authors in general positive-material rights, (2) provisions that subject foreign authors to the law of the adjudicating country, and (3) provisions that deny protection for foreign authors or stipulate certain restrictions on their rights. *Id.*

156. *Id.*

protection principle motivated the introduction of Article 19 during the Berlin conference held in 1908. In its old version, Article 19 stated: "The provisions of the present Convention shall not prevent a claim being made for the application of any wider provisions which may be made by the legislation of a country of the Union *in favour of foreigners in general.*"[157]

Baum considered this provision (which survived unchanged until the 1948 Brussels revision) as an important *limitation* on the power of Berne members to grant Berne-plus rights to the authors of other members *selectively*. Indeed, the main idea was to clarify that Berne does not stand in the way of members wishing to grant more protection than they must to foreignener.[158] At the same time, Baum argued the language of Article 19 (old version) muddied the water by restricting the scope of Article 4 (old version). To him, Article 19 (old version) illustrated a case in which Berne expressly *denied* protection by presenting a *prohibition* on local law to grant protection to foreign authors when Berne imposed substantive restrictions on such protection.[159] Otherwise, the existence of such Berne provisions could not be explained.[160] Alongside Article 19 (old version), Article 13(3) Berne Convention (Rome text) presented a specific example of such restrictions, reinforcing the general theory of maximum protection.

Hoffmann called the problem Baum has been grappling with "one of the most difficult interpretation question in the Berne Convention."[161] He supplemented Baum's legislative history and textual account with theoretical and teleological arguments. Hoffmann rejected the notion the essence of copyright had

---

157. *See* Art. 19 Berne Convention (1908), Berlin Text (emphasis added), *reprinted in* WILHELM NORDEMANN ET AL., INTERNATIONAL COPYRIGHT AND NEIGHBORING RIGHTS LAW (1990). All further translations to English of early Berne provisions cited hereinafter reprint this source.

158. *See* Baum, *supra* note 154, at 690–91.

159. *Id.* at 691. *See also* Alfred Baum, *Die revidierte Berner Übereinkunft und die günstigeren Landesgesetze*, 1930 UFITA 400 (1930). Historically, there was at least one explicit rule in Berne confirming the proposition foreign authors might sometimes receive less protection, namely in the case of duration. Article 7(2) in the Rome text denied foreign authors the entitlement of enjoying a duration lasting longer than life-plus-fifty when such longer protection was provided by the country in which protection was sought if the law in the country of origin secured a shorter term. *See* an unfair advantage to foreign authors as compared to their local counterparts Berne Convention (1928), Rome Text, Art. 7(2). The rationale was a desire to prevent an unfair advantage to foreign authors as compared to their local counterparts, and in that case, the country where protection was sought was not allowed to provide the longer protection; instead, local law had to apply the duration rule as stated in the country of origin.

160. *Id.* at 189 ff.

161. *See* Willy Hoffmann, *Berner Konvention und Landesgesetz*, 1928 GRUR 897, 897] (1928).

merely been to protect the rights of authors[162] and stressed the dualistic nature of copyright law having the mission of simultaneously protecting both the rights of authors and of the public.[163] To Hoffmann, the rights of the public were no less important than those of authors, and the provision in Berne that benefited the public must not be ignored, at least inasmuch as restrictions on the protection of foreign authors were concerned.[164]

Concurring with Baum's reading of Article 19 (old version) and the interpretation as to the limitation clause "in favour of foreigners in general," Hoffmann also rejected the view that would secure Berne-plus rights to foreign authors in all situations.[165] He believed the Berne Convention clearly stipulated the rights of the public in the form of explicit "exceptions" of which the public cannot be deprived. Among these rights, which constituted Berne's Magna Carta of maximum protection rules for the benefit of the public (as stipulated in the 1928 Rome text), he listed Article 7(2) (the shorter duration applies to foreign works in the case of a difference between the rule in the country of origin and the country of adjudication), Article 9(2) (exception to news of the day published by the press), and the above-mentioned Article 13(3) (prohibiting retroactive protections of the rights stipulated in Article 13(1) regarding mechanical reproductions of musical works).[166] In all those instances, the rights of the public should not be encroached upon by national laws, a principle Hoffmann underpinned with reference to copyright theory and the drafting history of the Berne Convention as well as its direct language.

But the maximum protection thesis also had fierce and able objectors. In his work published in 1938, Ladas rejected outright both Baum's reading of Article 19 (Rome text) and the more general idea of maximum protection under Berne. He stated the governing idea of Berne as "constitu[ting] a minimum protection only."[167] This emanated from the rationale of Article 4 (Rome text) and from Article 20 (Rome text) allowing members to enter a bipartite agreement

162. *See* Willy Hoffmann, Die Berner Übereinkunft Zum Schutze Von Werken Der Literatur Und Kunst 3 ff (1935).

163. *Id.* at 21–37; Hoffmann, *supra* note 162, at 899–900.

164. Hoffmann went so far to suggest that exceptions in favor of the public are not to be viewed as exceptions at all, but as a material part of copyright law. Hence, impinging on those provisions is a violation of the rights of the public. Hoffmann, *supra* note 162, at 900.

165. *See* Hoffmann, *supra* note 163, at 248–49.

166. *See* Hoffmann, *supra* note 162, at 900–01. He particularly emphasized the importance of non-voluntary licensing as an essential component of the copyright system. *Id.* at 899–900.]

167. *See* Stephen P. Ladas, 1 International Protection of Literary and Artistic Property 189 (1938).

granting greater protection to each other's authors.[168] Ladas argued that domestic laws' advantages, which went beyond the minimum secured in Berne, should be equally enjoyed by foreign and domestic authors alike.

Ladas returned to Article 19 (Rome version) and identified the problem with the phrase "*en faveur des étrangers en général*" ("in favour of foreigners in general"). He admitted this language was "somewhat restrictive";[169] however, drawing a conclusion allowing a differentiated application of Berne-plus protections would "limit the principle of the national-treatment clause of Article 4, and to that extent the amendment [Article 19 Rome text] does not seem in conformity with the spirit of the Convention."[170] Ladas dismissed the plausibility of differentiation by stating "[t]he foreign author is completely linked to the national." He considered a situation, in which foreign authors could not avail themselves of Berne-plus protections in the adjudicating country—particularly when non-Unionist authors *did* enjoy greater protection by virtue of a bilateral agreement Unionist authors could not enjoy—as "shocking."[171]

To support his view, Ladas returned to a specific example noted earlier by Baum and Hoffmann as setting a maximum protection bar (i.e., the issue of retroactive protection to mechanical reproductions of musical works).[172] The law of Great Britain at the time granted such retroactive protection to mechanical adaptations in some situations, in apparent conflict with the Berne stipulation denying all retroactive protections of musical works that had already been adapted mechanically before the entry of the Berlin Act into force on November 13, 1908.[173] Ladas told the story of French music editors who complained in 1927 about a refusal of Great Britain to apply the same provisions in their favor. The British Administration based its decision on Article 18 (Berlin Text), arguing these Berne-plus benefits were not granted to foreign authors "in general".[174]

Ladas was aware of efforts to strike out this problematic clause from Article 19 and the failure of the Rome conference to pass a corresponding amendment. He nonetheless remained confident a strict reading of the text of Article 19 as it stood was more appropriate. His most powerful argument went back to the basic question of whether Berne secured only a minimum level of protection or whether one should read into its text also dispositive maximum-protection rules. He favored the first alternative while essentially asserting that striking a balance between the interest of authors on the one hand, and the interest of the public on the other, was important—but not the task of the Berne Convention. To him,

168. *Id.*
169. *Id.* at 190.
170. *Id.*
171. *Id.* at 191.
172. *Id.* at 191–92.
173. *See* Berne Convention (1928), Art. 13(3) (Rome text).
174. *See* Ladas, *supra* note 168, at 192.

this striking of a proper balance was purely a matter of domestic legislation, which, in any event, must adhere to the substantive minimum and national treatment principles;[175] the reason he gave is "[t]he factors which enter into the actual compromise arrived at in a certain country are particular to that country."[176] In other words, to the extent Berne Convention provisions reflect a compromise, this compromise did not reflect a balance between the interests of authors and the public, but rather one between different national laws and governments having their own unique perspective on the issue. According to Ladas, such compromise could not furnish a basis for any affirmative entitlements in favor of the public.

Later, the Brussels revision of 1948 amended the text of Article 19, which now plainly states: "The provisions of this Convention shall not preclude the making of a claim to the benefit of any greater protection which may be granted by legislation in a country of the Union."[177]

Baum, who personally attended that Conference, considered this amendment the single most important change in the text of the Berne Convention brought about in the whole of the Brussels Conference.[178] He congratulated the Conference for passing this important clarification and finally bringing Article 19 into agreement with Article 4 (old version).[179] Baum applauded the amending of Article 19 for eliminating the *textual* treaty interpretation problem he had considered most troublesome two decades earlier. As to the principal question of maximum protection under Berne, however, he added an important reservation:

> Although the thought, which formed the basis of the Belgian proposal of 1908 has now been realized in its purest form, the decision on an important question which is connected with the subjective law of the Convention and its influence on national laws has regrettably been omitted . . .
>
> The question is: does the rule, that the rights given by the Berne Convention represent only the minimum protection, apply also in cases where a provision of the Convention expressly restricts or excludes protection? . . . This expression [of maximum protection] is not quite logical. It could possibly be

175. *Id.* ("The copyright law is a compromise between the interests of authors and those of the public. This is indeed true so far as domestic legislation is concerned, but it is hardly possible to introduce the same idea in the construction of an International Convention.").

176. *Id.*

177. *See* Berne Convention (1971), Art. 19.

178. *See* Alfred Baum, The Brussels Conference for the Revision of the Berne Convention 70 (1948). By comparison, Masouyé laconically noted that in Brussels, Art. 19 had been "slightly amended." *See* Claude Masouye, Guide to the Berne Convention for the Protection of Literary and Artistic Works ¶ 19 (1978).

179. *See* Baum, *supra* note 178, at 71.

> supported if the provisions merely limited the protection. But it is certainly impossible to speak of maximum protection if the protection is expressly excluded. The idea, on which the Austrian proposal [asking during the Rome Convention to clarify whether the Convention did not stipulate maximum protection in certain cases] was based, is of course correct . . .
>
> About the problem itself, nothing new can be said . . . A clarification would be desirable. Should it lead to the result that, when protection is limited or excluded by a provision of the convention, more favorable national laws are applicable, then there is no sense in writing restrictive provisions into the Convention, and the present provisions which exclude or limit protection should be annulled. If, however, the opinion represented by Hoffmann and myself since 1928 is to be followed, that in the before mentioned cases the more favorable national laws are not applicable, then that should be expressed in Art. 19.[180]

Baum's general position is nicely reflected in this quote. The fundamental question of maximum protection yes-or-no was not resolved as a result of the 1948 amendment of Article 19 in Brussels. Remaining provisions limiting or altogether excluding protection in the Berne Convention had to be somehow explained, especially after the main doubts concerning minimum protection and national treatment had been removed. Baum's suggestion—to either amend Article 19 to explicitly reflect the maximum protection theory, or alternatively, to remove language that explicitly prohibited or restricted authors' rights from Berne's text—went away in the passage of time.

In his influential Guide to the Berne Convention, Masouyé stated what came to be the standard interpretation of Article 19 (current version): "[T]he minimum rights prescribed by the Convention form the basis of the Union but if, under the national laws of member countries, Convention nationals and their successors in title can claim better copyright treatment, *nothing* stops them doing so."[181]

II. THE RICKETSON/GINSBURG ACCOUNT

Two leading copyright scholars have recently revisited the issue. Sam Ricketson and Jane C. Ginsburg identified in the current text of the Berne Convention two exceptions they described as "clear imperative restrictions of significance."[182] The reference is to the Berne provisions concerning "news of the day" and "mis-

180. *Id.* at 71–72.

181. *See* MASOUYE, *supra* note 178, ¶ 19.2 (emphasis added). *See also* VON LEWINSKI, *supra* note 2, § 5.94.

182. *See* RICKETSON & GINSBURG, *supra* note 75, § 6.111.

cellaneous facts" in Article 2(8),[183] and the quotation exception in Article 10(1).[184] Echoing Hoffmann's approach, Ricketson and Ginsburg explain the broad policy considerations behind these provisions, reflecting "[a] concern to maintain the free international flow of basic elements of information [which] appear to animate and unite these exceptions [and] reveal the Convention's solicitude for the broader public interest, notwithstanding the Convention's overall goal to protect the rights of authors."[185]

Ricketson and Ginsburg purport that the laws of Union members *must* entertain such exceptions, at least as applied to foreign authors. For one, there is no dispute Union members are free to create stringent copyright schemes having no exceptions at all, and this freedom is not affected by Berne so long as only domestic works (i.e., works with respect of which the jurisdiction is the "country of origin")[186] are fully controlled by such regime. For another, Ricketson and Ginsburg argue this is not so vis-à-vis foreign authors (i.e., rights-holders in non-"country of origin" works): "[I]f national legislation purports to grant protection to Union authors in such cases [where Berne explicitly either limits or denies protection] this must be contrary to the Convention."[187]

In assessing this observation, we may assume arguendo the provision in Article 10(1) Berne Convention in fact spells out a maximum protection rule. Accordingly, copyright laws must allow the making of "quotations from a work which has already been lawfully made available to the public, provided that their making is compatible with fair practice, and their extent does not exceed that justified by the purpose, including quotations from newspaper articles and periodicals in the form of press summaries."[188] Before we proceed, outlining a general analytical framework for the maximum protection thesis is necessary, in which four main scenarios of maximum protection rule affecting domestic laws

---

183. *See* Art. 2(8) Berne Convention (1971) ("The protection of this Convention *shall not apply* to news of the day or to miscellaneous facts having the character of mere items of press information.") (emphasis added).

184. *Id.* Art. 10(1) ("*It shall be permissible* to make quotations from a work which has already been lawfully made available to the public, provided that their making is compatible with fair practice, and their extent does not exceed that justified by the purpose, including quotations from newspaper articles and periodicals in the form of press summaries.") (emphasis added).

185. *See* Ricketson & Ginsburg, *supra* note 75, § 6.111. By comparison, Reinbothe and von Lewinski identified only one such "obligatory" exception, namely, the exception provided for in Art. 10(1) Berne Convention. *See* Reinbothe & von Lewinski, *supra* note 80, at 122 & n.23.

186. The term "country of origin" is defined in Art. 5(4) Berne Convention. *See also* Art. 5(3) Berne Convention ("Protection in the country of origin is governed by domestic law.").

187. *See* Ricketson & Ginsburg, *supra* note 75, § 6.111.

188. *See* Art. 10(1) Berne Convention (1971).

are considered. To simplify the analysis, a bilateral relationship between two Union members shall be assumed. Unless specifically stated otherwise, these countries do not have separate bipartite arrangements.

Scenario (1): Union Member *A* (*UMA*) *deprives* nonowners (or generally, "the public") in its jurisdiction of the ability to exercise the mandatory quotation exception with respect to *both domestic and foreign works*. As a result, both domestic and foreign authors enjoy greater protection. As noted, Berne cannot set a maximum protection bar in *UMA* regarding works of which *UMA* is the country of origin. Yet the maximum protection theory advocated by Ricketson and Ginsburg precludes the option of ignoring the mandatory exception as applied to works of which Union Member *B* (*UMB*) is the country of origin. This would namely violate *UMA*'s obligations under the Convention. Note that respecting the maximum protection approach would lead to compromising of the national treatment principle: as the quotation exeception cannot apply to them, domestic works would enjoy in some sense a greater protection. In contrast, according to a "pure" minimum protection approach á la Ladas, providing the same greater level of protection in both cases would not violate *UMA*'s obligations, as Berne cannot compel *UMA* to provide any exceptions for exclusive rights with respect to any works or authors in general.

Scenario (2): The law of *UMA grants* the said exception *uniformly regarding both domestic and foreign work*. This situation does not raise compliance problems so long as the substantive minimum protection to foreign authors is not thereby undermined.

Scenario (3): The law of *UMA discriminates* as between domestic and foreign authors in the following manner: Domestic works, as well as works of authors from Union countries with which *UMA* has special agreements, are *not* subject to a domestic exception mirroring Article 10(1) Berne Convention. However, this exception *applies* to works from *UMB*, which is a Union member without a special agreement with *UMA*. As a result, *UMB*'s authors receive inferior protection, with their situation being comparable to the one described in Scenario (1) if compliance with Article 10(1) were mandatory with respect to all foreign works. As noted, Ladas opined this would be impermissible.[189] In contrast, according to the approach advocated by Ricketson and Ginsburg, such discrimination appears permissible (i.e., discrimination against Union members), else granting Berne-plus protection to *UMB* authors would violate Article 10(1) Berne Convention.[190]

---

189. *See* LADAS, *supra* note 167, at 189–194.

190. *See* RICKETSON & GINSBURG, *supra* note 75, § 6.111 ("The Convention cannot prevent a member state from locally privatizing information its own authors generated—that is the consequence of article 5(3)—but it can require that member state preserve the freedom of these excluded elements when the works that contain them traverse borders.

Scenario (4): The law of *UMA discriminates* as between domestic and foreign authors in the following manner: domestic works are subject to the imperative exception of citation, whereas *UMB*'s works enjoy full exclusivity in this respect. This scenario would violate the Convention according to the maximum protection theory, but is unlikely to occur in reality. As Baum already noted in 1928, it would be naïve to expect domestic law would grant foreign authors better protection than it grants its own.[191] Either way, to the extent domestic rules can be interpreted as leading to such a result, according to the maximum protection thesis it would violate Berne obligations, which in turn leads to the following result: if the law of *UMA* initially treated foreign works/authors from all countries uniformly, application of the maximum protection rule would mean protection to *foreign Union* works must be "downgraded", whereas protection to non-Union works would remain unaffected. This is a scenario Ladas considered "shocking."

III. INTERMEDIARY COMMENTS

In Scenario (1), the law of *UMA* follows a protectionist copyright policy, which simply ignores Article 10(1) Berne Convention across-the-board. Under a working assumption the provision is imperative, it is important to assess in which way the rule might be violated by domestic law, which calls for a brief scrutiny of the scope and meaning of Article 10(1).

As Ricketson and Ginsburg explain, application of the Berne quotation exception in domestic law requires three main conditions to be fulfilled cumulatively: (1) The work in question must have been "lawfully made available to the public", (2) quoting it must be "compatible with fair practice", and (3) the quotation must "not exceed that justified by the purpose."[192] Their analysis shows each one of these requisites may receive either a broad or narrow interpretation. If the law of *UMA* followed a protectionist policy that read these requisites restrictively, the number of instances actually covered by the exception would become insignificant.[193] Put another way, restrictive domestic interpretation (which the language

---

Thus, if national legislation purports to grant protection to Union authors in such cases this must be contrary to the Convention.").

191. *See* Baum, *supra* note 154, at 691.

192. *See* Art. 10(1) Berne Convention (1971); Ricketson & Ginsburg, *supra* note 75, § 13.41.

193. For example, if the requisite of "fair practice" were said to conflate with the three-step test, as Ricketson and Ginsburg seem to suggest, the position of beneficiaries who seek quotation privileges would be limited to cases where the economic interests of rights-holders remain largely unaffected. Further, the ability to make quotations for the purpose of teaching is excluded from the scope of this provision as Art. 10(2), which specifically addresses this situation, grants Member States *full discretion* whether to provide such an exception or not. *See* Art 10(2) Berne Convention (1971) ("It shall be a matter for legislation in the countries of the Union, and for special agreements existing or to be concluded

of Article 10(1) perfectly permits) might seriously wither this provision. Consequently, the difference between having and not having this exception in domestic law (according to Berne's prescriptions) might have little impact on the actual freedom to quote. By extension, the choice between a maximum protection interpretation and pure minimum protection approach would seem in this case rather academic.

Moving to discuss Article 2(8) as yet another potential source of mandatory maximum norm,[194] Ricketson and Ginsburg explain the purpose of this exception is uncertain and that its scope is difficult to outline.[195] They allude to an intricate matter, namely, the question whether Article 2(8) stipulated an exception for works that are principally eligible for copyright protection (a so-called "public policy" exception), or alternatively, whether it is merely an expression of the idea/expression distinction that traditionally draws the line between protectable and nonprotectable elements of the work.[196]

Based on historical evidence and records related to the 1967 Stockholm Conference, in possibly throwing more light on the intention behind Article 2(8), Ricketson and Ginsburg seem to believe this provision still reflects the latter interpretation. Accordingly, it is a statement denying protection for news items that are *not eligible for copyright protection under Berne in the first place.*[197] It follows Article 2(8) should be read together with Berne's subject matter stipulations, namely, with Article 1 (providing the convention covers "the rights of *authors* in their *literary and artistic works*"), and with Article 2 (stating "[t]he expression 'literary and artistic works' shall include every production in the literary, scientific and artistic domain, whatever may be the mode or form of its expression, such as . . ."). According to this view, Article 2(8) merely stipulates a class of *negative categories* subject matter that is excluded from the copyright exclusivity regime.[198] The upshot is that though Berne cannot prevent *UMA* from granting exclusive

---

between them, to permit the utilization, to the extent justified by the purpose, of literary or artistic works by way of illustration in publications, broadcasts or sound or visual recordings for teaching, provided such utilization is compatible with fair practice.").

194. The "mandatory" language in Art. 2(8) Berne Convention is comparatively weaker, as it provides "protection of this Convention *shall not apply* to . . . ."

195. *See* RICKETSON & GINSBURG, *supra* note 75, § 8.104.

196. *Id.* § 8.105 (suggesting the latter interpretation might render the provision superfluous, as noncopyrightable information is excluded from the governance of the Berne Convention in the first place).

197. *Id.* § 8.106.

198. The notion of "negative categories" was explained in Chapter 1. *See* Chapter 1, Section V.A.1(c) *supra*. This is precisely how news of the day is classified under recent Israeli legislation. Section 5 of the Copyright Act of 2007 places news of the day (together with ideas, procedures, and methods of operation; mathematical concepts; and facts or data) outside the subject matter protected under copyright. *See* Israel Copyright Act (2007), Sec. 5(5).

rights in negative categories elements such as raw fact or even ideas, foreigners may not invoke the Convention while demanding such protection under the auspices of the national treatment principle. According to Ricketson and Ginsburg, this seems to be the function of Article 2(8) regarding "news of the day or to miscellaneous facts having the character of mere items of press information."

What is the contribution of this discussion to the maximum protection controvercy? It seems as a practical matter that even after accepting the mandatory maximum protection approach advocated by Ricketson and Ginsburg, each Union member can easily achieve the "Ladas result" by employing a simple strategy. To effectuate the "Ladas result" in Scenario (1), *UMA*'s law would stipulate that domestic works are unaffected by the quotation exception, whereas foreign works are subject to an extremely narrow quotation privilege. This exception could have only a marginal impact on the freedom to quote foreign works, but *UMA* could not be said to formally violate any Berne provisions under either approach. Furthermore, if *UMA* nonetheless stipulated a more vigorous quotation exception to comply with the maximum protection approach, but denied enjoyment of the same exceptions regarding domestic works, the danger is the law would discriminate against foreigners: domestic works would remain exception-free, whereas a generous Article 10(1)–based exception would apply to works with respect to which *UMA* is not the country of origin.

A legal scheme in which the application of important exceptions depends on country-of-origin questions would contravene notions of coherence and certainty. Consider for instance the legal uncertainty involved, the information cost burden on the public in *UMA*, and specifically, the information cost effect on potential beneficiaries of the Article 10(1)–based exception. The basic problem nonowners must deal with is making a decision whether to quote or not quote from copyrighted works without permission. If they are unsure about the country-of-origin issue, they cannot be certain, without investing time and money resources in legal inquiries, about the scope of their privilege. Consequently, nonowners might refrain ex ante from exercising the privilege altogether, thereby reducing the desired public benefits at the basis of the quotation exception and contrary to the policy objectives underlying the maximum protection appraoch. In short, a dichotomist exceptions structure might prove considerably less beneficial to the public interest at large.

IV. RESOLUTION: MAXIMUM PROTECTION AS A COMMITMENT TO THE PROTECTION OF *AUTHORSHIP*

Several recognitions emanating from the above analysis well illustrate why Hoffmann considered the issue "one of the most difficult interpretation question in the Berne Convention."[199] First, the Berne Convention has no influence on the protection granted to domestic authors in the adjudicating country.

199. *See* Hoffmann, *supra* note 161, at 897.

Second, Scenario (1) should be avoided as it ignores the arguably imperative Berne exceptions and enhances the risk of overprotection with respect to all works. Third, Scenario (2) should be discouraged as it might lead to undesirable discrimination against foreign authors.

Ladas rejected the notion of maximum protection in 1938, believing author-users balance issues should be resolved exclusively on the domestic level. His position must be revisited today. In a reality in which regional and global trade agreements directly address copyright minimum protection issues, and in which international and supranational regulatory instruments virtually dictate copyright provisions to domestic lawmakers, it turns less promising to trust the domestic legislative process to effectively correct overprotection situations. In many cases, the hands of national lawmakers are tied by virtue of international agreements and treaties acceded to by their governments that have much to do with protecting industry/sectoral interests in multinational negotiation fronts and less with proecting the interests of the public in accessing and using copyrighted works.

According to the current state of affairs (following the Ladas approach), Union members are encouraged to overprotect (Scenario (1)). Under the Ricketson/Ginsburg approach, Union members are encouraged to discriminate against foreign authors. A reasonable copyright policy should strive to avoid both situations. To break this vicious circle, one parameter should be modified, possibly the axiom that Berne (or international copyright law more generally) *can never affect domestic authors' protection*. This would require a modification of the national treatment principle to correct Scenario (2) situations and compel members to grant certain public policy exceptions (in rare situations) also vis-à-vis domestic works.

Admittedly, the proposed modification is not a minor one, and its rationale calls for further explanation.[200] The starting point is that the Ricketson and Ginsburg position and their concept of maximum protection is laudable at its core. The desire is to locate in the Berne Convention itself some *real* safeguards for the public interest. At the same time, the structure, language, and history of

---

200. Kur and Ruse-Kahn have recently examined the prospects of "ceilings" in the broader IP context, especially under TRIPS. *See* Annette Kur & Henning Grosse Ruse-Kahn, *Enough Is Enough: The Notion of Binding Ceilings in International Intellectual Property Protection* (2008) (available at http://papers.ssrn.com/sol3/papers.cfm?abstract_id=1326429). The idea of enforcing Berne maximum provisions via the TRIPS dispute resolution mechnism (as mentioned by these authors) is interesting in itself. But there is a fundamental difficulty in pointing Berne or TRIPS provisions (be they minimum or maximum oriented) *against domestic rights-holders*. The international instrument on limitations and exceptions proposed by Hugenholtz and Okediji appears to be designed to provide for, inter alia, a set of "mandatory" limitations and exceptions effective in the states that adopt such instrument with respect to all works. *See* Hugengoltz & Okediji, *supra* note 149, at *43–*44.

the Berne convention make the task of defining a maximum protection bar a serious ordeal. Ricketson and Ginsburg follow a route, which, like Baum's at the time, is based for the most part on specific provisions in the contemporary text of the Berne Convention itself. Whereas Baum initially deduced his maximum protection interpretation from an apparent internal conflict between various Berne provisions, Ricketson and Ginsburg deduce this insight from textual analysis of isolated exceptions provisions that echo an affirmative tone.

As we have seen, in reviewing his position in retrospect, Baum acknowledged that fixing the language of Article 19 could relax textual interpretation issues, but it could not solve the deeper riddle involved in the maximum protection problem. A more solid maximum principle should also consider Hoffmann's contribution to the debate. Hoffman, as noted, rejected the doctrinal-structural distinction between authors' exclusive right, norms that limited exclusive rights, and norms that safeguard the public interest.[201] Every substantive rule stipulated in Berne affects the interests of multiple stakeholders, and the higher the minimum protection bar is, the weaker the position of the public becomes.

This matter is reflected in the dilemma of interpreting Article 2(8) Berne Convention: at bottom, the classification of this norm, either as a public policy exception or a subject matter clarification should not bear on the protection of the public interest is concerned. Yet a maximum protection theory based on specific exceptions provisions might treat such public interest safeguards differently.

The maximum protection thesis obviously goes beyond stating Berne does not cover noncopyrightable subject matter, and in order to fulfill its policy objectives, the rationale behind it must overcome the literal wording while returning to the Convention's most fundamental vision: the preservation of fostering human creativity. This vision should stand at the basis of the efforst to consolidate among the three core Berne principles: (1) the ideal of adequately protecting authors' rights in general, (2) the desire to maintain a level of uniformity concerning minimum protection across the Union, and (3) the objective of effectively preserving the public interest. The maximum protection theory could and should become an important interpretation cannon in defining the scope of domestic obligations under Berne and the WCT. As its normative baseline, Berne's central project should be understood as being devoted to the protection of *authorship*, not contemporary "*authors*" in the narrow sense.[202]

201. *See* Hoffmann, *supra* note 163, at 7 ff, especially at 21 ff.

202. *Cf.* Paul Goldstein, Copyright's Highway—From Gutenberg to the Celestial Jukebox 61 (2003) ("Copyright is about authorship, about sustaining the conditions for creativity that enable an artist to create out of thin air and intense, devouring labor on *Appalachian Spring*, a *Sun Also Rises*, a *Citizen Kane*. In a culture that depends on the marketplace, creative authorship is central.").

The Berne Convention seeks to foster the vitality and richness of human creativity; like the information process in which it dwells, human creativity has an important dynamic dimension. Overprotection harms authorship in the long run, as Chapter 1 illustrates by showing how originators-authors on the one hand and recipients on the other are prone to change roles over different communication sequences.[203] Protecting authorship also means that when exclusory regimes go too far (reaching a level where the very institution of authorship is jeopardized), the maximum protection principle could be triggered. And one instance in which this principle should be applied is anticircumvention laws.

Before reaching this complexity, the three principles of the modified maximum protection thesis shall be restated. *First*, it is misleading to doctrinally separate minimum protection issues from the desire to secure public interests and entitlements to access information, as well as from the impact of exclusive rights on the ability to produce new works. *Second*, to the extent the maximum protection principle is necessary for preserving the copyright balance, the emergence of dichotomist regimes in which the scope of protection significantly depends on the country of origin should be discouraged. *Third* and most importantly, the normative foundation and application of the maximum protection principle in domestic law should not exclusively depend on the literal wording of various Berne provisions. This might lead to a perverse structure, enshrining the supremacy of "quotations from newspaper articles and periodicals in the form of press summaries" over other important exceptions such as ones fostering education, teaching or research, absent of policy reasoning supporting this hierarchy. In this respect, one may consider the maximum protection principle and its public policy character as deserving general acceptance beyond the narrow purview of Article 10(1) Berne Convention.

(c) The Maximum Protection Doctrine and Art. 11 WCT

The maximum protection principle may be thought of as a "soft" interpretation tool—perhaps as distinguished from the "hard" and more established minimum protection and national treatment principles. It is called to task in cases where overprotection clearly threatens to undermine the nature of copyright as protector of authorship.

More concretely on the issue of anticircumvention: As WCT signatories are committed to respect Article 10(1) Berne Convention, the question is whether domestic laws *must* protect the beneficiaries of Article 10(1) exceptions as the signatories comply with their obligations under Article 11 WCT. If domestic anticircumvention regimes substantially curtail the ability to benefit from that exception, we could read in Article 11 (read together with Art. 10(1) Berne

203. Chapter 1, Section V.C *supra*.

Convention) a material obligation to preserve it. Under the assumption technological protection measures might handicap quotation privileges,[204] arguably Article 1(4) WCT (in connection with the maximum protection principle) imposes an affirmative limitation on the freedom of domestic legislatures in designing anticircumvention schemes. Accordingly, whereas the adequate-and-effective clause sets a minimum protection bar, there is also a mandatory *maximum* bar, which means that the edifice of international obligations has both a floor and a ceiling. In the present context, compliance with Berne/WCT would prescribe a framework in which domestic anticircumvention law regimes can neither be too loose nor too restrictive. In addressing this specific problem, Ricketson and Ginsburg acknowledged the tension:

> [A]rticle 10(1) of the Berne Convention . . . is of mandatory character . . . [and] contracting states are obligated to adopt such an exception . . . anti-circumvention measures may cut across this exception, where the effect of such measures is either to deny users access to the works protected for the purpose of making quotation or is to prevent them from making the necessary reproduction or dissemination.[205]

If the work has been lawfully made available, and if the work is not available in analog, non-TPM-protected format, Ricketson and Ginsburg advise national legislatures to accommodate a specific anticircumvention exception. Alternatively, domestic law should provide that exceptions are applicable to digitally protected versions, and in general "there should be no restrictions placed on the making of quotations . . . in cases where a work is only available in digital protected formats."[206] According to this line, the crux of defining the *actual content* of an international obligation of that sort is in deciding what "lawfully made available to the public" means. If the very deployment of TPMs indicates rights-holders wished to *prevent* access, than perhaps an unauthorized access will not satisfy this clause, rendering the exception inapplicable.

---

204. Some commentators downplay the consequences of the inability of making digital quotations. For instance, Liebowitz writes: "Some might persist in arguing that pay-per-use DRM can lock up content inappropriately. What about when one simply wants to quote from a paragraph in an online article, for example? I don't understand why that's a problem. There is something called 'ink pen.'" *See* Stanley J. Liebowitz, *Copyright in the Post-Napstar World: Legal or Market Solutions?*, *in* COPY FIGHTS: THE FUTURE OF INTELLECTUAL PROPERTY IN THE INFORMATION AGE 203 (Adam Thierer & Wayne Crews eds., 2002). Obviously, we cannot assume the only subject matter of copyright is text, and that the legal-technological impossibility of making digital quotations (e.g., from a song or a movie) could be reduced merely to questions of convenience and costs of making the quotation.

205. *See* RICKETSON & GINSBURG, *supra* note 75, § 13.132.

206. *Id.*

The question is far from being merely theoretical. For instance, the German Copyright Act provides statutory exceptions for some quotations that comply with Article 10(1) Berne Convention.[207] However, TPMs circumvention for the purpose of exercising this privilege is apparently forbidden.[208] Further, rights-holders using TPMs are not obligated to facilitate enjoyment of this privilege as the quotation exception is not listed in the catalog of exceptions in Section 95b(1).[209] This might result in an inability to exercise the quotation privilege in some situations. If the work is considered to have been "lawfully made available to the public" but is unavailable in non-protected formats (which renders quotation technically impossible), according to Ricketson's and Ginsburg's approach Germany (as well as other E.U. members having a similar regulation)[210] would be violating its obligations under both Berne and the WCT. This would be a serious allegation indeed.

Without our having to decide whether the framework dictated by the EUCD conflicts with Berne, the more troublesome problem is in restricting the application of the maximum protection principle to the extremely narrow province of Article 10(1) Berne Convention. This limited application results from the unyielding reliance on textual interpretation, leading to the assumption that a restriction on domestic anticircumvention schemes applies only to Article 10(1)-based exceptions. But from a broad policy perspective, there is no justification for such a limited application. What makes Article 10(1)-based exceptions superior to all other copyright exceptions such as political speeches, law administration and proceedings, government/official texts of legislation, lectures, quotation for educational purposes,[211] and so on? The fear of "digital lockup" might equally affect these exceptions in the same way.

The doctrinal payoff of the maximum protection approach rests in furnishing a normative basis for expanding the rule by analogy to public policy exceptions beyond the instances covered by Article 10(1) Berne Convention. To the extent Berne/WCT members are committed to maintaining a balanced copyright

---

207. *See* § 51 UrhG. *See also* Gerhard Schricker, *in* URHEBERRECHT KOMMENTAR § 51 nr. 34 (Gerhard Schricker ed., 3d ed. 2006).

208. This according to § 95a UrhG. *See also* Horst-Peter Götting *in* URHEBERRECHT KOMMENTAR § 95a nr. (Gerhard Schricker ed., 3d ed. 2006) at 14 (no right to self-help circumvention); § 95b nr. 18 (Sec. 95b does not include the quotation privilege of § 51 UrhG).

209. *See* § 95b(1) UrhG (listing an exhaustive catalog of exceptions not including quotation).

210. The EUCD generally does not allow domestic laws to subject quotation exceptions (as described in Art. 5(3)(d)) to the "appropriate measures" mechanism. The EUCD anticircumvention regime is further reviewed in Section VI. *infra*

211. These and other exceptions are listed in Arts. 2, 2bis to the Berne Convention.

system by virtue of their membership in the international copyright community,[212] some key exceptions must be carried over to the domestic anticircumvention regime irrespective of the question whether those exceptions are explicit in the current text of Berne. Nor should it matter whether their articulation in Berne uses "obligatory" or "permissive" language. Article 20 Berne convention provides: "The Governments of the countries of the Union reserve the right to enter into special agreements among themselves, in so far as such agreements grant to authors more extensive rights than those granted by the Convention, *or contain other provisions not contrary to this Convention.* The provisions of existing agreements which satisfy these conditions shall remain applicable."[213] The WCT is a special agreement in the meaning of Article 20, and as argued above, the view submitted here is that overprotective anticircumvention regulations can clearly be considered "other provisions [] contrary to this Convention." The conclusion must be that Article 11 WCT can neither warrant nor justify anticircumvention overprotection, and to some extent, such overprotection might conflict with international obligations.

3. Right Management Information: Article 12 WCT

(a) Introduction

Article 12 WCT contains a rather detailed text addressing obligations concerning rights management information (RMI). The idea had been circulated in the mid-1990s in connection with the work on a new protocol to the Berne Convention.[214] Early proposals emphasized two basic rationales behind this regulation: First, RMI were said to be important for insuring successful functioning of global digital networks. Second, RMI regulation was intended to protect the public against manipulations and fraud.[215] Progress in this direction was no doubt influenced by the prediction stated in the 1995 U.S. White Paper:

> In the future, the copyright management information [CMI] associated with a work . . .may be critical to the efficient operation and success of the NII [the Internet]. [CMI] will serve as a kind of license plate for a work on the information superhighway, from which a user may obtain important information about the work. The accuracy of such information will be crucial to the ability of consumers to find and make authorized uses of copyrighted works on the

---

212. The fourth Recital to the WCT, which is the only occasion in this Treaty where the "public interest" is recited, refers back to the balance "as reflected in the Berne Convention." WCT (1996), fourth Recital.

213. *See* Art. 20 Berne Convention (emphasis added in text).

214. *See* REINBOTHE & VON LEWINSKI, *supra* note 80, at 148–49.

215. *Id.* at 149 (referring to the U.S. comment at the fifth session of the New Protocol Committee).

NII. Reliable information will also facilitate efficient licensing and reduce transaction costs for licensable uses of copyrighted works.[216]

Draft Article 14 to the WCT Basic Proposal articulated the proposed international RMI provision.[217] That text included basic prohibitions on the willful removal or altering of electronic RMI,[218] and prohibitions on the distribution and communication to the public of works with respect to which RMI has been removed or altered.[219] Draft Article 14 also proposed a definition of the term *rights management information.*[220] The Notes to Draft Article 14 emphasized, inter alia, that contracting parties should enjoy great latitude in implementing obligations under these provisions, implying that compliance should not necessarily warrant amending domestic copyright laws.[221] The proposed text to a RMI provision went through several amendments during the Diplomatic Conference; the final provision of Article 12 WCT reads:

(1) Contracting Parties shall provide adequate and effective legal remedies against any person knowingly performing any of the following acts knowing, or with respect to civil remedies having reasonable grounds to know, that it will induce, enable, facilitate or conceal an infringement of any right covered by this Treaty or the Berne Convention:
   (i) to remove or alter any electronic rights management information without authority;
   (ii) to distribute, import for distribution, broadcast or communicate to the public, without authority, works or copies of works knowing that electronic rights management information has been removed or altered without authority.

(2) As used in this Article, "rights management information" means infor-

---

216. U.S. White Paper (1995) at 239 & 191–94 (stating the policy rationale for protection). That report recommended amending the U.S. Copyright Act to include a special provision protecting the integrity of CMI against manipulations. *Id.* Appendix I at 6–7.

217. *See* WCT Basic Proposal (1996), Draft Art. 14.

218. *Id.* Draft Art. 14(1)(i).

219. *Id.* Draft Art. 14(1)(ii).

220. *Id.* Draft Art. 14(2) ("As used in this Article, 'rights management information' means information which identifies the work, the author of the work, the owner of any right in the work, and any numbers or codes that represent such information, when any of these items of information are attached to a copy of a work or appear in connection with the communication of a work to the public.").

221. *Id.* Note 14.04 ("Contracting Parties may design the exact field of application of the provisions envisaged in this Article taking into consideration the need to avoid legislation that would impede lawful practices. Having regard to differences in legal traditions, Contracting Parties may, in their national legislation, also define the coverage and extent of the liability for violation of the prohibition enacted according to paragraph (1).").

> mation which identifies the work, the author of the work, the owner of any right in the work, or information about the terms and conditions of use of the work, and any numbers or codes that represent such information, when any of these items of information is attached to a copy of a work or appears in connection with the communication of a work to the public.[222]

Article 12 WCT is supplemented with the following agreed statements:

> It is understood that the reference to "infringement of any right covered by this Treaty or the Berne Convention" includes both exclusive rights and rights of remuneration. It is further understood that Contracting Parties will not rely on this Article to devise or implement rights management systems that would have the effect of imposing formalities which are not permitted under the Berne Convention or this Treaty, prohibiting the free movement of goods or impeding the enjoyment of rights under this Treaty.[223]

Article 12 WCT[224] (accompanied by parallel Article 19 in the WPPT)[225] constitutes yet another unprecedented international norm. In 1996, RMI regulation was so novel that most contracting parties had not even begin to consider it before Article 12 was passed.[226] The threats Article 12 sought to combat were at the time quite abstract and nearly hypothetical—and rights-holders could not provide concrete indications that manipulation of RMI constituted a serious and immediate threat to their economic interests.[227] Against this reality backdrop, the policy argument supporting RMI had to make some very soft suppositions that bordered on mere speculations: it assumes (1) electronic RMI *could* be attached to works, (2) such information *could* help rights-holders to exploit their work, and (3) as offenders *could* willfully manipulate that information, (4) what in turn *could* result in a serious injury to rights-holders.[228] The following pas-

---

222. *See* WCT (1996), Art. 12.

223. *Id.* agreed statement concerning Art. 12.

224. For a more detailed commentary on Article 12 and its agreed statement, *see* REINBOTHE & VON LEWINSKI, *supra* note 80, at 151–60; RICKETSON & GINSBURG (2006), *supra* note 75, §§ 15.30–15.40.

225. *See* WPPT (1996), Art. 19.

226. *Cf.* REINBOTHE & VON LEWINSKI, *supra* note 80, at 151–52. The European Commission at that time expressed the intention to "continue studying the issue of management of rights in the light of the developments of the market with particular regard to the Information Society." *See* E.C. Follow-Up to the Green Paper (1996) at 26.

227. Reinbothe and von Lewinski stated Article 12 "may be considered as a rare example of a legal regulation which has largely preceded the developments on the factual level" (footnote omitted). *Id.* at 151.

228. *Cf.* REINBOTHE & VON LEWINSKI, *supra* note 80, at 152 (explaining the rationale behind the RMI provision).

sages discuss a number of selected issues relating to TPMs protections with a special emphasis on access entitlements.

(b) The Concept of Rights Management Information

Article 12 WCT by definition protects "information." Its text indicates both formal and material criteria describing the information covered. First, it must be "electronic"[229] and "attached to a copy of a work or appears in connection with the communication of a work to the public."[230] The terms "*electronic* information," "*attached* to a copy" and "*appears* in connection [with communication to the public]" all provide a fertile ground for interpretative excursions.[231]

The RMI *content* and *details* that are protected against manipulations and further dissemination are more precisely defined. It is important to distinguish between two types of RMI. The first is identification-information (called here *identification-RMI*), which "identifies the *work*, the *author* of the work, the *owner of any right* in the work."[232] The second type is permission-information (called here *permission-RMI*), indicating "the terms and conditions of use of the work."[233] The phrase in Article 12(2) that clarifies RMI may be "any numbers or codes that represent such information" refers to both types of RMI.

Generally speaking, and in conjunction with the suppositions mentioned earlier, legal protection of RMI intends to facilitate new business models for the digital environment:[234] More specifically, protecting identification-information and permission-information against unauthorized manipulation is meant to ensure works are used in accordance with the terms prescribed by the rights-holder, and that rights-holders who authorize use remain identifiable and continue to receive compensation according to the intended commercialization scheme. Preventing RMI manipulation is said to promote these goals, yet the connection to *copyright infringement* as expressed in Article 12 itself is only indirect; namely, the nexus to infringement is derivable from the language establishing liability *upon knowledge* accused acts "will induce, enable, facilitate or

---

229. Interestingly, the term *electronic* appears in both prohibitions under Art. 12(1) WCT (concerning (1) manipulation and (2) dissemination), but *not* in the second subsection providing the definition of "rights management information."

230. *See* WCT (1996), Art. 12(2).

231. For more discussion, *see, e.g.*, Reinbothe & von Lewinski, *supra* note 80, at 158–59 (discussing the "attached or appears" elements); Peter Wand, Technische Schutzmassnahmen und Urheberrecht 49 (2001) (discussing the issue of "physical" attachment of RMI to works); Ricketson & Ginsburg (2006), *supra* note 75, § 15.28 (interpreting the term "electronic") & §§ 15.32–15.33 (discussing the requirement the information should "come together with the work").

232. *See* WCT (1996), Art. 12(2), first sentence.

233. *Id.* Art. 12(2), second sentence.

234. *See* Ricketson & Ginsburg (2006), *supra* note 75, § 15.29.

conceal an infringement of any right covered by this Treaty or the Berne Convention."[235]

(c) RMI, Contracts, and Copyright Exemptions

I. RMI PROVISIONS ARE NOT A RESTATEMENT OF COPYRIGHTS

The term *rights* appears both in the caption of Article 12 ("Obligations concerning *Rights* Management Information") and in the definition provided in subsection (2). The language of "rights" and "rights management" might create some confusion.[236] RMI *itself* does not have to be protected under copyright; in fact, Article 12 implies that often RMI will not qualify as a copyrighted "work."[237] Further, entitlements under Article 12 are not an exposition of moral rights, so the prohibition related to the alteration or removal of the author's name is not a version of the right of paternity.[238] Similarly, the prohibition on altering RMI is not an extension of the right of integrity.[239] In the same vein, RMI provisions are not the electronic equivalent of traditional economic rights such as those of adaptation, distribution, or communication to the public.

Indeed, RMI may *assist* rights-holders to exercise their economic rights, and RMI manipulation might burden exploitation of economic rights. But the prohibitions expressed in Article 12 WCT materially detour from traditional infringement prohibitions both in the definition of violations and the motivation for enacting them. As mentioned, legal prohibition on RMI manipulation is a completely new species of copyright regulation, including the requirement the relevant information itself must not be copyrightable but must be "attached" to copyrighted works. In addition, its removal or alteration triggers liability that is distinguishable from infringement liability, and in this respect it is safe to say copyright infringement and RMI violations are two separate types of violations,

---

235. *See* WCT (1996), Art. 12(1).

236. A similar point was made in the explanation of the concept of DRM systems. *See* Chapter 3, Section IV.A.2 *supra*.

237. Identification-information may include names, titles, addresses, contacts and other information identifying works and rights-holders. *Cf.* REINBOTHE & VON LEWINSKI, *supra* note 80, at 157–58. Such details usually do not receive independent copyright protection, nor are permission-information texts classic exemplifications of originality and creativity. Either way, it is clear the aim of Article 12 is not to grant protection vis-à-vis RMI that are equivalent or similar to copyright protection vis-à-vis works of authorship.

238. *Cf.* RICKETSON & GINSBURG (2006), *supra* note 75, § 15.31 ("Article 12 is not a shadow right of attribution"); WAND, *supra* note 231, at 45 ff.

239. The copyright-protected work *itself* is not necessarily altered via RMI manipulation in a manner that would trigger the conventional moral right of integrity. In any event, though manipulating authorial details or altering contextual information might independently violate the author's moral rights, the RMI provision is not an alternative norm to secure the same type of interests. For more discussion, see Severine Dusollier, *Some Reflections on Copyright Management Information and Moral Rights*, 25 COLUM J.L. & ARTS 377, 389 ff (2003).

where the latter type of protection is designed to enable better enforcement of the former.

II. THE RIGHTS MANAGED ARE CONTRACTUAL

The "rights" managed by RMI systems are typically stipulated in contractual instruments, including voluntary and non-voluntary licensing of copyrighted works. As in the case of TPMs, the licensing terms do not always regulate acts covered by copyright exclusion entitlements. The inclusion of remuneration claims arising out of statutory or compulsory licensing as part of RMI, as well as claims raised out of private contracts, is clarified in the first sentence of the agreed statement.[240]

Contractual entitlements typically relate to the nature, scope, and price of using copyrighted materials. The conducts regulated by the license may overlap with conducts exclusively reserved to rights-holders or with acts covered by a statutory license. For instance, RMI that administrates the duration and cost of access based on payment models may have a weaker connection to core exclusive copyrights than RMI that supports a licensing term concerning the number of copies allowed to be made. In any case, violation of license terms administrated by RMI is not a synonym for copyright infringement.[241]

To generalize this observation a little, the stated mission of Article 12 is to *secure the enforcement of agreements and licensing terms* concerning the use of copyrighted works. Such terms may cover the following types of use: (1) use that, without authorization, would infringe on exclusive rights; (2) use that is explicitly privileged, subject to involuntary licensing or otherwise permitted by copyright law; and (3) use that implicates no exclusive right in the work. On the one hand, only the manipulation of permission-RMI that enforce terms of the first type would maintain a clear nexus to copyright infringement. On the other hand, attempting to make noninfringing use that falls under the second and third categories (which conflicts with contractual terms) will probably *not* excuse manipulation of permission-RMI. Users wishing to object to licensing terms, whether RMI-supported or not, are free to challenge the validity and enforceability of the

---

240. WCT (1996), agreed statement to Art. 12, first sentence. Importantly, the Agreed Statement mentions "rights of remuneration" in general, not exclusively remuneration rights based on copyright statutory provisions and international norms. *Cf.* RICKETSON & GINSBURG (2006), *supra* note 75, § 15.37 ("the term 'rights of remuneration' does not ineluctably evoke contractual obligations") (footnotes omitted).

241. For a different view, see REINBOTHE & VON LEWINSKI, *supra* note 80, at 156 ("the 'infringement' of a contractual remuneration right corresponds to an indirect infringement of the underlying exclusive right and is covered as such"). This statement might create the false impression that every contractual violation amounts to copyright infringement. Not every violation of a contractual obligation made possible by the removal or alteration of RMI will have a discernable linkage to infringement. *Cf.* RICKETSON & GINSBURG (2006), *supra* note 75, § 15.35.

underlying contract in court. But as long as the RMI-supported agreement is valid and enforceable, arguing that the contemplated use is *not* subject to exclusive rights would per se neither undermine the legitimacy of the license nor excuse RMI violations.

III. KNOWLEDGE AND THE IMPLICIT "PERMITTED BY LAW" CLAUSE

This result appears on its face quite harsh for licensees and nonowners in general. Yet where tension exists between acts permissible under copyright law but impermissible under RMI-supported control systems, relaxing Article 12 prohibitions is possible after examining further its liability terms.

Specifically, liability for RMI manipulation is subject to a material knowledge requirement. This requirement is crucial, as it states the connection between copyright infringement and RMI violations. The knowledge test is rigorous and operates on three levels.[242] At the *first level*, the *accused conduct* (unauthorized removal/alteration of RMI or dissemination of RMI-manipulated works) must be performed with the actor's knowledge.[243] At the *second level, dissemination* of RMI-manipulated works must be performed with knowledge that unauthorized manipulation took place.[244] The critical language is set forth at the *third level*: the actor (manipulator or disseminator) must have actual or constructive knowledge that *manipulation* "will induce, enable, facilitate or conceal infringement of any right" covered by WCT/Berne Convention.[245] In addition, acts of both manipulation and dissemination must be done "without authority."[246]

Two interlocked interpretation problems arise, with the first concerning the unauthorized *act*. From the text of the provision, it is not readily clear whether the act of RMI manipulation/distribution must be authorized or instead the act managed by the RMI system. Second, if the latter interpretation is correct, does "authorization" include acts that are permitted *by law*?[247] Plain reading of Article 12 suggests the "without authority" clause refers to activities of removing/altering RMI and the dissemination of RMI-manipulated works.[248] Hence, this clause is relevant for first- and second-levels knowledge analysis. It may follow that actors who remove/alter RMI or disseminate RMI-manipulated works must know, or have a reasonable ground to know, these acts are unauthorized.

---

242. *See* RICKETSON & GINSBURG (2006), *supra* note 75, § 15.34 ff.

243. Principally, the knowledge requirement is necessary to prevent punishing accidental or unintended conduct.

244. The rationale for this knowledge requirement is similar to the one underpinning the former type of knowledge. *Id.*

245. *See* WCT (1996), Art. 12(1).

246. *Id.* Art. 12(1)(i) & (ii).

247. Unlike Art. 11 WCT, the provision addressing RMI violations does not contain an explicit "permitted by law" clause.

248. *See* WCT (1996), Art. 12(1)(i)–(ii).

The authorization requirement may be interpreted in two ways. Strict interpretation would *always* require authorization by rights-holders. A more moderate interpretation would also negate liability when such conducts are permitted by law.[249] Some commentators follow the second approach, but the term "permitted by law" itself has more that one possible interpretation. For example, Reinbothe and von Lewinski suggest "if the work is already in the public domain, and not even perpetual moral rights are involved, the law permits the acts as set out in Article 12 WCT."[250] An alternative and broader interpretation purports that copyright exceptions permissible under Berne and the WCT could also be considered as being authorized.[251]

The next question is *what law* may permit conducts that are otherwise prohibited under Article 12. In the case of Article 11 WCT, acts covered by statutory copyright exceptions are often considered as "permitted by law."[252] A direct analogy to Article 12 prohibitions cannot be drawn, as RMI prohibitions do not address certain acts directly performed *with respect to works.*[253] Instead, Article 12 bans certain acts regarding *information attached to works.* Statutory copyright exceptions are incapable of legitimizing manipulation of noncopyrightable information, at least not directly. The "permitted by law" problem seems to emanate (at least partly) from the fact RMI bans are *not* a restatement of the exclusive rights, and RMI violations are *not equivalent* to copyright infringement. Furthermore, RMI manipulation and dissemination of RMI-manipulated works per se may not necessarily implicate any traditional exclusive right. As RMI provisions do not require infringement, it appears the inquiry whether such acts actually infringe, or rather are "permitted by law" by virtue of copyright exceptions, is immaterial for the question of liability under the RMI bans. The specific provisions of copyright law including exceptions to exclusive rights, as strange as it might sound, remain until this stage quite irrelevant. They could become relevant only in connection with third-level knowledge analysis under the assumption a "permitted by law" rule is applicable here.

The assumption a "permitted by law" clause is implied in the third-level knowledge requirement may have the following consequences: manipulations and disseminations generally prohibited under Article 12 shall be excused

---

249. *See* Reinbothe & von Lewinski, *supra* note 80, at 155; Wand, *supra* note 231, at 51 (arguing that acting under copyright exceptions could not be considered unauthorized in the context of RMI violations).

250. *Id.* at 155. This restrictive reading of "permitted by law" basically reiterates the basic entry requirement that content to which RMI is attached must be copyrighted.

251. *See* Wand, *supra* note 231, at 51.

252. *Cf.* Section IV.B.4 *supra.*

253. To clarify this point, it may be useful to recall the distinction between the concept of TPMs in the narrow sense (i.e., real-technical restrictions of behavior) and other DRM functions more broadly. *See* Chapter 3, Section IV.A.1 *supra.*

(1) upon a reasonable belief the work is not protected by copyright, or (2) upon a reasonable belief manipulation/dissemination will not advance infringement. In the later case, the actor's belief may be based on a reasonable assumption that potential "infringers" (including the actor himself) are shielded by copyright privileges.

Further complications arise after we realize the "without authority" requirement attaches to first- and second-level knowledge analysis, but not to third-level knowledge. As noted, third-level knowledge analysis asks whether the actor knew (or should have known) his conduct would induce, enable, facilitate, or conceal infringement of any right covered by WCT/Berne. If the "authorized by law" clause does not apply here (as the structure of Article 12 suggests), the question of reasonable assumption by the actor concerning copyright exceptions covering conduct his acts facilitated will become mute. The result is paradoxical, as copyright exceptions become powerless in the only situation in which they could influence liability analysis under RMI provisions. Differently stated, the "permitted by law" clause (implicitly derived from the "without authorization" clause) applies to cases where copyright exceptions are largely irrelevant, but not where copyright exemptions could be relevant.

To correct this, authorization requirement must be derived from the language of the third-level knowledge provision, namely from the phrase "infringement of any right covered by this Treaty or the Berne Convention." If the accused act facilitates noninfringing acts (which, by definition, are "permitted by law"), such knowledge will satisfy Article 12(1) WCT. This seems to be the only plausible route to negate third-level knowledge by showing the actor had a reasonable ground to believe the actions enabled by his alleged RMI violations were noninfringing. Practical, procedural, and evidentiary hurdles will surely surface when attempts are made to prove (or disprove) this kind of knowledge. For example, how can a plaintiff rights-holder prove in court that at the time of action, the defendant knew (or had reasonable grounds to know) his RMI-suspect act would promote infringement committed by others? In which circumstances should the actor be justified in believing that, whatever conducts were facilitated by his RMI removal, these conducts are shielded by copyright exceptions?[254] The difficulties involved might explain why in jurisdictions that have transposed these rules, the volume of litigation around them has remained so far quite marginal.

---

254. To eliminate this issue, Reinbothe and von Lewinski recommend a rather sweeping rule of thumb stipulating that merely performing the acts defined in Art. 12, when done deliberately, would already embody a strong presumption the "reasonable grounds to know" requirement about subsequent infringements was met. *See* Reinbothe & von Lewinski, *supra* note 80, at 156–57. This view would practically eliminate the third-level knowledge requirement and render the consideration of copyright exemptions utterly meaningless.

(d) The Proprietary Aspect of RMI Protections

The nexus between an RMI violation and the violation of copyrights is concealed within the third-level knowledge requirement. The actor must have actual or constructive knowledge the RMI-related act will induce, enable, facilitate, or conceal copyright infringement. The vocabulary of inducing and facilitating resembles circumstances where *indirect* liability for copyright infringement is imposed. An act that induces, enables, facilitates, or conceals copyright infringement is not infringing in itself, but is assumed to render infringement more likely.

In the context of Article 11 WCT, it has been argued contracting parties may determine if, and under which circumstances, preparatory conduct to actual circumvention (trafficking) shall be unlawful.[255] The same principle of broad national discretion is reflected in Article 12 WCT via a similar "adequate and effective legal remedies" clause.[256] Article 12 covers certain types of "preparatory act," but unlike trafficking under Article 11, this time the WCT expressly mandates RMI provisions. Contracting parties are committed to transpose Article 12 obligations in their respective copyright laws and grant rights-holders[257] remedies akin to in rem exclusion protections vis-à-vis information.

A potential violator of RMI provisions is a user who had initially acceded to stipulated license terms (e.g., via a click-wrap agreement), but later attempted to expand her use by altering permission-RMI (e.g., by altering the tariff she is charged through an automated payment system). In this scenario, the parties to a potential dispute are in contractual privity, and to enforce the original terms, plaintiff may invoke both contractual and copyright infringement claims, depending on the circumstances. A second type of defendant includes those who alter or remove RMI without initially acceding to any terms determined by the rights-holder.[258] Such manipulators and those who disseminate RMI-manipulated works are not in contractual privity with rights-holders, so the ability to hold them accountable is improved by the availability of property-like RMI provisions. This is especially important in cases where an independent infringement cannot be proved.

The discussion thus far illustrates that at least with respect to some violations covered by RMI provisions, the nexus between covered acts and copyright

---

255. *See* Section IV.B.6 *supra*.

256. *See* Art. 12(1) WCT (1996) ("Contracting Parties shall provide adequate and effective legal remedies . . .").

257. It is not clear from the language of Art. 12 WCT who are the beneficiaries of the norm. The logic of this provision implies that intended beneficiaries are persons who hold rights with respect to the work *and* who have attached RMI to the work in which they have rights.

258. Such a violation may involve a combination of TPMs circumvention and RMI manipulation, in case the terms are technologically enforced by the system.

violations is exceedingly abstract. At the same time, this addition to the arsenal of rights-holders certainly constitutes an expansion of their property-like entitlements secured under copyright law yet the shaky policy basis for these provisions only amplifies the interpretation quandaries they raise.

(e) The Interface between RMI and TPMs

TPMs and RMI protections are sometimes called "collateral" protections due to their indirect relationship to traditional copyright violations. Legal protection concerning TPMs and protections concerning RMI share a common rationale and some common features. The aim is to assist rights-holders to control and charge for use of copyrighted works in the digital environment, which is achieved by deploying DRMS that restrict access and use. Technological control facilitates the translation of legal rights into pecuniary advantages achieved through (at least theoretically) improved digital exploitation conditions.

It is interesting to note a certain "distribution of labor" between TPMs and RMI. The latter does not actually restrict access and use, which is the task of TPMs designed to *technically* prevent unauthorized conducts. RMI, particularly permission-RMI, provides TPMs with the data needed to enforce differentiations among users, fine-tune the system to accommodate various use platforms and consumer needs, and in the end, make use not only secure but also profitable and attractive for consumers. As anticircumvention laws do not always cover RMI manipulations, specific prohibitions were called for to secure the integrity of RMI. Because both TPMs and RMI systems are considered important components in a secure DRM environment, both became subject to legal protection against third-party interferences. Depending on the definition given to the respective regulated component, some coverage overlap may occur, invoking norm competition issues. The extent to which anticircumvention provisions offer solutions to the problems RMI provisions seek to remedy largely depends on the domestic regulative model and approach to TPMs definition. For instance, the broader the TPM concept, the greater the chance for simultaneous coverage becomes. By and large, the ability to distinguish fact situations in which TPMs regulation apply from RMI situations significantly hinges on domestic models and the statutory definition of the terms "TPMs" and "circumvention"—as compared to "RMI," "removing," and "altering."[259] The WCT for the most part leaves those questions unsettled.

259. As a general rule of thumb, it seems prohibited *circumventions* (controlled by Art. 11) likely cover tampering with the *restricting function* of TPMs, perhaps in the sense of "cracking" (breaking) the protecting system. RMI provisions would likely apply to alteration of the rules and policies enforced by TPMs, in the sense of "hacking" (bypassing) the system.

V. ANTICIRCUMVENTION LAW IN THE UNITED STATES

A. Introduction

The Digital Millennium Copyright Act of 1998 (DMCA) is a massive enactment amending the 1976 U.S. Copyright Act that addressed many important digital copyright issues. Specifically, Title I of the DMCA (captioned "WIPO Treaties Implementation") introduced new provisions designed to comply with the protection prescribed in the WIPO Treaties.[260] The new Section 1201, canvassing the U.S. anticircumvention scheme, was designed to bring U.S. law in conformity with obligations under Article 11 WCT.[261] The legislative motivation for enacting the DMCA has been to "facilitate the robust development and worldwide expansion of electronic commerce, communications, research, development, and education in the digital age."[262] As one congressional report explained:

> Due to the ease with which digital works can be copied and distributed worldwide virtually instantaneously, copyright owners will hesitate to make their works readily available on the Internet without reasonable assurance that they will be protected against massive piracy. Legislation implementing the [WIPO] treaties provides this protection and creates the legal platform for launching the global digital on-line marketplace for copyrighted works. It will facilitate making available quickly and conveniently via the Internet the movies, music, software, and literary works that are the fruit of American creative genius. It will also encourage the continued growth of the existing off-line global marketplace for copyrighted works in digital format by setting strong international copyright standards.[263]

The Court of Appeals for the Second Circuit further explained the policy goal: "Fearful that the ease with which pirates could copy and distribute a copyrightable work in digital form was overwhelming the capacity of conventional copyright enforcement to find and enjoin unlawfully copied material, Congress sought to combat copyright piracy in its earlier stages, before the work was even copied."[264]

The DMCA anticircumvention scheme sets forth three main prohibitions, several statutory exceptions, and a rulemaking process creating periodical exceptions in certain cases. It further includes some key definitions and several general provisions. The U.S. scheme reflects a number of important design choices. First, it resolved to comply with Article 11 WCT by amending the

---

260. *See* DMCA House Conference Report 105-796 (1998) at 63 ff.

261. *See* Melville B. Nimmer and David Nimmer, Nimmer on Copyright §§ 12A.02[A]–12A.04[B][3] (2006).

262. *See* DMCA Senate Report (1998) at 1–2.

263. *Id.* at 8.

264. *See* Universal City Studios, Inc. v. Corley, 273 F.3d 429, 435 (2d. Cir 2001).

copyright statute.[265] Second, preparatory conducts are codified as direct violations of statutory copyright law. Further, the U.S. scheme draws two basic distinctions. The first separates access-controls from copy-control TPMs, and the second separates acts of actual circumvention and preparatory conducts of trafficking. Third, the catalog of exceptions is detached from the copyright exceptions both structurally and substantively. The structural division here is complete: copyright exceptions do not apply to anticircumvention violations, and anticircumvention exceptions to not protect against infringement of exclusive rights. The catalog of anticircumvention exceptions is casuistic, exhaustive, and narrowly tailored to specific situations and beneficiaries. A general fair use exception is absent from the anticircumvention apparatus,[266] and as a partial substitute for the protection of fair use interests, the Librarian of Congress is granted a limited mandate to promulgate periodical exceptions applicable to certain anticircumvention violations.[267]

B. Substantive Prohibitions of Section 1201

Section 1201(a)(1)(A) (*the anticircumvention provision*) introduced the prohibition on actual *circumvention* of a technological measure that effectively controls *access* to a work protected by copyright. This provision plainly reads: "No person shall circumvent a technological measure that effectively controls access to a work protected under this title."[268] Section 1201(a)(2) (the anti-trafficking provision) outlaws *trafficking* in *access control* circumvention devices that fall under the three alternative settings stipulated in subsections 1201(a)(2)(A)–(C).[269] The DMCA anti-trafficking provision reads:

> No person shall manufacture, import, offer to the public, provide, or otherwise traffic in any technology, product, service, device, component, or part

---

265. The legislative history of the DMCA indicates that at a certain point, it was suggested anticircumvention laws be enacted that would be "free-standing" and external to the Copyright Act. The House of Representatives Commerce Committee Report opined: "The Committee on Commerce adopted an amendment that moves the anti-circumvention provisions out of Title 17 and establishes them as free-standing provisions of law. The Committee believes that this is the most appropriate way to implement the treaties, in large part because these regulatory provisions have little, if anything, to do with copyright law. The anti-circumvention provisions (and the accompanying penalty provisions for violations of them) would be separate from, and cumulative to, the existing claims available to copyright owners." *See* DMCA House Report 105-551 (II) (1998) at 23–24.

266. A recorded attempt during the legislative process of the DMCA to introduce such a general defense did not come to pass. *See id.* at 85–86 (separate statement of Representatives Klug and Boucher).

267. The intention was to create a "fail safe" administrative mechanism for the protection of fair use interests adversely affected by the anticircumvention bans. *Id.* at 36–38.

268. *See* 17 U.S.C. § 1201(a)(1)(A).

269. *Id* § 1201(a)(2)(A)–(C).

thereof, that—

(A) is primarily designed or produced for the purpose of circumventing a technological measure that effectively controls access to a work protected under this title;

(B) has only limited commercially significant purpose or use other than to circumvent a technological measure that effectively controls access to a work protected under this title; or

(C) is marketed by that person or another acting in concert with that person with that person's knowledge for use in circumventing a technological measure that effectively controls access to a work protected under this title.[270]

The statute provides in subsections 1201(a)(3)(A)–(B) definitions for the act of "circumvent[ing] a technological measure"[271] and for a technological measure that "effectively controls access to a work" in the meaning of Section (a), respectively.[272] Finally, Section 1201(b)(1) disallows *trafficking* in devices that circumvent *copy control*[273] in situations described under subsections 1201(b)(1)(A)–(C) (additional violations provision).[274] This provision reads:

No person shall manufacture, import, offer to the public, provide, or otherwise traffic in any technology, product, service, device, component, or part thereof, that—

(A) is primarily designed or produced for the purpose of circumventing protection afforded by a technological measure that effectively protects a right of a copyright owner under this title in a work or a portion thereof;

(B) has only limited commercially significant purpose or use other than to circumvent protection afforded by a technological measure that effectively protects a right of a copyright owner under this title in a work or a portion thereof; or

(C) is marketed by that person or another acting in concert with that person with that person's knowledge for use in circumventing protection afforded

270. *Id.*

271. *Id.* § 1201(a)(3)(A) ("to 'circumvent a technological measure' means to descramble a scrambled work, to decrypt an encrypted work, or otherwise to avoid, bypass, remove, deactivate, or impair a technological measure, without the authority of the copyright owner").

272. *Id.* § 1201(a)(3)(B) ("a technological measure 'effectively controls access to a work' if the measure, in the ordinary course of its operation, requires the application of information, or a process or a treatment, with the authority of the copyright owner, to gain access to the work").

273. *Id.* § 1201(b)(1) (the term "copy control" is shorthand for the exercise of any exclusive rights granted under Section 106); *see also* U.S. Copyright Office Summery, The Digital Millennium Copyright Act (1998) (explaining the two categories of technological measures that are subject to protection under the anti-circumvention rules).

274. *Id.* at § 1201(b)(1)(A)(C).

by a technological measure that effectively protects a right of a copyright owner under this title in a work or a portion thereof.[275]

The statute furnishes in subsections 1201(b)(2)(A)–(B) definitions of the act of "circumvent[ing] protection afforded by a technological measure" and of a technological measure that "effectively protects a right of a copyright owner under this title" within the meaning of Section 1201(b), which are similar to definitions provided in the context of the anticircumvention and anti-trafficking provisions.[276] Notably, the DMCA does not prohibit actual circumvention of copy controls that would have paralleled the anticircumvention provision relating to access controls. This omission was intended to reflect the position that illegitimate conducts restricted by copy controls are already prohibited by general infringement rules and should not be subject to additional restrictions under anticircumvention law.[277] It follows circumvention of copy controls is not a violation of copyright law if the restricted conduct is noninfringing (e.g., when shielded by statutory exceptions).

C. Statutory Anticircumvention Exceptions

The DMCA delineates a number of narrowly tailored exceptions relating to the three main prohibitions. Some exceptions focus on specific beneficiaries (such as libraries[278] or government law enforcement actors),[279] while others apply to all persons (such as the reverse engineering,[280] encryption research,[281] and security testing[282] exceptions). The exceptions are casuistic and kaleidoscopic. They sometimes apply selectively to one prohibition (anticircumvention) but not to the other (anti-trafficking).[283] Their coverage adheres strictly to the particular circumstances prescribed, and in any event, they apply *exclusively* to Section 1201 violations. Anticircumvention exceptions cannot shelter from infringement liability, and in fact, if the act of circumvention also involves copyright infringement (typ-

---

275. *Id.*

276. *See* 17 U.S.C. § 1201(b)(2)(A)–(B). The most importation distinction is that the definition applied to the additional violation provision refers to a measure that "in the ordinary course of its operation, prevents, restricts, or otherwise limits *the exercise of a right of a copyright owner under this title.*" *Id.* at § 1201(b)(2)(B) (emphasis added).

277. *See* DMCA Senate Report (1998) at 12; Chamberlain Group, Inc. v. Skylink Techs., Inc., 381 F.3d 1178, 1195 (Fed. Cir. 2004).

278. *See* 17 U.S.C. § 1201(d).

279. *Id.* § 1201(e).

280. *Id.* § 1201(f).

281. *Id.* § 1201(g).

282. *Id.* § 1201(j).

283. *Id.* §§ 1201(d)–(k); *see also* Nimmer, *supra* note 13, at 700–02 (2000) (enumerating the various statutory exceptions and noting "some of section 1201's exceptions apply to the basic provision [§1201(a)(1)(A)] alone, others to this provision along with the trafficking ban [§ 1201(a)(2)], and others still to all three anti-circumvention bans").

ically the reproduction right), some DMCA exceptions will not be available to a defendant even if all other conditions are met.[284]

D. Rulemaking Process

The DMCA delegates the power to promulgate triennial exceptions to the prohibition in Section 1201(a)(1)(A) (anticircumvention ban) to the Librarian of Congress,[285] where the relevant prohibitions might adversely affect beneficiaries' ability to make noninfringing use of a particular class of copyrighted works.[286] At the time the current study was prepared, the Librarian of Congress (upon recommendations of the Register of Copyrights) has completed three rulemaking processes followed by issuance of three sets of periodical exceptions. The 2000 Rulemaking announced two exceptions,[287] the 2003 Rulemaking announced four exceptions,[288] and the 2006 Rulemaking announced six exceptions.[289] Each Rulemaking delineates circumstances concerning specific classes of copyrighted works secured by access controls, where circumvention by certain beneficiaries is permissible for a given period, notwithstanding the general anticircumvention ban.[290] For example, the 2006 Rulemaking announced an exception concerning audiovisual works included in the educational library of a college or university's

---

284. *Id.* § 1201(f)(1)–(3) (in all three of the reverse-engineering situations, the applicability of the exceptions depends on lack of infringement).

285. The announcement of exceptions takes place every three years with exceptions being valid for the subsequent period of three years, unless extended after consideration de novo.

286. *See* 17 U.S.C. § 1201(a)(1)(B)–(D).

287. *See* DMCA Rulemaking (2000) (exempting (1) compilations consisting of lists of Web sites blocked by filtering software applications, and (2) literary works, including computer programs and databases, protected by access control mechanisms that fail to permit access because of malfunction, damage, or obsolesence).

288. DMCA Rulemaking (2003) (exempting (1) compilations consisting of lists of Internet locations blocked by commercially marketed filtering software applications that are intended to prevent access to certain domains, Web sites or portions of Web sites, (2) computer programs protected by dongles that prevent access due to malfunction or damage and that are obsolete, (3) computer programs and video games distributed in formats that have become obsolete and that require the original media or hardware as a condition of access, and (4) literary works distributed in e-book format when all existing e-book editions of the work (including digital text editions made available by authorized entities) contain access controls that prevent the enabling of the e-book's read-aloud function and screen readers to render the text into a specialized format).

289. *See* DMCA Rulemaking (2006). Shortly before this book went to press, a fourth rulemaking process was completed. See Exemption to Prohibition on Circumvention of Copyright Protection Systems for Access Control Technologies, 37 CFR Pt. 201, Vol. 75, No. 143 pp. 43825-39 (July 27, 2010).

290. *See* U.S. Copyright Office Memorandum concerning the 2003 DMCA Rulemaking (2003) 4-13 (providing a thorough explanation of the Rulemaking process).

film or media studies department, when circumvention is accomplished for the purpose of making compilations of portions of those works for educational use in the classroom by media studies or film professors.[291]

E. Other Provisions

Several additional DMCA provisions are noteworthy. Section 1201(c)(1) provides "[n]othing in [Section 1201] shall affect rights, remedies, limitations, or defenses to copyright infringement, including fair use, under this title."[292] Section 1201(c)(3) is the DMCA's "no mandate" provision, clarifying that equipment manufacturers are not obligated to conform to any specific TPMs standard.[293] The statute further stipulates special civil remedies and criminal sanctions for violating the three core prohibitions.[294]

Knowledge is irrelevant for the question of civil liability under the DMCA anticircumvention scheme. However regarding civil sanctions, courts are allowed to consider "innocent violations" as grounds for reducing or remitting awards of damages.[295] By comparison, criminal sanctions require violations be willful and done for the purpose of commercial advantage or private financial gain.[296] The mechanism of anticircumvention sanctions and remedies is wholly separate from and independent of the one applicable to copyright infringement. Additionally, Section 1202 was added to the Copyright Act to reflect prohibitions concerning right management information (RMI), called in the U.S. statute Copyright Management Information (CMI).[297]

F. DMCA Anticircumvention Critique

The copyright literature abounds with DMCA critiques, in which anticircumvention laws attract much of the fire. Various aspects of this legislation were subjected to strong criticism,[298] and the passages below summarize some of the main points relating both specific features of Section 1201 and the wisdom of

---

291. *See* DMCA Rulemaking (2006) at 68473–68474.

292. *See* 17 U.S.C. § 1201(c)(1). This provision does not seem to qualify fair use defense as directly applicable to anticircumvention and anti-trafficking violations.

293. *Id.* § 1201(c)(3) ("Nothing in this section shall require that the design of, or design and selection of parts and components for, a consumer electronics, telecommunications, or computing product provide for a response to any particular technological measure, so long as such part or component, or the product in which such part or component is integrated, does not otherwise fall within the prohibitions of subsection (a)(2) or (b)(1).").

294. *Id.* §§ 1203–1204.

295. *Id.* § 1203(c)(5).

296. *Id.* § 1204(a).

297. *Id.* § 1202.

298. For a summary covering the main objections, *see* Besek, *supra* note 6, at 467–69; Peter Yu, *Anticircumvention and Anti-Anticircumvention*, 84 Denv. U.L. Rev. 13, 34–40 (2006).

anticircumvention regulation in general. The objections targeting Section 1201 often exemplify fairly well the principal reservations concerning anticircumvention law in general.

1. Structural Issues: Complexity, Inconsistency, Transparency

Anticircumvention laws are complex and rich in detailed provisions. They draw fine distinctions that occasionally provide the basis for vague or ambivalent rules. Critics generally attack the DMCA for being highly complicated.[299] Overcomplexity is especially troublesome when the law affects ordinary citizens in the most direct sense, having application to and influence on their daily affairs. Section 1201's complexity is reflected, inter alia, in the long list of detailed exceptions and effect of the Rulemaking mechanism on the scope of permissible acts.

Awkward formulation of elaborate rules occasionally leads to logical inconsistencies and exceptions that cannot be reasonably exercised without risking being in violation of the anti-trafficking provision.[300] For example, when beneficiaries of statutory anticircumvention exceptions (e.g., libraries and archives)[301] themselves are technically unable to exercise their liberty to break access protection systems without assistance, providing them with services or tools is still prohibited under the anti-trafficking and possibly, the additional violations provisions.[302] Similarly, the authority to promulgate periodical exceptions does not extend to acts of providing beneficiaries with the circumvention tools they need to exercise their privileges. For instance, the law exempts media students and film professors as beneficiaries of the first 2006 Rulemaking exception. These specific beneficiaries are allowed to circumvent audiovisual works themselves for the purpose of educational or classroom use. However, the administrative Rulemaking lacks competence to exempt related violations of the anti-trafficking provision.

---

299. *See, e.g.*, Jessica Litman, Digital Copyright 142 (2001) ("Copyright bills never seen to get shorter, clearer, or less complicated when 'improved' through the negotiation process . . . By the time that the Digital Millennium Copyright Act passed the Senate, the legislation had ballooned to something in the neighborhood of ten thousand words . . . The legislation has been assembled in a hurry, and was riddled with ambiguities, internal inconsistencies, contradictions, and obfuscatory prose.") *See also* Nimmer, *supra* note 23, at 1342–43.

300. *See* Nimmer, *supra* note 13, 734–39.

301. *See* 17 U.S.C. § 1201(d)(1) ("A nonprofit library, archives, or educational institution which gains access to a commercially exploited copyrighted work solely in order to make a good faith determination of whether to acquire a copy of that work for the sole purpose of engaging in conduct permitted under this title shall not be in violation of subsection (a)(1)(A).").

302. Liability under the additional violation is possible when the scope of libraries' exceptions against infringement and the scope of their anticircumvention exceptions do not overlap.

One major risk related to overcomplexity is in blurring the line between acts that are controlled by the copyright statute and acts that are not, as well as uncertainty concerning the actual impact of regulation when it does apply. A complex legislation obscures the true effect of the law on the interests of stakeholders, making it easier to create a pretence of balance even though it is not really the case. When provisions devoted to protecting nonowners are numerous, but their application scope is extremely thin, it is more difficult to see why those protections are insufficient, which leads to a certain transparency problem. Perhaps the most significant dimension of the transparency problem is that anticircumvention laws generally (and despite statements to the contrary in legislative history records) *in fact create a new exclusive right,*[303] or more precisely, move the system of owners' protections closer to an access-right regime. Nevertheless, during the legislative process anticircumvention laws were rarely debated as adding a completely new weapon to the arsenal of copyright exclusory entitlements.

2. A Problematic Distinction: Access-Control versus Copy-Control TPMs

In the structure of Section 1201, the distinction between technological access-controls and copy-controls is crucial. Circumvention of copy-control TPMs is not at all prohibited. Further, the various DMCA exceptions apply selectively according to the classification of a certain TPM along the terms of this distinction. In addition, the Rulemaking process applies only to circumvention of access-control TPMs. The DMCA legislative history indicates access-control TPMs, covered by Sections 1201(a)(1)–(2), are TPMs that protect against unauthorized "initial access," whereas copy-control TPMs subject to Section 1201(b) are measures that "effectively protect [owners'] copyrights."[304]

This distinction is designed to play a key policy role in the attempt to create a balanced regime. According to the legislative intent, access controls generally receive greater protection and are subject to fewer exceptions.[305] If the distinction is murky, or worse, proves unworkable, the entire edifice of Section 1201 and its quest for equilibrium are jeopardized. Despite its cardinal importance, the statutory distinction between access controls and "copy" (or "rights") controls suffers from insufficient clarity. In the absence of a specific explanation about the

---

303. *See, e.g.*, Koelman & Helberger, *supra* note 100, at 201–02 (the DMCA has effectively added "a new 'right to control access' [] for the benefit of right-holders that apply [TPMs]").

304. *See* DMCA House Report 105-551 (II) (1998) at 39. *See also* DMCA Senate Report (1998) at 29. An earlier House Report would have inserted the phrase "initial access" into the statutory definition of access-control TPMs. *See* DMCA House Report 105-551 (I) (1998) at 19. But this phrase mysteriously disappeared in the course of the legislative process and is not included in Section 1201.

305. *See, e.g.*, R. Anthony, Reese, *Will Merging Access Controls and Rights Controls Undermine the Structure of Anticircumvention Law?* 18 BERKELEY TECH. L.J. 619, 631 (2003).

difference between measures that secure "initial" access and those that restrict "non-initial" access—as well as their distinction from other types of "use" controls—it becomes more difficult to decide which norm to apply in many borderline cases.

Indeed, critics argue the distinction might collapse in various real-life situations,[306] and this concern can only be exacerbated as the classic reproduction right virtually merges with the first access-right prong discussed in Chapter 4.[307] A broad conception of access-control TPMs can embrace nearly all TPMs as such, perhaps excluding some very basic copy controls such as the SCMS and similar mechanisms having today only a marginal significance, which call into question the logic behind drawing this distinction in the first place. It is important to recall the distinction is premised on a fairly clear division between copyright-implicating acts (e.g., reproduction, distribution, etc.) and access-conducts from which the division between different types of TPMs becomes derivable. The shakiness of this premise, however, seriously undermines Section 1201's structure and intended operation.

3. Overbroad Prohibitions and Narrow Exceptions

The Copyright Act outlines numerous statutory limitations, exceptions, and defenses to equilibrate the copyright regime and calibrate the scope exclusive control.[308] In addition, the case law furnishes a number of protections against direct infringement liability (e.g., reverse engineering),[309] as well as protections against indirect infringement liability (e.g., multipurpose devices).[310] Those exemptions are an important part of the copyright balance, yet some critics argue their expression in the anticircumvention scheme is far too modest. Interestingly, the early DMCA-proposed legislation bill mentioned nearly no exception at all.[311] Working its way through the legislative hearings, later Congressional reports and lobbying campaigns, additional anticircumvention exceptions and the Rulemaking mechanism found their way into the statutory text.[312] The result was

---

306. *Id.* at 647 ff (referring to the problem of "merged" technological protection measures that combine both access and "copy" controls); Jacqueline D. Lipton, *Solving the Digital Piracy Puzzle : Disaggregating Fair Use from the DMCA's Anti-Device. Provisions*, 19 HARV. J. L. & TECH. 111, 124–27 (2005) (reviewing the critique in the context of the fair use defense).

307. Chapter 4, Section VI *supra*.

308. *See* 17 U.S.C. §§ 107–122.

309. *See, e.g.*, Sega Enter. Ltd. v. Accolade, Inc. 977 F.2d. 1510 (9th. Cir 1993).

310. *See, e.g.*, Sony Corp. v. Universal City Studios, Inc., 464 U.S. 417 (1984).

311. *See* DMCA House Report 105-551 (I) (1998) at 4–5 (the text approved by the House Judiciary Committee listed only an extremely narrow exception for nonprofit libraries, archives, and educational institutions, as well as an additional exception for law enforcement and intelligence activities).

312. *See* David Nimmer, *Appreciating Legislative History: The Sweet and Sour Spots of the DMCA's Commentary*, 23 CARDOZO L. REV. 909 (2002) (providing a detailed account of the

a parallel, elaborate, standing-alone exceptions apparatus having the mission of counterweighting rights-holders' entitlements for the "limited" purpose of anticircumvention law. As unlawful circumvention is not infringement, an exemption concerning infringement liability cannot apply to circumvention violations. Furthermore, protections of indirect infringement liability developed by the case law are inapplicable to anti-trafficking violations and thus, statutory anticircumvention exceptions constitute the main instrument capable in theory of delimiting Section 1201 liability. The critique purports that the existing statutory exceptions are inadequately restrictive and ramshackle.[313]

4. Bending Copyright Subject Matter and Duration Rules

Copyright protection famously extends only to the original or creative elements of the expression. In the United States, protection is granted to "original works of authorship"[314] and not to "any idea, procedure, process, system, method of operation, concept, principle or discovery."[315] Also "facts" reside outside copyright exclusivity.[316] In addition, the duration of copyright protection is limited.[317] Nonoriginal messages, negative categories of message elements, and works for which the protection term has elapsed are completely free from copyright restrictions. Section 1201 (and copyright anticircumvention regulation in general) technically covers only TPMs that restrict access and use with respect to eligible copyright subject matter. To the extent TPMs control access to a copyrighted work, they also block access to the noncopyrightable elements of the message. And to the extent public domain works are restricted by the same technological protection together with works still under copyright, the new prohibitions might contribute to private enclosure trends on the public domain effectuated by punishing circumvention.[318]

This has been one of the most persistent critiques with respect to anticircumvention regulation in general, which calls for a short comment here. There is something naïve in the complaint technological means block access both to the

---

DMCA's legislative history).

313. *See, e.g.*, Pamela Samuelson, *Intellectual Property and the Digital Economy: Why the Anti-Circumvention Regulations Need to Be Revised*, 14 Berkeley Tech. L.J.. 519, 546–57 (1999); Dan L. Burk, *Anti-Circumvention Misuse*, 50 UCLA L. Rev. 1095, 1107 (2003).

314. *See* 17 U.S.C. § 102(a).

315. *See* 17 U.S.C. § 102(b).

316. *See* Feist Publishing, Inc. v. Rural Tel. Serv. Co., 499 U.S. 340 (1991). Defining noncopyrightable "facts" in this context is not as obvious as it may seem at first glance. For a critical analysis, see Justin Hughes, *Created Facts and the Flawed Ontology of Copyright Law*, 83 Notre Dame L. Rev. 43 (2007).

317. *See* 17 U.S.C. §§ 302–305.

318. *See, e.g.*, Yochai Benkler, The Wealth of Networks: How Social Production Transforms Markets and Freedom 415 ff (2006). *See also* Reto M. Hilty, *The Expansion of Copyright Law and its Social Justification*, *in* Copyright Law and the Information Society in Asia 12–13 (Christopher Heath & Kung-Chung Liu eds., 2007).

idea and to the expression. The idea/expression distinction is based on the assumption mere access is not directly affected by the exercise of copyright exclusivity, as opposed to acts such as reproductions, communications, and other types of conducts that involve information use and exploitation. Thereby, ideas are said to remain theoretically "free" from copyright constraints.

This idealized view must be confronted with the recognition that limited access both to expressions *and to their underlying ideas* will always be a more or less disturbing consequence of copyright regulation, depending on the actual effect of copyright law on access opportunities in general.[319] Formally denying negative categories (such as ideas, facts, or news items) of copyright protection operates to the benefit of nonowners if, and only if, alternative access avenues not subordinated to the veto power of rights-holders remain open.[320] Therefore, this line of critique in the context of anticircumvention regulation could be phrased in the following way: the danger is that anticircumvention laws would accelerate the migration from analog to digital TPM-protected formats, thereby rendering alternative (analog) access avenues comparatively scarcer. In that case, negative categories cannot fulfill their traditional balancing role, and the eminent distinction between original and nonoriginal work elements would lose much of its practical significance .[321]

5. Chilling and Cross Effects

Chilling effect is a term used to describe the DMCA's negative impact on innovation, creativity, and other socially desirable activities. Particularly in the context of the DMCA trafficking prohibition, critics contended technological innovations (as well as research and development in the area of cryptology, reverse engineering, and consumer electronics) might be substantially chilled by the fear of incurring DMCA liability.[322] Cryptologists who publish the results of their research about weaknesses and flows of protection measures might be held liable.[323] Product developers who distribute devices and technologies that can be used to bypass DRM permissions might be accountable for illicit trafficking.

The crux of the matter is that the actual effects of anti-trafficking provisions can hardly be channeled neatly in the desired direction to capture the "intended" violators. Those effects are difficult to predict, and the relevant restrictions on

---

319. *Cf.* Chapter 1, Section V.C *supra.*

320. This proposition will receive more discussion in the next chapter. *See* Chaper 7, Section II.B *infra.*

321. *Cf.* de Werra, *supra* note 100, at 118–19.

322. *See* the EFF Report, *Unintended Consequences: Seven Years under the DMCA* (2006) (criticizing the DMCA as, inter alia, chilling free speech and impeding competition and innovations).

323. For a detailed study on the DMCA's effect on software encryption, security, and research, see Deidre K. Mulligan & Aaron Perzanowski, *The Magnificence of the Disaster: Reconstructing the Sony BMG Rootkit Incident*, 22 BERKELEY TECH. L. J. (2007).

behavior never capture *only* infringement-relevant activities. The chilling effect argument is part of a broader spillover concern relating to the unintended consequences of anticircumvention bans that are undesired by the legislature and are said to be unwise as a matter of information policy.[324] The *Chamberlain* and *Lexmark* decisions revealed some of the possible unanticipated applications of the law on downstream competition in the secondary market for interoperable devices.[325] When certain products require "access" to a copyrighted computer program in the course of their normal operation, and when makers of such products (who are also copyright holders in the software) choose to employ a protection mechanism to block such "access" unless "authorized," competitors distributing components in the secondary market will be exposed to (hitherto largely unsuccessful) anti-trafficking allegations.[326]

6. Free Speech and Privacy Concerns

The term *chilling effect* is also conjured up in the context of the apprehension to exercise free speech privileges. The tension between free speech privileges and copyright exclusivity[327] is said to intensify when works are technologically protected.[328] An overarching private control over how and under which conditions nonowners are allowed to receive and produce information invoked concerns relating to the ability to exercise constitutional freedoms, intertwined with a warning that in the digital environment, traditional safeguards of fair use and the idea/expression distinction erode. The broad restrictions imposed by the DMCA on the distribution of circumvention information (which Section 1201 defines as trafficking violations) were said to abrogate free speech guarantees under the First Amendment to the U.S. Constitution.[329] Additionally, the surveillance capacity of DRMS and legal protection related to RMI components against interferences and manipulations raised anxiety concerning the harm to privacy interests.[330]

---

324. *See* Efroni, *supra* note 101; Jacqueline D. Lipton, *The Law of Unintended Consequences: The Digital Millennium Copyright Act and Interoperability*, 62 Washington & Lee L. Rev. 487 (2005).

325. The facts of these decisions are described in Chapter 3. *See* Chapter 3, Section II.B.2.

326. Section V.G *infra* (reviewing litigation that exemplified such attempts).

327. Chapter 3, Section III.B.2(c) (reviewing the tension between copyright law and free speech).

328. *See, e.g.*, Yochai Benkler, *Free as the Air to Common Use: First Amendment Constraints on Enclosure of the Public Domain*, 74 N.Y.U. L. Rev. 354, 415 ff (1999).

329. *See, e.g.*, L. Ray Patterson, *The DMCA: A Modern Version of the Licensing Act of 1662*, 10 J. Intell. Prop. L. 33 (2002).

330. *See, e.g.*, Bygrave & Koelman, *Privacy, Data Protection and Copyright: Their Interaction in the Context of Electronic Copyright Management Systems*, *in* Copyright and Electronic Commerce (P. Bernt Hugenholtz ed., 2000); Ian R. Kerr, *To Observe and Protect? How Digital Rights Management Systems Threaten Privacy and What Policy Makers*

7. Conflict with Social Norms and Practices

Traditional copyright rules mirror social norms and generally acceptable allocations of entitlements concerning informational resources. The ability of a book owner to read a book in private circumstances has been completely unaffected by copyright rules. If rights-holders hypothetically demanded to supervise the number of times an owner of a physical book may read it, such demand would probably be considered socially unacceptable and absurd, practically unenforceable, and clearly outside the "bargain" between authors and their readers copyright law is said to manifest.

The structure of copyright was shaped to correspond both to the technical limitations of analog media and social conventions as it drew the line between areas of freedom and the property regime.[331] Digital technology has been changing the rules of the game dramatically, and users are increasingly confronted with copyright restrictions, which are said to conflict with norms of behavior and general conventions about acts that are lawful and acts that are not.[332]

Imperfect enforcement of exclusivity in the analog information environment corresponded to and mirrored existing social norms to some extent by establishing informal yet effective boundaries to copyright control. These norms of permissible behavior also reflected a certain status quo that all stakeholders could accept. As part of this status quo, formal copyright rules covered only *some* communication-conducts, and the enforcement of exclusive rights has never been hermetic. These types of checks and balances in the analog information environment cannot operate in the same way as we shift to the digital setting, where rights-holders can better enforce their control over both activities within the province of copyright exclusivity and those traditionally outside the scope of their control in the first place.[333] The costs of such control become more manageable and the supervision of the behavior of users becomes more effective. Minor (or de minimis) "violations" engaged in by private persons in their intimate social and family circles that were ignored by rights-holders in the past (or activities that have been covered by non-voluntary licenses and certain exemptions) gradually came under a right-to-exclude regime. At bottom, there is a growing sense of

---

Should Do About It, in 1 INTELLECTUAL PROPERTY AND INFORMATION WEALTH: COPYRIGHT AND RELATED RIGHTS (Peter Yu ed., 2007).

331. *Cf.* Michael J. Madison, *Fair Use and Social Practices, in* INTELLECTUAL PROPERTY AND INFORMATION WEALTH: COPYRIGHT AND RELATED RIGHTS (Peter Yu ed., 2007) (arguing for a "social practices approach" to the fair use doctrine).

332. *See, e.g.*, Mark F. Schulz, *Copynorms: Copyright Law and Social Norms, in* INTELLECTUAL PROPERTY AND INFORMATION WEALTH: COPYRIGHT AND RELATED RIGHTS (Peter Yu ed., 2007).

333. *See, e.g.*, Ann Bartow, *Electrifying Copyright Norms and Making Cyberspace More Like a Book*, 48 VILLANOVA L. REV. 13 (2003).

frustration among nonowners leading to a serious legitimacy problem: novel legal rules overriding long-standing behavioral norms risk a clash between the grassroots' sense of fairness and copyright enforcement that ever more intrusively affects many aspects of their lives. As a consequence, the legitimacy of copyright law *in general* is called into question.

G. Section 1201 in Court

1. Overview

Past years yielded numerous court decisions in the United States addressing claims of unlawful circumvention and trafficking.[334] The bulk of the case law reveals two judicial patterns. The first pattern, predominant in earlier decisions, adheres generally to the black letter of the DMCA. First-pattern courts tend to support their analysis and conclusions by citing chapters from the DMCA legislative history, which explains the motivation for the new prohibitions in this area. Those courts exhibited a notable aversion to departing from the explicit statutory framework, which often led to a broad application and a high likelihood anticircumvention liability would be found.

By contrast, the second pattern of decisions demonstrates a higher degree judicial independence and less reliance on the literal language of Section 1201. Here, the anticircumvention provisions are applied in a fashion more compatible with the courts' vision of the boundaries of copyright liability.[335] Decisions falling in the purview of the second pattern are generally more sympathetic to defendants, as some courts proved more skeptical about the issue of access control and the proper match between DMCA liability and traditional copyright exceptions.[336] The watershed signifying the departure from the early (and more conservative) judicial approach was clearly the landmark decision of the Federal Circuit in *Chamberlain v. Skylink*.[337] In *Chamberlain*, the Federal Circuit was the

---

334. The anticircumvention prohibition entered into force in 2000 after two years' moratorium (counting from the date of enactment). *See* § 1201(a)(1)(A). The other two prohibitions (anti-trafficking and additional violations) became effective immediately in 1998. *See* Title I, Sec. 105 of the DMCA.

335. *See* Zohar Efroni, *Towards a Doctrine of "Fair Access" in Copyright: The Federal Circuit's Accord*, 46 IDEA 99 (2005). *See also* Timothy K. Armstrong, *Fair Circumvention*, 74 BROOK. L. REV. 1 (2008).

336. The distinction between the two patterns described above is based on the court's *approach* to the new anticircumvention bans and their appropriate scope. It is not necessarily guided by the end result (defendant's liability yes-or-no). Further, there is no clear chronological line separating the two patterns, though second-pattern decisions began to emerge comparatively late.

337. *See* Chamberlain Group, Inc. v. Skylink Techs., Inc., 381 F.3d 1178 (Fed. Cir. 2004).

first court to depart from a per se application of the DMCA anticircumvention provisions, which it later restated and expanded in *Storage Technology. v. Custom Hardware.*[338]

2. The Early (Conservative) Judicial Pattern

In one of the earliest anticircumvention decisions in the United States, the district court in *Realnetworks v. Streambox*[339] held that defendant's product, the Streambox VCR, likely violated Section 1201 in two respects. First, it allowed unauthorized access to the server transmitting media files, bypassing a "secret handshake" procedure that was supposed to take place between the RealServer and plaintiff's software, the RealPlayer.[340] Second, the function of a "Copy Switch" had been dismantled on the accused product; the switch prevented unauthorized copying (downloading) of files transmitted by streaming technology.[341]

In another early decision from 1999, the district court in *Sony v. Gamemasters*[342] held the distribution of a product—a video game modification device known as "Game Enhancer"—was likely to violate the DMCA anti-trafficking provision because it enabled users to overcome technological measures that restricted access from certain game consoles (the Sony PlayStation device) to certain game CDs according to the geographical origin of the CDs.[343] This mechanism allowed plaintiff Sony to control the geographical distribution of its games; regional access control was achieved by employing regional codes that matched the geographical origin of the game console with the CD-ROM played on it. As the Game Enhancer enabled consumers to play and import "non-territorial" video games,[344] the court accepted Sony's contention regarding the likelihood of violation of the anti-trafficking provision and issued an injunction.[345]

United States v. Elcom Ltd.[346] involved a criminal prosecution for violating the DMCA anti-trafficking provision directed against a Russian company and its owner for developing and selling a product (a Windows-based software program) that allowed a user to remove use restrictions from Adobe Acrobat PDF files and

---

338. *See* Storage Tech. Corp. v. Custom Hardware Eng'g, Inc. (Fed. Cir. 2005).

339. *See* Realnetworks, Inc. v. Streambox, Inc., 2000 WL 127311 (W.D. Wash. 2000).

340. *Id.* at 6–10 (finding it likely the defendant had violated the anti-trafficking provision).

341. *Id.* (finding it likely the defendant was liable under the additional violations provision). The court earlier explained at length the difference between streaming and downloading. *Id.* at 1–2.

342. *See* Sony Computer Entm't Am., Inc. v. Gamemasters, Inc., 87 F.Supp. 2d. 976 (N.D. Cal. 1999).

343. *Id.* at 987–88.

344. *Id.* at 981–82.

345. *Id.* at 989.

346. *See* United States v. Elcom Ltd., 203 F.Supp. 2d. 1111 (N.D. Cal. 2002).

files formatted for the Adobe eBook Reader. The program allowed a purchaser of an eBook Reader-formatted electronic book to convert the format to one readable in any PDF viewer without the use restrictions imposed by the publisher.[347] In this case, the court rejected, inter alia, various arguments challenging the constitutionality of DMCA.[348]

In *Universal City Studios v. Reimerdes*[349] the district court provided a detailed analysis of the DMCA anticircumvention provisions and concluded that online posting of source and object code of a software (DeCSS), which could defeat encryption technology for DVDs (CSS), as well as posting links to Web sites where such software was made available, violated the DMCA anti-trafficking provision.[350] This decision was later affirmed by the Court of Appeals for the Second Circuit in *Universal City Studios v. Corley*.[351]

Some time later, the district court in *321 Studios v. MGM Studios*[352] ruled the distribution of software designed to facilitate backup copies of DVDs protected by CSS, allowing consumers to bypass the CSS protection against copying of their legally acquired DVD, violated both the DMCA anti-trafficking and additional violations provisions.[353]

Another 2004 district court decision, *Davidson & Associates v. Internet Gateway*,[354] concerned plaintiffs who created and sold computer games played on personal computers, allowing users who logged in to their online gaming server (called Battle.net) to play and compete against each other over the Internet.[355] The service was freely available for purchasers of lawful copies of the games, but did not allow the playing of unauthorized game versions via the official Battle.net server by performing an authentication process.[356] When defendants, a group of volunteers and game enthusiasts who sought to improve the Battle.net service, created a competing service (called bnetd project) that allowed users to play unauthorized versions without being blocked by the authentication process,[357] the court

347. *Id.* at 1118.

348. *Id.* at 1122–42.

349. *See* Universal City Studios, Inc. v. Reimerdes, 111 F.Supp. 2d. 294, (S.D.N.Y. 2000).

350. *Id.* at 316–25.

351. *See* Universal City Studios, Inc. v. Corley, 273 F.3d 429 (2d. Cir. 2001).

352. *See* 321 Studios v. Metro Goldwyn Studios, Inc., 307 F.Supp. 2d. 1085 (N.D. Cal. 2004).

353. *Id.* at 1094–1199. *See also* Paramount Pictures Corp. v. 321 Studios, 2004 WL 402756 (S.D.N.Y. 2004).

354. *See* Davidson & Assoc. v. Internet Gateway, 334 F.Supp. 2d. 1164 (E.D. Mis. 2004).

355. *Id/* at 1168–69.

356. *Id.* at 1169.

357. *Id.* at 1171–74.

found them liable for violating both the DMCA anticircumvention and anti-trafficking provisions.[358] This decision was later affirmed by the Court of Appeals for the Eight Circuit in *Davidson & Associates v. Jung*.[359] The court refused to apply the codified DMCA reverse engineering exception because circumvention involved copyright infringement, in which case the reverse engineering exception in Section 1201(f) did not apply.[360]

More recently, in *Ticketmaster v. RMG Technologies*,[361] the district court upheld anticircumvention claims brought by a vendor (Ticketmaster) that sold tickets for entertainment and sports events on behalf of its clients to the general public through a variety of means, including its copyrighted Web site. Defendant RMG developed and marketed automated devices to access and navigate through Ticketmaster's Web site.[362] The court held the products RMG developed likely violated the anti-trafficking provision because they allowed users to bypass an identification and control system (known as CAPTCHA) designed to block automated devices from reaching the ticket purchase pages.[363] The court upheld Section 1201 liability after concluding the "CAPTCHA both *controls access* to a protected work because a user cannot proceed to copyright protected webpages without solving CAPTCHA, and *protects rights* of a copyright owner because, by preventing automated access to the ticket purchase webpage, CAPTCHA prevents users from copying those pages."[364]

This partial list of Section 1201 decisions generally demonstrates the high level of technical complexity and specificity of characteristics in disputes over TPMs circumvention. In the cases mentioned above and in many others, defendants failed to persuade the court their actions were shielded by DMCA statutory exceptions. Nor were defendants successful in invoking the fair use defense or constitutional challenges to the DMCA.[365] But despite their technically specific nature, many fact patterns share similar features: they typically involve

---

358. *Id.* at 1183–87.

359. *See* Davidson & Assoc. v. Jung, 422 F.3d. 630 (8th. Cir. 2005).

360. *Id.* at 641–42.

361. *See* Ticketmaster LLC v. RMG Tech., Inc., 507 F.Supp. 2d 1096 (C.D. Cal. 2007).

362. *Id.* at 1102.

363. *Id.* at 1111 ff. The CAPTCHA "presents 'a box with stylized random characters partially obscured behind hash marks.'. . . The user is required to type the characters into an entry on the screen in order to proceed with the request . . . Most automated devices cannot decipher and type the random characters and thus cannot proceed to the copyrighted ticket purchase pages." *Id.* at 1112.

364. *Id.* (italicization in original).

365. The district court in *Reimerdes* clearly rejected the application of the fair use defense to anticircumvention allegations: "Defendants . . . are not here sued for copyright infringement. They are sued for offering and providing technology designed to circumvent technological measures that control access to copyrighted works and otherwise violating Section 1201(a)(2) of the [Copyright] Act. If Congress had meant the fair use defense

entertainment and software products such as video games, music, and video or multimedia works that often have a dominant connection to network distribution and exploitation. Rights-holders attempt to technologically restrict unauthorized activities, and defendants (for reasons ranging from an "anarchist" view on copyright to an outright promotion of commercial self-interests) provided technological "solutions" to avoid those restrictions.

3. Second-Generation Case Law

In *Chamberlain v. Skylink*, the Federal Circuit held that trafficking in universal remote control devices that interoperated with plaintiff's products (automatic garage door openers) did not violate the anti-trafficking provision, despite the plaintiff employing a technological mechanism that "controlled access" to the computer program managing the operation of the doors.[366] Interestingly, in dismissing the anti-trafficking allegations, the court resorted neither to the DMCA special exceptions nor to traditional copyright limitations or exceptions. Instead, the court created a new threshold requirement for anticircumvention complaints: plaintiff must show a *reasonable relationship* between circumvention of TPMs and traditional copyright infringement.[367] Plaintiff's failure to show the alleged circumvention of the authentication sequence process taking place between remote control devices and the garage door software had any "reasonable relationship" to the protection of copyrights in the software led the court to dismiss the DMCA trafficking claims.[368]

In *Lexmark v. Static Control*, the Court of Appeals for the Sixth Circuit dismissed anti-trafficking allegations against a defendant manufacturing electronic chips that allowed consumers to use "unauthorized" toner cartridges for laser printers.[369] In reversing the lower court's decision and remanding for further proceeding, the Sixth Circuit indicated the TPMs applied by plaintiff (Lexmark) did not qualify as access-control TPMs within the meaning of Section 1201(a)(3),[370] and further indicated the DMCA exception covering reverse engineering for interoperability purposes in Section 1201(f)(3) could apply.[371]

---

to apply to such actions, it would have said so." *See* Universal City Studios, Inc. v. Reimerdes, 111 F.Supp. 2d. 294, 322 (S.D.N.Y. 2000).

366. *See* Chamberlain Group, Inc. v. Skylink Techs., Inc., 381 F.3d 1178 (Fed. Cir. 2004).

367. *See id.* at 1202 ("We conclude that 17 U.S.C. § 1201 prohibits only forms of access that bear a reasonable relationship to the protections that the Copyright Act otherwise affords copyright owners.").

368. *Id.* at 1203 ("Here, [plaintiff] can point to no protected property right that [defendant] imperils.").

369. *See* Lexmark Int'l Inc. v. Static Control Components, Inc., 387 F.3d 522 (6th Cir. 2004).

370. *Id.* at 546–50 (rejecting the assertion the authentication sequence verifying information on the cartridge chip qualified as an effective technological measure that controlled access to work within the meaning of Sec. 1201(a)(3)).

371. *Id.* at 550–51.

Later, the Federal Circuit in *Storage Technologies v. Custom Hardware* continued developing its "reasonable relationship" doctrine. In vacating and remanding the lower instance's decision, *Storage Technologies* dismissed Section 1201(a)(1) claims against a service company that repaired computerized data storage libraries while mimicking a certain password-protected process to identify system malfunctions.[372] Two elements underpinned the rejection of the circumvention allegations. First, based on the conclusion appellee Storage Technologies was unlikely to succeed on the merits of its *copyright infringement* claim (due to an available defense in Section 117 of the Copyright Act), the court concluded the entry requisite for a DMCA violation could not be established.[373] This assertion is remarkable as Section 117 provides a defense against copyright infringement—not against unlawful circumvention of access-control TPMs.[374] The possible implication is that when the act prevented by the access control TPM is privileged under a statutory copyright exception, circumvention of the measure is not unlawful under section 1201(a)(1)(A), which appears to contradict the logic and structure of the DMCA anticircumvention scheme.[375]

Second, even if Storage Technologies were able to prove the automatic copying of the maintenance software to the RAM *did* constitute non-excused copyright infringement, the court stressed appellee had still failed to prove appellant Custom Hardware's circumvention process *facilitated* that infringement.[376] The court held: "The activation of the maintenance code may violate [Appellee's] contractual rights vis-à-vis its customers, but those rights are not the rights protected by copyright law. There is simply not a sufficient nexus between the rights protected by copyright law and the circumvention of [Storage Tech.'s] system."[377]

The three decisions reviewed above established principles that are quite significant for the future development of anticircumvention laws in the United States. All three rulings share several common elements: The disputes involve computer programs as the copyrighted work protected by TPMs. Those computer programs performed specific and highly functional tasks, which were

---

372. *See* Storage Tech. Corp. v. Custom Hardware Eng'g, Inc., 421 F.3d. 1307, 1309–10 (Fed. Cir. 2005) (describing plaintiff's and defendant's systems and the software at issue).

373. *Id.* at 1318 ("To the extent that [Appellant's] activities do not constitute copyright infringement or facilitate copyright infringement, [Appellee] is foreclosed from maintaining an action under the DMCA.").

374. *See* 17 U.S.C. § 117(c). This subsection was added to the Copyright Act by Title III to the DMCA to release machine maintenance services and repair activities from infringement liability resulting from reproductions of computer programs.

375. For more discussion, see Efroni, *supra* note 335, at 137–39.

376. *See Storage Tech.*, 421 F.3d. at 1319.

377. *Id.* See also, MGE USP Systems Inc., v. GE Consumer et al., No. 08-10521 (5th Cir. 2010) (applying the reasonable relationship proviso to deny anticircumvention liability.)

related to securing and managing the operation of electronic devices and computer systems. Further, rights-holders asserting DMCA violations appeared much more concerned about preserving their position in the markets for goods and services than typical copyright plaintiffs who are worried about infringement, and in fact, the markets plaintiffs sought to control were not markets for creative expression, but rather for consumer electronics and services. In all cases, the nexus between the accused acts and copyright protections against unauthorized reproduction, distribution, or communication of creative works was exceedingly faint. Second-generation courts refused to grant anticircumvention protections in such circumstances, with policy motivation clearly guiding their analysis. Even though those courts did not always describe their rulings as such, they attempted to correct the results possible under a per se reading of the statute. It is hard to overlook the tension between the two judicial patterns of Section 1201 interpretation and application.[378]

VI. ARTICLE 6 OF THE E.U. INFORMATION SOCIETY DIRECTIVE

A. Overview

The EUCD marks an important junction in European lawmaking as it entered the era of "second-generation" copyright directives in 2001. That Directive sought to fill gaps left by first-generation directives, harmonize some aspects of domestic legal frameworks, increase legal certainty, and provide a high level of copyright protection.[379] The need for a greater degree of harmonization was explained by technological developments that "multiplied and diversified the vectors for creation, production and exploitation"[380] and by the requirement to implement "new international obligations" in the aftermath of the WIPO Treaties.[381]

The Directive expressed the view "[a] rigorous, effective system for the protection of copyright and related rights is one of the main ways of ensuring that European cultural creativity and production receive the necessary resources and of safeguarding the independence and dignity of artistic creators and performers."[382] At the same time, it pointed out "[a] fair balance of rights and

378. *See* Efroni, *supra* note 101, at 308–10.

379. *See* EUCD (2001), Recital 4 ("A harmonised legal framework on copyright and related rights, through increased legal certainty and while providing for a high level of protection of intellectual property, will foster substantial investment in creativity and innovation, including network infrastructure, and lead in turn to growth and increased competitiveness of European industry, both in the area of content provision and information technology and more generally across a wide range of industrial and cultural sectors. This will safeguard employment and encourage new job creation.").

380. *Id.* Recital 5.

381. *Id.* Recital 15.

382. *Id.* Recital 11.

interests between the different categories of rightholders, as well as between the different categories of rightholders and users of protected subject-matter must be safeguarded."[383]

The EUCD launched an ambitious attempt to provide Community-level solutions to technology's challenges in the field of copyright law. It instructed Member States to secure a broadly defined reproduction right,[384] provide for exclusive rights of communicating and making available to the public,[385] and safeguard the exclusive right of distribution.[386] The Directive further provides obligatory guidelines in the area of copyright exemptions. It articulates a uniform Community exhaustion rule;[387] prescribes a narrow mandatory exception to the reproduction right;[388] adds a catalog of permissible exceptions to the reproduction right;[389] and lists fifteen permissible exceptions to the reproduction, communication, and making- available rights.[390]

The Directive further embodies an "enforcement" provision, stating members must provide "appropriate sanctions and remedies in respect of infringements of the rights and obligations set out in this Directive."[391] Article 12(1) EUCD established a periodical review process concerning the application of the Directive, particularly regarding exceptions, technological protection measures, and the communication and making-available rights.[392] Implementing Article 12 WCT, the EUCD stipulates a framework for protecting rights management information.[393] Finally, obligations under Article 11 WCT concerning technological protection measures are regulated in Article 6 EUCD.

---

383. *Id.* Recital 31. It added that "existing exceptions and limitations to the rights as set out by the Member States have to be reassessed in the light of the new electronic environment." *Id.*

384. *Id.* Art. 2.

385. *Id.* Art. 3.

386. *Id.* Art. 4(1).

387. *Id.* Art. 4(2).

388. *Id.* Art. 5(1).

389. *Id.* Art. 5(2)(a)–(e).

390. *Id.* Art. 5(3)(a)–(o).

391. *Id.* Art. 8(1).

392. *Id.* Art. 12(1) ("Not later than December 22, 2004 and every three years thereafter, the Commission shall submit to the European Parliament, the Council and the Economic and Social Committee a report on the application of this Directive, in which . . . it shall examine in particular the application of Articles 5, 6 and 8 in the light of the development of the digital market. In the case of Article 6, it shall examine in particular whether that Article confers a sufficient level of protection and whether acts which are permitted by law are being adversely affected by the use of effective technological measures. Where necessary, in particular to ensure the functioning of the internal market pursuant to Article 14 of the Treaty, it shall submit proposals for amendments to this Directive.").

393. *Id.* Art. 7.

B. Article 6 EUCD

The anticircumvention framework stipulated in Article 6 EUCD is rather detailed.[394] Recital 47 explains the importance of TPMs in securing copyrights and the rationale for the Community-level harmonization necessity:

> Technological development will allow rightholders to make use of technological measures designed to prevent or restrict acts not authorised by the rightholders of any copyright, rights related to copyright or the sui generis right in databases. The danger, however, exists that illegal activities might be carried out in order to enable or facilitate the circumvention of the technical protection provided by these measures. In order to avoid fragmented legal approaches that could potentially hinder the functioning of the internal market, there is a need to provide for harmonised legal protection against circumvention of effective technological measures and against provision of devices and products or services to this effect.[395]

At the same time, Recital 48 states TPMs protection "should respect proportionality and should not prohibit those devices or activities which have a commercially significant purpose or use other than to circumvent the technical protection."[396] The anticircumvention scheme outlined in Article 6 EUCD does not apply to TPMs protecting computer programs,[397] a topic regulated in the relevant provision of the 1991 Software Directive.[398]

1. The Core Anticircumvention Prohibition: Article 6(1)

Article 6(1) prohibits actual acts of TPMs circumvention performed with actual or constructive knowledge: "Member States shall provide adequate legal protection against the circumvention of any effective technological measures, which the person concerned carries out in the knowledge, or with reasonable grounds to know, that he or she is pursuing that objective."[399] The wording is strongly reminiscent of Article 11 WCT, particularly the use of the terms "adequate legal protection" and "effective" TPMs covered by the norm. As in the WCT, the concept of "circumvention" remains undefined.

2. The Trafficking Prohibition: Article 6(2)

A broad prohibition on trafficking in, and commercial possession of, circumvention tools is set forth in Article 6(2):

> Member States shall provide adequate legal protection against the manufacture, import, distribution, sale, rental, advertisement for sale or rental, or

394. *Id.* Art. 6.
395. *Id.* Recital 47.
396. *Id.* Recital 48.
397. *Id.* Recital 50.
398. *See* E.C. Software Directive (1991), Art. 7(1).
399. *Id.* Art. 6(1).

> possession for commercial purposes of devices, products or components or the provision of services which:
> (a) are promoted, advertised or marketed for the purpose of circumvention of, or
> (b) have only a limited commercially significant purpose or use other than to circumvent, or
> (c) are primarily designed, produced, adapted or performed for the purpose of enabling or facilitating the circumvention of, any effective technological measures.[400]

3. Definitions: Article 6(3)

Article 6(3) importantly provides a definition of "technological measures" that are subject to the norms stipulated in the previous provisions:

> For the purposes of this Directive, the expression "technological measures" means any technology, device or component that, in the normal course of its operation, is designed to prevent or restrict acts, in respect of works or other subject-matter, which are not authorised by the rightholder of [any copyright, related right or sui generis rights].[401]

The second sentence of this provision explains the notion of an "effective" TPM:

> Technological measures shall be deemed "effective" where the use of a protected work or other subject-matter is controlled by the rightholders through application of an access control or protection process, such as encryption, scrambling or other transformation of the work or other subject-matter or a copy control mechanism, which achieves the protection objective.[402]

4. Anticircumvention Exceptions: Article 6(4)

Article 6(4) is organized into four main paragraphs. The first paragraph *obligates* Member States, in the absence of voluntary measures taken by rights-holders and notwithstanding the obligation in Article 6(1), to take "appropriate measures" to ensure rights-holders make available to beneficiaries of seven exceptions and limitations (to the extent they exist in national law) the means of benefiting from those exceptions and limitations, provided the beneficiaries have "legal access" to the protected subject-matter concerned.[403] The list of obligatory exemptions includes "analog" reproductions,[404] reproductions by publicly

---

400. *Id.* Art. 6(2).
401. *Id.* Art. 6(3), first sentence.
402. *Id.* Art. 6(3), second sentence.
403. *Id.* Art 6(4), para. 1.
404. *Id.* Art. 5(2)(a).

accessible institutions such as libraries and educational establishments,[405] ephemeral recordings by broadcasting organizations,[406] use for the sole purpose of illustration for teaching and scientific research,[407] and a quotation exception that somewhat resembles Article 10(1) Berne Convention.[408]

The second paragraph of Article 6(4) specifically addresses the exception in Article 5(2)(b) EUCD, which is not included in the list of obligatory exemptions. It *allows* Member States to create an anticircumvention exception to accommodate "private copying" exceptions to the reproduction right in domestic laws. The relevant exception may apply to "reproductions on any medium made by a natural person for private use and for ends that are neither directly nor indirectly commercial."[409] According to Article 5(2)(b), Member States may introduce such an exception to the reproduction right, provided rights-holders receive "fair compensation."[410] Member States *may* amend domestic anticircumvention laws to require rights-holders who use TPMs to provide beneficiaries of the private copying exception with the means to exercise their privilege, unless reproduction for private use has already been made possible by rights-holders.[411] This paragraph specifically refers to the three-step test articulated in Article 5(5) EUCD,[412] indicating domestic *anticircumvention* exceptions (not only the private copying exception itself) are directly subject to this test.[413]

In its third paragraph, Article 6(4) clarifies that TPMs that are applied "voluntarily" by rights-holders (including their exceptions accommodation features),[414] as well as TPMs applied in accordance with the "measures" taken by Member States to secure exceptions and limitations, shall enjoy the protection granted in Article 6(1).[415] This provision flatly prohibits legitimization of self-help actions by exceptions beneficiaries, and circumvention cannot be excused when the

405. *Id.* Art. 5(2)(c).

406. *Id.* Art. 5(2)(d).

407. *Id.* Art. 5(3)(a).

408. *Id.* Art. 5(3)(d).

409. *Id.* Art. 5(2)(b).

410. *Id.* By contrast to the obligatory exceptions in the first paragraph, the second paragraph of Art. 6(4) contains no additional requirement that beneficiaries have "legal access" to the copyrighted work.

411. *Id.* Art. 6(4), para. 2.

412. *Id.* Art. 5(5) EUCD ("The exceptions and limitations provided for in paragraphs 1, 2, 3 and 4 [of Art. 5 EUCD] shall only be applied in certain special cases which do not conflict with a normal exploitation of the work or other subject-matter and do not unreasonably prejudice the legitimate interests of the rightholder.").

413. In this respect the Directive clearly goes beyond the mandatory international minimum stipulated in Art. 11 WCT in connection with Art. 10 WCT. As shown, anticircumvention exceptions are not directly subject to the three-step test under the WCT regime. *See* Section IV.C.1(b) *supra*.

414. *Cf.* EUCD (2001), Recital 51.

415. *Id.* Art. 6(4), para. 3.

TPM-restricted activity is contractually permissible or when the TPM restriction is subject to the "appropriate measures" taken by Member States in accordance with the first paragraph of Article 6(4).[416]

Finally, the fourth paragraph of Article 6(4) provides the first and second paragraphs concerning measures compelling rights-holders to avail themselves of the means to exercise privileges "shall not apply to works or other subject-matter made available to the public on agreed contractual terms in such a way that members of the public may access them from a place and at a time individually chosen by them."[417]

C. Scope and Interpretation

1. The EUCD Anticircumvention Framework

The text of the directive reflects a number of noteworthy design choices that significantly narrow the margins left for domestic discretion under Article 11 WCT. To begin with, the core anticircumvention prohibition contains a knowledge requirement,[418] meaning that circumvention is only unlawful when the actor has actual or constructive knowledge concerning *the act of circumvention.* But despite the fact knowledge must attach to the act of circumvention, that act is not defined,[419] and the preambular text furnishes little guidance.[420]

Article 6 requires Member States to introduce a broad anti-trafficking provision covering a wide range of preparatory activities, including the mere possession of circumvention tools for commercial purposes.[421] The list of three alternative circumstances rendering preparatory activities unlawful articulates the nexus between these activities and unlawful circumvention within the meaning of Article 6(1). The formulation of circumstances is somewhat reminiscent of the parallel DMCA anti-trafficking text. Likewise, the relevant factor rendering a preparatory act unlawful is its relation to TPMs *circumvention*, not directly to

---

416. Recital 51 explains: "in order to prevent abuse of such measures taken by rightholders, including within the framework of agreements, or taken by a Member State, any technological measures applied in implementation of such measures should enjoy legal protection . . ."

417. *Id.* Art. 6(4), para. 4.

418. Knowledge text is not mentioned in Art. 11 WCT. It is also absent in the DMCA anticircumvention prohibitions.

419. By comparison, the DMCA defines *actionable circumventions* in §§ 1201(a)(3)(A) and 1201(b)(2)(A).

420. Bechtold suggested the term *circumvention* within the meaning of Art. 6 EUCD captures "[a] broad variety of activities . . .[including] exploration of passwords and decryption keys, the manipulation of authentication protocols as well as physical attacks on hardware protection mechanisms." *See* Stefan Bechtold, *in* CONCISE EUROPEAN COPYRIGHT LAW 388 (Thomas Dreier & P. Bernt Hugenholtz eds., 2006).

421. *See id.* at 389–90 (reviewing the scope of the trafficking prohibition).

copyright infringement. Unlike the DMCA, however, Article 6 does not distinguish between access-control TPMs and rights- (or copy-) control TPMs.[422]

At to exceptions, the anticircumvention exceptions regime set forth in Article 6(4) has several distinctive features. First, anticircumvention exceptions *must be tied to domestic exceptions against copyright infringement*, inasmuch as they exist in national laws. Unlike the DMCA (which, as noted, provides a separate and independent list), any permissible anticircumvention exception should relate to an existing copyright exemption. The limited freedom to craft domestic anticircumvention exceptions appears *not* to cover domestic anti-trafficking prohibitions.[423] The Directive precludes legalization of self-help acts of actual circumvention committed by exceptions beneficiaries as part of domestic "appropriate measures" taken to accommodate copyright exceptions. In this respect, the Directive clearly favors contractual arrangements to facilitate enjoyment from copyright privileges over compelling rights-holders to enable such privileges via the instrument of "appropriate measures."[424] This is derived primarily from the first paragraph of Article 6(4) containing the proviso "in the absence of voluntary measures taken by rightholders" and the second paragraph, which provides a similar requirement with respect to domestic exceptions under Article 5(2)(b).[425]

Perhaps most significantly, the fourth paragraph of section 6(4) EUCD overrides the regime of "appropriate measures" when the work is offered on-demand on a contractual basis. As noted, Article 6 arranges copyright exemptions into three groups. The first group includes exceptions Member States are *obligated* to facilitate by taking "appropriate measures" under the conditions of Article 6(4), first paragraph. The second group contains one *elective* exception for private copying. Under the third residual category fall all exceptions and limitations provided in national laws that are not mentioned in Article 6(4), in which cases Member States are *not allowed* to take "appropriate measures" in the absence

---

422. This observation is derived from the definition of "effective" TPMs provided in the second sentence of subsection (3) covering "access control or protection process."

423. This emanates from the text of Art. 6(4), which opens with the wording: "Notwithstanding the legal protection provided for in *paragraph 1* . . ." (emphasis added).

424. *See* EUCD (2001) Recital 51. ("Member States should promote voluntary measures taken by rightholders, including the conclusion and implementation of agreements between rightholders and other parties concerned, to accommodate achieving the objectives of certain exceptions or limitations provided for in national law in accordance with this Directive. In the absence of such voluntary measures or agreements within a reasonable period of time, Member States should take appropriate measures to ensure that rightholders provide beneficiaries of such exceptions or limitations with appropriate means of benefiting from them, by modifying an implemented technological measure or by other means.") *See also* EUCD (2001) Recital 52 (setting similar considerations with regard to the private copying exceptions).

425. "[U]nless reproduction for private use has already been made possible by rightholders to the extent necessary to benefit from [that exception.]" *Id.* Art. 6(4), para. 2.

of agreement.[426] Article 6 might be said to adopt a limited European "maximum protection" approach in the sense of commanding "Member States *shall* take appropriate measures."[427] However, this command concerns only first category exceptions. Observing that structure from the proper distance reveals only a quasi-maximum protection rule because when domestic law does not lodge the relevant copyright exception, the obligation to take appropriate measures drops.

There is only one obligatory copyright exception stipulated by the Directive, namely, for temporary reproductions according to Article 5(1) EUCD.[428] Curiously, this exception falls under the third category and therefore is not subject at all to the "appropriate measures" regime of Article 6(4). In addition, the entire "appropriate measures" scheme in Article 6(4) becomes irrelevant as soon as *access* to the TPM-protected work is offered over the Internet under conditions dictated by rights-holders.[429]

Article 6 EUCD provides that the catalog of domestic anticircumvention exceptions subject to "appropriate measures" is exhaustive. More precisely, the intervention of domestic law is allowed only to facilitate enjoyment from the copyright exemptions enumerated in the first and second paragraphs of Article 6. Having said that, the preambular language refers to additional instances in which anticircumvention protection gives way to other interests. One of them is the "no mandate" rule mentioned in Recital 48.[430] The same Recital further provides anticircumvention laws "[i]n particular . . . should not hinder research into cryptography."[431] Recital 50 leaves the door open for domestic reverse engineering/decompilation exceptions that would limit circumvention prohibitions in the case of computer programs by virtue of the saving clause preserving the arrangement set forth in the 1991 Software Directive.[432] Further, Recital 51 somewhat vaguely states "legal protection of technological measures applies without prejudice to public policy, as reflected in Article 5, or public security."[433]

2. The Issue of "Legal Access"

According to Article 6(4)(1), the obligation to take "appropriate measures" to secure first-category exceptions is subject to the condition "that beneficiary has

426. For an overview, see Bechtold, *supra* note 421, at 393–94.

427. *See* EUCD (2001), Art. 6(4), first para. (emphasis added).

428. *See* Chapter 4, Section V.B.2 *supra* (analyzing that provision).

429. EUCD (2001), Art. 6(4), para. 4.

430. *Id.* Recital 48 ("Such legal protection [to technological measures] implies no obligation to design devices, products, components or services to correspond to technological measures, so long as such device, product, component or service does not otherwise fall under the prohibition of Article 6.").

431. *Id.*

432. *Id.* Recital 50.

433. *Id.* Recital 51.

legal access to the protected work or subject-matter concerned."[434] The Directive is silent on the meaning of the phrase "legal access."[435] As rights-holders do not have a formal legal right to forbid unauthorized access to works, a systematic reading would derive a requirement that the beneficiary is not engaged in copyright infringement, somewhat similar to several DMCA exceptions that expressly stipulate such condition. In other words, "legal access" means access that has been achieved without violation of the exclusive rights secured under copyright law. It follows that to the extent access-conducts violate exclusive rights, the "appropriate measures" obligation will not apply.

To appreciate the complications involved with the legal access requirement, zooming out for a moment may prove helpful, as there are several "legal" ways to access a TPM-protected work. Most obviously, access is legal when rights-holders give permission, whether explicit or implicit. Note, however, that the very deployment of access controls predicts that more often an explicit permission would be required. A second alternative is to perform access-conducts that implicate one or more exclusive right(s), but which are fully shielded by one or more copyright exceptions. Though access may be considered "legal" as a matter of copyright infringement analysis, to the extent access-control TPMs block or restrict the necessary access-conducts, circumvention is strictly prohibited. If, as a consequence, access to the work was never achieved, it appears Article 6(4)(1) does not apply because "legal access" has never been accomplished. The third option to achieve "legal access" is by being granted *partial* access permission to the TPM-protected work. In the relevant scenario, the TPM allows some restricted form of access, but restricts further operations needed for exercising a first-category copyright privilege. In the case that all initial and subsequent avenues of access to the work are controlled by the TPM (e.g., legal, nonrestricted versions are not freely available in the market), this third (narrow) scenario seems to be the most important instance where the "appropriate measure" may have some positive impact on the position of beneficiaries.

The "legal access" aspect within the European scheme puts anticircumvention exceptions beneficiaries under the EUCD regime in a worse position than DMCA beneficiaries. Though DMCA anticircumvention exceptions also require that beneficiaries shall not commit infringement, this requirement applies sporadically, depending on the terms of the specific DMCA exception.[436] Should "legal access" mean that access achieved from infringing copies is excluded, the

---

434. *Id* Art. 6(4), para. 1 (emphasis added).

435. *Cf.* Bechtold, *supra* note 421, at 393 (suggesting beneficiaries do not have a right to "initial access" for the purpose of exercising their privileges. Nor does Art. 6(4)(1) extend protection to beneficiaries who obtained illegal copies).

436. This advantage is rather theoretical. Though the DMCA does not have a general "legal access" requirement, almost each and every specific exception separately stipulates that for the exception to be available to them, beneficiaries shall not infringe. A possible

condition becomes more stringent than the DMCA's requirement, asking merely that the beneficiary *himself* shall not infringe. This might beg the conclusion that in nearly any partial access situation falling under the third access scenario, beneficiaries still need to secure some explicit permission to cover additional uses to satisfy the "legal access" condition. Either way, in most real-life situations beneficiaries will depend on *some* level of individual authorization, and under the "legal access" clause, it is reasonable to assume the "appropriate measures" mechanism would be inapplicable in the case of access-control TPMs. The EUCD's "appropriate measures" instrument might assume some relevancy in case the TMP at question could clearly be classified as a "rights control" protection measure. Adding to this analysis the fact Article 6(4) does not apply to anti-trafficking bans leads to the conclusion that, from a practical viewpoint, the ground covered by Article 6(4)(1) is extremely narrow.

3. "Effective," "Technological Measures," and Nexus to Infringement

A scrutiny of Article 6's plain text leaves several key elements of the EUCD anticircumvention model unclear. The Directive defines two central concepts—"technological measures" and "effective"—that are crucial for ascertaining the nexus between unlawful circumvention and copyright protections against infringement. In essence, TPMs can be virtually anything ("any technology, device or component") that "in the normal course of its operation" is designed to prevent or restrict unauthorized acts in respect to copyright-protected subject matter.[437]

The reference to *unauthorized acts* restricted by technological protection is reminiscent of the language in Article 11 WCT, albeit with one critical difference. Though the act restricted by the technological measure must be unauthorized by rights-holders, the "in-connection" to the exercise of copyrights (or an equivalent) wording is missing.[438] The accompanying definition of *effective* addresses the notion of TPMs subject to the regime of the Directive. However, instead of clarifying matters, this definition unfortunately seems to spread more confusion. A TPM is effective "where the *use* of a protected work . . . is controlled by the rightholders."[439] The term *use* opened a debate as to whether both access-control and rights-control TPMs fall within the definition, or rather only the latter (i.e., only measures that restrict acts that implicate exclusive rights).[440] Read in context, however, the term "use" cannot be said to restrict the TPM definition only to rights control. Such an inference is significantly rebutted by

---

exception thereto is codified in 17 U.S.C. § 1201(i) (concerning personal identity information).

437. *See* EUCD (2001), Art. 6(3).

438. *See* Section IV.B.2 *supra*.

439. *See* EUCD (2001), Art. 6(3) (emphasis added).

440. *See* Stefan Bechtold, Vom Urheberrecht zum Informationsrecht 204 & n.1017 (2002).

the text immediately following: TPMs covered by Article 6 are described as falling under of four (occasionally overlapping) groups: (1) access-controls, (2) protection process, (3) "other transformation of the work," and (4) copy controls. To be considered "effective," these measures must "achieve [] the protection objective."[441] Thereby, a very broad range of TPMs (including access controls and copy controls) is captured by the anticircumvention prohibitions, and simultaneously, the relationship between the deployment of such measures and copyright protections against infringement remains quite loose. Article 6(3) states an effective measure "achieves the protection objective." One way to interpret this qualifier is to perceive "protection objective" as denoting *copyright* protection, including its underlying policy objectives. This could provide the essential nexus between anticircumvention bans and copyright infringement. However, this alternative conflicts with the syntax of the provision, which implies the intended protection at issue is reflected by protection *effectuated by the TPM*. It may follow "the protection objective" must not necessarily square with traditional copyright rationales. In the context of effectiveness, what matters is the manner in which the TPM serves the subjective protection goals of rights-holders. If this reading is correct, Article 6 EUCD contains *no indication whatsoever on how to address the nexus problem*. In fact, the plain text of Article 6, which lacks any version of the "in-connection" clause, suggests showing such a nexus is not required at all. If one still insists on articulating a nexus to copyright infringement, one is compelled to reach beyond the text of the anticircumvention provisions.[442]

4. Converting Copyright Exceptions into Contractual Duties

Article 6 does not contain text similar to the WCT's "or permitted by law" language.[443] As noted, this alternative affords WCT-contracting parties with the freedom to create anticircumvention exceptions to accommodate domestic copyright exemptions. Its omission from Article 6 is understandable in light of the Directive's intention to dictate with specificity what shall be considered permissible by law. At the EUCD's baseline there is the principle of clear priority to voluntary arrangements between rights-holders and exemptions beneficiaries over coercive steps directed against the former. Rights-holders are granted broad discretion to determine under which conditions to permit or restrict conducts that might affect copyright privileges. As long as *some* opportunity to exercise copyright privileges remains available, the obligation to take "appropriate measures" will not be triggered.

441. EUCD (2001), Art. 6(3), second sentence.

442. *See, e.g.*, Bechtold, *supra* note 421, at 387 ("Technological measures are only protected by art. 6 if they prevent or restrict acts that fall within the rightholder's power to authorize. If a technological measure prevents a certain activity that is neither protected by copyright law nor by any neighbouring right or the 'sui generis' database right, art. 6 does not forbid the circumvention of this technological measure, regardless of whether the 'rightholder' has authorized this activity.").

443. *Cf.* WCT (1996), Art. 11.

This basic principle receives a strong exposition in the case of on-demand transmission where the "appropriate measure" clause is wholly inapplicable.[444] The supremacy that contracts and licensing terms enjoy under the EUCD's anti-circumvention scheme is obviously perilous to the viability of copyright exemptions. Hohfeldian classification is a useful tool for describing the systematic alternation in the relevant legal positions: situations that traditionally represented privilege/no-right relations gradually migrate to the right/duty rubric.

The ramifications of this change are far-reaching. In the emerging reality anticipated by the EUCD regime, privilege beneficiaries may have a *contractual right-claim* to perform a given act, granted through a license. Alternatively, in the absence of a license they have a legal *duty* to abstain, which is the general default rule in property scenarios. For determining the legal position of the parties to a given dispute concerning a given use, it becomes less material what copyright law stipulates and more important what the contract says. The privilege scenario, in which rights-holders simply have a Hohfeldian "no-right" to interfere, becomes more rare. If the act in question (1) is blocked by TPMs, and, (2) circumvention is in any case prohibited, (3) there are no meaningful legal obligations to accommodate copyright exceptions, and (4) rights-holders offer beneficiaries the opportunity to purchase a license, there is not much room left for legal privileges.

In this reality, copyright exemptions become optional, a kind of cordial gesture or simply a component in a larger commercialization strategy—but in any event, not a meaningful balancing counterweight to the vigor of the exclusive rights. The extent to which the conversion process of privileges into duties will take place in practice largely depends on the answer to the following questions: Should Member States intervene to protect beneficiaries *even when they are offered a license,* and if so, under which circumstances? Should the law intervene in actual and potential contractual relations and "correct" licensing terms if found unreasonably or overly tilted in favor of licensors? What should be the criteria for such state intervention in the freedom of contracts?[445] The issue of *when* and *how* domestic laws may (or should) intervene is one of the most shadowy corners of Article 6. At least in the case of on-demand services, the question becomes substantially mute. When works are made available to the public "on agreed contractual terms in such a way that members of the public may access them from a place and at a time individually chosen by them," no state intervention is allowed. If this rule applied literally, and to the extent TPMs are widely deployed, copyright exceptions stand to disappear from perhaps the most important market for digital works in the future.[446]

---

444. *See* EUCD (2001), Art. 6(4), para. 4.

445. For a discussion on general interface questions between freedom of contracts and copyright exemptions, see LUCIE GUIBAULT, COPYRIGHT LIMITATIONS AND CONTRACTS: AN ANALYSIS OF THE CONTRACTUAL OVERRIDABILITY OF LIMITATIONS ON COPYRIGHT (2002).

446. The rhetoric often differs from reality in that context. Recital 3 promised that harmonization relates to "compliance with the fundamental principles of law and

D. EUCD Anticircumvention Critique

Many commentators are highly critical of the EUCD's framework,[447] with the main claims in the context of Article 6 relating to overprotection, ambiguity, or both.[448] Much of the critiques overlap with arguments advanced against the DMCA (and anticircumvention regulation in general) and shall not be repeated here.[449] In the particular context of European copyright lawmaking, it has been argued the Directive failed to achieve its main goal: to establish a high degree of harmonization and uniformity at the Community level.[450] Further, by its strongly emphasizing protection of rights-holders' economic interests, some questioned the soundness of the economic impetus of the Directive.[451]

Critics further accuse the Directive of being ambiguous on key matters, for instance, the definition provided of "effective" TPMs.[452] It is unclear when, under which circumstances, and how domestic laws must intervene in situations described by Article 6(4)(1).[453] It is also quite uncertain whether *any type* of contractual arrangement may satisfy the "voluntary measures" clause, determining the instances where the obligation to take "appropriate measures" is replaced

---

especially of property, including intellectual property, and freedom of expression and the *public interest.*" *See* EUCD (2001), Recital 3 (emphasis added). If "public interest" were another name for private ordering of digital information markets, the Directive indeed would be quite successful in securing it.

447. For a general critique, *see* P. Bernt Hugenholtz, *Why the Copyright Directive is Unimportant, and Possibly Invalid* 2000 Eur. Intell. Prop. Rev. 501 (2000). For a critique addressing the exemptions framework mandated by the Directive, see Reto M. Hilty, *Vergütungssystem und Schrankenregelungen–Neue Herausforderungen an den Gesetzgeber,* GRUR 2005, 824–25.

448. *Cf.* Reto M. Hilty, *Intellectual Property and the European Community's Internal Market Legislation,* 7 IIC 760, 773–74 (2004) ("the Directive sets the target (which is barely achievable) in such a loose manner and leaves such a wide margin to national legislators that it is natural that there are extreme differences in how the Directive has been transformed into national law.") (footnote omitted).

449. See Section V.F *supra.*

450. *See, e.g.,* Bechtold, *supra* note 221, at 392; Maria Martin-Prat, *The Relationship Between Protection and Exceptions in the EU "Information Society" Directive, in* Adjuncts and Alternatives to Copyright 466 (Jane C. Ginsburg & June M. Besek eds., 2002); Pierre Sirinelli, *The Scope of the Prohibition on Circumvention of Technological Measures: Exceptions, in* Adjuncts and Alternatives to Copyright 404 ff (Jane C. Ginsburg & June M. Besek eds., 2002); Urs Gasser & Michael Girsberger, *Transposing the Copyright Directive: Legal Protections of Technological Measures in EU-Member States—A Genie Stuck in a Bottle?,* Berkman Working Paper No. 2004-10 (2004).

451. *See* Kamiel J. Koelman, *Copyright Law and Economics in the EU Copyright Directive: Is the Droit d´Auteur Passé?,* 35(6) IIC 603, 637 (2004).

452. *See* Bechtold, *supra* note 221, at 387–88 (arguing the definition is tautological).

453. Recitals 51 and 52 speak in terms of "a reasonable period of time," during which the parties may reach an agreement before external intervention becomes an option. *See* EUCD (2001), Recitals 51–52. The question of what constitutes a "reasonable" period of time remained open.

with a *prohibition* to do the same.[454] The Directive indicates voluntary measures should "accommodate achieving the objectives of certain exceptions or limitations provided for in national law in accordance with this Directive."[455] In real-life disputes, the question whether this condition has been fulfilled is likely to be contested between rights-holders and beneficiaries. There is no indication in the Directive how to solve such disagreements in a uniform fashion.[456]

Finally, the nature of "appropriate measures" is left substantially open.[457] A repeating complaint is that the Directive has failed to formulate a balanced framework for domestic legislation.[458] Article 6 EUCD has become an example of overprotective legislation in which the maladies and flaws of anticircumvention regulation are served up in a concentrated dose. Whereas provisions concerning circumvention and trafficking bans are rigorous and plain,[459] the essential provisions that are supposed to furnish the counterweight to copyright exclusivity remain obscure, hesitant, and full of gaps and uncertainties.

VII. IMPLEMENTATION IN GERMANY

A. Overview

In light of the EUCD's ambiguity regarding some key features of the European anticircumvention framework, it is important to take a closer look at the manner in which its provisions were implemented in domestic law. This section reviews the adoption of anticircumvention law by German law. The EUCD obligated Member States to complete transposition in national laws by December 22, 2002,[460] but the process took many states much longer. Germany implemented

454. Other than mentioning "agreements" as an example of "voluntary measures," the Directive remains silent on the issue of what voluntary measures may or should be.

455. *See* EUCD (2001), Recital 51.

456. *Cf.* Ficsor, *supra* note 76, § C11.29 (suggesting the terms offered by rights-holders must be "sufficiently reasonable"). The capability of this criterion to solve concrete disputes is questionable. "Reasonable" may mean not unduly oppressive, yet again, this issue remained wide open for interpretation.

457. Shortly after enactment of the Directive, it had been commented: "We await impatiently to learn what these 'appropriate measures' might be." *See* Sirinelli, *supra* note 451, at 407. The German legislation described in the next section will review a particularly interesting model of "appropriate measures."

458. *See, e.g.*, Reto M. Hilty, *Rechtsschutz technischer Maßnahmen: Zum UrhG-Regierungsentwurf vom 31.7.2002, in* Ein Leber für Rechtskultur: Festschrift für Robert Dittrich zum 75. Geburtstag,578 (H. Tades et al. eds., 2002) (criticizing in particular Art. 6(4)(4) EUCD).

459. The Directive itself declared that rigid anticircumvention laws are an important component in "[a] rigorous, effective system for the protection of copyright and related rights." *See* EUCD (2001), Recital 11.

460. *See* EUCD (2001), Art. 13(1).

large parts of the EUCD (including Article 6) by passing on September 10, 2003 the so-called "first bundle" (*erster Korb*) of amendments to the 1965 German Copyright Act.[461] The German anticircumvention scheme is laid out in the new Sections 95a through 95d. Section 95a contains the anticircumvention prohibitions and relevant definitions, Section 95b articulates the domestic approach to the "appropriate measures" mechanism, Section 95c stipulates rights management information prohibitions, and Section 95d creates a unique rights-holders' identification duty.

B. The Substantive Anticircumvention Provisions

1. Section 95a UrhG.

Section 95a restates the provisions of Article 6(1)–(2) EUCD with some minor alterations. Subsection (1) prohibits the unauthorized circumvention of effective TPMs protecting subject matter covered by copyright, provided the actor knows (or under the circumstances should know) that circumvention is being performed to enable access to or use of works.[462] The law stipulates a series of new criminal sanctions for certain willful violations of this provision.[463] Subsection (2) recasts Article 6(3) EUCD almost verbatim. It defines effective technological protection measures as technologies and devices that, in the normal course of their operation, are intended to prevent or restrict unauthorized conducts with respect to copyright-protected works.[464] TPMs are "effective" (*wirksam*) if the use of copyright-protected works is restricted through access control; a mechanism such as encryption, scrambling, or other transformation; or a copy-control mechanism, which secures the achievement of the protection's objective.[465]

---

461. *See Gesetz zur Regelung des Urheberrechts in der Informationsgesellschaft* (2003).

462. *See* UrhG., § 95a(1). ("Effective technological measures for the protection of works protected by this law or of other subject-matter protected by this law may not be circumvented without authorization of the rightholder, if the actor knows or has a reason to know that the circumvention takes place in order to enable access to such a work or subject matter, or to enable its use.") Translations of Section 95 into English by Alexander Peukert (available at http://eurorights.cdfreaks.com/index.php/14/51).

463. *Id.* §§ 108b(1) nr. 1, 108b(3) UrhG. (prescribing imprisonment and criminal fines).

464. *Id.* § 95a(2) UrhG., first sentence. ("Technological measures for the purpose of this law are technologies, devices and components, which in the normal course of their operation, are designed to prevent or restrict acts, in respect of protected works or other subject-matter protected by this law, which are not authorized by the rightholder.").

465. *Id.* § 95a(2) UrhG., second sentence ("Technological measures are effective, if the use of a protected work or other subject-matter protected by this law is controlled by the rightholder through application of an access control, a protection process such as encryption, scrambling or other transformation, or a copy control mechanism, which achieves the protection objective.").

Subsection (3) outlaws trafficking in (as well as possession for commercial purposes of) devices and services under three alternative circumstances similar to those stated in the EUCD.[466] Violations of the trafficking prohibitions are subject to statutory administrative fines[467] and criminal sanctions.[468] Subsection (4) provides a special anticircumvention exception applying both to the circumvention and trafficking provisions that exempts prohibited acts for purposes of public security and criminal administration of justice. Certain trafficking activities connected to TPMs circumvention of computer programs are regulated separately.[469]

2. Section 95b UrhG.

The first sentence of Section 95b(1) obligates rights-holders who use TPMs to provide beneficiaries of certain exception the necessary means to make the privileged use, provided beneficiaries have legal access to the work.[470] The provision lists seven statutory exceptions subject to this rule.[471] In accordance with Article 6(4)(2) EUCD, the law included the private copying exception in this catalog,[472] albeit not all the circumstances covered by this exception are also subject to the duty to provide means. For instance, the privilege to make reproductions for private academic use is covered,[473] as well as the privilege to copy small portions of works for certain private educational purposes.[474]

---

466. *Id.* § 95a(3) UrhG. ("Prohibited are the manufacture, the import, the distribution, the sale, the rental, the advertisement for sale or rental and the possession for commercial purposes, of devices, products or components as well as the provision of services, which are (1) promoted, advertised or marketed for the purpose of circumvention of effective technical measures, or (2) have only a limited commercially significant purpose or use other than to circumvent effective technical measures, or (3) are primarily designed, produced, adapted or performed for the purpose of enabling or facilitating the circumvention of effective technological measures.").

467. *Id.* §§ 101a(1) nr. 1, 101a(2) UrhG.

468. *Id.* § 108b(2) UrhG.

469. *Id.* § 69a(5) UrhG. The Copyright Act stipulates a special rule concerning TPMs applied to computer programs in Section 69f(2). This rule gives effect to some of the remedies available to copyright holders in computer programs against infringement, and also with respect to means whose sole purpose is to facilitate unauthorized removal or circumvention of protection mechanisms. *Id.* at § 69f(2) UrhG.

470. *Id.* § 95b(1) UrhG., first sentence ("As far as a rightholder uses technological measures in accordance with the condition of this law, he is obligated to make available the necessary means which enable the use covered by the following limitations to the beneficiaries of those limitations, if they have legal access to the protected work or subject-matter . . .").

471. *Id.* § 95b(1) UrhG., first sentence nr. (1)–(7).

472. *Id.* § 53 UrhG. (defining exceptions covering copying for private use).

473. *Id.* § 95b(1) UrhG., first sentence nr. (6)(b).

474. *Id.* § 95b(1) UrhG., first sentence nr. (6)(e).

The rights-holders' duty to provide necessary means in the context of copying for private use under Sections 53(1) of the Copyright Act extends only to the ability of beneficiaries to make "analog" reproductions.[475] Other than some Section 53 private or educational reproductions, the rule of Section 95b also applies, inter alia, to the exception in Section 52a (making available to the public for educational and research purposes),[476] Section 55 (ephemeral reproduction by transmission organizations),[477] and Section 45a (exception to the benefit of persons with disabilities).[478]

The second sentence of Section 95b(1) explicitly prohibits any contractual arrangements that would release rights-holders from their obligation under the first sentence to provide means.[479] To secure the effective enforcement of the duty to provide necessary means, Section 95(b)(2) stipulates a special cause of action afforded to exceptions beneficiaries against rights-holders who violate their obligations under Section 95b(1).[480] The law also added new sanctions against violating rightholders.[481] The law creates a presumption that when the means offered by rights-holders corresponds to an agreement between rights-holders' associations and beneficiaries, the means is deemed sufficient.[482] In accordance with Article 6(4)(4) EUCD, the rights-holders' duty to provide means does not apply to situations where works were made available on a contractual basis so that members of the public may access them from places and times of their choice.[483]

3. Section 95d UrhG.

The anticircumvention model added special duties imposed on rights-holders who deploy TPM protections. First, rights-holders must clearly and visibly indicate that works are protected by TPMs, and similarly features of the technical

---

475. *Id.* § 95b(1) UrhG., first sentence nr. (6)(a).

476. *Id.* § 95b(1) UrhG., first sentence nr. (5), in connection with § 52a UrhG. The privilege in Sec. 52a was newly introduced by the 2003 reform as a counterweight to the new "making available" right in Sec. 19a UrhG.

477. *Id.* § 95b(1) UrhG., first sentence nr. (7), in connection with § 55 UrhG.

478. *Id.* § 45a UrhG.

479. *Id.* § 95b(1) UrhG., second sentence.

480. *Id.* § 95b(2) UrhG., first sentence.

481. *Id.* §§ 111a(1) nr. 2, 111a(2) UrhG. (stipulating administrative fines against rights-holders violating § 95b(2), first sentence). Injunctive relief is provided in the Injunctions Act of August 27, 2002, as amended on September 10, 2003; *see Gesetz über Unterlassungsklagen bei Verbraucherrechts- und anderen Verstößen, Unterlassungsklagengesetz* [ULlaG.] §§ 2a, 3a.

482. *See* § 95b(2) UrhG., second sentence.

483. *See* § 95b(3) UrhG. ("Paragraphs 1 and 2 shall not apply if works and other subject-matter are made available to the public on agreed contractual terms in such a way that members of the public may access them from a place and at a time individually chosen by them.").

protection (labeling duty).[484] Second, to facilitate legal actions under Section 95b(2), rights-holders must provide identification information such as name and address (identification duty).[485] Rights-holders who violate the identification duty commit misconduct,[486] but are not subject to the administrative fine in Section 111a.[487]

C. Scope and Interpretation

1. *The Anticircumvention and Trafficking Prohibitions*

Acts of actual circumvention and preparatory actions (trafficking) are regulated separately. The prohibitions on circumvention and trafficking follow the language of Article 6 EUCD nearly without alteration. Section 95a(1) is somewhat more elaborate as to knowledge requirements in the sense it requires knowledge regarding (1) TPM circumvention (2) for the purpose of enabling access to or use of a *copyrighted work*.[488] This said, there is no explicit statutory requirement that access/use must involve conduct covered by the exclusive rights.[489]

The anti-trafficking provision in Section 95a(3), like the parallel EUCD provision, reflects a very broad prohibition. At the same time, an explicit requirement is absent that the illicit preparatory act must be performed without the authority of rights-holders.[490] The text of Article 95a(3) adds no further clarification to the relationship between liability for preparatory acts and violation of copyrights.[491] Importantly, the three circumstances listed in Section 95a(3)(1)–(3) define the connection between the accused trafficking act (e.g., offering, advertising, or distribution) and *actual circumvention*. A direct linkage between unlawful trafficking and copyright violations is not expressed in the statute.

2. *Effective TPMs*

The wording of Section 95a(2) mirrors Article 6(3) EUCD, bringing into domestic law the entire plethora of interpretation issues and overbreadth concerns.[492] The TPM concept covers a broad range of both access controls and use controls.

---

484. *Id.* at § 95d(1) UrhG.

485. *Id.* at § 95d(2) UrhG.

486. *Id.* at § 111a(1)(3) UrhG.

487. *Id.* at § 111a(1)(2) UrhG.

488. *See* Thomas Dreier & Gernot Schulze, Urheberrechtsgesetz § 95a ¶ 12 (2006); Claudia Ohst, *in* Praxiskommentar zum Urheberrecht § 95a at ¶¶ 62–64 (Artur-Axel Wandtke & Winfried Bullinger eds., 2006). *See also* Horst Peter Götting *in* Urheberrecht Kommentar § 95a ¶ 12 (Gerhard Schricker ed., 2006).

489. *Cf.* Götting, *supra* note 489, § 95a ¶10; Ohst, *supra* note 489, § 95a ¶ 65.

490. *See* Ohst, *supra* note 489, § 95a ¶ 69 (opining this requisite is nonetheless implied).

491. *See* Thomas Dreier *in* Thomas Dreier & Gernot Schulze, Urheberrechtsgesetz § 95a ¶¶ 17–18 (2006).

492. *Id.* § 95a ¶¶ 14–15.

With respect to access controls, some commentators argue access prevention to works per se is not subject to prohibitions under Section 95a. According to this view, only access controls that are deployed to prevent acts connected to the exercise of the exclusive rights should be subject to the anticircumvention bans.[493] Put another way, only access controls that help rights-holders to exercise copyrights and concern acts covered by their exclusive veto power fall under the protection umbrella of Section 95a. The reasoning is not textual but normative-teleological: the objective of the provision, as the fruit of *copyright* legislation, cannot be other than to protect exclusive rights secured to rights-holders *under copyright law*. Anticircumvention entitlements are not independent protections but rather ones that derive both their legitimacy and legal force from the exclusive rights.[494] The exclusive copyrights define the material scope of legal powers granted to rights-holders in order to prevent some unauthorized conducts with respect to their works.[495]

3. The Exceptions Enforcement Mechanism of § 95b UrhG.

The implementation of Article 6(4) EUCD is one of the most interesting features of the German anticircumvention model. Section 95b(1) imposes an unprecedented legal *duty* on *rights-holders* to facilitate the exercise of copyright exceptions. The provisions spells out clear Hohfeldian rights-claims *granted to beneficiaries of some exceptions* (called *Begünstigten*)[496] to enforce their intention to

---

493. *See* Alexander Peukert *in* HANDBUCH DES URHEBERRECHTS § 34 nr. 2–3 (Ulrich Loewenheim ed., 2003); Ohst, *supra* note 489, § 95a ¶ 15 ("Aus dem Schutzzweck des § 95a ergibt sich allerdings, dass die Zugangskontrolle letztendlich nur zu schützen ist, wenn dadurch Handlungen verhindert werden sollen, die Ausschließlichkeitsrechte des Urhebers verhindern oder erschweren"); FREDERIKE HÄNEL, DIE UMSETZUNG DES ART. 6 INFO-RL INS DEUTSCHE RECHT 107 ff (2005).

494. *See* Günter Auer, *Rechtsschutz für technischen Schutz im Gemeinschaftsrecht* 14ff, *in* EIN LEBER FÜR RECHTSKULTUR: FESTSCHRIFT FÜR ROBERT DITTRICH ZUM 75. GEBURTSTAG,578 (H. Tades et al. eds., 2000) (analyzing the European norm that later influenced the formulation in German law).

495. As the law explicitly identifies access-controls as an example of covered TPMs, the question is how to determine whether access-control TPMs were attached to a copyrighted work *as part of an effort to prevent infringement* falling under the exclusive veto power of rights-holders. Though the commentary overwhelmingly favors the teleological interpretation, the answer to this question remains mostly vague. Because access-controls, as the name suggests, block access to the copyrighted work, whether they are part of a legitimate or illegitimate technological protection scheme cannot be based on their objective operation (i.e., blocking access), but on the subjective mental state of the rights-holder. A definition of covered TPMs that would depend solely on the subjective intention of rights-holders is obviously unattractive.

496. *See* § 95b(2) UrhG. *See also* Ohst, *supra* note 489; § 95b UrhG. nr. 11–12. The provision defines a cause of action, which technically can be distinguished from standing to file a lawsuit. *See* Gunda Dreyer *in* GUNDA DREYER ET AL., HEIDELBERGER KOMMENTAR ZUM URHEBERRECHT § 95b UrhG. nr. 38 (2004) .

benefit from their privileges despite TPMs. Self-help remains strictly unlawful, and beneficiaries must use legal means (i.e., file a suit) if they wish to have the technological barriers removed against the will of rights-holders.[497]

Despite the possible weakness and arguable ineffectiveness of this entitlement, this provision is a unique and novel development in copyright law where nonowners are granted affirmative causes of action against copyright holders. In this case, the opportunity to receive compensation for the use made possible by exercise of the privilege[498] comes at the price of rights-holders being *deprived of their right to exclude*, despite their TPMs being able to enforce exclusion, and despite those TPMs generally being protected against circumvention under Section 95a. The pioneering aspect of this rule within copyright law's landscape notewithstanding, the scope of the new beneficiaries' entitlements is quite limited, and the effectiveness of protection endowed has been questioned. Some of the important weaknesses of Section 95b are briefly noted below.

(a) Limited Catalog of Relevant Exceptions

The catalog of seven exceptions listed in Section 95b is exhaustive. Some important exceptions such as the news reporting privilege (Section 50 UrhG.) and the quotation privilege (Section 51 UrhG.) are *not* among them. The limited number of Section 95b exceptions is largely a consequence of European legislation, as in the case of news reporting, which is listed in Article 5(3)(c) EUCD but not in Article 6(4).[499] To reiterate, including such exceptions in Section 95b might put German law in conflict with the EUCD, as the relevant exception is not provided in the exhaustive list of Article 6(4) EUCD. The same is true with regard to some quotations specified in Article 5(3)(d) EUCD.[500] As argued in a different context, there is some tension between this regulation and Article 1(4) WCT in connection with Article 10(1) Berne Convention to the extent such restrictions apply to foreign works.[501] It appears beneficiaries who wish to challenge TPMs protections in the case of unlisted exceptions lack an articulable legal cause of action.

The position of those who pursue acts that do not trigger any exclusive rights but who find themselves nonetheless restricted by access-control TPMs is not

---

497. At the time of this writing, this provision has not yet been tested in the courts. Commentators predict beneficiaries who try to invoke it will face grave legal, technical, and procedural obstacles. *See* Dreyer, *supra* note 497, § 95b UrhG. nr. 39 ff.

498. Most of the exceptions listed in § 95b(1) mandate equitable remuneration.

499. For a critical evaluation, see Thomas Dreier, *Die Umsetzung der Urheberrechtsrichtlinie in Deutsches Recht*, 2002/1 ZUM, 28, 37–39 (2002).

500. *See* EUCD (2001), Art. 5(3)(d) (concerning "quotations for purposes such as criticism or review, provided that they relate to a work or other subject-matter which has already been lawfully made available to the public, that, unless this turns out to be impossible, the source, including the author's name, is indicated, and that their use is in accordance with fair practice, and to the extent required by the specific purpose").

501. Section IV.C.2(b) *supra*.

much better. Subjecting only TPM that facilitates *copyright relevant acts* to anticircumvention protections would not necessarily defeat rights-holders' argument that blocking access in a given case is part of their legitimate effort to curtail infringement. Consider the exception for persons with disabilities stipulated in Section 45a.[502] TPMs can block functions of software and other products (such as e-books) that are necessary for making works perceptible to disabled persons wishing to gain human-access (for instance, a read-aloud function). To the extent making the work perceptible to such persons for noncommercial purposes requires reproduction and/or distribution, Section 45a exempts the actors from liability under those specific exclusive rights. In fact, Section 95b(1)(2) subjects this exception to the *duty* to provide necessary means.[503] However, to the extent that making a work perceptible to disabled persons does *not* involve reproduction and/or distribution, Section 45a is *not* triggered, and by extension, Section 95b is inapplicable. In such situations, beneficiaries cannot demand necessary means be provided, yet circumvention remains unlawful—and this despite Section 45a being listed in Section 95b.[504] This juridical labyrinth and its unfortunate outcome for exceptions beneficiaries is a direct result of the modus operandi dictated by the EUCD of attaching rights-holders' duties to provide necessary means to traditional copyright exceptions, instead of possibly creating standing-alone duties to provide means.

(b) Limited Application to Private Copying Exceptions

Though the anticircumvention model accommodates exceptions for private, noncommercial copying stipulated in Section 53(1), it does so only to a limited degree. One important aspect of this limited application is that nonowners wishing to make a *digital* reproduction for private use (e.g., for backup purposes) of a copy-protected digital work have no cause of action against rights-holders under the provisions of Section 95b.[505]

---

502. *See* § 45a UrhG.

503. *Id.* § 95b(1) nr. 2 UrhG.

504. In the United States, the 2006 Rulemaking provided a special exception for "[l]iterary works distributed in ebook format when all existing ebook editions of the work (including digital text editions made available by authorized entities) contain access controls that prevent the enabling either of the book's read-aloud function or of screen readers that render the text into a specialized format." *See* DMCA Rulemaking (2006) at 68475. The exemption is not tethered to any exclusive right due to the different structure of the U.S. anticircumvention law.

505. For an analysis of the tension between private copyright exceptions and anticircumvention regulation in German law, see JAN POEPPEL, DIE NEUORDNUNG DER URHEBERRECHTLICHEN SCHRANKEN IM DIGITALEN UMFELD 285 ff (2006); CHRISTIAN ARLT, DIGITAL RIGHTS MANAGEMENT SYSTEMS: DER EINSATZ TECHNISCHER MASSNAHMEN ZUM SCHUTZ DIGITALER INHALTE 169 ff (2006).

(c) Access Provision On-Demand Not Covered

In conformity with Article 6(4)(4) EUCD, technologically restricted works that are offered to members of the public at times and places of their choice (on-demand and interactive services) are not subject to the duty to provide necessary means.[506] To the extent providing access falls under the (vague) concept of interactive services, licensing terms prevail over traditional copyright exceptions. In this context, commentators discussed the options of imposing some legal restrictions on the term that may control access via interactive services.[507] The calls made after the 2003 copyright reform to clarify the legal situation and improve the position of beneficiaries by extending the duty to provide necessary means to interactive services[508] did not find expression in the subsequent 2007 reform.

(d) Self-Help Impermissible

The weak position of beneficiaries resulting from the limited application of Section 95b is worsened by the flat prohibition imposed on any self-help circumvention measures to facilitate the exercise of copyright exceptions vis-à-vis TPM-protected works.[509] In addition, the broad bans against trafficking are not subject to any exceptions other than in two extremely narrow situations (i.e., public security and law enforcement),[510] which have absolutely nothing to do with safeguarding the interests of nonowners in reception and use of works. The combination of prohibitions both on actual circumvention and the expansive ban on preparatory acts creates a high degree of dependency on cooperation with rights-holders. Commentators expressed concerns the hurdles involved in litigation would prevent an effective application of mechanisms designed to protect beneficiaries.[511] To mitigate some of these concerns, the law allows collective actions (*Verbandsklage*) against rights-holders to enforce the duty to provide necessary means.[512] Nevertheless, the mechanism establishing a "duty" to provide means under German law has been strongly criticized for being, as a practical matter, a toothless tiger.

(e) The "Legal Access" Requirement

To execute the mechanism in Section 95b, beneficiaries must have already gained "legal access" to the work in line with Article 6(4)(1) EUCD. Here again, the burden of pondering this unfortunate legal requirement and its ramifications

---

506. *See* § 95b(3) UrhG. For a critical comment on the draft bill heralding this provision, see Hilty, *supra* note 459.

507. *See, e.g.*, Ohst, *supra* note 489, § 95b ¶ 47.

508. *See, e.g.*, Arlt, *supra* note 506, at 332–33.

509. *See* First Bundle Bill (2002) at 27. *See also* Dreier, *supra* note 492, § 95b ¶ 2.

510. *See* § 95a(4) UrhG.

511. *See, e.g.*, Arlt, *supra* note 506, at 129–33 (discussing, inter alia, the option of collective actions).

512. *See* Dreier & Schulze, *supra* note 489, § 95b nr. 53–54.

is an inevitable consequence of the Directive. The legislative history of Section 95b fails to illuminate this clause, and not much can be learned from the text of the EUCD either.[513] In fact, the German legislature has expanded this prerequisite also to cases of noncommercial reproductions made by a natural person for private use, which are *not* strictly subject to the "legal access" clause of the EUCD.[514] There is a dangerous likelihood the requirement of legal access attached to all the cases covered by Section 95b might render this provision too often simply meaningless (e.g., in the case of persistent access control).

D. Anticircumvention Provisions in the Courts

As of the time of writing, the number of reported anticircumvention cases in Germany is fairly small. Most of the puzzling interpretation and application issues entangled with Section 95a et seq still await judicial scrutiny. The court decisions presently available confront (for the most part) questions concerning the scope of the anti-trafficking provision in Section 95a(3). Courts have additionally discussed narrow aspects of the "effectiveness" requirement and mentioned in the margins some related constitutional issues.

1. Scope of the Anti-Trafficking Provision

(a) News Reporting is Not Trafficking: Heise-AnyDVD

In March 2005 the Munich District Court I issued an injunction against an online news agency (Heise Online) that had published a report about a new software update (AnyDVD) that enabled overcoming copy restrictions of DVDs. Heise provided a link to the Web site of the company that offered CD- and DVD-ripping tools (SlySoft).[515] The district court held that *downloading* the copy control circumvention software by users in Germany would constitute *importation and distribution* within the meaning of Section 95a(3) UrhG., and therefore, would violate the trafficking prohibition.[516] Based on this finding, the court held that by providing Internet linking to the SlySoft Web site, Heise Online was liable for willfully assisting that illegal act.[517] The court refused to declare linking in the context of news reporting as an activity that is principally secured under

513. *See* Section VI.C.2. *infra*. Dreier proposed the lawful possession of a material copy (*Werkexemplar*) would satisfy this precondition. *See* Dreier, *supra* note 492, § 95b nr. 9. As noted in a different context *supra*, possession of a material object that carries digital signals does not ensure human-access—and this is even less when access control TPMs are employed. Note the language of law speaks in terms of legal access to the *work* ("*rechtmäßig Zugang zu dem Werk*"), not legal access to a *copy*.

514. *Compare* EUCD (2001), Art. 6(4), para. 2 (in connection with Art. 5(2)(b)) *with* § 95b(1) nr. 6(a) UrhG. (in connection with § 53(1) UrhG).

515. *See* Munich District Court I, *AnyDVD*, 2005 GRUR-RR 214.

516. *Id.* at 215.

517. *Id.*

the constitutional freedom of the press.[518] However, the court held the journalistic report neither qualified as an "advertisement"[519] nor as the "provision of services"[520] within the meaning of Section 95b(3). Thus, Heise could not be found to be *directly* violating the anti-trafficking provision.

Both parties appealed to the Munich Regional Court (OLG), which dismissed both appeals.[521] The appellate court agreed that publishing the story about SlySoft qualified as news reporting (*Berichtserstattung*) rather than an advertisement or provision of service within the meaning of Article 95a(3).[522] As such, the activity enjoyed constitutional protection of the press.[523] The court disagreed with the lower court's analysis on the issue of secondary liability for assisting illicit importation/distribution. It left open the question whether Heise could be found liable as an accomplice to these acts.[524] However, Heise was found indirectly liable as a facilitator (*Störer*) regarding the *illegal infringing activities of SlySoft*.[525] In the view of the courts, freedom of the press did not legitimize the provision of the "additional service" of linking, and consequently, the injection was affirmed to remove the link to the SlySoft Web site.[526]

The *AnyDVD* litigation leaves the door open to constitutional protection being afforded to news publishers accused of trafficking allegations as long as their conduct remains within the boundaries of "news reporting." In addition, it appears a defendant could be found *secondarily* liable of *trafficking violations*. This result would radically expand the circle of actors theoretically affected by anticircumvention laws. In such scenarios, accountability reaches even further away from basic copyright violation and the intention to prevent actual infringement, obscuring even more the traditional core and purpose of the copyright law.[527]

---

518. *See* Grundgesetz [GG.], Art, 5(1)(2). At the same time, the court did not impose liability merely for *publishing the story* on SlySoft and its activities.

519. *See AnyDVD*, 2005 GRUR-RR at 216–17.

520. *Id.* at 217.

521. *See* Munich Regional Court (OLG), *AnyDVD*, 2005 GRUR-RR 372.

522. *Id.* at 373–74.

523. *Id.* (The court also referred to Art. 10 of the European Convention on Human Rights as a relevant norm securing freedom of the press).

524. *Id.* at 374.

525. *Id.* (Heise's linking was willful and had a sufficient causal connection in supporting illicit trafficking. At a minimum, that linking made it easier for SlySoft to distribute illicit software).

526. *Id*, at 374–75. Heise appealed this ruling before the German Federal Constitutional Court. Meanwhile, a later decision of the Munich District Court I on similar facts repeated the analysis and conclusion of the appellate court. *See* Munich District Court I, *AnyDVD II* (2006). The Constitutional Court dismissed the Heise appeal on procedural grounds. *See* BVerfG. (*AnyDVD*, 31.1.2007), 2007 MMR 576.

527. For a critique, *see* Thomas Hoeren, *Case Comment, OLG München, Urteil vom 28.7.2005—29 U 2887/05 (LG München I)*, 2005/11 MMR, *768, 773*; Gerald Spindler,

(b) "Private" Advertising in Auction Web Site is Trafficking

In 2005 a district court in Cologne was asked to decide a dispute concerning attorney's fees involving a pensioner defendant who offered DVD-burning/ripping software for sale over an online auction site (eBay). The defendant received a cease-and-desist letter demanding the removal of his offers on the ground the software was illegal.[528]

The relevant question was whether a private person offering such circumvention tools falls under the distribution/advertising prohibition in Section 95a(3). The court first determined that the software at issue—here again products of the company SlySoft—was covered by Section 95a(3).[529] Further, sale offers made by private persons were captured by the anti-trafficking ban, a conclusion corroborated by mere private possession for commercial purposes having been actionable.[530] Specifically, private sale offers were "advertising with the intention to sell" (*Werbung im Hinblick auf Verkauf*) within the meaning of Section 95a(3).[531] The court found a constitutionally oriented interpretation of this prohibition required a subjective mental state of at least simple negligence, a requirement that was satisfied under the circumstances at hand.[532] One interesting aspect of this holding is its confirming the primary remedies and sanctions for anticircumvention violations are similar to those relating to "conventional" copyright infringement.[533]

2. Effective TPM and the "Analog Hole"

In a case brought before the district court in Frankfurt am Main, the plaintiff, a provider of online music services, offered subscribers who paid a monthly fee the opportunity to download music files from a music repertoire.[534] The downloaded files were allowed to be played only as long as the user retained her subscription. The terms of use stipulated that users, who were not current subscribers, had no entitlement to use the data stored in their machines. A certain DRMS enforced these terms by blocking access to the files once the subscription elapsed. Defendant distributed a software tool (called N.DirectCut) that allowed former subscribers to listen to the downloaded songs despite the technological protection. The tool took advantage of the possibility of capturing and copying

---

Pressefreiheit im Internet und (Störer-) Haftung für Hyperlinks - Anmerkung zu OLG München, GRUR-RR 2005, 369, 372

528. *See* Cologne District Court, 2006 MMR 412 (2006).

529. *Id.* at 415.

530. *Id.* at 415–16.

531. *Id.*

532. *Id.* at 416.

533. *Id.* at 414 ff. (violation under § 95a ff. triggered conventional infringement provision under § 97 UrhG.). On appeal, the federal high civil court confirmed this decision. *See* BGH Az. I ZR 219/05 (17.7.08).

534. *See* Frankfurt District Court, 2006 MMR 766 (2006).

analog music signals and reconverting them to digital signals, thereby creating a digital copy playable without DRMS restriction.[535]

The court rejected plaintiff's anti-trafficking-based demand to enjoin defendant from possessing the N.DirectCut,[536] as the subject tool relied on *analog* signals against which DRM protection is not effective.[537] According to the same logic, songs could always be copied by external analog copying devices, so the court concluded it was immaterial whether recording analog signals was done by an external device or within the computer by means of the software application. The DRM system did not prevent the recording of the analog signals, and therefore, could not be considered "effective" within the meaning of Section 95a(2).[538]

3. Constitutionality of the Anticircumvention Law

Several courts touched in passing upon issues concerning the tension between anticircumvention laws and the constitutional norms. The Munich district court in *AnyDVD* suggested the anticircumvention provisions were in conformity with constitutional protections of freedom of the press.[539] Nonetheless, constitutional consideration guided the Munich regional court as it classified defendant's activities under the rubric of "news reporting," which, as such, escaped the statutory definition of the anti-trafficking bans.[540] Constitutional considerations led the Cologne district court to clarify that for liability to be established under the anti-trafficking provision, the actor must have a minimum mental state of negligence.[541]

In general, anticircumvention laws have proved so far quite insulated from constitutional attacks. On one occasion, the Federal Constitutional Court commented that claims of injury to the constitutionally protected property rights of purchasers of copy-protected DVDs would likely fail.[542] In 2007 the Constitutional

---

535. *Id.*

536. *Id*, 766–67.

537. *See* Sicker et al., *The Analog Hole and the Price of Music: An Empirical Story*, 5 J. TELECOMM. & HIGH TECH. L. 573, 575–78 (2007) (providing a technical background for the "analog hole" problem). *See also* Reto M. Hilty, *Der "zweite Korb"—ein erster Schritt in die richtige Richtung* 7 MMR 713–15 (2004) (explaining the technical and political pitfalls in the context of legislative initiatives in Germany).

538. *See* Frankfurt District Court (2006) at 766–67. The court nonetheless held defendant's distribution and advertising as violating the German Unfair Competition Law. *Id.* at 767. One district court in the United States evaluated similar facts and reached the opposite conclusion when applying the DMCA anti-trafficking bans. *See* Macrovision v. Sima Prod. Corp., 2006 WL 1063284 (S.D.N.Y. 2006).

539. *See* Munich District Court I, *AnyDVD*, 2005 GRUR-RR at 215–16.

540. *See* Munich Regional Court (OLG), *AnyDVD*, 2005 GRUR-RR at 373–74.

541. *See* Cologne District Court, 2006 MMR at 416–17.

542. *See* BVerfG. (*Kopierschutz*, 25.7.2005), 2005 MMR at 751 (obiter) The court limited the discussion to the constitutional property guarantee of the buyers, holding petitioner did not have standing that would justify a ruling on the merits. The court thus did not

Court had a rare opportunity to provide guidance concerning the interface between the anti-trafficking provision and constitutional guarantees such as freedom of speech and the press.[543] Yet the court declined to decide on the merits of the question of whether the requirement to remove the hyperlink to the SlySoft Web site was constitutionally impermissible as violating freedom of the press. The decision merely emphasized that subjecting hyperlinking to an injunction did not prevent dissemination of information about SlySoft and its products, and the related questions of secondary liability are yet to be resolved in the courts.[544] In a side comment, the court called the anticircumvention provision a "behavioral norm" (*Verhaltensnorn*)[545]—possibly as distinguished from rules typically prohibiting conventional copyright infringement. This classification is perhaps not without significance, though its concrete meaning remained somewhat cryptic.

VIII. ANTICIRCUMVENTION LAW AS ACCESS-RIGHT

A. Anticircumvention and the First Access-Right Prong

The enactment of anticircumvention laws was the single development that most distinctively triggered the academic debate over access rights under copyright. The abstract access-right paradigm (Chapter 3 supra) helps to identify the role and function of positive anticircumvention rules within the general access-right structure: TPMs enable the distribution of works to the public while simultaneously retaining *legal* control over access, as the necessary access-conducts for making works perceptible are *precisely the same acts the law subjects to the veto power of rights-holders*. This way, the first access-right prong has been materializing as part of positive copyright law. The role of TPMs in this scenario is cardinal: access-control technologies have been providing the logical and logistic conditions necessary for making proprietary control over conducts of access to information possible and enforceable in the first place. Importantly, this control is significantly divorced from questions of legal possession and use rights concerning physical data carriers. In the absence of such digital protection technologies, the first access-right prong would have remained largley hypothetical. The deeper technological access controls penetrate our information environment, the more realistic the access-right vision (or nightmare, if you will) becomes.

---

reach freedom of information issues and the conflict between the private copy privilege and anticircumvention law. *Id.* at 753.

543. *See* BVerfG (*AnyDVD*, 31.1.2007), 2007 MMR 576.

544. *Id.* at 577–78.

545. *Id.* at 577.

B. The Teleological School and *Chamberlain*

1. The Teleological School: A Doctrinal Earthquake or False Alarm?

The analysis underscores one persistent question of crucial importance concerning the nature of anticircumvention regulation and its place within the legal fabric of copyright. The statutory anticircumvention texts reviewed above do not provide straightforward answers to the *nexus problem*: the relationship between anticircumvention bans and conventional copyright infringement. Some courts have been trying to systematically classify anticircumvention laws within the more established framework of copyright protections and violations. Commentators also have identified the classification/nexus problem as a Punctum Archimedis that reflects on virtually every aspect of their scholarly attempts to analyze anticircumvention laws as copyright regulation.[546]

While commenting on the EUCD draft, Günter Auer offered an early account on the topic.[547] At the turn of the millennium, Auer reviewed the legislative history of European efforts to introduce anticircumvention provisions and showed how the nexus between anticircumvention violations and copyright infringement gradually vanished as drafts and proposals were being continuously discussed, revised, and rewritten.[548] He then turned to discuss the nature of legal protection encapsulated in the anticircumvention provisions, stressing the legislative intention to have them serve as mere auxiliary claims (*Hilfsansprueche*) for one—yet still make them an integral part of copyright regulation for another.[549] These inaugural provisions were not meant to create a new exclusive copyright; rather, they were supposed to help rights-holders to enforce their core copyrights. Auer noticed, however, the EUCD draft *already contained* a specific "enforcement" provision (presently expressed in Article 8 EUCD).[550] This provision was specifically designed to secure appropriate sanctions and remedies against infringements of the rights stipulated in the Directive's draft. Auer could not explain the difference between the two types of provisions and their separate loci in the EUCD draft.[551] Nevertheless, Auer importantly opined the

---

546. *Cf.* Haimo Schack, Urheber- und Urhebervertragsrecht § 732k (2007).

547. Auer had before him the latest EUCD draft from March 1, 2000, which contemplated the introduction of anticircumvention laws into European copyright law.

548. *See* Auer, *supra* note 495, at 6–12.

549. *Id.* at 12.

550. *See* EUCD (2001), Art. 8(1) ("Member States shall provide *appropriate sanctions and remedies* in respect of infringements of the rights and obligations set out in this Directive and shall take *all the measures necessary to ensure that those sanctions and remedies are applied.* The sanctions thus provided for shall be effective, proportionate and dissuasive.") (emphasis added).

551. Auer noted, however, that because anticircumvention laws did not create any subjective rights or duties, the said "enforcement" provision (today Art. 8 EUCD) did not apply to them. This conclusion makes sense, as designating an "enforcement" provision to secure the enforcement of other "enforcement" provisions would be an odd arrangement.

anticircumvention provisions covered only technological measures that *encumbered copyright infringement*.[552]

Subsequent copyright commentary in Europe (and especially in Germany) enthusiastically endorsed this approach.[553] Yet the nexus problem persisted: the text of the E.U. Copyright Directive lacks any language that could explain the (perhaps necessary) linkage between copyright violations and anticircumvention violations (called earlier the "in-connection" clause). This has led some domestic legislatures in Europe to adopt anticircumvention bans that do not clearly articulate their nexus to traditional copyright violations. Following Auer, and overwhelmed by the opaque formulation of the new anticircumvention provisions, many commentators endorsed the view that anticircumvention laws are only adjunct ("*flankierend*") to copyright infringement.[554] This ostensibly means rights-holders' entitlements extend only to stopping behaviors that implicate their core exclusive rights.[555] Consequently, access-controls are legally protected against circumvention if *and only if* they help to restrict infringing conducts, as opposed to TPMs that prevent access but do not implicate copyrights in any way.[556]

This interpretation relies on a narrow reading of the phrase "without authorization of the rightholder" (in the German statute–"*ohne Zustimmung des Rechtsinhabers*"). In accordance with Auer's reading, all the rights and powers granted to rights-holders under anticircumvention regulations draw their

---

He further opined that as far as draft Article 6 EUCD was concerned, Member States were free to decide whether or not to introduce *anti-trafficking* provisions. *See* Auer, *supra* note 495, at 13.

552. *Id.* at 15. Accordingly, Auer believed that unlawful circumvention did not include actions enabling the exercise of copyright exceptions such as the private copying exception. *Id.* at 17.

553. For an eloquent exposition of this line, see Alexander Peukert, *Der Schutzbereich des Urheberrechts und das Werk als öffentliches Gutt, in* Reto M. Hilty & Alexander Peukert, Interessenausgleich im Urheberrecht (2004). *See also* Cyril P. Rigamonti, *Schutz gegen Umgehung technischer Maßnahmen im Urheberrecht* 2005(1) GRUR-Int 1, 6 ff (2005).

554. For an early expression of this view, see Wand, *supra* note 231, at 165 ff. For post-first-bundle commentary, *see, e.g.*, Ohst, *supra* note 489, § 95a ¶ 4; Götting, *supra* note 489, Vor. §§ 95a ff. ¶11; Peukert, *supra* note 494, § 33 nr. 11.

555. Ohst, *supra* note 489, § 95a ¶ 15; *Cf.* Peukert, *supra* note 494, § 34 nr. 5 (not all access controls are governed by anticircumvention regulation, and to the extent Sec. 19a UrhG. (the German making-available provision) also included the acts involved in reception, access controls falling under the definition in Sec. 95a(2) UrhG. are only those that help to exercise the making-available right).

556. Peukert, *supra* note 494, § 34 nr. 10; Ohst, *supra* note 489, § 95a ¶ 11; Stefan Bechtold *in* Handbuch Multimedia-Recht ¶7.11 nr. 49 at 52–53; (Thomas Hoeren & Ulrich Sieber eds., 2007); *cf.* Dreyer, *supra* note 497, § 95a nr. 38; Götting, *supra* note 489, § 95a ¶¶ 14–22; Dreier, *supra* note 492, § 95a nr. 17-16.

legitimacy from the acts rights-holders *are entitled to prohibit under conventional copyright rules.* The teleological construction therefore purports that inasmuch as TPMs prevent noninfringing conducts, their circumvention remains outside the universe of things copyright law *can* regulate.[557]

One obvious problem with this approach is the rarity of instances in which access-controls circumvention would *not* involve any infringement aspect as access-conducts in the digital context (with or without TPMs) inevitably involve *at least some reproduction* likely to trigger the digital reproduction right. If access-conducts and conducts covered by the exclusive rights were inextricable,[558] how could the narrow teleological interpretation effectively tame the legal power to exclusively control access to works? How could it help in articulating the nexus between copyright infringement and anti-trafficking violations more judiciously? How could it explain the connection between *preparatory* acts (e.g., possession of TPMs) and *actual* circumvention?

2. Chamberlain's *"Reasonable Relationship" Theory*

The *Chamberlain* court, facing similar dilemmas, translated the teleological approach into important case law. In fact, the problem under the DMCA is even worse, as the statutory prohibition on circumvention of *access controls as such* is concise and unequivocal, and it also covers computer programs (as opposed to Article 6 EUCD). Further, the statutory definition of access-control TPMs leaves little room for creative interpretations. This notwithstanding, *Chamberlain* wished to establish a "teleological" reading to Section 1201 of the U.S. Copyright Act while being aware that an express in-connection clause was deliberately omitted from the statute, inter alia, to achieve the distinction between access controls and rights controls.[559] It is important to reiterate the facts in *Chamberlain* were quite unusual: the accused devices enabled acts that simply could not, under any circumstances, implicate any existing exclusive copyrights. Those "unauthorized" remote control devices that imitated the authentication sequence neither contained any software owned by the plaintiff nor created any reproduction of the software in the course of their use by consumers. Thus, it was virtually *impossible* to persuade the court that users of those devices did anything at all to put exclusive copyrights at risk, which directly reflected on the liability question of the defendant for providing them with the said "copyright-harmless" devices.

This peculiar fact pattern allowed the *Chamberlain* court to proceed in two steps. First, it created the "reasonable relationship" condition for which there was no trace in the wording of the DMCA. This "reasonable relationship" is simply an additional circumstance the court added to the statutory requirements of Section 1201 for showing prima facie violations. Second, and unsurprisingly,

557. *See, e.g.*, Bechtold, *supra* note 557, ¶11.7 nr. 52.
558. Chapter 4, Section VI.A *supra*.
559. Section V.B *supra*.

it held such "reasonable relationship" to infringement could not be established under the circumstances of the dispute. The facts of the case indeed exhibited *zero* relationship to copyright infringement, which is obviously less than whatever a *reasonable* relationship theory would require. For the same reason, the court did not feel obligated to specifically address the interplay between the reasonable relationship theory and conventional copyright exemptions. However, the opportunity to proceed to the next stage came shortly thereafter as the same court rendered its *Storage Technologies* decision.[560] That ruling, as discussed earlier, paved the way for more far-reaching, court-made exceptions to the anticircumvention bans based on the same "reasonable relationship" postulation.[561]

C. Anticircumvention Laws as Access-Right

In some way, the teleological interpretation of anticircumvention laws and the "reasonable relationship" or "in-connection" theories stand in contradiction to the access-right theory. Supposedly, the impetus behind the teleological objection to the emergence of an access-right regime is bringing copyright law "back to track" as it seems to have been veering off course and reaching too far beyond its original mission. This interpretative avenue doubtlessly could help courts mitigate some of the troubling aspects of anticircumvention laws in some cases. But the uncertainties and absurdities anticircumvention regulation brings with it will nonetheless continue to haunt copyright law.

The discussion above underscored that what makes anticircumvention regulation so objectionable is the combination of *overcomplexity* and the lack of adequate *offsetting mechanisms,* which increases the prospects of *overprotection.* These ingredients make up a dangerous mix that might prove deleterious to the integrity and legitimacy of copyright law. At the same time, simply proposing to abolish anticircumvention regulation would fall short of addressing the problems these laws were designed to solve in the first place—problems that today are as acute as ever before.

Unlike the teleological approach, the access-right model (Chapter 8 infra) will attempt to confront the challenge not by *denying* the access-based nature of digital copyright. Instead, the idea is to achieve a better match between copyright protection and the relentless market transition to access-based exploitations while adding the necessary safeguards. This model will endorse the legal and technological shift toward an access-right regime in a very real and radical sense, yet in combination with introducing new conditions to the enforcement of exclusivity over access-conducts and communication-conducts. Before this model is presented, the next chapter will review the impact of digital rights on the traditional copyright system and discuss the main approaches aimed at combating the perils of overprotection.

---

560. *See* Storage Tech. Corp. v. Custom Hardware Eng'g., Inc., 421 F.3d. 1307 (Fed. Cir. 2005).

561. *See* Efroni, *supra* note 335, at 137–141.

PART 3

THE PRESENT AND FUTURE OF THE ACCESS-RIGHT

7. THE PRESENT

I. INTRODUCTION

The access-right construct from Chapter 3[1] furnished a framework that helps to describe, explain, and assess recent developments in the positive copyright law. The previous three chapters showed how copyright has been conquering new territories that once belonged to the property-free realm colloquially referred to as "access to information" or "private enjoyment." It brought ample evidence from the realm of the positive law that reinforces the expansion thesis—and the consolidated analysis presented in the second part of this study (Chapters 3–6) supports the proposition that copyright law has been acquiring an ever-growing similitude to the access-right notion.

In some respects, the evolution of copyright protection in the digital networked environment reflects a surprising degree of coherence: though the details of a given copyright law might seem highly complex and confusing, the general trend is coherent in the sense it fits nicely within the logic of the access-right paradigm. As the same time, the institution of property-like rights that underpin rights-holders' control over access-conducts (never before considered illicit under traditional copyright rules) without there being a grand plan justifying this transition is surely alarming. No less troubling is the vast power copyright holders may exercise to block dissemination in the networked digital environment. Assessing these developments from a policy viewpoint necessitates first forming a very general picture that might explain the logic behind them. The core pattern may be analogized to a three-legged stool:

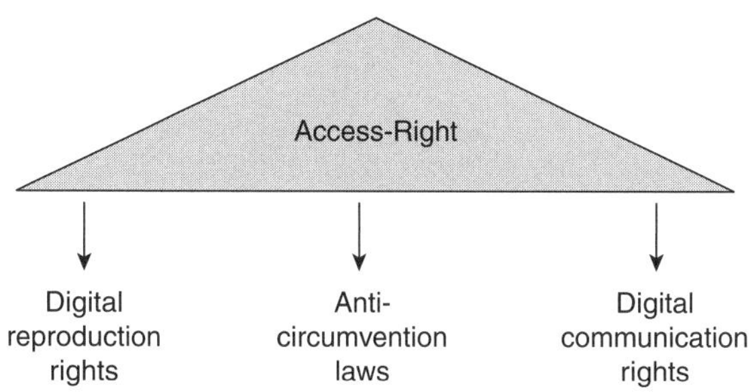

FIGURE 7.1 THE ACCESS-RIGHT IN THE POSITIVE LAW

1. Chapter 3, Section III *supra*.

The information model from Chapter 1 pointed to the intersections where the information *process* and information *regulation* meet.[2] One important point to be drawn from the model is that, in addition to regulating origination and media activities, access control could be perfected once the lawmakers turned to target *reception* activities. Anticircumvention regulation seems to furnish the missing piece in the puzzle for doing exactly that. Along with the three-legged stool pattern, the *type* of proprietary control TPMs and TPMs regulation make possible is not merely ancillary to copyright protection—it is at its core. Logically, the right to control access-conducts within the access-right framework can be the companion of more conventional copyrights to control certain disseminations (or communication-conducts) in the same way the right to receive information is a corollary of the rights to free speech.[3] Principally, living the normative aspect aside for the moment, there is nothing irrational or bizarre about an intellectual property apparatus that covers access-conducts while imposing access-related duties directly on recipients.

However, a *normative* evaluation of this pattern calls for a more careful analysis. This chapter will focus on that transition from a bundle of traditional copyrights toward a digital access-right. Should this transition be endorsed—or condemned? Considering the changing conditions and information infrastructure, as well as changes in human communicative and economic behavior that characterize digital information societies, could it be confidently said the shift is avoidable? What are the justifications for instituting and preserving a property system in information goods that is more oriented by access control and less by control over the making and distributing of physical copies?

The following discussion will evaluate the main arguments for and against the access-right regime, then turn to review contemporary approaches that seek to thwart overprotection hazards that emanate from the current structure of copyright law. This chapter sets the stage for the introduction of a model (Chapter 8) that premises digital copyright on the access-right thesis.

II. THE ARGUMENTS

A. The Case for the Access-Right

As the access-right appears to significantly upgrade copyright exclusory entitlements and consequently increase the impact of copyright law on our information society, the traditional justifications supporting copyright protection need to be revisited. The next passages first briefly review the three main contentions that together compose the principal argument in support of the shift towards an

---

2. Chapter 1, Section V.C *supra*.

3. *Cf.* Chapter 3, Sec. III.B.2(c) *supra*.

access-right regime: the historical function of copyright law, new threats related to digital technology, and the economic efficiency aspect.

1. Copyright's Historical Function

The claim is quite straightforward: copyright law essentially is said to be a form of access control with respect to the information subject matter it covers.[4] The gist of the argument is the transition towards an access-right regime is an *evolutionary* process having its roots in the core historical function of copyright restriction, its impact on information markets, and more generally, copyright law's place within information regulation policies. From this vantage point, the emergence of anticircumvention laws is said to be a natural response of the law to the shift from analog to digital information and communication infrastructure.

The discussion in previous chapters supports the general contention that any copyright regulation intervenes with the information process, and by extension has a restrictive impact on access opportunities in both the short and long run. Indeed, it cannot be denied copyright has always been restricting free circulation of messages and limiting the ability to create new messages based on pre-existing works. At the same time, the ability to translate the resulting access impediments into cash flowing directly into the pockets of rights-holders has been limited, and the formal coverage of the exclusive rights did not extend to access-conducts anyway. In the pre-digital era, there has never been a clear and direct relationship between copyright control and the ability to achieve human-access from a copy in one's possession. In this respect, traditional copyrights and access control are neither synonymous nor antonymous, and assertions about the historical function of copyright as a mechanism of access control is subject to important reservations.

2. The Threat Argument

The threat argument is a familiar and repeating theme, constituting the main driving force behind digital copyright lawmaking in recent years.[5] From the inception of WIPO's discussions concerning a possible Berne new protocol in the 1980s, in domestic and regional reports, through the adoption of the WIPO Treaties, and during implementation of those norms in the laws of many nations, one central narrative has dominated: the traditional scheme of copyright provided insufficient protections to the economic interests of rights-holders in the face of new digital technologies and communication opportunities. According to

4. *Cf.* Jane C. Ginsburg, *From Having Copies to Experiencing Works: The Development of an Access Right in U.S. Copyright Law*, 50 J. Copyr. Soc. 113, 131 (2003) ("The access right is, I would contend, a necessary and integral component of copyright law"); Michael Landau, *Has the Digital Millennium Copyright Act Really Created a New Exclusive Right of Access?: Attempting to Reach a Balance Between Users' and Content Providers' Rights*, 49 J. Copyright Soc'y 277 (2001).

5. In the case of anticircumvention law, see Chapter 6, Sec. III *supra*.

this line, the inadequacy of the traditional regime posed a severe and immediate threat to the livelihood of individuals, corporations, and entire industries whose ability to generate revenues from exploitation of copyrighted works came under great risk.

Of course, there is little dispute digital technology has had a profound impact on information societies and markets. For one, works in digital form can be easily detached from the tangible objects in which they are embodied, then duplicated and diffused worldwide within seconds at minimal cost. The physical bond between the work and the tangible medium is no longer sufficiently strong to ensure a reasonable degree of control by supervising the primary markets for copies; thus, controlling distribution of copies upstream may no longer ensure a sustainable demand after initial release to the market. This explains why the issue of technological fencing has assumed crucial importance for offering a mechanism that facilitates *logical* control over the process of rendering digital data perceptible. TPMs and DRMS have been considered self-help measures for controlling works after their initial release and for preserving revenue streams for rights-holders.[6]

3. The Economic Efficiency Argument and Discriminatory Pricing

The threat argument notwithstanding, it is equally clear digital technology can contribute to significant reductions in production, promotion, and distribution costs.[7] In addition, perhaps the most powerful reasoning in support of TPMs is based on economic efficiency considerations and certain assumptions concerning the opportunities for price discrimination. To the extent that under an access-right regime rights-holders are in a better position to manage discriminatory pricing strategies that would enhance the market values of works, this could entail a positive social welfare impact. Simultaneously, it is often argued that access controls directly benefit users who enjoy a greater quantity and variety of works priced in a way that better matches their usage needs, preferences, and payment capacity.[8]

(a) Discriminatory Pricing: In General

Discriminatory pricing is one of a firm's strategies for maximizing profits. As most commercial firms seek to do exactly that, we should expect firms would

---

6. *See* Kenneth W. Dam, *Self-Help in the Digital Jungle*, 28 J. Legal Studies 2 (1999).

7. *See* Reto M. Hilty, *Copyright Law and the Information Society—Neglected Adjustments and Their Consequences*, 38 Int'l Rev. Industrial Prop. & Copyright L. 135, 136 (2007) (noting the reduction in production and distribution costs of academic publications in electronic media, which stands in sharp contrast to the notable surge in subscription fees publishers charge.) *See also* Reto M. Hilty, *The Expansion of Copyright Law and Its Social Justification, in* Copyright Law and the Information Society in Asia 12–13, 14 ff (Christopher Heath & Kung-Chung Liu eds., 2007).

8. *See, e.g.*, Michael A. Einhorn, Media, Technology and Copyright 49 ff (2004).

price discriminate if they can. To the extent access controls facilitate successful price discrimination (and assuming such strategies increase social welfare), anticircumvention laws could be considered justified from a pure economic viewpoint.

It is common to say discriminatory pricing occurs when the firm sells two identical or similar products having the same marginal cost of production at different prices.[9] In other words, the firm charges a different price for different groups of consumers for an identical good or service for reasons not associated with costs. Most economists agree for the firm to successfully practice price discrimination and maximize revenues, three conditions must be fulfilled: (1) consumers differ in their demand for a given good or service, (2) the firm has a certain market power, and (3) the firm can limit or prevent arbitrage.[10] The first condition means that there should be a difference in the elasticity of the demand curve among consumers.[11] Certain consumers will be willing to pay more than others for a certain product, and their reaction to the change in price will have a different impact on the quantity sold. The second condition means a limitation on competition that confers some market power. This market power inhibits the ability of the consumer to obtain the same (or substitute) products from a competitor at a lower price. The third condition has a similar anticompetition character, according to which trading between the consumers (whose willingness to pay varies) should be prevented. If arbitrage transactions are possible, consumers will compete with the firm and distort its pricing strategy.

Consider the following simple example: *A*, *B*, and *C* are consumers willing to pay 3, 4, and 5 respectively for the same product *X*. If the firm offers the product to everyone at a uniform price 4, its revenues will be 8 as only *B* and *C* will purchase the product. If it adopts discriminatory pricing, the revenues will increase to 12. However, if *A*, *B*, and *C* can trade with each other, the revenues will decrease, for example, if *A* (who bought the product for 3) offers it to B and C for a price lower than 4 and 5, respectively.[12]

---

9. *See* Mark Armstrong, *Price Discrimination* 1 (2006) (available at http://mpra.ub.uni-muenchen.de/4693) (attributing the definition to GEORGE J. STIGLER, THEORY OF PRICE (1987); *Cf.* MASSIMO MOTTA, COMPETITION POLICY 491, n.106 (2004) (adding a cautionary note concerning the precise economic definition of the term).

10. *See* R. Preston McAfee, *Price Discrimination, in* ISSUES IN COMPETITION LAW AND POLICY 1–2 (2008).

11. Elasticity of demand measures the responsiveness of the demand to price, represented by the expression:

$$\varepsilon = -\frac{pq'(p)}{q(p)}$$

where p is price, q is quantity, and $q(p)$ is the quantity the firm can sell for the price p.

12. A number of market conditions may limit that *actual* ability for arbitrage, such as high transportation costs, legal restrictions on resale, thin markets, and information

Pigou offered the distinction between the three "degrees" of price discrimination.[13] First-degree price discrimination (perfect price discrimination) occurs when each unit of the good is sold to the individual who values it most highly at the maximum price this individual is willing to pay.[14] Each consumer who is willing to pay a maximal price *P* per unit for a given quantity pays exactly that price, and the firm absorbs the entire consumer surplus, which drops to zero. Optimal pricing will generate maximum revenues for the firm, represented by the entire area below the demand curve, as Figure 7.2 demonstrates. Under the assumption of zero marginal cost (an assumption often associated with production of information goods),[15] the marginal consumer should be able to buy the product at zero marginal price. Otherwise, there will be utility loss for consumers who subjectively value the good but are not willing to pay the uniform market price for it. The welfare loss is represented by the black triangle in Figure 7.2:

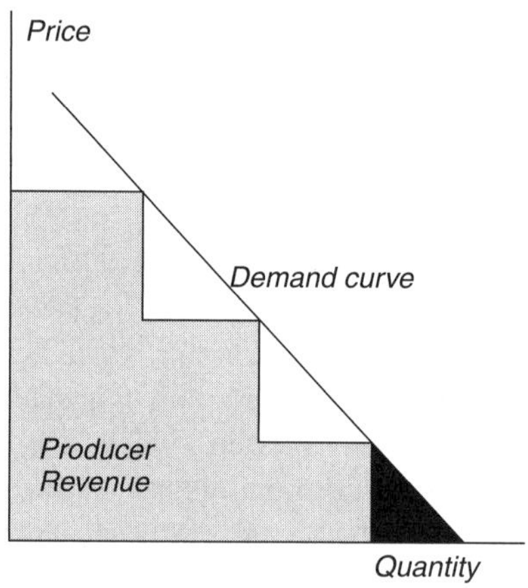

FIGURE 7.2 WELFARE LOSS IN NON-PERFECT PRICE DISCRIMINATION[16]

First-degree price discrimination is merely a theoretical option. In real market conditions, the firm does not have perfect information about individual consumers' willingness to pay. However, this option is important for illustrating the

problems. *See* Preston R. McAfee, *Price Discrimination, in* Issues in Competition Law and Policy (2008), at *3–*4 (page numbers follow the current online draft (available at http://vita.mcafee.cc/PDF/ABAPriceDiscrimination.pdf).

13. Arthur C. Pigou, The Economics of Welfare (MacMillian 1932) (1920) at Part II, Ch. XVII(1) ff.

14. Hal R. Varian, Intermediate Microeconomics 439–41 (2003).

15. Chapter 2, Section IV.B.3(b) *supra*.

16. Reprinted from: Hal R. Varian, *Differential Pricing and Efficiency* 5 (1996) (available at http://www.firstmonday.dk/issues/issue2/different).

theoretical efficiency gains possible under discriminatory pricing.[17] Second-degree price discrimination (nonlinear pricing) means the price per unit of output is not constant but depends on the quantity (or quality) bought.[18] Common examples are discounts for quantities (different price quantity packages) or two-part tariffs, which allow consumers to self-select between various options, thereby revealing their willingness to pay. The third degree of price discrimination is considered the most common form. Here, the firm slices the market into segments and charges consumers belonging to certain segment a differentiated price according to assessments about the willingness to pay among the members of those more-or-less homogeneous groups.[19]

The advantages of discriminatory pricing to the firm are obvious. At the same time, the actual impact on social welfare is more ambiguous, partly because there are different ways to measure social welfare (e.g., as the entire gain of trade, or alternatively, as a factor of consumer surplus).[20] On the one hand, the ability to price discriminate anticipates that more consumers will be served, particularly those with elastic demand curves and niche markets. On the other hand, discriminatory pricing usually results in reduction of consumer surplus as many consumers will now pay a price high over the marginal cost of production. Returning to the numerical example above, if the firm has a monopoly in the market for product *X*, consumers such as *C* will have to pay the higher price 5. At the same time, consumers such as *A* will benefit, as without discriminatory pricing (i.e., under a uniform price 4) they would not be able to buy the product at all. The changes in consumer surplus and producer surplus resulting from discriminatory pricing may provide some indication of the aggregate welfare effect, possibly in connection with their impact on total output. Some economists adopted a rule of thumb stating that when price discrimination increases total production, there is a good chance for an increase in net social welfare.[21]

(b) Discriminatory Pricing and Information Goods

Discriminatory pricing is expected to be a particularly effective strategy to maximize revenues when the products or services show an increasing return on scale, when there are large fixed and sunk costs involved but low marginal costs, and

---

17. *See* Armstrong, *supra* note 9, at 3.

18. *See* Varian, *supra* note 14, at 441–45; Motta, *supra* note 9, at 494–95.

19. Varian, *supra* note 14, at 445–46. *See* McAfee (2008), *supra* note 12, at 4–5 (arguing third-degree price discrimination is actually an imperfect form of the first degree. Thus, an alternative distinction between direct price discrimination (first and third degrees) and indirect price discrimination (second degree) is possible).

20. *See* Armstrong, *supra* note 9, at 6–7.

21. *See* Varian, *supra* note 16; *cf.* Armstrong, *supra* note 9, at 10–11 (arguing that using changes in output as an indication for welfare effects of price discrimination is capable of delivering only "bad news"—namely, when production does *not* increase, the welfare impact is necessarily negative).

when economics of scope are significant.[22] Two archetypical examples are telecommunication services and information goods and services. Assuming consumers have differential willingness to pay, if copyright holders can preserve their market power by depressing competition in a purely competitive market,[23] and if they can substantially prevent arbitrage, discriminatory pricing will become attractive for copyright holders.[24] A common form of third-degree price discrimination is prevalent in the market for books in which early releases of hardcover editions are more expensive than later paperback copies. Thus, publishers discriminate between keen readers and price-sensitive readers who are willing to wait longer for the cheaper version to become available.

Also in its traditional sense, copyright law can be said to preserve market conditions that allow price discrimination by prohibiting competitors from selling at a marginal price equal to the cost of producing a marginal copy. In other words, copyright law generally secures some market power that is necessary for price discrimination of works. However, copyright law assists rights-holders to prevent arbitrage dealing only to a very limited degree. For example, exhaustion rules (perhaps with the exception of rental rights) explicitly delimit the power of the rights-holder to influence transactions in secondary marks for copies.

Concurrently, developments outside the law have been changing that landscape: new technologies help price discrimination to be more effective with or without the assistance of legal entitlements. DRMS dramatically contribute to the ability to price discriminate effectively at least in the following two respects: First, DRMS improve rights-holders' ability to collect and analyze personal information about consumers' identity, behavior, purchase habits, and preferences. As noted, this information is important for designing a workable, profit-maximizing pricing strategy. Second, to the extent access and use permissions become tethered to individual users or devices, technological measures that enable such tethering help to limit arbitrage opportunities and dealing between nonowners. As noted, from an economic standpoint, whether legal protections against TPMs circumvention are advantageous or not would depend on their overall welfare effect, yet economists agree the welfare effects of price discrimination

---

22. *See* Hal R. Varian et al., The Economics of Information Technology: An Introduction 12–21 (2004) (analyzing discriminatory pricing for information producers).

23. *See* Hal R. Varian, *Pricing Information Goods* 1 (1995) (available at http://people.ischool.berkeley.edu/~hal/Papers/price-info-goods.pdf) (purely competitive markets exist where there are several producers of an identical commodity such as corn or company shares traded in financial markets). Clearly, copyright protection extends also to products that are not identical to the work, such as adaptations and partial copying.

24. For two recent empirical studies, see Julie Holland Mortimer, *Price Discrimination, Copyright Law, and Technological Innovation: Evidence from the Introduction of DVDs*, 122 Q.J. Econ. 1307 (2006) (studying price discrimination in the market for DVDs); Philip Leslie, *Price Discrimination in Broadway Theatre*, 35 Rand J. Econ. 520 (2004).

are ambiguous.[25] This observation applies also to markets for copyrighted works. Alone the fact more consumers are served (assuming such effect of discriminatory pricing) is not a *guarantee* of a rise in general welfare. And by extension, the causal connection between anticircumvention regulation and a positive welfare effect resulting from better legal conditions to carry out price discrimination strategies is far from being clear-cut.[26]

B. The Case Against the Access-Right

1. Empirical Objections

The empirical objection to anticircumvention laws mainly relates to the problem of assessing the net welfare impact of those regulations as well as other negative side effects of strong copyright protection more generally. Assuming the initial choice between regulation and nonregulation is guided by the expected impact of both options of net social welfare, there is no clear evidence the net effect of copyright protection in general is positive.[27] It is perhaps even more difficult to buttress the threat argument with hard data proving that expanding exclusivity in this form or the other could remedy the problem and be more socially beneficial than the alternatives.[28]

The empirical question looms large, as strengthening copyright protection essentially is premised on anticipated harms to the economic interests of rights-holders. High-protection proponents argue that without legal adjustments, those harms would never be outweighed via market forces alone, including the advantages of digital technology to rights-holders. The threat argument purports that the economic damages facing rights-holders would ultimately also harm users, as consumers of content rights-holders might not be able to continue producing without being granted stronger rights in digital works. The empirical objection essentially is that premising the argument for expanding exclusive rights on unproved (or even worse, *unprovable*) assumptions[29] should fail, especially if we accept utilitarian-economic principles as providing the overriding justification

---

25. *See* Armstrong, *supra* note 9, at 33; Varian et al., *supra* note 22, at 17–18 (welfare effect in the context of third-degree price discrimination might be native if consumer groups are heterogeneous).

26. *See* John A. Rothchild, *Economic Analysis of Technological Protection Measures*, 84 Or. L. Rev. 489, 504 ff (2005) (reviewing the detriments of anticircumvention laws); John A. Rothchild, *The Social Costs of Technological Protection Measures*, 34 Fla. St. U. L. Rev. 1181, 1198 ff (2007) (reviewing the issue of negative externalities created by TPMs).

27. Chapter 2, Section IV.B.3(b) *supra*.

28. *See* Peter K. Yu, *Anticircumvention and Anti-Anticircumvention*, 84 Denv. U.L. Rev. 13, 50–53 (2006) (noting the lack of empirical evidence in the debate over anticircumvention laws in the United States).

29. *See* David McGowan, *Copyright Neoconsequentialism*, 69 Mo. L. Rev. 1, 2 (2004) ("the legal endgame is to place the burden of proof on the other side. Whoever has to prove the unprovable facts is likely to lose").

for copyright regulation in the first place. In other words, the absence of a clearer nexus between higher level of protection and net social gain undermines the normative force of the threat argument.

2. The Issue of "Overprotection"—A Normative Objection

What does the phrase *overprotection* actually mean? As we have seen, warnings against overprotection effects resulting from new copyright legislation capture center stage in the debate surrounding the digital dilemma, juxtaposed alongside assertions the shift towards access-right disturbs the "delicate balance" in copyright law.[30]

Upon closer inspection, the term *overprotection* encapsulates at least two interrelated assumptions. First, there should be an articulable way to gauge the level of protection and determine a situation of balance within the copyright system, where overprotection represents a different situation in which exclusive rights exceed the desirable level. Second, according to the same logic, a situation of *under*protection is also thinkable, at least in theory. This simply calls attention to the obvious point "overprotection" is a *relative* term that requires a point of reference or a concept to which it can *relate.*[31]

One such possible point of reference is the level of protection available to works in analog formats, for example, comparing protection to literary works embodied in books with that given to digital texts.[32] However, it is not readily

---

30. *Cf.* P. Bernt Hugenholtz, *Copyright, Contract and Code: What Will Remain of the Public Domain?* 26 Brook. J. Int'l. L. 77, 87 (2000) ("the large-scale application of licenses and technological measures will undoubtedly disturb the delicate balance between intellectual property protection and information freedoms, which is presently codified in the copyright law"); Séverine Dusollier, *Tipping the Scale in Favor of the Right Holders, in* Digital Rights Management. Technological, Economic, Legal and Political Aspects 470 (Eberhard Becker et al. eds., 2003) ("Technical locks can jeopardize the legitimate exercise of exceptions to copyright and the whole balance of the copyright regime.").

31. It is possible to conceptualize overprotection differently, somewhat in more "absolute" terms, particularly when it can be clearly stated the objectives or interests meant to be promoted by copyright law are curtailed as a result of an excessive exclusory regime. For example, consider a situation where some sort of non-voluntary licensing would better serve the interest of authors as compared to exclusion rights, which are often transferred in advance and actually enforced by derivative rights-holders. In legal systems that focus on protecting the human creative author, liability rule exceptions are sometimes preferable for achieving the clear objectives of copyright law to protect authors. *Cf.* Reto M. Hilty, *Vergütungssystem und Schrankenregelungen—Neue Herausforderungen an den Gesetzgeber,* 10/2005 GRUR 820, 823 ff (2005). If exclusive rights, which authors in reality cannot efficiently exploit themselves for their own benefit, obscure their ability to draw pecuniary benefits from their works, we may argue the system "overprotects" derivative rights-holders.

32. *See, e.g.,* Ann Bartow, *Electrifying Copyright Norms and Making Cyberspace More Like a* Book, 48 Villanova L. Rev. 13 (2003).

obvious that direct analogies between analog and digital protections are always informative as the markets they regulate are very different in some important respects. Concurrently, the traditional copyright regime seems to constitute the sole concrete reference point available, and from that perspective, the overprotection argument is powerful: if traditional copyright protection presented a reasonable and balanced arrangement, going far beyond traditional protections in the case of digital works would seriously jeopardize that balance. But it is equally clear that though the level of traditional protection *could* be considered arguendo a constant point of reference, the technological and economic conditions under which it operates are by no means constant.

A slightly different notion of overprotection would point out that digital copyright protections cover vaster territories than they used to in the analog environment.[33] The exclusory regime inflates and spills over to control conducts that did not implicate exclusive rights in the analog setting. In addition, due to TPMs and the laws that protect against unlawful circumvention and trafficking, enforcement vis-à-vis individual users becomes more direct, vigorous, and effective. This way, anticircumvention laws affect the traditional balance in copyright law in two respects. First, TPMs can undermine or abolish free spheres of access opportunity that were unregulated under the old regime (e.g., private enjoyment). Consequently, the *formal* restrictions of copyright law are triggered almost every time a nonowner wishes to achieve access to copyrighted information secured in digital formats. Second, once copyright law is triggered, anticircumvention regulation distorts the operation of traditional statutory exceptions, thereby undermining their capacity to provide a proper balancing counterweight to the exclusory regime. The point is illustrated in Figure 7.3 below:

In this depiction, Zone A encompasses all the subjectively valuable actions vis-à-vis copyrighted works in analog formats nonowners can perform. Actions that fall outside the definitions of copyright's exclusive rights are located in Zone A, acts covered by exclusive rights are located in Zone B, whereas statutory exemptions are indicated as Zone C. Accordingly, free zones independent of rights-holders' authorization power are represented by Zone A and Zone C.

Figure 7.4 illustrates the *qualitative* expansion of the area captured by the exclusivity zone, formally determined by the broad digital reproduction and communication rights. Its expansion is a result of changes in the positive law through which the exclusivity zone (Zone B) captures a relatively larger area.

33. The argument is presented here in qualitative, not quantitative terms. Saying "more acts" are covered must obviously take into consideration the fact that perhaps *more acts* vis-à-vis works in digital format have become possible. The important expansion is qualitative (evaluating the nature of the act), not necessarily quantitative (counting the number of covered acts), though it is not unlikely a quantitative focal point would also confirm the same point.

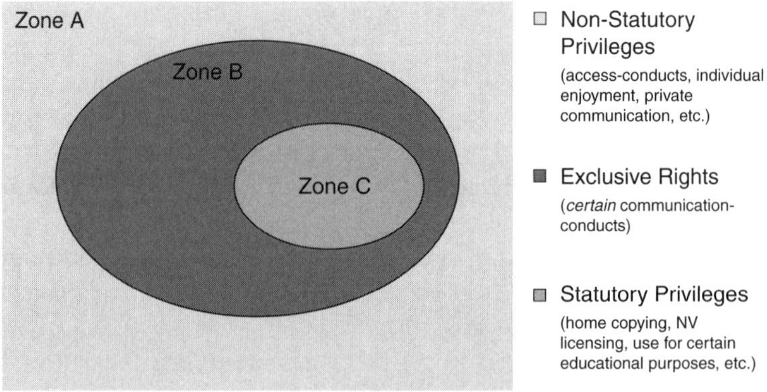

FIGURE 7.3 COPYRIGHT PROTECTION FOR ANALOG WORKS

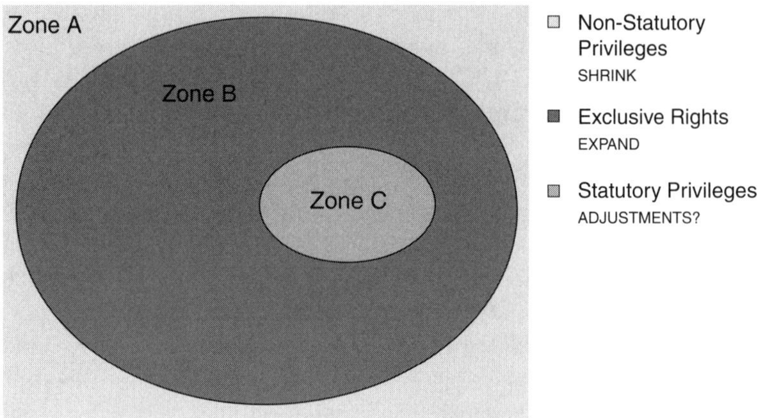

FIGURE 7.4 THE EFFECT OF "DIGITAL COPYRIGHT" PROTECTIONS

This expansion comes at the price of shrinking privileges of Zone A, which stands for the negative freedoms to perform communication and communication-related acts with respect to copyrighted works.

Figure 7.5 illustrates the impact of anticircumvention regulation. The grid represents the area of activities vis-à-vis a work that can be restricted by technological measures.[34] Zone D denotes activities exempted *both* from copyright infringement liability and anticircumvention liability. Only freedoms to engage in such acts remain unaffected by copyright and anticircumvention restrictions.

34. The fact the grid does not cover the *entire* Zone A is meant to express the possibility of "analog holes" in technological protection, and more generally, to recognize the imperfection of DRMS protection in theory and practice.

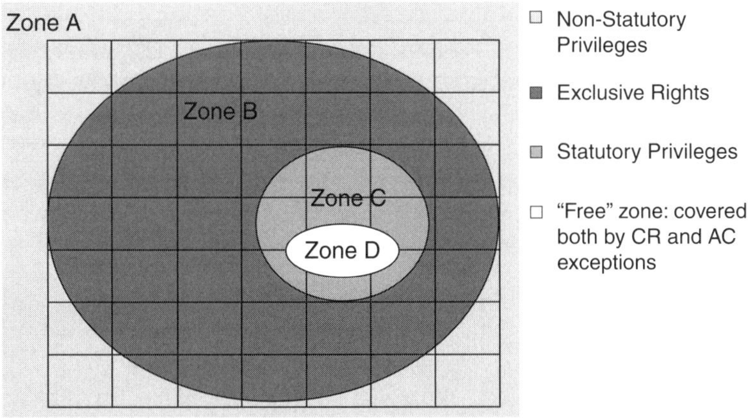

FIGURE 7.5 THE EFFECT OF ANTICIRCUMVENTION LAWS

The free zones are therefore represented by the part of Zone A that is *not* covered by the grid, as well as by the inner Zone D. The overprotection argument essentially points to an alteration in the exclusivity/freedom ratio in favor of rights-holders as we move from a Figure 7.3 situation to a Figure 7.5 situation.

(a) The Impact on Free Spheres: Non-Statutory Privileges and Implicit Limitations

The discussion now proceeds to examine the overprotection argument in greater detail. *Non-statutory privileges* by definition are not regulated directly by copyright law. Access-conducts in the pre-digital information environment largely belonged to this category.[35] Leaving non-statutory privileges outside the regulative scheme of copyright law filled an important function in achieving the "copyright balance" as non-statutory privileges to perform access-conducts established (by default) copyright-free zones. The freedom to read a book in one's possession as many times as one wishes is an example of copyright-free zone conducts.

In turn, the access-right regime inevitably causes such copyright-free zones to shrink, which is related to the nature of anticircumvention regulation and the legal protection to access controls. Also *copyright statutory privileges,* which outline explicit copyright-free zones, lose much of their influence. Statutory privileges are specific stipulations in the copyright law bringing some acts in certain circumstances outside the realm of the exclusory regime. For instance, it is usually lawful to trade in copies of copyrighted works after their initial consensual release without the need to obtain permission, it is lawful to use "negative categories" elements (such as ideas, methods, or abstract concepts), and it is often

35. Recall the definition given to access-conducts in Chapter 3. *See* Chapter 3, Section II.C.1 *supra.*

lawful to make a private noncommercial reproduction of a work without suffering infringement consequences. To assess the impact of new copyright regulations on those free zones, it is necessary to examine the application of the exceptions to the broad reproduction and communication rights, as well as the relationship between copyright exceptions and anticircumvention exceptions. In the end, the actual net effect of this transition on the copyright balance will depend on the specific anticircumvention model in a given jurisdiction and the nexus it creates between copyright infringement and anticircumvention violations.

(b) Impinging on Explicit Copyright Exceptions

It would be logical to assume preserving the level of balance would require access-conducts necessary for exercising explicit copyright exemptions to fall in Zone D in Figure 7.5. However, the reality is different where copyright's anticircumvention protections cover access-control TPMs. One of the main points emphasized in Chapter 6 was that due to structural interface discrepancies, Zone D in reality is smaller than Zone C, denoting exceptions to copyright infringement.[36] This result is particularly troublesome in the face of shrinking nonstatutory privileges, as the role of express limitations to copyright exclusivity become even more important. Despite this danger, Chapter 6 has also shown positive exceptions apparatuses went through only minor adjustments in comparison to exclusion apparatuses.[37]

Under anticircumvention restrictions, nonowners must satisfy the conditions set by the two sets of exceptions—namely, the conduct must neither infringe nor violate anticircumvention bans. For instance, showing a certain circumvention act is excused by a relevant anticircumvention exception might not suffice; to escape liability, the actor must further show the act does not infringe conventional exclusive rights. The answer to the copyright infringement question will often depend on the applicability of a relevant copyright exception. Due to the structural asymmetry between the two sets of exceptions, it is plausible to conclude the net effect on copyright-free zones in general will be negative.

This depiction suggests a certain hierarchy between copyright exceptions and anticircumvention exceptions that emanates from the common course of events and the way access and use relate to one another. To the extent access-control TPMs are in place, as a technical matter nonowners must first gain access

---

36. Figure 7.5 assumes that anticircumvention exceptions always refer to activities covered by copyright exceptions. This is clearly the case under the EUCD model. However, under the U.S. model, it is theoretically possible a given anticircumvention exception would allow the performance of a given conduct that is covered neither by the exclusive rights nor by the exceptions thereto. In such a hypothetical reality, some of Zone D freedoms would have to reside *outside* Zone C.

37. This assessment is represented by Zone C maintaining its formal scope of coverage, whereas Zone B substantially grows as we move from Figure 7.3 through Figure 7.4 to Figure 7.5.

without violating anticircumvention prohibitions. As a result, if DRMS become widespread, anticircumvention exceptions (and *not* copyright exceptions) will likely dominate the digital landscape. If they are tailored too narrowly, concerns about the declining *legal* position of nonowners in the copyright scenario in general become eminent. Both actual and legal opportunities to perform acts vis-à-vis copyrighted works without permission substantially decrease as compared to the situation described in Figure 7.3. In conclusion, should rights-holders resolve to pursue the full range of tools and rights at their disposal, the formal coverage of their entitlements (and the effect on the position of nonowners) enables them to exercise a level of control that goes far beyond their control opportunities concerning works in analog formats.

Before turning to examining existing approaches to minimizing overprotection effects on the copyright balance, it should be noted the notion of overprotection described above obviously also has a normative side. It would be perhaps misleading to stick to a pure quantitative assessment of the expansion of exclusive rights as digital technology might add use opportunities that are not available for analog works (for instance, global access to online libraries that provide access to millions of digitized books).[38] The regulatory decision whether and under which circumstances new digital access opportunities should be subject to copyright exclusivity must inevitably incorporate normative and policy considerations (as distinguished from nominally comparing the scope of exclusivity under analog conditions to the scope of exclusivity under digital conditions). This recognition seems to be woven through many of the approaches described and evaluated in the next passages.

III. APPROACHES ADDRESSING OVERPROTECTION

The prospects of copyright overprotection in the digital environment and concerns about the eroding position of nonowners have triggered numerous calls to restore the shaken copyright balance.[39] Many proposals seek to correct the current legal structure by focusing on some narrow, relatively specific aspects of the present system. It appears possible to organize many of the current proposals into two general categories. One category shall be referred to as "copyright neoconservatism" and the other as "copyright reformism." The difference between the two categories rests on their degree of fidelity to the traditional entitlements structure. In general, neoconservative approaches continue to cherish the right

38. *See, e.g.*, Pamela Samuelson, *Google Book Search and the Future of Books in Cyberspace*, 94 MINN. L. REV.1308 (2010).

39. Among many others, *see, e.g.*, Pamela Samuelson, *Preliminary Thoughts on Copyright Reform*, 2007 UTAH L. REV. 551 (2007) (proposals to amend the current U.S. copyright law).

to exclude as the centerpiece of the copyright system, whereas reformist approaches are prepared to significantly deviate from the exclusivity principle while considering measures to adjust and rebalance the system.

A. Neoconservative Approaches

Copyright neoconservatism is a name used in this study to generally describe approaches that premise necessary adjustments to the traditional structure of copyright law. The basic allocation of legal entitlements is unquestioned, based on the assumption the pre-digital structure can successfully cross over to regulate digital information markets. Accordingly, the familiar copyright principles and concepts (perhaps with some necessary accommodations) provide the essential basis for adequate solutions to overprotection concerns in the digital setting. To the extent the current structure needs to be fixed, it should be possible to achieve the desired results via a series of casuist and sporadic fine-tuning amendments.

Accordingly, the catalog of the conventional exclusive rights (possibly with the necessary adjustments and clarifications) should be preserved and further applied. Similarly, the traditional apparatus of exemptions shall continue to protect the interests of nonowners, and explicit statutory exceptions shall continue to operate as the principal instrument limiting traditional exclusive rights. The diminishing force of non-statutory privileges may require offseting by expressly expanding the privileges' scope secured under statutory exceptions and possibly adding new "digital" exceptions. Concurrently, a narrower reading of existing exclusive rights may be required for reaching a more balanced copyright regulation. However, neoconservatives generally reject the need for a more fundamental revision of the law as it stands today.

Some concrete examples of neoconservative approaches have been already discussed throughout this study, and it is now possible to fit them within a more general theoretical scheme reflecting the agenda they promote for the future of copyright.

1. A Restrictive Reading of Exclusive Rights

Under the present Berne/WCT framework, it is still possible in some cases to adopt a relatively narrow reading of exclusive rights by employing teleological, rational, and textual interpretation techniques. A clear example is the reproduction rights secured in Article 9(1) Berne Convention and the WIPO Treaties. As argued earlier, the international provisions may tolerate a minimalist approach to digital reproduction leaving some instrumental, temporary, access-facilitating copying outside its scope.[40] Historically, the reproduction right had little to do with restricting individual access-conducts, and further attempts can be made to replicate similar outcomes in the digital context as well.

---

40. Chapter 4, Section III.B *supra*.

Moving to copy-unrelated rights, in light of the broad language of Article 8 WCT, a similar strategy in the case of the communication and making-available rights would have a smaller chance of success. On the margins, the making-available right could be narrowed by clarifying the right covers only *acts of actively making the work available* and not the acts of intermediators (including hyper-linking) and end-recipients.[41] The text of Article 8 WCT (possibly also the parallel provision in Article 3 EUCD) does not necessarily cover semi-interactive services,[42] and certain classifications could possibly narrow exclusivity application, at least in the case of the making-available prong. Excluding from its scope instances where end users are required to make selection decisions before the work is actually made accessible could be an example of such strategy. However, as already emphasized in Chapter 5, a restrictive reading of the making-available right would achieve little if the general exclusive communication rights—which are not subject to non-voluntary licensing permissible under the Berne Convention—could simultaneously apply to the same act.[43]

2. *A Restrictive Reading of Anticircumvention Rules*

(a) Narrow Anticircumvention Bans

An additional component in a neoconservative strategy could be to limit the effect of anticircumvention law via restrictive interpretation of the relevant prohibitions. For example, the previous chapter showed anti-trafficking bans are not mandatory under Article 11 WCT.[44] Requiring plaintiffs to meet a heavier burden of proof in legal actions against traffickers under indirect liability theories could substantially reduce the risk of overusing such claims against the "wrong" defendants.

In addition, the general approach to anticircumvention law can be the one advocated by the teleological school: anticircumvention regulations do not give rise to a new independent right to exclusively control access to TPM-protected works.[45] Accordingly, plaintiffs would have to establish a necessary (and strong) minimum linkage between the accused circumvention and risks of copyright infringement.[46] At this junction, much will depend on articulating clear and workable linkage (or "reasonable relationship") provisions.

---

41. Chapter 5, Section III.B *supra*.

42. Semi-interactive services require further approval by the provider after the initial request from the user has been initiated.

43. Chapter 5, Section V.A *supra*.

44. Chapter 6, Section IV.B.6 *supra*.

45. Chapter 6, Section VIII.B *supra*.

46. The *Chamberlain* decision can help to develop this idea. Accordingly, to violate anticircumvention provisions, the accused act must be one that "infringes or facilitates infringing a right protected by the [copyright statute]." *See* Chamberlain Groups, Inc. v. Skylink Techs., Inc., 381 F.3d 1178, 1203 (Fed. Cir. 2004) (emphasis in original).

To the extent anti-trafficking activities are directly prohibited, the law would require showing a manifest causality between the accused acts and likelihood of copyright violations. A possible way to monitor the scope of anti-trafficking provisions is via a heightened requirement of mental state—for example, the showing of intent, recklessness, or (sole) purpose of facilitating infringement.[47] In addition, the law may add a negative clause stating that to be illicit, the device, technology, or service at issue must have only a limited (or no) commercially significant purpose or use other than to circumvent covered TPMs.

In combination with the above, the concept of covered TPMs could be narrowly defined. For example, Article 6(3) EUCD states TPMs are considered "effective" only "where the use of a protected work . . . is controlled by the rightholders through application of an access control . . . which achieves the protection objective."[48] Inasmuch as domestic implementation margins so permit, Member States may read the phrase "protection objectives" as referring to the objectives of *copyright* protection, including policy objectives.[49] In this case, the subjective protection objectives of rights-holders should not always enjoy priority even when robust TPMs are in place to enforce them.[50]

Finally, recalling the conceptual distinction between technological-access and human-access explained in Chapter 3,[51] anticircumvention laws that protect access-controls should apply to the latter but not to the former. In other words, TPMs that effectively restrict technological-access but have nothing to do with restricting human-access to a copyrighted message (or intellectual content) are denied anticircumvention protections. The distinction is particularly important in U.S. law, where software is governed by the DMCA anticircumvention provision (Section 1201(a)(1)(A)), including software that technically speaking is highly functional. In this vein, measures that block technological-access but have no connection to the ability to achieve human-access to the technologically protected works could be denied protection under copyright anticircumvention provisions.[52]

---

47. *Cf.* § 95a(3) UrhG. (stipulating two types of connections between preparatory acts and actual circumvention: (1) The tools should be "promoted, advertised or marketed for the purpose" of TPMs circumvention; or, (2) tools should be "*primarily designed, produced, adapted or performed for the purpose of* enabling or facilitating the circumvention of effective technological measures") (emphasis added).

48. *See* EUCD (2001), Art. 6(3).

49. Chapter 6, Section IV.B.1 *supra*.

50. In this context, it is advisable to adopt a normative interpretation approach to the effectiveness qualifier in various definitions of "effective" TPMs. *Id.*

51. Chapter 3, Section II. *supra*.

52. *Cf.* Lexmark Int'l Inc. v. Static Control Components, Inc. 387 F.3d 522, 547–48 (6th. Cir. 2004). *See also* Chapter 3, Section II.B.2(b)(ii) *supra*. In addition, the courts can develop an "analog hole" doctrine that would declare measures susceptible to unrestricted analog

(b) Modifying Anticircumvention Exceptions

An obvious strategy to reduce overprotection effects is to open and expand the apparatus of statutory exceptions to anticircumvention violations. To illustrate, European law should allow domestic exceptions accommodating the quotation privilege,[53] and U.S. law should expand the narrow DMCA exceptions for reverse engineering, encryption research, and security testing.[54] An (imperfect) example of an open and modifiable exceptions structure is the Rulemaking process created by the DMCA.[55] Though the specific mandate stipulated in Section 1201(a) is quite narrow, this must not remain the case. Instituting an administrative process that receives communications from the public and promulgates periodical exceptions to anticircumvention bans according to changing conditions and needs could fulfill an important function in this context.

3. Revising Copyright Exemptions

(a) Copyright Exceptions as a Correction Mechanism

The apparatus of copyright exemptions (statutory exceptions, limitations on exclusive rights, defenses to infringement allegations, etc.) is the most important policy instrument to counerbalance the impact of exclusive rights on individual nonowners and the information process at large. In combination with a restrictive reading of exclusive rights as indicated above, neoconservative approaches might consider a certain change in exemptions models as well. Consider Article 5(2)–(3) of the EUCD: Such exceptions catalogs as listed in the Directive could be amended to embody more exceptions and/or define existing exceptions more broadly, but in any event, the formulation remains tightly tailored around the traditional exclusive rights.[56] This means that such provisions could excuse access-conducts or communication-conducts (as defined in Chapter 3) only to the extent they overlap with excused copyright infringement.

Nor can these provisions apply directly to anticircumvention violations. A good illustration of such an approach and its contours is found in the EUCD model: All permissible exceptions to the relevant exclusive rights are listed in Section 5 EUCD, which, insofar as they exist in domestic laws, may only apply to the exclusive rights yet not to "access-conducts" in the abstract. Though some

---

access ineffective for the purpose of anticircumvention protection. *Cf.* Cologne District Court, 2006 MMR 412 (2006).

53. *Cf.* Chapter 6, Section VI.C.1 *supra.*

54. For a proposal in this spirit, see Deidre Mulligan & Aaron K. Perzanowski, *The Magnificence of the Disaster: Reconstructing the Sony BMG Rootkit Incident*, 22 Berkeley Tech. L. J. 1157, 1221 ff (2007).

55. Chapter 6, Section V.D *supra.*

56. For a critiquue of this approach in the context of new copyright legislation in Germany, see Reto M. Hilty, *Der "zweite Korb"—ein erster Schritt in die richtige Richtung*, 11/2004 MMR 713, 714 (2004).

minor adjustments in the context of digital works are permissible, Member States are not allowed to breach the closed framework of Article 5, which mandates a more or less faithful rendition of traditional exceptions models.

(b) The Three-Step Test

A neoconservative approach to copyright reform could also reflect on the interpretation and implementation of the three-step test. The three-step test is designed to instruct legislatures in countries bound by international copyright instruments in case they choose to exercise the discretion afforded to them under the relevant treaties and tailor domestic limitations to exclusive rights that affect foreign rights-holders. The common approach to applying the three-step test examines a given limitation against the three "steps" progressively and cumulatively. This means a given limitation is first scrutinized under the conditions imposed by the first step (certain special cases). If these conditions are satisfied, the evaluation continues to examine conformity to the second step (no conflict with a reasonable exploitation). Finally, and only upon concluding the limitation passed the first and second steps, we would turn to apply the proportionality evaluation pursuant to the third step.[57]

However, the text and structure of the three-step test do not prescribe this particular methodology. Nor do the relevant drafting histories indicate that a specific test procedure is more appropriate than others.[58] Indeed, the literature on the three-step test has been exploring several alternatives to the conventional step-by-step procedure,[59] the impetus for which has been the strong impression that conventional reading is too restrictive, lending a disproportional weight to the commercial interests of copyright holders. Consequently, it was feared the leeway left to national legislatures to strike a proper balance has become too

---

57. The WTO Panel reporting on U.S. § 110(5) applied a similar methodology. *See* WTO Panel Report on § 110(5) U.S. Copyright Act (2000) ¶¶ 6.97–6.98. ("The three conditions apply on a cumulative basis, each being a separate and independent requirement that must be satisfied. Failure to comply with any one of the three conditions results in the Article 13 exception being disallowed.").

58. For example, the Records of the 1967 Stockholm Conference indicate an application procedure that begins with the second step, continues to the third step, and concludes with the first step: "If it is considered that reproduction does not conflict with the normal exploitation of the work, the next step would be to consider whether it does not unreasonably prejudice the legitimate interests of the author. Only if such is not the case would it be possible in certain special cases to introduce a compulsory license, or to provide for use without payment." The WCT Basic Proposal followed suit. *See* WCT Basic Proposal (1996), Note 12.05.

59. *See, e.g.*, Daniel J. Gervais, *Towards a New Core International Copyright Norm: The Reverse Three-Step Test*, 9 Marq. Intell. Prop. L. Rev. 1 (2005); Christophe Geiger, *The Three-Step Test, a Threat to a Balanced Copyright Law?* 6 Int'l Rev. Intel. Prop. & Comp. L. 683, 697 ff (2006); Kamiel J. Koelman, *Fixing the Three-Step Test*, 28 Eur. Intel. Prop. Rev. 407 (2006).

narrow, handicapping their efforts to adjust the copyright system to the changing conditions of the information society.[60]

It is important to mention in this context proposals that favor a "holistic" approach to the three-step test and that would, inter alia, cement the role of proportionality evaluation within it.[61] Such approaches to the method in which the test is applied would not prioritize any "step" over another, neither as a matter of sequential order nor of weight. Drawing on the model of the U.S. fair use doctrine, some alternative approaches call for transforming the steps procedure into a multifactor standard. Accordingly, each factor is evaluated separately and independently irrespective of order. Such analysis might have a better chance to generate a balanced result that would judiciously integrate all the important parameters needing consideration. The Declaration on A Balanced Interpretation of the "Three-Step Test" in Copyright Law[62] articulates the basic principles that underlie many advanced approaches to the three-step test. The Declaration manifests:

> When correctly applied, the Three-Step Test requires a comprehensive overall assessment, rather than the step-by-step application that its usual, but misleading, description implies. No single step is to be prioritized. As a result, the Test does not undermine the necessary balancing of interests between different classes of rightholders or between rightholders and the larger general public. Any contradictory results arising from the application of the individual steps of the test in a particular case must be accommodated within this comprehensive, overall assessment. The present formulation of the Three-Step Test does not preclude this understanding.[63]

The Declaration further challenges the principle of narrow interpretation to copyright limitations, which constituted a central tenet within the traditional approach to copyright limitations, especially in Europe.[64] The Declaration calls for taking into consideration the legitimate interests of third parties that are only implicit in the text of the three-step test. This includes public and private

---

60. For a critique in the context of the three-step test as applied in the Information Society Directive (2001), see Reto M. Hilty, *Intellectual Property and the European Community's Internal Market Legislation—Copyright in the Internal Market*, 7 IIC 760, 765 ff (2004).

61. *See, e.g.*, Martin Senftleben, Copyright, Limitations and the Three-Step Test 243 (2004) (proposing to expand the proportionality principle to the first and second steps).

62. *See* Declaration on the "Three-Step Test" in Copyright Law (2008).

63. *Id.* at 2.

64. *Id.* at 4 ("The Three-Step Test does not require limitations and exceptions to be interpreted narrowly. They are to be interpreted according to their objectives and purposes.").

interests nestled within principles of fundamental freedoms and commercial competition, as well as interests in scientific, cultural, and social progress.[65]

In connection with the previous subsection concerning more expansive copyright exemptions models, a liberal reading of the three-step text might be part of a neoconservative agenda to reduce the danger of overprotection. Combating overprotection with copyright exemptions as weapons under conditions of rapid changes in markets and technologies requires a certain degree of flexibility, but flexibility is precisely what the commonplace reading of the three-step test might stifle.[66] Especially after the inclusion of the three-step test as an obligation under TRIPS[67]—and liberal constructions of the test notwithstanding—the vast majority of the world's national legislatures cannot simply restructure their exemptions apparatuses as they see fit to the extent those exceptions apply to foreign works. As a practical matter, any new strategy to remodel these apparatuses would have to consider the provisions of the three-step test and develop an interpretative framework (whether broad or narrow) for its application.[68]

(c) Fair Use

I. FLEXIBILITY AND WEIGHT

The calls for more flexibility and adaptability in the area of exceptions bring the U.S. fair use doctrine to mind. It is said to be an "open" mechanism that is principally capable of shielding against any infringement accusation. Fair use is not a statutory exception in the strict sense. Courts apply its four prongs on a case-by-case basis, and in its current state, the fair use doctrine provides access-seeking recipients only a very thin defense, especially in the digital setting.[69]

In situations of access to digital works, access-conducts significantly converge with reproduction,[70] and reproduction of the *entire* work in the course of digital access weighs against fair use.[71] In the context of communication-conducts, the "transformativeness" examination dominating the application of the doctrine in recent years amplifies the danger of excluding numerous legitimate acts that do

---

65. *Id.* at 4–5.

66. *Cf.* WTO Panel Report on § 110(5) U.S. Copyright Act (2000) (declaring a certain U.S. Copyright Act exception allowing some public performances without compensation did not meet the requirements of the three-step test). For a critique, see Jane C. Ginsburg, *Toward Supranational Copyright Law? The WTO Panel Decision and the Three-Step Test for Copyright Exceptions,* 187 *Revue Internationale du Droit D'Auteur* (2001).

67. For further commentary, see Daniel Gervais, The TRIPS Agreement ¶¶ 2.121–2.136 (2003).

68. *See, e.g.,* Senftleben, *supra* note 61, at 304–11 (proposing an interpretative framework).

69. Chapter 3, Section III.B.2(a)ii *supra.*

70. Chapter 4, Section VI.A *supra.*

71. *See* 17 U.S.C. § 107(3) (instructing courts to take into consideration "the amount and substantiality of the portion used in relation to the copyrighted work as a whole").

not necessarily build on or transform an existing work. In addition, the unpredictability associated with the application of fair use exacerbates the chilling effect potential, as risk-averse (fair) users fear the consequences of having their defense ultimately dismissed by the court.[72]

The first fair use factor (checking purpose and nature of use) carries the promise of flexibility, yet the second prong of the same factor ("including whether such use is of a commercial nature or is for nonprofit educational purposes") casts doubts concerning its overall robustness in practice, as many legitimate access-conducts are not inherently "for nonprofit educational purposes."[73] Together with the fourth fair use factor (checking "the effect of the use upon the potential market for or value of the copy-righted work")—which has been considered most crucial—it is likely fair use would provide only scanty security for access-conducts that could be said to affect the commercial interests of rights-holders.

To improve the position of nonowners in a meaningful way, the fair use doctrine will have to undergo some modifications. Normative and qualitative aspects surrounding the targeted act should assume more weight in the overall assessment. For instance, more significance can be attributed to the *purpose* of that act, and simultaneously, less significance to the commercial/noncommercial inquiry. When the *sole* purpose of the act is to *gain access* to the copyrighted work, fair use analysis perhaps should be more sympathetic to the defendant even when real or speculative impacts on rights-holders' revenues are conceivable.

The language of section 117(a)(1) of the U.S. Copyright Act could inspire a neoconservative approach that seeks to lend more weight to fair use as part of the larger mission of rebalancing the system. This provision furnishes a model exempting reproduction or adaptations that are "created as an essential step in the utilization of the computer program in conjunction with a machine and that it is used in no other manner."[74] The principle highlighted in this exception is adaptable and can extend beyond the narrow scope of that specific context, perhaps even as a general fair use principle exempting prima facie violations that are *purely instrumental to access*. Current proposals seeking to address fair use uncertainty problems such as introduction of "fair use harbors"[75] that would predetermine situations where certain uses are fair per se could also inform the

---

72. *See* James Gibson, *Risk Aversion and Rights Accretion in Intellectual Property Law*, 116 YALE L. J. 882, 887–95 (2007) (noting "[f]air use's adaptability, however, is a double-edged sword"); William W. Fisher, *Reconstructing the Fair Use Doctrine*, 101 HARVARD L. REV. 1659, 1667 ff (1988).

73. *See, e.g.*, Fisher, *supra* note 72, at 1672–74 (criticizing the distinction between commercial and noncommercial use for the application of the fair use defense).

74. *See* 17 U.S.C. § 117(a)(1).

75. *See* Gideon Parchomovsky & Kevin A. Goldman, *Fair Use Harbors*, 93 VA. L. REV. 1483 (2007).

debate about remodelling fair use law within the purview of neoconservative approaches. [76]

II. FAIR USE AND ANTICIRCUMVENTION

Those who trust that a modified and viable fair use defense for the digital environment should play a central role in achieving balance must also address its tense interplay with anticircumvention regulation. Currently, this interface is highly contentious. The legal commentary on the relationship between section 1201 of the U.S. Copyright Act and fair use grapples with two types of questions. The first is what the law *de lege lata* states, and the second is what it should state *de lege ferenda*.

The basic question is whether the fair use defense may excuse certain anticircumvention violations in cases where the accused act is necessary for effectively exercising fair use privileges. With respect to the additional violations provision (section 1201(b)), it is fairly undisputed the circumvention of "rights controls" is allowed for fair use purposes, as circumvention is allowed any other lawful, noninfringing purpose. The difficult riddle is whether fair use applies to circumventions of *access*-controls.

In this context, several key points are rather uncontested. First, codified fair use (section 107), by its stipulated terms is applicable only to violations of the *exclusive rights* listed in sections 106 and 106A. Second, the anticircumvention "saving clause" provides *fair use is not affected* by the anticircumvention regulation set forth in section 1201.[77] Third, the anticircumvention scheme contains a unique rulemaking mechanism to ensure the exercise of fair use under the terms of the mandate delegated to the Librarian of Congress and the U.S. register of Copyrights.

Against this statutory backdrop, at least three main interpretation approaches have developed. The first approach posits the fair use defense in section 107 as wholly inapplicable to section 1201 violations.[78] This view has been widely followed by many first-generation anticircumvention cases in the United States, including *Reimerdes* and *Corley*.[79] The second approach purports that fair use shields certain circumventions of access-control TPMs (e.g., when circumventions are aimed at making a noninfringing use of a lawfully obtained copy of

76. *Id.* at 1502 ff (the aim is to "increase clarity and certainty for users of copyrighted works by enacting clearly defined, nonexclusive fair use safe harbors. Uses that fall within these harbors would be considered per se fair").

77. *See* 17 U.S.C. § 1201(c)(1) ("Nothing in this section shall affect rights, remedies, limitations, or defenses to copyright infringement, including fair use, under this title.").

78. *See, e.g.*, David Nimmer, *A Riff on Fair Use, in the Digital Millennium Copyright Act*, 148 U. PENN. L. REV. 673 (2000). This interpretation appears most plausible considering the language, structure, and legislative history of § 1201.

79. Chapter 6, Section V.G.2 *supra*.

a work).[80] A middle ground approach would apply fair use limitations to the anti-circumvention scheme indirectly under a broader fair use concept, in which fair use is understood as a general common law doctrine going beyond the exact wording of section 107.[81] However, no matter what approach one chooses to follow, the structural discrepancies between fair use and anticircumvention regulation remain. As the next subsection suggests, this casts doubts on whether a neoconservative approach following the second or the third interpretation lines could be sufficiently effective.

(d) Copyright Exemptions and Anticircumvention Law: The Troubled Interplay
The tension between fair use and anticircumvention law is a special case of a more general and so far insoluble problem: the interplay between traditional copyright exemptions and anticircumvention regulation. A neoconservative line would attempt to preserve as much as possible the ability to exercise traditional privileges despite TPMs and to keep them in harmony with anticircumvention prohibitions.

As noted, the problem is first structural. The interests of copyright exceptions beneficiaries are best served when no technological means stand in their way; one way to promote such a situation would be to remove legal incentives to install TPMs (i.e., abolish anticircumvention laws), or perhaps more radically, to create legal incentives to remove TPMs (i.e., ban technological measures that contravene the policy behind copyright privileges).[82] As neoconservatives attempt to come to terms with anticircumvention regulations, their strategy remains centered around tying anticircumvention exceptions to some traditional copyright exceptions (as the EUCD does).

There are several practical ways to safeguard the interest of beneficiaries under such a framework. For example, beneficiaries of copyright exceptions may be granted a legal privilege to circumvent TPMs ("self-help circumvention") either explicitly or implicitly. In the former case, the law stipulates provisions allowing circumvention under certain circumstances. In the latter, anticircumvention bans do not cover certain types of technological protections or operations in the first place.[83] Alternatively, when self-help is disallowed, rights-holders may incur a legal duty to facilitate privileges under certain terms. As part of such a solution (principally adopted in Article 6(4) EUCD), the law may designate a

80. *See, e.g.*, Pamela Samuelson, *Intellectual Property and the Digital Economy: Why the Anti-Circumvention Regulations Need to Be Revised*, 14 BERKELEY TECH. L.J.. 519, 539–40 (1999).

81. *See, e.g.*, Jane C. Ginsburg, *Copyright Use and Excuse on the Internet*, 24 COLUM.-VLA. J.L. & ARTS 1, 8–9 (2000). *See also* Timothy K. Armstrong, *Fair Circumvention*, 74 BROOK. L. REV. 1 (2008).

82. *Cf.* Section III.A.5(c)ii *infra*.

83. For example, U.S. law supports an implicit privilege to circumvent TPMs in the case of rights-controls.

third party having authority to compel rights-holders to provide necessary means, or having itself the technical and legal capability to facilitate exceptions.[84] A U.S.-style rulemaking process is yet a third alternative for preserving analog privileges in a digital world. The Rulemaking represents a middle ground compromise between the two competing philosophies of anticircumvention exceptions. On the one hand, it is designed to facilitate the enjoyment of fair use protections *as they stand*—i.e., it does nothing to effectively alter the content or scope of fair use. On the other hand, it creates special permissions to circumvent access-control TPMs under a narrow statutory mandate delegated to an administrative agency. The procedure bypasses formal legislation and thereby might offer a streamlined response to acute fair use concerns on a more elastic basis. As noted, a similar (yet improved) mechanism could fashion exceptions with respect to *all* anticircumvention bans and for *any* legitimate purpose or use.

4. Private Ordering, Free Licensing, and Nonproprietary Approaches

(a) Underlying Principles

This category covers a cluster of approaches that do not directly collide with copyright orthodoxy; instead, it includes various strategies that run parallel to conventional copyright rules. Some of them introduce mechanisms that in fact rely on the existence of conventional copyright protection with their declared mission not being to overhaul positive copyright law, or at least not directly. Instead, the primary mission is to relax the restrictive grip of copyright rules by persuading certain classes of rights-holders to change and coordinate their behavior in certain ways.

Most initiatives mentioned in the following discussion consider overprotection a great peril to cultures, markets, and societies. To thwart those risks, some initiatives lead organized campaigns designed to provide rights-holders with information and tools to mitigate the effect of a strong exclusive right they do not intend to exercise. This is obviously premised on the recognition many rights-holders do not need (or do not want) to exercise control to the maximum level afforded by law. Accordingly, the focus is on providing convenient and effective tools allowing such rights-holders to license their works under permissive conditions.

Free licensing and open access initiatives identify—and attempt to alleviate—the public choice problem involved that creates significant costs (such as transaction costs and information costs relating to rights clearance and figuring out the legality of a certain use and the status of a certain work), as well as unnecessary

84. See, e.g., Terese Foged, *U.S. v EU Anti Circumvention Legislation: Preserving the Public's Privileges in the Digital Age*, 24 Eur. Intell. Prop. Rev. 525, 538–42 (2002) (discussing a proposal to implement Art. 6(4) in Danish law. In one version of that proposal the third party is a governmental agency that fulfills an escrow function by keeping an unprotected copy of the work).

restrictions on individual behavior: In the normal case, risk-averse nonowners who seek to make use of copyrighted material must assume the work is protected to the extent stipulated by law. To carry forth the desired use, they need to identify the rights-holders and negotiate a license. The transaction costs involved are often prohibitively high *even when rights-holders are willing to grant a free license.* This is where arrangements such as open source and creative commons licensing come into play, seeking to coordinate (and to some degree standardize) rights-holders' readiness to grant nonindividual permissions.

(b) Free Software, Open Access, and Creative Commons

As concerns about overbroad exclusivity surged in recent years, many initiatives set their general objective as providing or facilitating broad access to information and knowledge opportunities, thereby mitigating the negative effect of copyright law.[85] Open access movements promote the dissemination of knowledge in the online environment.[86] Through voluntary and collaborative efforts, rights-holders create platforms in which nonowners enjoy comparatively more freedom and legal certainty concerning access to and use of copyrighted material. The seminal project launched by the Free Software Foundation/GNU movement was pathbreaking. Free software[87] is a social-political movement that began its activity in the early 1980s.[88] Its bedrock idea is that certain informational resources (in the specific case of software) should remain free from nondisclosure agreements, over-restrictive licensing, and private copyright exclusion entitlements.[89] Accordingly, the free software movement advances the principle of "freedom" in connection with using and developing computer programs. As famously coined by Richard Stallman, to understand the ideology of free software, *freedom* should be thought of as in the way of "free speech," not "free beer."[90] According to the Free Software Foundation (FSF)'s definition, four basic parameters qualify software as free: (1) the freedom to run the program; (2) the freedom to study how the program works and adapt it to individual needs (with access to the source

---

85. *See* Amy Kapczynski, *The Access to Knowledge: Mobilization and the New Politics of Intellectual Property*, 117 Yale L.J. 804 (2008).

86. *See, e.g.*, Berlin Declaration on Open Access to Knowledge (2003). For background and comment, see Reto M. Hilty, *Five Lessons about Copyright in the Information Society*, 53 J. Copyright Soc'y U.S.A. 103, 127–29 (2006).

87. Terms such as *copyleft* and *open source* are often mentioned in this context as well. Name variations sometimes indicate ideological difference. *See, e.g.*, The Open Source Definition (available at http://www.opensource.org/docs/osd) (proposing a definition of "open source" software). For more discussion on open source/open software terminology, see Till Jaeger & Axel Metzger, Open Source Software 1–7 (2006).

88. Jaeger & Metzger, *supra* note 87, at 11–13.

89. *See* The Free Software Definition (available at http://www.gnu.org/philosophy/free-sw.html).

90. *Id.* ("Free software is a matter of liberty, not price. To understand the concept, you should think of free as in free speech, not as in free beer.").

code being a precondition for exercising this freedom); (3) the freedom to redistribute copies; and (4) the freedom to improve the program and release improvements to the public for the collective benefit of the whole community, preconditioning access to the source code.[91] These freedoms are secured by a special license, the General Public License (GPL),[92] which is designed to ensure these freedoms shall "run with the software" and apply to distribution and adaptations achieved by taking advantage of the GPL terms.

Adhering to similar ethical motivations, a number of other initiatives have been seeking to underpin the freedoms of knowledge and information, including freedom from copyright restrictions in other contexts. Among others are Wikimedia projects,[93] educational programs,[94] scientific and academic peer-view enterprises,[95] and open-access archives. These and similar projects wish to promote access, use, reuse, adaptations, and sharing of informational resources by creating a more lax legal framework.[96] One of the most important projects has been the Creative Commons (CC), which seeks to expand the free software principle to other types of creative works.[97]

In its institutional incarnation, CC is a U.S. nonprofit organization that launched its first project in December 2002. Strongly under the impression that the law provides too much copyright protection in too many unnecessary cases, CC endeavors to replace the default set of rules by creating more liberal permission platforms based on a special type of licensing, thereby enriching the "effective" public domain.[98] Creative Commons endeavors to replace the "all rights

---

91. *Id.*

92. *See* GNU General Public License, version 3 (available at http://www.gnu.org/licenses/gpl-3.0.html).

93. Wikimedia (available at http://wikimedia.org/) (including its thus-far most successful free encyclopedia project, Wikipedia (available at http://www.wikipedia.org)).

94. *See, e.g.*, Wikimedia, open educational resources (available at http://en.wikipedia.org/wiki/Open_educational_resources).

95. *See, e.g.*, Science Commons (available at http://sciencecommons.org/); Social Sciences Research Network (available at http://www.ssrn.com).

96. For example, Creative Commons' stated mission is "to promote an ethos of sharing, public education, and creative interactivity." *See* Creative Commons Web site (available at http://creativecommons.org/about/legal).

97. *See* Creative Commons History (available at http://creativecommons.org/about/history). ("Unlike the GNU GPL, Creative Commons licenses are not designed for software, but rather for other kinds of creative works: websites, scholarship, music, film, photography, literature, courseware, etc.").

98. "Creativity and innovation rely on a rich heritage of prior intellectual endeavor. We stand on the shoulders of giants by revisiting, reusing, and transforming the ideas and works of our peers and predecessors. Digital communications promise a new explosion of this kind of collaborative creative activity. But at the same time, expanding intellectual property protection leaves fewer and fewer creative works in the 'public domain'—the body of creative material unfettered by law and, to quote Supreme Court Justice Louis

reserved" mentality and legal regime with the notion of "some rights reserved."[99] The set of default rules formulated in CC licenses challenges the hegemony of formal lawmaking in regulating digital information markets for creative works. A bottom-to-top dynamics of change becomes conceivable as numerous rights-holders voluntarily choose to adopt the alternative default rules simply because these rules better serve their needs and expectations.[100]

CC licensing appeals predominantly to authors whose primary interest is providing broad access and who are willing to grant a certain amount of freedom to communicate and reuse their works. Creative Commons provides authors with a set of legal and technological tools from which they can choose their favorite variation to license their works.[101] The central instrument is the *CC license*. The licensing platform consists of several core terms that can be combined in a given license, thereby affording a certain level of flexibility corresponding to licensor preferences.[102] The key features common to all variations is the grant of a worldwide, royalty-free, nonexclusive, and perpetual (for the life of copyright protection) permission to perform acts that are usually subject to exclusion rights such as reproduction, public display, public performance, and distribution of works. Attribution is always required, and use of technological protection measures by licensees is strictly foreclosed.

(c) Creative Commons Critique

CC critics focus on three interrelating points. They complain about a certain ambivalence concerning CC's ideological agenda, they argue the strategy and

---

Brandeis, 'free as the air to common use.'" (available at http://creativecommons.org/about/legal).

99. *Id.* ("Creative Commons provides free tools that let authors, scientists, artists, and educators easily mark their creative work with the freedoms they want it to carry. You can use CC to change your copyright terms from 'All Rights Reserved' to 'Some Rights Reserved.'") (available at http://creativecommons.org).

100. *See* Lawrence Lessig, *The Creative Commons*, 65 MONT. L. REV. 1, 11 (2004) ("The idea here is that we need to build a layer of reasonable copyright law, by showing the world a layer of reasonable copyright law resting on top of the extremes. Take this world that is increasingly a world by default regulating all and change it into a world where once again we can see the mix between all, none, and some, using the technology of the Creative Commons.").

101. Creative Commons tools come in three layers: (1) the Commons Deed (the "human-readable code") explaining in simple words the nature of the license); (2) the "Legal Code" (the "lawyer-readable code"), which is the full and legally binding license; and (3) the metadata (the "machine readable code") that is customized to accommodate search engines to identify CC-licensed works. *See* http://wiki.creativecommons.org/FAQ.

102. Creative Commons currently provides six basic types of licenses that combine the following core terms: *Attribution, Non-Commercial, No Derivative Works,* and *Share Alike. See* http://creativecommons.org/about/licenses/meet-the-licenses. It further offers several special arrangements such as Sampling Licenses, Public Domain Dedication, Founders Copyright, licenses concerning music sharing, and Developing Nations licenses. *Id.*

tools of CC are ill-fitted to achieve its goals, and they further question the workability of the licensing scheme as a stable alternative to formal legislation.

I. THEORETICAL CRITIQUE

Some accuse CC of ideological fuzziness.[103] CC presents itself as a social movement striving toward a social change. On the one hand, it celebrates sharing, creative interaction, expansion of the public domain, and enrichment of the pool of free informational resources. On the other, it sends a clear proprietary message that authors should continue to govern their works.[104] It gives noncommercially minded individuals both legitimacy and tools to apply more or less restrictive terms premised on their basic proprietary entitlements. For example, unsophisticated CC licensors may easily impose explicit prohibitions on commercial use and/or reuse in a derivative work at near zero costs and without needing the assistance of lawyers.[105] As a result, property might become even more prevalent, and violation of the license would trigger conventional copyright rules.[106] In this vein, Niva Elkin-Koren argued CC might encourage trends of information commodification and magnify the social ramifications of those trends.[107]

A second and related critique attacks CC's strategy of relying on property rights as the baseline, then encouraging authors to choose a license and "disclaim" those rights.[108] To the extent CC seeks to alter the meaning of copyright, or at least to "subvert" property conceptions as applied to creative works, it has

---

103. *See* Niva Elkin-Koren, *What Contracts Cannot Do: The Limits of Private Ordering in Facilitating a Creative Commons* 74 FORDHAM L. REV. 375, 387–90 (2005).

104. *Id.* at 390.

105. For a relatively restrictive variation, see Attribution-NonCommercial-NoDerivs 3.0 license (available at http://creativecommons.org/licenses/by-nc-nd/3.0/legalcode). For convenience, subsequent references to specific provisions are based on the text of this license (cited as CC Legal Code) unless indicated otherwise.

106. *See* Elkin-Koren, *supra* note 103, at 400.

107. *Id.* at 399 ("Exchanging ideas is not a transaction. The conceptual framework of property does not capture this complexity. Property rules do not merely define rights and duties. They further carry a normative message, announcing which values deserve protection and how. Therefore, CC's reliance on property rights in creative works is likely to reinforce the belief that sharing these works is always prohibited unless authorized. To the extent this normative framework affects our behavior, it may distort our natural practices related to information.") *See also* weblog post by Richard Stallman, *Fireworks in Montreal* ("I used to support Creative Commons, but then it adopted some additional licenses which do not give everyone that minimum freedom, and now I can no longer endorse it as an activity.") (available at http://www.fsf.org/blogs/rms/entry-20050920.html) (posted 2.9.2005).

108. *Cf.* Robert P. Merges, *A New Dynamism in the Public Domain*, 71 U. CHI. L. REV. 183, 197 (2004) (suggesting CC licensing "publicly disclaim property rights").

been argued that relying on copyright itself is misguided.[109] In this respect, some argue CC licensing does not help to undercut the "property metaphor" applied to informational assets, being the wrong tool for undermining property-like protections enshrined by that metaphor.[110]

II. INTERPRETATION AND APPLICATION PROBLEMS

A third layer of critique is more practically oriented: it scrutinizes the legal nature of the CC instruments and their enforceability, interpretation, and related policy issues. To succeed, the CC terms *must be enforceable against the licensor, the licensee, and "third parties."* The instrument obviously needs to have binding force to attract licensors and persuade third parties to rely on the permission it grants. Enforceability is essential for the stability of the system, and in this context, it is possible to analyze the CC license as a contract.[111] However, its classification as a formal contract bears multiple implications and complications, including issues of formation and remedies.[112]

(aa) Enforceability against licensees

The formation of a contract normally requires, inter alia, an offer and an acceptance of the offer by the offeree. The CC Legal Code stipulates that *exercising* any right provided in the license constitutes acceptance.[113] Technically, no specific procedure (such as clicking on a click-wrap version of the license) is

---

109. *See* Elkin-Koren, *supra* note 103, at 376 ("Creative Commons advocates the use of copyrights in a rather subversive way that would ultimately change their meaning. It introduces an innovative way of exercising legal rights to bring about social change.") *See also* Thomas Dreier, *Creative Commons, Science Commons—Ein Paradigmenwechsel im Urheberrecht?*, *in* PERSPEKTIVEN DES GEISTIGEN EIGENTUMS UND WETTBEWERBSRECHTS 298 (2006).

110. *See* Elkin-Koren, *supra* note 103, at 397–402; *see also* Séverine Dusollier, *The Master's Tools v. The Master's House: Creative Commons v. Copyright*, 29 COLUM. J.L. & ARTS 271, 282–85 (2006).

111. *See, e.g.*, Merges, *supra* note 108, at 198 (suggesting "the Creative Commons is a copyright license. Thus the entire scheme operates by virtue of contract"). The preamble to the CC license itself notes the possibility the CC instrument will *not* be treated as a contract ("[t]o the extent this license may be considered to be a contract . . .") *See* CC Legal Code under the caption "License."

112. The analysis of many issues may differ according to the controlling contract law and its rules concerning formation, enforcement, remedies, etc. The discussion here mostly refers to U.S. contract law principles. From the perspective of some European systems, fundamental questions concerning the legal nature of the CC instrument would probably have different focal points. *Cf.* RETO M. HILTY, LIZENZVERTRAGSRECHT 107 ff (2001) (discussing the nature of the license in Continental European systems).

113. *See* CC Legal Code under the caption "License" ("BY EXERCISING ANY RIGHTS TO THE WORK PROVIDED HERE, YOU ACCEPT AND AGREE TO BE BOUND BY THE TERMS OF THIS LICENSE.").

necessary to attest acceptance. Simply performing an act covered by its terms should automatically place the actor under the regime stipulated in the relevant license. Contract law sometimes terms such formation "acceptance by performance": in this case, when a specific action expresses the willingness to be bound by the CC license.[114] This mechanism appears reasonable only when the actor is *informed* about the existence of the CC license and its terms before acceptance begins to bind her.[115] Several features of the CC license aim at putting potential licensees on immediate notice concerning the legal status of the work and the core terms attached. This includes the presentation of visual symbols, the use of simple "commons deeds," and the obligations to attach a notice to all distributed copies.[116] As knowledge is established, an actor having such knowledge who performs an act covered by the license could be bound under the "acceptance by performance" theory.

A crucial feature of CC licenses is the *automatic termination of material obligations upon breach by the licensee.* This feature inserts an interesting twist in the conventional legal analysis dealing with breach of contract, enforcement of terms, and available remedies. Upon breach by the licensee, all the permissions under the CC grant terminate automatically.[117] Further, the restrictions on the exercise of those permissions expire as well, and the parties substantially revert back to conventional copyright rules. To the extent the license stipulates certain duties that go *beyond* conventional copyright law, it appears such extra-copyright obligations *cannot be affirmatively enforced without consensual cooperation of the licensee.* For example, assuming the rights of attribution and integrity (as defined and covered in the license) are not secured by the controlling copyright law, CC terms are legally unenforceable (for instance, obligating the licensee to name

---

114. *See* Burt A. Leete, *Contracts Formation Under the United Nations Convention on Contracts for the International Sale of Goods and the Uniform Commercial Code: Pitfalls for the Unwary*, 6 TEMP. INT'L & COMP. L.J. 193, 207–08 (1993) (discussing the acceptance-by-performance provision (Art. 18(3)) in the Convention on Contracts for the International Sale of Goods (1980)).

115. *See* Lydia Pallas Loren, *Building a Reliable Semicommons of Creative Works: Enforcement of Creative Commons Licenses and Limited Abandonment of Copyright*, 14 GEO. MASON L. REV. 271, 311–12 (2007). Arguably, as a meeting of the minds cannot extend to unknown terms, acceptance upon exercising a reserved act must be coupled with knowledge.

116. For example, the CC Legal Code obligates licensees to "keep intact all notices that refer to this License and to the disclaimer of warranties with every copy of the Work You Distribute or Publicly Perform." *See* CC Legal Code, Sec. 4(a). *See also* Sec. 4(c) (obligating licensees to "keep intact all copyright notices of the Work").

117. *Id.* Sec 7(a) ("This License and the rights granted hereunder will terminate automatically upon any breach by You of the terms of this License. Individuals or entities who have received Collections from You under this License, however, will not have their licenses terminated provided such individuals or entities remain in full compliance with those licenses. Sections 1, 2, 5, 6, 7, and 8 will survive any termination of this License.").

the authors). Breaching those obligations throws the parties back to their initial position and leads to the replacing the license terms with conventional copyright, effectively annulling any extra-copyright provisions.[118] In general, extra-copyright provisions are unenforceable against the licensee even if the license itself is considered a perfectly binding contract at the outset.[119] For example, the U.S. Court of Appeals for the Federal Circuit upheld a free software license against a violating licensee, holding violation of the special terms reinstated copyright rules.[120] Accordingly, the plaintiff (who was a developer of the software subject to the license) was eligible for copyright infringement remedies.[121] This fairly recent decision is an important milestone that is likely to influence interpretation of CC licenses and the validity of their provisions regarding the mechanism reverting back to copyright rules upon breach.

(bb) Enforceability against licensors

Another subset of questions concerns licensees and their ability to enforce the terms against rights-holders/licensors. Rights-holders may change their minds about CC licensing or the specific terms of the license. For example, they may want to shift from a license allowing unrestricted commercial use to one that reserves commercial use, or from CC licensing to conventional copyright. In such situations, the licensee (who has already "accepted" the terms) should be able to rely on the license to protect him against copyright infringement allegations.[122] To this end, the CC licenses proclaim their "perpetual" effect

---

118. If the license is analyzed as a contract, a claim of breach technically remains available to the initial licensor, instead of (or concurrent to) copyright infringement claims. *See* Loren, *supra* note 115, at 305. However, the language of the license seems to preclude positive enforcement as a remedy. The provision in Sec. 7 does terminate the deal, but it does not invalidate *itself*.

119. This result could be mitigated by providing that certain obligations survive termination, as Sec. 7 does with respect to general provisions (not rights and obligations). But such a strategy of rendering material obligations automatically non-terminable upon breach would open up a plethora of new and difficult issues.

120. *See* Jacobsen v. Katzer, 535 F.3d 1373 (Fed. Cir. 2008).

121. *Id.* at 1381–82 ("Copyright licenses are designed to support the right to exclude; money damages alone do not support or enforce that right. The choice to exact consideration in the form of compliance with the open source requirements of disclosure and explanation of changes, rather than as a dollar-denominated fee, is entitled to no less legal recognition. Indeed, because a calculation of damages is inherently speculative, these types of license restrictions might well be rendered meaningless absent the ability to enforce through injunctive relief.").

122. In general, the CC license does not preclude parallel licensing of the same CC-licensed work under different terms. *See* CC Legal Code, Sec. 7(b). Nor does the license prevent the licensor from stopping distribution altogether or participating in collective administration and distribution of royalties. *Id.* Sec. 4(d).

(i.e., for the duration of copyrights) subject to termination upon breach.[123] By the terms of the license, the grant of permissions thereunder is "irrevocable." It follows (inasmuch as the license is a contract) a licensor would "breach" it if attempted to enforce copyrights already "disclaimed" under the CC license. It is likely in some situations (for example, as demand for the work suddenly surges) the licensor would seek to avoid the CC license, or at least to regain exclusive control prospectively. Under a contract law framework, a licensor could attempt to argue that a binding contract has never been formed (for instance, due to lack of consideration).[124] Alternatively, the licensor can argue the instrument is a "bare" license—as such, it is granted unilaterally and is revocable at will.[125] One basic difficulty is specifying licensor's *acts* that would constitute "breach" of the agreement. Several options that come to mind are issuing a demand to pay royalties for past activities, demanding to cease performing a use covered by the license, or filing a copyright infringement suit. As the legal position of licensees in such situations is unclear, there is a certain legal and economic risk involved in relying on the CC license.[126]

(cc) Enforceability against third parties

Third-party problems can have a considerable impact on the practical side of the CC project. Several possible scenarios call for attention. When copyrights change hands— either via a voluntary transaction or by operation of law such as bankruptcy or death—the question is whether the new owner in automatically bound by the permissions granted by its predecessor. As to third-party licensees, the preliminary problem is to *define* what a "third party licensee" is to a CC license. The CC license, by its own definition, grants a quasi-public license: it binds every person who exercises rights covered by the grant. The issue therefore is to distinguish between "initial" licensees and more distant (or "subsequent") licensees located further downstream in the distribution chain. For the present purpose, initial (or direct) licensees can be thought of as recipients whose access is a direct result of communication or facilitation acts performed by the licensor,

123. *See* CC Legal Code, Sec. 7(b) (license is perpetual, subject to automatic termination upon breach by licensee).

124. In some jurisdictions consideration is a material requirement for the formation of a contract.

125. A "bare" license could generally stand for a unilateral allowance to use a resource revocable by will, subject to equitable limitations on its revocation such as promissory estoppel or detrimental reliance.

126. In many jurisdictions the legal uncertainty is considerable. As of the time of this writing, there seem to be no reported cases dealing with such questions in the United States or Germany. Two decisions from Spain and Holland upheld the conditions of the CC. license. *See* Reto Mantz, *Creative Commons-Lizenzen im Spiegel Internationaler Gerichtsverfahren*, 2008 (1) GRUR-Int. 20, 21–23 (2008) (reviewing those decisions).

whereas subsequent (or "third party") licensees are those whose access is facilitated by someone other than the licensor himself. Third parties may encounter the work as originally created or as incorporated in a compilation or derivative work.

This proposed analytical distinction between the prototypical actors in a CC licensing scenario is not sterile, however. Assuming "subsequent" licensees know about the CC status of the work, their position is identical for most (or all) purposes to that of "initial" licensees. This situation is most likely to occur when the work is further disseminated and communicated in its original form and with the CC notice attached. Matters can turn more complex in the case of derivative works or other modifications. For instance, an initial licensee receives the work from the licensor and then creates (under the permission of the license) a derivative work based on the original one. First, it should be determined whether the *entire* derivative work is now subject to the CC license, and whether subsequent recipients of that work have the same permissions and obligations as stipulated in the license.[127] Second, to the extent the license so holds, can recipients who did *not* have knowledge of the CC license benefit from its permissions even if they assumed they were infringing at the time the act took place?[128] Are uninformed recipients generally affected by the license, and if so, to what extent? Can recipients "violate" a special CC term (e.g., the Share-Alike (SA) or the attribution (BY) provisions) without being aware of its existence?[129]

An additional third-party problem is whether extra-copyright terms stipulated in the CC license are (or should be) enforceable "in rem" against every user of the work.[130] Some of the third-party issues involve interpretation of specific provisions in the license. For instance, it is unclear whether incorporating a CC-Share-Alike-licensed element (e.g., a CC-licensed photo) within a larger compositing (say, a slide show or a movie) obligates licensee to distribute the

---

127. This hypothetical assumes the license permits the making of derivative works.

128. Sec. 4(c) requires licensees who distribute or perform the work to "keep intact all copyright notices for the Work." Failure to do so (or to give notice about the controlling license) might launch the automatic termination provision, *but only against the violators personally. See* CC Legal Code, Sec. 7(a). Thus, it is conceivable subsequent recipients will access that work without knowing about its legal status and trigger the license by exercising the rights provided therein.

129. For further discussion on this question, see Elkin-Koren, *supra* note 103, at 404–07.

130. Some commentators warn against the creation of a new type of property, a replication of the "click-wrap" problem prevalent in online licensing. *See, e.g.*, Dusollier, *supra* note 108, at 284–05. However, such concerns appear overstated as extra-copyright terms cannot be involuntarily enforced against licensees due to the termination clause. (Paradoxically, their "violation" rescinds their legal force.) Alternatively, if "violators" did not have knowledge, under some contract theories they cannot be considered bound by the terms in the first place.

derivative work under the Share-Alike license.[131] It is further difficult to consolidate the "perpetuity" of the license and nonwaivable termination rights. For example, the U.S. statutory termination rule provides that rights-holders are generally entitled to terminate a grant of rights after thirty-five years, notwithstanding voluntary agreements to the contrary.[132] If CC permissions are subject to termination, the grantee will *not* be able to rely on the promise the license is valid for the entire duration of copyrights.[133] The termination issue underscores a more general problem manifest in situations where the law imposes some legal restrictions on the alienability of copyrights.[134]

III. CREATIVE COMMONS—A SEISMOGRAPH WITHIN THE NEOCONSERVATIVE LANDSCAPE

There is some dissonance between neoconservatism on the one hand and the socio-political agenda of the FSF, CC, and similar projects on the other. Free licensing movements grew out of a deepening discomfort with the traditional legal structure. At the same time, they are classified here as "neoconservative" for one simple reason explained at the outset: free licensing, open content, open access, access to knowledge, and the like merely offer an optional layer of standardized voluntary permissions on top of mandatory copyright rules as they currently exist.

Free Software, Open Source, and CC have enjoyed considerable popularity among certain classes of rights-holders, and there is little reason to doubt they

---

131. The problem is alluded to in Educause, *7 Things You Should Know About Creative Commons* (Mar. 2007) (available at http://www.educause.edu/ir/library/pdf/ELI7023.pdf) (asking whether incorporating a Share-Alike photo in a PowerPoint presentation renders the whole presentation a SA-licensed work). Lessig opined the answer is no. *See* Lessig Blog, weblog post from March 13, 2007 (available at http://www.lessig.org/blog/archives/003733.shtml). ("The example considered is of a BY-SA photo included in a report. Does the whole report have to be BY-SA? My view is no—including a picture is not a derivative work of the picture.").

132. *See* 17 U.S.C. § 203(a)(3).

133. To solve the problem of statutory termination, it has been suggested the CC license be regarded as a "partial abandonment" of copyrights. *See* Loren, *supra* note 115, at 319–27. The abandonment is "partial" in the sense rights-holders do not irrevocably relinquish all the rights they have in the works. According to this theory, abandonment is not a "grant," and therefore is not subject to termination rules. However, it is far from being clear whether partial abandonment doctrines are applicable to *horizontal* relinquishment in the sense that all economic rights are disclaimed for the life of copyright unless certain licensing terms are violated.

134. Recently, it has been proposed CC licenses be considered as a new type of servitude. *See* Molly S. Van Houweling, *The New Servitudes*, 96 GEO. L.J. 885, 926 ff (2008). This taxonomy of the CC licenses could influence the analysis of termination questions, as well as other issues discussed above.

will continue to flourish alongside conventional copyright laws in the future. Though the CC option is primarily attractive for noncommercial actors, it also offers licensing alternatives to authors who wish to retain control over commercial exploitations.[135] It is less clear whether the influence of free licensing initiatives can ultimately revolutionize copyright by reversing the exclusivity default across-the-board, and skeptical voices question the capability of free licensing to bring about a real shift in the current legal reality.[136]

From a broad policy perspective and while considering the hovering danger of overprotection, the main significance of CC and similar projects is symbolic, and more importantly, diagnostic. These tools and the authors' choice of using them underscore crucial flaws and weaknesses of the current copyright system. It is perhaps true CC licensing works best where property rights should not have been granted in the first place.[137] But this is precisely the point: where CC is most successful, these are exactly the meeting points where the system is broken, and thus, should attract the attention of lawmakers. The topography of permissive public licensing applications brings to the surface typical situations in which the formal system of entitlements most fundamentally fails to correspond to the real needs of a great many stakeholders.

5. Technology-Based Approaches

(a) The Problem of Regulatory Design

I. TECHNOLOGY AS A FORM OF REGULATION

The tension between legal norms and technological systems designed to regulate and control behavior came under sharp focus in the digital age.[138] Automated code-based processes capable of managing access and use requests cannot accurately mirror legal positions, and no current technology can perfectly mimic the complex structure of entitlements organized by copyright law.[139]

---

135. There is a lot of vagueness concerning the definition of the commercial/noncommercial distinction. *See* CC Legal Code, Sec. 4(b) (preclusion of commercial use includes "any manner that is primarily intended for or directed toward commercial advantage or private monetary compensation").

136. *See, e.g.*, Dreier, *supra* note 109, at 297–98.

137. *Cf.* Merges, *supra* note 108, at 203 ("Rather than a perfect counterbalance, it is just as likely in a given case that these new initiatives represent a creative response to a second-best situation, one where property rights ought never have been granted in the first place.").

138. *See* Lawrence Lessig, Code V.2 61–75 (2006) (discussing the regulative capacity of technology). Regulative design is a general problem having both digital and analog aspects. Both speed bumps and self-eliminating DVDs are examples of regulatory design in which the physical attributes of artifacts (the construction of roads or versatile discs) dictate behavior and use. *See* Dan L. Burk, *Legal and Technical Standards in Digital Rights Management Technology*, 74 Fordham L. Rev. 537, 540–46 (2005).

139. *See* Edward W. Felten, *A Skeptical View on DRM and Fair Use*, 46 Commun. ACM 57 (2003).

An important aspect of the problem is the distinction between two types of regulative instruments: *standards* and *rules*. Rules are sometimes defined as relatively detailed and specific provisions defining the regulated act with a high degree of precision, and which enable prediction of the legal outcome ex ante. By contrast, standards tend to be more open and less precise, requiring the adjudicator to exercise discretion beyond mere processing of factual information. Hence, the legal result (or the specific "content" of the law) is determined ex post, and the degree of predictability is comparatively low.[140] The rules/standards distinction has important applications to issues of regulative design and specifically, technological protection measures. DRMS self-help measures better mirror situations dominated by rules rather than by standards.[141] At the same time, law and legal norms often apply regulative strategy that is dominated by standards. Put another way, legal norms assume various levels of precision and predictability. The law often leaves a fair amount of discretion for the adjudicating authority to consider the particular circumstances.

The difference between legal norms and DRM permission platforms does not end here. Legal norms are products of a public lawmaking process, and many stakeholders may participate in determining their content and design. Legal norms can create exceptions to legal rules to promote the legislative policy. Further, there is a structural and institutional separation between a prohibitive rule and its enforcement. The law articulates sanctions that attach to violations meant to deter illicit behavior, but the final decision whether to take the risk of incurring sanctions and other consequences of such behavior is ultimately left in the hands of the actor. Adjudicators are often required to consider the actor's mental state in evaluating the lawfulness of the suspect behavior. Applying a legal norm to a factual situation commonly invites a complex analysis, and copyright norms are no different.

Regarding all these aspects, technologies designed to regulate behavior differ substantially. DRMS are better at reflecting clear-cut, binary-style rules, but they fare much worse in processing legal standards. DRMS platforms are usually designed by private actors for the purpose of serving private commercial interests. Some DRMS both *define* the rule and simultaneously *enforce* it by the

---

140. *Cf.* Louis Kaplow, *Rules Versus Standards: An Economic Analysis*, 42 DUKE L.J. 557 (1992) (drawing the distinction between rules and standards as a question of whether to give content to the law before (rules) or after (standards) an individual act). Note the terminology and definitions related to the rules/standards distinction may vary. Extensive discussion on this subject goes beyond the scope of the present study.

141. *Cf.* Burk, *supra* note 138, at 549 (considering "rules" as providing bright-line decisional criteria, as opposed to "standards" that are more flexible, taking case-by-case circumstantial factors into consideration). The term *standards* in this context should not be confused with the rather opposite meaning of "standards" in the sense of *technical specifications* denoting common design features for a product or a process. *Id.* at 551.

deployment of TPMs. Enforcement of prohibitions is effective before the act can take place, and often, DRM authorization system set <*denial*> as its default rule. In contradiction to some liberal political philosophy and modern concepts of freedom, in the DRM world each access or use that is not expressly permitted is automatically disallowed.[142] Finally, the capacity of the system to consider contextual information is limited, and integration such information in the operation of DRMS might come at the price of high complexity, inefficiency, and vulnerability.

At the same time, DRMS (as well as other regulative design products) are advantageous for offering a low-cost alternative to policing behavior, enforcing rights, and preventing violations. Regulative design is disadvantageous when it is more important to allow individuals to deviate from the formal stipulation of the legal norm. This option is important where violating the rule serves a higher value or purpose (e.g., driving through a red light in an emergency situation).[143] But before reaching exceptional situations, the most troublesome and frequent issues emerge in non-exceptional circumstances in which the law and regulative design disagree. The danger of overriding the public legal order via private regulative design is especially potent in the digital information environment. The fear is that privately designed technologies would assume more regulative power and effect than they should, as code indeed might become law.[144]

II. DRM ARCHITECTURE

There is a notable tension between common DRM architecture and the law, specifically in the context of copyright law. The problematic interface with DRMS is rooted in structural limitations of that particular type of regulative design. DRMS policies stipulate permission rules often written in Right Expression Language (REL). A common method of expressing permission models is by employing markup tags based on Extensible Markup Language (XML). Common XML-based systems are the eXtensible right Markup Language (XrML)[145] and the eXtensible Access Control Markup Language (XACML).[146] An XrML authorization logarithm considers up to eight parameters such as a "principal" (the

---

142. *See, e.g.*, Barbara L. Fox & Brian A. LaMacchia, *Encouraging Recognition of Fair Uses in DRM Systems*, 46 Commun. ACM 61 (2003).

143. *See* John S. Erickson & Deidre K. Mulligan, *The Technical and Legal Dangers of Code-Based Fair Use Enforcement*, 92 Proc. IEEE 985, 992 (2004).

144. *Cf.* Joel R. Reidenberg, *Lex Informatica: The Formulation of Information Policy Rules Through Technology*, 76 Tex.L.Rev. 553, 583 (1988) ("Lex Informatica may constrain law's ability to deal with a problem. As seen with the present Internet architecture and the very existence of the world wide web, infrastructure decisions that enable multiple paths of communication diminish the territorial authority to address social policy choices unilaterally. Lex Informatica may also substitute for law when technological rules are better able to resolve policy issues.") (footnote omitted).

145. *See* XrML Web site (available at www.xrml.org).

146. *See* XACML Web site (available at www.xacml.org).

entity issuing the request), a "right" (requested act expressed as a verb such as "view," "copy," or "print"), a "resource" (i.e., the content against which access is attempted), time interval, and sets of licenses.[147] Such RELs enable a broad variety of permission models at a high level of flexibility and granularity to accurately correspond to the requirements of content owners.[148]

Upon request, the XrML policy evaluates the relevant parameters and produces a determination whether to deny, permit, or transfer the request to an intermediate, which follows a predetermined authorization scheme. As a technical matter, only policies that can reliably be reduced to yes/no decisions may be automated successfully.[149] This means numerous exemptions and conditions are difficult or impossible to automate with existing DRM architecture.[150] In addition, the information relevant for the evaluation of a request and the production of a decision usually flows in one direction, namely from the policy decision point (PDP) to the policy enforcement point (PEP).[151] This type of one-way, top-to-bottom information flow normally cannot facilitate a dynamic exchange of information between the PDP and the principal issuing the request. The possibility of exchange is substantially eliminated when the authorization process is performed locally (i.e., when no communication with an external authority takes place). Within static permission architecture, the end user cannot communicate with the authorization system in real time and thereby influence predetermined access rules.

These features (or bugs, if you will) exhibit a manifold tension between DRMS architecture and copyright exemptions. XML-languages essentially express access controls, and each access request not explicitly stipulated in and affirmed by the policy is denied by default. As opposed to the non-DRM environment, *each and every access is regulated*, regardless of whether the use it enables is privileged under a copyright exemption. In this architecture, nothing remains "unregulated" and there is not much room left for "free zones."[152] As often noted

147. *See* John S. Erikson, *Fair Use, DRM and Trusted Computing*, 46 COMMUN. ACM 34, 36 (2003). For a more detailed technical overview on XrML, see XrML 2.0 Technical Overview, Version 1.0 (Mar. 8, 2002) (available at http://www.xrml.org/reference/XrMLTechnicalOverviewV1.pdf).

148. *See* XrML and Emerging Models of Content Development and Distribution (Apr. 23, 2002) (available at http://www.xrml.org/reference/GRWP042302.pdf).

149. *See* Erikson, *supra* note 147, at 37.

150. *Id. See also* Erickson & Mulligan, *supra* note 143, at 992.

151. The policy enforcement point (PEP) is described as an intermediary situated between user applications and the policy-setting authority, or the policy decisions point (PDP). Its mission is to permit or deny the request based on applicable policy. *See* Erickson & Mulligan, *supra* note 143, at 987.

152. *Cf.* Section II.B *supra*.

in this context,[153] to the extent the applicability of copyright exemptions depends on contextual information about the user and his intentions, the purpose of the use, its consequences, and so on, DRMS cannot adequately incorporate these variables into the authorization process. There is no mathematical algorithm available that could evaluate all the relevant parameters concerning all copyright exceptions vis-à-vis all potential beneficiaries.[154] The issue is especially thorny with respect to "open" exemptions systems such as the fair use model.[155] Acts shielded by fair use may be performed without authorization or compensation, and fair users remain effectively anonymous.[156] No ex ante permission is needed before fair use can take place, which is a crucial feature in providing meaningful safeguards to fair users. No transaction needs to take place through which compensation is paid and users' identities disclosed. It is quite clear the legal doctrine of fair use, which essentially reflects a legal *standard*, cannot be imitated in the DRM environment.[157]

(b) Technology-Based Solutions

Paraphrasing Charles Clark,[158] technology-based solutions trust machines to address the overprotection problem caused by the use of those (or other) machines that were originally designed to solve the problem of digital infringement. Technology-based approaches essentially challenge the notion that DRMS, due to their basic architecture, cannot be designed to better reflect

---

153. *See, e.g.*, Pamela Samuelson, *DRM {and, or, vs.} the Law*, 46 COMMUN. ACM 41 (2003); Thomas C. Vinje, *A Brave New World of Technical Protection Systems: Will There Still Be Room for Copyright*, 18 EUR. INTEL. PROP. REV. 431 (1996).

154. Even if a DRM system that could almost perfectly mimic the results of a judicial fair use analysis existed, fair users would still be worse off. In such a technological environment, they are deprived of their liberty to consciously violate copyrights when they consider violation, despite its possible legal consequences, as more beneficial or economically efficient.

155. *See* Felten, *supra* note 139, at 58 ("The legal definition of fair use is, by computer scientists' standards, maddeningly vague"); *id.* at 59 ("Fair use is one of the starkest examples of the mismatch between what the law requires and what technology can do.") *See also* Fox & LaMacchia, *supra* note 142, at 63 (mathematically modeling fair use is infeasible); Deidre K. Mulligan & Aaron Burstein, *Implementing Copyright Limitations in Rights Expression Languages* at 7 (2002) (available at http://crypto.stanford.edu/DRM2002/mulligan_burstein_acm_drm_2002.doc) (it is "impractical to expect the rights expression language component of a DRM system to support the machine-readable expression of a fair use").

156. *See* Timothy K. Armstrong, *Digital Rights Management and the Process of Fair Use*, 20 HARV. J. L. & TECH. 49, 59 (2006).

157. *See* Felten, *supra* note 139 (noting the difficulty in technically expressing the four fair use factors in evaluating the impact of the use on the potential market or impact of the use on the value of the copyrighted work).

158. *See* Charles Clark, *The Answer to the Machine is in the Machine*, *in* THE FUTURE OF COPYRIGHT IN A DIGITAL ENVIRONMENT (P. Bernt Hugenholtz, ed., 1996).

the copyright balance.[159] The various proposals essentially attempt to provide several layers of security to users' privileges. The *first layer* approximates situations in which use is likely covered by a privilege. Then it creates a casuistic list of instances for which the technological protection system would automatically grant permission.[160] For instance, it has been suggested that making one backup copy of a work for personal use is likely to be lawful, and such exceptions could be easily programmed into DRM code.[161] This layer, stipulating a subset of authorized uses, should be built into the system in advance to eliminate users' dependency on individual permissions or legal proceedings. The idea is to mitigate the denial-by-default feature of technological protection systems and replace the default for a number of lawful uses with *<approval>*.[162]

A *second layer* of architectural modifications involves a remote (possibly human) decision maker.[163] Accordingly, an impartial third party having the necessary expertise and technical capacity to facilitate access to TPM-protected works would have the discretion to do so in cases likely covered by fair use. Such third party may be a specialized government agency or a sort of streamlined semi-judicial decision maker. In this scenario, permission to perform a certain use is not dependent only on precoded permissions programmed into the REL. Instead, the request is electronically transmitted to the remote authority, which decides requests on a case-by-case basis.[164] Flexibility is thereby enhanced, as the management of permissions is separate (both in time and space) from the rendering machine (e.g., the personal computer or the digital device) and *from the*

---

159. *See, e.g.*, Stefan Bechtold, *The Present and Future of Digital Rights Management—Musing on Emerging Legal Problems*, *in* DIGITAL RIGHTS MANAGEMENT—TECHNOLOGICAL, ECONOMIC, LEGAL AND POLITICAL ASPECTS 602 (Eberhard Becker et al. eds., 2003) ("Nothing in the 'nature' of DRM requires that DRM be only used for restricting access to protected content or suppressing fair use privileges. Properly understood, DRM is a much more neutral technology than commonly acknowledged.") (footnote omitted).

160. *See* Dan L. Burk & Julie E. Cohen, *Fair Use Infrastructure for Rights Management Systems* 15 HARV. J.L. & TECH. 41, 55–58 (2001) (proposing "to build into rights management systems some level of discretionary access for users that would fall within a range that would almost always constitute fair use"); Fox & LaMacchia, *supra* note 142, at 63 (proposing a pragmatic engineering approach that would focus on modeling a useful subset of fair uses in a policy language embedded into DRMS).

161. *See* Fox & LaMacchia, *supra* note 142; Burk & Cohen, *supra* note 160, at 58 (mentioning the U.S. Audio Home Recording Act as a precedent supporting a technological solution for lawful use).

162. *See* Mulligan & Burstein, *supra* note 155, at 8 (suggesting changing the syntax of XrML to include default rights such as "Play," "Excerpt," and "Copy").

163. *See* Burk & Cohen, *supra* note 160, at 59–65 (proposing to entrust a publicly funded institution with escrow access keys and the authority to provide them to users for the purpose of engaging in fair use activity).

164. *Id.* at 63.

content itself.[165] Permission may depend on "obligations" which must be fulfilled prior to issuing access permission.[166] In this context, XACML-based policies offer an additional layer of flexibility (as compared to XrML) as all policies, attributes, and decisions may be remotely sourced.[167] This feature substantially alters the static nature of permission policies, as an XACML policy supplemented with optional specifications of "obligations" to be fulfilled before the policy enforcement point (PEP) allows or denies access could relax the rigidness of a fully pre-programmed system.[168] Such architecture should also help to integrate contextual parameters.[169]

At the *third layer,* DRMS should facilitate bi-directional communication channels between request-issuing users and the policy decision point (PDP). Possibly by deploying rights messaging protocol (RMP),[170] users will be able to negotiate the terms with the PDP within an open and dynamic DRMS environment. In such systems, users are able to "assert" rights rather than being granted permission.[171] To open the deterministic ex ante permission structure and to unwind the binary mechanism of automated systems, it has been further proposed to allow users to "challenge the code."[172] Some futuristic DRMS models envision a "rich dialogue" between users and the licensing authority: that authority could process in real time yet-unspecified actions for yet-unspecified purposes.[173] This feature could be combined with the idea of an intermediate third party to handle challenges and issue decisions.[174]

Building on these proposals, it has also been suggested the system should adopt a policy in which a range of fair uses is permitted by default. However, when a particular use is *not* accommodated, a remote authority should be able to supply the license and issue digital keys upon evaluation of contextual

---

165. *See* Erickson & Mulligan, *supra* note 143, at 987–88.

166. *Id.* at 986 (distinguishing between authorization policies, which are intended to protect against unauthorized use, and obligation policies, which define actions that must or must not be performed when a particular event occurs).

167. *See* Erikson, *supra* note 147, at 36–37.

168. *See* Erickson & Mulligan, *supra* note 143, at 991.

169. The technical possibility of integrating supplemental obligations into a remote authority issuing access permissions based on contextual information suggests this authority must not necessarily be human.

170. *See* Mulligan & Burstein, *supra* note 155, at 4.

171. *Cf.* Erickson & Mulligan (2004), *supra* note 143, at 988–90 (describing a system based on Security Assertion Markup Language (SAML) that enables communication between the DRM client and the license servers via right messaging or transaction protocol).

172. *Id.* at 992.

173. *Id.* at 993–94.

174. *Id.* at 993–95.

information.[175] After receiving a denial, the user should still be able to challenge the code via a rights assertion procedure upon which use should *always* be enabled, possibly in exchange for supplying identification information.[176] Accordingly, access will eventually be granted upon assertion, but will create an audit trail that will enable rights-holders to trace the user.[177] This mechanism shall be designed to support a multilayer, complex, and flexible DRM architecture that endeavors to recreate freedom zones akin to those available in a non-DRM environment.

(c) Some Reservations

One problem architecture and design approaches do not solve (and may even worsen) is users' privacy and the ability to benefit from exceptions anonymously. It is further unclear what compromises such advanced systems might entail in terms of security, trusted computing, and technical standards. As to security, complex and flexible DRM architecture (possibly supported by remote authorization mechanism) is more risky and likely to raise efficiency and cost objections.[178] This point relates also to trusted computing issues. To enhance security, all components of the DRMS must operate in a secure domain in which all trusted components adhere to the specifications of the policy.[179] The more complex and multi-component the DRMS is, the more difficult it becomes to create a secure environment in which security increasingly depends on effective remote attestation.[180] As regards technical standards, DRM components use technical standards that must speak a language "understood" by all other components. Multi-component systems give rise to interoperability issues when not all components are designed by the same maker—hardly a rare situation in the market reality of digital devices and platforms. Interoperability and standardization

---

175. *See* Armstrong (2006), *supra* note 156, at 100–02.

176. *Id.* at 101.

177. This proposal would create an infrastructure in which initial access is granted as the system creates a "trail" of requests attached to a certain work initiated by users. The implied idea of a quid-pro-quo between privacy interests and fair use interests is intriguing but cannot be addressed here at length. It should only be noted that asking users to voluntarily surrender personal information in exchange for being able to perform use that (supposedly) is already covered by copyright exceptions might play to the hands of rights-holders. Rights-holders who use DRMS might value personal consumers' information much more than whatever they could actually charge for the single access or use at issue, whether or not covered by fair use.

178. *Cf.* Fox & LaMacchia, *supra* note 142, at 62 (a system based only on affirmative grants of the content owner is less likely to "make a mistake").

179. *Cf.* Electronic Frontier Foundation, *Trusted Computing: Promise and Risk* 10–11 (2003) (explaining the interface between trusted computing and DRM.) *See also* Jonathan T. Weinberg, *Hardware-Based ID, Rights Management, and Trusted Systems,* 52 STAN. L. REV. 1251 (2000).

180. *See* Electronic Frontier Foundation, *supra* note 179.

invoke further complications that cannot be discussed in detail here. Some commentators believe DRM technology will eventually converge toward common and widely used standards.[181] This could perhaps mitigate the problem of interoperability, but at the same time aggravate concerns of privacy, technology lock-ins, competition, and strategic behavior.

(d) Evaluation

I. THE TRUE NATURE OF "KEY ESCROW" MODELS

Involving a remote or external decision maker in the technical authorization process carries the promise of reintroducing human intelligence into the DRM environment. The underlying objective of such proposals is to avoid situations in which fair use and users are governed solely by DRM codes and the whims of content providers. A subset of precoded authorizations is important, but alone it cannot suffice as the sole balancing mechanism. Human intelligence should further prevent precoded authorizations from becoming a ceiling by determining the de facto scope of copyright exemptions in the DRM environment. Most technology-based approaches essentially seek to preserve analog exceptions, defenses, and limitations in the digital realm. This observation underlies their classification here as roughly falling within the rubric of "neoconservatism" despite their highly innovative character.

That said, determining the true nature of technology-based approaches might turn tricky. Consider for example the key escrow proposal that would introduce external decision making into the technological process of permission granting: to the extent the key escrow authority can authorize copyright-relevant use against the will of copyright holders, this may lead to some erosion in their traditional power to proscribe such activities. To the extent that under such framework, rights-holders lose some of their *legal* power to veto the said activities (according to the taxonomy explained earlier), the key escrow proposal shifts closer to the reformist camp.[182] This illustrates that occasionally, the distinction between neoconservatism and reformism turns blurry, and much would depend on the scope of powers delegated to the key escrow agent and the level of correspondence between what the law permits on the one hand, and the kind of permissions issued by the agent on the other.

In addition, proposals that nominally falls under the caption "technology-based solutions" having no aspiration to change the legal regime itself might result in de facto *upgrading nonowners' positions* as their entitlements become *enforceable* against rights-holders. Inasmuch as technology-based strategies aim at striking a *new* balance (i.e., alter the content align themselves with compared to their position in the analog space), they copyright reformism and

181. *Cf.* Erickson & Mulligan, *supra* note 143, at 995; Burk, *supra* note 138, at 554.

182. The cardinal question is whether using such systems could become obligatory by virtue of a legal duty or an equivalent measure.

should be analyzed as such, and not as merely a technical element in an architectural solution.

Consequently, the proponents of such solutions must explicitly outline their policy and then define the technological solutions as a means to achieve the stated ends.[183] In the model proposed by Burk and Cohen, for instance, the need for an external decision maker emanated from the authors' skepticism regarding the capability of a precoded subset of permissions to encompass all fair uses. For example, they wish to preserve fair use protections against private censorship vis-à-vis technologically protected works.[184] The assumption is "the point of fair use is to provide low cost or free access to content."[185] If so, the task of the key escrow agent is simply to *facilitate* existing rights of access,[186] not establish new ones:

> In order to avoid difficult ex ante judgments about particular uses, and to approximate as nearly as possible the cost and incentive structure of traditional fair uses, the third party would not be required, and would not attempt, to make a determination about the bona fides of the access application. Rather, the *third party would simply issue keys to applicants via a simple online procedure.*[187]

The reality this model seeks to emulate is one in which access to copyrighted content is often inadvertent, spontaneous, anonymous, and authorization-independent. It seems, however, that the Burk/Cohen proposal nicely illustrates that preserving fair use conditions in the DRM environment is *practically impossible without materially changing the content of rights.* The key escrow agent will undercut rights-holders' control in a way that goes beyond mere restoration of long-standing users' privileges: it will inevitably tilt the system toward an explicit rights-of-access regime.

In addition, implementation of architectural approaches should take into consideration at least two types of further complications, namely, the interplay with current copyright protection provisions and issues of enforcement against rights-holders. Consider the question whether user-friendly DRMS pass the effectiveness muster stipulated in Article 11 WCT.[188] Does the TPM remain "effective" when denial of access can turn into permission simply upon issuing

183. *See* Reidenberg, *supra* note 144 (proposing to use technological architecture and infrastructure explicitly as a means to achieve stated policy goals).

184. *See* Burk & Cohen, *supra* note 160, at 59–61.

185. *Id.* at 66.

186. The term *rights-of-access* corresponds to its meaning in Chapter 3 *supra.*

187. *See* Burk & Cohen, *supra* note 160, at 63 (emphasis added).

188. Chapter 6, Section IV.B.1 *supra.*

an application,[189] or when the system technically *does not really block anything*?[190] And if so, can such regime further satisfy the international obligation to provide "adequate legal protection and effective legal remedies"[191] against the circumvention of effective TPMs? After all, if permission is granted upon request, there would be no need to circumvent anything, and anticircumvention provisions would seem rather superfluous.

A related question concerns the nature and scope of rights-holders' obligations under the proposed regime. It would be naïve to expect rights-holders to voluntarily adopt a permissive DRM architecture only to preserve fair use conditions and the opportunity to exercise statutory exceptions. One option is to fashion a legal *obligation* to use certain systems and not others (*coercion strategy*); the second is to provide incentives to *voluntarily* deploy exceptions-friendly DRMS (*incentives strategy*). Burk and Cohen proposed to punish noncompliance by depriving rights-holders of the ability to enforce their copyrights.[192] They admit, however, that such rules could not apply vis-à-vis foreign authors due to the current scope of international obligations.[193] Denying noncomplying rights-holders their anticircumvention claims is a milder alternative, which in itself is not entirely unproblematic in light of the tension with international obligations to provide anticircumvention protections.[194] Instead of pursuing a strategy of imposing direct obligations to install only approved systems (coupled with legal sanctions or deprivation of legal claims in case on noncompliance), the law alternatively could provide positive incentives designed to encourage voluntary implementation of the desired DRM scheme, as discussed briefly below.

II. ADDITIONAL COMPLICATIONS

The sheer technological challenge involved in developing an exceptions-friendly DRM architecture should not be understated. Assuming such systems become available, it is important to ensure rights-holders would actually use them.[195] One scenario envisions such systems will become an industry standard; then, as

---

189. *See* Burk & Cohen, *supra* note 160, at 63.

190. *Cf.* Armstrong, *supra* note 156, at 68 ff.

191. Chapter 6, Section IV.B.6 *supra*.

192. *See* Burk & Cohen, *supra* note 160, at 65.

193. *Id.* at 72.

194. Creating an explicit direct privilege to circumvent systems that do not accommodate copyright exceptions to a sufficient degree would not per se violate obligations under Art. 11 WCT but would likely be in conflict with the EUCD.

195. Fox and LaMacchia argued that focusing on content owners' incentives to accommodate fair uses in DRM architecture is misplaced. Instead, DRM builders should be incentivized to develop conflict-resolution algorithms and expression of fair uses in policy systems. *See* Fox & LaMacchia, *supra* note 142, at 62. However, they do not explain how incentives should be created, nor do they address the "market failure" in this sector due to DRMS being ordered and paid for by content owners whose commercial interests typically rank higher than their fair use concerns.

a practical matter, content owners, DRM builders, service providers, and device manufacturers would be committed to DRM standards that accommodate copyright exceptions. Yet it is questionable those standards will emerge and take over the industry only via private contracting and market forces.[196] A more affirmative, regulation-based incentive might be required.

Government intervention in the DRM industry and satellite markets can take several forms. The less likely option is to create a legal *duty* to use only recommended DRM systems that conform to certain legal and technical standards.[197] Under that regime, use of noncomplying systems would be flatly prohibited.[198] The coercion strategy implies the government or its regulative agency (assisted by technical and legal experts) would develop, periodically adapt, and enforce the standards with which rights-holders should comply for content protection objectives. But the objections to strict regulation of DRM markets in general are equally strong, making it an unattractive option indeed, special efforts were made to clarify that anticircumvention laws do not mandate adherence to any specific technological standard.[199]

The principal alternative to the coercion strategy is the incentive strategy: granting monetary incentives to use preferred systems comes to mind (for instance, instituting participation rights in collective administration revenues under levy systems). Another tactic is to impose a special tax on noncomplying systems and direct the money collected to research and development of exceptions-friendly systems—or even distribute direct grants to complying rights-holders to carry forth advances in this area. Indeed there are many thinkable way to encourage voluntary adoption of preferred systems, and the package of incentives and disincentives to rights-holders may assume various shapes and forms. Further scrutiny is perhaps advisable as the concept of exceptions-friendly DRMS and their industrial application became more solid and realizable.

B. Copyright Reformism

The crucial difference between copyright neoconservatism and reformism is the degree to which one is prepared to compromise the exclusivity principle. Reformists are ready for a deeper and more painful operation. They assert the

---

196. *Cf.* Samuelson, *supra* note 153, at 4.

197. The standards do not have to be purely technical or technology-specific. For example, the XrML model defines the interactions between a request issuer (principal), a resource, a *condition*, and a *right*. The legal standard for preferred DRMS could theoretically provide a framework for the content of the latter two parameters, forming a minimum level of prima facie fair uses. Alternatively, or in conjunction with this, the standard could compel a feature of remote attestation outsourcing the decisions on requests to a third-party authorization body.

198. *Cf.* Armstrong, *supra* note 156, at 117–18 (noting this option with reservation).

199. *See, e.g.*, 17 U.S.C. § 1201(c)(3); EUCD (2001), Recital 48.

digital reality necessitates a fundamental change that shall influence some key features of the copyright system. But reformists are not copyright anarchists—they do not seek to abolish copyright regulation completely. They challenge neither the basic idea of intellectual property nor the long-standing theoretical underpinnings of copyright. However, reformists believe a substantial reconstruction must take place to achieve a better fit between copyright theory, its policy goals, and its actual effect in the information environment. The point of departure for reformist approaches is that more powerful weapons than the ones offered by neoconservatives are needed to combat the perils of overprotection.

1. Shifting to Liability Rules

(a) Introduction

The right to exclude enshrines property rights-holders' veto power to prevent unauthorized use of works in some circumstances.[200] It is the core principle of copyright law and the default rule controlling reserved use of copyrighted material. Nonowners must generally assume unauthorized reserved use might be unlawful unless exceptions apply, in which case they effectively reverse the default rule from exclusivity to freedom (or a Hohfeldian privilege.) Some exceptions replace the duty to obtain permission with one to compensate rights-holders for the use at issue. Such exceptions can be called liability rule exceptions, or simply liability rules.[201] They define special situations to which the veto power to prohibit use does not apply.

A shift from a property rule to a liability rule can be described as follows: liability rules alter both the *quality* and *content* of the legal positions between the parties. In a given fact situation defined by the exception, the owners' right-claim to enjoin reserved acts is reduced to a monetary claim. Correlatively, the nonowners' default duty to refrain from acting without authorization is replaced by a privilege to act (possibly) coupled with a duty to pay. In practice, the jural analysis is more complex and involves more parties. To facilitate large-scale circulation of works and reduce transaction costs, sometimes an intermediary actor absorbs rights and duties by entering into the shoes of the principal parties. So, for instance, the duty to pay equitable remuneration is not owed directly by end users to rights-holders, and rights-holders' remuneration claims are not applicable directly against end users. Thereby, the circle of persons who hold copyright-relevant entitlements expands, which explains why often not only the *content* of the entitlement changes but also its *holder*. Intermediaries play a crucial role in liability rule scenarios in current copyright systems. Collection societies in particular have professional and organizational capacities (and also the relevant

---

200. *Cf.* Chapter 2, Section III.B.2 *supra* (discussing the right to exclude in the general property context).

201. *See* Chapter 2, Section III.B.5 *supra* (discussing the general distinction between property rules and liability rules).

legal position) to assume the task of collecting royalties from numerous disperse users and distributing them among multiple participating rights-holders.

There are two archetypical mechanisms to facilitate liability rules in the copyright system. One is based on imposition of levies on equipment and media, and the second covers more broadly performances to which a set of non-voluntary licensing schemes applies. Roughly speaking, levy payments are meant to compensate rights-holders for exceptions that undercut their *copy-related rights*, primarily the reproduction right.[202] It is a quid pro quo designed to compensate rights-holders for losing their exclusory power by burdening third parties who stand to profit from the ability to use works under a liability rule scheme. The revenues collected from the levies on transactions in certain media, products, and equipment flow to the pockets of rights-holders.

More broadly, under non-voluntary licensing, the property rule is converted into the liability rule in various ways and the license may apply to *copy-unrelated* usage such as public performances, broadcasting, and other communications to the public.[203] According to the same principle, the ability to engage in certain communications does not depend on individual licensing, and rights-holders are usually compensated via collective administrators (or collection societies), which actually charge fixed license fees to the relevant parties.

It is possible to further refine the distinction between a *statutory* license and a *compulsory* license: the former usually creates an unconditional privilege to engage in the reserved act according to specific terms stipulated in the law. In contrast, the latter compels rights-holders (or their representatives) to negotiate the specific terms of use with the privilege beneficiaries (or their representatives).[204]

We may arrange the relevant liability rule provisions into three groups. The first category covers acts, which upon fulfillment of the statutory conditions are privileged without any duty of compensation. Otherwise, the property rule returns to govern the act. Such type of copyright exceptions (or licenses) does not stipulate liability rules in the strict sense as those provisions do not create a legal duty of monetary compensation. In other words, there is no "liability" involved.

---

202. *See* P. Bernst Hugenholtz et al., *The Future of Levies in a Digital Environment: Final Report* 10ff (2003) (reviewing the history of levy systems in Europe and their current structure and applications).

203. Some copy-related rights may also be covered by non-voluntary licensing (e.g., provisions that allow recording cover versions of sound recordings, or provisions allowing ephemeral recording by broadcasting organizations.) *See, e.g.*, 17 U.S.C § 115 (granting certain licenses for making and distributing phonorecords containing nondramatic musical works).

204. *See* Reto M. Hilty, *Verbotsrecht vs. Vergütungsanspruch*, *in* PERSPEKTIVEN DES GEISTIGEN EIGENTUMS UND WETTBEWERBSRECHTS 333–34 (2005) (explaining the nature of "actual" compulsory licenses and the distinction from statutory licenses).

The second category allows noncompensated use so long as the statutory conditions are fulfilled; otherwise, it creates a claim for compensation. Such norms represent a sort of *conditional* liability rule. Finally, the third category stipulates situations in which the use covered by the norm is always permissible under an unconditional duty to pay remuneration.[205]

In all examples and variations of liability rule, exclusion rights are restricted in a similar way. Rights-holders are unable to enjoin the covered acts, which otherwise would trigger the conventional exclusive rights. Liability rules legitimize unauthorized use, and at the same time, seek to prevent injustice while ensuring compensation where individual exercise of exclusive rights is impractical. Rights-holders benefit from this arrangement mostly in market situations where they cannot enforce their formal entitlements efficiently and translate exclusivity entitlements into royalties.

Economic analysis suggests the liability rule is justified when market failures render voluntary transactions prohibitively costly or practically impossible.[206] The privilege secured under a liability rule facilitates valuable uses and enhances the utility derived from works when parties cannot negotiate an efficient transaction, thereby reducing the social costs of copyright. From an economic perspective, the duty to pay remuneration in exchange for exercising privileges helps rights-holders to internalize some of the externalities they are not able to internalize themselves under the property rule's regime. Those externalities typically emerge as a result of market structural deficiencies and the special nature of information subject matter.

Copyright collectives are most commonly designated administrators of liability rules. Those associations have deep roots in Continental European systems, performing the traditional role of securing compensation to dispersed and uncoordinated authors and of strengthening authors' collective bargaining position vis-à-vis commercial exploiters such as theaters.[207] The rule of the copyright collective gained more significance in the early twentieth century with the advent of radio broadcasting, mechanical reproductions, and later, widespread home recording. In those and many other cases, effective enforcement of exclusive rights on an individual basis appeared neither possible nor desirable. In addition, copyright collectives traditionally considered themselves protectors of the

---

205. *Id.* at 334–35 (applying the taxonomy to German law, which nicely demonstrates the flexibility in structuring duties and privileges under liability rules).

206. *See* Mark A. Lemley & Phil Weiser, *Should Property or Liability Rules Govern Information?* 85 TEX. L. REV. 783, 786–89 (2007) (discussing the economic rationale and its application in Internet-related cases).

207. *See* Daniel J. Gervais, *The Evolving Role(s) of Copyright Collectives, in* DIGITAL RIGHT MANAGEMENT—THE END OF COLLECTING SOCIETIES? 28–29 (Christoph Beat Graber, ed., 2005).

artistic profession as such.[208] Parallel to fostering the pecuniary interest of authors, societies sometimes seek to promote social and cultural ends by designating portions of their budgets to cultural projects.[209] The function of rights-holders' societies as collection agents of authors is deeply woven into the structure of copyright, and the law sometimes allocates to such parties *exclusive* causes of action to receive royalties under the various non-voluntary licensing schemes.[210]

(b) Liability Rule and Overprotection

I. THE PRINCIPLE

Many copyright reformists believe that if copyright overprotection is the disease, a shift to broader liability rules may be (at least part of) the cure. The principle is usually the same: the scope of liability rules should expand and the scope of exclusory powers should respectively shrink, especially concerning various Internet activities. Liability rules are conceived as a means against overprotection by weakening the level of control rights-holders may exercise. The phrase "Compensation Without Control" is often used to compactly express this idea.[211] The goal is to have non-voluntary licensing models cover much more ground than they presently do. Some proposals would go as far as subjecting all (or a substantial portions of) Internet communication activities to modules of fixed compensation or "flat rates."[212] Proposals to expand the governance of liability rules far beyond their traditional boundaries shall be called hereinafter "***broad** **liability rules***" (*BLR*) approaches.

II. THE BENEFITS

Alongside correcting overprotection situations, it has been argued liability rule regulation can help to correct market distortion concerning the distribution of royalties between creative authors on the one hand and commercial exploiters on the other.[213] When the gap between the bargaining power of individual authors and derivative rights-holders is great (especially in close-knit communities and industries), dependency relationships lead to situations in which authors are

208. *See* Cohen Jehoram, *The Future of Copyright Collecting Societies,* 23 EUR. INTELL. PROP. REV. 134, 137 (2001).

209. *Id.* at 137–38.

210. For example, collecting societies in Germany have exclusive standing to bring claims under numerous provisions ensuring equitable remuneration that accompanies copyright exceptions. *See* Gerhard Schricker *in* URHEBERRECHT KOMMENTAR, *Einleitung,* nr. 25. (Gerhard Schricker, ed., 3d ed. 2006).

211. *See* LAWRENCE L. LESSIG, THE FUTURE OF IDEAS THE FATE OF THE COMMONS IN A CONNECTED WORLD 201–02 (2001); *see also* Berlin Declaration on Collectively Managed Online Rights: Compensation Without Control (2004).

212. *See, e.g.,* Philipp Runge, *Die Vereinbarkeit einer Content-Flatrate für Musik mit dem Drei-Stufen-Test,* 2/2007 GRUR. INT. 130 (2007) (describing the debate and evaluating the legal ramifications of flat rate proposals in the music sector).

213. *See* Hilty, *supra* note 31, at 345 ff.

under-compensated. Additionally, abusive exercise of exclusion entitlements by derivative rights-holders driven by narrow commercial interests might harm both authors and the public interest in terms of broad access.[214] In this context, a liability rule regime puts checks and balances on the power of derivative rights-holders. It endeavors to restrict the opportunities for overusing exclusivity to the detriment of other copyright stakeholders.

Most BLR proponents are hostile to broad deployment of TPMs restrictions.[215] They reject the argument that in digital information markets the need diminishes for resorting to liability "second best" solutions such as levies and crude mass licensing mechanisms. Taking the point even further, some proponents question the utilitarian-economic justification of copyright exclusivity *in general,* and argue the case for exclusive rights is even *weaker* in the digital environment.[216] They stress compensation for creative activities (inasmuch as it is justified and necessary for securing investments) should be achieved largely by alternative means than exclusive copyrights.

III. SPECIES

Several patterns of liability rule proposals have been emerging in recent years. The first, which cannot really be classified as "reformist," would adopt a *voluntary* mechanism to which rights-holders could opt in if they wanted to. Opting-in has no general impact on the system and content of copyright entitlements; exclusion remains the default rule.[217] Those proposals (and BLR proposals in general) often count on sophisticated, technology-based collective rights administration designed to accommodate the needs of rights-holders who elect to join in.

A second approach would create a similar mechanism *but reverse the default rule.* Accordingly, certain works in certain scenarios (as defined by the specific model) are generally governed by the liability rule. However, rights-holders can take affirmative steps to opt out of that liability framework, and upon fulfillment

---

214. *Cf.* Reto M. Hilty, *The Expansion of Copyright Law and Its Social Justification, in* Copyright Law and the Information Society in Asia 1, 29 (2007) (noting "[t]he real hazard to the creators comes from their direct contractual partners").

215. *See, e.g.,* Berlin Declaration on Collectively Managed Online Rights (2004) ("The digital revolution holds the potential of a semiotic democracy, the reuse and remix culture being one of its most promising innovative aspects. Content locked under DRM will destroy the potential of this culture.").

216. *See, e.g.,* Glynn S. Lunney, *The Death of Copyright: Digital Technology, Private Copying, and the Digital Millennium Copyright Act,* 87 Va. L. Rev. 813 (2001).

217. *See* Alexander Peukert, *A Bipolar Copyright System for the Digital Network Environment,* 28 Hastings Comm. & Ent. L.J. 1 (2005); *cf.* Daniel J. Gervais, *The Price of Social Norms: Towards a Liability Regime for File-Sharing,* 17 Harv. J.L. & Tech. 1, 71–73 (2003).

of certain opting-out requirements, property rules shall be reinstated.[218] In such models, liability becomes the general rule and property the "exception." This is obviously a far-reaching change in the system of copyright, as rights-holders are no longer granted exclusive rights automatically; instead, they need to take affirmative steps to establish exclusivity.

A third variation would convert the initial situation from property rules to liability rules but *eliminate the possibility of earning exclusivity on an individual basis*. A liability regime would then cover all (or most) copyright-related communications and activities, whether in a certain medium (e.g., over the Internet) or for all existing and future digital media.[219] This solution is even more radical, as it contemplates rights-holders shall be denied veto power permanently and irreversibly. Fisher, for instance, advocated for an extended version of the latter approach, which would substantially abolish proprietary control over works in the digital environment. He proposed replacing major portions of traditional copyright rules and anticircumvention models with a governmentally administrated reward system.[220] Instead of exclusive rights, creators and other rights-holders shall be entitled to monetary compensation via a centralized mechanism to be financed through general taxation.[221]

Netanel drafted a proposal having somewhat narrower application. It addressed specifically the problem of unauthorized distribution of music over peer-to-peer (P2P) networks by imposing new levies. The levy system should broadly cover devices, media, and communication services that facilitate P2P activities. Affected candidates are Internet service providers, P2P services, and related software makers, computer hardware, consumer electronics, and storage media.[222] In exchange for levy revenues, individual noncommercial activities of file swapping and related copyright violations (such as large-scale private copying of music files) should become lawful. The revenues generated from

---

218. *Cf.* Jessica Litman, *Sharing and Stealing*, 27 HASTINGS COMM. & ENT. L.J. 1, 40 (2004) ("So long as shareable is the legal default, we don't need to make sharing compulsory. We can allow creators who would like to prevent their music from being shared to make that election, without encouraging them to do so.").

219. *Compare* WILLIAM W. FISHER, PROMISES TO KEEP: TECHNOLOGY, LAW, AND THE FUTURE OF ENTERTAINMENT, 199 ff (2004), *with* Neil W. Netanel, *Impose a Noncommercial Use Levy to Allow Free Peer-to-Peer File Sharing*, 17 HARV. J.L. & TECH. 1 (2003).

220. *See* FISHER, *supra* note 219, at 203.

221. *Id.* at 204–23.

222. Netanel, *supra* note 219, at 4. ("'Noncommercial Use Levy,' or 'NUL,' would be imposed on the sale of any consumer product or service whose value is substantially enhanced by P2P file sharing (as determined by a Copyright Office tribunal). Likely candidates include Internet access, P2P software and services, computer hardware, consumer electronic devices (such as CD burners, MP3 players, and digital video recorders) used to copy, store, transmit, or perform downloaded files, and storage media (like blank CDs) used with those devices.").

collection of levies (Netanel proposed an average rate of 4 percent of the retail price) shall be channeled to compensate rights-holders.[223] Importantly, the liability rule shall cover only *noncommercial* activities of copying, distributing, streaming, adapting, etc.[224]

In a similar vein, Ku attacked the current structure of copyright as designed to preserve profitability of intermediaries that was largely no longer necessary in the digital environment.[225] Ku, drawing on the statutory model stipulated in the U.S. AHRA, proposed substantially abolishing copyright exclusivity but imposing a levy capturing ISP services and computer hardware equipment.[226] Levy revenues shall be allocated to creators, inasmuch as creation required additional financial incentives that remained unsatisfied by the market.[227] Lunney likewise proposed that taxing technology and media used for private copying (instead of exclusive rights governance) could better serve the utilitarian aspiration of consequentialist copyright systems.[228]

(c) Objections

Objections to BLR approaches have both theoretical and practical focal points. We may criticize the theoretical soundness of a broad liability rule and its appropriateness under traditional copyright philosophy, invoking related questions of fairness and ethics. We may further cast doubts upon the economic rationale supporting a liability rule regime and its interplay with DRMS and anticircumvention law. Finally, the question of conformity with international copyright obligations calls for consideration. Some of these concerns are briefly addressed in the following passages.

I. THEORETICAL AND ECONOMIC OBJECTIONS

Opposition to the BLR regime questions its wisdom on copyright theory grounds.[229] A broad liability rule regime covering substantial segments of

---

223. *Id.* at 35–59.

224. *Id.* at 37–40. Netanel considers "noncommercial" any situation where "the individual is not selling copies of, access to, or advertising in connection with the copyright-protected work or any modification of the work." *Id.* at 42–43.

225. *See* Raymond Shih Ray Ku, *The Creative Destruction of Copyright: Napster and the new Economics of Digital Technology*, 69 U. Chi. L. Rev. 263 (2002).

226. *Id.* at 293–311.

227. *Id.* at 312.

228. *See* Lunney, *supra* note 216, at 910–12.

229. It is assumed the liability rule regime does not substantially affect moral rights, or at least is designed to have minimal effect on moral rights. *Cf.* Netanel, *supra* note 219, at 39 (noting in passing the application of his proposal regarding the attribution rights under the contemplated general privileges to make derivative works). Gervais indirectly touched upon this issue by asking: "What should the copyright holder's main focus be: *To maximize authorized uses of protected material or to minimize unauthorized uses?* There is a world of difference here." *See* Gervais, *supra* note 217, at 58 (emphasis in original) (footnote

information markets would obviously generate tension with law-and-economics orthodoxy. That orthodoxy assumes the best way to achieve efficiency is via proper interaction among the three "Golden Oldies" of property rights, contracts, and markets.[230] Property rights are not only central players in achieving market efficiency—in the case of information goods, exclusory entitlements in fact *define* the subject of the market transaction, thereby making efficient transactions possible in the first place. Take away exclusory rights, and works (or more broadly, proprietary "messages"[231]) become something inherently different, more akin to "pure public goods" or "commons."

Legal fencing in the form of exclusory entitlements renders information capable of being exchanged via market transactions toward a greater societal utility. If rights-holders could contractually transfer exclusive rights in work because everyone can use the information under non-voluntary licensing, the market value of the work would drop, and with it, general social welfare. BLR opponents conceive as dreadful the idea of substantially replacing the market mechanism with a centralized bureaucracy that would compensate creative endeavors and substitute for property rights-based incentives.[232] They argue that some BLR

---

omitted). The same question can be asked concerning the main focus of the *copyright system itself*. Even if the economic efficiency argument for a BLR model could be proven beyond doubt with empirical data, it would be hard to persuade a copyright monist (or perhaps even a dualist) who believes in individuality-based foundations of copyright protection to accept that model. One possible way to somewhat ease the tension between BLR proposals and droit d'auteur traditions is to make a clear separation between moral and economic rights, and articulate a corresponding distinction concerning protections granted to human authors on the one hand and derivative rights-holders on the other. *Cf.* Hilty, *supra* note 204, at 345–46.

230. *See* Robert P. Merges, *Compulsory Licensing vs. the Three "Golden Oldies": Property Rights, Contracts, and Markets*, Cato Institute, Policy Analysis No. 508 (2004). For a thorough analysis presenting a skeptical view on non-voluntary licensing, see Robert P. Merges, *Contracting Into Liability Rules: Intellectual Property Rights and Collective Rights Organizations*, 84 CALIF. L. REV. 1293 (1996).

231. Use of the term *message* here corresponds to its definition in Chapter 1.

232. *See* Stanley J. Liebowitz, *Copyright Reconsidered: A Review of Promises to Keep*, 21 ISSUES IN SCI. & TECH. 92 (2005) ("The most difficult economic problem with [Fisher's proposed] system is determining the total amount of money the government should spend on artistic creations. Fisher largely sidesteps how this is to be accomplished . . . that the process can be quite capricious . . . Remarkably, [Fisher] states that a 'socially optimal output' should be rejected as a goal, because it would 'draw an excessively large number of workers into the industry'. . . After discarding the goal of market efficiency, Fisher suggests replacing it with the goal of a 'flourishing entertainment industry.' How would the government office charged with managing intellectual property make this assessment? He states: 'If . . . the industry seemed starved, the office would enrich . . . if it seemed flush, the office would constrict . . . the flow of money.' These murky rules are likely to lead to battles between taxpayers and copyright owners that will make our current copyright problems look quaint in comparison.").

models fundamentally diverge from Western capitalistic principles and the role market efficiency plays in the political economy and society in general.

Opponents suggest existing BLR proposals fail to provide satisfactory substitution to property rights as the engine of market efficiency in the exchange and trade of valuable information goods. As a partial rejoinder, some moderate BLR proponents integrate a more refined "utilitarian" stance in their argument: they do not wish to do away with exclusive rights in general and their trade in economic markets. They also admit centralizing the mechanism of compensating for creative production might harm rights-holders in the short run. At the same time, the argument is that the harm is economically justified due to the resulting increase in net social utility achievable in the longer run,[233] to which opponents generally object on empirical grounds. They often stress that collective administration mechanisms are very costly in the long run—costs that are not likely to be outweighed by the supposed benefits of the BLR system.[234]

II. FAIRNESS ISSUES

Every BLR model must address two basic questions: how should royalties be collected, and how should they be distributed among claimants (or participating members)? Faintness and justice in collection and distribution has always been a thorny issue under existing liability models.[235] Should liability arrangements expand to assume the magnitude of the general rule, possible unjust results might move from the margins to the midpoint of the copyright system. More specifically, the fairness critique questions the ability of the system to achieve the appropriate correlation between the value of artistic contribution and the level of compensation transferred to its creators. Further, it questions the capacity to correlate between the amount paid under levy systems and the benefits those who bear levy costs will actually enjoy. For instance, levy systems artificially

---

233. *See* Gervais, *supra* note 217, at 57 ff.

234. *See* Merges, *supra* note 230, at 4 ("Compulsory licenses, being creatures of federal statute, tend to be less flexible and more susceptible to political manipulation than market-based transactions. The costs that are saved by a compulsory license in the short run are usually more than offset by the inefficiencies that it causes over time.") Some additional costs are associated with coordination among societies, standardization, and reciprocity arrangements at the domestic and international levels.

235. In Germany, for instance, the law obligates collection societies to set appropriate conditions (*angemessenen Bedingungen*) for materializing rights and claims under the statutory collective administration framework. *See* Urheberrechtswahrnehmungsgesetz (1965), § 6(1). *Appropriate conditions* is an open term that seems to impose a general reasonableness duty rather that providing specific instructions. For further discussion, see Jörg Reinbothe *in* URHEBERRECHT KOMMENTAR § 6 WahrnG. nr. 13 (Gerhard Schricker, ed., 3d ed. 2006). For historical background and analysis, see Wilhelm Nordemann, *Der Begriff der "angemessenen Bedingungen" in § 6 Absatz 1 Wahrnemungsgesetz* (1973).

increase the price of goods and services uniformly and without sensitivity to the intensity of actual use of copyrighted works.[236]

Either way, the sum of the transaction increases irrespective of whether copyright relevant activity facilitated by that transaction actually takes place or of the intensity of copyright-relevant activities performed by individual consumers. Levy systems inevitably result in cross-subsidization between low-volume users of copyrighted material (or those who are not engaged in copyright-relevant activity at all) and high-volume users.[237] Levies are imposed broadly on a variety of goods, including multipurpose devices *capable* of being used for copyright-related activities such as home copying of copyrighted material. There is no direct relationship between actual copyright relevant use and compensation paid. Further, affected parties such as media and device manufacturers (as well as consumers) cannot simply "opt out" from the system if they have no intention whatsoever of engaging in any copyright-relevant activity.

Expanding the levy framework to cover more commercial activities is expected to exacerbate such incommensurability concerns. At the stage of revenue distribution, the "egalitarian" (or "solidarity") principle governing the operation of copyright collectives has been increasingly under attack.[238] Traditionally, the tariffs paid to collective members are principally fixed and uniform. Formulas that merely calculate the aggregate number of performances or broadcasts of a given work are to some degree indifferent to quality, popularity, demand, or other parameters that reflect value to consumers.[239] Critics also attack the traditional copyright collectives' practice of designating a certain percentage of their budget to promote social and cultural projects as it is arguably inappropriate to use

---

236. In theory, intermediaries (e.g., retailers) shoulder the levy burden. In practice, it is believed most of the price difference is eventually rolled over to consumers. *See* Hugenholtz et al., *supra* note 202, ¶ 4.1.2 ("As a rule, the obligation to pay the remuneration imposed on recording or reprographic equipment as well as on blank recording media does not lie on the consumer, but rather on the manufacturers, importers, or intra-community acquirer of such devices and media. . . In the majority of cases, manufacturers and importers of reproduction equipment or media pass the charge on to the consumers by means of the sales price of such equipment or media . . . we note that the obligation to pay the proportional remuneration for reprographic activities generally lies with the legal person under whose supervision, direction, or control the reprographic equipment is used.").

237. *Id.* at 40–41. For a discussion and response to this critique, see Netanel, *supra* note 219, at 67–74.

238. *See, e.g.*, Roger Wallis et al., *Contested Collective Administration of Intellectual Property Rights in Music: The Challenge to the Principles of Reciprocity and Solidarity* 14 EUR. J. COMM. 5 (1999).

239. Matters get worse and more complicated at the regional and international levels. *Id.* at 19 ff.

collected monies for ends other than compensating members for use of their works covered by non-voluntary licensing schemes.[240]

There are several standard replies to the fairness critique. Perhaps the most prevalent one is seeing the "rough justice" achieved by collective rights administration as the lesser evil.[241] Otherwise, private copying and certain performances would never be compensated at all due to impossibility of enforcement or prohibitively high costs. Second, to the extent creative works boost the sales of levied equipment and media, imposing costs of levies on makers and sellers to the benefit of authors is not unjustified in principle. Recent proposals to "phase out" levies and undercut collective rights administration build on the argument that new digital technologies significantly undermine the justification for "rough justice" measures as technology now permits "fine justice" based on market transactions (as discussed immediately below).

III. LIABILITY RULE, DIGITAL TECHNOLOGY, AND DRMS

This aspect of BLR criticism purports that new technologies, which facilitate individual low-cost transactions and private enforcement of licensing terms, may eliminate the principal justification for liability rules under copyright. (In turn, this tension between technological protection measures and collective licensing explains BLR proponents' hostility to DRMS, and anticircumvention laws in particular.)[242] Inasmuch as BLR opponents are correct that new technological protection systems can alleviate the problems traditional collective licensing was designed to solve, the first question is whether both could (or should) coexist within the current legal system. If the answer is negative, which one should give way to the other?

As a practical matter, it is quite difficult to slice the market into sub-markets in a way so that some activities are governed exclusively by non-voluntary licensing and others by TPM-supported individual licensing, which gives rise to the danger of double compensation.[243] Accordingly, it is conceivable rights-holders would receive collection royalties in their right pocket and private licensing fees in their left for the same copyright-implicating act.[244] Taking into account new

---

240. *See* Jehoram, *supra* note 208, at 137–38.

241. *See* Constanze Ulmer-Eilfort, *Private Copying and Levies for Information and Communication Technologies and Storage Media in Europe*, *in* DIGITAL RIGHTS MANAGEMENT. TECHNOLOGICAL, ECONOMIC, LEGAL AND POLITICAL ASPECTS 453–54 (Erhard Becker et al. eds., 2003).

242. *See, e.g.*, Fisher, *supra* note 219, at 247 ff.

243. *See* Jeremy F. DeBeer, *Locks & Levies*, 84 DENV. U.L. REV. 143, 177–78 (2006).

244. The EUCD is quite ambivalent on this point. *See* EUCD (2001), Recital 35 ("The level of fair compensation [compensating for exceptions or limitations] should take full account of the degree of use of technological protection measures referred to in this Directive. In certain situations where the prejudice to the rightholder would be minimal, no obligation for payment may arise.") *See also* Recital 39. The German legislature

technological opportunities (and in light of the growing potential for double compensation), two opposite responses may come under scrutiny. The reformist response is to *expand* the mandate of non-voluntary licensing at the expense of exclusive rights while restricting (or completely abolishing) anticircumvention laws.[245] An opposite response has been to "phase out" levies and similar rough justice mechanisms.[246] A middle ground approach posits that both regimes can nonetheless coexist. Its proponents advance three main arguments: (1) they take note of the double compensation problem, (2) they voice skepticism about the prediction DRMS will conquer the entire spectrum of acts presently covered by statutory remuneration duties/compulsory licensing, and (3) they underline the importance of the existing mechanisms in protecting authors and performers as opposed to DRM-enthusiastic industry players.[247]

It is important to approach this contested topic carefully. Most of the arguments for and against BLR revolving around the "new technologies" axis rely on factual assumptions that are not simple to prove. Some BLR promoters implicitly assume most DRMS will eventually disappear from the market by virtue of market forces and/or legislative intervention in order to give way to broad tax or blanket licensing arrangements. This could prevent the double compensation side effect of BLR from assuming astronomic dimensions.[248] As mentioned earlier in a different context, however, both expectations appear at the moment quite unrealistic. At the opposite pole of the debate, those wishing to see levies and similar collective royalties administration mechanisms vanish with individual licensing as their substitute tend to assume new technologies are (or soon will be) capable of solving most market failures and structural deficiencies such traditional mechanisms were intended to ameliorate, at least with respect to digital markets.[249] As of yet, this assumption is far from being shown to be correct either. Proponents of the hybrid approach purport that the copyright system can have it both ways—that is, accommodate both "locks and levies" simultaneously[250]–and

---

attempted to prevent double compensation by clarifying that in the course of evaluating certain claims under nonvoluntary licensing, the fact that TPMs (protected under anticircumvention law) are deployed should be taken into account. *See* UrhG., §§ 54a, 54h(2). This explicit rule applies only in certain limited instances, however.

245. *Cf.* Netanel, *supra* note 219, at 77–80 (criticizing and rejecting the "digital lock-up" option).

246. *Cf.* Hugenholtz et al., *supra* note 202, at 41 ff.; Copyright Levies Reform Alliance, *Copyright Levies Backgrounder* (2007) (presenting the campaign run by the Copyright Levies Reform Alliance calling, inter alia, to freeze E.U. private copying levies).

247. *See* Silke von Lewinski, *Stakeholder Consultation on Copyright Levies in a Converging World*, 38 IIC. 65, 67–68 (2007). *See also* DeBeer, *supra* note 243, at 177.

248. Section III.A.5(d)ii *supra*. Theoretically, a possible solution is creating a rule that would destroy the participation claim of a rights-holder who uses DRMS.

249. *Cf.* Hugenholtz et al., *supra* note 202, at 46–47.

250. *See* DeBeer, *supra* note 243.

still provide appropriate security to the concerns of all stakeholders. Though a hybrid approach is not objectionable on its face, it is still hard to see how such system could operate smoothly within the current structure of copyrights and anticircumvention entitlements.

IV. INTERNATIONAL COPYRIGHT LAW AND THE THREE-STEP TEST

(aa) Background

Finally, BLR proposals should be scrutinized against core international law obligations in the area of copyright. The Berne Convention's principal approach is that liability rules for acts that implicate exclusive rights are the rare exception, not the general rule. Berne currently allows compulsory licenses with respect to works that have already been embodied in sound recordings with the permission of rights-holders under certain conditions.[251] In such case, Berne explicitly foresees "reservations and conditions on the exclusive right granted to the author of a musical work and to the author of any words" for works incorporated in sound recordings with permission.[252]

Historically, this norm was part of a bargain formulated during the 1908 Berlin revision. On the one hand, the language of Berne was then modified to explicitly recognize the exclusive right to authorize the making of mechanical reproductions and public performance by means of mechanical instruments.[253] On the other, Berne countries were allowed to impose "[r]eservations and conditions" applied to these rights in domestic law.[254] Berne further allows compulsory licenses pertaining to certain broadcasting and public performances. Compulsory licenses are currently allowed with respect the exclusive rights to authorize (1) wireless broadcasting and similar communication to the public, (2) wired rebroadcasting, and (3) public communication via loudspeakers and similar equipment.[255] Article 11bis in which these cases are listed was originally adopted during the 1928 Rome Conference in response to a then-novel and

251. *See* Berne Convention (1971), Art. Art. 13(1) ("Each country of the Union may impose for itself reservations and conditions on the exclusive right granted to the author of a musical work and to the author of any words, the recording of which together with the musical work has already been authorized by the latter, to authorize the sound recording of that musical work, together with such words, if any; but all such reservations and conditions shall apply only in the countries which have imposed them and shall not, in any circumstances, be prejudicial to the rights of these authors to obtain equitable remuneration which, in the absence of agreement, shall be fixed by competent authority.").

252. *Id.*

253. *See* Berne Convention (Berlin text, 1908), Art. 13, first para.

254. *Id.* Art. 13, second para. For a historical overview, see STEPHEN P. LADAS, 1 THE INTERNATIONAL PROTECTION OF LITERARY AND ARTISTIC PROPERTY 419–22 (1938).

255. *See* Berne Convention (1971), Art. 11bis(2).

revolutionary communication technology called radio broadcasting.[256] This provision, like many other key Berne provisions, was a child of a compromise. It reflected the fundamental disagreement between voices that favored a broad exclusive right to cover the new radio technology and those insisting local legislatures should be allowed to permit unrestricted radio broadcasting due to the strong public interest at stake.[257] The Berne three-step test, which is also relevant to the institution of non-voluntary licensing as applied to foreign works, came much later (in 1967 in Stockholm) to accompany the newly introduced Berne reproduction right.[258]

(bb) BLR versus the three-step test

Subsequent developments in international copyright law have transformed the Berne three-step test into a ubiquitous yardstick, which makes the tension between this limitation on domestic regulation and a BLR regime appear irreconcilable. We may argue a broad liability rule does not *necessarily* unreasonably prejudice the legitimate interests of the author (third three-step test factor), for example, when the alternative to the revenues stream it facilitates means much less income to rights-holders—or no income at all. Further, we perhaps can go out on a limb and argue the BLR regime does "not conflict with a normal exploitation of the work" (second three-step test factor). This view may draw on the premise that "normal exploitation" is a relative qualifier having no ipso facto fixed meaning, as markets rapidly change and evolve.[259]

A historical anecdote regarding the major radio debate that predated the three-step test (but shows similar outlines) could corroborate this position. In the 1920s and 1930s, the highly innovative radio broadcasting could hardly be considered "normal exploitation."[260] Despite loud protests from the tribunes of

256. The original text read: "Authors of literary and artistic works shall enjoy the exclusive right of authorising the communication of their works to public by radiocommunication." *See* Berne Convention (Rome text, 1928), Art. 11bis(1). Subarticle (2) allowed introduction of domestic compulsory licenses to that exclusive right. In the current text of the Convention, compulsory licenses are expressly prohibited with respect to the making, reproducing, and distributing of cinematographic adaptations of literary and artistic works, as well as public performance and communication to the public of such adaptations and reproductions. *See* Berne Convention (1971), Art. 14(3).

257. *See* Ladas, *supra* note 254, at 475–77.

258. *See* SAM RICKETSON & JANE C. GINSBURG, INTERNATIONAL COPYRIGHT AND NEIGHBORING RIGHTS: THE BERNE CONVENTION AND BEYOND § 3.58 (2006).

259. The WTO Panel reporting on § 110(5) of the U.S. Copyright Act suggested "*normal exploitation*" ordinarily could imply both an inquiry that is empirical in nature and one that is more normatively oriented. *See* WTO Panel Report on § 110(5) U.S. Copyright Act (2000) ¶ 6.166.

260. For a historical background on that period, see LADAS, *supra* note 254, at 470–506. Using the framework of the WTO Panel above, radio was neither something regular/

copyright maximalists, Article 11bis as initially adopted during the 1928 Rome Conference did expressly allow compulsory licensing. This begs the following question: why was such a ground-breaking technological advancement (which had already begun to reveal its huge significance to exploitation opportunities by rights-holders) placed very shortly after its inauguration under the prospects of domestic compulsory licensing?[261]

The answer seems to have something to do with the fact certain participants attending the Rome Conference demanded to *exclude* ratio broadcasting from copyright *completely*.[262] Their strong opposition to copyright exclusivity in radio broadcasting was based on public interest considerations and the value of the emerging technology to the enrichment and expansion of cultural and social horizons. Ladas indicated "[t]he Australian and New Zealand delegations saw in radio a means of national education and culture, and did not desire to prevent its development by a rigid text in the Convention."[263] Ultimately, radio broadcasting was generally subjected to copyright but Berne members remained free to impose compulsory licensing that should not prejudice the authors' right to "obtain an equitable remuneration which shall be fixed, failing agreement, by the competent authority."[264] Ever since, there has been no serious attempt to change that result, and entire markets were created, shaped, and continued to flourish under the framework of non-voluntary licensing. Returning to the contemporary debate, it appears plausible to recast similar arguments in support of a BLR regime for (most) online environment exploitations in the context of the three-step test's "normal exploitation" prong.

Even so, passing the third "special cases" criterion (which is actually the "first" factor and is considered sometimes the test's "threshold")[265] seems especially challenging. One way to go about this hurdle is simply to ignore or underplay the

---

usual/typical in terms of its portion of the total exploitation revenues in the market of those days, nor did it squarely conform to a normative standard. *But see* WTO Panel Report (2000) ¶ 6.180 ("It appears that one way of measuring the normative connotation of normal exploitation is to consider, in addition to those forms of exploitation that currently generate significant or tangible revenue, those forms of exploitation which, with a certain degree of likelihood and plausibility, *could acquire considerable economic or practical importance*.") *Id.* (emphasis added).

261. It is true the three-step test did not exist in 1928, but the general Berne principle stating exclusive rights as the rule and liability provisions as the exception did.

262. *See* Ladas, *supra* note 254, at 476–77 (reciting views of delegations from Australia, New Zealand, and Norway).

263. *Id.* at 477.

264. *See* Berne Convention (Rome text, 1928), Art. 11bis(2).

265. *See* P. Bernt Hugenholtz & Ruth L. Okediji, *Conceiving an International Instrument on Limitations and Exceptions to Copyright*, Final Report 22 (Mar. 6, 2008).

"special cases" factor.[266] Otherwise, it is hard to see how the three-step test, according to its conventional reading, could be reconciled with the BLR philosophy and political agenda. The BLR regime, by its terms, seeks to reverse the default rule concerning the use of copyrighted material, according to which property rule is replaced by a liability rule, and a veto power by a compensation claim. How could this agenda conform to the "special cases" factor without doing violence to its literal words?

At the most fundamental level, it strikes one as an entirely misguided endeavor to apply an exceptions-and-limitations threshold standard to a regime in which non-voluntary licensing *is the general rule*. Despite its relatively late arrival, the three-step test belongs to the old legal order, or, in terms of this chapter, to conservative or neoconservative approaches to copyright protection by virtue of its quest to preserve the scope of the *traditional exclusivity norms* as they stand.

2. (Re-)Introducing Copyright Formalities

The discussion now veers to another central topic on the reformist agenda. The term *formalities* ordinarily stands for the state-created conditions and requirements rights-holders must satisfy to obtain and fully enjoy their copyrights.[267] Formalities may be classified according to their function and the consequences of noncompliance. *Constitutive formalities* (typically registration) precondition the vesting of copyright in the first place. Other formalities must be followed to legally enforce copyrights, sometimes called *enforcement formalities*. A third type of formalities are necessary for preserving the duration of protection for the maximum period afforded by the law (typically by renewal procedure), sometimes called *maintenance formalities*.[268] Familiar types of formalities are duties as to placement of a copyright notice, initial registration and registration of transfer, renewal, payment of fees, deposit of copies, and making certain declarations.

(a) Formalities and the Berne Convention

At the time of the original 1886 Berne Act, most national copyright laws stipulated some kinds of formalities requirements (FR).[269] FR changed from one jurisdiction to another and the consequences of noncompliance were not uniform, varying from a technical inability to enforce rights until compliance was

266. *Cf.* SENFTLEBEN, *supra* note 61, at 126–27 (discussing and critiquing some tendencies to reduce the three-step test to its latter two criteria).

267. *Cf.* Jane C. Ginsburg, *A Tale of Two Copyrights: Literary Property in Revolutionary France and America*, 64 TULANE L. REV. 991, 994 (1990) ("Formalities are state-imposed conditions on the existence or exercise of copyright.").

268. Renewal requirements are sometimes discussed separately from provisions concerning registration, deposit, or notice. Despite this distinction, renewal is covered by the concept of copyright formalities in the broad sense.

269. *See* RICKETSON & GINSBURG, *supra* note 258, § 1.19.

achieved (e.g., in France) to denial of copyright altogether.[270] The text of the original Berne Act specifically allowed Berne members to practice "conditions and formalities."[271] The basic rule of Article 2(2) stipulated a rather straightforward reciprocity principle: the adjudicating country must acknowledge the fulfillment of FR in the country of origin.[272]

The concept of "conditions and formalities" was broadly conceived to cover everything that had to be complied with to ensure the rights of authors came into existence.[273] During the 1908 Berlin revision, the original text was replaced by a specific prohibition imposing formalities on rights in foreign works.[274] The abolishment of formalities soon became a "fundamental principle" of Berne,[275] and the current binding text of the Convention stipulates "[t]he enjoyment and the exercise of [Berne] rights shall not be subject to any formality; such enjoyment and such exercise shall be independent of the existence of protection in the country of origin of the work."[276] Article 5(2) Berne Convention obviously does not prohibit Berne members from imposing FR affecting copyright protection of national authors.[277] Further, a formality-free regime does not mean *any* procedural or technical requirement imposed on foreign rights-holders would violate the rule against formalities.[278]

It is important to remember the principal reason behind the mandatory removal of formalities was not a copyright-material objection to FR in general. Before the Berlin revision, depriving foreign authors of copyright protection in case they could not show compliance with FR in the country of origin did not violate the national treatment principle per se. Removing FR on the Berne Union level was rather a matter of convenience, and to some extent, devoted to making the procedure for copyright protection work more smoothly. As a matter of

270. *Id.*

271. *See* Berne Convention (Original Act of 1886), Art. 2, second para.

272. *See* Ernst Röthlisberger, Berner Übereinkunft zum Schutz von Werken der Literatur und Kunst 105 (1906).

273. *Id.* at 101 (quoting Dr. Meyer from the German delegation to the 1884 Diplomatic Conference, who, under the express approval of the chairman, formulated a broad formalities concept).

274. *See* Ricketson & Ginsburg, *supra* note 258, § 6.103 (noting the text of the Berlin Act used the term "any formality" in lieu of "conditions and formalities" and suggesting the meaning remained unchanged).

275. *See* Claude Masouye, Guide to the Berne Convention for the Protection of Literary and Artistic Works ¶ 5.5 at 33 (1978). Several more recent international and regional instruments explicitly adopted Berne's rule against formalities. *See, e.g.*, WPPT (1996), Art. 20 ("The enjoyment and exercise of the rights provided for in this Treaty shall not be subject to any formality.").

276. *See* Berne Convention (1971), Art. 5(2).

277. Masouye, *supra* note 275, ¶ 5.6 at 33.

278. For further discussion, see Ricketson & Ginsburg, *supra* note 258, §§ 6.105–6.106.

adjudicative economy, FR proved particularly burdensome in the early years of the Berne Union.[279] Showing compliance with FR created additional costs, and failure to do so (due to ignorance, mistake, or impossibility) could have disastrous consequences for authors, as grave as the complete annulment of copyrights in the adjudicating country.

Before and during the Berlin Conference, several initiatives sought to simplify compliance for foreign authors. A special effort was made to eliminate an interpretative option to Article 2—one purporting foreign authors must comply with the FR *of the adjudicating country* by virtue of the national treatment principle. Toward this end, the French delegation attending the Paris 1896 Conference proposed to amend Article 2(2) to expressly clarify that only compliance with country-of-origin FR would be a condition to granting material protections under Berne.[280] During the Berlin Conference, it was proposed to make protection in the adjudicating country completely independent of FR in the country of origin.[281] The main obstacle was the possible effect of that proposal on the efforts to amend Article 2(2) to reflect a uniform copyright protection term.[282]

The compromise reached as stipulated in the then-new Article 4(2) of the Berlin text removed FR completely, and Article 7(1) created a minimum duration rule (life-plus-fifty) coupled with a reciprocity requirement in case the term in the country of adjudication exceeded that in the country of origin. Accordingly, foreign authors did not enjoy the longer duration in the adjudication country if the country of origin stipulated a shorter term, which in any event could not be shorter than life-plus-fifty. This way, the so-called "rule of the shorter term" could be preserved irrespective of the question whether foreign authors had complied with FR in the country where protection was sought.

(b) Formalities in the United States

U.S. law has a long tradition of formalities.[283] The earliest versions of the copyright statute stipulated most common types of formalities, including

279. *See* Ladas, *supra* note 254, § 124 (citing a 1910 estimate by the Berne International Bureau, which reckoned that about seven percent of all legal disputes concerning the Berne Convention were related to questions of compliance with formalities in the country of origin).

280. *See* Ricketson & Ginsburg, *supra* note 258, § 6.85. For a detailed historical background to the pre-Berlin situation, see Röthlisberger, *supra* note 272, at 100–02.

281. Ricketson & Ginsburg, *supra* note 258, § 6.87 (citing the proposal of the German delegation).

282. *Id.* (noting the French delegation's concern a radical national treatment approach, also subjecting copyright duration to domestic law, might lead to a lack of uniformity in this area).

283. *See* Richard Mose Bracey, *Searching for Substance in the Midst of Formality*, 14 J. Intel. Prop. Law 111, 123–26 (2006) (reviewing the history of the U.S. registration requirement); Christopher Sprigman, *Reform(aliz)ing Copyright*, 57 Stan. L. Rev. 485, 491–94 (2004) (providing a general overview).

registration, notice, deposit, and renewal. Noncompliance was a serious matter; for instance, failure to register the work meant a copyright did not arise, and failure to comply with renewal procedures meant the work fell into the public domain much earlier than the maximum copyright duration available.[284] Before the 1976 copyright reform, formalities characterized the U.S. copyright protection under federal law as an "opt-in" system,[285] meaning copyright did not automatically vest in authors at the moment of creation or fixation. Instead, authors were required to actively bring their works under copyright protection.[286] Authors were further required to maintain copyright protection by affirmatively renewing their registration.[287]

The 1976 copyright reform introduced important changes to the formalities system.[288] Among other things, the registration requirement was dropped and replaced with a rule attaching copyright protection automatically upon fixation of the work in a tangible medium of expression.[289] However, formalities are not completely absent from the current statute. Compliance with FR is mostly optional, and the main motivation rests on some technical and procedural advantages conferred upon rights-holders choosing to do so.[290] Registration became optional, though owners (of U.S. works only) must register in order to file an infringement action.[291] According to the 1992 amendment, renewal is no longer required.[292] To comply with the Berne Convention's formalities ban, the Berne Convention Implementation Act of 1988 lifted those requirements as regards foreign works.[293] However, the change did not apply retroactively to foreign work that had not complied with U.S. formalities and consequently belonged

284. *See* Sprigman, *supra* note 283, at 493.

285. This argument and terminology were invoked by appellants in Kahle v. Gonzales, 487 F.3d. 697 (9th. Cir. 2007). Though the court dismissed the appeal, it did not dispute appellants' description of the U.S. copyright system in the pre-Copyright Act (1976) era as an "opt-in" system.

286. According to the first U.S. federal Copyright Act (1790), copyright vested upon registration. *See* William Patry, 2 Patry on Copyright § 6:19 (2007).

287. Initial protection of fourteen years upon registration under the 1790 Act could be extended up to an additional fourteen years upon compliance with renewal procedure. *See* William Patry, 1 Patry on Copyright § 1:19 (2007).

288. For a detailed overview, see *id.* § 6:74 ff.

289. *See* 17 U.S.C. §102(a).

290. Formalities are currently regulated mainly by Chapter 4 of the 1976 U.S. Copyright Act, in which § 408 makes registration optional, and § 410(c)) creates a presumption the information in the certificate of registration constitutes prima facie evidence of the validity of the copyright and the facts stated in the certificate. According to § 401(a), placing a copyright notice is optional, and § 401(d) stipulates that doing so could destroy the "innocent infringement" defense that can mitigate actual or statutory damages.

291. *See* 17 U.S.C. § 411(a).

292. *See* U.S. Copyright Renewal Act (1992) (amending Sec. 304).

293. *See* U.S. Berne Convention Implementation Act (1988).

automatically to the public domain. To correct this result, the 1994 Uruguay Round Agreements Act (URAA)[294] created a complex procedure called *restoration.*[295] Importantly, the Court of Appeals for the Tenth Circuit in *Golan* v. *Gonzales* has identified a tension between the First Amendment protection of speech and the retroactive coverage of copyright for works already in the public domain made possible under the URAA.[296]

(c) Advantages and Disadvantages of Formalities

I. OBJECTIONS TO FORMALITIES

A number of standard objections to copyright formalities has been raised in this context. Formalities suffer from a reputation of constituting technical and unnecessary encumbrances on the exercise of copyrights[297] as they involve bureaucracy, administration, and direct costs borne primarily by rights-holders. The agency responsible for the administration of formalities also creates public costs that arguably cannot be fully recovered from fees alone. In this context, it is argued formalities interfere with the very system of incentives promoted by copyright protection.[298] Another repeating complaint against formalities focuses on their unfairness: FR create the potential for a partial or complete loss of copyright entitlements, which may result from ignorance, mistake, or impossibility.

Some of these problems are amplified in the international arena. A rule of reciprocity such as the one governing the Berne Union before the 1908 Berlin revision was said to impose unjustified costs and procedural hurdles on foreign authors. The risks FR posed to Berne's core principles of national treatment, substantive minima, and independence of protection in the adjudicating country have been considerable. And indeed, a broad consensus formed a hundred yeas ago in Berlin led to the abolishment of FR from the relationship between foreign authors and domestic administration of justice in all Berne Union members.[299]

---

294. *See* U.S. Uruguay Round Agreement Act (1994).

295. *See* 17 U.S.C. § 104A. *See also* PATRY, *supra* note 287, § 6:80 ("Section 514 of the URAA, which was effective on January 1, 1995, contains an amendment granting protection, retroactively, to preexisting works from 'eligible countries' that fell into the public domain in the United States for reasons other than expiration of terms").

296. *See* Golan v. Gonzales, 501 F.3d. 1179, 1197 (9th. Cir. 2007) ("[if] § 514 [of the URAA] altered the traditional contours of copyright protection in a manner that implicates plaintiffs' right to free expression, it must be subject to First Amendment review"). But see, *Golan v. Holders*, 609 F.3d 1076 (10th. Cir. 2010)

297. *See* Shira Perlmutter, *Freeing Copyright from Formalities*, 13 CARDOZO ARTS & ENT. L.J. 565, 581–87 (1995) (presenting the case against formalities in the United States).

298. *Id.* at 582.

299. *Cf.* RICKETSON & GINSBURG, *supra* note 258, § 3.12 (noting also countries that practiced formalities in 1908 (such as the U.K.) agreed to the establishment of an international formalities-free system).

II. ADVANTAGES OF FORMALITIES

(aa) An information cost argument

Notwithstanding these common objections, formalities could have advantages from both morality and efficiency standpoints. Some formalities (such as registration and notice) help to delineate and mark the information subject matter with respect to which rights-holders assert claims. They help duty holders to identify *what* is the subject of a property-like regime and to ascertain *whether* a given work is subject to a copyright, and if so, by *whom* (tracing/search costs).[300] FR can reduce information and search costs and thereby contribute to a sharp reduction in the overall transaction costs and enhancement of efficiency. All the actors who bear information costs are potentially served by such formalities: it becomes cheaper for "avoiders" to know what materials they cannot use, for "transactors" to evaluate transactions, and for "challengers" to formulate their claims.[301] Rights-holders as well can benefit from the formalities apparatus as it may provide them with an institutional platform to signal their ownership claims and intentions to enforce them.

(bb) FR as an efficiency buffer

It has been argued the historical U.S. mandatory registration requirement (an "opt-in" system) created an important "buffer" moderating the effect of copyright exclusivity.[302] Authors who have no interest in enforcing a copyright may simply not comply—and the costs of singling out such an intention *not* to enforce exclusive rights are zero. Simultaneously, nonowner-avoiders can quickly and cheaply inform themselves and exercise their privileges more effectively. Studies launched in the United States show that under the mandatory formalities system, a substantial number of rights-holders did not comply with constitutive and renewal formalities.[303] As a result, many works fell immediately into the public domain.[304]

Standard economics would suggest that rational rights-holders are expected to comply if the expected present value of future income under copyright protection outweighs the direct costs of compliance (e.g., registration fees). As costs of compliance are relatively low, rights-holders who decline to comply likely do

---

300. Chapter 2, Section III.C.2 *supra* (reviewing the information cost analysis).

301. The terminology of avoiders, transactors, and challengers was explained in Chapter 2. *See* Chapter 2, Section III.C.2(a) *supra*.

302. *See* Sprigman, *supra* note 283, at 526 ff. (discussing formalities as a buffer in the context of free speech rights).

303. *See* William M. Landes & Richard A. Posner, *Indefinitely Renewable Copyright*, 70 U. Chi. L. Rev. 471, 498–507 (203).

304. Sprigman concluded that as a result of noncompliance with formalities, only a little more than fifty percent of the copyrightable works in the United States were actually under copyright between 1801–1870. *See* Sprigman, *supra* note 283, at 504–510.

not expect the work to have more than insignificant commercial value. In economic terms, such works can be classified as "nonmarket goods" (or "nonmarket works").[305] There is a significant potential for social gain (positive externalities) if nonmarket works never receive copyright protection, and this potential can be best materialized if nonowner-avoiders have available a low-cost mechanism helping them to distinguish the copyrighted "goats" from noncopyrighted "sheep" crowding their information environment. As a result, the social costs of the copyright system could decrease dramatically without harming rights-holders economically. Rights-holders who decline to comply likely reckon that possible exploitation profits are zero or near zero. Importantly, works are not driven out of the copyright regime arbitrarily as only those works rights-holders consider commercially worthless would suffer such a fate. Further, it is reasonable to assume the incentives provided under copyright law, which are intended to foster creativity, have little to do with the production of nonmarket works in the first place. It follows markets for informational resources can become more efficient under a formalities regime.

(cc) Renewal and copyright duration

A system of renewal can help rights-holders to correct their predictions and assumptions over time. Renewal formalities delegate some of the discretion concerning the effective duration of copyright in works to their authors. Under a mandatory renewal system, declining to renew functions both as a signal and a buffer. In that case, rights-holders "correct" the situation where continuing copyright protection up to the maximum possible duration does not benefit anybody. In opt-in systems, the decision not to renew is guided by similar considerations to those informing the initial decision to comply with constituting formalities. If at the point renewal becomes due, the costs and trouble involved exceed the present value of expected future revenues for the remainder of the protection term, rights-holders would decline to renew and the work would enter the public domain earlier than otherwise would occur. Studies from the United States show a relatively low renewal rate after the initial period (about 15 percent), presumably related to pessimistic estimates about the ability to further commercially exploit most of the works under copyright that enjoyed the initial term.[306]

---

305. *See* Brett M. Frischmann, *An Economic Theory of Infrastructure and Commons Management*, 89 U. MINN. L. REV. 917, 265 (2005) (referring to nonmarket goods as "those goods that are neither provided nor demanded through the market mechanism"). Obviously, terming nonmarket works as being such does not necessarily mean they do not have *any* value whatsoever to recipients.

306. *See* Sprigman, *supra* note 283, at 519–22; *See also* Landes & Posner, *supra* note 303.

Based on renewal data collected in the United States, Sprigman concluded the "real" term of copyright protection was on average 34.2 years.[307] Proponents argue a system of renewal can help rights-holders to fine-tune the scope of protection. To the extent renewal requirements are placed *on top* of an opt-in mechanism, rights-holders receive additional opportunities to separate the wheat (commercially valuable works) from the chaff (nonmarket works.) Their renewal decisions will be based on revised assessments concerning the commercial future of their works. As a general matter, whether a formalities-based system *actually* promotes efficiency will significantly depend on the accuracy of rights-holders' assessments. By renewing (or declining to renew), rights-holders are invited to reevaluate the decisions they made in the past, now guided by the experience gathered during the previous protection period that gives them more indications about the prospects of commercializing their works.

(dd) A rejoinder to unfairness complaints

Finally, formalities approaches offer a reply to the fairness objection. It is possible to begin addressing the challenge with a question: why is it justified to subject the bulk of human creativity expressed in digital formats and the operation of digital communication media to full-blown exclusive rights without giving rights-holders the proper legal means to publicly disclaim exclusivity if they do not need it, and without giving nonowner-avoiders reasonable tools to be informed about such decisions?[308] The role of recipients in the information process is no less important than of originators, as they are all essential players in the same complex dynamism.[309] Inasmuch as formalities can largely prevent situations where protection is granted when its impact is mostly (or solely) inhibitive (bringing no payoffs to anyone), a formalities system should be justified also on moral grounds.

More than securing a windfall to authors, the automatic grant of copyright often blocks valuable uses of works that will never become successful in the marketplace. This state of affairs perhaps could be tolerated in the analog information environment where those primarily affected by copyright restrictions were commercial actors (or professional "free riders"), who typically position themselves in direct competition with copyright holders. Generally speaking, it appears more appropriate to burden *such actors* with a duty to clear exclusive rights under a system that endows exclusivity automatically without asking rights-holders to signal out their claims. In the online setting, however, users

307. Sprigman, *supra* note 283, at 521.

308. As discussed earlier, some relevant extra copyright law instruments do exist, most importantly, Creative Commons licensing. Section III.4 *supra*. The assumption here is that providing similar opportunities is a task for the *legislature* as part of its duty to pursue a healthy public policy.

309. Chapter 1, Sec. V.C(2) *supra*.

routinely engage in copyright-implicating behaviors as an essential part of their communication activities and social life.[310] Without putting them on notice—- and without installing judicious mechanisms to enable cheap and simple rights clearing—subjecting entire digital communities and communication media used by a rapidly growing portion of the world's population to automatic property rules would seem both *unreasonable and unfair*. Certainly, legal doctrines of implied license, copyright exceptions, non-voluntary licensing, and lack of perfect enforcement could mitigate some of the implications of automatic exclusivity grants. Yet proponents of formalities have a point when stating their solution to the problem of overprotection could prove far more elegant and efficient.

(d) Formalities and Overprotection

In 1908, delegations attending the Berlin Conference were concerned about problems of *under*-protection. They wished to ensure a minimum level of protection to Berne Union authors in every other Member State. Realizing formalities might curtail effective enjoyment from substantive rights, they faced three basic options: The first was to adopt a radical national treatment approach, fully subjecting foreign authors to domestic formalities. The second option was to maintain the reciprocity rule, where authors are required to comply with formalities in the country of origin, if and inasmuch as they existed. The third option was to abolish formalities from the framework of international copyright relations under Berne. In electing the third alternative, Berlin delegates were not so much concerned with the question of how to prevent copyright exclusivity from getting out of control. Today, proponents argue formalities can be part of the solution to overprotection,[311] challenging the common Pavlovian reaction to the notion and function of such restrictions on copyright exclusivity. In their eyes, formalities could function as an important check on the copyright system, where constitutive formalities substantially reduce the rate of works controlled by exclusive rights in the first place. Further, they would effectively shorten the average duration of exclusivity rights, reduce transaction and social costs, relax tensions between copyright and free speech law, practically sidestep the problem of orphan works,[312] and in general, make the copyright system more balanced and reasonable. Proponents further argue new technologies can substantially alleviate concerns about the administrative inefficiency involved.[313] Online registration,

---

310. *See* John Tehranian, *Infringement Nation*, 2007 UTAH L. REV. (2007)

311. *See, e.g.*, LAWRENCE LESSIG, FREE CULTURE 287–93 (2004); Litman, *supra* note 218, at 16 ("What we miss when we dismiss the formalities as characteristic of a provincial and outmoded attitude is that the formalities were the principal method embodied in U.S. copyright law for preserving the public domain and encouraging the public to use, reuse, and share potentially copyrightable material.").

312. *See* U.S. Copyright Office Report on Orphan Works (2006).

313. Lessig proposed to instate a registration system akin of the online registration of domain names. LESSIG, *supra* note 311, at 289–90.

electronic databases, and telecommunication channels along with payment and coordination systems can render compliance with FR and rights-clearing tasks uncomplicated and cost-effective.

I. REPEALING THE RULE AGAINST FORMALITIES

Overprotection concerns have recently led some commentators to revisit the wisdom of formalities-based copyright. As a practical matter, reintroducing formalities must overcome Berne's rule against formalities, inasmuch as formalities are to be applied also to foreign works. Sprigman advocated a modified reciprocity approach under which domestic formalities shall be tolerated and rights-holders able to choose to fulfill either the rules of their home country or those of the country of first publication.[314] Such reciprocity is expected to work best between two nations that have formalities systems in place. Problems may arise when only one of two (Berne Union Member *A*, or *UMA*) requires compliance with FR, and the other (Berne Union Member *B*, or *UMB*) does not. In that case, there are no formalities requirements to which *UMA* can give reciprocity. If *UMA* granted automatic protection to *UMB* authors, it would end up discriminating against its own authors. Sprigman thus considered introducing a certain degree of standardization at the international level by creating a standardized system that would stipulate a uniform formalities model. The FR stipulated in the model would be recognized by all Berne members as sufficient. In practice, FR countries would recognize compliance either with the standardized model or formalities in the country of origin/first publication.[315] An additional (and more complex) question concerns renewal. Should Member States be allowed to apply to foreign authors an initial protection term shorter that the existing life-plus-fifty rules stipulated in Article 7(1) Berne Convention?[316] How could reciprocity function efficiently in a world of divergent renewal regulation?[317]

II. NEW-STYLE FORMALITIES

(aa) Sprigman's proposal

Sprigman interestingly proposed to introduce what he named "new-style" formalities. The idea is quite simple: formalities in national laws (such as registration, notice, recordation of transfer, and so on) shall become "voluntary" in the sense failure to comply would not destroy copyright entitlements completely. Instead, noncompliance would subject the work to a default license stipulating

---

314. *See* Sprigman, *supra* note 283, at 546–47.

315. *Id.* at 547. Arguably, this proposal worsens the position of rights-holders as it existed before the Berlin revision. According to the old Berne regime, in the case *UMB* had no FR at all, *UMA* could not obligate *UMB*'s authors to comply with *any* FR.

316. Sprigman seems to hold that granting an initial protection term shorter than life-plus-fifty would not violate Berne as long as it applied uniformly to all authors. *Id.* at 549

317. *Cf. id.* at 549–51.

predetermined royalty rates.[318] The law would fix a relatively low rate of statutory compensation for authors who did not comply, with the rates being modest to encourage authors to comply if they are interested in reaping financial exploitation benefits. Rights-holders who look forward to commercial gains are likely to choose a property rule if they expect copyright exploitation revenues to exceed the statutory rates.[319]

According to a liberal reading of the wording "enjoyment and exercise" in Article 5(2) Berne Convention, the model arguably does not conflict with the rule against formalities as applied to foreign authors.[320] Failure to comply would not result in forfeiture of rights, as the important question to ask in the context of Article 5(2) Berne Convention is whether the formalities requirements *actually* undermine rights-holders' abilities to enjoy and exercise Berne rights. In cases where liability rules better serve authors' *overall* ability to exploit their works, setting liability rules as the default is also defensible under the traditional framework. Giving rights-holders the option to choose whether to comply is arguably the best way to receive an accurate indication of whether the property rule indeed best serves their interests.[321]

(bb) Critique

This argument is plausible both on the theoretical and normative levels, but problem areas concerning its implementation remain nonetheless. There is a real difficulty in reconciling it with the plain language of Article 5(2) Berne Convention, which stipulates in its first sentence "[t]he enjoyment and the exercise of these rights shall not be subject to any formality; such enjoyment and such exercise shall be independent of the existence of protection in the country of origin of the work."[322] To understand what "*these*" right are, we should read the provision in tandem with Article 5(1) referring to "the rights [in] their respective laws . . . as well as the rights specially granted by this Convention."[323] Domestic laws may replace property rules with liability rules if they wish, but the Berne substantive minima ("rights specifically granted under this Convention") must be preserved with regard to foreign authors. (A different question, which will not

318. *Id.* at 555.

319. Sprigman argues that rights-holders can best assess whether the expected return from exercising exclusive rights would justify investment in FR compliance. Rights-holders who are unsure are nonetheless advised to comply as a form of "insurance." *Id.* at 558.

320. *Id.* at 554–58.

321. *Id.* at 559.

322. *See* Berne Convention (1971), Art. 5(2) (emphasis added).

323. *Id.* Art. 5(1) (emphasis added).

be explored here, is whether new-style formalities conform to the three-step test.)[324]

The idea of a new-style formalities regime is further based on debatable assumptions. The economic rationale behind it rests on the presupposition that rights-holders are rational decision makers and that they have full (or at least sufficient) information. In reality, the decision not to comply with FR may result from accident or lack of knowledge; accordingly, subjecting the work by default to non-voluntary licensing would have little to do with making rational decisions reflected in the economic behavior of rights-holders. Consequently, the efficiency buffer would not operate as intended. Furthermore, in cases where such works become commercially attractive, the economic damage to rights-holders who initially failed to "opt in" or renew their registration might be considerable.[325]

A different type of complication emerges on the multinational scale. Assuming many countries adhered to such structure, an affirmative compliance with domestic FR in each country (or perhaps an international standardized model) would be necessary for bringing the work under the governance of the exclusive rights. It is not unlikely that in some counties, a liability rule would make good economic sense from the perspective of the individual copyright holder, but in other countries it would not. To maximize revenues, rights-holders would then have to conduct a separate (and costly) market analysis for each country or region.

All these concerns about a given formalities regime need to be considered, but overall (and posed against the alternatives), reasonable formalities in conjunction with default liability rules could play a central role in the legal framework of copyright protection in the digital environment. This thread shall be further developed in the last chapter of the book.

3. Upgrading Nonowners' Privileges and Rights of Access

Lending rights-of-access a formal and explicit acknowledgement in copyright laws is another reformist pattern that can be mentioned here only briefly.

---

324. Sprigman argues that even if the new-style model violated Berne's rule against formalities, it would nonetheless be permissible under the three-step test. *See* Sprigman, *supra* note 283, at 560. The implicit assertion that conformity to the three-step test (assuming that the case is so) could legitimize a violation of Article 5(2) Berne Convention is problematic. These are two separate questions: a new-style formalities model might be impermissible by either one, the other, or both. As to the three-step test inquiry, it must first be resolved whether the statutory licensing involved in Sprigman's proposal falls under the exceptions or limitations controlled by that test. *Cf.* Hugengoltz & Okediji, *supra* note 265, at 18–19. In fact, it appears the three-step test cannot be applied to a system that dramatically reverses the default rule of copyright. As argued above, the two are structurally incompatible.

325. This flaw can perhaps be corrected by allowing rights-holders to "opt in" after an initial period of time in which the work is subject to non-voluntary licensing.

Chapter 3 showed rights of access under the current copyright system are only implicit and have been served indirectly, principally via copyright exemptions.[326] Concerns about the position of nonowners in the digital setting underlie approaches calling for "upgrading" the status of nonowners' copyright entitlements.[327] Concrete efforts in this direction seek to stipulate certain situations where performing access and privileged conducts are *enforceable* against persons who interfere with use of privileges[328]—most relevantly, copyright holders who impose strict contractual and technological restrictions. Specifically (and in order to avoid relying only on statutory interpretations by the courts), we may consider the option of expressing clear rights-of-access in the copyright statute.[329] In contrast to current statutory exemptions, such rights-of-access perhaps should explicitly use the term *access* while anchoring in express terms the privileges of both gaining and providing access to copyrighted works. Within the anticircumvention regulation framework, rights-of-access may assume the form of statutory "privileges to hack" or even a duty on rights-holders to provide or facilitate privileged access and use.

IV. NEOCONSERVATISM OR REFORMISM?

This chapter revisited the oft-voiced argument of copyright overprotection. The discussion opened with an inquiry about the nature of this claim while tinkering with the meaning of the term *overprotection*. The term and claim invoking it can be perceived in at least in two ways: either contemporary copyright law covers *quantitatively* more activities than before (e.g., private enjoyment

---

326. Chapter 3, Section III.B.2(a) *supra*.

327. For an implicit call for such a reform to combat the negative effects of private ordering, see Niva Elkin-Koren, *Copyright in Cyberspace—Rights Without Laws?* 73 CHI-KENT L. REV. 1155, 1200 (1988) ("regulating access to information by private ordering alone would be inadequate . . . private ordering should not be immune from government regulation under freedom of contract doctrine . . . there is sufficient justification for setting limits on the abilities of information providers to propertize information in the public domain . . . terms of access that were privately generated by the parties should be subject to public regulation to the extent they affect public interest . . . private ordering should be subject to scrutiny under the copyright framework . . . Subjecting contracts to copyright principles may . . . allow the incorporation of public policy into the emerging private ordering regime") (footnote omitted).

328. *See e.g.*, Wendy J. Gordon & Daniel Bahls, *The Public's Right to Fair Use: Amending Section. 107 to Avoid the "Fared Use" Fallacy*, 2007 UTAH L. REV. 619 (2007).

329. *Cf.* Jacques de Werra, *Moving Beyond the Conflict Between Freedom of Contract and Copyright Policies: In Search of a New Global Policy for On-Line Information Licensing Transactions*, 25 COLUM. J.L. & ARTS 329, 349–51 (2003) (discussing proposals to introduce "fair access" protections, especially in the context of anticircumvention laws).

of TPMs-protected works or acts previously excused under the exhaustion rules), or copyright covers *qualitatively too much* from the universe of possible acts in a manner that subverts its ability to achieve its goals and live up to its justification as a legal institution.[330] The expansion of proprietary control in recent years as reflected in the positive copyright law supports both types of overprotection claims, giving rise to concerns about the ability of the system to reflect and preserve the balance so essential in areas of information regulation.

The sheer quantity of proposals for improving copyright law is in itself a sort of evidence of the "crisis" we are facing.[331] This chapter offered a taxonomy arranging existing proposals in two main categories, namely, *neoconservative* and *reformist* approaches. The principle difference between the two concerns the future role and operation of the exclusion principle in copyright: whereas neoconservatives generally would maintain exclusivity as the centerpiece of copyright law, copyright reformists would rather downgrade the level of exclusivity rights-holders are able to exercise, possibly by introducing broad liability rues in this area. Whereas neoconservatives would address the mismatch between the digital reality and the regulative apparatus by fine-tuning the current system to better accommodate the legitimate needs of all stakeholders, reformists would rather introduce more drastic changes that implicate the nature of protection copyright law affords. According to the reformist vision, copyright law must become much less "trespassory" in nature and effect. As of yet, legislative efforts to adjust the law to the digital environment have been largely painted with neoconservative colors, despite critical voices in the literature that would rather see a reformist agenda being pursued to achieve a proper equilibrium.

This chapter reviewed both neoconservative and reformist proposals with a skeptical eye. Neoconservatives will need to continue their tedious project of fixing and adjusting a giant maze of complex, lengthy, and inconsistent rights and exceptions originally designed to regulate the information reality of the past. Reformists, on their part, still have a long way to go to persuasively demonstrate that measures such as broad liability rules are superior to the flawed system they want to replace.

Neoconservatism and reformism are not the only options, however. A third avenue explored in the next chapter will combine insights from both patterns to create a completely new solution. On the one hand, the access-right approach would uphold the principle of exclusivity as the centerpiece of the copyright system.

---

330. Of course, this alternative assumes copyright law *has* articulable "goals," or at least a solid normative support for the allocation of entitlements in information subject matter. No matter how defined, and irrespective of its geographical, cultural, and political tradition, copyright law *must* have some goals or justifications excusing legal interventions in the information process that are potentially harmful for this process.

331. *See, e.g.*, Paul Edward Geller, *Beyond the Copyright Crisis: Principles for Change*, 55 J. COPYRIGHT SOC'Y U.S.A. 165, 166–74 (2008).

On the other hand, the proposed approach would redefine copyright entitlements in a manner that would make copyright exclusivity more rare and contingent (as opposed to automatic and omnipresent). The ensuing chapter will explain the structure, intended operation, and comparative advantages of such an access-right system.

8. THE FUTURE

I. INTRODUCTION

A. The Project

The access-right model (ARM) is a proposal for redesigning copyright rules as applied and enforced in the realm of digital media and communication networks. The need for a new "digital copyright" model is multifaceted. As this study has shown, the traditional arrangement of copyright entitlements fails to provide a reasonable and efficient legal platform for the operation of digital information markets. This recognition is today widespread, and the objective of this chapter is to supplement the abundance of critical commentary with a comprehensive and theoretically solid approach.

The discussion in Chapter 7 suggested neoconservative approaches to dealing with the digital dilemma have been dominating the legislative agenda in recent years.[1] Alas, inasmuch as issues such as social costs, overcomplexity, and overprotection are concerned, little progress has been achieved thus far. Overall, neoconservative initiatives to amend the law neither alleviated the major concerns nor prepared copyright law for the challenges of future advancements in communication technologies. Rather, Internet-related regulation rendered the law even more intricate, non-transparent and murky in some key areas where the ability of ordinary citizens to use and benefit from digital technology is directly affected. Simply expanding the existing exclusive rights through legislation did not (and indeed, cannot) sidestep the problem, and many contemporary observers agree the answer to cheap and easy copying and the diffusion opportunities digital technology facilitates does not rest in mechanically inflating the good old reproduction and distribution rights. In their haste to formulate such ad hoc amendments, lawmakers have often instead exacerbated the crisis.[2]

The ARM's approach is antithetical to the neoconservative pattern in the sense it seeks to confront the incompatibility between traditional rules and the digital reality already at the fundamental level of defining basic legal rights and duties. The current legal structure works more as a splint (or as a Procrustean bed, if you will) that *inhibits* the constructive adaptation of law to technological progress rather than facilitating proper and timely responses to changes in the information environment. For that reason, the ARM does not frame its task

1. The notion of "neoconservative" approaches (as distinguished from "reformist" approaches) is explained in Chapter 7. Chapter 7, Section III ff, *supra*.

2. Chapter 7, Section IV, *supra*.

in terms of finding ways to improve the existing structure of entitlements. The vantage point is that some of copyright's most basic concepts, doctrines, and assumptions are irreconcilable with modern life. The mission is therefore not to repair a broken legal system, but to develop an alternative that would lend digital copyright the opportunity for a fresh start. Toward this end, the following passages will outline the contours of a copyright system that is designed *for* the digital environment from the outset.

B. The Boundaries

Despite its fairly ambitious project, the ARM leaves some familiar and established elements of the copyright system unaffected. First, the model does not directly address the legal definition of copyright subject matter.[3] Second, the ARM does not challenge the core justifications for copyright protection in general, whether economically or morally based. Copyright law continues to be necessary and socially valuable in digital network settings for its role in encouraging creative undertakings and for protecting the legitimate interests of creative individuals and enterprises. The model's assumptions do not dispute the *potential* of copyright protection to provide a reasonably workable system of incentives. That potential capacity to effectively enhance the level of creative production and contribute to intellectual and informational prosperity remains unchallenged. Third, the proprietary nature of copyright, enshrining the right to exclude in rem,[4] remains a keystone of the system. The private right to exclude continues to provide the ideological and doctrinal axis around which legal positions are to be arranged. The transition from the analog to the digital does not undermine these fundamental premises, which lead to this underlying observation: rather than the very idea of copyright, it is the *technique in which it seeks to achieve its goals* that should undergo a drastic revision.

---

3. For the purpose of determining copyrightability, existing legal thresholds such as originality, creativity, etc. may continue to fill their ordinary role. This being said, the discussion in Chapter 1 (especially the deliberations on the "message" concept) may contribute to the subject matter debate and the theoretical limitations of "work," as well as to related questions such as the legal notion of a derivative work and the merger doctrine. Some basic recognitions drawn from the information model in Chapter 1 are integrated into the proposed framework without addressing in detail the range of implications the model might have on specific subject matter questions.

4. Chapter 2, Section III.B *supra*. The model does not propose to apply the "property metaphor" to intellectual property on a strict basis. Instead, incorporating *some carefully selected* principles of private property into the copyright regime would be appropriate. As noted earlier, a blind reliance on property principles is inherently suspicious, and thus, any drawing on property principles must be subject to a studied, nuanced scrutiny rather than based on instinctive assimilations between tangible and intangible property rights.

C. The Idea

The ARM articulates an alternative method for defining and allocating entitlements under copyright law. The basic idea behind the ARM is quite simple indeed: both exclusive rights and the exemptions thereto[5] shall be tailored around the concept of *access*[6] in a *direct and explicit manner*. The break with the present copyright system in this respect is profound. Whereas current statutes design exclusive rights around notions of reproduction, distribution, communication, or public performance, the ARM is oriented expressis verbis by the concept, operation, and implications of *access to information*. In the digital information environment, access is the "name of the game." As such, it should receive clear recognition and expression in the structure of copyright law. As the necessary terminology does not yet exist in the respective legal vernacular, it needs to be invented, and in this respect the proposed model strongly relies on the vocabulary and taxonomies developed throughout this study, particularly the access paradigm set forth in Chapter 3. This vocabulary serves both to define exclusive rights and to formulate rules limiting their reach and effect. As stressed during this study, attaching proper *checks and breaks* to exclusive rights in information subject matter is no less important than properly defining the exclusive rights themselves.[7] In accordance with this maxim, the model integrates certain mechanisms that are specifically designed to delimit and monitor the application and enforcement of exclusory norms. The aim is to achieve a reasonable and balanced legal apparatus via the systematic application of a new toolbox of elements and techniques. This toolbox should facilitate a smoother and more direct treatment of the deficiencies of copyright exclusivity without dismantling its potential virtues.

D. The Form

The central concept of the model is the *access-right*.[8] As used in this chapter, the access-right is not an amorphous legal principle; instead, it furnishes an ordered program for legislative action. Most importantly, the access-right anticipates positively enacted, exclusory-*negative* entitlements by which the rights-holder is legally entitled to prevent *others* from acting. The essence of the controlled acts

---

5. The term *exemptions* in this context denotes (as throughout this study) all types of copyright rules that delimit the scope of exclusive rights called exceptions, limitations, defenses, etc.

6. Chapter 3, Section II *supra*.

7. *See also* ALEXANDER PEUKERT, GÜTERZUORDNUNG ALS RECHTSPRINZIP 895 ff (2008) (in the general context of designing property systems, advocating for strengthening the principle of negative freedoms to limit the positive freedom of exclusivity rights-holders as an essential component of the property system itself).

8. The theoretical notion of the "access-right" as used in this study is defined and explained in Chapter 3. *See* Chapter 3, Section III.A.2 *supra*.

intimately relates to the notion of access (or more accurately, the narrower notion of *human-access*).[9] Due to the special nature of access to information as the regulated "conduct"[10]—and in contrast to the existing copyright model—exclusive rights cannot attach to things such as "works" (or more generally, "messages")[11] as an automatic legal consequence of their creation. Differently put, an original expression in digital form cannot receive strict property-like protections immediately upon and by virtue of its existence in the world. This normative position is reflected in the following trade-off: On the one hand, the exclusive access-right supports a comprehensive substantive protection for the works to which it applies (Sections III.B.1 and III.C.1 infra). On the other hand, authors who wish to enjoy that protection must *actively assert* their rights. This means rights-holders, as a condition to enforcing various aspects of the access-right, must take certain affirmative steps to attest to their inclinations. This is the ARM's *assertion principle*. As explained in Chapter 3, the access-right rests on two pillars, which are represented by the two prongs of that right: The *first prong* grants exclusivity with regard to access-conducts performed vis-à-vis copyrighted works. The *second prong* grants exclusive rights to prevent communication-conducts in the broad sense.[12] The assertion principle basically means each one of these prongs must be asserted independently by fulfilling different requirements.

Figure 8.1 provides a graphic illustration of the access-right model, depicting among other things the two exclusive access-right prongs and their respective assertion mechanisms.

The two red boxes represent the two access-right prongs, and the two blue boxes to their right represent the assertion requirements attached respectively. These requirements emanate from the assertion principle and are depicted under the column captioned "Structural Limitations." Figure 8.1 demonstrates how these structural limitations correlate to the exclusivity prongs of the access-right. Structural limitations essentially encourage rights-holders to roughly "self-select" the scope of protection according to their individual needs and expectations, and thereby moderate the impact of undesired-by-owners (thus superfluous)

---

9. Chapter 3, Section II.A, *supra* (defining the notion of "human-access," as distinguished from mechanical access performed by machines). As noted previously, access to information, as a subjective-mental procedure, is essentially non-regulatable. Nonetheless, the law might attempt to regulate access by imposing legal restrictions on access-conducts and communication-conducts.

10. Chapter 1, Section IV.C *supra*.

11. Chapter 1, Section V.A *supra*. As explained in Chapter 1, the notion of medial message could help to conceptualize IP subject matter in very general terms. An original work in the meaning of copyright law can be viewed as a subcategory (or a special case) of the message concept.

12. The notions of communication-conducts in both the strict and the broad sense are explained in Chapter 3. *See* Chapter 3, Section II.C.2 *supra*.

exclusivity on the freedom to access and use works.[13] In addition to these limitations, the ARM also provides for exceptions to exclusive rights. The two green boxes (located under the column captioned "Exceptions") represent these provisions. They illustrate how designated exception mechanisms may attach respectively and apply separately to each exclusivity prong. Finally, in order to maintain a level of flexibility and adaptability, the extreme left column (captioned "Monitoring") consists of two blue boxes. These boxes represent build-in mechanisms designed to adjust the scope of exceptions according to changing needs, conditions, specific circumstances, and broad policy goals.

II. THREE PRELIMINARY DISTINCTIONS

A. Moral Rights Unaffected

The problem of copyright's overprotectiveness in the digital environment concerns primarily (if not exclusively) the scope and effect of the *economic* rights.[14] As the heart of the matter is how to maintain a reasonable structure of economic exclusive rights, the model seeks to reconstruct the legal, exclusivity-based platform for commercialization of digital works while paying due consideration to the access and communication interests of users and noncommercial actors. The anticipated correction thus targets economic rights only. But in order to overhaul the structure of economic rights while simultaneously leaving authors' moral/personality rights untouched, both species of rights should be protected *independently* from the other, somewhat in line with dualist doctrinal traditions of copyright.[15] The model assumes moral rights regimes can *co*exist with the

---

13. The term *self-selection* is borrowed from the economic discourse on price discrimination, where consumers, by virtue of their choices between alternative products, packages, or intensity of services, single out their preferences and willingness to pay.

14. *See* Chapter 7, Section II.B.2 *supra*. Digitization of the information environment also raises moral rights-related issues. *See, e.g.*, Guy Pessach, *The Author's Moral Right of Integrity in Cyberspace—A Preliminary Normative Framework*, 34 IIC 2003 (2003). The ARM is not designed to address such questions, at least not directly.

15. In a "copyright" system, in which the protection of moral rights does not belong within the theoretical-ideological core of the copyright order, the separation issue remains marginal. In droit d'auteur traditions, however, the problem must be confronted at the outset. It would be more difficult to introduce the assertion principle in monist copyright jurisdictions (such as the German copyright system) where moral and economic interests are dogmatically inextricable. *Cf.* Elizabeth Adeney, The Moral Rights of Artists and Performers §§ 9.12–9.23 (2006) (explaining the distinction between German monism and French dualism); Silke von Lewinski, International Copyright Law and Policy §§ 3.01–3.80 (2008) (providing a comparative overview). This said, the philosophical tradition of copyright systems in Continental Europe has never been too insensitive to perceive the fundamental difference between (mainly publishers') economic rights on the one hand, and the authenticity interests of the authors on the other. *Cf.* Karl Nikolaus Peifer,

access-right framework, and most importantly, with the assertion principle. According to this vision, the legal system must tolerate some considerable restrictions on the exercise of exclusive economic rights in case rights-holders fail to assert those rights. At the same time, these restrictions should not influence authors' ability to exercise moral rights to their full extent.[16] The exclusivity prongs (the two red boxes in Figure 8.1) are meant to substitute existing economic rights *only*. In this respect, the access-right is an economic right par excellence.

B. Subject Matter Unaffected

As noted, the model does not interfere with copyrightability questions. The access-right may principally apply to creative works of authorship, secure "neighboring rights" to producers and performers, cover sui generis entitlements in databases, and so on.[17] Circumscribing the outer limits of copyright subject matter involves making some fundamental choices with which the model is not concerned. The proposal thus should not affect legal thresholds such as creativity, originality, or individuality as they exist in various copyright systems.[18] By the

---

The Return of the Commons—Copyright History as a Helpful Source? 2008 IIC 679, 685–86 (2008).

16. It is possible to imagine cross-effects between the ARM rights' structure and moral rights. For instance, when rights-holders want to enjoin initial dissemination over the Internet, the ability (or inability) to do so via enforcement of economic rights might influence the enforcement of certain moral rights. In other words, a strong economic right to prevent communication-conducts also serves indirectly authors' personality interests of controlling first publication or determining the media and channels through which the work is being made available to the public. Surely, the same partial overlap is traceable under current law. *See, e.g.,* Harper & Row v. Nation Enter. 471 U.S. 539, 548–49 (1985) ("In using generous verbatim excerpts of Mr. Ford's unpublished manuscript to lend authenticity to its account of the forthcoming memoirs, The Nation effectively arrogated to itself *the right of first publication,* an important marketable subsidiary right.") (emphasis added). With this caveat in mind, a careful design of assertion requirements should minimize their impact on the exercise of moral rights, because, as it shall be explained below, the rationale of assertion is overwhelmingly economic.

17. The same constitutional tenets that *guarantee* property rights (and specifically, copyrights) and that influence their substance, scope, and limits will continue to guide the formulation of explicit, positively acknowledged entitlements under the access-rights regime. For an elaborate analysis of the role (and *limits*) of the constitutional property guarantee in German law in connection with the allocation of subjective-exclusive entitlements, *see* PEUKERT, *supra* note 7, § 11. For a perspective on the U.S. Intellectual Property Clause's limits on the legislative power, see Dotan Oliar, *Making Sense of the Intellectual Property Clause: Promotion of Progress as a Limitation on Congress's Intellectual Property Power,* 94 GEO. L.J. 1771 (2006).

18. The same applies to fixation, inasmuch as fixation reflects on subject matter questions, as is the case under U.S. law. *See* 17 U.S.C. 102(a) ("Copyright protection subsists, in accordance with this title, in original works of authorship fixed in any tangible medium of expression.") Because the access-right applies only to works in digital form (*infra*),

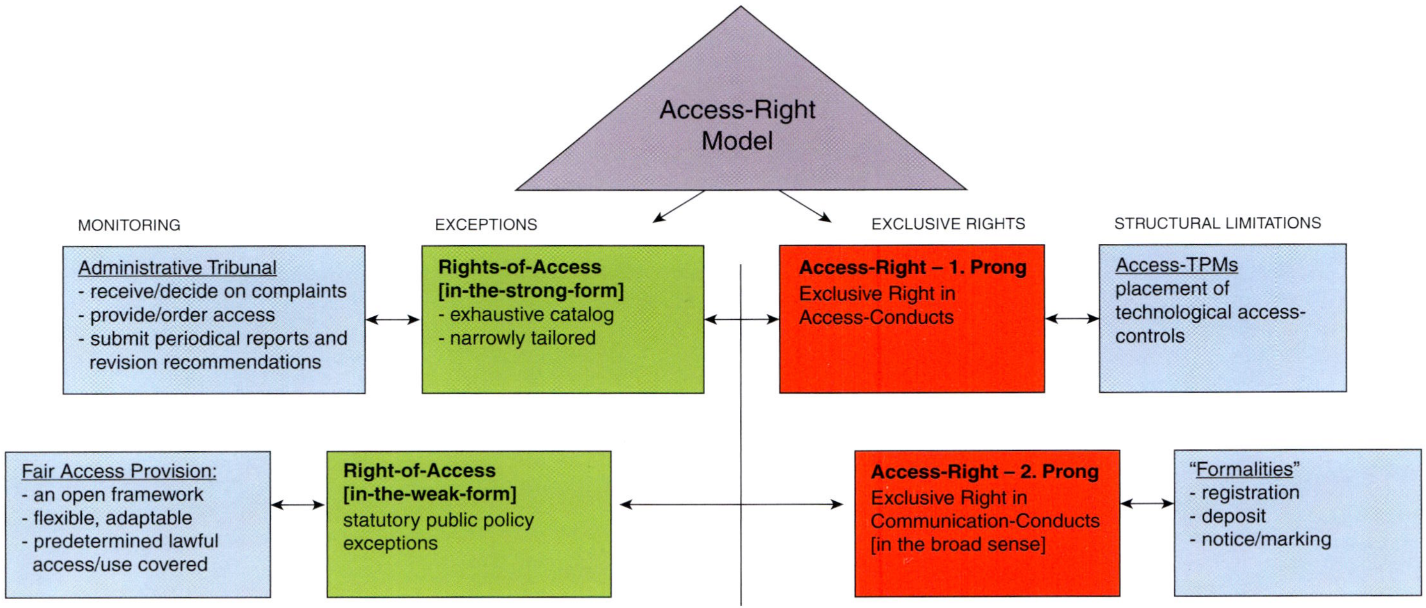

FIGURE 8.1 THE ACCESS-RIGHT MODEL

same token, to the extent certain types/categories of information are *excluded* from copyright subject matter (ideas, concepts, facts, processes, etc.),[19] those restrictions continue to hold also for determining the substantive scope of the access-right. Finally, the model does not contain a developed program for altering the minimum or maximum longevity of exclusive copyrights.[20]

Admittedly, as a practical matter the model *might* indirectly affect subject matter issues. The first access-right prong relies on the use of technological access controls (Section III.B infra), and its second prong is premised on concepts (Section III.C.1 infra) that indeed might de facto erode some traditional distinctions between protectable and non-protectable elements. To be sure, a sterile division between the limitative effect of copyright restrictions and actual opportunities to access or communicate *unprotected* elements such as ideas or concepts has always been beyond reach. This is not surprising considering the analysis presented in Chapter 1: there is absolutely nothing in the nature of communicative acts or in the ontological conditions of message creation that can explain (or even anticipate) copyright's subject matter distinctions. These legal distinctions, like the very state-supported protection against "infringements" itself, are from information and communication theories' viewpoints purely artificial, and there is something pretentious (or at best, naïve) about saying copyright law has no negative effect on the dissemination of ideas, concepts, and other non-original elements.

So there is an unavoidable gulf spreading between the utopian copyright system that extends only to original elements and the operation of any copyright regime in reality, no matter how copyright rules are formulated and construed. Copyrighted works *always* contain unprotectable elements, and to the extent copyright law burdens communication of works, it inevitably burdens access to ideas. Having a copyright system in place necessarily entails some disturbances and obstacles on accessing noncopyrightable information as well. Arguably, this gulf between theory and practice will widen further under a regime that directly targets individual access-conducts.[21] As the argument might go, the significance

---

fixation as a copyright subject matter requisite will mostly take place anyway, at least under a generous fixation notion.

19. Chapter 1, Section V.A.1(c) *supra*.

20. A variant of the model that would accommodate renewal formalities (*infra*) is likely to shorten the *effective* duration of economic rights on the average. Yet such "maintenance formalities" (as opposed to constitutive registration) are not an absolutely essential element of the model. As with subject matter issues, determining the optimal duration of copyrights is a fundamental decision that is not necessarily inherent to the basic formulation of exclusive rights' coverage. At the same time, as the difference between the duration of patents and copyrights suggests, a broader scope of substantive coverage might entail a correspondingly shorter protection.

21. To the extent TPMs block access to ideas, concepts, facts, etc., the objections to anticircumvention law are expected to reemerge. The argument that premising rights on

of excluding things such as ideas, concepts, formulas, facts, or data from substantive copyright protection would continue to decline in tandem with the capacity of the idea/expression dichotomy to effectively counterbalance exclusory entitlements and foster the creation of new works.

Traditional subject matter distinctions such as the idea/expression dichotomy surely play an important rule in achieving balance.[22] The assumption that under an access-right regime such distinctions would not function as intended does not yet mean their *spirit* cannot be preserved. The answer to the critique of the vanishing distinctions may run along the following lines: insofar as the proposed access-right structure further undermined nonowners' safeguards enshrined by the idea/expression dichotomy and similar mechanisms, it would be a modest sacrifice for a worthy cause, because (1) such safeguards have never provided solid, reliable, and predictable subject matter limitations to exclusivity due to their fuzziness (which is inevitably reflected in some case law applying them in real-life disputes), (2) the traditional distinctions are becoming even less effective in the digital environment for various reasons reviewed in this study, and most importantly (3) the model would preserve their spirit and purpose by establishing additional and more robust limitations on exclusivity. As shall be explained, the proposed system would compensate for the deficit in balancing power with instruments such as structural limitations (formalities), effective exceptions, explicit rights-of-access, and a monitoring authority to supervise the enforcement of the first access-right prong (infra).

C. Only Digital Works Affected

The ARM is designed to regulate digital information markets. It is unnecessary to apply it to markets for analog works for the same reasons an access-right regime has not been thinkable, plausible, or needed thus far. The class of works to which the ARM applies can be determined according to two related criteria (or distinctions). The first is between works expressed in digital form and works that are not (the digital/nondigital distinction). The second is between works that were made available over digital computer networks and works that were not (the online/offline distinction). The former distinction (ARM applies only to

---

assertion via access TPMs could erode users' safeguards, though legitimate, is not dispositive because the model relies on additional instruments to preserve a proper balance, as explained in Section III *infra*.

22. The U.S. Supreme Court (especially in the *Eldred* decision) even enshrined the constitutional significance of the idea/expression dichotomy in U.S. law and its important role in delimiting copyright subject matter: "As we said in *Harper & Row*, this 'idea/expression dichotomy strike[s] a definitional balance between the First Amendment and the Copyright Act by permitting free communication of facts while still protecting an author's expression' . . . Due to this distinction, every idea, theory, and fact in a copyrighted work becomes instantly available for public exploitation at the moment of publication." *See* Eldred v. Ashcroft, 537 U.S. 186, 219 (2003) (citations omitted).

digital works) captures a larger pool of works that obviously includes all those falling in the online works class. Choosing here between the two distinctions does not appear essential for the general presentation of the model; for convenience, this chapter often draws on the digital/nondigital distinction to discuss the scope and technical limits of the access-right regime. Accordingly, the exclusivity prongs apply *only to works expressed digitally*.[23] Nondigital works (or, according to the second distinction, offline works)[24] will continue to be governed by traditional copyright rules. This principle provokes two types of issues briefly subsumed below as the practical question and the normative question. The practical question asks whether it is at all *possible* to design a workable dualistic[25] copyright system that applies different sets of rules to digital and nondigital works. The normative question asks whether it would be *justified*.

1. The Normative Question

The access-right, when fully asserted, strikes one as having an extremely broad mandate, moving certainly beyond the protection secured under the current copyright system. This difference is a direct consequence of the transition from traditional exclusive rights in the direction of access-based regulation. Digital expressions need a different type of protection as they differ fundamentally from nondigital expressions. The difference is not merely technical or formal: digital media radically change virtually all the parameters lawmakers need to take into consideration as they seek to calibrate a balanced regime. Digital technology influences anything from circumstances of reception and meaning of messages to efficiency of communication, its costs, objective and subjective value, and utility effects.[26] These changes have a profound impact on the copyright system as digital technology renders messages *qualitatively* distinguishable from messages expressed in nondigital media. The economics of digital information markets runs along different vectors, forming unique analytical perspectives and focal points.[27] Electronic mail or Instant Messaging (IM) are dissimilar to a letter

---

23. For that matter, a digital work is an original message expressed in binary code, which is detectable and readable by machines that can process its electric, magnetic, or optical signals.

24. Offline works also include digital works that were never made available over computer networks with the permission of the copyright holder.

25. Dualism in this context means the law distinguishes between exclusivity interests in analog and digital works.

26. Chapter 1, Section IV.D.2 *supra*. From the perspective of communication theories, content and context are both important parameters in the meaning-making process. Even when messages in digital and nondigital forms have the same "content," this tells only part of the story of communication and the way a message is analyzed and evaluated. For an early and still felicitous analysis, see M. ETHAN KATSH, LAW IN A DIGITAL WORLD 212–26 (1995).

27. *See* HAL R. VARIAN ET. AL, THE ECONOMICS OF INFORMATION TECHNOLOGY: AN INTRODUCTION 49 ff (2004).

written with a pen on a sheet of paper that is delivered by post in any number of ways. The same applies to an MP3 file or an e-book, as compared to a vinyl record plate or a hard copy of the book, respectively. This is the crux of the digital dilemma after all, and there is little new about its far-reaching impact on information markets to be added at this point.

Furthermore, a host of fairly recent phenomena that are now considered valid copyright subject matter such as computer programs, content of Internet Web sites, computer games, electronic music, or electronic art *do not at all exist outside the digital realm* to begin with. Digital technology furnishes both logical and logistic media for making various messages perceptible, transferable, and comprehensible. The medium determines not only the physical incarnation of the expression but its interpretation and usage as well.[28] And if McLuhan's observation "the medium is the message"[29] has the gist of truth in it, the same logic can certainly buttress a legal distinction between expressions that are perceived and communicated through fundamentally different types of media.

In recent times, many kinds of information goods have been undergoing a medial transition to "digital only" or "digital mostly" formats. Music, text publishing, news reporting, broadcasting, film, and entertainment (to name a few) are increasingly available in digital formats, which come to underlie their most basic forms of use and exploitation. As digital formats and business models premised on digital dissemination become more prevalent, the deficiencies of traditional rules become more visible, and from normative and regulative standpoints, more disturbing. The impact of digital technology on both market and

---

28. As noted, digital technology determines not only what recipients can do with the message, it also alters the circumstances of reception, its speed, appearance, quality, and costs, as well as idiosyncratic value and market value factors. In some way, it is not the same "message" once translated into binary code and ushered into the digital online universe.

29. *See* Marshall McLuhan, Understanding Media: The Extensions of Man (1964). McLuhan wrote more than four decades ago:

> In a culture like ours, long accustomed to splitting and dividing all things as a means of control, it is sometimes a bit of a shock to be reminded that, in operational and practical fact, the medium is the message. This is merely to say that the personal and social consequences of any medium—that is, of any extension of ourselves—result from the new scale that is introduced into our affairs by each extension of ourselves, or by any new technology . . . Many people would be disposed to say that it was not the machine, but what one did with the machine, that was its meaning or message. In terms of the ways in which the machine altered our relations to one another and to ourselves, it mattered not in the least whether it turned our cornflakes or Cadillacs. The restructuring of human work and association was shaped by the technique of fragmentation that is the essence of machine technology. The essence of automation technology is the opposite. It is integral and decentralist in depth, just as the machine was fragmentary, centralist, and superficial in its patterning of human relationships.

Id. at 7–8.

nonmarket activities has been so deep that the need to devise new copyright models to replace the one that has been serving society in past centuries is now compelling.

Importantly, though the proposed model seeks to sketch the structure of an alternative system, it is not suggested that it completely displace the traditional system with one strike. The old regime will continue to regulate analog markets. In sectors where analog communication media become marginal or disappear completely over time, the old regime will turn irrelevant and vanish with them.[30] Digital recording or broadcasting is not a perfect substitute to attending a live musical performance, and for that matter, conventional public performance rights may continue to apply to this particular avenue of exploitation.[31] Traditional copyrights could and should continue to regulate nondigital (or, according to the second distinction, "offline") expressions alongside the access-right prongs.

Maintaining a dualistic system essentially means digital and nondigital works enjoy different sets of protection. Market forces of supply and demand will indicate which format is superior with respect to which type of exploitation, and in places where analog media perish of natural causes, the traditional regime will effectively be replaced by the access-right system. This would allow the existing system to expire precisely in those segments of creative production where it is no longer needed. In conclusion, a sort of "discrimination" between digital and nondigital works (or between online and offline works) is not only unobjectionable on normative and policy grounds, it even appears to be warranted.[32]

---

30. To be sure, there will always be room for the traditional exclusive rights. Many works will remain to some extent "nondigitizable." Further, it is likely some works that are technically "digitizable" will continue to be distributed and consumed in analog media, at least in the short run.

31. In a nutshell, experiencing a digital representation of "nondigitizable" works differs substantially from experiencing it directly without the digital medium. "Nondigitizable" messages can be thought of as works that cannot be initially expressed in digital form when access to digital representation of such messages is not a perfect substitute to being exposed to them directly. Patent examples are works of visual arts and similar creative expression where direct access to the original exemplar (i.e., a sculpture or a painting) is particularly important. As mentioned, nondigitizable messages are also live performances, of which digital recording is not comparable to physically attending the performance.

32. In fact, already under current law nondigital works are "discriminated against" is some way, because anticircumvention protections are available only with respect to *works in digital form* with effective TPMs attached. A dualistic copyright regime seeks to translate the intrinsic differentiations between digital and nondigital works into differentiations in the nature of copyright protection in a more systematic, transparent, and justifiable manner.

2. The Practical Question

The answer to the normative question is that a law treating digital and nondigital works differently is not implausible on its face—quite the opposite is true. Next, we should consider the implications of a split system from a legal-pragmatic standpoint, namely, whether and how the dualistic system could work in practice. Although the present exposition cannot address all the details, the question should receive at least an initial response. One of the most important challenges of a dualistic system would be to set criteria determining what works are controlled by which protection regime. In principle, traditional copyright rules should continue to apply to works expressed in nondigital formats (including unfixed works) for the reasons explained above. The access-right regime would apply in three prototypical scenarios: it will control works (1) initially produced and distributed digitally,[33] (2) works digitized (and digitally distributed) by, or with the permission of the copyright holder,[34] and (3) works that had been initially digitized without permission, of which the rights-holder subsequently endorsed this unauthorized act by asserting the access-right prongs.

The general rule emerging from the first and second scenarios is that works that are expressed, marketed, and exchanged digitally (and predominantly, works that are made available with permission over computer networks) are controlled *exclusively* by the access-right regime. The difficult interface question concerns situations where the work had been initially created and distributed with permission only in analog format and was later digitized and further disseminated without permission in a manner that potentially infringes the rights of reproduction, adaptation, distribution, transmission, etc.

To begin with, the model does not dispute the established doctrine that considers digitization of an analog work and dissemination of the digital representation without permission actionable infringements of incumbent exclusive copyrights. As the work has never been digitized *with the permission of the rights-holder*, digitization itself—and diffusion of the work digitally—would continue to be considered violations of traditional copyright rules.[35]

---

33. Such works would fall automatically under the ARM regime.

34. Such digitized versions will be subject to the ARM regime upon digitization and dissemination with the permission of the rights-holder.

35. As a matter of policy, legal certainty, and information costs, third parties without knowledge of the illegal digitization who access the work over computer networks should be able to regard these works as controlled by the access-right. This means, inter alia, that innocent third parties who perform copyright-implicating conducts that are permissible under the access-right regime but prohibited under traditional rules shall not incur infringement liability. Legal certainty and simple rules determining the legal status of the work are important. This requires persons who receive or encounter a work in digital format to be able to assume the access-right regime applies. Rights-holders who see their works leak to digital markets without their consent may wish simply to assert their access-right prongs and enjoy the broad protections afforded thereby. Again, moral rights remain

The next question concerns the *status* of a work that, as a result of conventional infringement, has "leaked" to the digital space and became available over computer networks without permission. Once the work diffuses to cyberspace as a consequence of such infringement, the rights-holders will face the following choice: either reverting to the legal scheme controlling analog formats or endorsing the option to continue exploitation digitally. In the first case, the rights-holder shall have the legal right to seize, block access to, and withdraw from the market all illicit digital copies and communication sources of the work to the extent eliminating its digital existence is reasonably achievable.[36] Alternatively, the rights-holder may elect to assert the access-right prongs, and from that point onwards, the work migrates to cyberspace and is controlled by the access-right regime. But what if the rights-holder declines to pursue one of these options within a reasonable time after becoming aware of the unauthorized digitization? It would be possible to consider a default to act as an implicit consent to the new digital life the work has acquired, and consequently, the law could consider the work a non-asserted digital work subject to the access-right regime. As we shall see, such works are subject to a non-voluntary license allowing access and communication without exclusivity restrictions, securing the rights-holder a claim to receive remunerations according to prefixed rates under the liability rule mechanism described in Section III.B.3 infra.

III. THE ACCESS-RIGHT REGIME

A. An Overview

The discussion now turns to explain the structure of entitlements depicted in Figure 8.1. The two red boxes on the right side of the chart's central axis stand for the core copyrights. These two prongs prescribe the substantive scope of copyright exclusivity entitlements under the ARM. The language expressing the

unaffected by the imposition of assertion requirements. For instance, if rights-holders consider unauthorized digitization also a violation of their right of integrity, there is nothing stopping them from vindicating that right before the court with or without having to comply with any assertion prerequisites.

36. In the case a complete reversion to the analog medium is not practically doable, the rights-holder will have to assert the relevant access-right prongs in order to maintain effective exclusory entitlements. This may seem unfair to those rights-holders who never wanted to exploit digitally but were "forced" into the access-right regime, possibly via an unlawful act. The rationale supporting this apparent injustice is the desire to prevent a greater injustice. Namely, innocent third parties who are exposed to the digital work as a consequence of unauthorized acts of digitization should be able to rely on the access-right notice mechanisms when considering the lawfulness of their own acts (infra).

exclusivity prongs uses the terminology of "access-conducts" and "communication-conducts"—two concepts Chapter 3 explored at length.[37] Both prongs are needed because (as shown previously), premising digital copyright protection on the idea of access implies the legal power to enjoin both actions of individual access to works and communications of works to others.[38] Introducing the access-right prongs into the positive copyright law should *replace* the traditional exclusive rights as applied to digital works. This is the essence of the *principle of substitution*. A fully asserted access-right confers upon its rights-holder entitlements that come *instead of* the set of enumerated exclusive rights provided under current law.

The *principle of independent assertion* means that rights-holders are free to choose whether they wish to assert the first prong alone, the second prong alone, or both. As the two prongs are subject to separate assertion prerequisites, rights-holders may pick the protection framework that better suits their needs. For example, a copyright holder may prefer to assert the second prong (securing exclusivity in various forms of communication) but decline to assert the prong furnishing control over individual access conducts. In such case and *regarding that specific work*, access-conducts to the work remain outside the territory governed by copyright exclusivity.[39] Owners who seek maximal copyright protection would likely want to assert and enforce both prongs. In situations where these prongs apply in either combination, nonowners are bound by the correlative Hohfeldian duties, which emanate from the definition of the right-claims based on the concepts of access-conducts and communication-conducts.

In order to give duty holders a fair opportunity to act in accordance with their duties, the law must afford them with clear and cost-effective indicators (or signals) concerning the exclusivity they must respect. Unsophisticated users should have convenient ways to find out whether (1) they can freely access and use the work without being subject to copyright restrictions, (2) if copyright restrictions do control the work, whether it is controlled by the access-right or traditional copyright regime,[40] and finally (3) if the former regime applies, which access-right prongs the rights-holder intends to enforce.

The principal mechanism designed for achieving this objective is the above-mentioned principle of assertion—a crucial feature of the model. Assertion means rights-holders must affirmatively proclaim the access-right prongs in

37. Chapter 3, Section II.C.1 *supra* (providing the relevant definitions).

38. Chapter 3, Section II.C.2 *supra*.

39. The opposite combination is technically possible but less likely to occur in practice. In that scenario, the copyright holder wishes to control access-conducts but allow unrestricted communications once authorized access has been achieved. As a practical matter, asserting at least the second access-right prong would be important for securing a meaningful level of protection in online commercial settings.

40. Section II.C.2 *supra*.

order to render them fully operative and binding vis-à-vis third parties. Accordingly, the model stipulates two independent assertion mechanisms that apply respectively to the exclusivity prongs. These mechanisms have two main functions. First, they mark the outer limits of the exclusivity (i.e., they serve as *structural limitations* on the right.) Second, they are designed to signal to the world the intentions of rights-holders. Such limitations are designed to place nonowners in a better position to quickly comprehend property signals, facilitating clear and straightforward indications on whether only the first, only the second, neither, or both prongs of the access-right control the work at issue.

B. The First Prong: Control over Access-Conducts

1. The Property Rule and Its Rationale

Chapter 3 defined the term *access-conducts* and its meaning in connection with exclusive rights in information. Accordingly, access-conducts are actions performed in order to gain human-access to (i.e., to perceive) the work. Access-conducts have both objective and subjective dimensions: Objectively, those acts furnish human-access to the actor, or bring the actor closer to achieving access. Subjectively, the intention or motivation behind the action (mental state) relates to achieving access.[41]

The first access-right prong is designed to endow rights-holders exclusivity over such conducts under certain circumstances. The rationale of this rule relates partly to the problems anticircumvention laws have been trying to tackle.[42] Under the assumption copyright exclusivity is principally justified, TPMs can play an important role in securing revenues in certain markets and segments of commercial exploitation (e.g., on-demand services). The basic economic reasoning in support of using TPMs for the purpose of improving discriminatory pricing strategies has some important merits.[43] However, private legal rights to control access to information are just an empty shell in the absence of a facilitative technological infrastructure and self-help.[44] From the perspective of property law in general, "access to information" is an evasive abstractum that challenges the application of common legal principles to its peculiar constellation of subject matter and relevant act. The ability to conceptualize this notion and consolidate it with property principles hinges greatly on the actual conditions of communication surrounding the message to be considered as property subject matter. If a communication infrastructure suitable for access control is in place, the first access-right prong predicts a certain degree of fusion between the *material-substantive*

---

41. This aspect implies the actor is initially aware of the existence of the work, and further, that some affirmative steps need to be taken to actually "receive" the message. Chapter 3, Section II.C.1 *supra*.

42. Chapter 6 *supra*.

43. Chapter 7, Section II.A.3.(b) *supra*.

44. Chapter 3, Section 3.A *supra*.

content of the right and *self-help measures* performed by the rights-holder.[45] This way, self-help achieved via access TPMs receives legal-substantive content that influences the reach and enforceability of copyrights.

2. Assertion: Attaching Access-Control TPMs

The first access-right prong must be asserted by its claimant in order to become enforceable. Generally, attaching to the work a technological measure that affectively controls access-conducts would fulfill this requirement. Legal rules alone (without any involvement of claimants) can hardly secure subjective-exclusive, property-like rights that regulate individual access to information subject matter. Moreover, rights-holders cannot legitimately expect to enforce such exclusivity when works are widely available in unrestricted digital formats. Assertion via access controls is this context is the only reasonable way to effectuate such right by its own terms, which, at the same time, functions as an essential "stop sign" for duty holders.

Without attempting here a model definition of "effective" access controls,[46] the TPM concept generally embraces any digital mechanism used by rights-holders to restrict unfettered access to the digital work.[47] Using such access control TPMs is the essential precondition to legal protection against unauthorized access under the first prong. In turn, a third party who dismantles access restrictions the relevant TPMs seek to achieve would violate the protection secured under the first prong, as thereby the actor gains (or may gain) access to the work rights-holders wished to prevent or condition.[48] The correlative duty imposed on

---

45. Regulative design theorists would consider such relationship between the content of legal rights and the relevant environmental infrastructure neither novel nor surprising. As Reidenberg proposed, it is possible and sometimes plausible to use infrastructure and technology to achieve public policy goals that are typically achieved via pure legal norms, provided, of course, that it is done thoughtfully. *See* Joel R. Reidenberg, *Lex Informatica: The Formulation of Information Policy Rules through Technology*, 76 TEX. L. REV. 553 (1988).

46. The "effectiveness" requisite is a relatively modest one. The measure should not be highly vulnerable to trivial circumvention attempts, and its primary objective is to inhibit inadvertent access. The definition of technological measures does not need to be complex or elaborate. An access-control TPM is any technical mechanism used by the rights-holder, which, in blocking access, singles out the intention to control it via the imposition of actual obstacles on the possibility to gain human-access.

47. Inasmuch as one adopts the online/offline distinction (Section II.C. *supra*), the relevant TPM would impose restrictions on the accessibility of the work over computer networks.

48. It is a difficult question whether exploiting "analog holes" (Chapter 6, Section VII.D.2 *supra*) to bypass DRMS protections without technically interfering with the operation of the (for our purposes "effective") digital access control mechanism would violate the first prong. A possible answer is that in most "analog hole" scenarios, initial access to the digital work is available to the actor, who, in fact, aims at overcoming further *use*

nonowners is therefore very simple: they are generally required not to tamper with access-TPMs. The flipside of this principle is also simple: when individual access to works is unrestricted by digital access controls, human-access must by lawful.[49]

The principle of asserting the first access-right prong by means of deploying an effective access-TPM virtually sidesteps the turbulent interface between conventional copyright regulation and anticircumvention provisions, a pressing issue under the current system. In fact, current anticircumvention provisions become wholly redundant and thus should be abolished under the ARM system.[50] The removal of this appendage from the copyright statute will be complete, including its controversial anti-trafficking provisions. Activities presently covered by statutory anti-trafficking bans imposing direct liability will become subject to indirect liability analysis. As explained in Chapter 6, one of the worst shortcomings of the anti-trafficking provisions is the vanishing ties between acts they make punishable and conventional copyright infringement.[51] The first prong here would restore the nexus between the legal (copyright) violation and the act under discussion, while drawing a clearer line between infringement analysis for primary and indirect violations. Providing someone with tools to defeat technological access control *might* give rise to (secondary) infringement liability under certain conditions and according to the applicable doctrines, but is never a direct violation of copyright.[52] This should provide the better framework

---

restrictions imposed by the DRMS. In that case, it is not the first but the second prong that is possibly triggered.

49. The presumption of lawful access by innocent users to technologically unrestricted works must hold also when a circumventor previously removed access restrictions unlawfully. Such users should be in the position to presume the lack of a "stop sign" means their own individual access is lawful. Importantly, this does not imply a license to *recommunicate* the work; asserting and violating the second access-right prong is a separate question. As noted above, in case of unlawful circumvention and distribution in unprotected format, rights-holders should have the right to seize unlawful versions and "relock" future authorized distribution channels.

50. Some elements are expected to survive the transition from existing anticircumvention laws to the first access-right prong. Providing a legal definition of an "effective" access control and of the act of "circumvention" will probably remain relevant. However, the proposed rights' structure will eliminate the interface problem entirely, and at the same time, dramatically simplify the law.

51. Chapter 6, Section VIII.B *supra*.

52. While attacking objections to the effect of indirect liability as chilling innovation (the "Chilled Innovation conjecture"), one commentator observed "the influence of indirect copyright liability upon technological innovation is multi-dimensional. Several countervailing forces—such as the relatively low capital requirements associated with the technology at issue, the nature of the many established research environments, the philosophical and cultural orientation of many digital technology researchers, various liability-insulating institutions, the ability of investors and technology companies to manage risk,

for dealing with actors who assist or facilitate violations of the first prong[53] while establishing a more direct and transparent nexus between principal and secondary "bad acts."[54] At the same time, it should be easier to moderate the reach and chilling effects of secondary infringement liability via the judicial application of relatively flexible doctrines, as compared to the current statutorily fixed bans on trafficking or preparatory acts.

Finally, it is possible to improve the signaling function of assertion by requiring rights-holders to supplement TPMs with notice. The notice would clarify for users the copyright nature of access restrictions and possibly warn against unlawful circumvention.[55] This way, users who encounter access obstacles are unambiguously informed about the sort of copyright claims/restrictions concerning that work and are given information on how to contact the respective rights-holders.[56]

C. The Second Prong: Control over Communication-Conducts

1. The Property Rule and Its Rationale

As reviewed in Chapter 5, conventional rights covering communications to the public have a long pedigree in copyright law. The core rationales, justifications,

---

and the importance of technological advance in fields unaffected by copyright law–suggest that the effects of indirect copyright liability on innovation in replication and distribution technologies will be both less dire and more complex than the Chilled Innovation conjecture suggests. The Chilled Innovation conjecture downplays the beneficial effects of indirect copyright liability on the development of balanced technologies (those that tend to balance incentives to create copyrighted works with advances in information dissemination) while ignoring the adverse effects of broad immunity, which fosters deployment of parasitic technologies that tend to drive out balanced technologies." *See* Peter S. Menell, *Indirect Copyright Liability and Technological Innovation*, 32 Colum. J.L. & the Arts (2009), 375, 399.

53. Indirect liability doctrines apply tests such as contributory liability, vicarious liability, or "inducement." In the context of the first access-right prong, such doctrines may serve to evaluate the lawfulness of behaviors such as facilitation, encouragement, promotion, or generating revenues from *assisting others* to circumvent relevant TPMs.

54. This seemingly aesthetic improvement would in fact help to flatten some troubling wrinkles in existing law. As a result of different definitions of copyright infringement, establishing secondary liability under the ARM is necessarily based—indeed dependent on—convincing the court the primary violation has taken place, or that it is very likely to take place as a result of the accused behavior (e.g., selling circumvention tools). The current situation, in which trafficking liability substantially loses touch with the question of actual copyright infringement, is a structural discrepancy the ARM would ameliorate. The shift the proposed model encourages is from regulation of *devices* to regulation of *harmful acts*.

55. Such notice requirement is not unprecedented in domestic anticircumvention schemes. A notice requirement that further indicates the rights-holders' identity and type of technological protection exists already in the German anticircumvention model. *See* UrhG., § 95d.

56. *Id.*

and intended effects of granting limited exclusivity in various communications do not need to be reiterated here. The ARM proposal, while drawing on the notion of communication-conducts, mindfully expands the substantive scope of exclusivity, an expansion that goes perhaps even beyond the digital communication and making-available right evinced by WIPO's "umbrella solution"[57] and its avatars in European Community and domestic laws.[58] At the same time, it must be stressed the philosophy behind the second prong is fundamentally different. Recall the umbrella solution was a neoconservative attempt to stretch the coverage of traditional copyrights over various digital transmissions and communication situations by letting domestic laws decide which specific exclusive right(s) shall apply.[59] In sharp contrast to the neoconservative pattern, the ARM cuts off reliance on traditional exclusive rights such as public performance or distribution rights by replacing them with a new "access provision right" in digital works. The explicit foundation of this right is the notion of communication.

In the process of moving away from the catalog of multiple, fragmented and relatively narrow exclusive rights (the "bundle" of copyrights) to a single overarching right, the ARM mindfully eliminates the current distinctions between the various exclusive rights. Among other things, this approach should undercut the possibility of parallel application of multiple rights to the same behavior and its troubling implications on use privileges.[60] A uniform and coherent communication prong would offer a far less complicated and fragmented basis for copyright exclusivity.[61] Separate legal definitions of multiple exclusive rights will no longer nurture complicated classifications and subclassifications that link certain work categories to certain exclusive rights and certain rights to certain exceptions/limitations, which, in turn, selectively apply to some rights but not to others.[62]

---

57. Chapter 5, Section III.A(4) *supra*.

58. Chapter 5, Section IV *supra*.

59. Chapter 5, Section III *supra*.

60. Chapter 5, Section V *supra*.

61. An exemplary provision that seems to reflect a similar approach is § 10(1) of the Swiss Copyright Act of 1992 (URG), granting to authors the exclusive right to determine if and how the work shall be exploited ("*verwendet*"). *See* URG (Switzerland, 1992), § 10(1) ("Der Urheber oder die Urheberin hat das ausschliessliche Recht zu bestimmen, ob, wann und wie das Werk verwendet wird.") The general clause granting exclusivity in "exploitations" could be paralleled with the second access-right prong granting exclusivity in digital communications in general. As shown in Chapter 1, all potentially infringing acts copyright law cares about involve communicative aspects.

62. Obviously, also under the ARM regime classifications will not disappear completely. The model would provide an opportunity to design necessary classifications more sensibly. For instance, subject matter classifications of works of "high" authorship, works of "low" authorship, neighboring rights, software, sui generis, and so on could provide a basis for reasonable differentiations in the context of duration.

The principle of substitution again underlies the intended operation of the second access-right prong: with such core right in place, all existing economic rights become superfluous. This approach would end (at least for the foreseeable future) the relentless pressure to incrementally expand existing rights[63] and contribute to shifting the focus to carving proper limitations to exclusivity and zones of freedom within it. In this context, it is crucial to understand a solid and uniform right based on the concept of communication does not come to serve the interests of one group of stakeholders or the other. Its impetus is to improve the system *as a whole* by allowing lawmakers to significantly simplify the signals of property, both when a certain use is subject to exclusivity and when it is privileged or located outside copyright in the first place.

Communication-conducts covered by the second prong are affirmative actions performed to communicate or transfer a message containing copyrightable elements. As we have seen, communication is a broad concept, both in the general sense and more specifically in the copyright context. It encapsulates some very basic restrictions on behavior derived from the nature of works as informational artifacts—and it is the essential meeting point between the information process and private property principles. In theory, the digital communication right captures all (public) externalizations or transfer of works (to the public) by means of digital media and computer networks.[64] The notion of *communication-conducts in the broad sense* covers mere facilitation of access via a communication act (the communicator does not alter the content) as well as re-communication of copyrighted materials embodied in a new derivative work.[65] Among other things, this notion also breaks with the long-standing distinction in copyright law between copy-related and copy-unrelated rights because (also) embodying work signals in tangible media from which the work can be perceived has a potential communicative quality.[66] In other words, to the extent digital reproduction actually

---

63. Chapter 5, Section III.C *supra* (reviewing the scope of Art. 8 WCT).

64. The communication concept principally engulfs both private and public communications. However, also under the ARM, the law should preserve the private/public distinction, leaving private communications (e.g., person-to-person e-mail, or generally, point-to-point communication procedures) outside the reach of the second prong. While formulating such distinction, it is important to keep in mind its eroding capacity to impose clear and stable limitations on the scope of the digital communication right. *See* Chapter 5, Section 5.B *supra*. That is to say, in calibrating the copyright balance, the role this distinction can play is limited by virtue of the technology at issue and the difficulty of separating the public from the private in the networked environment.

65. As a practical matter, lawmakers may elect whether to subject to direct or indirect liability mere facilitation of access by operating as a passive conduit (e.g., communication service provides). In either case, the law may preserve the instrument of safe harbors for service providers and other passive conduits that are structured similarly to existing arrangements.

66. Chapter 3, Section II.C.2 *supra*.

facilitates (or can facilitate) relevant (public) communications, making reproductions is a copyright-relevant act. In this light, the second prong principally embraces various reproductions and/or distributions of digital duplicates that operate as a means of communicating the work to the public.

The last point is critical for understanding the scope of the second prong and the structural change it would institute. As shown in Chapter 4, current exclusive rights are modeled around the distinction between copy-related and copy-unrelated rights, whether explicitly or implicitly. Under current law, the concepts of "copy" and "fixation" still assume enormous theoretical and practical significance for courts deciding on infringement disputes.[67] However, compelling evidence from the case law repeatedly confirms digital technology has brought legal notions such as fixation to the verge of a conceptual breaking point.[68] A key rationale for modeling exclusive rights in the image of the second prong is the need to do away with fixation-based classifications in digital network settings. Among other things, the new right should sidestep the vexing problem of temporary digital reproductions in computer components and network operations, as more-or-less stable fixation would no longer play a decisive role in the infringement test and the application of copyright law more generally.

2. *Assertion: Registration, Deposit, and Notice Formalities*

(a) The Principle

The ARM incorporates a proposal to institute copyright formalities. By its terms, the second access-right prong might become ubiquitous in the digital information environment, thereby aggravating the danger of overprotection. To mitigate this risk and channel nonmarket works (or works whose authors are not interested in enforcing copyrights) directly to the public domain, a structural barrier (or "screen") to exclusivity should be built into the system. Such structural limitation on second-prong exclusivity mainly seeks to achieve two things: (1) avoid in rem exclusivity (or "property rule") when rights-holders have neither an interest in, nor intention to enforce their claims; and (2) reduce net information, search, and tracing costs the property system entails. For the present purpose, "formalities" are legal requirements imposed on rights-holders who wish to vindicate their exclusivity claims. According to the principle of assertion, such rights-holders must assert exclusivity claims over communication-conducts by means of compliance with a set of statutory formalities. The ARM integrates such requirements into the copyright system as part of a new quid pro quo: rights-holders receive generous exclusive entitlements in digital communications and communication-facilitating acts, but their entitlements *cannot vest automatically from the moment a work is expressed digitally*. The strong powers the

---

67. *See, e.g.*, The Cartoon Network v. CSC Holdings, 536 F.3d 121, 127–34 (2d. Cir. 2008).

68. Chapter 4, Section VI.A *supra*.

second prong confers simply cannot come into existence unconditionally, because recognizing an automatic exclusivity over communications would impose an intolerable burden on the information process. To avoid this stifling effect, the ARM forges the said structural limitations that generally operate as *prerequisites* to the enforceability of economic exclusive rights.

The need to comply with basic formalities should encourage rights-holders to participate in drawing boundaries around the information they call their "property." As noted, the design of limitations around exclusive rights should be sensitive to information cost and efficiency considerations, and one of the things formalities rules should result in is an effective reduction in net information costs.[69] Another related effect of formalities would purge exclusivity claims when their possibility serves no defendable purpose.[70] It is true formalities themselves involve expenses, including new ones borne by owners (e.g., filing fees) and administrative costs. Having that in mind, the model is premised on the assumption positive externalities generated by freeing the majority of works from exclusivity restrictions would far outweigh the social costs of having a formalities mechanism in place. A simple formalities model that sets forth modest compliance requirements can prove both just and efficient as complying rights-holders gain more robust protection in the digital space under the "new deal" the ARM proposal promotes. It is also efficient because the net social gains from alleviating monopoly (and other exclusivity-related) costs precisely where exclusive rights are nothing but a burden on creation are expected to render the property system as a whole less costly and more goal-oriented.

(b) The Advantages of Formalities

As reviewed in Chapter 7, formalities have important efficiency advantages.[71] Those advantages should be assessed jointly with the increasing dominance of digital technology and computer networks in the modern information environment. In this environment, cybercitizens are exposed to a dazzling quantity and variety of conveniently accessible information as an integral part of their daily lives. People wish for, and now have real and fascinating opportunities to participate in the culture in which they live, which means opportunities for becoming active speakers (rather than passive listeners) are much more meaningful and realizable.[72] Every culture participant may legitimately desire to take advantage of the new social and economic opportunities of enhanced connectivity and interaction venues and avenues digital technology now offers. As many observers

69. Section VII.B.1 *infra*.

70. Chapter 2, Section III.C.2.(a) *supra*.

71. Chapter 7, Section III.B.2(c)ii *supra*.

72. *See* Lawrence Lessig, Remix: Making Art and Commerce Thrive in the Hybrid Economy 36 ff (2008) (describing the reemergence of the "read-write" culture in digital space).

have noted before, the clash between a highly participative, decentralized information culture and copyright law is unavoidable; copyrighted content constitutes an essential part of our collective vocabulary, and copyrighted elements of speech and discourse are often the indispensable currency of basic communication. This recognition—that copyrighted messages remain essentially exchangeable and shareable speech—must be consolidated with the "property" status of works and the potentially beneficial role exclusion might play in societal progress.[73]

To somewhat relax this tension (or paradoxical[74] relationship) between private property principles and the personal right to communicate, and to facilitate a defendable operation of an intangible property system in the network environment, ordinary people (the paradigmatic "users") should be able to answer for themselves two basic questions: (1) *What information* is protected under copyright? and (2) *What acts* with respect to copyrighted material require authorization? A set of reasonable formalities could bring the copyright system closer to achieving more certainty in these areas. The aim is to establish a built-in, low-cost *filtering mechanism* that would create a more visible distinction between cases where exclusivity is potentially beneficial (or even necessary) and those where its burden on communication is disproportionate, unduly, and normatively objectionable.

By virtue of their affirmative actions, and guided by the free choices they make, rights-holders themselves should be encouraged to participate in maintaining that filtering mechanism by feeding it with information about their individual preferences and expectations. Ideally, users should be able to benefit from this filtering mechanism and find quick answers to the two basic questions noted above. In essence, the ARM foresees a small yet important shift in the burdens the copyright system imposes on stakeholders. Requiring rights-holders to make a relatively minor "extra" effort (beyond merely creating/fixing messages or the acquisition of legal rights from their actual originators) to "assist" nonowners in respecting copyright appears neither unfair nor unreasonable. In the digital information reality, instructing rights-holders to *identify* the messages with respect to which they intend to enforce exclusive rights is intimately related to and almost a natural consequence of the major medial transformation of our age (Section II.C supra).

In this vein, the law "expects" rights-holders to *mark*[75] copyrighted information they (legitimately) *expect* to have exclusivity in—and which they *expect* the state apparatus to kindle and enforce. Satisfying this set of mutual expectations

---

73. For a recent analysis of the intricate tension between copyright and free speech through a U.S. law lens, see Neil W. Netanel, Copyright's Paradox (2008).

74. *Id.* at 3–12.

75. *Cf.* Lawrence Lessig, Free Culture: How Big Media Uses Technology and the Law to Lock Down Culture and Control Creativity 290–91 (2004) (advocating

is all the more necessary in light of the dramatic influx in available informational resources that pass common copyrightability thresholds and which thereby are being automatically (and sometimes senselessly) "allocated" to private individuals and firms.

To summarize, formalities must be carefully designed with one central goal in mind: they should help put parties affected by the property system on notice with regard to the implications of private property rights as regards the lawfulness of their behavior. When designing a formalities model, it is further important to ensure the technicalities of compliance do not overcomplicate the system to a degree that might obscure their efficiency advantages. This goal and admonition should be the beacon that guides the drafting of copyright formalities such as registration, notice, and possibly deposit as noted below.

(c) Application

I. REGISTRATION

The purpose of registration is to create a publicly accessible database of copyrighted works, including the persons/entities who are legally entitled to exercise exclusive rights and grant use permissions. Registration under the ARM system is cardinal in the sense that rights-holders wishing to enforce the second access-right prong are required to register their works with a central registration authority. Recent proposals to introduce a registration requirement draw significantly on enhanced efficiency advantages of new technologies and their potential contribution to simplifying the operation and administration of the mechanism. For example, simple online procedures can facilitate both registration by rights-holders and information retrieval about the status of a given work by users.[76]

It is important to keep the burden on rights-holders modest, and compliance (ideally performed and administrated online) should involve only a low-cost and trivial procedure. For example, rights-holders would be required to provide the name of the author, the title of the work, a short description thereof, year and place of first publication, and contact information (in accordance with reasonable privacy policies). Registration could entail the payment of a modest fee; the money collected should be channeled to cover administrative costs. Copyright registration information should be made freely accessible to the public over the Internet, allowing users to (1) ascertain the copyright status of the work and, when relevant, (2) find rights-holders for purposes of requesting use permissions, negotiating a license or transfer of rights, and so forth.

---

for a marking requirement, where the consequence of failure to mark is an implied permission to "use unless someone complains").

76. *Id.* at 289–90.

II. COPYRIGHT NOTICE/MARKING

The theoretical advantages of copyright notice/marking should be translated into practice.[77] Rights-holders may satisfy the notice requirement in many different ways, such as by attaching to the work a symbol (such as the well-known © symbol introduced by Art. III of the Universal Copyright Convention) or other visual, audio, or audiovisual emblem, texts, or even tones, depending on the nature of the work and the media used for its dissemination.[78] In the digital networked environment, tags, flags, visual symbols, audio notices, and computer codes may notify human users (and also rendering machines) about the copyright status of that work.[79] The form of notice/marking is immaterial so long as the test guiding the formulation of the legal requirement is *functional*, namely, whether the measures can reasonably fulfill the purpose of effectively informing users about the copyright status of the digital work and the legal restrictions involved. In general, a failure to give proper notice might result in a presumption in favor of users (Section III.C.3 infra).

III. DEPOSIT

In principle, a deposit duty could have important advantages. As the access-right applies only to works in digital form, it should be relatively easy as a technical matter to deposit a digital, TPMs-free version of the work with the registration authority. There are at least two benefits to including a deposit obligation as part

---

77. *Cf.* EUCD (2001), Recital 55 ("Technological development will facilitate the distribution of works, notably on networks, and this will entail the need for rightholders to *identify better the work* or other subject-matter, the author or any other rightholder, and to *provide information about the terms and conditions of use* of the work or other subject-matter in order to render easier the management of rights attached to them.") (emphasis added). An additional economic advantage of digital marking that has not been discussed above at length is in helping rights-holders to estimate usage intensity and fine-tune their reaction to market demand.

78. In the end, the specific method of giving effective notice or effectively marking the work will likely depend on the type of work, the circumstances in which it becomes perceptible, the communication/network channel through which it travels, and most importantly, the way it ultimately arrives for users.

79. It is crucial to understand the difference between notice-facilitating systems on the one hand and access-control TPMs on the other. The latter (restricting) type of measures does not belong here, whereas the former type merely serves to provide information, not to block use. Copyright Management Information (CMI) systems themselves, including machine-oriented technologies such as digital watermarking, fingerprinting, HASH function identification etc., do not impose technical restrictions on use, though they can help rights-holders to trace usage (both legitimate and infringing). Two important points should be clarified: first, installing rights management systems is *not* an integral part of any assertion requirement. It is optional, and in light of the principal goal of giving notice to *end users*, it is secondary in importance. Second, neither prong of the access-right defines manipulation of digital notice-giving systems as a direct violation of copyrights, as opposed to the CMI provisions discussed in Chapter 6.

of the assertion mechanism. The first is evidential: the deposited version, in combination with registration, serves as evidence that exclusive copyrights cover the specific content subject to an infringement suit. Second, if a TPM-protected work is subject to an administrative dispute resolution process that results in a grant of access (infra), the adjudicating authority shall have the power to facilitate access to the deposited version according to the terms of access it orders. At the same time, a deposit requirement might be less advantageous in cases where online content (e.g., of an Internet Web site) is being frequently modified and updated. Demanding rights-holders to deposit all versions of the work they constantly alter might place a heavy burden and overcomplicate the administration of the formalities system. For that reason, a strict deposit requirement should be relaxed in instances it proves too cumbersome or remain in some cases optional.[80]

3. Consequences of Noncompliance

(a) In General

The effect of formalities requirements (FR) on exclusivity under the ARM is crucial, as compliance is a condition precedent to exercising the second access-right prong. What then should be the consequences of noncompliance? Opponents to formalities accuse them of unjustifiably harming authors by depriving them of their rights in cases of mistake, ignorance, or impossibility. Without disputing the earnestness of these concerns, the idea of formalities as an integral element of the ARM—as opposed to simply instituting formalities within the present regime—requires a reevaluation of these objections. As a general matter, the model seeks to avoid situations in which a failure to comply with FR results in stripping authors of any potential economic advantage whatsoever. Noncompliance would result instead in the inability to exercise exclusivity, but rights-holders should still have the opportunity to be compensated for uses they cannot proscribe. To be sure, the consequence of noncompliance is *not* the total forfeiture of rights. Rather, it shifts the nature of recourse to a liability rule mechanism.

---

80. Deposit could make sense in the case of films, music, books, visual works, and even software or computer games. As noted, in cases where rights-holders constantly change the content of the work (add, edit, improve, revise, modify, combine, etc.) it might be too burdensome to require a separate deposit every time a change or update has taken place. A possible solution would be to make an *initial* deposit mandatory, which then would cover future modifications of and additions *to the same work by the same rights-holder.* A similar principle could also apply to the registration of content in the dynamic Internet environment: registration of the initial work and its source (e.g., a Web site operating under a certain unique domain name) could cover its content even as the content is being changed over time.

(b) Liability Rule

The logic of the ARM's solution to this problem is the same that underlies modern "broad liability rule" proposals as well as historical regulations (such as the old Canadian copyright statute mentioned below). As discussed in Chapter 7, some academics propose to subject copyright exclusivity to registration formalities where the default arrangement in case of noncompliance is a liability rule mechanism.[81] These proposals would create a sort of non-voluntary licensing regime for non-registered works; for users, these works would be free from exclusivity claims, but rights-holders could still demand compensation, which would take place in a centralized form (e.g., by filing a claim with collection societies) rather that through enforcing claims individually.

Past chapters in the history of copyright indicate that requiring rights-holders to fulfill a statutory requirement (formality) with noncomplying works being subject to a non-voluntary license is not without precedence. For example, historical Canadian legislation stipulated an interesting arrangement: its statutory license essentially applied to works whose rights-holders did not provide reasonable access to the public.[82] According to Section 13(1) of the Canadian Copyright Act of 1921, every person was entitled to apply for a license to print a book under copyright published in Canada or provide copies of such book to satisfy the demand for the book in Canada.[83] Applicants were required to deposit with the Minister an amount of no less than 10 percent of the retail selling price of one thousand copies (but no less than one thousand dollars).[84] Upon application, the Minister had to notify the rights-holder immediately.[85] In case the rights-holder failed to respond in a specific manner after a fixed period of time, the Minister had discretion to grant the applicant a license to print and publish the book under terms determined by the Minister.[86] A license issued this way conferred upon the licensee the sole right to print and publish the book in Canada for a maximum period of five years.[87] The licensee was required to pay royalties on the retail sale price of every copy printed under the license at a rate determined by the Minister.[88]

---

81. *See*, e.g., Christopher Sprigman, *Reform(aliz)ing Copyright*, 57 STAN. L. REV. 485, 554–57 (2004).

82. *See* Canadian Copyright Act (1921). This demonstrates the problem of books that are both under copyright and out-of-print is not new, nor is the need to address it through legislation—which in this case could have even more drastic consequences for rights-holders as compared to various orphan works arrangements.

83. *Id.* § 13(1).

84. *Id.* § 13(3).

85. *Id.* § 13(4).

86. *Id.* § 13(5).

87. *Id.* § 13(7).

88. *Id.* § 13(8).

This mechanism underscores two important points unrelated directly to the specific structure of the historical Canadian rule. First, it basically teaches the *consequence* of rights-holders' failure to *affirmatively act in a certain way* (in that case, to provide sufficient access to books) might lead to the creation of a non-voluntary license. Second, giving this principle a distinctive twist, modern proposals (discussed in Chapter 7) suggest the affirmative act necessary to trigger the property rule could be compliance with formalities—with a liability rule arrangement as the default option.

The ARM combines formalities and a broad liability rule in one scheme. Accordingly, a failure to register brings the work under a liability rule mechanism for a certain fixed period (for instance, five years from the release of the digital work). During that period, the rights-holder may file a claim with the administrator[89] invoking the entitlement to receive remunerations. To the extent possible, the payment should correlate to the intensity/frequency of use, calculated according to predetermined rates that undergo periodical evaluations and updates.[90] During the governance of the license, all the acts the second exclusivity prong covers (i.e., various communications, reproductions, and disseminations in electronic form) are not subject to exclusivity.[91] The remunerations paid according to the distribution scheme, though modest, will ameliorate to some degree any negative financial consequences of the inability to enforce exclusive rights. Importantly, the status of a work as subject to a non-voluntary license should not be irreversible at least for the period of the license. Fairness and economic efficiency considerations would advise allowing rights-holders to revise their initial decision not to comply with formalities and continue benefiting from collective remunerations. Whether noncompliance in a given case has been deliberate (i.e., a conscious decision to take the liability rule track) or not (i.e., error, lack of knowledge, inability etc.), the rights-holder should be able to switch to the property rule track and "activate" the second exclusivity prong after the initial release of the digital work. It is thus proposed that, at any time during the period of the license (say, five years from the initial distribution), rights-holders

---

89. The administrator of the royalties distribution system could be a consortium of collection societies or a non-for-profit organization operating under the supervision of a government agency.

90. The yearly sum paid to rights-holders should be commensurate with the approximate intensity of use. The budget for maintaining the system may be generated through modest levies on devices and/or a modest flat-rate on connectivity services. The administrator of this mechanism will create a database open to the public listing all works/rights-holders that benefit from this arrangement.

91. In contrast to the historical Canadian law (which regulated a reality in which professional competing publishers and printers were the worst enemies of rights-holders), there shall be no need to file any formal application before using a work subject to the license, and use permissions will not depend on individual grants from the sovereign.

are able to "opt in" by registering the work and complying with other mandatory formalities.[92]

One of the main purposes of this mechanism is to encourage rights-holders to assess the commercial viability of their works and elect a copyright arrangement (property rule or liability rule) accordingly. At any point during the collective license, rights-holders may compare their assessment of expected revenues from licensing exclusive rights individually with the expected remunerations under the statutory license. Especially in the case of a noncomplying work that becomes extremely popular and thus lucrative in the years subsequent to its initial release, its rights-holder might consider a property rule superior.[93] But the "opt in" option should be limited in time and remain available no longer than the duration of the statutory license. If the rights-holder declines to opt in during the period of the license (five, ten, or fifteen years—the term could depend on the type/class of work), the option to elect a property rule will expire and the work will enter the public domain.

Finally, complete inaction on the part of rights-holders would create a "public domain presumption" according to which the work is not subject to exclusivity restrictions, and further, that rights-holders are not entitled to collective remunerations. The law would consider such completely passive rights-holders—those who decline to comply with formalities *and* do not file a claim for statutory remuneration during a reasonable period after the initial authorized release of the works—as persons who are not interested in exploiting their work economically in any way, unless the rights-holders can rebut this presumption in the particular case and justify their omission.

IV. THE EXEMPTIONS

A. Rights-of-Access

The structure described in the previous sections affords rights-holders significant influence on the scope and effect of their copyrights. The maximum level of protection resulting from full assertion is likely to sporadically emerge in the

---

92. Obviously, the registration of information should be instantly changed to reflect the new status of the work as subject to copyright exclusivity. In such case, the property rule will apply only prospectively from the effective date of registration and compliance with other relevant formalities. The term during which the rights-holder has benefited from collective remunerations will be subtracted from the applicable duration of copyright exclusivity.

93. An opposite switch is also thinkable. In the initial phase of the commercial life of a work that is under a property rule, its rights-holder may switch to a liability rule by erasing the registration, removing the work from the database of works under exclusivity, and filing a claim under the collective license scheme.

case of works held by commercial entities and industry players. The structural limitations described above provide only initial buffers against excessive exclusivity: they draw the outer boundaries of the property rule, but they do not interfere with the exercise of copyright exclusivity once it stands. Yet the copyright system also needs mechanisms that would oversee the operation and effect of exclusivity on occasions where it is principally enforceable to the full extent permitted by law. The model strongly supports positive-relative access entitlements as the salient mechanism to moderate copyright-based control. It is proposed namely to positively institute rights-of-access. These newly created provisions will cement the legal position of their beneficiaries while guarding the interests of nonowners and counterweighing asserted exclusivity.

Under the access-right regime, hence, *rights-of-access* receive for the first time in the history of copyright an explicit recognition, as the two green boxes in Figure 8.1 illustrate. The structure of ARM exemptions is consistent with the exclusive rights. Exemptions fall under two general categories, and the model maintains the systematic distinction between rights-of-access in both the weak and in the strong form. This distinction, in turn, parallels the distinction between the two access-right prongs explained earlier. Rights-of-access in the strong form (here, *strong ROA*) mean the beneficiary holds an affirmative right-claim against the opponent:[94] This position is subjective-positive, meaning the opponent is *legally obliged* to make works under his control accessible to the rights-of-access holder (who, in this case, is *not* the copyrights holder).[95] In comparison, rights-of-access in the weak form (here, *weak ROA*) refer to situations in which certain copyright-relevant acts are privileged and the privilege beneficiary is not exposed to copyright infringement liability.[96] In other words, weak ROA recognizes the negative freedom of beneficiaries to act and communicate. In the proposed structure, strong ROA applies to the first exclusivity prong whereas weak ROA applies to the second exclusivity prong. As shown in Figure 8.1, each exemptions apparatus connects solely to its designated exclusivity prong, and each category of rights-of-access connects to a unique monitoring mechanism.

1. Rights-of-Access in the Strong Form

(a) The Exemptions Apparatus

Exclusivity over access-conducts (actions covered by the first access-right prong) is not absolute; an exhaustive catalog of exceptions will enumerate instances in

---

94. Chapter 3, Section III.B.1 *supra*.

95. The situation, in which the law grants *authors* the right to access *their* work placed under the actual control of someone else, was discussed in Chapter 3. *See* Chapter 3, Section III.A.3(a) *supra*.

96. Recall that (in line with the Hohfeldian concept of a legal privilege), privileged acts are lawful by definition, but other persons (including the proprietors) are under no legal obligation *not to interfere* with the exercise of the privilege.

which beneficiaries may also gain lawful access to the asserted work *without the rights-holders' consent.* The purpose of this instrument is to guard against the emergence of lockout scenarios in connection with rights-holders misusing their legal and technological arsenal to overly throttle access to information and unduly curtail competition.

When can such exemptions become necessary? Current anticircumvention laws highlight a number of situations where putting breaks on the technical ability and legal right to control access should receive high priority. To name a few, such exemptions could cover actions performed by libraries and educational institutions for promoting their mission, law enforcement operations, encryption researchers, reverse engineering, software security testing, software maintenance and servicing, and so on. To the extent the freedom to perform acts covered by those exceptions is curtailed as a result of the use of access-control TPMs, the law should nonetheless find ways to secure access *when appropriate.*

Of course, the appropriateness of such powerful legal positions held by non-owners and their scope are loaded with difficult policy decisions. Beyond stating its necessity and explaining its general pattern of operation, the current proposal does not specify the precise content of entitlements within the strong ROA apparatus. Creating the relevant catalog is a task for the lawmaker to tackle, who in any case should stick to the following general guidelines: First, the list remains exhaustive (not exemplary), which means inter alia that courts do not have a charter to expand it as they see fit. The statutory list will narrowly specify situations where *compelling public policy considerations* necessitate deviation from the exclusivity principle despite satisfaction of the assertion requirement.[97] Strong ROA norms will describe in detail the class of beneficiaries, the nature/purpose of the acts covered, and the circumstances where beneficiaries are entitled to demand access. When applicable, these entitlements will secure to their beneficiaries access to the technologically restricted content despite rights-holders'

97. For example, an exception is necessary when the ratio between the quantity of original content and public domain material restricted by access-TPMs is strikingly disproportional, and consequently, the TPM mainly blocks access to public domain material and other non-protected elements. In such case, the "digital envelope" in fact contains very little original expression compared to other noncopyrightable information. This diminishes the justification for copyright protection. Carving strong ROA could also be important when TPMs control access to copyrighted information that is objectively very difficult or impossible to obtain in alternative routes, and which is essential for the creation of new works of social, political, or artistic significance. A third ground for creating a duty to provide access to locked-up information is where TPMs are used to smother competition and enforcing the first prong shows little nexus to safeguarding *copyright* interests.

objections and possibly prevail over contractual provisions (or waivers) to the contrary.[98]

(b) Monitoring: The Copyright Tribunal

To function properly, strong ROA mechanisms need a monitoring authority to fulfill two main tasks: it should (1) enforce the ROA exceptions against rights-holders in specific situations, and (2) broadly monitor the enforcement of the first prong and oversee actual impacts of technological access controls on the relevant industries, competition, innovation, and consumers. The closed list of narrow ROA must sustain some degree of flexibility in order to keep up with technology and respond to pointed concerns that surface over time. To achieve this, consider the creation of a specialized *copyright tribunal* as responsible for the administration and enforcement of strong ROA.[99] To this end, the law will delegate to the tribunal several adjudicative and administrative powers:

- The tribunal shall receive complaints filed by beneficiaries who assert that strong ROA applies in their case. It will then perform a streamlined adjudicative procedure and issue a decision. If the tribunal finds a relevant ROA applies, it will award the beneficiary access (possibly to the deposited exemplar directly) according to the scope of the access entitlement it has recognized. If a deposited exemplar is not available and the rights-holder refuses to enable access, the tribunal may issue a decree instructing the rights-holder to do so.[100]
- The tribunal may receive communications from rights-holders and access claimants who are affected by strong ROA. Claimants may wish to assert existing ROA are too narrowly formulated or that new exceptions to the first prong should be created. Parties may prefer to have their disagreements resolved via an alternative dispute resolution process. The tribunal will have the authority to launch (or refer the parties to) such a process. If the parties cannot resolve the dispute this way, the door shall remain open to filing a formal complaint before the tribunal, or alternatively, filing a conventional lawsuit.

---

98. As strong ROA play an essential balancing role, we may consider creating a presumption the contractual waiver of such rights is invalid, particularly in consumer protection situations. The copyright tribunal (discussed *infra*) should have authority to decide on such matters.

99. The copyright tribunal, as an institutional subsidiary of the registration authority, could help in reducing coordination costs and simplifying the procedure of providing access to the extent a TPMs-free version of the work has been deposited with the registry. *Supra* Section III.C.2(c).

100. The tribunal may also resolve challenges to the validity of contractual waivers on exercising the rights ROA secure. After a decision on the dispute has been issued and before executing the operative order, either party should be able to appeal the administrative decision to a conventional court of law.

- The tribunal may receive communications from stakeholders, interest groups, organizations, government agencies, and members of the public concerning issues of DRMS, technical standards, technological access controls, and related topics. Those communications will contain critiques and proposals on how to modify certain existing provisions, abolish certain ROA, or create new ones. The tribunal will prepare a periodical report and submit it to the responsible governmental agency or ministry.[101] If the report includes a recommendation to modify the list, it could provide the basis for legislative initiatives to amend the law on the relevant points.

2. Rights of Access in the Weak Form

The operation and effect of the weak ROA apparatus is similar to current copyright exceptions. It provides a list of statutory privileges that legitimize unauthorized acts covered by the second access-right prong. The statutory catalog will identify and define situations in which the general rule of exclusivity over communications in asserted works gives way to privileged uses and users. Lawmakers may partly premise the privileges mechanism on instances of use privileges available under current copyright laws.[102] For example, many copyright systems contain exemptions concerning libraries, research institutions, teaching, news reporting, criticism, private copying, computer users, persons with disabilities, and so on. The core mission of this mechanism within the ARM structure is not necessarily to reinvent categories of beneficiaries and scenarios where communication-related behaviors should be lawful and respective exceptions are warranted. A long tradition of copyright exceptions already points out the regions of tension where relaxation of proprietary rules is essential for maintaining a reasonable balance of interests. However, there is one crucial difference: the conceptual and normative basis for exemptions under the ARM is the idea of access to information. Applying the model's terminology should assist in *re*formulating traditional copyright exceptions and furnishing a more flexible, access-oriented framework. Use privileges are no longer limited to the scope of traditional exclusive rights; rather, they may apply to whatever form of communication or communication-related behavior the second prong governs.

The implications of this principle on the positive law should not be underestimated. To illustrate, current law contains exceptions for the reproduction or the public performance rights, which are specific forms of communication or communication-related acts. But the law usually does not secure access interests in a more direct fashion that is detached from acts governed by exclusive rights. As a result, copyright regulation is ill-equipped when it comes to

---

101. An existing example of a monitoring agency that supervises the effect of anticircumvention rules is stated in § 39(b) of the Swiss Copyright Act [URG] (ver. 01.07.2008).

102. To illustrate, the EUCD sketches some prototypical situations where current laws excuse certain copyright-implicating acts. *See* EUCD (2001), Art. 5(1)–(3).

effectively correcting actual control that spills beyond the formal coverage of legal exclusivity. This is a significant flaw the ARM endeavors to correct. As the range of activities covered by the second prong largely ignores legal (thus artificial) distinctions between certain forms of communication, exceptions may theoretically assume almost any shape and form. Specifically, they may legitimize various digital *communications* of copyrighted material and the freedom to *receive such communications*, directly or indirectly. Put slightly differently and in the spirit of the access-right approach, the weak ROA apparatus will permit the legislature to tailor privileges around the concept of access *as such*. A series of statutory permissions will allow beneficiaries both to *access* and *provide access* to copyrighted works under the terms stipulated therein. The mechanism would promote principles (and effectively secure interests) of free speech, access to knowledge, cultural participation, education and research, and the like.

B. A Fair Use/Fair Access Privilege

The weak ROA apparatus is static in the sense that its privileges are statutorily fixed. To insert the necessary degree of flexibility and delegate a more significant role to the judiciary, the proposal supports the creation of a monitoring mechanism in the form of an "open" legal standard. This mechanism would encourage courts to exercise discretion, fine-tune the scope of exclusivity, and make corrections on a case-by-case basis. Thus, alongside fixed exceptions, consider the formulation of a general fair use/fair access clause inspired by the framework of the U.S. fair use provision.[103]

The parallel ARM clause will differ from section 107 of the U.S. Copyright Act in several important respects, however. First, the range and types of behaviors the proposed clause would be able to legitimize is broader than what U.S. fair use permits. Again, in line with the access-right approach, fair use/access might extend to cover whatever activity is principally subject to private exclusivity in asserted works. And again, in contrast to current U.S. fair use law (or at least to the way in which courts usually apply it), ARM fair use is not formally limited to defend solely against prima facie violations of traditional exclusive rights. The proposed clause should also provide the basis for developing doctrines of

---

103. Fair use is distinctively a U.S. concept and legal doctrine, of which international expansion/plausibility has been drawing some academic attention. *See, e.g.*, Ruth L. Okediji, *Toward an International Fair Use Doctrine*, 39 Colum. J. Transnat'l L. 75 (2000); Richard J. Peltz, *Global Warming Trend? The Creeping Indulgence of Fair Use in International Copyright* Law, 27 Tex. Intell. Prop. L.J. 267–68 (2009) (observing that in recent years the fair use concept "has escaped its disfavored status as a U.S. peculiarity and achieved some traction in international legal circles"). In any event, the common association of fair use with U.S. law does not mean the idea behind it cannot be incorporated in other copyright systems, and importantly, at point here is not U.S. fair use in its present form, but rather the ARM's variation.

privileged communications beyond the boundaries of "static" exceptions.[104] The range of conducts it *might* legitimize (after a careful fair use/access analysis according to the applicable legal standard) would spread over *anything* the second access-right prong can prohibit.

Similar to the current U.S. fair use provision, the clause might include preambular language to describe the common situations or circumstances in which fair use/fair access is likely.[105] In addition, a multi-prong examination modelled after the U.S. provision could form an attractive and adaptable standard. Consider Israeli legislation of a fair use provision that is unmistakably styled after the U.S. formula. Section 19 of the 2007 Israel Copyright Act reads:

> (a) Fair use of a work is permitted for purposes such as: private study, research, criticism, review, journalistic reporting, quotation, or instruction and examination by an educational institution.
> (b) In determining whether a use made of a work is fair within the meaning of this paragraph the factors to be considered shall include, inter alia:
> (1) The purpose and character of the use;
> (2) The character of the work used;
> (3) The scope of the use, quantitatively and qualitatively, in relation to the work as a whole;
> (4) The impact of the use on the value of the work and its potential market.
> (c) The Minister may make regulations prescribing conditions under which a use shall be deemed a fair use.[106]

Drawing on this language, the ARM clause would permit the courts to consider certain lawful prima facie violations of the second access-right prong after passing them through a multifactored scrutiny.[107] The fair access/use clause should allow courts to consider the special circumstances of a given act before imposing liability—for instance, the purpose and nature of providing or facilitating access, the character of the copyrighted work, and qualitative and quantitative

---

104. It would, of instance, allow the court to absolve all the operations the actor must perform to attain individual access to a digital work (assuming no access-TPMs)—even when the operations necessarily involves some kind of reproduction.

105. The preambular language of the U.S. provision describes such situations according to the purpose of the potentially infringing use, namely, "for purposes such as criticism, comment, news reporting, teaching (including multiple copies for classroom use), scholarship, or research." *See* § 107 U.S.C.

106. *See* Israel Copyright Act (2007), Sec. 19 (unofficial translation).

107. The ARM fair use/fair access provision would replace the word "use" with the term "communication-conducts" or simply "communications and provision of access" for achieving a better match with the scope of the exclusive rights. The court, in turn, would be able to recognize respective privileges to access and communicate using precisely these terms.

parameters related to the scope of access provided, as well as the impact of the suspect act on the commercial interests of rights-holders.

Interestingly, the first Israeli fair use factor differs from the parallel U.S. factor by omitting the language ". . . including whether such use is of a commercial nature or is for nonprofit educational purposes."[108] A comparative interpretation of this factor supports the conclusion the Israeli fair use standard is perhaps less dominated by commercial/noncommercial distinctions, and consequently, is less prone to subordination to commercial interests of rights-holders.[109] In a similar vein, ARM fair use/fair access protections should not a priori be crippled by the prospects of prejudice to rights-holders' economic affairs when the suspect activity is done for profit. In addition, subsection (c) of the Israeli provision offers a (partial) response to one of the most vexing problems associated with the U.S. fair use defense, namely, the fairly low security it offers ex ante due to the unpredictability of its application by the courts.[110] An effective protection of fair use/fair access interests requires some ex ante security, which is reflected in the Israeli solution that integrates an administrative promulgation of uses to be considered privileged per se. In a similar way and for similar reasons, the corresponding ARM clause may entrust to the hands of the legislature or an executive agency (ministry, copyright office) the authority to compose a list of acts that *presumptively* pass the multifactor test and thus, are lawful on their face. The list may be modified and updated over time (at the discretion of the promulgating authority) to the extent necessary for keeping pace with technological developments and market trends.

V. INTERNATIONAL ASPECTS

As copyright lawmaking turns more internationalized,[111] evaluation of the ARM as an operative substitute to current copyright regimes cannot ignore international aspects, in particular, international *restrictions* on the design of domestic laws. There are multiple interface areas between the ARM proposal and international copyright law; this section can address only some of them

108. *Cf.* 17 U.S.C. § 107(1).

109. It could be said, a contrario, the Israeli fair use framework permits more leeway for the courts in cases where the use clearly affects commercial exploitation opportunities.

110. There are several recent proposals to enact fair use "safe harbors" and similar instruments designed to mitigate this problem. *See, e.g.*, Gideon Parchomovsky & Kevin A. Goldman, *Fair Use Harbors*, 93 VA. L. REV. 1483 (2007).

111. *See, e.g.*, Jane C. Ginsburg, *Toward Supranational Copyright Law? The WTO Panel Decision and the Three-Step Test for Copyright Exceptions*, 187 *REVUE INTERNATIONALE DU DROIT D'AUTEUR* (2001).

(mainly formalities-related questions) and devote only a cursory discussion to the complex legal issues involved. The brief discussions below center around two related propositions: (1) international copyright treaties principally would not preclude the institution of the proposed system, and (2) international harmonization in some fundamental areas of copyright law (such as the structure of exclusive rights and the mechanism of formalities) is a welcome and perhaps inevitable development. Of course, there is a latent connection between the two statements, as the ARM could provide the basis for a tighter and more systematic international harmonization.

A. Formalities

1. Standardization

One obvious tension point is the mechanism of assertion attached to the second access-right prong. It invokes at least two important questions, one legal and one pragmatic. To begin with, the model of formalities advocated for in the previous sections might contravene Berne's rule against formalities. A related question is how to coordinate compliance with domestic formalities requirements internationally and how to efficiently administrate the system on the transnational level.

At to the latter, pragmatic question, some level of standardization in the area of formalities would be unavoidable. To achieve this, consider the following suggestion: a specialized organization (such as WIPO) will create an international registry and draft a uniform formalities model specifying registration, notice, and possibly deposit provisions. All WIPO signatories will grant reciprocity to that model.[112] The compliance procedure with the international model will take place online. A consolidated registry will provide information about all national and international copyright registrations, making that information accessible over the Internet. In a parenthetical clause, it should be noted a variety of domestic *renewal* schemes[113] (assuming that renewal requirements are applicable to foreign works) might complicate matters. Requiring international authors to comply with divergent renewal models practiced in the various nations in order to enjoy the minimum protection the treaty stipulates (and when applicable, the

112. To make it simpler for foreign authors, compliance with at least one of the following three models must be shown: (1) formalities in the country of origin, (2) formalities in the country of adjudication, or (3) the WIPO formalities model. This set of alternatives should encourage all rights-holders to simply comply with the formalities of their home countries for purposes of domestic protection, and with WIPO formalities for enforcement in other countries. As the ARM formalities model is based on two to three simple requirements, the difference between the WIPO model and various national schemes should not be great.

113. For a discussion on the efficiency advantages of renewal from the perspective of domestic laws, see Chapter 7, Section III.B.2.c(ii)(cc) *supra*.

maximum duration afforded by the domestic law) might turn unreasonable and possibly violate Berne obligations. Therefore, inasmuch as domestic law contains renewal formalities, it seems advisable foreign works/authors would enjoy a uniform minimum protection term such as the minimum duration rules stated in Art. 7 Berne Convention (or even better, a shorter one, a change that would require modification of the present international scheme).[114]

The broader question concerning the (dis)advantages of international harmonization *in the area of exclusive rights* (possibly following the model of the access-right's exclusivity prongs) can receive only a very short and surely incomplete reference here. Saying the Internet does not "acknowledge" or "respect" international borders between state and geographical sovereignty regions has long been a cliché, but the private-international law problems to which the global nature of the Net has given rise (e.g., questions of personal jurisdiction, applicable law, appropriate forum and forum shopping, and enforcement of foreign rights and judgments) are as disquieting and puzzling as ever.[115] The ARM, as a model designed with the Internet reality in mind, could principally replace any given domestic copyright law. It is attractive precisely because of the demonstrated effort to eliminate the friction between national laws that emanates from the different ways in which they define and apply various exclusive rights. At least in the areas of *substantive coverage* and *structural limitations*, the ARM could establish a rather uniform exclusivity platform upon which domestic legislatures may continue to build their respective protection regimes.[116]

---

114. As renewal formalities may play an important role in optimizing the efficient duration of copyrights, a best-practice model concerning renewal could be developed. Such a best-practice model will consider local and global economic parameters and market analysis for various works and exploitation patterns. The purpose is to achieve a more or less uniform scheme of initial and subsequent protection periods to be voluntarily adopted by various countries concerning protection of domestic works. In the case the model enjoys considerable success among members of the international community, an initiative to standardize, harmonize, and internationalize renewal formalities can become a real possibility.

115. In the area of international copyright law, *see, e.g.*, Paul E. Geller, *Rethinking the Berne-Plus Framework: From Conflicts of Law to Copyright Reform*, 8 EUR. INTELL. PROP. REV. 391 (2009); for an anlysis in the context of international trademark law and domain names, see Zohar Efroni, *A Barcelona.com Analysis: Toward a Better Model for Adjudication of International Domain Name Disputes* 14 FORDHAM INTEL. PROP. MEDIA & ENTM'T J. 29 (2003).

116. Geller argued a "core right" should have important advantages over the current model of domestic bundles of rights from the perspective of protecting copyright internationally and elevating choice-of-law problems and discrepancies among national legislation. *See* Geller, *supra* note 115. Interestingly, Geller explains his use of the term *core right* in the following way: "What do I mean by a 'core right' in copyright law? Such a right is technology-neutral, applying, for example, to the distribution of hard copies and to electronic transmission. A core right is also self-limiting: a right of communication or making

2. Berne's Rule against Formalities

The tension between the ARM's assertion principle and Berne's rule against formalities should receive an initial response here. According to a lenient interpretation of Article 5(2) Berne Convention, imposing domestic formalities in tandem with a liability rule mechanism as a default would not *necessarily* violate international obligations. This reading argues in essence that subjecting property rule-style protections to formalities requirements—yet otherwise offering rights-holders the opportunity to enjoy collective remuneration under a liability rule-style mechanism—would not contravene the obligation not to subject the "enjoyment and the exercise" of foreign rights to any formalities.[117] First, "enjoyment" is not affected, as the proposed formalities do not influence the *initial recognition* in rights with respect to works of authorship and the *vesting of rights* in authors.[118] Second, the commitment not to burden the "exercise"[119] of Berne rights does not mean *exclusivity* is warranted in any event and under any circumstances. By comparison, a stricter reading of the phrase "enjoyment and exercise" might suggest a different conclusion: to the extent foreign rights-holders must comply with *whatever* formalities model in order to enforce *exclusive entitlements* stated in Berne, this would plainly violate the rule against formalities.

Which approach would be more apt for addressing the pressing needs to adapt the copyright system to the networked environment? The former, less rigid view would advocate for revisiting the old wisdom and rationale behind an unconditional and absolutistic rule against formalities. The Berne Convention did not prohibit formalities from its inception,[120] and presently, the digital revolution and its impact on the copyright system points toward consideration of a more permissive international arrangement.

---

available to members of the public, by definition, would not include any right to control private activities; if the core right is conceived as a right of commercial exploitation, it would not definitionally include any right to control non-commercial activities." (footnotes omitted), *id.* at 393. Of course, it is possible to think about the access-right as a "core right" with two exclusivity prongs and other distinctive features that could, among other things, provide the basis for international harmonization in the area of coverage.

117. Chapter 7, Section III.B.2(d)(i) *supra.*

118. In Berne parlance, *enjoyment* is one's eligibility to be legally considered the copyright holder in the work. Enjoyment formalities burden the core entitlement to have exclusive rights vested in that person. The eligibility to be recognized as an author (or as a holder of exclusive rights more generally) should not be subject to any conditions and prerequisites, and the ARM does not conflict with this directive.

119. Adding the word "exercise" to Article 4(2) BC during the 1908 Berlin Revision (today Art. 5(2) BC) clarified the *vindication of vested rights* (similarly to their recognition) should remain formalities-free, so a formalities-free "enjoyment" would not turn merely theoretical. The term *exercise* refers primarily to the opportunity of foreign authors to harness the legal system in the jurisdiction to give effect to their copyrights (e.g., by filing an infringement lawsuit).

120. Chapter 7, Section III.B.2(a) *supra.*

In this vein, the argument for relaxing the rule against formalities may be structured along the following outlines: (1) A central purpose of the Berne Convention is to preserve and promote a viable and rich process of creative authorship by securing the rights of authors from one Member State in another Member State.[121] (2) The process of authorship necessitates adequate access and communication opportunities; the authorial freedom to create works, which in turn awards the author exclusive copyrights in those works, is not a priori superior to (aspiring) authors' rights to gain ample access to the works of their predecessors.[122] (3) It should follow that Berne implicitly obligates its members to avoid overprotection that results in the curtailment of reasonable access opportunities.[123] (4) The access-right model is designed to reduce the danger of overprotection, which, as shown in this study, is a result of a strict and mechanical application of traditional exclusivity norms in the modern information reality. (5) The international obligation to avoid overprotection is *material* in nature, whereas the obligation to avoid formalities has dominant *technical-formal* characteristics. (6) As a matter of treaty interpretation and in line with common legal principles, in the case of a contradiction between material and formal obligations, the material obligation should prevail. (7) Thus, Berne should not be read to prohibit assertion requirements modeled after the ARM to the extent: (i) The assertion requirements are not overly burdensome, (ii) statutory license remunerations are available to noncomplying rights-holders, (iii) rights-holders may choose to opt in to the property rule arrangement at any time during the governance of the statutory license, and (iv) the model as a whole provides effective and comprehensive copyright protection, which, at the same time, opens access avenues where exclusivity has little merits and/or where its benefits to rights-holders are virtually nonexistent.

B. General Conformity to International Minimum Standards

Extenuating the tension with Article 5(2) Berne Convention addresses only one (though quite prickly) problem among the range of interface issues between the ARM and international minimum obligations. As far as *substantive minimum* copyright protection is concerned, a fully asserted access-right would cover all the rights the Berne-TRIPS-WIPO scheme secures—and beyond. The next question is whether the arrangement of a broad liability rule as a default conflicts with the three-step test.

In approaching this complex issue, we should begin by asking whether the ARM's structural limitations fall under "exceptions" or "limitations" in the

121. Chapter 6, Section IV.C.2(b)(iv) *supra*.
122. Chapter 1, Section V.C. *supra*.
123. Chapter 6, Section IV.C.2(b)(iv) *supra*.

meaning of the three-step test in the first place.[124] This is largely a question of interpretation which, in any event, appears rather misplaced within the general project the ARM seeks to mobilize. The theory advocating for an *alternative* system is not in a good position to encourage efforts to consolidate the proposed new structure with the three-step test, as this test is antithetical to the ARM approach for potentially arresting the development of copyright exceptions at the domestic level.[125] The structure and application of the three-step test are premised on the set of Berne-TRIPS-WIPO exclusive rights, and this standard by design applies only to exceptions and limitations *to the traditional exclusive rights*. Further, this test is premised on the conjuncture the efficacy and breadth of traditional exclusivity norms should be preserved and carried forward into the digital future (a "neoconservative" approach). As explained earlier, the ARM approach draws on quite different assumptions, namely, that stagnancy and stiffness are harmful, and that a structural change in the law must take place in order to adjust it to the digital reality. Any change begins with remodeling the same basic exclusive rights the three-step test would perpetuate,[126] not with artificial conservation of a mechanism that was invented in the late 1960s to secure an international basis for the protection of the reproduction right.

VI. ACCESS-BASED REGULATION AS A BALANCING INSTRUMENT

A. Technological Measures as the Service of Many Masters?

A number of possible policy-driven objections exist to the access-right model. One of them would surely target the grant of an explicit right to control access to TPM-protected works (the first access-right prong). This critique is likely to run along the lines of familiar objections to anticircumvention laws. Delegating too

---

124. A negative answer to this question would obviate the need to scrutinize the ARM under the three-step test because only copyright exceptions and limitations are subject to its provisions. Even a positive answer, suggesting the broad liability rule *is* a "limitation" on the exercise of exclusive rights, would not compel the conclusion that instituting such a limitation violated the three-step test, at least not under the "holistic" approach to interpreting and applying it. *Cf.* Declaration on the "Three-Step Test" in Copyright Law (2008).

125. Chapter 7, Section III.B.1(c)(iv)(bb) *supra*.

126. It is perhaps possible to interpret a three-step test in a manner that would permit the liability rule to be the default model of compensation and exclusivity subject only to formalities. Also ARM exceptions instruments (ROA in the weak and strong form) are not inherently incompatible with the three-step test and other international norms. Pointed questions concerning the formation, scope, and interpretation of such rights of access—perhaps in connection with *the general aim* behind the three-step test—may be evaluated as part of erecting the access-right regime and relevant concerns vis-à-vis the proper breadth of protection.

much power to the content industry, the emergence of lockout scenarios, suppression of users' rights, and curtailment of robust competition are some of the most predictable allegations raised in this context.[127] The most important response to the "disturbance of copyright balance" objection is this: current anticircumvention law is squeezed into an already cluttered, skewed, inconsistent, and dysfunctional system, whereas the ARM's approach would rewrite the key entitlements in an attempt to strike a new and better (though different) balance. In their present form, anticircumvention laws *on top* of the traditional set of exclusive rights and exceptions have been facing a deep lack of enthusiasm—and rightfully so. However, the ARM would replace that messy arrangement with a newly drafted legal apparatus that sees the advantages in access-based copyright protection for digital works in some cases on the one hand, but remains mindful of the inherent perils of proprietary access control to information on the other.[128]

Perhaps the most dominant aspect of the "disturbance of copyright balance" critique is the focus on industry players and the fear they would enforce (or even misuse) their legal position to the disadvantage of other stakeholders, primarily end users. Even worse, as the argument might continue, creative individuals—the talents who give originality in copyright its genuine meaning—have seen little improvement in their situation despite the introduction of "para-copyright" protections and other expansions of exclusive rights. DRMS, above all, are widely conceived as tools that serve the interests of derivative rights-holders and large, already powerful commercial actors. Should the law recognize an unequivocal right to control individual access to works and various forms of digital communications, these actors might be encouraged to continue pursuing their interests even more forcibly at the expense of other interest groups.

---

127. For an early expression of these concerns, see James Boyle *Cruel, Mean, or Lavish? Economic Analysis, Price Discrimination and Digital Intellectual Property*, 53 VANDERBILT L. REV. 2007, 2010–11 (2000) ("The plan is fairly easy to work out. After claiming new, larger and longer intellectual property rights, the next step is to engage in much more fine-grained regulation of how that intellectual property can be used. Owners of content will rely on shrinkwrap contracts and technological restraints to strip users of the standard rights offered by intellectual property systems: the right of fair use, first sale and so forth. Software, music, e-texts, and movies will be licensed rather than sold to users. As a result, some of the privileges people take for granted with a book—the ability to lend it, resell it, criticize it, parody it and so on—will be explicitly waived by contract. Technological encryption and watermarking schemes will be used to tie digital objects to particular people and computers, so that there are physical as well as legal restraints on the use of those objects. These schemes will prevent (or at least hamper) not only black market 'piracy' of intellectual property, but also 'gray market' resale, non-market gift, or loan transactions and competitive attempts at decompilation and reverse engineering.") (footnote omitted).

128. As explained earlier, the model addresses overprotection concerns very differently than the way it has been done under current law. *See* Section IV.A.1 *supra*.

As to the author-publisher interface, the ARM admittedly does not offer a silver bullet to resolve the basic tension between the interests of authors and publishers (or generally, derivative rights-holders).[129] But would it be correct to conclusively assume anticircumvention protections necessarily assist only commercial corporate actors and do virtually nothing for authors? Indeed, there is a stubborn assumption prevailing among copyright "pessimists"[130] that technological protection measures primarily serve the narrow interests of commercial derivative rights-holders.[131] Based on that premise, many observers consider the outlawing of TPMs' circumvention a straightforward boon to the content (mainly entertainment) industry.[132] The legislative history of anticircumvention laws, the lobbying groups behind them,[133] and the resulting legal norms surely justify this reputation. At the same time, the fundamental question is not whether *current* anticircumvention laws are good or bad, but whether premising the entire copyright edifice on access-based entitlements could do a better job in ordering the digital communication reality. Neither conceptually nor functionally is TPM

---

129. It is frequently argued that publishers and other derivative rights-holders are prone to take advantage of their superior bargaining position vis-à-vis authors. For an analysis of widely criticized legislative attempts in Germany to improve the position of authors and some extraterritorial implications of that regulation, see Reto M. Hilty & Alexander Peukert, *"Equitable Remuneration" in Copyright Law: The Amended German Copyright Act as a Trap for the Entertainment Industry in the U.S.?* 22 CARDOZO ARTS & ENTM'T L.J. 401 (2004).

130. *See* PAUL GOLDSTEIN, COPYRIGHT'S HIGHWAY—FROM GUTENBERG TO THE CELESTIAL JUKEBOX 11 (rev. ed. 2003) ("[C]opyright pessimists . . . accept that copyright owners should get some measure of control over copies as an incentive to produce creative works, but they would like copyright to extend only so far as is necessary to give this incentive, and treat anything more as an encroachment on the general freedom of everyone to write and say what they please.").

131. *See, e.g.*, Pamela Samuelson, *DRM {and, or, vs.} the* Law, 46 COMM'CN. ACM 41, 42 (2003) ("An alternative phrase for DRM is 'digital restrictions management,' given its use by copyright industries to restrict users' right.") (footnote omitted).

132. *See* Reto M. Hilty, *Intellectual Property and the European Community's Internal Market Legislation—Copyright in the Internal Market* 7 IIC 760, 764 (2004) ("Regarding this new [anticircumvention] protection, however, one should be aware that today (and probably also in the future) it is extremely rare for a creator to be able to utilise such devices him or herself. It is rather the producer who wants to protect his own investments . . . it would be an illusion to believe that the effect of implementing technical measures could help safeguard 'the independence and dignity of artistic creators and performers.'") (citing Recital 11 of the EUCD).

133. *See* Pamela Samuelson, *The U.S. Digital Agenda at* WIPO, 37 VA. J. INT'L L. 369, 409–10 (1997) ("An important part of the U.S. digital agenda at WIPO was establishment of a new international norm to regulate technologies and services likely to be used to circumvent technological protection for copyrighted works . . . The impetus for this provision came largely from the U.S. motion picture industry, which has for many years been keen on the idea of regulating technologies that enable infringement.") (footnotes omitted).

technology itself inherently disadvantageous from a broad copyright perspective and the obvious need to balance conflicting interests. The remainder of this section will point out some possible advantages to individual authors and to the regulative system as a whole.

B. Technological Measures and the Individual Author

The often-occurring conflict of interests between authors and publishers and the uneven bargaining powers typical to their relationships should encourage copyright policy makers to help authors reduce their chronic dependency on middlemen. Indeed, digital technology raised hopes for such a practice of "cutting out the middleman" to occur.[134] In the Internet reality, more often than before authors no longer need to contract with publishers to make their works available to local and global audiences; at the same time, commercially minded authors might also want to secure ways to earn money from making their works available *by* and *for* themselves. Despite the undeniable association of technological measures with big enterprises, authors principally are not prevented from applying technological protections for their sole benefit.[135] Not only complex and expensive DRMS but also a basic encryption scheme (possibly supplemented by an electronic payment system) could serve to assert the first prong.[136] Using "author-friendly" measures should not require astronomic investments or high technical skills. In the end, simple-to-use access control measures and legal protection against circumvention could serve a class of independent authors who are interested in online distribution, but at the same time (and unlike authors using open licenses) being more sensitive to exploiting the commercial value of their works.[137]

---

134. *Cf.* Gregory F. Lastowka, *Free Access and the Future of* Copyright, 27 RUTGERS COMPUTER & TECH. L.J. 293, 304 (2001) (musing on the "End of the Middleman" in the digital environment "who makes money by producing and selling hard copies") (footnote omitted).

135. It is true the development, deployment, and maintenance of highly sophisticated DRMS require a considerable investment. Many private individuals cannot afford such expenditures. But asserting the first access-right prong does not say anything about using *highly sophisticated* DRMS; it merely requires rights-holders who wish to enforce the first prong to release the work in a digital format that prevents inadvertent access.

136. The model adopts a liberal interpretation of the requirement the measure should "effectively" prevent access to the work. *Cf.* Kamiel J. Koelman & Natali Helberger, *Protection of Technological Measures, in* COPYRIGHT AND ELECTRONIC COMMERCE 172 (P. Bernt Hugenholtz ed., 2000) (suggesting "effective" under current provisions could mean "that only measures that actually require intentional acts of circumvention" are covered by anticircumvention norms).

137. Also authors who initially assert the access-right prongs (especially the second prong) have the option to license the work under Creative Commons, open source, GFDL, and similar permissive licensing. The difference under the ARM is the property platform

Some market structures that have been preserving publishers' hegemony and perpetuating authors' dependency on the services of derivative rights-holders during the twentieth century are becoming increasingly shaky in the digital environment. Commons-based production structures, occasionally supported by various kinds of open licensing, emerge and thrive alongside commercialization platforms in the hybrid economy the Net makes possible.[138] The ARM does nothing to discourage nonproprietary models for works' dissemination and use as freely adopted by their creators. At the same time, there is no necessity that commercialization of information products continue to be dominated by large firms, at least with regard to some segments of creative production where individual initiatives could lead to individual, decentralized gains. Independent writers, photographers, musicians, digital artists, and programmers who are not dependent on the deep pockets and coordination expertise of publishers for producing their own commercializable content to which they can sell access (i.e., low start and production-capital, and easily distributable works) might welcome the opportunity to do so as being economically attractive, even emancipating.[139]

Of course, such opportunities are already available under present regimes of anticircumvention laws. Yet the deficiencies of current law and the structural incompatibility of the exclusive rights with digital markets and the new ways copyrighted material are being delivered and consumed tend to obscure the possible advantages of an access-based regulation. The ARM challenges the instinctive aversion against circumvention prohibitions under copyright by suggesting a reasonable scheme would not necessarily serve the agenda of Hollywood or the recording industry alone. Under the changing technological and market parameters of the digital information environment, access-based exclusive rights could become beneficial for individual authors as well in a more significant way, and the law should remain attentive and receptive to such developments.

---

upon which permissive licensing is based will depend on initial assertion of the relevant prongs.

138. *See* Yochai Benkler, The Wealth of Networks 35–127 (2006).

139. Authors who prefer not to engage in operating access-control systems themselves may want to hire professional services or cooperate with derivative rights-holders on a more equitable basis. Commercial exploiters, on their part, might deploy in some cases sophisticated control schemes to support their business model. One example of newly formed cooperation between authors and commercial distributors that is based on DRM technology is Amazon's Kindle platform for e-books. It allows individual authors to publish their content digitally over Kindle's platform and receive thirty-five percent of the retail sales price Amazon charges its customers for accessing the content. *See* Digital Publication Distribution Agreement (available at http://forums.digitaltextplatform.com/dtpforums/entry.jspa?externalID=2&categoryID=12).

C. Locking Up the Information Society?

Though individual authors might find ways to translate access-based regulation into personal monetary gains and exercise more sovereignty in dealing with publishers, we cannot be so naïve as to suggest legal protection to access TPMs would *primarily* assist struggling artists and autonomous creators. Use of various models of digital access control will probably continue to be associated with established content industries, possibly in cooperation with network infrastructure operators and connectivity providers. Commercial entities that invest heavily in creative productions and whose main marketable asset is their intellectual property are likely to continue pursuing infringers, with or without explicit rights to control access. Yet industry players are not the only players around, and their strategies do not follow any universal law of cyberspace. The networked hybrid economy accommodates various models of benefiting from connectivity.[140] Side by side with free sharing and open communications, proprietary strategies for commercializing copyrighted content are not objectionable per se, even when "Big Media" actors stand behind them. After all, amortizing for publishers and producers has long been a fundamental tenet of both utilitarian and authors' rights-based copyright systems.[141] In a legal-technological landscape that accommodates multi-platform and cross-platform informational exchange, locking content behind "electronic fences" as a strategy for generating revenues will inhabit its own (predictably limited) ecological niche.

Having said that, a careful examination of the model should reveal the ARM is not designed to create optimal conditions for the emergence of digital lockup scenarios. The model aims, inter alia, at proliferating options and enabling rights-holders to navigate their own course and tailor the package of legal protection in a more nuanced manner to fit their individual needs. The model does not dispute the basic point that there is a price for technologically blocking access to information, but—perhaps counterintuitively—this price is not being paid exclusively by information consumers or by those interested in as broad a public domain as possible; access control, nearly by definition, lowers exposure and prevents *authors and rights-holders in general* from taking full advantage of the Internet, the most powerful platform for information distribution ever invented by man. Global diffusion of accessible content helps authors to influence, build

---

140. The term *hybrid economy* or *hybrid economies* basically means that both proprietary and nonproprietary economic and social frameworks can simultaneously apply *to the same "information."* They may coexist and even synergistically supplement one another. *Cf.* Lessig, *supra* note 72, at 225 ff. To be sure, a good copyright law should encourage such synergy, not suppress it.

141. Also Kant, considered as one of the founding fathers of individualistic justifications for copyright, supported exclusive rights for *publishers* as coming "in the shoes" of the authors (*"ein Geschäft eines andern (des Autors.)"*) *See* Emmanuel Kant, *Von der Unrechtmäßigkeit des Büchernachdrucks*, 5 Berlinische Monatsschrift 403–17 (1785).

their reputation, and have their works noticed and acknowledged. TPMs and DRMS are in essence technologies designed to *complicate* communication procedures. The artificial complication might sometimes also be fatal from the perspective of paradigmatic industry players who are initially keen about TPMs, but then discover TPMs-supported business models ultimately do not work well for them.

The logic behind these observations translates into evidence from the last decade of anticircumvention protections in the United States and elsewhere. None of the early doomsday scenarios depicting a segregated information society, in which every access costs money and DRMS are everywhere, has ever materialized. Even under the assumption TPMs will become cheaper and easier to manage at the individual author's level, creative individuals will continue to exhibit reluctance for using such measures when distributing the work under permissive licensing better serves their material and spiritual needs (or even their social-political views). As compared to commercial exploiters, authors who are in the position to make strategic decisions of this kind are more likely to reject TPMs on the average, with the reason being simple: individual originators of messages (to use the terminology of Chapter 1) are far more sensitive to the advantages of an unbridled communication with their audience, and more generally, to the advantages of effective communication that has little or nothing to do with monetary gains. At bottom, the option available to *all* types of authors and rights-holders to assert the exclusivity prongs remains an *option* that requires an affirmative action, rather than constituting a legal default.

VII. CONCLUSION

A. The Access-Right Model: An Alternative Framework

This chapter presented a theoretical framework for copyright regulation in the digital twenty-first century. The seeking of alternatives to the current law is motivated by two related propositions. The first is that gaining, providing, and controlling *access* to works becomes the very crux of copyright protection in the digital environment. The second is that restructuring the system of entitlements accordingly appears a more beneficial strategy than adjusting the existing system. The technology-driven transformation in copyright law mirrors a new, challenging reality in which the basic background conditions for the consumption, communication, and commercialization of works shift and evolve. This transformation is fundamental—and so should be the approach to copyright reform. Rethinking the way in which copyright entitlements can be defined and formulated is not merely an academic exercise performed for the sake of the intellectual challenge involved; it is vital for the constructive development of the law.

In this respect, the access-right model may be regarded as a thought experiment rather than a full-bodied, mature and ready-to-use model law. Building specific legal provisions—the flesh around the skeletal structure represented in Figure 8.1—remains to be done. Still, at the early stage of developing a new way of thinking about copyright law, the model ventures to demonstrate how the access-right concept may provide an alternative basis for a workable copyright regime. The argument is that an access-based strategy for regulating digital content is not only thinkable in theory and achievable in practice, it could also be better than the alternatives. One key advantage of this strategy resides in the opportunity to achieve a property system that is simpler to understand and apply. The access-right model envisions an entitlements structure that is more coherent, consistent, transparent, adaptable, and efficient than the cluster of anachronistic rules could ever hope to become in the digital milieu. This chapter has already touched upon several key advantages of an access-based approach, and by way of concluding this installment, the next passages will highlight some of its strengths in more detail.

B. Selected Advantages

1. Reducing Information Costs

Copyright regulation today directly affects individual members, sectors, and communities of modern society in a much more straightforward and sharper manner than ever before. This renders the challenge of designing a sensible law both acute and complex. Achieving policy goals via copyright regulations in the digital environment requires some understanding of the technology; the matrix of markets for digital content; the dramatic social, cultural, and aesthetic changes the digital revolution has been mobilizing; the transitions in consumption habits and business models; and primarily, the potential and actual impact of regulation on all the above. Legislatures and policy makers could therefore benefit from solid theoretical approaches to guide their endeavors.

Chapter 2 provided an overview on some basic theories and rationales for copyright law. It concluded that though the application of property principles to intangible resources is not objectionable on its face, the art of attaching property-style rules to information subject matter demands caution and some degree of foresight. The discussion mentioned, inter alia, information cost theory as a possible framework that could provide some guidance in this respect.

It has been noted a given property scheme can be positioned somewhere on a continuum stretching between an "exclusion strategy" on the one end and a "governance strategy" on the other end.[142] Using this terminology, traditional copyright is located closer to the governance pole, meaning it stipulates relatively detailed, specific, and finely grained property rights. An information cost-sensitive approach might advocate for a simpler structure of exclusive rights that would produce clearer signals to be processed and observed by duty holders.

142. Chapter 2, Section III.C.2(a) *supra*.

The access-right model attempts to make the system more efficient and transparent first by "pushing" the property apparatus somewhat closer to the "exclusion" pole.[143] Simplifying the structure of exclusive rights in accordance with the ARM is expected to have two implications on the scope and effect of exclusivity. On the one hand, the *potential coverage* of exclusive rights will expand. A fully asserted access-right hovers over the most basic ways in which copyrighted information can be utilized. On the other hand, the exclusivity signals become clearer, socially cheaper, and perhaps most importantly, *dispositive*: non-asserted works, from their inception, are not subject to exclusivity constraints, a feature that is expected to offset the overall restrictive impact of the property system on the information process. Making affirmative assertion a precondition to exclusivity (especially in the context of the second prong dealing with communication-conducts) would not only diminish information costs, but is expected to reduce monopoly costs and the chilling effect on lawful activity.

Obviously, the idea is not to reduce copyright to the level of an absolutistic, trespass-like mechanism. It would be impossible and absurd to simplify the system down to binary clarity, sending always "NO" signals as long as the work is under copyright and always "YES" signals when it is not. Exceptions are inherent in the copyright system, and by their very nature, they "pull" the system in the opposite direction, namely toward the "governance" end. Also under the proposed model, exceptions cannot be other than relatively detailed and specific, which might attenuate the property signals assertion wants to make more conclusive. It is equally clear the information cost of any property system cannot be eliminated completely. Under this caveat, a property structure based on *one* principal and fairly comprehensive right that is subject to assertion requisites (as opposed to several, granulate, and more limited rights that vest automatically) might facilitate a significant improvement both in lowering net information costs entailed by the system and in channeling exclusivity in the (subjectively) desired and (socially) desirable directions.

2. Legitimizing Technological Access-Control Measures: Threats and Opportunities

Asserting the first access-right prong (which, as indicated, would furnish copyright control over individual access-conducts) is an affirmative action that converges with the deployment of TPMs. As discussed in Chapter 7, price discrimination strategies supported by technological access and use restrictions

143. From an information cost perspective, exclusion strategy is likely to be advantageous when duty holders are numerous, dispersed, and unspecified. In this context, the more people affected directly by copyright regulation, the more pressing is the need to simplify property rules and signals. Chapter 2, Section III.C.2(b) *supra*. As the sheer number of affected duty holders dramatically rises (every Internet user must consider copyright law while performing daily tasks), the copyright system becomes more costly because more people must know, understand, and respect copyright restrictions.

might sometimes help rights-holders to better serve the market and culminate in win-win situations.[144] The observation that access in fact becomes the true gravity center of the copyright system must correspond to an economic and technological reality in which the smallest marketable unit of utility that underlies transactions is the opportunity to achieve human-access to works, or in other words, to perceive works on an individual basis at a certain time and place. It is important to remember, however, the mere availability of such form of exploitation does not yet mean such granular commercialization will happen all the time, even when the rights-holder is a commercial, profit-oriented entity. As noted, DRMS have significant disadvantages to which commercial exploiters must remain sensitive. There is presently a broad awareness of the fact DRMS might quickly turn into a double-edged sword: instead of opening new markets and maximizing profits, an ill-advised use of technological measures might destroy existing markets, scare away consumers, and smear a company's reputation—a lesson some players in the music industry learned in the course of their rootkit experiment.[145]

The ARM regime indeed would allow rights-holders to experiment with more or less complex, restrictive, expensive, and effective technological protections. Granting a direct (yet qualified) legal right to control access is not likely to dramatically increase the use of DRMS overall, as the same market-based incentives and disincentives involved should continue to moderate the spread of technological measures and inform rights-holders' strategies on that matter.[146] To the extent business decisions and market forces fail to prevent excessive private information dominance in a manner undesirable on policy grounds, the legal system will accommodate mechanisms to guard against the potential harms of access restrictions. To inhibit various forms of overenforcement, the model proposed a number of offsetting tools that are designed to ameliorate the *actual effect* of technological measures on the information ecosystem. In the end, individual access to digital works will remain free from copyright restrictions when

144. Chapter 7, Section II.A.3 *supra*. As noted, however, the relationship between price discrimination and net welfare is in many cases ambivalent.

145. The scandal of Sony BMG's rootkit protection to music compact discs (CDs) has become a classroom example of the potential devasting impact of an unwise deployment of TPMs. For a Wikipedia article dedicated to this incident, see http://en.wikipedia.org/wiki/Rootkit.

146. For certain types of works and markets (e.g., software products, computer games, on-demand services, or cellular communication/devices), TPMs may continue to play an important role in firms' pricing strategies. The access-right model would encourage commercial rights-holders to adjust their strategies to the changing conditions of digital markets without discouraging them from adopting TPMs-free strategies that build on the advantages of free access (e.g., larger volume of Internet traffic and greater advertising revenues, as well as the sale of related products/services that benefit from broad and unrestricted access to works).

it makes economic sense to their rights-holders, when economic considerations are irrelevant, and when *formal and sufficiently powerful rights-of-access could legally defeat technological access limitations*. The proposed model neither encourages rights-holders to use digital locks more extensively nor assumes business models alone could amply safeguard elementary freedoms to access and communicate information.

3. Assertion, Formalities, and "Informal Formalities"

It is important to have a clear view of the thread linking (1) the practical enforceability of an exclusivity claim, (2) the need to affirmatively communicate that claim to duty holders, and (3) the normative legitimacy of the property right on which the claim is based. The less a property right is noticeable, the less is it enforceable; this issue inevitably projects on the normative legitimacy of an exclusivity claim that duty holders cannot easily comprehend—a situation especially common in the case of intangible property. This logic is woven through the ARM's structure of exclusive entitlements. A key assumption is that in the absence of a logical and logistic infrastructure that permits effective notice and enforcement, the access-right structure cannot function. The *intellectual property* right to exclusively control individual access to works becomes quite illusory where physical control over the medium (say a book, record, or even personal computer) guarantees access to the information it carries or delivers. The first access-right prong—as an aspect of copyright protection—is neither enforceable nor defendable when the communication channel or platform would not facilitate access control as a practical matter. But this easy access feature of the medium has been a characteristic of analog communication infrastructures serving humanity in past centuries. In the digital age, however, we need to grapple with the legitimacy of an access-based exclusivity rule, which entirely rests on the ability and readiness of rights-holders to affirmatively announce (or single out) their property claim, a statement that is carried over via the placement of access locks. As noted, the assertion requirement in the context of the first prong consists of two elements: notice ("this is my property—get permission or keep away!") and prevention (actual access restrictions), both encapsulated in the notion of an "effective" access TPM. Technological measures that satisfy this effectiveness requirement operate simultaneously as a sign and as a fence.

The same communication infrastructure that renders this aspect of copyright protection practically thinkable also affects old and new communication rights. In the Internet reality, mechanically attaching exclusive rights to a great bulk of the content available online is largely meaningless as these rights often remain unenforceable with legal tools alone. In addition, the lack of workable notice mechanisms burdens duty holders who wish to respect copyright law *but only as far as it goes*. Thus, in the networked information environment, effectively signaling property claims will play a central role at the very core of the arguments that seek to justify exclusivity in disseminations and communication-related activities.

Formal property rights that are largely unenforceable are quite useless to their holders, and the widening gap between de jure rights and the level of respect these rights enjoy pushes organized rights-holders into private, cross-industrial arrangements that demonstrate a surprising similarity to formalities systems. Such private arrangements between large IT sector-companies (such as major search engines, ISPs, Internet platform operators, and online forum providers) on the one side, and corporate, coordinated copyright holders on the other, actually have begun to emerge. Among other things, the parties establish schemes of voluntary registration and marking that the rights-holders carry out on their own initiative (so-called "informal formalities").[147]

Inasmuch as registration and digital marking of copyrighted content became a *practical prerequisite* to effective enforcement in the networked environment, many major rights-holders would probably "comply" irrespective of any legal requirement to do so.[148] One problematic aspect of an industry-driven system of registration, marking, and monitoring might be the involvement of filtering technologies at the ISP level. Systems of content registration, identification, monitoring, and filtering are usually designed to serve the private interests of the entities that create them.[149] Their operation lacks the checks and balances that would characterize the studied and publicly debated enactment of a sensible "formal" formalities mechanism. Private formalities coupled with network traffic filtering present the lurking, comparatively unattractive alternative to statutory formalities. In contrast, an official, public system of reasonable and low-cost formalities could achieve several things at once: it will function as an efficiency

---

147. *See* Zohar Efroni, *Informal Formalities* (2007) (available at http://cyberlaw.stanford.edu/node/5208). *Cf.* Rebecca Tushnet, *Informal Formalities* (2007) (available at http://tushnet.blogspot.com/2007/09/informal-formalities.html). Private initiatives by large rights-holders to digitally market their works and monitor online traffic and use would fill up the regulative vacuum. Some industry players (in cooperation with RMI and DRM developers) have been making efforts to establish private registration databases, supported by agreements with Internet service providers and search engines to monitor traffic in such works. The idea is to create a secure environment based on self-help measures involving work-ID and filtering technologies. These mechanisms require some sort of private "assertion" to *preemptively* prevent infringement. The trouble is that communication is blocked before one has the chance to determine whether it would indeed violate copyrights. Efroni, *supra*.

148. A striking example is the Google Books Registry, a product of the settlement agreement between Google, the American Authors Guild, and the American publishing industry. Authors who want to benefit from that class action settlement (that is currently under court review and possible antitrust examination) must register their claim in accordance with Arts. V and VI to the agreement. *See* Google Book Search Agreement (2008). The same arrangement survived the recent amendment of the Google settlement. *See* Amended Settlement Agreement (2009).

149. Consider the variety of services a company such as Audible Magic Corp. offers to rights-holders (available at http://www.audiblemagic.com/index.asp).

buffer that remains attentive to the needs of the public and the public interest; it will apply uniformly to *all* works, not just works owned by the parties to voluntary pacts; and it should inhibit the incentive of commercial actors to design and run parallel schemes in the first place.

C. A Closing Note

The access-right model aspires beyond establishing a more economically efficient system as it is equally sensitive to fairness and broader balance considerations. This chapter could not attend to the many questions and numerous details involved in devising a better-working copyright protection in the digital age. However, as concerning the fundamental issues the model does address, its core solutions appear attractive and worthy of further discussion. Studying Figure 8.1 from some distance now might pour new content into the overused "copyright balance" cliché: suddenly, the notion of balance assumes a vivid configuration and presence that is nearly perceptible to the touch.

BIBLIOGRAPHY

Adeney, Elizabeth
THE MORAL RIGHTS OF AUTHORS AND PERFORMERS (Oxford University Press 2006)
Adeney, MORAL RIGHTS (2006)

Alexander, Larry A.
Trouble on Track Two: Incidental Regulation of Speech and Free Speech Theory, 44 HASTINGS L.J. 921 (1993)
Alexander, *Trouble on Track Two* (1993)

Alston, Phillip
Out of the Abyss: The Challenges Confronting the New U.N. Committee on Economic, Social and Cultural Rights, 9 HUM. RTS. Q. 332 (1987)
Alston, *Out of the Abyss: The Challenges Confronting the New U.N. Committee on Economic, Social and Cultural Rights* (1987)

Arlt, Christian
DIGITAL RIGHTS MANAGEMENT SYSTEMS: DER EINSATZ TECHNISCHER MASSNAHMEN ZUM SCHUTZ DIGITALER INHALTE (H.C. Beck 2006)
Arlt, *Digital Rights Management Systems: Der Einsatz Technischer Massnahmen zum Schutz Digitaler Inhalte* (2006)

Armstrong, Mark
Price Discrimination, Munich Personal RePEc Archive (MPRA) Online Paper No. 4693 (2006) (available at http://mpra.ub.uni-muenchen.de/4693) (posted Nov. 7, 2007)
Armstrong, *Price Discrimination* (2006)

Armstrong, Timothy K.
Fair Circumvention, SSRN Paper (available at http://papers.ssrn.com/sol3/papers.cfm?abstract_id=1095876, 2008)
Armstrong, *Fair Circumvention* (2008)

Armstrong, Timothy K.
Digital Rights Management and the Process of Fair Use, 20 HARV. J.L. & TECH. 49 (2006)
Armstrong, *Digital Rights Management and the Process of Fair Use* (2006)

Arrow, Kenneth J.
Economic Welfare and the Allocation of Resources for Invention, Reproduced by the RAND Corporation, Ca. (1959)
Arrow, *Economic Welfare and the Allocation of Resources for Invention* (1959)

Auer, Günter
Rechtsschutz für technische Schutz im Gemeinschaftsrecht, *in* EIN LEBER FÜR RECHTSKULTUR: FESTSCHRIFT FÜR ROBERT DITTRICH ZUM 75. GEBURTSTAG 3–19 (H. Tades et al. eds., 2000)
Auer, *Rechtsschutz für technischen Schutz im Gemeinschaftsrecht* (2000)

Austin, Graeme W. & Zavidow, Amy G.
Copyright Law Reform Through a Human Rights Lens, in INTELLECTUAL PROPERTY AND HUMAN RIGHTS (Paul L. C. Torremans ed.) (Kluwer 2008)
Austin & Zavidow, *Copyright Law Reform Through a Human Rights Lens* (2008)

Barlow, John P.
The Economy of Ideas, A Framework for Patents and Copyrights in the Digital Age, WIRED 2.03 (Mar. 1994), republished, John P. Barlow, *Selling Wine Without Bottles, in* THE FUTURE OF COPYRIGHT IN A DIGITAL ENVIRONMENT 169–87 (P. Bernt Hugenholtz ed.) (Kluwer 1996)
Barlow, *Selling Wine Without Bottles* (1996)

Bartow, Ann
Electrifying Copyright Norms and Making Cyberspace More Like a Book, 48 VILLANOVA L. REV. 13 (2003)
Bartow, *Electrifying Copyright Norms and Making Cyberspace More Like a Book* (2003)

Barzel, Yoram
ECONOMIC ANALYSIS OF PROPERTY RIGHTS (Cambridge University Press 1989)
BARZEL, ECONOMIC ANALYSIS OF PROPERTY RIGHTS (1989)

Bauckhage, Tobias
The Basic Economic Theory of Copying, in DIGITAL RIGHTS MANAGEMENT: TECHNOLOGICAL, ECONOMIC, LEGAL AND POLITICAL ASPECTS 234–49 (Eberhard Becker et al. eds.) (Springer 2003)
Bauckhage, *The Basic Economic Theory of Copying* (2003)

Baum, Alfred
Berner Konvention und Landesgesetze, 1928 GRUR 684 (1928)
Baum, *Berner Konvention und Landesgesetze* (1928)

Baum, Alfred
Berner Konvention und Landesgesetze, 1929 GRUR 186 (1929)
Baum, *Berner Konvention und Landesgesetze* (1929)

Baum, Alfred
Die revidierte Berner Übereinkunft und die günstigeren Landesgesetze, 1930 UFITA 400 (1930)
Baum, *Die revidierte Berner Übereinkunft und die günstigeren Landesgesetze* (1930)

Baum, Alfred
THE BRUSSELS CONFERENCE FOR THE REVISION OF THE BERNE CONVENTION, The Library of Congress, Washington D.C. (William S. Strauss trans. 1948)
BAUM, THE BRUSSELS CONFERENCE (1948)

Bechtold, Stefan
VOM URHEBERRECHT ZUM INFORMATIONSRECHT: IMPLIKATIONEN DES DIGITAL RIGHTS MANAGEMENT (C.H. Beck, 2002)
BECHTOLD, VOM URHEBERRECHT ZUM INFORMATIONSRECHT (2002)

Bechtold, Stefan
Digital Rights Management in the United States and Europe, 52 AM. J. COMP. L. 323 (2004)
Bechtold, *Digital Rights Management in the United States and Europe* (2004)

Bechtold, Stefan
The Present and Future of Digital Rights Management—Musing on Emerging Legal Problems, in DIGITAL RIGHTS MANAGEMENT: TECHNOLOGICAL, ECONOMIC, LEGAL AND POLITICAL ASPECTS 597–654 (Eberhard Becker et al. eds.) (Springer 2003).
Bechtold, *The Present and Future of Digital Rights Management—Musing on Emerging Legal Problems* (2003)

Becker, Eberhard et al., *DRM as an Interlocking Challenge for Different Scientific Disciplines: Introduction, in* DIGITAL RIGHTS MANAGEMENT: TECHNOLOGICAL, ECONOMIC, LEGAL AND POLITICAL ASPECTS 1–2 (Eberhard Becker et al. eds.) (Springer 2003)
Becker et al., *DRM as an Interlocking Challenge for Different Scientific Disciplines: Introduction* (2003)

Bell, Abraham & Parchomovsky, Gideon
A Theory of Property, 90 CORNELL L. REV. 531 (2005)
Bell & Parchomovsky, *A Theory of Property* (2005)

Bell, Tom W.
Copyright as Intellectual Property Privilege, 58 SYRACUSE L. REV. 532 (2008)
Bell, *Copyright as Intellectual Property Privilege* (2008)

Bell, Tom W.
Indelicate Imbalancing in Copyright and Patent Law, in COPY FIGHTS: THE FUTURE OF INTELLECTUAL PROPERTY IN THE INFORMATION AGE 1–6 (Adam Thierer & Wayne Crews eds.) (CATO Institute 2002)
Bell, *Indelicate Imbalancing in Copyright and Patent Law* (2002)

Benkler, Yochai
Free as the Air to Common Use: First Amendment Constraints on Enclosure of the Public Domain, 74 N.Y.U. L. REV. 354 (1999)
Benkler, *Free as the Air to Common Use* (1999)

Benkler, Yochai
From Consumers to Users: Shifting the Deeper Structures of Regulation Toward Sustainable Commons and User Access, 52 FED. COMM. L.J. 561 (2000)
Benkler, *From Consumers to Users* (2000)

Benkler, Yochai
THE WEALTH OF NETWORKS (Yale University Press 2006)
BENKLER, THE WEALTH OF NETWORKS (2006)

Bentham, Jeremy
THEORY OF LEGISLATION (Étienne Dumont trans.) (Weeks, Jordan 1840)
BENTHAM, THEORY OF LEGISLATION (1840)

Bentham, Jeremy
Anarchical Fallacies, in 2 THE WORKS OF JEREMY BENTHAM 489–534 (John Bowring 1843)
Bentham, *Anarchical Fallacies* (1843)

Berlo, David K.
THE PROCESS OF COMMUNICATION: AN INTRODUCTION TO THEORY AND PRACTICE (Holt, Rinehart 1960)
BERLO, THE PROCESS OF COMMUNICATION (1960)

Besek, June M.
Anti-Circumvention Laws and Copyright: A Report from the Kernochan Center for Law, Media and the Arts, 27 COLUM.-VLA J.L. & THE ARTS 385 (2004)
Besek, *Anti-Circumvention Laws and Copyright* (2004)

Bing, Jon
The New Evolving "Access Right", *in* ADJUNCTS AND ALTERNATIVES TO COPYRIGHT (ALAI-USA 2002)
Bing, *The New Evolving "Access Right"* (2002)

Birch, Stanley F.
Copyright Fair Use: A Constitutional Imperative, 54 J. COPYRIGHT SOC'Y U.S.A. 139 (2007)
Birch, *Copyright Fair Use* (2007)

Birkinshaw, Patrick
FREEDOM OF INFORMATION: THE LAW, THE PRACTICE AND THE IDEAL (2d ed.) (Butterworths 1996)
BIRKINSHAW, FREEDOM OF INFORMATION (1996)

Birnhack, Michael
The Copyright Law and Free Speech Affair: Making-Up and Breaking-Up, 43 IDEA: J.L. & TECH. 233 (2003)
Birnhack, *The Copyright Law and Free Speech Affair* (2003)

Birnhack, Michael
Copyright Law and Free Speech after Eldred v. Ashcroft, 76 S. CAL. L. REV. 1275 (2003)
Birnhack, *Copyright Law and Free Speech after Eldred v. Ashcroft* (2003)

Blackstone, William
COMMENTARIES ON THE LAWS OF ENGLAND (W. E. Dean 1838) (1765–1769)
BLACKSTONE, COMMENTARIES (1838/1765–1769)

Bone, Robert & Gordon, Wendy J.
Copyright, *in* 2 ENCYCLOPEDIA OF LAW AND ECONOMICS (Boudewijn Bouckaert & Gerrit de Geest eds.) (Edward Elger 2001)
Bone & Gordon, *Copyright* (2001)

Boyle, James
A Politics of Intellectual Property: Emvironmentalism for the Net?, 47 DUKE L.J. 87 (1997)
Boyle, *A Politics of Intellectual Property* (1997)

Boyle, James
Cruel, Mean, or Lavish? Economic Analysis, Price Discrimination and Digital Intellectual Property, 53 VAND. L. REV. 2007 (2000)
Boyle, *Cruel, Mean, or Lavish? Economic Analysis, Price Discrimination and Digital Intellectual Property* (2000)

Bracey, Mose
Searching for Substance in the Midst of Formality, 14 J. INTEL. PROP. L. 111 (2006)
Bracey, *Searching for Substance in the Midst of Formality* (2006)

Bracha Oren
Owning Ideas: A History of Anglo-American Intellectual Property (2005) (J.S.D. Dissertation, Harvard University)
Bracha, Owning Ideas (2005)

Brandeis, Louis D. & Warren, Samuel D.
The Right to Privacy, 4 HARV. L. REV. 193 (1890)
Brandeis & Warren, *The Right to Privacy* (1890)

Breyer, Stephen
The Uneasy Case for Copyright: A Study of Copyright in Books, Photocopies, and Computer Programs, 84 HARV. L. REV. 281 (1970)
Breyer, *The Uneasy Case for Copyright* (1970)

Brown, Abbe E.L.
Guarding the Guards: The Practical Impact of Human Rights on Protection of Innovation and Creativity, Conference Paper, 20th BILETA Conference: Over-Commoditised; Over-Centralised; Over-Observed: the New Digital Legal World? (Apr. 2005) Queen's University of Belfast
Brown, *Guarding the Guards* (2005)

Buhse, Willms & Wetzel, Amélie
Creating a Framework for Business Models for Digital Content, *in* DIGITAL RIGHTS MANAGEMENT: TECHNOLOGICAL, ECONOMIC, LEGAL AND POLITICAL ASPECTS 271–87 (Eberhard Becker et al. eds.) (Springer 2003)
Buhse & Wetzel, *Creating a Framework for Business Models for Digital Content* (2003)

Burk, Dan L.
Legal and Technical Standards in Digital Rights Management Technology, 74 FORDHAM L. REV. 537 (2005)
Burk, *Legal and Technical Standards in Digital Rights Management Technology* (2005)

Burk, Dan L.
Anti-Circumvention Misuse, 50 UCLA L. REV. 1095 (2003)
Burk, *Anti-Circumvention Misuse* (2003)

Burk, Dan L.
Method and Madness in Copyright Law, 2007 UTAH L. REV. 587 (2007)
Burk, *Method and Madness* (2007)

Burk, Dan L. & Cohen, Julie E.
Fair Use Infrastructure for Rights Management Systems, 15 HARV. J.L. & TECH. 41 (2001)
Burk & Cohen, *Fair Use Infrastructure for Rights Management Systems* (2001)

Bygrave, Lee A. & Koelman, Kamiel J.
Privacy, Data Protection and Copyright: Their Interaction in the Context of Electronic Copyright Management Systems, *in* COPYRIGHT AND ELECTRONIC COMMERCE 59–124 (P. Bernt Hugenholtz ed.) (Kluwer 2000)
Bygrave & Koelman, *Privacy, Data Protection and Copyright: Their Interaction in the Context of Electronic Copyright Management Systems* (2000)

Calabresi, Guido & Melamed, Douglas A.
Property Rules, Liability Rules, and Inalienability: One View of the Cathedral, 85 HARV. L. REV. 1089 (1972)
Calabresi & Melamed, *Property Rules, Liability Rules, and Inalienability* (1972)

Callaos, Nagib & Callaos, Belkis de
Definition of Education and Meta-Design of Educational Systems, *in* COMPREHENSIVE SYSTEMS DESIGN: A NEW EDUCATIONAL TECHNOLOGY, (Charles M. Reigeluth et al. eds.) (NATO ASI Series, Computer and Systems Science, Vol. 95 1993)
Callaos & Callaos, *Definition of Education and Meta-Design of Educational Systems* (1993)

Campbell, Tom D.
Introduction to LEGAL POSITIVISM (Tom D. Campbell ed.) (Ashgate Dartmouth 1999)
Campbell, *Introduction* to LEGAL POSITIVISM (1999)

Carlson, David G.
How to Do Things with Hegel, 78 TEX. L. REV. 1377 (2000)
Carlson, *How to Do Things with Hegel* (2000)

Cass, Roland A.
The Perils of Positive Thinking: Constitutional Interpretation and Negative First Amendment Theory, 34 UCLA L. REV. 1405 (1987)
Cass, *The Perils of Positive Thinking* (1987)

Chapman, Audrey R.
Intellectual Property and the Right to Culture, in INTELLECTUAL PROPERTY AND HUMAN RIGHTS, WIPO Panel Discussion to commemorate the 50th Anniversary of the Universal Declaration of Human Rights, Geneva, Nov. 9, 1988 (1999)
Chapman, *Intellectual Property and the Right to Culture* (1999)

Cherry, Colin
ON HUMAN COMMUNICATION: A REVIEW, A SURVEY AND A CRITICISM (3d ed.) (MIT Press 1978)
Cherry, On Human Communication (1978)

Clark, Charles
The Answer to the Machine is in the Machine, in THE FUTURE OF COPYRIGHT IN A DIGITAL ENVIRONMENT 139–45, Proceedings of the Royal Academy Colloquium, Amsterdam (P. Bernt Hugenholtz ed.) (Kluwer Law International 1996)
Clark, *The Answer to the Machine is in the Machine* (1996)

Clarke, Alison & Kohler, Paul
PROPERTY LAW: COMMENTARY AND MATERIALS (Cambridge University Press 2005)
CLARKE & KOHLER, PROPERTY LAW (2005)

Coase, Harold R.
The Problem of Social Cost, 3 J.L. & ECON. 1 (1960)
Coase, *The Problem of Social Cost* (1960)

Cohen Jehoram, Herman
The Future of Copyright Collecting Societies, 23 EUR. INTEL. PROP. REV. 134–39 (2001)
Cohen Jehoram, *The Future of Copyright Collecting Societies* (2001)

Cohen, Felix S.
Transcendental Nonsense and the Functional Approach, 35 COLUM. L. REV. 809 (1935)
Cohen, *Transcendental Nonsense* (1935)

Cohen, Julie E.
The Place of the User in Copyright Law, 74 FORDHAM L. REV. 347 (2005)
Cohen, *The Place of the User* (2005)

Cohen, Julie E.
Cyberspace and/as Space, 107 COLUM. L. REV. 210 (2007)
Cohen, *Cyberspace and/as Space* (2007)

Cohen, Morris R.
Property and Sovereignty, 13 CORNELL L.J. 8 (1927)
Cohen, *Property and Sovereignty* (1927)

Cohon, Rachel
Hume's Moral Philosophy, THE STANFORD ENCYCLOPEDIA OF PHILOSOPHY, (Edward N. Zalta ed. 2004)
Cohon, *Hume's Moral Philosophy* (2004)

Cole, Daniel H. & Grossman, Peter Z.
The Meaning of Property Rights: Law vs. Economics?, 78 LAND ECON. 317 (2002)
Cole & Grossman, *The Meaning of Property Rights* (2002)

Cornish, William R.
Senior Chair's Remarks, in ADJUNCTS AND ALTERNATIVES TO COPYRIGHT 80–81, (ALAI-USA 2002)
Cornish, *Senior Chair's Remarks* (2002)

Cotter, Thomas F.
Fair Use and Copyright Overenforcement, 93 IOWA L. REV. 1271 (2008)
Cotter, *Fair Use and Copyright Overenforcement* (2008)

Croskery, Peter
Institutional Utilitarianism and Intellectual Property, 68 CHI-KENT L. REV. 631 (1993)
Croskery, *Institutional Utilitarianism and Intellectual Property* (1993)

Cunningham, Roger et al.
THE LAW OF PROPERTY (West 1984)
CUNNINGHAM ET AL., THE LAW OF PROPERTY (1984)

Dahlman, Carl J.
The Problem of Externalities, 22 J.L. & ECON. 141 (1979)
Dahlman, *The Problem of Externalities* (1979)

Dam, Kenneth W.
Self-Help in the Digital Jungle, 28 J. LEGAL STUD. 393 (1999)
Dam, *Self-Help in the Digital Jungle* (1999)

Darwin, Charles
THE ORIGIN OF SPECIES (Signet 2003) (1859)
DARWIN, THE ORIGIN OF SPECIES (2003/1859)

Davies, Gillian
COPYRIGHT AND THE PUBLIC INTEREST (2d. ed.) (Sweet & Maxwell 2002)
DAVIES, COPYRIGHT AND THE PUBLIC INTEREST (2002)

Dawkins, Richard
THE SELFISH GENE (2d. ed.) (Oxford University Press 1989)
DAWKINS, THE SELFISH GENE (1989)

de Werra, Jacques
Access Control or Freedom of Access?, *in* DIGITAL RIGHTS MANAGEMENT: THE END OF COLLECTING SOCIETIES?, 111–22 (Christoph Beat Graber et al. eds.) (Staempfli 2005)
de Werra, *Access Control or Freedom of Access?* (2005)

de Werra, Jacques
Moving Beyond the Conflict Between Freedom of Contract and Copyright Policies: In Search of a New Global Policy for On-Line Information Licensing Transactions, 25 COLUM. J. LAW & ARTS 329 (2003)
de Werra, *Moving Beyond the Conflict Between Freedom of Contract and Copyright Policies* (2003)

DeBeer, Jeremy F.
Locks & Levies, 84 DENV. U.L. REV. 143 (2006)
DeBeer, *Locks & Levies* (2006)

Demsetz, Harold
The Private Production of Public Goods, 13 J.L. & ECON. 293 (1970)
Demsetz, *The Private Production of Public Goods* (1970)

Demsetz, Harold
Toward a Theory of Property Rights, 57 AM. ECON. REV. 347 (1967)
Demsetz, *Toward a Theory of Property Rights* (1967)

Denicola, Robert C.
Copyright and Free Speech: Constitutional Limitations on the Protection of Expression, 67 CALIF. L. REV. 283 (1979)
Denicola, *Copyright and Free Speech* (1979)

DeRose, Keith
What is Epistemology?: A Brief Introduction to the Topic, online publication (2005) (available at http://pantheon.yale.edu/%7Ekd47/What-Is-Epistemology.htm)
DeRose, *What is Epistemology?* (2005)

DeRose, Keith
Responding to Skepticism, Introduction to SKEPTICISM: A CONTEMPORARY READER (Keith DeRose & Ted A. Warfield eds.) (Oxford University Press 1999)
DeRose, *Responding to Skepticism* (1999)

Dietz, Adolf
The Artist's Right of Integrity under Copyright Law—A Comparative Approach, 25 INT'L REV. INDUS. PROP. & COPYRIGHT L. 177 (1994)
Dietz, *The Artist's Right of Integrity* (1994)

Drahos, Peter
The Universality of Intellectual Property Rights: Origins and Development, in INTELLECTUAL PROPERTY AND HUMAN RIGHTS, WIPO Panel Discussion to commemorate the 50th Anniversary of the Universal Declaration of Human Rights, Geneva, Nov. 9, 1988 (1999)
Drahos, *The Universality of Intellectual Property Rights: Origins and Development* (1999)

Drahos, Peter
A PHILOSOPHY OF INTELLECTUAL PROPERTY (Dartmouth, Aldershot 1996)
DRAHOS, A PHILOSOPHY OF INTELLECTUAL PROPERTY (1996)

Dreier, Thomas
Copyright Digitized: Philosophical Impacts and Practical Implications for Information Exchange in Digital Networks, *in* WIPO Worldwide Symposium on the Impact of Digital Technology on Copyright and Neighbouring Rights, Geneva 1993 at 187–211 (WIPO ed. 1993)
Dreier, *Copyright Digitized* (1993)

Dreier, Thomas
Die Umsetzung der Urheberrechtsrichtlinie 2001/29/EG in Deutsches Recht, 2002/1 ZUM 28–43 (2002)
Dreier, *Die Umsetzung der Urheberrechtsrichtlinie in Deutsches Recht* (2002)

Dreier, Thomas
Creative Commons, Science Commons–Ein Paradigmenwechsel im Urheberrecht?, *in* PERSPEKTIVEN DES GEISTIGEN EIGENTUMS UND WETTBEWERBSRECHTS, FESTSCHRIFT FÜR GERHARD SCHRICKER ZUM 70. GEBURTSTAG (H.C. Beck 2006)
Dreier, *Creative Commons, Science Commons—Ein Paradigmenwechsel im Urheberrecht?* (2006)

Dreier, Thomas & Hugenholtz, P. Bernt (eds)
CONCISE EUROPEAN COPYRIGHT LAW (Kluwer 2006)
DREIER/HUGENHOLTZ, CONCISE EUROPEAN COPYRIGHT LAW (2006)

Dreier, Thomas & Schulze, Gernot
URHEBERRECHTSGESETZ (2d. ed.) (Beck 2006)
DREIER/SCHULZE, URHEBERRECHTSGESETZ (2006)

Dreyer, Gunda et al.
HEIDELBERGER KOMMENTAR ZUM URHEBERRECHT (C.F. Müller 2004)
DREYER ET AL., HEIDELBERGER KOMMENTAR ZUM URHEBERRECHT (2004)

Druey, Jean Nicolas
INFORMATION ALS GEGENSTAND DES RECHTES (Schulthess Polygraphischer 1995)
DRUEY, INFORMATION ALS GEGENSTAND DES RECHTES (1995)

Durham, Alan L.
Copyright and Information Theory: Toward an Alternative Model of "Authorship", 2004(1) BYU L. REV. 69 (2004)
Durham, *Copyright and Information Theory* (2004)

Dusollier, Séverine
Electrifying the Fence: The Legal Protection of Technological Protection Measures for Protecting Copyright, 21 EUR. INTEL. PROP. REV. 285–97 (1999)
Dusollier, *Electrifying the Fence* (1999)

Dusollier, Séverine
Tipping the Scale in Favor of the Right Holders: The European Anti-Circumvention Provisions, *in* DIGITAL RIGHTS MANAGEMENT: TECHNOLOGICAL, ECONOMIC, LEGAL AND POLITICAL ASPECTS 462–78 (Eberhard Becker et al. eds.) (Springer 2003)
Dusollier, *Tipping the Scale in Favor of the Right Holders* (2003)

Dusollier, Séverine
Some Reflections on Copyright Management Information and Moral Rights, 25 COLUM. J. L.& ARTS 377 (2003)
Dusollier, Some Reflections on Copyright Management Information and Moral Rights (2003)

Dusollier, Séverine
Situating Legal Protections for Copyright-Related Technological Measures in the Broader Legal Landscape: Anti-Circumvention Protection Outside Copyright, *in* ADJUNCTS AND

ALTERNATIVES TO COPYRIGHT 123–54, proceedings of the ALAI Congress, June 13–17, 2001 (Jane C. Ginsburg & June M. Besek eds., 2002)
Dusollier, Situating Legal Protections for Copyright-Related Technological Measures in the Broader Legal Landscape (2002)

Dusollier, Séverine
The Master's Tools v. The Master's House: Creative Commons v. Copyright, 29 COLUM. J.L. & ARTS 271 (2006)
Dusollier, The Master's Tools v. The Master's House: Creative Commons v. Copyright (2006)

Efroni, Zohar
A Momentary Lapse of Reason: Digital Copyright, the DMCA and a Dose of Common Sense, 28 COLUM. J.L. & THE ARTS 249 (2005)
Efroni, A Momentary Lapse of Reason: Digital Copyright, the DMCA and a Dose of Common Sense (2005)

Efroni, Zohar
Towards a Doctrine of "Fair Access" in Copyright: The Federal Circuit's Accord, 46 IDEA 99 (2005)
Efroni, Towards a Doctrine of "Fair Access" in Copyright (2005)

Efroni, Zohar
A Barcelona.com Analysis: Toward a Better Model for Adjudication of International Domain Name Disputes, 14 FORDHAM INTEL. PROP. MEDIA & ENTM'T L. J. 29 (2003)
Efroni, A Barcelona.com Analysis: Toward a Better Model for Adjudication of International Domain Name Disputes (2003)

Einhorn, Michael A.
MEDIA, TECHNOLOGY AND COPYRIGHT (Edward Elgar 2004)
Einhorn, Media, Technology and Copyright (2004)

Elkin-Koren, Niva
Making Room for Consumers Under the DMCA, 22 BERKELEY TECH. L.J. 1119 (2007)
Elkin-Koren, Making Room for Consumers under the DMCA (2007)

Elkin-Koren, Niva
What Contracts Cannot Do: The Limits of Private Ordering in Facilitating a Creative Commons, 74 FORDHAM L. REV. 375 (2005)
Elkin-Koren, What Contracts Cannot Do: The Limits of Private Ordering (2007)

Elkin-Koren, Niva
Copyright in Cyberspace—Rights Without Laws?, 73 CHI.-KENT L. REV. 1155 (1988)
Elkin-Koren, Copyright in Cyberspace—Rights Without Laws? (1988)

Emerson, Tomas I.
THE SYSTEM OF FREEDOM OF EXPRESSION (Random House 1970)
EMERSON, THE SYSTEM OF FREEDOM OF EXPRESSION (1970)

Epstein, Richard A.
Liberty versus Property? Cracks in the Foundations of Copyright Law, 42 SAN DIEGO L. REV. 1 (2005)
Epstein, *Liberty versus Property?* (2005)

Epstein, Richard A.
Possession as the Root of Title, 13 GA. L.J. 1221 (1979)
Epstein, *Possession as the Root of Title* (1979)

Erickson, John S.
Fair Use, DRM and Trusted Computing, 46 COMMUN. ACM 34–39 (2003)
Erikson, *Fair Use, DRM and Trusted Computing* (2003)

Erickson, John S. & Mulligan, Deidre K.
The Technical and Legal Dangers of Code-Based Fair Use Enforcement, 92(6) Proceedings of the IEEE 985 (2004)
Erickson & Mulligan, *The Technical and Legal Dangers of Code-Based Fair Use Enforcement* (2004)

Eriksson, Owen
Communication Quality: Towards an Intersubjective Understanding of Quality, Conference Paper presented at Quergo'99 International Conference on TQM and Human Factors, June 15–17, 1999, Linköping (available at http://users.du.se/~oer/forskning/rapporter/er99arap.pdf)
Eriksson, *Communication Quality* (1999)

Felten, Edward W.
A Skeptical View on DRM and Fair Use, 46(4) COMMUN. ACM 56 (2003)
Felten, *A Skeptical View on DRM and Fair Use* (2003)

Ficsor, Mihály
Copyright for the Digital Era: The WIPO "Internet" Treaties, 21 COLUM.-VLA J.L. & ARTS 197 (1997)
Ficsor, *Copyright for the Digital Era: The WIPO "Internet" Treaties* (1997)

Ficsor, Mihály
THE LAW OF COPYRIGHT AND THE INTERNET: THE 1996 WIPO TREATIES (Oxford University Press 2002)
FICSOR, THE LAW OF COPYRIGHT AND THE INTERNET (2002)

Fischman-Afori, Orit
Human Rights and Copyright: The Introduction of Natural Law Consideration into American Copyright Law, 14 FORDHAM INTEL. PROP. MEDIA & ENTM'T L.J. 497 (2004)
Fischman-Afori, *Human Rights and Copyright* (2004)

Fisher William W. III
PROMISES TO KEEP: TECHNOLOGY, LAW AND THE FUTURE OF ENTERTAINMENT (Stanford University Press 2004)
FISHER, PROMISES TO KEEP (2004)

Fisher, William W. III
Theories of Intellectual Property, *in* NEW ESSAYS IN THE LEGAL AND POLITICAL THEORY OF PROPERTY (Stephen R. Munzer ed.) (Cambridge University Press 2001)
Fisher, *Theories of Intellectual Property* (2001)

Fisher, William W. III
Reconstructing the Fair Use Doctrine, 101 HARV. L. REV. 1659 (1988)
Fisher, *Reconstructing the Fair Use Doctrine* (1988)

Fisher, William W. III et al.
AMERICAN LEGAL REALISM (William W. Fisher et al. eds.) (Oxford University Press 1993)
FISHER ET AL., AMERICAN LEGAL REALISM (1993)

Foged, Terese
US v EU Anti Circumvention Legislation: Preserving the Public's Privileges in the Digital Age, 24 EUR. INTEL. PROP. REV. 525–42 (2002)
Foged, *US v EU Anti Circumvention Legislation: Preserving the Public's Privileges in the Digital Age* (2002)

Fox, Barbra L. & LaMacchia, Brian A.
Encouraging Recognition of Fair Uses in DRM Systems, 46 COMMUN. ACM 61 (2003)
Fox & LaMacchia, *Encouraging Recognition of Fair Uses in DRM Systems* (2003)

Frischmann, Brett, M.
Evaluating the Demsetzian Trend in Copyright Law, 3 REV. L. & ECON. 649 (2007)
Frischmann, *Evaluating the Demsetzian Trend in Copyright Law* (2007)

Frischmann, Brett, M.
An Economic Theory of Infrastructure and Commons Management, 89 MINN. L. REV. 917 (2005)
Frischmann, *An Economic Theory of Infrastructure and Commons Management* (2005)

Fuchs, Christine
AVANTGARDE UND ERWEITERTER KUNSTBEGRIFF (Nomos 2000)
FUCHS, AVANTGARDE UND ERWEITERTER KUNSTBEGRIFF (2000)

Fuks, Hugo & Assis, Rodrigo Lemos de
Facilitating Perception on Virtual Leaningware Based Environment, 5 J. SYS. & INFOR. TECH. 93–113 (2001) (available at http://139.82.24.161/groupware/publicacoes/jositFUKS.pdf)
Fuks & Assis, *Facilitating Perception on Virtual Leaningware Based Environment* (2001)

Garvey, John H. & Schauer, Frederick
THE FIRST AMENDMENT: A READER (2d. ed.) (West 1996)
GARVEY & SCHAUER, THE FIRST AMENDMENT (1996)

Gasser, Urs, & Girsberger, Michael
Transposing the Copyright Directive: Legal Protection of Technological Measures in EU-Member States—A Genie Stuck in the Bottle?, Berkman Working Paper No. 2004-10 (Nov. 2004)
Gasser & Girsberger, *Transposing the Copyright Directive* (2004)

Geiger, Christophe
Right to Copy v. Three-Step Test: The Future of the Private Copy Exception in the Digital Environment, 2005(1) COMP. L.REV. INT'L 7–13 (2005)
Geiger, *Right to Copy v. Three-Step Test* (2005)

Geiger, Christophe
The Three-Step Test, a Threat to a Balanced Copyright Law?, 6 IIC 683 (2006)
Geiger, *The Three-Step Test, a Threat to a Balanced Copyright Law?* (2006)

Geller, Paul E.
Inquiry into Justice in Copyright Law: Toward a Core Author's Right, in INTELLECTUAL PROPERTY AND THEORIES OF JUSTICE (Axel Gosseries & Alain Strowel eds.) (Palgrave Macmillan 2008)
Geller, *Inquiry into Justice in Copyright Law: Toward a Core Author's Right* (2008)

Geller, Paul E.
Beyond the Copyright Crisis: Principles for Change, 55 J. COPYRIGHT SOC'Y U.S.A. 165 (2008)
Geller, *Beyond the Copyright Crisis: Principles for Change* (2008)

Geller, Paul E.
Rethinking the Berne-Plus Framework: From Conflicts of Law to Copyright Reform, 8/2009 EUR. INTEL. PROP. REV. 391–95 (2009)
Geller, *Rethinking the Berne-Plus Framework: From Conflicts of Law to Copyright Reform* (2009)

Gettier, Edmund L.
Is Justified True Belief Knowledge?, ANALYSIS 23, 121–23 (1963)
Gettier, *Is Justified True Belief Knowledge?* (1963)

Gervais, Daniel J.
THE TRIPS AGREEMENT: DRAFTING HISTORY AND ANALYSIS (2d ed.) (Sweet & Maxwell, 2003)
Gervais, *The TRIPS Agreement* (2003)

Gervais, Daniel J.
Towards a New Core International Copyright Norm: The Reverse Three-Step Test, 9 MARQ. INTEL. PROP. L. REV. 1 (2005)
Gervais, *Towards a New Core International Copyright Norm: The Reverse Three-Step Test* (2005)

Gervais, Daniel J.
The Evolving Role(s) of Copyright Collectives, in DIGITAL RIGHTS MANAGEMENT: THE END OF COLLECTION SOCIETIES? 27–56, Christoph Beat Graber et al. eds.) (Staempfli 2005)
Gervais, *The Evolving Role(s) of Copyright Collectives* (2005)

Gervais, Daniel J.
The Price of Social Norms: Towards a Liability Regime for File-Sharing, 12 J. INTEL. PROP. L. 39–74 (2003)
Gervais, *The Price of Social Norms: Towards a Liability Regime for File-Sharing* (2003)

Gibson, James
Risk Aversion and Rights Accretion in Intellectual Property Law, 116 YALE L.J. 882 (2007)
Gibson, *Risk Aversion and Rights Accretion in Intellectual Property Law* (2007)

Ginsburg, Jane C.
Essay: From Having Copies to Experiencing Works: The Development of an Access Right in U.S. Copyright Law, 50 J. COPYRIGHT SOC'Y U.S.A. 113 (2003)
Ginsburg, *The Development of an Access Right in U.S. Copyright Law* (2003)

Ginsburg, Jane C.
A Marriage of Convenience? A Comment on the Protection of Databases, 82 CHI.- KENT L. REV. 1171 (2007)
Ginsburg, *A Marriage of Convenience? A Comment on the Protection of Databases* (2007)

Ginsburg, Jane C.
A Tale of Two Copyrights: Literary Property in Revolutionary France and America, 64 TULANE L. REV. 991 (1990)
Ginsburg, *A Tale of Two Copyrights* (1990)

Ginsburg, Jane C.
Authors and Users in Copyright, 45 J. COPYRIGHT SOC'Y U.S.A. 1 (1997)
Ginsburg, *Authors and Users in Copyright* (1997)

Ginsburg, Jane C.
Copyright and Control Over New Technologies of Dissemination, 101 COLUM. L. REV. 1613 (2001)
Ginsburg, *Copyright and Control Over New Technologies of Dissemination* (2001)

Ginsburg, Jane C.
Creation and Commercial Value: Copyright Protection of Works of Information, 90 COLUM. L. REV. 1865 (1990)
Ginsburg, *Copyright Protection of Works of Information* (1990)

Ginsburg, Jane C.
Toward Supranational Copyright Law? The WTO Panel Decision and the Three-Step Test for Copyright Exceptions, 187 RIDA 2 (2001)
Ginsburg, *Toward Supranational Copyright Law? The WTO Panel Decision and the Three-Step Test* (2001)

Ginsburg, Jane C.
News from the US, 1999 R.I.D.A. 179 (1999)
Ginsburg, *News from the US* (1999)

Ginsburg, Jane C.
Copyright Use and Excuse on the Internet, 24 COLUM. J.L. & ARTS 1 (2000)
Ginsburg, *Copyright Use and Excuse on the Internet* (2000)

Goldstein, Bruce E.
SENSATION AND PERCEPTION (6th. ed.) (Wadsworth 2002)
GOLDSTEIN, SENSATION AND PERCEPTION (2002)

Goldstein Paul
COPYRIGHT'S HIGHWAY—FROM GUTENBERG TO THE CELESTIAL JUKEBOX (rev. ed.) (Stanford University Press 2003)
GOLDSTEIN, COPYRIGHT'S HIGHWAY—FROM GUTENBERG TO THE CELESTIAL JUKEBOX (2003)

Goldstein Paul
Copyright and the First Amendment, 70 COLUM. L. REV. 983 (1970)
Goldstein, *Copyright and the First Amendment* (1970)

Goldston, James A. et al.
A Nation Less Secured: Diminished Public Access to Information, 21 HARV. C.R.- C.L. L. REV. 409 (1986)
Goldston et al., *A Nation Less Secured: Diminished Public Access to Information* (1986)

Gordon, Wendy J.
Authors, Publishers, and Public Goods: Trading Gold for Dross, 36 LOYOLA L.A. L. REV. 159 (2002)
Gordon, *Authors, Publishers, and Public Goods* (2002)

Gordon, Wendy J. & Bahls, Daniel
The Public's Right to Fair Use: Amending Section 107 to Avoid the "Fared Use" Fallacy, 2007 UTAH L. REV. 619 (2007)
Gordon & Bahls, *The Public's Right to Fair Use* (2007)

Gordon, Wendy J.
Fair Use as Market Failure: A Structural and Economic Analysis of the Betamax Case and its Predecessors, 82 COLUM. L. REV. 1600 (1982)
Gordon, *Fair Use as Market Failure* (1982)

Gordon, Wendy, J.
A Property Right in Self-Expression: Equality and Individualism in the Natural Law of Intellectual Property, 102 YALE L.J. 1533 (1993)
Gordon, *A Property Right in Self-Expression* (1993)

Gordon, Wendy J.
Intellectual Property, in THE OXFORD HANDBOOK OF LEGAL STUDIES (Peter Cane & Mark V. Tushnet eds.) (Oxford University Press 2003)
Gordon, *Intellectual Property* (2003)

Gordon, Wendy J.
An Inquiry into the Merits of Copyright: The Challenges of Consistency, Consent and Encouragement Theory, 41 STANFORD L. REV. 1343 (1989)
Gordon, *An Inquiry into the Merits of Copyright* (1989)

Gower, Andrew
GOWER'S REVIEW OF INTELLECTUAL PROPERTY (HM Stationary Office, U.K. 2006)
GOWER'S REVIEW OF INTELLECTUAL PROPERTY (2006)

Graham, Daniel
Heraclitus, STANFORD ENCYCLOPEDIA OF PHILOSOPHY (Edward N. Zalta ed., Spring ed. 2007)
Graham, *Heraclitus* (2007)

Graham, Gordon
PHILOSOPHY OF THE ARTS: AN INTRODUCTION TO AESTHETICS (Routledge 1997)
GRAHAM, PHILOSOPHY OF THE ARTS (1997)

Greenawat, Kent
O'er the Land of the Free: Flag Burning As Speech, 37 UCLA L. REV. 925 (1990)
Greenawalt, *O'er the Land of the Free* (1990)

Grey, Thomas C.
The Disintegration of Property, in PROPERTY: NOMOS XXII (J. Roland Pennock & John W. Chapman eds.) (NYU Press 1980)
Grey, *The Disintegration of Property* (1980)

Grotius, Hugo
THE RIGHTS OF WAR AND PEACE (Cosimo 2007) (1625)
GROTIUS, THE RIGHTS OF WAR AND PEACE (2007/1625)

Guibault, Lucie
COPYRIGHT LIMITATIONS AND CONTRACTS (Kluwer 2002)
GUIBAULT, COPYRIGHT LIMITATIONS AND CONTRACTS (2002)

Ha, Louisa et al.
Broadcast via the Internet: Technology, Market, and the Future, 11 TRENDS IN COMMUN. 155–68 (2003)
Ha et al., *Broadcast via the Internet* (2003)

Ha, Louisa
Webcasting, in 3 THE INTERNET ENCYCLOPEDIA 674–86 (Hossein Bidgoli ed.) (Wiley 2004)
Ha, *Webcasting* (2004)

Stuart Haber et al.
If Piracy is the Problem, Is DRM the Answer?, in DIGITAL RIGHTS MANAGEMENT 224–33 (Springer 2003)
Haber et al., *If Piracy is the Problem, Is DRM the Answer?* (2003)

Hamilton, Marci A.
The TRIPS Agreement: Imperialistic, Outdated, and Overprotective, 29 VANDERBILT J. TRANSNAT'L L. 613 (1996)
Hamilton, *The TRIPS Agreement: Imperialistic, Outdated, and Overprotective* (1996)

Hamilton, Marci A. & Kohnen, Clemens G.
The Jurisprudence of Information Flow: How the Constitution Constructs the Pathways of Information, 25 CARDOZO L. REV. 267 (2003)
Hamilton & Kohnen, *The Jurisprudence of Information Flow* (2003)

Hänel, Frederike
DIE UMSETZUNG DES ART. 6 INFO-RL (TECHNISCHE SCHUTZMASSNAHMEN) INS DEUTSCHE RECHT (Peter Lang 2005)
HÄNEL, DIE UMSETZUNG DES ART. 6 INFO-RL INS DEUTSCHE RECHT (2005)

Hansmann, Henry & Kraakman, Reiner
Property, Contract, and Verification: The Numerus Clausus Problem and the Divisibility of Rights, 31 J. LEGAL STUD. 373 (2002)
Hansmann & Kraakman, *Property, Contract, and Verification* (2002)

Harris, Jim W.
PROPERTY AND JUSTICE (Oxford University Press 1996)
HARRIS, PROPERTY AND JUSTICE (1996)

Harris, Jim W.
Is Property a Human Right?, in PROPERTY AND THE CONSTITUTION 64–87 (Jean McLean ed.) (Hart 1999)
Harris, *Is Property a Human Right?* (1999)

Hauser, Tobias & Wenz, Christian
DRM Under Attack: Weaknesses in *Existing Systems, in* DIGITAL RIGHTS MANAGEMENT206–23 (Eberhard Becker et al eds.) (Springer 2003)
Hauser & Wenz, *DRM Under Attack: Weaknesses in Existing Systems* (2003)

Heath, Robert L. & Bryant, Jennings
HUMAN COMMUNICATION THEORY AND RESEARCH: CONCEPTS, CONTEXTS AND CHALLENGES (2d. ed.) (Lawrence Erlbaum 2000)
HEATH & BRYANT, HUMAN COMMUNICATION THEORY (2000)

Hegel, Georg Wilhelm Friedrich
PHILOSOPHY OF RIGHT (S.W. Dyde trans.) (Batoche Books 2001 (1896)
HEGEL, PHILOSOPHY OF RIGHT (Dyde trans.) (2001/1896)

Hegel, Georg Wilhelm Friedrich
GRUNDLINIEN DER PHILOSOPHIE DES RECHTES 1821
HEGEL, GRUNDLINIEN (1821)

Heide, Thomas
Copyright in the EU and U.S.: What "Access Right"?, 48 J. COPYRIGHT SOC'Y U.S.A. 363 (2001)
Heide, *What "Access Right"?* (2001)

Heide, Thomas
Approach to Innovation under the Proposed Copyright Directive, 2000(3) INTEL. PROP. Q. 215–33 (2000)
Heide, *Approach to Innovation under the Proposed Copyright Directive* (2000)

Heide, Thomas
Access Control and Innovation Under the Emerging EU Electronic Commerce Framework, 15 BERKELEY TECH. L.J. 993 (2000)
Heide, *Access Control and Innovation Under the Emerging EU Electronic Commerce Framework* (2000)

Helfer, Laurence R.
Toward a Human Rights Framework for Intellectual Property, 40 U.C. DAVIS L. REV. 971 (2007)
Helfer, *Toward a Human Rights Framework for Intellectual Property* (2007)

Helfer, Laurence R.
Human Rights and Intellectual Property: Conflict or Coexistence?, 47 MINN. INTEL. PROP. L. REV. 47 (2003)
Helfer, *Human Rights and Intellectual Property: Conflict or Coexistence?* (2003)

Heller, Michael A.
The Tragedy of the Anticommons: Property in the Transition from Marx to Markets, 111 HARV. L. REV. 621 (1998)
Heller, *The Tragedy of the Anticommons* (1998)

Herdin, Garret
The Tragedy of the Commons, 162 SCIENCE 1243 (1968)
Herdin, *The Tragedy of the Commons* (1968)

Heverly, Robert A.
The Information Semicommons, 18 BERKELEY TECH. L.J. 1127 (2003)
Heverly, *Information Semicommons* (2003)

Hilty, Reto M.
LIZENZVERTRAGSRECHT—SYSTEMATISIERUNG UND TYPISIERUNG AUS SCHUTZ—UND SCHULDRECHTLICHER SICHT (Stämpli 2001)
HILTY, LIZENZVERTRAGSRECHT (2001)

Hilty, Reto M.
Urheber in der Informationsgesellschaft: "Wer will was von wem woraus?" Ein Auftakt zum "zweiten Korb", ZUM SONDERHEFT, 983–1005 (2003)
Hilty, *Wer will was von wem woraus?* (2003)

Hilty, Reto M.
Eldred v. Ashcroft: Die Schutzfrist im Urheberecht—eine Diskussion, die auch Europäer interessieren sollte, 2003(3) GRUR-INT. 201 (2003)
Hilty, *Eldred v. Ashcroft: Die Schutzfrist im Urheberecht—eine Diskussion, die auch Europäer interessieren sollte* (2003)

Hilty, Reto M.
Rechtsschutz technischer Maßnahmen: Zum UrhG-Regierungsentwurf vom 31.7.2002, 2002(9) MMR 577 (2002)
Hilty, *Rechtsschutz technischer Maßnahmen: Zum UrhG-Regierungsentwurf vom 31.7.2002* (2002)

Hilty, Reto M.
The Expansion of Copyright Law and Its Social Justification, in COPYRIGHT LAW AND THE INFORMATION SOCIETY IN ASIA 1–31, 26 IIC Studies (Christopher Heath & Kung-Chung Liu eds.) (Hart 2007)
Hilty, *The Expansion of Copyright Law and its Social Justification* (2007)

Hilty, Reto M.
Intellectual Property and the European Community's Internal Market Legislation—Copyright in the Internal Market, 7 IIC 760 (2004)
Hilty, *Intellectual Property and the European Community's Internal Market Legislation—Copyright in the Internal Market* (2004)

Hilty, Reto M.
Der "zweite Korb"—ein erster Schritt in die richtige Richtung, 2004(11) MMR 713 (2004)
Hilty, *Der "zweite Korb"—ein erster Schritt in die richtige Richtung* (2004)

Hilty, Reto M.
Vergütungssystem und Schrankenregelungen—Neue Herausforderungen an den Gesetzgeber, 10 GRUR 819 (2005)
Hilty, *Vergütungssystem und Schrankenregelungen—Neue Herausforderungen an den Gesetzgeber* (2005)

Hilty, Reto M.
Verbotsrecht vs. Vergütungsanspruch: Suche nach den Konsequenzen der tripolaren Interessenlage im Urheberrecht, in PERSPEKTIVEN DES GEISTIGEN EIGENTUMS UND WETTBEWERBSRECHTS 325–52, Festschrift für Gerhard Schricker zum 70. Geburtstag (H.C. Beck 2005)
Hilty, Verbotsrecht vs. Vergütungsanspruch (2005)

Hilty, Reto M.
Five Lessons about Copyright in the Information Society, 53 J. COPYRIGHT SOC'Y U.S.A. 103 (2006)
Hilty, Five Lessons about Copyright in the Information Society (2006)

Hilty, Reto M.
Copyright Law and the Information Society—Neglected Adjustments and Their Consequences, 2 IIC 135 (2007)
Hilty, Copyright Law and the Information Society—Neglected Adjustments and Their Consequences (2007)

Hilty, Reto M. & Peukert, Alexander
"Equitable Remuneration" in Copyright Law: The Amended German Copyright Act as a Trap for the Entertainment Industry in the U.S.?, 22 CARDOZO ARTS & ENTM'T L.J. 401 (2004)
Hilty & Peukert, "Equitable Remuneration" in Copyright Law: The Amended German Copyright Act as a Trap for the Entertainment Industry in the U.S.? (2004)

Hoeren, Thomas
Access Right as a Postmodern Symbol of Copyright Deconstruction?, *in* ADJUNCTS AND ALTERNATIVES TO COPYRIGHT 348–63, proceedings of the ALAI Congress, June 13–17, 2001 (Jane C. Ginsburg & June M. Besek eds. 2002)
Hoeren, *Access Right* (2002)

Hoeren, Thomas
INTERNETRECHT SKRIPTUM (Institut für Informations-, Telekommunikations- und Medienrecht Universität Münster 2007)
Hoeren, Internetrecht (2007)

Hoeren, Thomas & Sieber, Ulrich (eds.)
HANDBUCH MULTIMEDIA-RECHT (H.C. Beck 2007)
Hoeren/Sieber, Handbuch Multimedia-Recht (2007)

Hoffmann, Willy
Berner Konvention und Landesgesetz, 1928 GRUR 897 (1928)
Hoffmann, Berner Konvention und Landesgesetz (1928)

Hoffmann, Willy
DIE BERNER ÜBEREINKUNFT ZUM SCHUTZE VON WERKEN DER LITERATUR UND KUNST (Springer 1935)
Hoffmann, Die Berner Übereinkunft zum Schutze von Werken der Literatur und Kunst (1935)

Hofweber, Thomas
Logic and Ontology, THE STANFORD ENCYCLOPEDIA OF PHILOSOPHY (Edward N. Zalta ed., Fall ed. 2008)
Hofweber, Logic and Ontology (2008)

Hohfeld, Wesley N.
Some Fundamental Legal Conceptions as Applied in Judicial Reasoning, 23 YALE L.J. 16 (1913)
Hohfeld, Some Fundamental Legal Conceptions as Applied in Judicial Reasoning (1913)

Hohfeld, Wesley N.
Fundamental Legal Conceptions as Applied in Judicial Reasoning, 26 YALE L.J. 710 (1917)
Hohfeld, Fundamental Legal Conceptions as Applied in Judicial Reasoning (1917)

Honoré, A. M.
Ownership, *in* OXFORD ESSAYS IN JURISPRUDENCE (Oxford University Press 1961)
Honoré, *Ownership* (1961)

Hume, David
A TREATISE OF HUMAN NATURE (eBooks@adelaide 2006) (1739)
HUME, TREATISE OF HUMAN NATURE (2006/1739)

Hugenholtz, P. Bernt
Why the Copyright Directive is Unimportant, and Possibly Invalid, 22 EUR. INTEL. PROP. REV. 499–505 (2000)
Hugenholtz, *Why the Copyright Directive is Unimportant, and Possibly Invalid* (2000)

Hugenholtz, P. Bernt
Copyright and Freedom of Expression in Europe, in INNOVATION POLICY IN AN INFORMATION AGE 343–64 (Rochelle Cooper Dreyfuss et al. eds.) (Oxford University Press 2002)
Hugenholtz, *Copyright and Freedom of Expression in Europe* (2001)

Hugenholtz, P. Bernt
Copyright, Contract and Code: What Will Remain of the Public Domain?, 26 BROOK. J. INT'L L. 77 (2000)
Hugenholtz, *Copyright, Contract and Code: What Will Remain of the Public Domain?* (2000)

Hugenholtz, P. Bernt & Okediji, Ruth L.
Conceiving an International Instrument on Limitations and Exceptions to Copyright, Final Report (Mar. 6, 2008)
Hugengoltz & Okediji, *Conceiving an International Instrument on Limitations and Exceptions to Copyright* (2008)

Hughes, Justin
The Philosophy of Intellectual Property, 77 GEO. L.J. 287 (1988)
Hughes, *The Philosophy of Intellectual Property* (1988)

Hughes, Justin
Created Facts and the Flawed Ontology of Copyright Law, 83 NOTRE DAME L. REV. 109 (2007)
Hughes, *Created Facts and the Flawed Ontology of Copyright Law* (2007)

Hurt, Robert M. & Schuchman, Robert M.
The Economic Rationale of Copyright, 56 AM. ECON. REV. 421–32 (1966)
Hurt & Schuchman, *The Economic Rationale of Copyright* (1966)

Jackson, Matt
From Broadcast to Webcast: Copyright Law and Streaming Media, 11 TEX. INTEL. PROP. L.J. 447 (2003)
Jackson, *From Broadcast to Webcast* (2003)

Jaeger, Till & Metzger, Axel
OPEN SOURCE SOFTWARE (2d. ed.) (C.H. Beck 2006)
JAEGER & METZGER, OPEN SOURCE SOFTWARE (2006)

Jaszi, Peter & Woodmansee, Martha
Introduction to THE CONSTRUCTION OF AUTHORSHIP: TEXTUAL APPROPRIATION IN LAW AND LITERATURE (2d. ed.) (Peter Jaszi & Martha Woodmansee eds.) (Duke University Press 1999)
Jaszi & Woodmansee, *Introduction* to THE CONSTRUCTION OF AUTHORSHIP (1999)

Jefferson, Thomas,
Letter from Thomas Jefferson to Isaac McPherson (Aug. 13, 1813) *in* 13 THE WRITINGS OF THOMAS JEFFERSON (Andrew A. Lipscomb ed. 1903)
Jefferson, *Letter to Isaac McPherson* (1903/1813)

Johnstone, David R.
Debunking Fair Use and Copyduty Under U.S. Copyright Law, 52 J. COPYRIGHT SOC'Y U.S.A. 345 (2005)
Johnstone, *Debunking Fair Use* (2005)

Jumarie, Guy
RELATIVE INFORMATION: THEORY AND APPLICATION (Springer 1990)
JUMARIE, RELATIVE INFORMATION (1990)

Juola, James F.
Pattern Recognition, in COGNITIVE PSYCHOLOGY AND INFORMATION PROCESSING: AN INTRODUCTION 489–523 (Lawrence Erlbaum 1979)
Juola, *Pattern Recognition* (1979)

Kant, Emmanuel
Von der Unrechtmäßigkeit des Büchernachdrucks, 5 BERLINISCHE MONATSSCHRIFT 403–17 (1785)
Kant, *Von der Unrechtmäßigkeit des Büchernachdrucks* (1785)

Kapczynski, Amy
The Access to Knowledge Mobilization and the New Politics of Intellectual Property, 117 YALE L.J. 804 (2008)
Kapczynski, *The Access to Knowledge Mobilization* (2008)

Kaplan, Benjamin
AN UNHURRIED VIEW OF COPYRIGHT (Columbia University Press 1967)
KAPLAN, AN UNHURRIED VIEW OF COPYRIGHT (1967)

Kaplow, Louis & Shavell, Steven
Fairness versus Welfare, 114 HARV. L. REV. 961 (2001)
Kaplow & Shavell, *Fairness versus Welfare* (2001)

Kaplow, Louis
Rules versus Standards: An Economic Analysis, 42 DUKE L.J. 557 (1992)
Kaplow, *Rules versus Standards: An Economic Analysis* (1992)

Katsh, Ethan M.
LAW IN A DIGITAL WORLD (Oxford University Press 1995)
KATSH, LAW IN A DIGITAL WORLD (1995)

Kerr, Ian
To Observe and Protect? How Digital Rights Management Systems Threaten Privacy and What Policy Makers Should Do about It, in 1 INTELLECTUAL PROPERTY AND INFORMATION WEALTH 321–343 (Peter K. Yu ed.) (Praeger 2007)
Kerr, *To Observe and Protect?* (2007)

Kerr, Orin S.
A Lukewarm Defense of the Digital Millennium Copyright Act, in COPY FIGHTS, THE FUTURE OF INTELLECTUAL PROPERTY IN RHE INFORMATION AGE 163–70, Adam Thierer & Wayne Crews (eds.), CATO Institute, Washington D.C. 2002
Kerr, *A Lukewarm Defense of the Digital Millennium Copyright Act* (2002)

Kieff, Scott F.
The Case Against Copyright: A Comparative Institutional Analysis of Intellectual Property Regimes, Working Paper, Hoover Institution, Stanford University (2004) (available at http://papers.ssrn.com/sol3/papers.cfm?abstract_id=600802)
Kieff, *The Case Against Copyright* (2004)

Kitch, Edmund W.
Elementary and Persistent Errors in the Economic Analysis of Intellectual Property, 53 VAND. L. REV. 1727 (2000)
Kitch, *Elementary and Persistent Errors in the Economic Analysis of Intellectual Property* (2000)

Knight, Graham
Internet Architecture, *in* 1 THE INTERNET ENCYCLOPEDIA 244–63 (Hossein Bidgoli ed.) (Wiley 2004)
Knight, *Internet Architecture* (2004)

Klein, Peter D.
Epistemology, *in* ROUTLEDGE ENCYCLOPEDIA OF PHILOSOPHY (Edward Craig ed.) (Routledge 1998, 2005) (available at http://www.rep.routledge.com/article/P059)
Klein, *Epistemology* (2005)

Koelman, Kamiel J.
Copyright Law and Economics in the EU Copyright Directive: Is the Droit d´Auteur Passé?, 35 IIC 603–38 (2004)
Koelman, *Copyright Law and Economics in the EU Copyright Directive* (2004)

Koelman, Kamiel J.
A Hard Nut to Crack: The Protection of Technological Protection Measures, 22 EUR. INTEL. PROP. REV. 272–88 (2000)
Koelman, *A Hard Nut to Crack* (2000)

Koelman, Kamiel J.
Fixing the Three-Step Test, 2006 EUR. INTEL. PROP. REV. 407 (2006)
Koelman, *Fixing the Three-Step Test* (2006)

Koelman, Kamiel J. & Helberger Natali
Protection of Technological Measures, *in* COPYRIGHT AND ELECTRONIC COMMERCE (P. Bernst Hugenholtz ed.) (Kluwer 2000)
Koelman & Helberger, *Protection of Technological Measures* (2000)

Krippendorff, Klaus
Information Theory, *in* COMMUNICATION AND BEHAVIOR 351–89 (Gerhard J. Hanneman & William J. McEwen eds.) (Addison-Wesley 1975)
Krippendorff, *Information Theory* (1975)

Ku, Raymond Shih Ray
The Creative Destruction of Copyright: Napster and the New Economics of Digital Technology, 69 U. CHI. L. REV. 263 (2002)
Ku, *The Creative Destruction of Copyright: Napster and the New Economics of Digital Technology* (2002)

Kur, Annette & Ruse-Kahn, Henning Grosse
Enough is Enough—The Notion of Binding Ceilings in International Intellectual Property Protection (Dec. 2008) (available at http://papers.ssrn.com/sol3/papers.cfm?abstract_id=1326429)
Kur & Ruse-Kahn, *Enough is Enough* (2008)

Kvanvig, Jonathan L.
Nozickian Epistemology and the Value of Knowledge in Epistemology, in PHILOSOPHICAL ISSUES 14/2004 (Ernest Sosa & Enrique Villanueva eds.) (Blackwell 2004)
Kvanvig, *Nozickian Epistemology and the Value of Knowledge* (2004)

Kwall, Roberta R.
Copyright and the Moral Rights: Is an American Marriage Possible?, 38 VAND. L. REV. 1 (1985)
Kwall, *Copyright and the Moral Rights* (1985)

Lachman, Roy et al.
COGNITIVE PSYCHOLOGY AND INFORMATION PROCESSING: AN INTRODUCTION (Lawrence Erlbaum 1979)
LACHMAN ET AL., COGNITIVE PSYCHOLOGY (1979)

Ladas, Stephen P.
THE INTERNATIONAL PROTECTION OF LITERARY AND ARTISTIC PROPERTY (Macmillan 1938)
LADAS, THE INTERNATIONAL PROTECTION OF LITERARY AND ARTISTIC PROPERTY (1938)

Landau, Michael
Has the Digital Millennium Copyright Act Really Created a New Exclusive Right of Access?, 49 J. COPYRIGHT SOC'Y U.S.A. 277 (2001)
Landau, *Has the Digital Millennium Copyright Act Really Created a New Exclusive Right of Access?* (2001)

Landes, William M. & Posner, Richard A.
THE ECONOMIC STRUCTURE OF INTELLECTUAL PROPERTY LAW (Harvard University Press 2003)
LANDES & POSNER, THE ECONOMIC STRUCTURE OF INTELLECTUAL PROPERTY LAW (2003)

Landes, William M. & Posner, Richard A.
An Economic Analysis of Copyright Law, 18 J. LEGAL STUD. 325–63 (1989)
Landes & Posner, *An Economic Analysis of Copyright Law* (1989)

Landes, William M. & Posner, Richard A.
Indefinitely Renewable Copyright, 70 U. CHI. L. REV. (2003)
Landes & Posner, *Indefinitely Renewable Copyright* (2003)

Lastowka, Gregory F.
Free Access and the Future of Copyright, 27 RUTGERS COMP. & TECH. L.J. 293 (2001)
Lastowka, *Free Access and the Future of Copyright* (2001)

Leete, Burt A.
Contracts Formation Under the United Nations Convention on Contracts for the International Sale of Goods and the Uniform Commercial Code: Pitfalls for the Unwary, 6 TEMPLE INT'L & COMP. L.J. 193 (1993)
Leete, *Contracts Formation Under the United Nations Convention on Contracts for the International Sale of Goods and the UCC* (1993)

Leistner, Matthias & Hansen Gerd

Die Begründung des Urheberrechts im digitalen Zeitalter—Versuch einer Zusammenführung von individualistischen und utilitaristischen Rechtfertigungsbemühungen, 2008(8) GRUR 479 (2008)

Leistner & Hansen, *Die Begründung des Urheberrechts im digitalen Zeitalter* (2008)

Lemley Mark A. & Reese, Anthony R.

Reducing Digital Copyright Infringement Without Restricting Innovation, 56 STAN. L. REV. 1345 (2004)

Lemley & Reese, *Reducing Digital Copyright Infringement Without Restricting Innovation* (2004)

Lemley, Mark A. & Weiser, Philip J.

Should Property or Liability Rules Govern Information?, 85 TEX. L. REV. 783 (2007)

Lemley & Weiser, *Should Property or Liability Rules Govern Information?* (2007)

Lemley, Mark A.

Dealing with Overlapping Copyrights on the Internet, 22 U. DAYTON L. REV. 547 (1997)

Lemley, *Dealing with Overlapping Copyrights on the Internet* (1997)

Lemley, Mark A.

Property, Intellectual Property, and Free Riding, 83 TEX. L. REV. 1031 (2005)

Lemley, *Property, Intellectual Property, and Free Riding* (2005)

Leslie, Phillip

Price Discrimination in Broadway Theatre, 35(3) RAND J. ECON. 520–41 (2004) (available at http://www.stanford.edu/~pleslie/broadway.pdf)

Leslie, *Price Discrimination in Broadway Theatre* (2004)

Lessig, Laurence

Does Copyright Have Limits: Eldred v. Ashcroft *and Its Aftermath,* 5 QUEENSLAND U. TECH. L. & JUST. J. 219 (2005)

Lessig, *Does Copyright Have Limits* (2005)

Lessig, Laurence

THE FUTURE OF IDEAS: THE FATE OF THE COMMONS IN A CONNECTED WORLD (Random House 2001)

LESSIG, THE FUTURE OF IDEAS (2001)

Lessig, Laurence

REMIX: MAKING ART AND COMMERCE THRIVE IN THE HYBRID ECONOMY (Penguin Press 2008)

LESSIG, REMIX (2008)

Lessig, Laurence

FREE CULTURE (Penguin Press 2004)

LESSIG, FREE CULTURE (2004)

Lessig, Laurence

The Creative Commons, 65 MONT. L. REV. 1 (2004)

Lessig, *The Creative Commons* (2004)

Lethem, Jonathan

The Ecstasy of Influence: A Plagiarism, HARPER'S, Feb. 2007, 59–71

Lethem, *The Ecstasy of Influence* (2007)

Levi, Leonard W.
Property as a Human Right, 5 CONSTITUTIONAL COMMENTARY (1988)
Levi, *Property as a Human Right* (1988)

Liebowitz, Stan J.
Copyright Reconsidered: A Review of Promises to Keep, 21 ISSUES IN SCIENCE AND TECHNOLOGY 92–95 (2005)
Liebowitz, *Copyright Reconsidered: A Review of Promises to Keep* (2005)

Liebowitz, Stan J.
Copyright in the Post-Napstar World: Legal or Market Solutions?, in COPY FIGHTS, THE FUTURE OF INTELLECTUAL PROPERTY IN THE INFORMATION AGE 197–204 (Adam Thierer & Wayne Crews eds.) (CATO Institute 2002)
Liebowitz, *Copyright in the Post-Napstar World: Legal or Market Solutions?* (2002)

Lipton, Jacqueline D.
Solving the Digital Piracy Puzzle, Disaggregating Fair Use from the DMCA's Anti-Device Provisions, 19 HARV. J.L. & TECH. 111 (2005)
Lipton, *Solving the Digital Piracy Puzzle* (2005)

Lipton, Jacqueline D.
The Law of Unintended Consequences: The Digital Millennium Copyright Act and Interoperability, 62 WASH. & LEE L. REV. 487 (2005)
Lipton, *The Law of Unintended Consequences: The Digital Millennium Copyright Act and Interoperability* (2005)

Litman, Jessica
The Exclusive Right to Read, 13 CARDOZO ART & ENTM'T L.J. 29 (1994)
Litman, *The Exclusive Right to Read* (1994)

Litman, Jessica
The Public Domain, 39 EMORY L.J. 965 (1990)
Litman, *The Public Domain* (1990)

Litman, Jessica
Sharing and Stealing, 27 HASTINGS COMMUN. & ENTM'T L. J. 1 (2004)
Litman, *Sharing and Stealing* (2004)

Litman, Jessica
DIGITAL COPYRIGHT (Prometheus Books, 2001)
Litman, DIGITAL COPYRIGHT (2001)

Liu, Joseph P.
Copyright Law's Theory of the Consumer, 44 B.C. L. REV. 397 (2003)
Liu, *Copyright Law's Theory of the Consumer* (2003)

Locke, John
TWO TREATISES OF GOVERNMENT AND A LETTER CONCERNING TOLERATION (Ian Shapiro ed.) (Yale University Press 2003)(1689)
LOCKE, TWO TREATISES OF GOVERNMENT (2003/1689)

Locke, John
AN ESSAY CONCERNING HUMAN UNDERSTANDING (13th. ed.)
(Willian Tegg 1849)
LOCKE, AN ESSAY CONCERNING HUMAN UNDERSTANDING (1849)

Loewenheim, Ulrich (ed.)
HANDBUCH DES URHEBERRECHTS (C.H. Beck 2003)
LOEWENHEIM, HANDBUCH DES URHEBERRECHTS (2003)

Long, Clarisa
Information Costs in Patent and Copyright, 90 VA. L. REV. 465 (2004)
Long, *Information Costs in Patent and Copyright* (2004)

Loren, Lydia P.
Building a Reliable Semicommons of Creative Works, 14 GEO. MASON L. REV. 271 (2007)
Loren, *Building a Reliable Semicommons of Creative Works* (2007)

Lunney, Glynn S., Jr.
The Death of Copyright: Digital Technology, Private Copying, and the Digital Millennium Copyright Act, 87 VA. L. REV. 813 (2001)
Lunney, *The Death of Copyright* (2001)

Madison, Michael J.
Law as Design: Objects, Concepts and Digital Things, 56 CASE W. RES. L. REV. 381 (2005)
Madison, *Law as Design* (2005)

Madison, Michael J.
Fair Use and Social Practices, *in* 1 INTELLECTUAL PROPERTY AND INFORMATION WEALTH 177–99 (Peter K. Yu ed.) (Praeger 2007)
Madison, *Fair Use and Social Practices* (2007)

Mantz, Reto
Creative Commons-Lizenzen im Spiegel Internationaler Gerichtsverfahren, 2008 (1) GRUR-INT. 20 (2008)
Mantz, *Creative Commons-Lizenzen im Spiegel Internationaler Gerichtsverfahren* (2008)

Martin-Prat, Maria
The Relationship between Protection and Exceptions in the EU "Information Society" Directive, *in* ADJUNCTS AND ALTERNATIVES TO COPYRIGHT 466–76, ALAI-USA (2002)
Martin-Prat, *The Relationship between Protection and Exceptions in the EU "Information Society" Directive* (2002)

Masouyé, Claude
GUIDE TO THE BERNE CONVENTION FOR THE PROTECTION OF LITERARY AND ARTISTIC WORKS (WIPO 1978)
MASOUYÉ, GUIDE TO THE BERNE CONVENTION (1978)

McAfee, Preston R.
Price Discrimination, *in* ISSUES IN COMPETITION LAW AND POLICY (American Bar Association 2008)
McAfee, *Price Discrimination* (2008)

McCrudden, Christopher
The Future of the EU Charter of Fundamental Rights, Jean Monnet Working Paper No. 10/01 (2002)
McCrudden, *The Future of the EU Charter of Fundamental Rights* (2002)

McEwen, William
Communication Innovation and Change, in COMMUNICATION AND BEHAVIOR 197–207 (Gerhard J. Hanneman & William J. McEwen eds.) (Addison-Wesley 1975)
McEwen, *Communication Innovation and Change* (1975)

McGowan, David
Copyright Neoconsequentialism, 69 MO. L. REV. 1 (2004)
McGowan, *Copyright Neoconsequentialism* (2004)

McLuhan, Marshall
UNDERSTANDING MEDIA: THE EXTENSIONS OF MAN (MIT Press 1964)
MCLUHAN, UNDERSTANDING MEDIA (1964)

Menell, Peter
Intellectual Property: General Theories, in 2 ENCYCLOPEDIA OF LAW AND ECONOMICS (Boudewijn Bouckaert & Gerrit de Geest eds.) (Edward Elger 2001)
Menell, *Intellectual Property: General Theories* (2001)

Menell, Peter S.
Indirect Copyright Liability and Technological Innovation, 32 COLUM. J.L. & ARTS 375
Menell, *Indirect Copyright Liability and Technological Innovation* (2009)

Merges, Robert P. et al.
INTELLECTUAL PROPERTY IN THE NEW TECHNOLOGICAL AGE (4th. ed.) (Aspen 2006)
MERGER ET AL., INTELLECTUAL PROPERTY IN THE NEW TECHNOLOGICAL AGE (2006)

Merges, Robert P.
A New Dynamism in the Public Domain, 71 U. CHI. L. REV. 183 (2004)
Merges, *A New Dynamism in the Public Domain* (2004)

Merges, Robert P.
Compulsory Licensing vs. the Three "Golden Oldies": Property Rights, Contracts, and Markets, Cato Institute, Policy Analysis No. 508, Jan. 15, 2004
Merges, *Compulsory Licensing vs. the Three "Golden Oldies": Property Rights, Contracts, and Markets* (2004)

Merges, Robert P.
Contracting into Liability Rules: Intellectual Property Rights and Collective Rights Organizations, 84 CA. L. REV. 1293 (1996)
Merges, *Contracting into Liability Rules: Intellectual Property Rights and Collective Rights Organizations* (1996)

Merrill, Thomas W.
Property and the Right to Exclude, 77 NEB. L. REV. 730 (1998)
Merrill, *Property and the Right to Exclude* (1998)

Merrill, Thomas W.
Property Rules, Liability Rules, and Adverse Possession, 79 NW U. L. REV. 1122 (1984)
Merrill, *Property Rules, Liability Rules, and Adverse Possession* (1984)

Merrill, Thomas W. & Smith, Henry E.
The Property/Contract Interface, 101 COLUM. L. REV. 773 (2001)
Merrill & Smith, *The Property/Contract Interface* (2001)

Merrill, Thomas W. & Smith, Henry E.
Optimal Standardization in the Law of Property: The Numerus Clausus Principle, 110 YALE L.J. 1 (2000)
Merrill & Smith, *The Numerus Clausus Principle* (2000)

Merrill, Thomas W. & Smith, Henry E.
What Happened to Property in Law and Economics?, 111 YALE L.J. 357 (2001)
Merrill & Smith, *What Happened to Property?* (2001)

Michelman, Frank I.
Property, Utility, and Fairness: Comments on the Ethical Foundations of "Just Compensation" Law, 80 HARV. L. REV. 1165 (1967)
Michelman, *Property, Utility, and Fairness: Comments on the Ethical Foundations of "Just Compensation" Law* (1967)

Miller, Ernest & Feigenbaum, Joan
Taking the Copy Out of Copyright, Digital Rights Management Workshop 233–44 (2001) (available at http://www.cs.yale.edu/homes/jf/MF.pdf)
Miller & Feigenbaum, *Taking the Copy Out of Copyright* (2001)

Milgate, Murray
Goods and Commodities, in THE NEW PALGRAVE: A DICTIONARY OF ECONOMICS (John Eatwell et al. eds.) (Macmillan 1987)
Milgate, *Goods and Commodities* (1987)

Mills, John G. et al.
PATENT LAW FUNDAMENTALS (Thomson-West 2008)
MILLS ET AL., PATENT LAW FUNDAMENTALS (2008)

Mortimer, Julie H.
Price Discrimination, Copyright Law, and Technological Innovation: Evidence from the Introduction of DVDs, National Bureau of Economic Research, NBER Paper No. 11676 (2006) (available at http://mortimer.fas.harvard.edu/06dvd1117.pdf)
Mortimer, *Price Discrimination, Copyright Law, and Technological Innovation* (2006)

Mossoff, Adam
Who Cares What Thomas Jefferson Thought About Patents? Reevaluating the Patent "Privilege" in Historical Context, 92 CORNELL L. REV. 953 (2007)
Mossoff, *Who Cares What Thomas Jefferson Thought About Patents?* (2007)

Mossoff, Adam
Is Copyright Property?, 42 SAN DIEGO L. REV. 29 (2005)
Mossoff, *Is Copyright Property?* (2005)

Mossoff, Adam
What Is Property? Putting the Pieces Back Together, 45 ARIZ. L. REV. 371 (2003)
Mossoff, *What Is Property?* (2003)

Motta, Massimo
COMPETITION POLICY: THEORY AND PRACTICE (Cambridge University Press 2004)
MOTTA, COMPETITION POLICY (2004)

Mulligan, Deirdre & Burstein, Aaron
Implementing Copyright Limitations in Rights Expression Languages, online paper (2002) (available at http://crypto.stanford.edu/DRM2002/mulligan_burstein_acm_drm_2002.doc)
Mulligan & Burstein, *Implementing Copyright Limitations in Rights Expression Languages* (2002)

Mulligan, Deirdre & Perzanowski, Aaron K.
The Magnificence of the Disaster: Reconstructing the Sony BMG Rootkit Incident, 22 Berkeley Tech. L.J. 1157 (2007)
Mulligan & Perzanowski, *The Magnificence of the Disaster: Reconstructing the Sony BMG Rootkit Incident* (2007)

Munzer, Stephan R.
A Theory of Property (Cambridge University Press 1990)
Munzer, A Theory of Property (1990)

Netanel, Neil W.
Copyright Alienability Restrictions and the Enhancement of Author Autonomy: A Normative Evaluation, 24 Rutgers L.J. 347 (1993)
Netanel, *Alienability Restrictions* (1993)

Netanel, Neil W.
Impose a Noncommercial Use Levy to Allow Free Peer-to-Peer File Sharing, 17 Harv. J.L. & Tech. 1 (2003)
Netanel, *Impose a Noncommercial Use Levy to Allow Free Peer-to-Peer File Sharing* (2003)

Netanel, Neil W.
Copyright's Paradox (Oxford University Press 2008)
Netanel, Copyright's Paradox (2008)

Nicholson, Bradley, J.
The Ghost in the Machine: MAI Systems Corp. v. Peak Computer, Inc. and the Problem of Copying in RAM, 10 High Tech. L. J. 147 (1995)
Nicholson, *The Ghost in the Machine: MAI Systems and the Problem of Copying in RAM* (1995)

Nimmer, David
A Riff on Fair Use in the Digital Millennium Copyright Act, 148 U. Pa. L. Rev. 673 (2000)
Nimmer, *A Riff on Fair Use* (2000)

Nimmer, David
Appreciating Legislative History: The Sweet and Sour Spots of the DMCA's Commentary, 23 Cardozo L. Rev. 909 (2002)
Nimmer, *Appreciating Legislative History: The Sweet and Sour Spots of the DMCA's Commentary* (2002)

Nimmer, David
Codifying Copyright Comprehensibility, 51 UCLA L. Rev. 1233 (2004)
Nimmer, *Codifying Copyright Comprehensibility* (2004)

Nimmer, David
Ignoring the Public, Part I: On the Absurd Complexity of the Digital Audio Transmission Right, 7 UCLA Entm't L. Rev. 189 (2000)
Nimmer, *Ignoring the Public, Part I: On the Absurd Complexity of the Digital Audio Transmission Right* (2000)

Nimmer, Melville B. & Nimmer, David
Nimmer on Copyright (Matthew Bender 2006)
Nimmer on Copyright (2006)

Nimmer, Melville B.
Does Copyright Abridge the First Amendment Guarantees of Free Speech and Press?, 17 UCLA L. Rev. 1180 (1970)
Nimmer, *Does Copyright Abridge the First Amendment Guarantees of Free Speech and Press?* (1970)

Nimmer, Melville B.
New Technologies and the Law of Copyright: Reprography and Computers, 15 UCLA L. Rev. 931 (1968)
Nimmer, *New Technologies and the Law of Copyright* (1968)

Nimmer, Raymond T.
Information Law (West 2007)
Nimmer, Information Law (2007)

Nordemann, Wilhelm et al.
International Copyright and Neighboring Rights Law, VCH (Weinheim 1990)
Nordemann et al., International Copyright (1990)

Nordemann, Wilhelm
Der Begriff der „angemessenen Bedingungen" in § 6 Absatz 1 Wahrnehmungsgesetz, (6–7) 1973 GRUR-Int. 306 (1973)
Nordemann, *Der Begriff der „angemessenen Bedingungen "in § 6 Absatz 1 Wahrnehmungsgesetz* (1973)

Nozick, Robert
Anarchy, State and Utopia (Basic Books 1974)
Nozick, Anarchy, State and Utopia (1974)

Nyquist, Chris
Teaching Wesley Hohfeld's Theory of Legal Relations, 52 J. Legal Educ. 238 (2002)
Nyquist, *Teaching Wesley Hohfeld* (2002)

Ogden, C.K. & Richards, I.A.
The Meaning of Meaning (Harcourt Brace Jovanovich 1989) (1923)
Ogden & Richards, The Meaning of Meaning (1989/1923)

Ohly, Ansgar
Gibt es einen Numerus clausus der Immaterialgüterrechte?, in Perspektiven des Geistigen Eigentums und Wettbewerbsrechts, Festschrift für Gerhard Schricker zum 70. Geburtstag (H.C. Beck 2005)
Ohly, *Gibt es einen Numerus Clausus der Immaterialgüterrechte?* (2005)

Okediji, Ruth
Toward an International Fair Use Doctrine, 39 Colum. J. Transnat'l L. 75 (2000)
Okediji, *Toward an International Fair Use Doctrine* (2000)

Oliar, Dotan
Making Sense of the Intellectual Property Clause: Promotion of Progress as a Limitation on Congress's Intellectual Property Power, 94 Geo. L.J. 1771 (2006)
Oliar, *Making Sense of the Intellectual Property Clause* (2006)

Olson, James M. & Zanna, Mark P.
Attitudes and Attitude Change, 44 Ann. Rev. Psychol. 117–54 (1993)
Olson & Zanna, *Attitudes and Attitude Change* (1993)

Olswang, Simon
Accessright: An Evolutionary Path for Copyright into the Digital Era, 17 EUR. INTEL. PROP. REV. 215–18 (1995)
Olswang, *Accessright* (1995)

Otto Palandt
BÜRGERLICHES GESETZBUCH (66th. ed.) (C.H. Beck 2007)
Palandt, *Bürgerliches Gesetzbuch* (2007)

Palmer, Tom G.
Intellectual Property: A Non-Posnerian Law and Economics Approach, 12 HAMLINE L. REV. 261 (1989)
Palmer, *Intellectual Property: A Non-Posnerian Law and Economics Approach* (1989)

Palmer, Tom G.
Are Patents and Copyrights Morally Justified? The Philosophy of Property Rights and Ideal Objects, in COPY FIGHTS, THE FUTURE OF INTELLECTUAL PROPERTY IN THE INFORMATION AGE (Adam Thierer & Wayne Crews eds.) (CATO Institute 2002)
Palmer, *Are Patents and Copyrights Morally Justified? The Philosophy of Property Rights and Ideal Objects* (2002)

Parchomovsky, Gideon & Goldman, Kevin A.
Fair Use Harbors, 93 VA. L. REV. 1483 (2007)
Parchomovsky & Goldman, *Fair Use Harbors* (2007)

Paskin, Norman
Components of DRM Systems— Identification and Metadata, in DIGITAL RIGHTS MANAGEMENT: TECHNOLOGICAL, ECONOMIC, LEGAL AND POLITICAL ASPECTS 26-61 (Eberhard Becker et al. eds.) (Springer 2003)
Paskin, *DRMS Identification and Metadata Components* (2003)

Patry, William F.
PATRY ON COPYRIGHT (Thomson-West 2007)
PATRY ON COPYRIGHT (2007)

Patterson, Lyman R.
Understanding the Copyright Clause, 47 J. COPYRIGHT SOC'Y U.S.A. 365 (2000)
Patterson, *Understanding the Copyright Clause* (2000)

Patterson, Lyman R.
The DMCA: A Modern Version of the Licensing Act of 1662, 10 J. INTEL. PROP. L. 33 (2002)
Patterson, *The DMCA: A Modern Version of the Licensing Act of 1662* (2002)

Patterson, Lyman R.
COPYRIGHT IN HISTORICAL PERSPECTIVE (Vanderbilt University Press 1968)
PATTERSON, COPYRIGHT IN HISTORICAL PERSPECTIVE (1968)

Patterson, Lyman R.
THE NATURE OF COPYRIGHT: A LAW OF USERS' RIGHTS (University of Georgia Press 1991)
PATTERSON, THE NATURE OF COPYRIGHT: A LAW OF USERS' RIGHTS (1991)

Peifer, Karl-Nikolaus
The Return of the Commons—Copyright History as a Helpful Source?, 6 IIC 679–88 (2008)
Peifer, *The Return of the Commons—Copyright History as a Helpful Source?* (2008)

Peltz, Richard J.

Global Warming Trend? The Creeping Indulgence of Fair Use in International Copyright Law, 17 TEX. INTELL. PROP. L.J. 267 (2009)

Peltz, *Global Warming Trend? The Creeping Indulgence of Fair Use in International Copyright Law* (2009)

Penner, James E.

THE IDEA OF PROPERTY IN LAW (Oxford University Press, 1997)

PENNER, THE IDEA OF PROPERTY (1997)

Perlmutter, Shira

Freeing Copyright from Formalities, 13 CARDOZO ARTS & ENTM'T L.J. 565 (1995)

Perlmutter, *Freeing Copyright from Formalities* (1995)

Pessach, Guy

The Author's Moral Right of Integrity in Cyberspace—A Preliminary Normative Framework, 3 IIC 250–70 (2003)

Pessach, *The Author's Moral Right of Integrity in Cyberspace—A Preliminary Normative Framework* (2003)

Peukert, Alexander

Der Schutzbereich des Urheberrechts und das Werk als öffentliches Gut, insbesondere: Die urheberrechtliche Relevanz des privaten Werkgenusses, in INTERESSENAUSGLEICH IN URHEBERRECHT 11–46 (Reto K. Hilty & Alexander Peukert eds.) (Nomos 2004)

Peukert, *Der Schutzbereich des Urheberrechts und das Werk als öffentliches Gut* (2004)

Peukert, Alexander

A Bipolar Copyright System for the Digital Network Environment, 28 HASTINGS COMMUN. & ENTM'T L.J. (2005)

Peukert, *A Bipolar Copyright System for the Digital Network Environment* (2005)

Peukert, Alexander

GÜTERZUORDNUNG ALS RECHTSPRINZIP 138 (Mohr Siebeck 2008)

PEUKERT, GÜTERZUORDNUNG ALS RECHTSPRINZIP (2008)

Pierce, John R.

AN INTRODUCTION TO INFORMATION THEORY: SYMBOLS, SIGNALS AND NOISE (2d ed.) (Dover 1980)

PIERCE, AN INTRODUCTION TO INFORMATION THEORY (1980)

Pigou, Arthur C.

THE ECONOMICS OF WELFARE (4th ed.) (Macmillan 1932) (1920)

PIGOU, THE ECONOMICS OF WELFARE (1932/1920)

Poeppel, Jan

DIE NEUORDNUNG DER URHEBERRECHTLICHEN SCHRANKEN IM DIGITALEN UMFELD (V&R 2006)

POEPPEL, DIE NEUORDNUNG DER URHEBERRECHTLICHEN SCHRANKEN IM DIGITALEN UMFELD (2006)

Posner, Richard A.

ECONOMIC ANALYSIS OF LAW (7th. ed.) (Wolters Kluwer 2007)

POSNER, ECONOMIC ANALYSIS OF LAW (2007)

Radin, Margaret Jane
Incomplete Commodification in the Computerized World, in THE COMMODIFICATION OF INFORMATION 3–21 (Neil W. Netanel & Niva Elkin-Koren eds.) (Kluwer 2002)
Radin, *Incomplete Commodification* (2002)

Radin, Margaret Jane
Property and Personhood, 34 STAN. L. REV. 957 (1982)
Radin, *Property and Personhood* (1982)

Rauterberg, Matthias
About a Framework for Information and Information Processing of Learning Systems in Information System, in INFORMATION SYSTEM CONCEPTS 54–69, IFIP Working Group 8.1, (Eckhard D. Falkenberg & Wolfgang Hesse eds.) (Chapman & Hall 1995)
Rauterberg, *Framework for Information* (1995)

Reese, Anthony
Will Merging Access Controls and Rights Controls Undermine the Structure of Anticircumvention Law?, 18 BERKELEY TECH. L.J. 619 (2003)
Reese, *Will Merging Access Controls and Rights Controls Undermine the Structure of Anticircumvention Law?* (2003)

Reidenberg, Joel R.
Lex Informatica: The Formulation of Information Policy Rules through Technology, 76 TEX. L. REV. 553 (1998)
Reidenberg, *Lex Informatica: The Formulation of Information Policy Rules through Technology* (1988)

Reinbothe, Jörg & von Lewinski, Silke
THE WIPO TREATIES 1996: COMMENTARY AND LEGAL ANALYSIS (Butterworths Lexis Nexis 2002)
REINBOTHE & VON LEWINSKI, THE WIPO TREATIES 1996 (2002)

Reinbothe, Jörg
Protection of Digital Content and DRM Technologies in the European Union, European Copyright—Yesterday, Today, Tomorrow, in DIGITAL RIGHTS MANAGEMENT: TECHNOLOGICAL, ECONOMIC, LEGAL AND POLITICAL ASPECTS 405–17 (Eberhard Becker et al. eds.) (Springer 2003)
Reinbothe, *European Copyright—Yesterday, Today, Tomorrow* (2003)

Ricketson, Sam & Ginsburg, Jane C.
BERNE CONVENTION AND BEYOND: INTERNATIONAL COPYRIGHT AND NEIGHBOURING RIGHTS (2d ed.) (Oxford University Press 2006)
RICKETSON & GINSBURG, BERNE CONVENTION (2006)

Ricketson, Sam
THE BERNE CONVENTION FOR THE PROTECTION OF LITERARY AND ARTISTIC WORKS (Center for Commercial Law Studies, Queen Mary College 1987)
RICKETSON, THE BERNE CONVENTION (1987)

Rigamonti, Cyrill P.
Deconstructing Moral Rights, 47 HARV. INT'L L.J. 353 (2006)
Rigamonti, *Deconstructing Moral Rights* (2006)

Rigamonti, Cyrill P.
Schutz gegen Umgehung technischer Maßnahmen im Urheberrecht aus internationaler und rechtsvergleichende Perspektive, 2005(1) GRUR-Int. 1 (2005)
Rigamonti, *Schutz gegen Umgehung technischer Maßnahmen im Urheberrecht* (2005)

Rose, Carol M.
Possession as the Origin of Property, 52 U. Chi. L. Rev. 73 (1985)
Rose, *Possession as the Origin of Property* (1985)

Rosenberg, Alexander
Philosophy of Science: A Contemporary Introduction (2d ed.) (Routledge 2005)
ROSENBERG, Philosophy Of Science (2005)

Rothchild, John A.
Economic Analysis of Technological Protection Measures, 84 Or. L. Rev. 489 (2005)
Rothchild, *Economic Analysis of Technological Protection Measures* (2005)

Rothchild, John A.
The Social Costs of Technological Protection Measures, 34 Fla. St. U.L. Rev. 1181 (2007)
Rothchild, *The Social Costs of Technological Protection Measures* (2007)

Röthlisberger, Ernst
Berner Übereinkunft zum Schutz von Werken der Literatur und Kunst und die Zusatzabkommen (A. Francke Bern 1906)
Röthlisberger, Berner Übereinkunft zum Schutz von Werken der Literatur und Kunst (1906)

Rump, Niels
Digital Rights Management: Technological Aspects, *in* Digital Rights Management: Technological, Economic, Legal and Political Aspects 3–15 (Eberrhard Becker et al. eds.) (Springer 2003)
Rump, *Digital Rights Management: Technological Aspects* (2003)

Runge, Philipp
Die Vereinbarkeit einer Content-Flatrate für Musik mit dem Drei-Stufen-Test, 2007(2) GRUR. Int. 130 (2007)
Runge, *Die Vereinbarkeit einer Content-Flatrate für Musik mit dem Drei-Stufen-Test* (2007)

Sadeghi, Ahmad-Reza & Schneider, Markus
Components of DRM Systems—Electronic Payment Systems, *in* Digital Rights Management: Technological, Economic, Legal and Political Aspects 113–37 (Eberhard Becker et al. (eds.) (Springer 2003)
Sadeghi & Schneider, *DRM Electronic Payment Systems* (2003)

Samuelson, Pamela
CONTU Revisited, The Case Against Copyright Protection for Computer Programs in Machine-Readable Form, 1984 Duke L.J. 663 (1984)
Samuelson, *CONTU Revisited, The Case Against Copyright Protection for Computer Programs in Machine-Readable Form* (1984)

Samuelson, Pamela
Google Book Search and the Future of Books in Cyberspace, 94 Minn. L. Rev.1308 (2010)
Samuelson, *Google Book Search and the Future of Books in Cyberspace* (2010)

Samuelson, Pamela
Intellectual Property and the Digital Economy: Why the Anti-Circumvention Regulations Need to Be Revised, 14 Berkeley Tech. L.J. 519 (1999)
Samuelson, *Why the Anti-Circumvention Regulations Need to Be Revised* (1999)

Samuelson, Pamela
The U.S. Digital Agenda at WIPO, 37 Va. J. Int'l L. 369 (1997)
Samuelson, *The U.S. Digital Agenda at WIPO* (1997)

Samuelson, Pamela
Why Copyright Law Excludes Systems and Processes From the Scope of its Protection, 85 Tex. L. Rev. 1921 (2007)
Samuelson, *Why Copyright Excludes Systems?* (2007)

Samuelson, Pamela
Legally Speaking: The NII Intellectual Property Report, 37 Commun. ACM 21–27 (1994)
Samuelson, *The NII Intellectual Property Report* (1994)

Samuelson, Pamela
Preliminary Thoughts on Copyright Reform, 2007 Utah L. Rev. 551
Samuelson, *Preliminary Thoughts on Copyright Reform* (2007)

Samuelson, Pamela
The Copyright Grab, Wired 4.01, Jan. 1996
Samuelson, *The Copyright Grab* (1996)

Samuelson, Pamela
DRM {and, or, vs.} the Law, 46 Commun. ACM 41 (2003)
Samuelson, *DRM {and, or, vs.} the Law* (2003)

Samuelson, Paul A.
The Pure Theory of Public Expenditure, 36 Rev. Econ. & Stat. 387 (1954)
Samuelson, *The Pure Theory of Public Expenditure* (1954)

Schack, Haimo
Urheber- und Urhebervertragsrecht (4th ed.) (Mohr Siebeck 2007)
Schack, Urheber- und Urhebervertragsrecht (2007)

Schiller, Dan
How to Think about Information (University of Illinois Press 2007)
Schiller, How To Think About Information (2007)

Schricker, Gerhard
Urheberrecht Kommentar (3d ed.) (C.H. Beck 2006)
Schricker, Urheberrecht Kommentar (2006)

Schricker, Gerhard et al. (eds.)
Konturen eines Europäischen Urheberrechts (Nomos 1996)
Schricker et al., Konturen eines Europäischen Urheberrechts (1996)

Schulz, Mark F.
Copynorms: Copyright Law and Social Norms, in 1 Intellectual Property and Information Wealth 201–35 (Peter K. Yu ed.) (Praeger 2007)

Schulz, *Copynorms: Copyright Law and Social Norms* (2007)

Shannon, Claude E.
A Mathematical Theory of Communication, 27 BELL SYS. TECH. J. 379 ff. (1948)
Shannon, *A Mathematical Theory of Communication* (1948)

Shannon, Claude E. & Weaver, Warren
THE MATHEMATICAL THEORY OF COMMUNICATION (2d ed.) (University of Illinois Press 1963)
SHANNON & WEAVER, MATHEMATICAL THEORY OF COMMUNICATION (1963)

Shapiro, Ian
Introduction: Reading Locke Today, *in* TWO TREATISES OF GOVERNMENT AND A LETTER CONCERNING TOLERATION (Ian Shapiro ed.) (Yale University Press 2003)
Shapiro, *Introduction: Reading Locke Today* (2003)

Schauer, Frederick
Must Speech Be Special?, 78 NW L. REV. 1284 (1983)
Schauer, *Must Speech Be Special?* (1983)

Schroeder, Jeanne L.
Unnatural Rights: Hegel and Intellectual Property, 60 U. MIAMI L. REV. 453 (2006)
Schroeder, *Unnatural Rights: Hegel and Intellectual Property* (2006)

Senftleben, Martin R.F.
COPYRIGHT, LIMITATIONS AND THE THREE-STEP TEST: AN ANALYSIS OF THE THREE-STEP TEST IN INTERNATIONAL AND EC COPYRIGHT LAW (Kluwer 2004)
SENFTLEBEN, COPYRIGHT, LIMITATIONS AND THE THREE-STEP TEST (2004)

Sherman, Brad & Bently, Lionel
INTELLECTUAL PROPERTY LAW (2d ed.) (Oxford University Press 2004)
SHERMAN & BENTLY, INTELLECTUAL PROPERTY LAW (2004)

Shiffrin, Seana V.
Lockean Arguments for Private Intellectual Property, *in* NEW ESSAYS IN THE LEGAL AND POLITICAL THEORY OF PROPERTY 138–67 (Stephen R. Munzer ed.) (Cambridge University Press 2001)
Shiffrin, *Lockean Arguments for Private Intellectual Property* (2001)

Shiffrin, Steven H. & Choper, Jesse H.
THE FIRST AMENDMENT (3d ed.) (West 2001)
SHIFFRIN & CHOPER, THE FIRST AMENDMENT (2001)

Sprigman, Christopher
Refrom(aliz)ing Copyright, 57 STAN. L. REV. 485 (2004)
Sprigman, *Refrom(aliz)ing Copyright* (2004)

Sicker, Douglas C. et al.
The Analog Hole and the Price of Music: An Empirical Study, 5 J. TELECOMMUN. & HIGH TECH. L. 573 (2007)
Sicker et al., *The Analog Hole and the Price of Music* (2007)

Simmonds, Nigel E.
Introduction, *in* FUNDAMENTAL LEGAL CONCEPTIONS AS APPLIED TO JUDICIAL REASONING (Wesley Newcomb Hohfeld) (Ashgate Dartmouth 2001)
Simmonds, *Introduction* to FUNDAMENTAL LEGAL CONCEPTIONS (2001)

Simpson & Weiner
THE OXFORD ENGLISH DICTIONARY (2d ed) (Clarendon Press 1989)
OXFORD ENGLISH DICTIONARY (1989)

Smith, Adam
THE WEALTH OF NATIONS (Penguin 1970) (1776)
SMITH, THE WEALTH OF NATIONS (1970/1776)

Smith, Henry E.
Property and Property Rules, 79 N.Y.U. L. REV. 1719 (2004)
Smith, *Property and Property Rules* (2004)

Smith, Henry E.
Exclusion versus Governance: Two Strategies for Delineating Property Rights, 31 J. LEGAL STUD. 453 (2002)
Smith, *Exclusion versus Governance* (2002)

Smith, Henry E.
Intellectual Property as Property: Delineating Entitlements in Information, 116 YALE L.J. 1742 (2007)
Smith, *Intellectual Property as Property* (2007)

Singer, Joseph W.
The Legal Rights Debate in Analytical Jurisprudence from Bentham to Hohfeld, 1982 WIS. L. REV. 975 (1982)
Singer, *The Legal Rights Debate* (1982)

Sirinelli, Pierre
Exception and Limits to Copyright and Neighboring Rights, WIPO document WCT-WTTP/IMP/1, Workshop on Implementation Issues of the WCT and the WPPT, Dec. 3, Geneva 1999
Sirinelli, *Exception and Limits to Copyright* (1999)

Sirinelli, Pierre
The Scope of the Prohibition on Circumvention of Technological Measures: Exceptions, in ADJUNCTS AND ALTERNATIVES TO COPYRIGHT 384–414, ALAI-USA & Kernochan Center for Law, Media and the Arts, Columbia University Law School, New York 2002
Sirinelli, *The Scope of the Prohibition on Circumvention of Technological Measures: Exceptions* (2002)

Smolla, Rodney, A & Nimmer, Melville B.
SMOLLA & NIMMER ON FREEDOM OF SPEECH (Thomson-West 2008)
SMOLLA & NIMMER, FREEDOM OF SPEECH (2008)

Sobel, Lionel S.
Copyright and the First Amendment: A Gathering Storm?, 19 Copyright Law Symposium (ASCAP) 43 (1971)
Sobel, *Copyright and the First Amendment: A Gathering Storm?* (1971)

Spenger, Gabriele
Authentication, Identification Technique, and Secure Containers, in DIGITAL RIGHTS MANAGEMENT: TECHNOLOGICAL, ECONOMIC, LEGAL AND POLITICAL ASPECTS 62–80 (Eberhard Becker et al. eds.) (Springer 2003)
Spenger, *Authentication, Identification Technique, and Secure Containers* (2003)

Stallberg, Christian G.
URHEBERRECHT UND MORALISCHE RECHTFERTIGUNG (Duncker & Humbolt 2006)
STALLBERG, URHEBERRECHT UND MORALISCHE RECHTFERTIGUNG (2006)

Stein, Peter
ROMAN LAW IN EUROPEAN HISTORY (Cambridge University Press 1999)
STEIN, ROMAN LAW IN EUROPEAN HISTORY (1999)

Steiner, Christine
Intellectual Property and the Right to Culture, in INTELLECTUAL PROPERTY AND HUMAN RIGHTS, WIPO Panel Discussion to commemorate the 50th Anniversary of the Universal Declaration of Human Rights, Geneva, Nov. 9, 1988 (1999)
Steiner, *Intellectual Property and the Right to Culture* (1999)

Steup, Matthias
The Analysis of Knowledge, in STANFORD ENCYCLOPEDIA OF PHILOSOPHY (Edward N. Zalta ed., Winter ed. 2005) (available at http://plato.stanford.edu/archives/win2005/entries/knowledge-analysis)
Steup, *The Analysis of Knowledge* (2005)

Stillman, Peter G.
Property, Freedom, and Individuality in Hegel's and Marx's Political Thought, in NOMOS XXII, PROPERTY 130 (J. Roland Pennock & John W. Chapman eds. (NYU Press 1980)
Stillman, *Property, Freedom, and Individuality in Hegel's and Marx's Political Thought* (1980)

Strowel, Alain & Dusollier, Séverine
Legal Protection of Technological Systems, WIPO document, WCT-WTTP/IMP/2—Workshop on Implementation Issues of the WIPO WCT and the WPPT, Dec. 6–7, 1999, Geneva 1999
Strowel & Dusollier, *Legal Protection of Technological Systems* (1999)

Sun, Andy Y.
The Law on Anti-Circumvention and Digital Rights Management, in COPYRIGHT LAW AND THE INFORMATION SOCIETY IN ASIA, 26 IIC Studies (Heath & Liu eds.) (Hart 2007)
Sun, *The Law on Anti-Circumvention and Digital Rights Management* (2007)

Tehranian, John
Infringement Nation, 2007(3) UTAH L. REV. 537 (2007)
Tehranian, *Infringement Nation* (2007)

Torremans, Paul L.C.
Copyright as a Human Right, in COPYRIGHT AND HUMAN RIGHTS 1–20 (Paul L. C. Torremans ed.) (Kluwer 2004)
Torremans, *Copyright as a Human Right* (2004)

Trayer, Martin
TECHNISCHE SCHUTZMASSNAHMEN UND ELEKTRONISCHE RECHTEWAHRNEHMUNGSSYSTEME (Nomos 2003)
TRAYER, TECHNISCHE SCHUTZMASSNAHMEN (2003)

Treiger-Bar-Am, Kim
Kant on Copyright: Rights of Transformative Authorship, 25 CARDOZO ARTS & ENTM'T L.J. 1059 (2008)

Treiger-Bar-Am, *Kant on Copyright: Rights of Transformative Authorship* (2008)

Tushnet, Rebecca
Copy This Essay: How Fair Use Doctrine Harms Free Speech and How Copying Serves It, 114 YALE L.J. 535 (2004)
Tushnet, *Copy This Essay* (2004)

Tuttle, Herbert
Video Streaming, in 3 THE INTERNET ENCYCLOPEDIA 554–66 (Hossein Bidgoli ed.) (Wiley 2004)
Tuttle, *Video Streaming* (2004)

Tyerman, Barry W.
The Economic Rationale for Copyright Protection for Published Books: A Reply to Professor Breyer, 18 UCLA L. REV. 1100 (1971)
Tyerman, *The Economic Rationale for Copyright Protection for Published Books: A Reply to Professor Breyer* (1971)

Ulmer, Eugen
Copyright Problems Arising from the Computer Storage and Retrieval of Protected Works, 8 COPYRIGHT 37–59 (1972)
Ulmer, *Copyright Problems Arising from the Computer Storage* (1972)

Ulmer, Eugen
URHEBER- UND VERLAGSRECHT (3. AUF.) (Springer 1980)
ULMER, URHEBER– UND VERLAGSRECHT (1980)

Ulmer-Eilfort, Constanze, *Private Copying and Levies for Information and Communication Technologies and Storage Media in Europe, in* DIGITAL RIGHTS MANAGEMENT: TECHNOLOGICAL, ECONOMIC, LEGAL AND POLITICAL ASPECTS 447–61 (Eberhard Becker et al. eds.) (Springer 2003)
Ulmer-Eilfort, *Private Copying and Levies for Information and Communication Technologies and Storage Media in Europe* (2003)

Van Houweling, Molly Shaffer
The New Servitudes, 96 GEO. L.J. 885 (2008)
Van Houweling, *The New Servitudes* (2008)

Varian, Hal R.
INTERMEDIATE MICROECONOMICS (6th. ed.) (W. W. Norton 2003)
VARIAN, INTERMEDIATE MICROECONOMICS (2003)

Varian, Hal R.
Differential Pricing and Efficiency, First Monday, Issue 2, online publication (available at http://www.firstmonday.dk/issues/issue2/different)
Varian, *Differential Pricing and Efficiency* (1996)

Varian, Hal R.
Pricing Information Goods, online paper (available at http://people.ischool.berkeley.edu/~hal/Papers/price-info-goods.pdf)
Varian, *Pricing Information Goods* (1995)

Varian, Hal R. et al.

THE ECONOMICS OF INFORMATION TECHNOLOGY: AN INTRODUCTION (Cambridge University Press 2004)
VARIAN ET AL. THE ECONOMICS OF INFORMATION TECHNOLOGY (2004)

Vinje, Thomas C.
A Brave New World of Technical Protection Systems: Will There Still Be Room for Copyright, 18 EUR. INTEL. PROP. REV. 431–40 (1996)
Vinje, *A Brave New World of Technical Protection Systems: Will There Still Be Room for Copyright* (1996)

Vivant, Michel
Le droit d'auteur, un droit de l'homme, [1997] 174 R.I.D.A. 60
Vivant, *Le droit d'auteur, un droit de l'homme* (1997)

von Lewinski, Silke
Stakeholder Consultation on Copyright Levies in a Converging World—Response of the Max Planck Institute for Intellectual Property, Munich, 1 IIC 65 (2007)
von Lewinski, *Stakeholder Consultation on Copyright Levies in a Converging World* (2007)

von Lewinski, Silke
Der EG-Richtlinienvorschlag zum Urheberrecht und zu verwandten Schutzrechten in der Informationsgesellschaft, (8–9) 1998 GRUR INT. 637 (1998)
von Lewinski, *Der EG-Richtlinienvorschlag zum Urheberrecht und zu verwandten Schutzrechten in der Informationsgesellschaft* (1998)

von Lewinski, Silke
INTERNATIONAL COPYRIGHT LAW AND POLICY (Oxford University Press 2008)
VON LEWINSKI, INTERNATIONAL COPYRIGHT LAW AND POLICY (2008)

Waldron, Jeremy
THE RIGHT TO PRIVATE PROPERTY (Oxford University Press 1988)
WALDRON, THE RIGHT TO PRIVATE PROPERTY (1988)

Waldron, Jeremy
From Authors to Copiers: Individual Rights and Social Values in Intellectual Property, 68 CHI.-KENT L. REV. 841 (1993)
Waldron, *From Authors to Copiers: Individual Rights and Social Values in Intellectual Property* (1993)

Wallis, Roger et al.
Contested Collective Administration of Intellectual Property Rights in Music: The Challenges to the Principles of Reciprocity and Solidarity, 14 EUR. J. COMMUN. 5–35 (1999)
Wallis et al., *Contested Collective Administration of Intellectual Property Rights in Music* (1999)

Walter, Michael M. (ed.)
EUROPÄISCHES URHEBERRECHT KOMMENTAR (Springer 2001)
WALTER, EUROPÄISCHES URHEBERRECHT KOMMENTAR (2001)

Wand, Peter
TECHNISCHE SCHUTZMASSNAHMEN UND URHEBERRECHT (C.H. Beck 2001)
WAND, TECHNISCHE SCHUTZMASSNAHMEN UND URHEBERRECHT (2001)

Wandtke, Artur-Axel & Bullinger, Winfrid (eds.)
PRAXISKOMMENTAR ZUM URHEBERRECHT (2d. ed.) (Beck 2006)

WANDTKE/BULLINGER, PRAXISKOMMENTAR ZUM URHEBERRECHT (2006)

Weber, Rolf H.
Press Art—Kunst als Botschaft, in WIRTSCHAFT ZU BEGINN DES 21. JAHRHUNDERTS, Fs für Peter Nobel zum 60. Geburtstag 1143–55 (Stämpfli 2005)
Weber, *Press Art—Kunst als Botschaft* (2005)

Weinberg, Jonathan
Constitutional Protection of Commercial Speech, 82 COLUM. L. REV. 720 (1982)
Weinberg, *Constitutional Protection of Commercial Speech* (1982)

Weinberg, Jonathan
Hardware-Based ID, Rights Management, and Trusted Systems, 52 STAN. L. REV. 1251 (2000)
Weinberg, *Hardware-Based ID, Rights Management, and Trusted Systems* (2000)

Westkamp, Guido
Transient Copying and Public Communication: The Creeping Evolution of Use and Access Rights in European Copyright Law, 36 GEO. WASH. INT'L L. REV. 1057 (2004)
Westkamp, *Transient Copying and Public Communication: The Creeping Evolution of Use and Access Rights in European Copyright Law* (2004)

Whelan, Frederick, G,
Property as Artifice: Hume and Blackstone, in PROPERTY: NOMOS XXII 101–29 (J. Roland Pennock & John C. Chapman eds.) (New York University Press, 1980)
Whelan, *Property as Artifice: Hume and Blackstone* (1980)

Wolfe, Jeremy et al.
SENSATION AND PERCEPTION (Sinauer 2006)
WOLFE ET AL., SENSATION AND PERCEPTION (2006)

Wood, Allen, W.
HEGEL'S ETHICAL THOUGHT (Cambridge University Press 1990)
WOOD, HEGEL'S ETHICAL THOUGHT (1990)

Wood, Allen, W.
Editor's Introduction, in Georg Wilhelm Friedrich Hegel, ELEMENTS OF THE PHILOSOPHY OF RIGHT (Allen W. Wood ed.) (Cambridge University Press 1991)
Wood, *Editor's Introduction to Hegel's* ELEMENTS OF THE PHILOSOPHY OF RIGHT (1991)

Wu, Timothy,
Copyright's Communication Policy, 103 MICH. L. REV. 278 (2004)
Wu, *Copyright's Communication Policy* (2004)

Yoo, Christopher S.
Copyright and Public Good Economics: A Misunderstood Relation, 155 U. PA. L. REV. 635 (2007)
Yoo, *Copyright and Public Good Economics* (2007)

Yu, Peter K.
Intellectual Property and the Information Ecosystem, 2005 MICH. ST. L. REV. 1 (2005)
Yu, *Intellectual Property and the Information Ecosystem* (2005)

Yu, Peter K.
Reconceptualizing Intellectual Property Interests in a Human Rights Framework, 40 U.C. Davis L. Rev. 1039 (2007)
Yu, *Reconceptualizing Intellectual Property Interests in a Human Rights Framework* (2007)

Yu, Peter K.
Anticircumvention and Anti-Anticircumvention, 84 Denv. U. L. Rev. 13 (2006)
Yu, *Anticircumvention and Anti-Anticircumvention* (2006)

Zemer, Lior
The Idea of Authorship inn Copyright (Ashgate 2007)
Zemmer, The Idea of Authorship (2007)

Zimmerman, Diana L.
Information as Speech, Information as Goods: Some Thoughts on Marketplaces and the Bill of Rights, 33 Wm. & Mary L. Rev. 665 (1992)
Zimmerman, *Information as Speech* (1992)

TABLE OF REFERENCES

CITATION FORM	REFERENCE
Amended Settlement Agreement (2009)	Amended Settlement Agreement, The Authors Guild, Inc. & Association of American Publishers, Inc., et al., v. Google Inc., Case No. 05 CV 8136-DC (S.D.N.Y.) (signed Nov. 13, 2009)
Architectural Works Copyright Protection Act (1990)	Architectural Works Copyright Protection Act, Title VII of the Judicial Improvements Act of 1990, Pub. L. No. 101-650, 104 Stat. 5089, 5133, enacted Dec. 1, 1990
Audio Home Recording Act (1992)	U.S. Audio Home Recording Act of 1992, Pub. L. No. 102-563, 106 Stat. 4237, enacted Oct. 28, 1992
Berlin Declaration on Collectively Managed Online Rights: Compensation without Control (2004)	Berlin Declaration on Collectively Managed Online Rights: Compensation without Control, Wizard of OS 4, a communication to Jörg Reinbothe, The European Commission June 21, 2004 (available at http://wizards-of-os.org/index.php?id=1699)
Berlin Declaration on Open Access to Knowledge (2003)	Berlin Declaration on Open Access to Knowledge, Conference on Open Access to Knowledge in the Sciences and Humanities, 20-22 Oct. 2003, Berlin
Berne Convention (1971)	Berne Convention for the Protection of Literary and Artistic Works, as last amended in Paris, July 24, 1971
Canadian Copyright Act (1921)	An Act to amend and consolidate the Law relating to Copyright, 11-12 George V., Chapter 24, assented June 4, 1921
CONTU Final Report (1978)	Final Report of the National Commission on New Technology Uses of Copyrighted Works, July 31, 1978, Library of Congress (1978)
Copyright Amendment, Pub. L. No. 96-517 (1980)	U.S. Copyright Amendment of 1980, Pub. L. No. 96-517, Pub. L. No. 96-517, 94 Stat. 3015, 3028 (amending §101 and §117, title 17, U.S. Code, regarding computer programs), enacted Dec. 12, 1980
Copyright Levies Backgrounder (2007)	Copyright Levies Backgrounder, Copyright Levies Reform Alliance, Feb. 8, 2007

Declaration on the "Three-Step Test" in Copyright Law (2008)	Declaration: A Balanced Interpretation of the "Three-Step Test" in Copyright Law, Max Planck Institute for Intellectual Property, Competition and Tax Law, Munich (available at http://www.ip.mpg.de/shared/data/pdf/declaration_three_step_test_final_english.pdf)
Digital Performance Right in Sound Recordings Act (1995)	Digital Performance Right in Sound Recordings Act, Pub. L No. 104-39, 109 Stat. 336, Nov. 1, 1995
DMCA (1988)	Digital Millennium Copyright Act, Pub. L. No. 105-304, 112 Stat. 2860 ff., enacted Oct. 28, 1998
DMCA House Conference Report 105-796 (1998)	DMCA House Conference Report 105-796, U.S. House of Representatives Conference Report No. 105-796, 105th Congress, 2d. Session, Oct. 8, 1998
DMCA House Report 105-551 (I) (1998)	DMCA House Report (I), U.S. House of Representatives Report Nr. 105-551 (II), 105th Congress, 2nd. Session, July 22, 1998
DMCA House Report 105-551 (II) (1998)	DMCA House Report (II), U.S. House of Representatives Report Nr. 105-551 (II), 105th Congress, 2nd. Session, July 22, 1998
DMCA Rulemaking (2000)	DMCA Rulemaking 2000, Rules and Regulations, Library of, Congress, 37 CFR Part 201, 65 F.R. 64556-01, Oct. 27, 2000
DMCA Rulemaking (2003)	DMCA Rulemaking 2003, Rules and Regulations, Library of Congress, 37 CFR Part 201, 68 F.R. 62011 ff., Oct. 31, 2003
DMCA Rulemaking (2006)	DMCA Rulemaking 2006, Rules and Regulations, Library of Congress, 37 CFR Part 201, 71 F.R. 68472 ff., Nov. 27, 2006
DMCA Senate Report (1998)	DMCA Senate Report, U.S. Senate Report No. 105-1May 90, 11, 1998
E.C. Conditional Access Directive (1988)	Directive 98/84/EC of the European Parliament and of the Council of November 20, 1998 on the legal protection of services based on, or consisting of, conditional access, Official Journal L 320, 28/11/1998 P. 0054 - 0057
E.C. Directive on Public Access to environmental Information (2003)	Directive 2003/4/EC of the European Parliament and of the Council of January 28, 2003, Directive on public access to environmental information, 2003/4/EC (Jan. 28, 2003)
E.C. Follow-Up to the Green Paper (1991)	Follow-Up to the Green Paper—working program of the Commission in the field of copyright and neighbouring rights, Commission of the European Communities, COM (90) 584 final, Jan. 17, 1991, Brussels

E.C. Follow-Up to the Green Paper (1996)	Follow-Up to the Green Paper on Copyright and Related Rights in the Information Society, Commission of the European Communities, Nov. 20, 1996, Brussels
E.C. Green Paper (1988)	Green Paper on Copyright and the Challenges of Technology–Copyright Issues Requiring Immediate Action, Commission of the European Communities, COM (88) 172 final, June 7, 1988, Brussels
E.C. Green Paper (1995)	Green Paper, Copyright and Related Rights in the Information Society, Commission of the European Communities, COM (95) 382 final, July 19, 1995, Brussels
E.C. Rental Directive (1992)	E.C. Rental Directive, Council Directive 92/100/EEC of November 19, 1992 on rental right and lending right and on certain rights related to copyright in the field of intellectual property, Official Journal L 346, 27.11.1992, 61–66
E.C. Software Directive (1991)	E.C. Software Directive, Council Directive 91/250/EEC of May 14, 1991 on the legal protection of computer programs, Official Journal L 122, 0042–0046
E.C. Television Broadcasting Directive 2007/65/EC (2007)	E.C. Television Broadcasting Directive 2007/65/EC, Directive 2007/65/EC of the European Parliament and of the Council of December 11, 2007, amending Council Directive 89/552/EEC on the coordination of certain provisions laid down by law, regulation or administrative action in Member States concerning the pursuit of television broadcasting activities, Official Journal L 332, 18.12.2007, 27–45
E.C. Television Broadcasting Directive 89/552/EEC (1989)	E.C. Television Broadcasting Directive 89/552/EEC, Council Directive 89/552/EEC of October 3, 1989 on the coordination of certain provisions laid down by Law, Regulation or Administrative Action in Member States concerning the pursuit of television broadcasting activities, Official Journal L 298, 17/10/1989, 0023–0030
EFF Report: Unintended Consequences: Seven Years under the DMCA (2006)	Unintended Consequences: Seven Years under the DMCA, Electronic Frontier Foundation, version Apr. 4, 2006
EUCD (2001)	Directive 2001/29/EC of the European Parliament and of the Council of May 22, 2001 on the harmonisation of certain aspects of copyright and related rights in the information society, Official Journal L 167, 22/06/2001, 0010–0019

European Charter of Fundamental Rights (2000)	Charter of Fundamental Rights of the European Union, Official Journal of the European Communities C. 364/1, 18.12.2000
European Convention on Human Rights (1950)	European Convention on Human Rights Council of Europe, Convention for the Protection of Human Rights and Fundamental Freedoms, as amended by Protocol No. 11, Rome, 4.11.1950
Exemption to Prohibition on Circumvention of Copyright Protection Systems for Access Control Technologies (2010)	37 CFR Pt. 201, Vol. 75, No. 143 pp. 43825-39 (July 27, 2010).
First Bundle Bill (2002)	Entwurf eines Gesetzes zur Regelung des Urheberrechts, in der Informationsgesellschaft, Gesetzentwurf der Bundesregierung, Drucksache 15/38, Nov. 6, 2002
Gesetz zur Regelung des Urheberrechts in der Informations-gesellschaft (2003)	Gesetz zur Regelung des Urheberrechts in der Informationsgesellschaft, enacted 1.9.2003, 2003 Bundesgesetzblatt Part I No. 46, Sept. 12, 2003 s. 1774 ff.
House Report 94-1476 (1976)	U.S. House of Representatives Report 94-1476, H.R. Report 94-1476, 94th Congress, 2nd, Session, Sept. 3, 1976
Google Book Search Agreement (2008)	The Authors Guild, Inc. et al, v. Google Inc., NO. 05 CV 8136, (SDNY), dated Oct. 28, 2008
Hübner, Angenehm Sinnfrei (2004)	Angenehm Sinnfrei, die Tageszeitung (TAZ), by Karl Hübner, (available at : http://www.taz.de/index.php?id=archivseite&dig=2004/11/27/a0265) (published 27.11.2004)
ICESCR Committee General Comment No. 17 (2005)	U.N. ICESCR, General Comment No. 17, Economic and Social Council, E/C.12/GC/17, 12 Jan. 2006, U.N. Committee on Economic, Social and Cultural Rights, 35th Sess., Geneva 7-25 Nov. 2005
ICESCR Committee Statement on Human Rights and Intellectual Property (2001)	U.N. ICESCR, Statement on Human Rights and Intellectual Property, Economic and Social Council, E/C 12.2001/15, Dec. 14, 2001, U.N. Committee on Economic, Social and Cultural Rights, 27th Sess., Geneva 12–30 Nov. 2001

International Covenant on Economic, Social and Cultural Rights (1966)	International Covenant on Economic, Social and Cultural Rights, U.N. General Assembly Resolution 2200A, 21st Session, Supp. No. 16, at 49, U.N. Doc. A/6316 (1966)
Israel Copyright Act (2007)	Israel Copyright Act of 2007, Sefer Ha'chukim 2119 at 38, Nov. 25, 2007
NAFTA (1992)	North American Free Trade Agreement (NAFTA), signed Dec. 17, 1992
OECD Music Report (2005)	OECD Report on Digital Broadband Content: Music, Organization for Economic Co-operation and Development, Committee for Information, Computer and Communications Policy, Working Party on the Information Economy, June 8, 2005, DSTI/ICCP/IE (2004) 12/FINAL (2005)
Records of the WIPO 1996 Diplomatic Conference (1999)	Records of the Diplomatic Conference on Certain Copyright and Neighboring Rights Questions, World Intellectual Property Organization, WIPO Publications No. 348(E), Geneva 1999
Request for Comments, U.S. Department of Commerce (1993)	Request for Comments on Intellectual Property Issues involved in the National Information Infrastructure Initiative, U.S. Department of Commerce, Patent and Trademark Office, 58 Federal Reporter at 539, Oct. 17, 19, 1993
Restatement (First) of Property (1936)	Restatement (First) of Property, American Law Institute 1936
Second Expert Committee Report on Copyright Problems (1982)	Report of the Second Committee of Governmental Experts on Copyright Problems Arising from the Use of Computers for Access to or the Creation of Works, [1982] Copyright 239 ff. June 1982
Senate Report 102-294 (AHRA 1992)	U.S. Senate Report 102-294, Senate Report 102-294, Audio Home Recording Act, June 9, 1992
Sonny Bono Copyright Term Extension Act (1998)	Sonny Bono Copyright Term Extension Act, title I of Pub. L. No. 105-298, 112 Stat. 2827, enacted Oct. 27, 1998
THE DIGITAL DILEMMA (2000)	THE DIGITAL DILEMMA–Intellectual Property in the Information Age, Committee on Intellectual Property Rights and the Emerging Information Infrastructure, National Research Council, National Academy Press, Washington D.C. 2000

The Future of Levies in a Digital Environment: Final Report (2003)	The Future of Levies in a Digital Environment: Final Report, Institute for Information Law, P.B. Hugenholtz et al., Mar. 2003, Amsterdam 2003
TRIPS (1994)	TRIPS Agreement, Agreement on Trade-Related Aspects of Intellectual Property Rights, April 15, 1994, Marrakesh Agreement Establishing the World Trade Organization, Annex 1C (1994) 33 ILM 1197 (1994)
Trusted Computing: Promise and Risk (2003)	EFF White Paper–Trusted Computing: Promise and Risk Electronic Frontier Foundation, White Paper–Trusted Computing: Promise and Risk, by Seth Schoen (2003), (available at http://www.eff.org/wp/trusted-computing-promise-and-risk)
U.S. Berne Convention Implementation Act (1988)	Berne Convention Implementation Act of 1988, Pub. L. No. 100-568, 102 Stat. 2853, 100th Congress, Second Session, enacted Oct. 31, 1988
U.S. Copyright Office Memorandum concerning the 2003 DMCA Rulemaking (2003)	U.S. Copyright Office Memorandum concerning the 2003 DMCA Rulemaking, Memorandum from Marybeth Peters, Register of Copyrights, to James H. Billington, Librarian of Congress, Recommendation of the Register of Copyrights in RM 2002-4, Oct. 27, 2003
U.S. Copyright Office Report on Orphan Works (2006)	Report on Orphan Works (2006), Report on Orphan Works–A Report of the Register of Copyrights, Jan. 2006, U.S. Copyright Office, Washington D.C. 2006
U.S. Copyright Office Section 104 DMCA Report (2001)	Report of the Register of Copyrights Pursuant to § 104 of the Digital Millennium Copyright Act, U.S. Copyright Office, the Librarian of Congress, Aug. 29, 2001, Washington D.C. 2001
U.S. Copyright Office Summery, The Digital Millennium Copyright Act (1998)	The Digital Millennium Copyright Act of 1998, U.S. Copyright Office Summary, Dec. 1998
U.S. Copyright Office, Circular No. 34 (2006)	Circular 34, U.S. Copyright Office, Library of Congress, Copyright Office, (available at http://www.copyright.gov/circs/circ34.html), revised: Feb. 2006
U.S. Copyright Renewal Act (1992)	U.S. Copyright Renewal Act of 1992, Pub. L. No. 102-307, 106 Stat. 264, 102nd Congress, 2nd Session, June 26. 1992
U.S. Green Paper (1994)	A Preliminary Draft of the Report of the Working Group on Intellectual Property Rights, Intellectual Property and the National Information Infrastructure, July 1994

U.S. Senate Concurrent Resolution 87 (2006)	Concurrent Resolution Expressing the sense of Congress that United States intellectual property rights must be protected globally, U.S. Congress, Concurrent Resolution, S. CON. RES. 87, 109th Congress 2nd. Sess., Apr. 5, 2006
U.S. Uruguay Round Agreement Act (1994)	Uruguay Round Agreement Act of 1994, Pub. L. No. 103-465, 108 Stat. 4809, 103rd Congress, 2nd Session, Jan. 25, 1994
U.S. White Paper (1995)	The Report of the Working Group on Intellectual Property Rights, Intellectual Property and the National Information Infrastructure, the Working Group on Intellectual Property Rights, Bruce Lehman, Chair, Sept. 1995
UNESCO Recommendation on Participation by the People in Cultural Life (1976)	UNESCO Recommendation on Participation by the People at Large in Cultural Life and their Contribution to It, in RECORDS OF THE GENERAL CONFERENCE UNESCO, 19th Session, Annex I at 29 ff., Art. I.2(a), Nairobi, 26 Nov. 1976
Universal Declaration of Human Rights (1948)	Universal Declaration of Human Rights, G.A. Reg. 217, U.N. GAOR, 3rd Sess. (1948)
URG (Switzerland 1992)	Bundesgesetz über das Urheberrecht und verwandte Schutzrechte (URG Switzerland), Law of October 9, 1992, as lastly amended in June 13, 2006
Urheberrechts-wahrnehmungsgesetz (1965)	Gesetz über die Wahrnehmung von Urheberrechten und verwandten Schutzrechten (Urheberrechtswahrnehmungsgesetz), BGBl. I S. 1294, enacted Sept. 9, 1965, as lastly amended in Oct. 26, 2007, BGBl. I S. 2513
WCT Basic Proposal (1996)	Basic Proposal for the Substantive Provisions of the Treaty on Certain Questions Concerning the Protection of Literary and Artistic Works to be Considered by the Diplomatic Conference, World Intellectual Property Organization, Diplomatic Conference on Certain Copyright and Neighboring Rights Questions, WIPO CRNR/DC/4, Geneva, Aug. 30, 1996

WPPT Basic Proposal (1996)	Basic Proposal for the Substantive Provisions of the Treaty for the Protection of the Rights of Performers and Producers of Phonograms to be Considered by the Diplomatic Conference, World Intellectual Property Organization, Diplomatic Conference on Certain Copyright and Neighboring Rights Questions, WIPO CRNR/DC/5, Geneva, Aug. 30, 1996
WTO Panel Report on § 110(5) U.S. Copyright Act (2000)	WTO Panel Report Concerning Section 110(5) of the US Copyright Act, World Trade Organization, United States–Section 110(5) of the US Copyright Act, WT/DS160/R, June 15, 2000
Zugangskontroll-diensteschutz-Gesetz-ZKDSG (2002)	Gesetz über den Schutz von zugangskontrollierten Diensten und von Zugangskontrolldiensten (Zugangskontrolldiensteschutz-Gesetz-ZKDSG) 1090 BGBl from 22.03.2002, Bundesgesetzblatt Jahrgang 2002 Teil I Nr. 19, ausgegeben zu Bonn am 22. März 2002, Seite 1090
Zweites Gesetz zur Regelung des Urheberrechts in der Informations-gesellschaft (2007)	Zweites Gesetz zur Regelung des Urheberrechts in der Informationsgesellschaft, enacted 26.1.2007, 2007 Bundesgesetzblatt Part I No. 54, Oktober 31, 2007 at 2513 ff.

CASE CITATION TABLE

CITATION FORM	NAME	FULL CITATION	YEAR
321 Studios *v.* MGM (N.D. Cal. 2004)	321 Studios *v.* Metro Goldwyn Studios, Inc.	307 F.Supp. 2d 1085 (N.D. Cal. 2004)	2004
Abrams *v.* United States (1919)	Abrams *v.* United States	250 U.S. 616	1919
Advanced Computer Services *v.* MAI Systems (E.D. Va. 1994)	Advanced Computer Services of Michigan, Inc., *v.* MAI Systems Corp.	845 F.Supp. 356 (E.D. Va. 1994)	1994
Anachronistischer Zug (1984)	German Constitutional Court (*Anachronistischer Zug*)	BVerfGRE 67, 213 (July 17, 1984)	1984
Apple Computer *v.* Formula (C.D. Cal. 1984)	Apple Computer, Inc., v. Formula Int'l, Inc.	594 F.Supp. 617 (C.D. Cal. 1984)	1984
Arnstein *v.* Porter (2d. Cir. 1946)	Arnstein *v.* Porter	154 F.2d 464 (2d. Cir 1946)	1946
Atlantic Recording Corp. *v.* Howell (D. Ariz. 2008)	Atlantic Recording Corp. *v.* Howell	District of Arizona, No. CV-06-02076-PHX-NVW, decided Apr. 29, 2008, 2008 WL 1927353 (D. Ariz.)	2008
Bilski *v.* Kappos (S.Ct. 2010))	Bernard L. Bilski & Rand A. Warsaw *v.* David J. Kappos	Bilski *v.* Kappos, No. 08-964, 130 S.Ct. 3218 (2010)	
BGH Paperboy decision (2003)	Bundesgerichtshof I ZR 259/00 (*Paperboy*)	Bundesgerichtshof, I ZR 259/00, GRUR 2003, 958	2003
BGH, V ZB 43/93 (1994) (Erwerberhaftung für Wohngeldrückstände)	Bundesgerichtshof V ZB 43/93 (Erwerberhaftung für Wohngeldrückstände)	(BGH), V ZB 43/93, decision from 24.2.1994	1994

Bleistein *v.* Donaldson (S.Ct. 1903)	Bleistein *v.* Donaldson Lithographing Company	188 U.S. 239, No. 117	1903
Board of Education *v.* Pico (S.Ct. 1982)	Board of Education, Island Trees Union Free School Dist. No. 26 *v.* Pico	457 U.S. 853 (1982)	1982
Burrow-Giles *v.* Sarony (1884)	Burrow-Giles Lithographic Company *v.* Sarony	111 U.S. 53 (1884)	1884
BVerfG (*AnyDVD*, 31.1.2007), 2007 MMR 576	German Constitutional Court, 1 BvR 1936/05	Bundesverfas-sungsgerichtshof (BVerfG), decision from 3.1.2007, 1 BvR 1936/05, reprinted in 2007 MMR 576	2007
BVerfG (*Kopieschutz*, 25.7.2005), 2005 MMR 751	German Constitutional Court, 1 BvR 2181/04	Bundesverfas-sungsgerichtshof (BVerfG), decision from 25.7.2005, 1 BvR 2181/04, reprinted in 2005 MMR 751	2005
California Satellite Systems *v.* Seimon (9th. Cir. 1985)	California Satellite Systems *v.* Seimon	767 F.2d 1364 (9th. Cir. 1985)	1985
Campbell *v.* Acuff-Rose (S.Ct. 1994)	Campbell *v.* Acuff-Rose Music, Inc.	510 U.S. 569 (1994)	1994
Capitol Records *v.* Thomas (D. Minn. 2008)	Capitol Records, Inc. et al. *v.* Jammie Thomas	2008 WL 4405282 (D.Minn.), decided 24.9.2008	2008
CCH *v.* Law Society of Upper Canada (2004)	CCH Canadian Ltd. *v.* Law Society of Upper Canada	2004 SCC 13, March 4, 2004	2004
Chamberlain I (N.D. Ill. 2003)	Chamberlain Group, Inc. *v.* Skylink Techs., Inc.	292 F. Supp. 2d 1023 (N.D. Ill. 2003)	2003

Chamberlain II (N.D. Ill. 2003)	Chamberlain Group, Inc. v. Skylink Techs., Inc.	292 F. Supp. 2d 1040 (N.D. Ill. 2003)	2003
Chamberlain *v.* Skylink (6th. Cir. 2004)	Chamberlain Group, Inc. v. Skylink Techs., Inc.	381 F.3d 1178 (Fed. Cir. 2004)	2004
Cologne District Court, 2006 MMR 412 (2006)	Cologne District Court Az: 28 S 6/05	Landgericht Köln, decision from 23.11.2005, Az: 28 S 6/05, reprinted in 2006 MMR 412	2006
CoStar, *v.* Loopnet (4th. Cir. 2004)	CoStar Group, Inc., *v.* Loopnet, Inc.	373 F.3d 544 (4th. Cir. 2004)	2004
Davidson & Assoc. *v.* Internet Gateway (E.D. Mo. 2004)	Davidson & Assoc. *v.* Internet Gateway	334 F.Supp. 2d 1164 (E.D. Mo. 2004), *aff'd,* Davidson & Assoc. *v.* Jung, 422 F.3d 630 (8th Cir. 2005)	2004
Davidson & Assoc. *v.* Jung (8th Cir. 2005)	Davidson & Assoc. *v.* Jung	422 F.3d 630 (8th Cir. 2005)	2005
DSC Communications *v.* Pulse Communications (Fed. Cir. 1999)	DSC Communications Corp. *v.* Pulse Communications, Inc.	170 F.3d 1354 (Fed. Cir. 1999)	1999
Eldred *v.* Ashcroft (S. Ct. 2003)	Eldred *v.* Ashcroft	537 U.S. 186 (2003)	2003
Eldred *v.* Reno (D.C. Cir. 2001)	Eldred *v.* Reno	239 F.3d 372 (D.C. Cir. 2001)	2001
Elektra *v.* Barker (S.D.N.Y. 2008)	Elektra Ent. Group Inc. et al. *v.* Barker	No. 05-CV-7340 (KMK), March 31, 2008, Slip Copy, 2008 WL 857527	2008
Feist *v.* Rural (1991)	Feist Publishing, Inc. *v.* Rural Tel. Serv, Co.	499 U.S. 340 (1991)	1991

First Nat'l Bank *v.* Bellotti (S.Ct. 1978)	First National Bank *v.* Bellotti	435 U.S. 765 (1978)	1978
Folson *v.* Marsh (C.C.D. Mass. 1841)	Folson *v.* Marsh	9 F.Cas. 342, Case No. 4,901, (C.C.D Mass. 1841)	1841
Food Lion, Inc., *v.* Capital Cities (4th Cir. 1999)	Food Lion, Inc., *v.* Capital Cities	194 F.3d 505 (4th Cir. 1999)	1999
Frankfurt District Court, 2006 MMR 766 (2006)	Frankfurt District Court, 2-06 O 288/06	Landgericht Frankfurt a.M., decision from 31.5.2006, 2-06 O 288/06, *rep'd* MMR 2006 766	2006
Golan v. Gonzales (9th Cir. 2007)	Golan v. Gonzales	501 F.3d 1179 (9th Cir. 2007)	2007
Graham *v.* John Deere Company (1966)	Graham *v.* John Deere Company	383 U.S. 1 (1966)	1966
Harper & Row *v.* Nation Enterprises (1985)	Harper & Row *v.* Nation Enterprises	471 U.S. 539 (1985)	1985
Helsinki District Court Case No. R 07/1004 (25.5.2007)	Helsinki District Court	Judgment 07/4535, Case No. R 07/10May 04, 25, 2007	2007
Jacobsen v. Katzer (Fed. Cir. 2008)	Jacobsen *v.* Katzer & Kamind Assoc., Inc.	535 F.3d 1373 (Fed. Cir. 2008)	2008
Jacque *v.* Steenberg Homes (Wis. 1997)	Harvey and Lois Jacque *v.* Steenberg Homes, Inc.	Supreme Court of Wisconsin, No. 95-1028, 207 Wis. 2d 605	1997
Kahle *v.* Gonzales (9th. Cir. 2007)	Kahle *v.* Gonzales	487 F.3d 697 (9th. Cir)	2007
Kleindienst *v.* Mandel (1972)	Kleindienst *v.* Mandel	408 U.S. 753	1972

Lexmark District Decision (E.D. Ky. 2003)	Lexmark Int'l, Inc. v. Static Control Components, Inc.,	253 F.Supp. 2d 943 (E.D.Ky. 2003), *vacated and remanded* by 387 F.3d 522 (6th Cir. 2004)	2003
Lexmark *v.* Static Control (6th Cir. 2004)	Lexmark Int'l, Inc. v. Static Control Components, Inc.	387 F.3d 522 (6th Cir. 2004)	2004
London-Sire *v.* Doe (D. Mass. 2008)	London-Sire Records, Inc. *v.* Doe 1 et al.	No. 04cv12434-NG., March 31, 2008, 2008 WL 887491 (D. Mass.)	2008
Los Angeles News Service *v.* Tullo (1992)	Los Angeles News Service *v.* Tullo	973 F.2d 791 (9th Cir. 1992)	1992
Luck's Music *v.* Ashcroft (D.D.C. 2004)	Luck's Music *v.* Ashcroft	321 F.Supp. 2d 107 (D.D.C. 2004)	2004
Macrovision *v.* Sima (S.D.N.Y. 2006)	Macrovision *v.* Sima Products Corp.	No. 05 Civ. 5587 (OR), not reported in F.Supp., 2006 WL 1063284 (S.D.N.Y.)	2006
MAI Systems *v.* Peak Computer (9th Cir. 1993)	MAI Systems Corp. *v.* Peak Computer	991 F.2d 511 (9th Cir. 1993), *cert. denied,* 510 U.S. 1033 (1994)	1993
Mazer *v.* Stein (S.Ct. 1954)	Mazer *v.* Stein	347 U.S. 201 (1954)	1954
Mephisto (1971)	German Constitutional Court (*Mephisto*)	BVerfGRE 30, 173 (Feb. 24, 1971)	1971
Miller *v.* California (1973)	Miller *v.* California	413 U.S. 15 (1973)	1973
Muholland Drive Case (2006)	French Supreme Court (Mulholland Drive Case)	French Supreme Court (*Cour de Cassation*) 1st Civil Chamber, No. 549	2006
Munich District Court I, *AnyDVD* (2005), 2005 GRUR-RR 214	Munich District Court I	Landgericht München I, decision from 7.3.2005, 21 O 3220/05, reprinted in 2005 GRUR-RR 214	2005

Munich District Court I, *AnyDVD II* (2006)	Munich District Court I	Landgericht München I, decision from 11.1.2006, 21 0 2004/06	2006
Munich Regional Court (OLG), *AnyDVD* (2005), 2005 GRUR-RR 372	Munich Regional Court	Oberlandesgericht München, decision from 28.7.05, 29 U 2887/05, reprinted in 2005 GRUR-RR 372	2005
New York Times *v.* Sullivan (1964)	New York Times Co. *v.* Sullivan	376 U.S. 254 (1964)	1964
Osborn *v.* Ohio (1990)	Osborn *v.* Ohio	495 U.S. 103 (1990)	1990
Paramount Pictures *v.* 321 Studios (S.D.N.Y 2004)	Paramount Pictures Corp., *v.* 321 Studios	2004 WL 402756 (S.D.N.Y. March 3, 2004)	2004
Peek & Cloppenburg KG v. Cassina SpA, ECJ Case C-456/06 (April 17, 2008)	Peek & Cloppenburg KG v. Cassina SpA	ECJ Case C-456/06 (April 17, 2008)	2008
Realnetworks *v.* Streambox (W.D. Wash. 2000)	Realnetworks, Inc., *v.* Streambox, Inc.	2000 WL 127311, (W.D. Wash 2000), No. 2:99CV02070 (not reported in F.Supp.), Jan. 18, 2000	2000
Reiss *v.* National Quotation Bureau (S.D.N.Y. 1921)	Reiss *v.* National Quotation Bureau, Inc.	276 F. 717 (S.D.N.Y 1921)	1921
Renne *v.* Geary (S.Ct. 1991)	Renne *v.* Geary	501 U.S. 312 (1991)	1991
RIAA *v.* Diamond (9th Cir. 1999)	Recording Industry Association of America *v.* Diamond Multimedia Systems Inc.	180 F.3d 1072 (9th Cir.)	1999
Richmond Newspapers *v.* Virginia (1980)	Richmond Newspapers, Inc., *v.* Virginia	448 U.S. 555 (1980)	1980

Scholz Design Inc. *v.* Larue et al., (E.D. Ark. 2008)	Scholz Design Inc. *v.* Wayne & Julie Larue, Don Mallory and Quality Design, Inc.	2008 WL 3827993 (E.D. Ark. 2008)	2008
Sega *v.* Accolade (9th Cir. 1993)	Sega Enterprises LTD *v.* Accolade, Inc.	977 F.2d 1510 (9th Cir.)	1993
Sheldon *v.* Metro-Goldwyn (1936)	Sheldon *v.* Metro-Goldwyn Pictures	81 F.2d 49 (2d. Cir. 1936), *aff'd*, 309 U.S. 390 (1940)	1936
Sheldon *v.* Metro-Goldwyn (1939)	Sheldon *v.* Metro-Goldwyn Pictures Corp.	106 F. 2d 45 (2d. Cir. 1939), *aff'd*, 309 U.S. 390 (1940)	1939
Sony Computers *v.* Gamemaster (N.D. Cal. 1999)	Sony Computer Entertainment America, Inc., *v.* Gamemasters, Inc.,	87 F.Supp. 2d 976 (N.D. Cal. 1999)	1999
Sony Corp., *v.* Universal City Studios (1984)	Sony Corporation of America et. al. *v.* Universal City Studios, Inc., et. al.	464 U.S. 417 (1984)	1984
Stanley v. Georgia (1969)	Stanley v. Georgia	394 U.S. 557 (1969)	1969
Storage Technology, *v.* Custom Hardware (Fed. Cir. 2005)	Storage Technology Corp., *v.* Custom Hardware Engineering, Inc.	421 F.3d 1307 (Fed. Cir.)	2005
SunTrust Bank *v.* Houghton Mifflin Co. (11th Cir. 2001)	SunTrust Bank *v.* Houghton Mifflin Co.	268 F.3d 1257 (11th Cir. 2001)	2001
Texas *v.* Johnson (1989)	Texas *v.* Johnson	491 U.S. 397 (1989)	1989
The Cartoon Network *v.* CSC Holdings (2d Cir. 2008)	The Cartoon Network LP and Cable News Network L.P., *v.* CSC Holdings, Inc. & Cablevision Systems Corp.	536 F.3d 121 (2d. Cir. 2008), *cert denied*, 129 S. Ct. 2890 (June 29, 2009)	2008
The Florida Star *v.* B.J.F. (1989)	The Florida Star *v.* B.J.F.	491 U.S. 524 (1989)	1989

Ticketmaster *v.* RMG Technologies (C.D. Cal. 2007)	Ticketmaster LLC, *v.* RMG Technologies, Inc.	507 F.Supp. 2d 1096 (C.D. Cal.)	2007
Triad Systems *v.* Southeastern Express (N.D. Cal 1994)	Triad Systems Corp. *v.* Southeastern Express Co.	31 U.S.P.Q.2d 1239, 1994 WL 446049 (N.D.Cal. 1994), *affirmed in part, reversed in part on other grounds*, Triad Systems Corp. *v.* Southeastern Exp. Co., 64 F.3d 1330 (9th Cir. 1995)	1994
United States *v.* Elcom (N.D. Cal. 2002)	United States *v.* Elcom Ltd.	203 F.Supp. 2d 1111 (N.D. Cal. 2002)	2002
United States *v.* O'Brien (1968)	United States *v.* O'Brien	391 U.S. 367 (1968)	1968
Universal City Studios *v.* Reimerdes (S.D.N.Y 2000)	Universal City Studios *v.* Reimerdes	111 F. Supp. 2d 294, (S.D.N.Y. 2000), *aff'd sub nom.* Universal *v.* Corley, 273 F.3d 429 (2d. Cir. 2001)	2000
Universal City Studios, Inc. *v.* Corley (2d Cir. 2001)	Universal City Studios, Inc. *v.* Corley	273 F.3d 429 (2d Cir.)	2001
Viacom *v.* YouTube (S.D.N.Y. 2008)	Viacom Int'l Inc., et al., *v.* YouTube Inc., et al.	U.S. District Court, S.D.N.Y., No. 07 Civ. 2103(LLS), 07 Civ. 3582(LLS), 2008 WL 2627388 (S.D.N.Y.)) 2.7.2008	2008
Virginia State *v.* Virginia Citizens Consumer Council (1976)	Virginia State Board of Pharmacy *v.* Virginia Citizens Consumer Council, Inc.	425 U.S. 748 (1976)	1976
White-Smith *v.* Apollo (1908)	White-Smith Music Publishing Company *v.* Apollo Company	209 U.S. 1, 18 (1908)	1908
Wooley *v.* Maynard (1977)	Wooley *v.* Maynard	430 U.S. 705 (1977)	1977

TABLE OF CASES

INDEX

Note: Page numbers followed by "*f*" and "*t*" denote to figures and tables, respectively.